Outline of a Phenomenology of Right

Outline of a
Phenomenology of Right

Alexandre Kojève

Translated, with an introductory essay and notes,
by
BRYAN-PAUL FROST AND ROBERT HOWSE

EDITED BY BRYAN-PAUL FROST

ROWMAN & LITTLEFIELD PUBLISHERS, INC.
Lanham • Boulder • New York • Oxford

ROWMAN & LITTLEFIELD PUBLISHERS, INC.

Published in the United States of America
by Rowman & Littlefield Publishers, Inc.
4720 Boston Way, Lanham, Maryland 20706
http://www.rowmanlittlefield.com

12 Hid's Copse Road
Cumnor Hill, Oxford OX2 9JJ, England

British Library Cataloguing in Publication Information Available

Library of Congress Cataloging-in-Publication Data

Kojève, Alexandre, 1902–1968.
    [Esquisse d'une phénoménologie du droit. English]
    Outline of phenomenology of right / Alexandre Kojève ; translated, with an
introductory essay and notes, by Bryan-Paul Frost and Robert Howse ; edited by
Bryan-Paul Frost.
      p. cm.
    Includes bibliographical references and index.
    ISBN 0-8476-8922-0
    1. Law—Philosophy.   2. Phenomenology.   I. Frost, Bryan-Paul, 1961-
II. Title
K350.K6513 2000
340′1.—dc21   00-020217

Printed in the United States of America

♾ ™ The paper used in this publication meets the minimum requirements of American
National Standard for Information Sciences—Permanence of Paper for Printed Library
Materials, ANSI/NISO Z39.48—1992.

From Robert to Denyse

From Bryan-Paul to Cathy

Contents

A Note from the French Publisher

Alexandre Kojève wrote these pages during the summer of 1943 in Gramat (Lot), where he had gone to see the family of Eric Weil.[1] Although the author declared himself satisfied with it, this work has remained unpublished and has kept its original form.

The first page of the typed text bears the comment "Marseille, 1943."

---

1. [Ed. Eric Weil (1904–1977) was deeply influenced by the revival of Hegelian studies in France, and he attended Kojève's famous series of lectures on the *Phenomenology of Spirit* during the 1930s. The author of numerous books and articles, he held several academic posts in France, including professorships at the Universities of Nice and Lille. Although Weil was a German prisoner during the war, his wife and sister-in-law, Catherine Mendelson (a German Jew), were hiding out near Gramat. Kojève went to visit them in 1941 or 1942, and fell in love with the village; he later returned there in 1943 and composed the entire manuscript that summer. For a fuller description of the events leading up to and after the writing of the *Esquisse*, see Dominique Auffret, *Alexandre Kojève: La philosophie, l'Etat, la fin de l'Histoire* (Paris: Bernard Grasset, 1990), 265–92.]

Acknowledgments

With a project of this size, there are many people to thank. Ed Andrew, A. David Barry, Peter Benson, Maurice Boesch, Larry Cooper, David Dyzenhaus, Jacques Henry, Daniel J. Mahoney, and Catherine Valcke read over portions of the translation and made many valuable corrections and suggestions. Thomas L. Pangle also read over portions of the manuscript as well as helped to bring it to the attention of publishers. Peter Berkowitz, Kalypso Nicolaidis, and Susan Shell read over the introductory essay and provided several constructive observations and criticisms, as did the students in Professor Howse's fall 1999 seminar at the University of Michigan. Nina Ivanoff, Kojève's literary legate, provided us a personal description of the time during which the *Outline* was written as well as checked the original manuscript to answer questions we had about the text. The editor of the journal *Interpretation*, Hilail Gildin, helped to bring to publication a slightly modified version of Part One, chapter 3, "The Specificity and Autonomy of Right" (Fall 1996), and we believe that this helped to generate interest in the book itself. Kassi Patrick diligently tracked down a few of Kojève's more obscure references, and this during final exam week at law school. Bryan-Paul Frost would like to thank everyone in the Department of Political Science at the University of Louisiana at Lafayette for their moral support and encouragement, and especially Janet Frantz, who as chair of the department made life as comfortable as possible for a newly appointed professor. Robert Howse was first introduced, as an undergraduate at the University of Toronto, to the work of Kojève by the late Allan Bloom and to that of Hegel by Emile Fackenheim. These remarkable teachers communicated a sense of the depth, vitality, and relevance of the thinkers in question, without which Howse finds it difficult to imagine that he would have acquired the motivation to undertake the present project. Much of his work on this project was done while a visiting professor at Harvard Law School and the University of Michigan Law School: both institutions provided superb and generous administrative and research resources for this project. And finally, the translators would also like to thank the many folks at Rowman & Littlefield who have been associated with this project over the course of the past few years, and who were willing to secure the rights to the translation before the translation was even complete. We would like to single out, however, Mary Carpenter for her technical assistance, and Steve Wrinn, who was instrumental in sheparding the project along from start to finish. Mary and Steve are truly author's editors.

A Note about the Translation

The most obvious or perhaps striking feature of the translation is that the word *droit* has been left untranslated throughout. Since *droit* can mean both "right" and "law," and since Kojève uses the word in both senses depending on the context, we have decided to allow readers the chance to judge for themselves the meaning that Kojève attributes to this key concept. Two frequently used phrases involving the word *droit*, however, have been translated: *règle de droit* has been translated as "legal rule," and *système du droit* as "legal system." Unless otherwise indicated, the word "law" in the text is always a translation of *loi*. We have translated *justiciable* as "litigant," although this word also has the much broader meaning of "those who are subject to law."

Although we have included several editorial notes explaining how we have translated a series of related words and phrases, several others need to be mentioned here at the outset. As *supprimer* is the French equivalent of the German *aufheben*, it has generally been translated as "overcome" in order to preserve its Hegelian flavor; however, when the context required, we also translated it as "suppress," and less frequently as "do away with" and "eliminate." *Léser* is translated as "infringe upon" or "injure" in order to distinguish it from *nuire*, meaning "harm" or "hurt": *léser* often refers to dignitary injury or an infringement of one's rights, whereas *nuire* generally refers to a tangible harm. *Effectif* and *effectivement* are translated as "effective" and "effectively," even when the words "actual" and "actually" might seem more appropriate; but we preferred to do this rather than cause any confusion when Kojève speaks about actual *droit* (*actuelle*) or *droit* in actuality (*en acte*) (in contrast to potential *droit* or *droit* in potentiality). *Tribunal* as well as *cour* have generally been translated as "court"; however, when *tribunal* refers to an administrative type of body, for example, a body reviewing the decisions of civil servants or handing out military justice, it has been translated as "tribunal." Kojève often uses the word *particulier* as a noun in the sense of a "private person," and as an adjective in the sense of "personal." Nevertheless, Kojève also uses the word *personne privée*, and we have put the original French word in square brackets to show when Kojève changes from one to the other. Kojève often uses the expression *faire appel au juge* or *au tiers* in the sense of "appealing to the services or offices of a judge or neutral third person." However, the use of the word "appeal" in this case may cause some readers to confuse the request (or appeal) by a litigant for a judge to intervene in a particular case with actually appealing a decision made in a lower court to a higher court. To eliminate any possible confusion, we have rendered this phrase as "have recourse to," and less frequently as "resort to." And finally, while *châtiment* and *punition* are translated as "punishment," *peine* is translated as "sentence" or "penalty," and occasionally as "punishment." Indeed, Kojève sometimes uses all of these words to mean "punishment," with no apparent difference in meaning. When we thought it would be helpful, we have included the original French word or phrase in square brackets.

We have retained all of Kojève's stylistic oddities, such as his frequent use of capitals, italics, and quotation marks. In order to indicate those instances when Kojève has put the word *droit* in italics, we have put it in bold typeface: **droit**. When Kojève uses a less familiar Latin or German word or phrase whose meaning is not clear from the context, we have translated it into English the first time it appears, and then left it in Latin or German if it reappears again. We have not used gender-neutral language as Kojève did not; therefore, we have translated *l'homme* as man (or the man) in order to distinguish it from *être humain,* human being. We must stress, however, that Kojève hardly believed that women were any less "human" than men or inferior to them in respect to rights and duties: all of Kojève's arguments and observations apply with equal vigor to women. Indeed, it is clear throughout the *Outline* that the lack of equal rights and duties for women and men at the time Kojève was writing was an indication that the concept of right was not adequate to its essence, that the absolute right at the end of history had not been manifested in the here and now. All of Kojève's footnotes are contained within the text while our explanatory notes are in square brackets.

We have corrected without comment some very minor omissions and errors in the text. For example, when Kojève begins a parenthetical expression but fails to supply the second parenthesis, we have done so; or again, when Kojève refers to an incorrect page number in a footnote, we have supplied the correct one. We have indicated in the notes those few instances when our reading differs from that in the published Gallimard text, and Nina Ivanoff (Kojève's literary legate) was kind enough to check the original handwritten manuscript to see if these readings were correct (or not). In those places where the manuscript differed from the published text, we have indicated this with the phrase "as in the original manuscript"; in those places where the manuscript and the text were in harmony, but where we nevertheless believed that Kojève made a small error of some sort, we have supplied in the notes both our alternative reading and the original without further comment. (We hope that the above remarks make clear that we have not seen the original manuscript itself and are relying on the accuracy of the Gallimard text.) As for references that Kojève himself makes to other works, when the edition of a book or text that we had available to us differed from Kojève's, we simply substituted our reference for his and changed the page numbers accordingly. Where possible, we have tried to indicate English translations of the works to which Kojève refers. When Kojève refers to a writer without indicating the specific text(s) he has in mind, we have indicated the work(s) to which he might be referring (where possible). Kojève refers to G.W.F. Hegel (and Karl Marx) several times throughout the book (indeed, he even assumes that the reader is familiar with the former), and readers may find it useful to consult his powerful and provocative interpretation of the *Phenomenology of Spirit*, an abridged English translation of which is *Introduction to the Reading of Hegel*, ed. Allan Bloom, trans. James H. Nichols Jr. (Ithaca: Cornell University Press, 1980). All other changes and variant readings have been identified in the notes.

Overall, we have striven for a literal translation, and we have tried whenever possible to render all words and phrases consistently by a single English word or phrase. We have also endeavored to convey a sense of Kojève's style by retaining his sentence structure and punctuation, although we have had to break up or combine sentences in order to render them into proper English. Numbers within square brackets refer to the pagination of the original French text published in 1981 by Gallimard. We have also profited greatly by previous translators of Kojève's works, in particular the work of James H. Nichols Jr., cited above.

Introductory Essay
The Plausibility of the Universal and Homogenous State

Robert Howse and Bryan-Paul Frost

IN THE ENGLISH-SPEAKING WORLD of ideas, to which this translation is directed, Alexandre Kojève is a figure known largely by reputation. The two main sources of this reputation are Kojève's dialogue with Leo Strauss about tyranny and philosophy and, more recently, the adaptation and popularization of Kojève's idea of the "end of history" by Francis Fukuyama.[1] In the dialogue with Strauss, Kojève stated with blunt force, bare of all obfuscating humanist sentimentality, the position of Marxist historicism—violent collective struggle, even periods of brutal dictatorship, are merely necessities of the historical process in its inexorable march toward socialist utopia, which Kojève calls the "universal and homogenous state." Any trans-historical moral judgment of the means or personalities through which this process works itself out is philosophically incoherent. Several decades later, at the moment when history seemed least to be going Kojève's way, as it were—namely, the collapse of Soviet communism and the apparent triumph of the market at the end of the 1980s—Fukuyama, a relatively unknown policy analyst at the time, catapulted himself to global fame by (apparently)[2] turning Kojève's idea on its head—with the collapse of communism, violent political struggle between alternative social visions was at an end, since one vision had now triumphed and need struggle violently no longer, namely the vision of liberal democracy. Of course, as Fukuyama wisely admitted before the war in Yugoslavia in the 1990s, violence would persist in many places and for a long time, but such conflicts simply reflected degrees of backwardness in the evolution toward liberal democracy in particular countries.

In his debate with Kojève about tyranny, Strauss had made two central criticisms of Kojève's idea of the universal and homogenous state. First, it would have to be a tyranny, because centralized rule of the whole world could only be achieved through brutal means. Second, it would not satisfy fundamental human longings, since by Kojève's own definition, in such a state there would no longer be any reason to struggle, or risk one's life, for anything higher or greater than one's own animal existence. Fukuyama saved Kojève from the first criticism by reinterpreting the universal and homogenous state as the American Empire after the death

---

1. Leo Strauss, *On Tyranny*, revised and expanded edition, including the Strauss-Kojève correspondence, ed. Victor Gourevitch and Michael S. Roth (New York: Free Press, 1991); Francis Fukuyama, *The End of History and the Last Man* (New York: Free Press, 1992).
2. Apparently since, as will be discussed *in extenso* in this essay, Kojève's position was in fact that, ultimately, "socialism" would be achieved through the modification and adaptation of capitalism, not its revolutionary downfall in the West.

of communism,[3] but he embraced the latter. In the universal and homogenous state, every citizen would be recognized as free and equal, without need for further violent political struggle; but what if "man's satisfaction, as opposed to his happiness, arose not from the goal itself, but from the struggle and work along the way"?[4] This objection gained credibility from rather famous remarks by Kojève in revised editions of his lectures on Hegel's *Phenomenology of Spirit*, which suggested, by turns, that human beings would either live and play like animals at the end of history or engage in empty exercises of self-overcoming—snobbery, perfection of forms, and so on—which Kojève claimed to have observed in Japan.[5]

Fukuyama's idea of the end of history was based on a transformation or attempted perfection of Kojève's thought as presented in his *Introduction to the Reading of Hegel*, and perhaps even more so, in the dialogue with Strauss concerning tyranny. In this exercise, Fukuyama never attempted to come to grips with the *Outline*, despite its more comprehensive and rigorous treatment of the universal and homogenous state.[6] This has resulted in an impoverishment of the entire debate about the end of history that Fukuyama provoked; for, as the leftist

---

3. Albeit with the constituent parts of that empire retaining the status of independent "statehood."

4. Fukuyama, *End of History*, 312.

5. Alexandre Kojève, *Introduction à la lecture de Hegel*, 2nd edition, ed. Raymond Queneau (Paris: Gallimard, 1968), 436–37.

6. In Fukuyama's defense, one might well point to the fact that Kojève's exchange with Strauss, and his famous footnote to later editions of his Hegel book, are works that were published after the *Outline*, and are therefore more representative of Kojève's fundamental position. In the case of the exchange with Strauss, however, Strauss himself characterized some of the arguments the interlocutors were making as "exoteric." For Strauss, exotericism denotes a public or popular presentation of the truth with the deeper teaching concealed between the lines: see Robert Howse, "Reading Between the Lines: Exotericism, Esotericism, and the Philosophical Rhetoric of Leo Strauss," *Philosophy and Rhetoric* 32 (1999), 60–77. In the shadow of McCarthyism, the exchange between Strauss and Kojève instructed Strauss's American students that the position of Marxism was one worthy of genuine philosophical engagement at the highest level, and that the appropriate response to communist ideas was thought, not suppression of thought, even if Kojève had, in his own thinking, moved beyond the publicly presented position. On Strauss's concern about McCarthyism, see Robert Howse, "From Legitimacy to Dictatorship and Back Again: Leo Strauss's Critique of the Anti-Liberalism of Carl Schmitt," in *Law as Politics: Carl Schmitt's Critique of Liberalism*, ed. David Dyzenhaus (Durham: Duke University Press, 1998), 73–74. With respect to Kojève's footnote to later editions of his *Introduction* concerning the life of posthistorical man, Jacques Derrida's comment that this might not have been intended entirely seriously is worth pondering. Moreover, Derrida points to a sentence in these remarks, uncommented by Fukuyama, that suggests that obligation or duty applies in the posthistorical condition. See Jacques Derrida, *Specters of Marx: The State of the Debt, the Work of Mourning, and the New International*, trans. Peggy Kamuf (New York: Routledge, 1994), 66–75. Yet these speculations are only the beginning point for reflection on the puzzle of the divergence between Kojève's postwar public persona as a Marxist existentialist intellectual and the argument of the *Outline*. Of course, Kojève's *other* postwar public persona was that of a negotiator of international trade and economic integration arrangements, including both the European Community and the GATT; and the argument of the *Outline* is quite consistent with *that* public persona. But for us, the overriding consideration in taking the *Outline* seriously as the possible core of Kojève's thought is very simply that it is the only work that presents in his own name a sustained, comprehensive philosophical argument for the plausibility of the universal and homogenous state.

social critic Perry Anderson notes, the *Outline* reveals a very different Kojèvean agenda, one that is not present in Kojève's exchange with Leo Strauss (and that is obscured in the remarks about posthistorical man that so impressed Fukuyama).[7] The *Outline* presents the universal and homogenous state as something to be achieved, not through tyranny or empire, but through legal integration between states that results in a kind of supranational constitutional order, informed and unified by a single, definitive concept of justice. Far from being beasts, nihilists, or even playful snobs, the inhabitants of this final order will be citizens, workers, and members of families, with reciprocal rights and duties appropriate to these human roles, whose distinctively human needs are met through recognition in work and love in the family. The final order will be the achievement of what one might call the hyper-liberal goal of the full replacement of the rule of men by the rule of law. Indeed, the political and the state in Carl Schmitt's sense will no longer exist—all economic and social relations, even those traditionally thought of as relations between sovereign states, will be ordered juridically. Moreover, the concept of justice on the basis of which this universal juridical order will realize itself will be a synthesis, bringing together elements of the bourgeois justice of the market and elements of socialist egalitarianism.

The *Outline of a Phenomenology of Right*, which Anderson rightly describes as Kojève's richest, if least discussed, book, is indispensable for a full appreciation of the idea of the end of history and its implication for the fate of the human. Can there be a genuine human social order that transcends the nation-state, or does globalization necessarily entail the yielding of the embattled (progressive) state to the (dis)order of the global marketplace? Must world law sacrifice the political to the technocratic? Can or should one throw in one's cards with the nationalist communitarian resistance to the apparent weakening of the nation-state? Or, as Jürgen Habermas has recently argued, should one rather attempt to realize social justice transnationally, on the same territorial scale claimed by markets themselves?[8] For legal and social theory today these are surely central questions, implicating fundamental choices of commitment and strategy. Kojève's idea of the universal and homogenous state as a perfected legal order, and especially the concept of justice animating this state as a synthesis of equality (equal status under the law) and equivalence (reciprocal social and economic benefits and burdens), has the potential to deepen significantly, and perhaps substantially reframe, the central contemporary debates about globalization, law, and the fate of the political.

The Definition of Right

Kojève's claim that the *telos* of right itself is the universal and homogenous state emerges from the "phenomenological" or "behaviorist" definition of

---

7. Perry Anderson, "The Ends of History," in *A Zone of Engagement* (New York: Verso, 1992), 320–21, especially note 102.
8. Jürgen Habermas, "Does Europe Need a Constitution? Response to Dieter Grimm," in *The Inclusion of the Other: Studies in Political Theory* (Cambridge: MIT University Press, 1998), 155–61.

right that he articulates and refines in the opening chapter of the *Outline*. There is right when an impartial and disinterested third, C, intervenes in the interaction between two subjects of right, A and B, to annul an act of one that has suppressed, or purports to suppress, the act of the other. We know that A had a right to do the act in question, and B had a duty to let her do that act without suppressing it, only because the intervention to annul B's act is of a specific character—it is the intervention of one who is "impartial and disinterested" (page 39).[9] The third's intervention is impartial because even if A and B switched places, the third would intervene all the same; and the intervention is disinterested because one third would intervene in the interaction just like any other third, meaning that the third could be "anyone at all" and is therefore intervening from the interest of right alone (page 79ff). The definition claims to be phenomenological or behaviorist in that it does not begin from an attempt to analyze the rights and duties of A and B as *essences*,[10] nor from the *being* of A or B, but rather infers these rights and duties from the manifest behavior, or action in the world, of the third in reaction to the *acts* of A and B themselves. But of course, this phenomenological definition contains, at first glance, one kind of ontological claim, namely concerning the existence of beings who act from an interest of right alone. We can know phenomenologically that human beings accept the authority of the third as juridical because the third *appears* to them to act from the interests of right alone. But as Kojève himself notes, there are theories of right that always posit some other end, whether economic welfare or interest of state, as the real motivation for the intervention of the third.[11] Kojève accepts, with Immanuel Kant, that we cannot know the heart. Thus, in order to establish right as an *authentic,* specific, and autonomous phenomenon, Kojève is compelled to add a further stipulation or condition for the appearance of right—the third must act in conformity with a given concept of justice (page 85). In a world where there are multiple states, this concept of justice will be the concept of justice of the "exclusive juridical group" of the state in question. The act of the third that conforms with this concept can therefore be *deemed* to be "disinterested"—in other words, not motivated by an interest of the third herself in the result of her intervention (or nonintervention, as the case may be) (pages 88–91).

At this point, Kojève's purportedly phenomenological account of right would appear to collapse into a more conventional Marxist account. Right is only a product of disinterested action in the attenuated sense that it is not the interests

---

9. All page references in the text are to the translation in this volume.
10. In this sense, the method that Kojève describes here differs from that which Husserl developed under the name "phenomenology," which involves the intuition or discernment of essences, and which Kojève identifies with Plato rather than Hegel. See Strauss, *On Tyranny*, 256. See also the *Introduction*, 470, where Kojève emphasizes certain commonalities between Hegelian and Husserlian phenomenology, even taking Husserl to task for opposing his method to that of Hegel.
11. And, of course, such accounts have typified Marxist theories of law. See, generally, Christine Sypnowich, *The Concept of Socialist Law* (Oxford: Clarendon Press, 1990).

of the individual lawmaker or adjudicator that are reflected in her actions, but the interests of the ruling class; for is the concept of justice of the "exclusive juridical group" anything other than the interests of the ruling class? Kojève makes matters much more complex by the suggestion that, while in a politically and socially stable state, the "exclusive juridical group" will usually coincide with the "exclusive political group," these are not necessarily identical (page 156). Indeed, should the "exclusive political group" seek to impose a concept of justice at variance with that of the "exclusive juridical group," it would have to resort to brute force; this would ultimately fail, or more precisely, would ultimately provoke a change in the state itself, either revolutionary or evolutionary (page 156ff). Of course, this leads directly to the question of who Kojève might be intending by the notion of the "exclusive juridical group." In the best or ideal case, Kojève suggests that this group would be the one that could give law the authority to demand obedience from others "excluded" from this very group without the exclusive group having to resort to violence.[12] Although much more can be said on this subject, Kojève does seem to reaffirm the distinction between law as legitimate authority and law as the application or vehicle of political force or violence (pages 160–61).[13]

At the same time as asserting the distinction between legal authority and political violence, Kojève insists that right requires or implies the state. For right to be a real, authentic *phenomenon,* manifest in and through real behavior in the world—to be something more or other than the mere Kantian thing-in-itself—the intervention of the third must be irresistible, at least in principle: the third must be *really* capable of annulling B's negation of A's rightful act, and not merely wishing it. Real right therefore implies the existence and effectiveness of police power: only the state's monopoly of violence can guarantee the reality of annulling B's act, as opposed to A's own efforts of resistance, and those of her private friends and allies (page 127). But in a world of many states, each a potential enemy of the other (à la Schmitt), A can escape the intervention of the third, C, by leaving her own state for another. Right is real, therefore, only inasmuch as A remains a citizen of a given state, the state in which the third is a member of the "exclusive juridical group." But even if right is real in this case, it is not fully *actual,* since as a matter of right the third cannot compel the intervention once A is outside the state. She could make it irresistible, but without right, as for example through military action on the territory of the other state (the abduction of Adolf Eichmann would be an example); or she could exhort or wish that the other state make her inter-

---

12. Similarly, the exclusive political group would be that group that could compel obedience from those "excluded" from this group in order to govern the state in an authoritative manner. Kojève calls this exclusive group that of the "governors," as opposed to the excluded group, the "governed" (pages 134–36).

13. Compare, on the Right, Carl Schmitt, *The Concept of the Political,* trans. George Schwab (New Brunswick, N.J.: Rutgers University Press, 1976), and on the Left, Walter Benjamin, "Critique of Violence," in *Selected Writings: Volume I 1913–1926* (Harvard: Harvard University Press, 1996), 236–52.

vention irresistible, or even seek this result, for example through extradition treaties or conventions on recognition of legal judgments. But, ultimately, this is contingent upon the political decision of the other state—it cannot follow necessarily from the juridical character itself of the third's intervention. In this sense, we can see how right is able to actualize itself fully only in the universal (and homogenous) state, one that encompasses the territory of the entire globe: only in such a state will the actual irresistibility of the third's intervention follow *necessarily* from the character of that intervention as right (page 126).

But this is not all. As long as C applies the concept of justice specific to the exclusive juridical class of a particular state, the intervention of the third will be disinterested only in the attenuated sense discussed above—most importantly, it will not appear simply disinterested either to those excluded from the exclusive juridical class in her own state or to the exclusive juridical classes of other states. The achievement of the universal and homogenous state requires, in fact almost by definition, the triumph of a single concept of justice (page 94). Now Kojève admits that this has not yet happened; but he also accepts, with Hegel, that history has ended, in the specific sense that collective violent struggle is no longer necessary to establish any decisive principle of the ultimate and final human social order. How then do we get from the point where history is in principle complete (where there is no new idea or concept left to struggle for) to the universal and homogenous state that fully realizes the end of history (where absolute *droit* will actually reign on earth)?

From the End of History to the End State

In order to understand the solution proposed by Kojève—to understand how, dynamically, the posthistorical universal and homogenous state emerges from the point where history is in principle complete (even some centuries later!)— we must first of all explore a seeming *paradox* in the very idea of the universal and homogenous state as Kojève presents it. As we have seen, right needs the state in order to realize itself through the irresistibility of the third's intervention; but this irresistibility only becomes fully actual once the state extends to the entire globe. At the same time, Kojève accepts the definition of the state and the political offered by Carl Schmitt: the state's very existence, and that of the political, implies the existence of *other* territorial states who are mutual enemies (in the sense that their relations can always become those of adversaries struggling to the death) as well as the internal political division between the governors and those governed (page 134ff).

How can Kojève build the universal and homogenous state beginning from this Schmittean conception of the political? Here at the outset one should note an important disagreement between Schmitt and Kojève: for Schmitt, the only really meaningful internal divisions in the state are based upon the recognition of the state's *external* enemies. All other divisions are pseudo-political products of bourgeois "pluralism." For Kojève, the socialist differences or divisions of class have at least a semiautonomous political significance; the determination of who is in or who is out of the "exclusive political or juridical group" within the state is not merely a function of its external enemies (pages 134–35).[14] For Kojève, a merely universal state could nevertheless preserve the fundamental friend-enemy character of the political by *internalizing* the friend-enemy struggle. In this case, however, violent class struggle (albeit within a *universal* state) would still seem necessary before arriving at the posthistorical condition. Indeed, such a state could lose its universal character: the excluded class, if it achieved sufficient military and economic power, could not be stopped from claiming a part of the globe as its "own" territory. In other words, this class could become the "exclusive" political class of that territory and thereby found a new state, robbing the hitherto "universal" state of its "universality."

This leads to the question of how the posthistorical condition can be achieved without necessitating further violent collective struggle, and if so, how this condition can be described as a state. According to Kojève, what has been settled about justice with the end of history is that any concept of justice adequate to the state and the subpolitical societies within it (above all, economic society and familial society), must be a *synthesis* of equality (formal equality in entitlement) and equivalence (reciprocity of rights and duties, of contribution to society and benefit to oneself) (page 268). These categories—(aristocratic) equality and (bourgeois) equivalence—emerge from the Master-Slave dialectic itself and are in fact needed to make sense of its outcome (page 243ff). After the French Revolution and Napoleon, it has been decisively established that no human social order that allows for human satisfaction can be simply based on static equality between Masters, without taking into account equivalence of rights and duties, benefits and burdens. And as Napoleon's building of the state upon the foundations of the revolutionary justice of (bourgeois) equivalence shows, the modern state itself can also not do without some elements of aristocratic equality—the equal status of all citizens before the law (for Kojève, this idea of equality is aristocratic in its root, originating in the sameness in status of Masters, who recognize each other as equally Masters) (page 266). But, so far, no stable synthesis has yet been achieved of these two elements within any state. Once such a synthesis were achieved it would represent the final form of the concept of justice—there could be no opposition based in *right* to an intervention of a third, anywhere on earth, based on this concept of justice. The third can now *really* be anyone at all, that is, someone whose act is unqualifiedly impartial and disinterested, because it is seen to conform to this universally accepted concept of justice. Law would have the perfected character of state law, in being irresistible everywhere, but there would be no political in the Schmittean sense—in other words, no *Schmittean* state. The achievement of the *Rechtsstaat*, contra Hegel, implies the end of the (national) state (page 126).

---

14. Kojève does suggest, however, that the existence of foreign enemies first causes a state to bifurcate internally and to create the division between governors and the governed (page 158).

More particularly, where the third can be anyone at all, the third can intervene in a disinterested and impartial manner between those entities that have hitherto been called states. Relations between "states" are no longer a matter of politics in the shadow of war, but are ordered juridically. As Kojève suggests, traditional international law could not actualize itself as *right* as long as such law remained at the level of an intervention of a third state in the form of a diplomatic compromise of the conflict between the other two: since every state is at least potentially an enemy of every other, such intervention could never be disinterested in the sense required by right (page 316ff). But Kojève also notes that international law is no longer simply a product of states; it is also in part a product of expert jurists and publicists (*opinio juris*). Now, once the third can be anyone at all, the third can settle by right (at least in principle) any conflict between states; but then, these states are no longer sovereign and, in the Schmittean sense, therefore no longer states (pages 323–25).

The universal and homogenous state *is* sovereign, but only in the sense that the intervention of the third is irresistible throughout, at least in principle (there are always, as Kojève acknowledges, outlaws who will elude the police in practice, even within a traditional state). This means that in the universal and homogenous state it is the third who is sovereign—it is the third who "decides" in the Schmittean sense. There is no particular group of individuals whose relations with some other group cannot be determined by right, and so *must* be settled by (potentially) violent political struggle (pages 91–92). We can see why the universal and homogenous state is an end state, in fact, by imagining the following scenario: suppose some group of individuals decides to "secede," that is, to assert their own "sovereignty," refusing the intervention of the third as the decisive settlement of their relations with others. These individuals would simply be common criminals, or outlaws (a gang or mob, whose territory is no different from a biker clubhouse): having no alternative concept of justice to which they could appeal in establishing an "independent" state, it would be a philosophically uninteresting empirical question as to when and to what extent, in practice, the police forces of the universal and homogenous state could suppress the resistance of these individuals to the intervention of the third.

If it is the third who is sovereign, in the sense that the third is "she who decides" in the universal and homogenous state, it is not the individual in question who is sovereign, but the third acting in her capacity as third by applying the single, universal concept of justice, and therefore appearing to act impartially and disinterestedly. Schmitt's attack on liberal constitutionalism, it will be recalled, was aimed at showing the personalistic character of all rule, despite the liberal illusion or myth of the rule of "law." Schmitt sought to save the state as sovereign in the strong sense from the liberal dilution of sovereignty through constitutionalism. Kojève shows how liberal constitutionalism cannot fulfill itself within a state, agreeing with Schmitt that as long as the state is sovereign in his sense, constituted by relations of enmity to other states, there will be a personalistic dimension to all even apparently legal rule, the third not being "disinterested" simply (page 88). But now Kojève turns Schmitt on his head—the realization of the liberal constitutionalist idea of completely depersonalized rule, the rule of right simply and not of "men," requires the project of an effective transnational, transpolitical human social order, where the third can be anyone at all (pages 91–92). This, ironically, is a project even more offensive to Schmitt's sensibilities than the liberal (nation)-state, but one that he cannot *speak* against; since Schmitt presents the friend-enemy distinction as the *ground* of his attack against liberal constitutionalism, how can he say anything against the disappearance of the ground itself?[15]

In the *Outline*, this turning upside down of Schmitt becomes most evident in the section on public law. Kojève begins on an apparently Schmittean note—*contra* liberalism, there is nothing juridical about relations between the individual citizen and the state. No impartial and disinterested third exists, since in these relations the state is necessarily a party, and thus cannot act also as third (page 297). As for the constitution, it is nothing other than a description of how the state (or the exclusive political class of the state) organizes itself. It has nothing to do with right, and everything to do with what is best for the self-preservation of the state. Indeed, in Schmittean fashion, Kojève largely dismisses the notion of the separation of powers as an illusion of liberalism (pages 85–87, 327–28).

However, as Kojève further notes, the state acts on its citizens through civil servants. But Kojève ultimately draws opposite conclusions than those of Schmitt from this conception of the state as only able to act through others, who are persons. The very *autonomy* of the state requires that these others (legislators, bureaucrats, and so on) act as its mere agents, as "civil servants," and not as private individuals with interests of their own separate from those of the state. Thus, however many or few the governors are, in their relations with citizens *within* the state, they are mere civil servants or functionaries of the state they have created (the description of which is the constitution). As long as the civil servants act as civil servants on others within the state as citizens—as long as they do not exercise the power conferred on them as agents of the state for private purposes and over others taken as private individuals—there can be no right governing the relationship between the state or its civil servants and the individual citizen: the state would be acting as party and therefore cannot be the third required for juridical intervention in the relations in question (pages

---

15. Schmitt, *Concept of the Political*, 57–58. In fact, the response Schmitt gives seems rather polemical. He asks: "The acute question to pose is upon whom will fall the frightening power implied in a world-embracing economic and technical organization. This question can by no means be dismissed in the belief that everything would then function automatically, that things would administer themselves, and that a government by people over people would be superfluous because human beings would then be absolutely free. For what would they be free? This can be answered by optimistic or pessimistic conjectures, all of which finally lead to an anthropological profession of faith." On the gap here in Schmitt's case against liberalism, see Robert Howse, "From Legitimacy to Dictatorship and Back Again," 66–67. As we shall argue later in this essay, Kojève's philosophical answer to this rhetorical question is to be found in the account of recognition in the *Outline*.

136, 333). But should the civil servant not be acting in her capacity as agent of the state, but from private interests, the state *can* be a third: in effect, the conflict is not between the state and the citizen, but between two private individuals. The civil servant is an "impostor," purporting to act on behalf of the state when in fact she is acting for her own personal advantage (pages 337–38). Now, how is it possible to *know* whether, in a given case, a civil servant is acting in her official capacity or as an "impostor"? Since one cannot, on the phenomenological approach adopted by Kojève, determine this by insight into the heart of the civil servant, one must determine it by what is manifest externally—and here the constitution does become of central importance to right. Phenomenologically, the civil servant is acting in her official capacity when her action conforms to the description of the state in the constitution (page 339).

This is a remarkable intellectual move, since Kojève would appear to have reestablished the idea of constitutionalism and the rule of law on the basis of the very premises of Schmitt's polemic against them. Kojève's argument is all the more remarkable in that it reintroduces something of the classical understanding of legitimacy in order to defend constitutionalism against the Schmittean attack on liberalism. Thus, on Kojève's view, who the exclusive political group is (whether one, few, or many) does not matter as such from the perspective of legitimacy, but rather whether the members of that group are perceived as acting in the interest of the whole (the state) or self-interestedly (pages 337–38). Yet, of course, Kojève differs from the classics in insisting, "phenomenologically," that this question can only be answered through judging the behavior of the governors as civil servants against a fixed description of the state in constitutional rules, and not through an investigation of the *character* of the governors. At the same time, as noted earlier in this essay, Kojève raises the possibility that a constitution may itself be considered, in some circumstances, unjust, as in the case where the exclusive juridical group does not coincide with the exclusive political group. In such a case, one possible outcome is revolution, but revolution is not the only possible outcome. It could be that the "juridical group can 'educate' the political group and induce it to accept the *Droit* appropriate to the juridical group" (page 157). This account of the possibility of "education" of the political group comes closer to the spirit of the Nocturnal Council in Plato's *Laws* than any other account in modernity of the relationship between law and legitimacy; it certainly differs from the first impression of bold or shocking indifference to legitimacy in the public, "exoteric" presentation of the philosopher as helper-adviser to the tyrant in Kojève's debate with Strauss on tyranny.[16]

Kojève's reformulation of constitutionalism is crucial to understanding his articulation of the dynamics by which the universal and homogenous state will tend to realize itself. As Kojève suggests, the unification of private law among different states is not sufficient to bring into being the universal and homogenous state, even when animated by agreement on a single concept of justice, as

---

16. See page 2, note 6, and accompanying text above.

long as the state itself, and its relation to the citizens, is determined purely polit-ically or nonjuridically, by the friend-enemy distinction; for it is the individual state that determines, through its constitution, what matters concern the private "status" of the individual, and which her status as "citizen" (pages 343–44). For instance, as Kojève explicitly argues, the practices we know as criminal law are in some cases the realization of penal right, but in others represent purely political acts, concerned with the self-preservation of the state. If states cannot agree on the division between the juridical and the political, then a state in which a given practice is understood as political would not enforce on its territory a judgment that emanates from a state where the practice in question is a matter of right. This implies that some genuinely juridical judgments will be denied irresistible force unless *public* law can also be harmonized.[17]

But all genuine acts of the state, as opposed to acts of impostors purporting to act on behalf of the state, are either juridical (the intervention of the third) or political (the relation of state to citizen as described in the constitution). Thus, if there can be universal agreement on the proper sphere of the juridical (which is in principle certainly possible if a there were a single concept of justice), then there must be, by implication, agreement on what remains properly "political" as well. This makes a supranational *constitution* possible, which would define whether any given civil servant acts genuinely for the state or as an "impostor." But, in the end, this constitution will make the (Schmittean) political itself disappear—since there is nothing now that cannot be settled through the intervention of a third in accordance with the definitive concept of justice. With a supranational constitution, agreement about the "political" really means the end of the political—the elimination of the friend-enemy struggle between and within sovereign states (page 325).

As was early observed among jurists by Eric Stein,[18] this is precisely the trajectory of the European Union, to which Kojève dedicated a significant part of his life after World War II. The Union began as a set of treaties, or to use Kojèvean language, at most as right in potentiality, since there was no irresistible intervention of the third, it being a case of a mere armistice between enemies in purely political relation to one another.[19] However, as the jurisprudence of the European Community evolved, the European Court of Justice came to understand the treaties as containing legally enforceable rights and obligations against member states; in other words, the Court invalidates any purported state act that does not conform to the specifics of the constitutional framework. Thus, no member state is any longer completely sovereign, and European law is something more than international law. This displays exactly the logical sequence proposed by Kojève: *political* unification occurs through the creation

---

17. And, in fact, it is a traditional rule of private international law that foreign penal and taxation judgments are not recognized or enforced.
18. "Lawyers, Judges, and the Making of a Transnational Constitution," *American Journal of International Law* 75 (1981), 1–27.
19. A notion well expressed in the slogan that the member states are the "*Herren der Vertrage* [lords of the compact]."

of a *juridical* union (pages 326–27). One can thus understand why, in the decision over the ratification of the Maastricht Treaty, the German Constitutional Court balked at the explicit endorsement of this logic. The Court, as Joseph Weiler has suggested, was in the grip of Schmittean thinking: to admit that the last word on the legality of acts of the German state is to be had by the European third is to admit that the (Schmittean) state no longer exists in Europe.[20]

In understanding the end of classic state sovereignty as the result of constitutionalization, and not vice versa, Kojève also closed a gap, or solved a dilemma, in Kant's account of "perpetual peace." The dilemma of perpetual peace is as follows: if a permanent federation were achieved, then the state would no longer need to worry about surrendering its sovereignty because it would have nothing to fear for its security from other "states"; but until such a point, what state would voluntarily renounce sovereignty permanently in the hopes that other states would forever join it in such a union? Thus, for Kant, the leap from treaty law, where states remain "*Herren der Vertrage,*" to federal union could only be imagined as a matter of faith or hope.[21] But, as we have seen, for Kojève, at a certain point the logic of juridical unification leads to a common public law, and therewith the constitutional basis for a federation in which states are no longer sovereign. Moreover, this unification and federalization, while beginning with a limited subset of states, tends toward universalization.[22]

Writing to Leo Strauss over a decade after drafting the *Outline*, Kojève would be able to make the meaning even more concrete: "If the Westerners remain capitalist (that is to say, also nationalist), they will be defeated by Russia, and *that* is how the End-State will come about. If however, they 'integrate' their economies and policies (they are on the way to doing so), then *they* can defeat Russia. And *that* is how the End-State will be reached (the *same* universal and homogenous State)."[23] The European Community was the universal and homogenous state *en herbe.* But Kojève's reference to the abandonment of "capitalism" (by which he means nineteenth-century *laissez-faire* capitalism)[24] reminds us that it is not a mere *harmonization* of positive right that leads to the

---

20. Joseph H. H. Weiler, "The State '*Uber Alles*': Demos, Telos and the German Maastricht Decision," in *Festschrift für Ulrich Everline,* ed. Ole Due et al. (Baden-Baden: Nomos Verlagsgesellschaft, 1995), 1651–88.
21. See a recent and very thoughtful essay by Habermas on Kant's idea of "perpetual peace" and the Schmittean challenge to it: "Kant's Idea of Perpetual Peace: At Two Hundred Years' Historical Remove," in *The Inclusion of the Other: Studies in Political Theory* (Cambridge: MIT University Press, 1998), 165–201.
22. The crucial passage is as follows: the state "tends to create a *Federation* of States or a federal State . . . having for a base and for a result the existence of a unique *Droit,* common to all the federated States, and implying—in its 'public *Droit*' aspect—an element of 'federal *Droit,*' regulating the relations of the federated States among themselves, [and] in particular the federal organization of justice" (page 327).
23. Strauss, *On Tyranny,* 256, and see the text of note 6, page 2 above.
24. See particularly Kojève's Dusseldorf lecture, "Kolonialismus in europäischer Sicht [Colonialism in European Perspective]," in *Schmittiana,* Band VI, ed. Dr. Piet Tommissen (Berlin: Duncker & Humblot, 1998), 126–40.

universal and homogenous state, but a unification made possible by agreement on a particular concept of justice—the synthesis of equality and equivalence in (socialist) equity. It is through the realization of this concept of justice that the universal and homogenous state is able to provide for the human satisfaction of all its citizens (page 479).

Mastery, Slavery, and the Family

To understand how Kojève is able to make this claim on behalf of the universal and homogenous state, we have to consider what equality, equivalence, and their synthesis in equity actually mean. But since these terms only gain their meaning in and through social relations—they have no transcendent but only a social-anthropological meaning—we first need to examine Kojève's understanding of man as a social being. According to Kojève, human beings live their lives and seek to fulfill themselves as members of various sub- or transpolitical societies, of which the most important (at least for understanding the potential of the universal and homogenous state) appear to be familial and economic society. Right is the application by the third of a given principle of justice to relations within these various societies, including the relationship of the individual to the society in question as a whole (page 167). The state comes into the picture as the guarantor of the irresistibility of the third's intervention; and yet, as we have already seen, the state is also the product of a group of political "friends" who unite against "enemies," this exclusive "political group" making nonjuridical demands on the citizens for the sake of the state (page 129). But there is no foundation in any permanent human need for the opposition of collectivities (i.e., the friend-enemy struggle that constitutes, for Schmitt, the political); the uniting of individuals against one another, on the purported grounds of "race," "language," and so on, is purely conventional, a function of the inability to achieve so far the universal and homogenous state. (Indeed, in a certain way, Schmitt himself prepared this anti-Schmittean conclusion by emphasizing that the friend-enemy distinction was defined existentially and could be based on any kind of opposition at all.)

Thus, according to Kojève, while man first humanizes himself through violent struggle and, for the first time, seeks recognition in this way, the permanent human need thus manifested and established is not the need for *struggle* but the need for *recognition* (pages 211–12). This is one of the most important, but least understood, assumptions in Kojève's argument for the universal and homogenous state. It has been obscured by commentators such as Fukuyama and Shadia B. Drury, who appear to identify the human, as understood by Kojève, with the struggle itself. As well, the appropriation of the Hegelian language of recognition to characterize the goal of groups, such as ethnic groups, in struggling for political status (most obviously by Charles Taylor), makes it more difficult to appreciate that for Kojève the recognition that finally satisfies human beings is neither recognition of a collective identity nor achieved *politically*.[25] It is achieved juridically, when the state loses its political character and simply becomes the universal guarantor of right based on a definitive concept of justice. Once so guaranteed, right can assure the recognition of the individual need for universal human satisfaction (pages 474–79).

Marx, of course, had predicted the withering away not only of the state, but also of law in the posthistorical condition: the coordination of production in order to provide for universal satisfaction of human needs would become a purely technical problem.[26] While Kojève preserves right, he clearly thinks that the process of collective decision-making entailed in *politics,* as distinguished from the administration of justice, is not based in any permanent human need: once all relations are determined by justice, political struggle is no longer necessary or possible (page 94). For those on the Left who are radical democrats this will be hard to swallow—yet it is a necessary implication of the wish for the perfect realization of an absolute, definitive concept of justice. The postmodernist and critical turns in Left thought indicate a keen awareness of the problem—one defends the contestability of the terms of social life against the (capitalist) consensus about (market) justice, and one speaks of plasticity, resistance, and opposition to false necessity. One increasingly sounds as if democratic contestability and political struggle in themselves are the human goods worth fighting for—which goes far toward explaining the otherwise bizarre interest in Carl Schmitt by the contemporary Left.[27]

How could Kojève (with Hegel) see struggle as fundamental to the emergence of the human, and yet propose an end state where human satisfaction would actually be achieved *after* the definitive abolition of such struggle? In the *Outline,* Kojève actually provides a clearer and richer account of the Master-Slave dialectic than in his *Introduction;* and this account, when read carefully, allows us to see exactly the place of struggle in the human. Man becomes human by negating his animal existence. In risking his animal existence in the struggle the Master seeks to assert, and achieve recognition of, his humanity. He does not seek mastery per se, but rather recognition. He only becomes Master because of the existential attitude of the opponent in the struggle, who decides to renounce the struggle to the death, and put himself at the mercy of the Master (page 212). There are no natural Masters or Slaves—in fact, the struggle itself, or rather its human meaning for justice, presupposes, in the manner of Thomas Hobbes, that men are equal in the sense of having roughly equal capacities to defend their lives in physical struggle with other men (pages 219–20). The Master does not kill his opponent: to do so would be self-destructive with respect to his goal of recognition. He spares the opponent's life in return for the opponent offering his labor to the Master. But recognition from the Slave is not humanly satisfying to the Master because it cannot

25. See Fukuyama, *End of History,* 312; Shadia B. Drury, *Alexandre Kojève: The Roots of Postmodern Politics* (New York: St. Martin's Press, 1994), 17–78; and Charles Taylor, "The Politics of Recognition," in *Multiculturalism and "The Politics of Recognition,"* ed. Amy Gutmann (Princeton: Princeton University Press, 1994), 25–73.
26. Sypnowich, *The Concept of Socialist Law,* 1–2.
27. See Chantal Mouffe, *The Return of the Political* (London: Verso, 1993).

be mutual—the Master cannot recognize the Slave as human, but only as a tool or means to his own needs, and therefore he is unable to satisfy the need to be recognized by one whom he can recognize in turn (pages 212–13). But through work—initially for the Master—the Slave finds a way to become human himself, but without risk of life in struggle; he negates animal existence through the mastery of nature itself that is entailed in work (pages 431–33). In renouncing the struggle, the Slave gives up his claim to be considered the equal of the Master, who recognizes as equal only other Masters who themselves have been prepared to fight the struggle to the end. However, from the Slave's point of view there is *equivalence*—a kind of contractual justice—in the exchange of the Slave's work for his life. This equivalence cannot, however, be recognized as justice by the aristocratic Society of Masters; for recognizing the Slave's work as human, as the product of a bargain (which *implies* a kind of equality), would undermine the very principle of aristocratic Society—the right only of Masters to human recognition (pages 223–24). The struggle thereby engendered results that allows the establishment of equivalence as a genuine principle of justice, and ultimately the synthesis of the justice of equivalence and that of equality in socialist equity, in what Kojève calls the justice of the citizen (page 224).

Therefore, it is because the primordial struggle leads to the possibility of recognized humanity through work that it provides the means of human satisfaction. Such recognition is based on the justice of equivalence but implies equality, since in a crucial sense to recognize someone as *human,* even on the basis of equivalence, is to recognize him as equal (the Slave is unequal to the Master because of his nonrecognized humanity). Because work can lead to a recognition that is mutual and universal, it is, in comparison to struggle and mastery themselves, a more adequate path to human satisfaction. In the posthistorical condition of the universal and homogenous state, men will reasonably want to work, but will not want or need to struggle: for the desire to work is not limited by the need to preserve one's life; work also creates new needs (pages 433, 477).[28]

Kojève makes this picture of human satisfaction even richer in his presentation of the family. According to Kojève, man needs not only to be recognized

---

28. In his Dusseldorf lecture, Kojève will note that it is in the first place because some have continued to work long after even their most extreme material desires were satisfied, namely the capitalists, that productivity gains have been realized through technological innovation, such that—in principle—the basic animal needs of everyone in society can be satisfied through work, which was the original objective, as Kojève recalls, of Marxian *communism.* For Kojève, it is the bourgeoisie that is the real revolutionary class, not the proletariat, for it is the bourgeoisie that demands to be recognized as human on account of its work, and does not merely stake a claim that work should entitle it to the satisfaction of material, animal needs. But work as well gives rise to new and greater material desires, as the possibilities of exchange are realized through recognition of the justice of equivalence (market justice). As will be discussed shortly, this will generate new inequalities that can only be resolved through new syntheses of equality and equivalence. But it is through this very process—that looks like the trajectory of social democracy and certainly not at all like the revolutionary process imagined by most Marxian socialists—that progress toward socialist equity occurs.

for his action, but to be loved for what he *is*. This second need is connected in a particular way to man's consciousness of his finitude, his mortality; he seeks to be loved, to *be*, past his death as an animal being. Thus, in the family, propagation is not simply the product of the animal, but also a distinctive human need (pages 408–13). Humanization through the family is in the first instance a sort of conquest or overcoming of man's brute or animal sexuality. Thus, while humanization through work entails mastery or domination of nonhuman nature, humanization in the family involves man restraining himself: indeed, human education within the family comes to light in the first instance as the teaching of taboos or limits (pages 403–4).[29] Here we are farthest from the image of wild licentiousness and full liberation of brute desire presented in Drury's caricature of Kojève, and far also from the macho view of real humanity as violent struggle in Fukuyama's revival of Kojève.[30] Indeed, how without self-restraint would recognition through justice and right be possible? Absent an element of self-constraint or self-overcoming, it is not easily imaginable that men would submit their conflicts to the intervention of a third, whose authority is recognized, rather than reverting to violent struggle. In fact, this restraint is already revealed or manifest in the willingness of Masters to apply justice among themselves, rather than simply continuing to struggle to the death; and it is this which is the origin, according to Kojève, of the right of (equal) property in aristocratic society (pages 245–49).

In a crucial passage Kojève in fact recognizes that the state has an interest, from the perspective of citizenship, in the education of children; but the borderline between the family, the state, and economic society is hard to draw, especially with respect to the education of children (pages 425–26). Because the family responds to a distinctive human need, namely to be loved for who one *is* (in principle forever), Kojève rejects any solution that does not give the family an important measure of autonomy in the education of children. But pedagogical authority within the family must respect the concept of justice that animates right in the state, and thus in the universal and homogenous state, the synthesis of equality and equivalence in equity. Thus, the members of the family can have different rights and duties provided both that these are equivalent and that they do not violate the element of equality in the synthesis—that is, the differentiation of rights and duties must be consistent with the recognition of each member of the family as equal in their *humanity* (pages 415, 424). Thus, Kojève's conception of the family is based on sexual equality and would not permit any differentiation of roles that is inconsistent with the recognition

---

29. One can understand the deeper disagreement between Strauss and Kojève if one considers that Kojève believed that these taboos or limits would not depend on the sacred, or piety, but that they would continue to be taught, on a purely human basis, in a fully atheistic society; Strauss, *On Tyranny*, 275, emphatically doubted, however, whether the socialization in question could occur without religion.

30. In particular, see Drury, *Alexandre Kojève*, 17–78, as well as Fukuyama's chapter "Men without Chests," 300–312, where he seems to lament that there is nothing after history for which it is worth fighting to the death.

of women as equal in their *humanity* to men. As Kojève emphasizes, sexual inequality persists as long as humanity is established only through violent struggle between males and the work of the (male) slave; once humanization occurs through the family itself, the equal humanity of men and women is established (pages 402n96).

Now that we have understood Kojève's account of human needs, and their origin in the struggle, only two more crucial steps remain in tracing the path to the universal and homogenous state. The first, already mentioned in the preceding discussion on the family, is how the dynamic relationship of equality and equivalence tends toward a synthesis in equity. The second is how a concept of justice that is a *stable* synthesis of these two elements can become *universal*, given that, hitherto, every such synthesis has not been stable and has produced a concept of justice that pertains to a given state.

On Kojève's phenomenological approach, which rejects natural right or natural law, one cannot articulate ahead of time, as it were, the synthesis of equality and equivalence that is capable of becoming stable and universal. Thus, it is not a sign of the incompleteness of the *Outline* that it fails to provide the details of such a synthesis or a code for the positive right of the universal and homogenous state; rather, it only makes clear certain possibilities and logical necessities implicit in the definition of right itself and its historical evolution.[31] Indeed, the description of the work in the title as an "*Outline*" (*Esquisse*) does not reflect the state of the manuscript but the philosophical impossibility of a definitive, complete phenomenology of right before the positive right of the universal and homogenous state manifests itself (page 268).

But once again, given that no advance blueprint is available of the positive right that emerges as the final synthesis of equality and equivalence, and given that one begins only from different national systems of positive *droit*, how can we imagine that such a final, universal concept could be arrived at? Almost by definition, the concept could not be inferred from the positive right of any particular existing state. Now if Kojève does not have an adequate account of how, through human action in the phenomenological world, the concept of justice can be arrived at as absolute, the *Outline* would have to be considered as philosophically inadequate on its own terms. One possibility is, of course, that through conquest a single state would be able to impose its own positive *droit* everywhere. But this possibility raises several problems, given the overall structure of Kojève's argument. One problem is connected with Kojève's insistence on the end of history thesis of Hegel. How can history be over if the definitive concept of justice remains to be resolved by violent struggle? And why would such a resolution be permanent or stable? If some group or class of men within the empire preferred the positive *droit* that predated imperial conquest, what would there be to stop them in seceding and (re-) creating a state based on that

---

31. Thus, there is much exaggeration, and some distortion as well, in Perry Anderson's suggestion (*A Zone of Engagement*, 321) that "The political conclusion of the book is in effect a set of proposals for the civil code of the universal and homogenous state."

droit? One could therefore envisage, not a stable and permanent universal and homogenous state, but rather the normal historical cycles of imperial action and nationalistic reaction.

Now we have already suggested that Kojève is successful at showing how a universal and homogenous state could be a *Rechtsstaat*—namely, through transnational constitutionalism, which overcomes the limits of traditional international law as a form of supranational juridical order. The further question is how this can, or must, come about, taking as a *point de depart* a world of nation-states, each with its own national positive *droit*, other than through the uncertain and tenuous route of conquest.

The answers depend on Kojève's understanding of man's satisfaction as based in his membership in, above all, economic society and familial society. Much of right is preoccupied with the ordering of man's relations within and with these societies. But neither of these societies is intrinsically co-extensive with the state—they can be subpolitical or, more importantly, transpolitical (pages 133–34). For right to actualize itself, it must be capable of ordering all relations within these societies; but, as well, for right to actualize itself, the intervention of the third must be irresistible. Now what happens when A and B interact as members of the same (transnational) economic society, but are members of different states? It is, first of all, not obvious whether the third of A's nationality or B's should intervene in the interaction. Second, whichever the third is that intervenes, her intervention will not be irresistible with respect to one or the other of the litigants. One kind of (unsatisfactory) answer is traditional comity—one state, as a courtesy or a political act about which there is nothing juridical, yields to the other, either accepting the application of the other state's right to its own national, or rendering the intervention of the other state's third irresistible on its territory. But because the recognition is political, the recognition of another sovereign as equal, it cannot really bring about what Kojève calls juridical union (page 326).

Juridical Unification through Mutual Recognition of National Laws

What, however, if such recognition could be juridical and not political? What if there were a process by which, in order to settle precisely those situations where the relations of A and B in a given society span more than one state, the third in one state recognized the right of the other state as equivalent to its own? Such a phenomenon could indeed justify Kojève's claim that right's very tendency to actualize itself, in regulating relations between members of different states who are members of the same transpolitical society, can lead to a juridical union.

How this is possible has now been described in the work of two scholars of our own generation, Anne-Marie Slaughter and Kalypso Nicolaidis. Slaughter has described how judicial cooperation across national boundaries has become a widespread and often successful solution to the problems of conflicts of national laws created by globalization. Slaughter has the central insight that, while such cooperation might have always occurred, when states now recognize foreign judgments, what judges are doing is recognizing judges in other states as *like them*—as acting as authentic thirds, to use Kojèvean language. However, Slaughter also observes that such cooperation occurs most intensely and adequately among liberal nations; with respect to other nations, recourse to recognition of political sovereignty remains the rule.[32] One could thus say that there is a relationship of recognition between thirds of different states: they recognize that the concept of justice underlying the right of the different states is the same or tends to be the same, even if positive right remains apparently different. However, the result of this recognition is that thirds end up applying (and thereby developing) the positive right of other states (strictly possible because of conscious, or implicit, recognition of a similar concept of justice); and in the end, one can imagine that differences in positive right due to purely idiosyncratic features of each national culture tend to erode and a single positive right emerges, if enough of these situations where A and B are from different states present themselves. Now this does not mean that there is a single positive *law;* there are differences in law (detailed legal rules) that are due to different physical or other nonjuridical conditions in different places (heating and insulation standards for housing will not be the same in the north as in the tropics). But there will be a single positive *right,* since the remaining differences between national *laws* will be understood as unrelated to differing (national) positive *droits,* and thus as having nothing to do with right in the strict sense (page 327).

One might say that from the point of view of understanding the concrete possibility of the creation of a juridical union, there is one very severe constraint in Slaughter's idea, at least from the socialist perspective of Kojève. The dynamic just described seems to apply forcefully to law (such as basic contract and tort law) that is to a large extent evolved through judicial decision (in common law countries) and elsewhere through codes that are as much the work of jurists as of politicians. But (socialist) justice as a synthesis of equality and equivalence also certainly implies redistributive and regulatory measures (consumer protection law, labor law, and so on). For Kojève, the third is not just the judge, but also the legislator and the police. And one would think that, since legislation and regulation is (apparently, if only apparently) more directly political than juridical, this might constrain juridical recognition of thirds to the judicial cooperation emphasized by Slaughter. Kalypso Nicolaidis has, however, developed a theory of recognition of legislation and regulations among different states.[33] Unlike the traditional understanding of this practice, as a purely political contract or treaty that *respects* sovereignty, Nicolaidis has sought to explain mutual recognition as based on trust between the regulators, that is, the legislators or civil servants of different states, whom Kojève would likely describe as the exclu-

---

32. Anne-Marie Slaughter, "International Law in a World of Liberal States," *European Journal of International Law* 6 (1995), 503.
33. "Mutual Recognition of Regulatory Regimes," in OECD, *Regulatory Reform and International Market Openness* (Paris: OECD, 1996), 171–203. Professor Nicolaidis has stated in conversation that she undertook her studies of the phenomenon of mutual recognition of law and regulations in awareness of Kojève's understanding of Hegelian recognition.

sive juridical class broadly understood. Such mutual recognition is possible precisely because the exclusive juridical class of each state can be confident that differences in positive laws and regulations do not matter—which is the more or less conscious recognition that these differences do not emanate from different concepts of justice between the states in question.

The possibility of juridical recognition of laws between states that still remain Schmittean states is in fact prepared by Kojève's interpretation of public law, as discussed earlier in this essay. Schmitt admitted that enmity among states was not *personal;* and Kojève's account of public law stresses that the state only acts through its civil servants. While these are usually part of the exclusive political class, which is in a political relation of enmity to the political class of the other states, precisely because (pro Schmitt) this enmity is not personal hatred, the actual *persons* in question, when acting as civil servants on behalf of the state (and not as its exclusive political class as such), need not be in a relation of enmity with each other. In cooperating in cases of transnational regulatory impacts, civil servants of different states recognize each other as civil servants and indeed, juridically, as legislative thirds; and for such ("friendly") recognition to be possible while each civil servant is acting for a potentially enemy state, it is necessary for that interstate enmity not to penetrate into the essential role the civil servant is playing. The civil servants of the different states do not feel enmity when they undertake their cooperative effort of mutual recognition; and yet, they are acting for different, potentially hostile states. There are, then, two possibilities: either they are acting as "impostors" (colluding with the other state's civil servants for personal advantage), or each is able to play her particular role as civil servant without enmity. The realization of this last possibility (the trust between civil servants as civil servants identified by Nicolaidis) can only imply one thing. A legislative third of state A can juridically recognize a third of state B because, more or less consciously, each recognizes the other's concept of justice as the same. We should remember the claim that the third appears to intervene as a genuinely disinterested third—as a civil servant and not an impostor—when the third applies the concept of justice of the state. Now if she can be sure that the concept of justice of state B is, in all essential or relevant respects, the same as that of her own, she can be confident of acting as a genuine third while (juridically) recognizing the right of B. This will be true despite the subsistence of difference in positive law that remains with mutual recognition: once again, through cooperation, exchange of ideas, information, and so on, the thirds of both states have confidence that these differences do not matter to right. In this very way, justice and right work themselves pure, as it were, of incidental or contingent differences between national laws, without the need for violent struggle and conquest, and without the end result of an imposition of a single positive law on the whole world, which would entail a tyrannical suppression of real, nonjuridical differences (climate, language, and so on).[34] Indeed, in the European Union, there is now even

---

34. This would seem to take care of Kant's objection in *Perpetual Peace* to a world state as a solution to the limits of traditional international law as a federalizing device.

a word for the acceptance or preservation of such differences under conditions of juridical unification: "subsidiarity."

It is thus possible to discern in the various phenomena identified by Slaughter and Nicolaidis how a single concept of justice can manifest itself beginning from the existence of apparently diverse national concepts of justice. And this is precisely due to the dynamic that Kojève identified in the *Outline:* right seeks to actualize itself even when ordering relations among members of transpolitical societies; but to actualize itself, it must come to grips with other states, since to do so is to make the intervention of the third irresistible everywhere. For the argument of the *Outline* to be complete, it is not necessary to show how fast the tendency in question is occurring or is spreading to all—it is sufficient to identify the possibility of this occurring, and why its occurrence is driven by the logic of right itself.

The Synthesis of Equality and Equivalence in (Socialist) Equity

What Kojève means by the dynamic of a synthesis of equality and equivalence in equity is most clearly articulated in his discussion of the right of economic society. We have already seen that, after the bourgeois revolution, both equality and equity become accepted as indispensable elements of justice. He provides the following illustration of the interaction between equality and equivalence:

> If it is a matter of sharing food for dinner between two persons, one of whom had lunch and the other not, we will say that the share will be just if the latter receives more. And we will say that it is just to give a child a slice of cake that is larger than the slices of the adults. It is also just that the weak carry less than the strong, and it is from an ideal of Justice that the practice of the handicap was born. From all of this, one need only go one step further in order to assert that it would be just to give a thing to the one who desires it the most. And one commonly says that it is just to give it to the one who needs it the most (cf. the principle of "communist" Society: to each according to his needs). Or once again, one will say that it is just to give the thing to the one who has made the most effort to have it (cf. the principle of "socialist" Society: to each according to his merits)—and so on.
>
> In all these cases, a Master would be struck by the injustice of inequality from the start. Thus, a poor but proud man will hide the fact that he has not had lunch in order to see the Justice of equality alone applied. And a weak person may through pride or amour-propre (the Bourgeois will say vanity) carry the same weight as the strong. . . . And there are athletes who prefer to forfeit a match when the Justice of equivalence requires that others be handicapped. In short, the Master can require equality without taking account of equivalence, of the compensation of his inequality with others. By contrast, the Bourgeois or the Slave will be satisfied by the equivalence of conditions, without taking account of their inequalities. (See page 254 in this volume.)

The way in which this tension between justice as equality and justice as equivalence can be resolved in a synthesis is suggested in this passage by the "socialist" idea of "to each according to his merits"; this notion embodies equivalence, since it can be just to give different shares to different persons, as well as equality of opportunity. The former differences of conditions and rewards (above all, of work) can only be attributed to differences of merit, if we can be sure that they are not fundamentally affected by accidents of birth or other contingencies. The socialist synthesis of equity is possible, therefore, through making chances or opportunities equal, such that different conditions and rewards are just in their equivalence. Absent equal entitlements (education, and so on) to secure equality of opportunity (a matter of the "status" of the citizen in the socialist state), there will always remain a more or less severe tension between equality and equivalence.

Kojève describes such a tendency to synthesis, picking up again on the dinner example.

> The principle of equality will require a share of equal portions between those having *droit*, and it will no longer be concerned about anything else. But the principle of equivalence will ask if the equal portions are truly equivalent. If one observes that some are more hungry than others, one will see [to it] that this is not so. One will then share the food differently, making the portions proportional to the hunger of each one. The principle thus being satisfied, one will leave matters there. But the other principle will be offended by the inequality of shares, and it will try to eliminate it. However, in order not to offend the principle of equivalence, it will be necessary to eliminate the inequality of the participants. One will therefore ask why some are more hungry than others. And if one observes that this difference results from the fact that some have had lunch and others not, one will see to it such that from now on all might have lunch. (See page 269 in this volume.)

In moving to synthesis one uses equivalence to address the limits of equality, and vice versa. And indeed, such a tendency is recognizable in the evolution of the contemporary welfare state practically everywhere. Take the example of gender equality, which Kojève himself raises (pages 269–70). A social consequence of the biological differentiation of men and women is the tendency of women to bear an inordinate burden for the care of children; because of this, men and women, while formally equal, lack equal opportunity in the workplace—women face constraints on achieving equal recognition through work that men do not. It will therefore be necessary to provide some means of equalizing the burdens on men and women that are present at the "starting gate" in the workplace. But what if women also earn less than men even if this "starting gate" problem is solved? To the extent that they are denied equal access to the same professions and trades as men, one will require antidiscrimination law; but one will still find women undercompensated for work of apparently equal value, perhaps due to historical assumptions about women's inequality. One will also need pay equity as well, a perfection of equivalence. Women will then have both equality of opportunity and equivalence of rewards with merits. The tendency to synthesis is in fact the realization that neither policy on its own can correct the problem—one can only correct injustice by attending to both equality and equivalence in their interaction.

Being a dynamic process, the achievement of such a synthesis cannot occur without some elements of inequality or inequivalence tending to be exacerbated in the short run. Pointing to these very disturbances, both the Right and the Left today tend to be highly dissatisfied with the condition of the regulatory and welfare state. In the equality policies of the contemporary state, the Right sees excessive leveling, treating unequals equally; they often do not see that the end result could in fact be a synthesis that allows *differences* in condition and result to be considered, definitively, as just. Likewise, the traditional Left tends to lament the extent to which unequal market outcomes are now tolerated, even by those who label themselves liberals or progressives. However, perhaps one simply realizes that in many cases a stable, just solution cannot be obtained by manipulating the outcomes of the market, but rather by equalizing the chances or opportunities that individuals bring to the market. As the intellectual Right and Left look over the same, evolving social welfare and regulatory state, they claim to see more of the inequalities and inequivalences that each of them does not like. The typical prognostication, or interpretation from this phenomenon, is that of increasing fragmentation and social division, or even an impasse in the project of liberal democratic politics. But for both the Right and the Left, it is worthwhile at least to consider and address Kojève's challenge: the fundamental tendency, through these various disturbances and adjustments, is toward synthesis (pages 263–68). It is, of course, beyond the scope of this essay to consider how this challenge plays itself out in the various areas of economic and social policy characteristic of the modern welfare and regulatory state. But one particular dimension of the problem should be noted: many on the Left see the progressive state as in retreat because of the globalization of markets. Kojève simply accepts as a truth that economic society has an inherently transpolitical character, but what this means is that a stable synthesis of equality and equivalence in these relations will never be achievable within the bounds of the state (pages 272–76). There is nothing regressive, then, about the expansion of economic relations beyond the state, and the great intensification of such relations; and there is nothing surprising that the initial result should be new inequalities and equivalences of the kind that the Left has identified. But why might the end result not be the removal of a basic limit on the realization of the socialist ideal imposed by the (nation) state itself? One blames globalization for slave labor in China or Myanmar, for example: but before globalization who, with any effective capacity to do something about it, really cared? Because economic Society increasingly includes members of both the states that have already come to a recognition of the injustice of these practices and those that have not, one can see that there is a *real* basis for the global propagation of socialist right, which does not, again, seek to or tend to eliminate all differences in outcomes from the market, but simply to conserve only those that are *just*. In any case, there is nothing that has happened so far that is inconsistent with, or that refutes, Kojève's understanding of the dynamics by which the synthesis of equality and equivalence proceeds, and universalizes itself. At a minimum, Kojève's view is a powerful challenge to those on the Left who have thrown in their chips with culture and the nation, as supposed sources of a still viable resistance to the "injustices" of globalization.

Toward a Critical Engagement with Kojève's *Outline*

In the preceding, we have sought to lay bare some of the core argument of Kojève's *Outline* in order to facilitate access to that argument for readers in the Anglo-American intellectual world, where, generally speaking, the view of Kojève and his project has been formed by reputation and distorted by a few dominant misinterpretations and misappropriations of his work. In attempting to illustrate the completeness of the philosophical argument of the *Outline,* we have been particularly concerned to avoid English-speaking readers turning to the *Outline* in the spirit that one usually turns to works that are incomplete or "drafts"—in other words, as marginalia of secondary or peripheral importance in discerning the fundamental thought of the author.

This does not mean that we think that Kojève's thought as presented in the *Outline* is a completely adequate account of the human situation. Kojève's undoubted original contribution in this work is to show how the *Rechtsstaat* need not, and indeed to realize fully its own ideal, *cannot* be a nation-state. He has also shown how one can begin by taking Schmitt's premises about the state and the political seriously and end up in a very different place, which is entirely congenial to constitutionalism and the rule of law.[35]

Of course, whether one is persuaded that human beings will be satisfied in the universal and homogenous state ultimately depends on the plausibility of Kojève's account of human needs. Fukuyama has suggested that there is a human need for what he calls *megalothymia* (high-mindedness or great-spiritedness), by which he intends something like rank-order—the need to esteem greatness or superiority, and the need for certain human beings to be esteemed unequally. Let us assume, with Fukuyama, that some such need existed. Because his view of Kojève is not informed by the *Outline,* Fukuyama misconstrues the idea of equal universal recognition as a kind of absolute and complete homogenization and leveling, and thus can claim that such a need could not be satisfied if the project of universal recognition were completed in the universal and homogenous state. But, as we have seen, since equity—which is the basis in justice of such recognition—is a synthesis of equality and equivalence, there can be, in the universal and homogenous state, significant differential recognition of talents—but only to the extent that this is compatible with recognizing the equal *humanity* of everyone. There is, thus, no intrinsic reason why in such a state the need to esteem excellence, and the need of the excellent for esteem, would not be satisfied by recognition on the basis of the socialist synthesis of equality and equivalence.

A deeper question would concern the contentless or formal character of universal recognition in the universal and homogenous state (already dis-

---

35. Which, it is argued, Leo Strauss did, or attempted to do, in a very different way. See Howse, "From Dictatorship to Legitimacy and Back Again."

cerned in Kojève's *Introduction* by Derrida and others). Kojève acknowledges that human beings seek to be recognized in their particularity. Now the universal and homogenous state secures such recognition, in the first place, because it does not recognize individuals merely as members of collectivities, such as classes or races or religious groupings, but as individuals with their own particular ends. But no recognition, at least direct, of the content of those particular ends is possible—as intrinsically superior to or different from those of others. Work is recognized through exchange and money, and—in the case of civil servants—rank and official position, that is, through a neutral medium of value. What is observable, at least in contemporary liberal democracies, is a widely felt need for some more personalistic kind of social recognition, one related to the specific "content" of the individual. Consequently, there is a celebrity culture. Yet the "ruling" elite of the liberal democracies, including politicians, technocrats, and businesspeople, are mostly not celebrities, though of course there are exceptions; for the most part, the celebrity culture operates independently of the sphere of management. Those who manage the conditions of social, legal, and economic life in the late twentieth century do not manifest a need to dominate or impose a particular personal content on society, nor are they typically the objects of the worship afforded celebrities. Yet there are some human beings who clearly need to be celebrities or celebrity worshipers, and there are many who deeply resent a public life dominated by a faceless elite.

As we have seen, trust between elites, between the juridical classes of different states, is central to the emergence of a definitive concept of justice, against which differences in positive law may be explained, to the extent they remain, as adaptations to different nonjuridical conditions and contexts (climate, language, and so on). Yet can one be so sure that people themselves will come to see it that way? The ability of the elites to "solve" complex problems of the management of economic relations through global law, that is, through technique, is of course evident, but the resistance of others to such solutions is also evident. Recently, for instance, the dispute between the United States and the European Union concerning the latter's ban on hormone-fed beef proved incapable of resolution through the technocratic/scientific tools of risk assessment and analysis entrenched in global economic law, with majoritarian European public opinion refusing to change its skeptical attitude toward the manipulation of nature in this way, and a resulting reversion to retaliation by the United States against European exports—in other words, to Schmittean sovereignty. Kojève, as we have pointed out, places no value on self-government or democratic self-determination as ends in themselves. Yet even if one were to discern the emergence of a single concept of justice, its interpretation and implementation in context could well result in enough disagreements about the meaning of this concept, albeit at a concrete level, so as to make politics indispensable to legitimacy. If so, then we are back to the indispensability of a genuine level of *governance* below that of the universal and homogenous state. And then, the question of who is the ultimate decider of the correct *interpretation* of the definitive concept of justice, whether the particular *demos* applying it in context, or the third of the universal and homogenous state, is pointedly political in the Schmittean sense—it is a (re)formulation of the Schmittean question of who decides. In sum, Kojève's admission that positive law will not be fully harmonized in the universal and homogenous state raises more difficulties than his faith in the technocratic management of difference would seem to allow. This being said, Kojève might respond that while the differences in question might still lead to occasional moments where the old sovereignty breaks through, it does not really break through: raising tariffs is not the same thing as struggling to the death, which is fundamental to the Schmittean concept of the political and sovereignty. This points to a possible problem with Kojève's entire treatment of politics— he operates entirely within the Schmittean understanding of the political, and while brilliantly overcoming Schmittean sovereignty from the inside, as it were, he may not have given politics its due. There may be some human differences that are best resolved politically, even if they do not seem to be worthy of, or require struggle to the death, in the last analysis. Influenced by Schmitt, Kojève does not believe that there can be a truly *liberal* politics, premised on political struggle that does not intensify to the potential level of violent confrontation. If Schmitt may have been wrong to say farewell to liberalism, Kojève may have been wrong to say farewell to politics, simply accepting Schmitt's terms for the debate and the choices.

A different challenge to the trajectory sketched by Kojève is that not all states are even liberal democracies, and one has such types as Slobodan Milosevic and Muammar Qaddafi. Nonetheless, such persons are increasingly described and treated as mere "criminals" (perhaps somewhat insane): violent measures against them are—in more sophisticated circles at least—put in terms of police action to enforce certain universal norms.

As for criminals, the persistence of right (including penal right) in the posthistorical condition suggests that these will not disappear. There will always be individuals who seek to make others the means to their particular ends. Unlike the young Marx, and much more in the manner of Sigmund Freud, Kojève admits that no social state can simply eliminate the possibility of frustrated desire as a pathology. What Kojève would deny is that the discontents could rally behind any alternative concept or claim of *justice,* for which it would be reasonable to engage in violent struggle against the universal and homogenous state.

But this, in short, is to say that human beings ought, rationally, to be satisfied in the universal and homogenous state. And does not Kojève claim a fundamental break with the Kantian "ought," with what he regards as the normative, aspirational character of *all* philosophy from Plato to Kant? Even if it were not reasonable for them to do so, how can one know that the discontents will not break up the universal and homogenous state by violence, if there are enough of them, and if their subjective dissatisfaction is intense enough? Without an alternative principle of justice, Kojève might respond, they will not be able to disturb the authority of the universal and homogenous state; for it is on this principle, much more than its actual police resources, that its durability depends. But did Adolf Hitler have an alternative principle of justice? Kojève would deny this, countering that Hitler failed on his own terms (to create a new sempiternal Reich) and succeeded only in helping to clear the ground, so to speak, for the building of the universal and homogenous state.[36] Yet, what if Hitler had, at the outset, possessed a nuclear arsenal capable of global destruction?

Posing this question gives us a window into Kojève's particular philosophical sensibility. Kojève dispenses with Hegel's philosophy of nature—nature is to be negated, from the human perspective, and is at one with itself. The universal and homogenous state is the culmination of the human project, but there is nothing that guarantees that it will not be destroyed—this project is fully rational on human terms, but it still remains a mere artifice of man. It could be swept away by any manner of accidents, even those provoked by man himself (a nuclear catastrophe). Or, as Fukuyama has recently speculated, through genetic manipulations man could become something different; he could even become a Schmittean man, genetically programmed to dominate violently or be so dominated.[37] But this would not affect the completeness of *human* history as defined by the anthropogenic struggle. As a socialist, Kojève could understand the project of the universal and homogenous state as worth completing—as worthy of serious effort. As a philosopher he could face its artificial, or constructed, character, unsupported by nature, God, or the cosmos. Kojève could accept this conclusion—a radical atheism—without the fright or despair that accompanies it in its original existentialist versions. He could be a good socialist worker, while recognizing that the end of this work, being made by man, could simply be swept away. It is this complex sensibility that has led so many of Kojève's interpreters and critics down wrong paths, while it made Kojève himself a source of such fascination, and even frustration and mystery, to the smartest of his contemporaries. It is summarized best by Kojève himself, who according to Raymond Aron said: "Human life is a comedy; once must play it seriously."[38]

---

36. See Kojève's letter to Schmitt, 16 May 1955, in *Schmittiana*, 103–4.
37. Francis Fukuyama, "Second Thoughts," *National Interest,* Summer 56 (1999), 16–33.
38. Raymond Aron, *Memoires: 50 ans de réflexion politique* (Paris: Julliard, 1983), 99.

Preliminary Remarks

Alexandre Kojève

§ 1

[9] IT IS IMPOSSIBLE to study human reality without sooner or later coming up against the phenomenon of *Droit,* particularly if one considers the political aspect of this reality, and especially when one is concerned with questions relative to the Constitution of the State, since the notion of a Constitution is itself a notion just as much political as it is juridical.

Unfortunately, the phenomenon of *Droit* has still not found a universally accepted and truly satisfying definition. As well, one can read in legal treatises phrases like this one: "In the present state of the science, a fully satisfying definition of the concept of '*Droit*' is out of the question."[1] Now, to speak about a thing without being able to define it is basically to speak without knowing what one is speaking about. And in these conditions the discourse has little chance of being convincing, or indeed, of conforming to the thing about which one speaks.

One must say, however, that one finds oneself in an analogous situation every time that one deals with a specifically human phenomenon: whether it is *Droit,* or the State, Religion, Art, and so on, a satisfying definition is generally lacking. But this remark does not at all excuse the search for a correct definition of *Droit*—on the contrary.

*

It would be easy to give an arbitrary definition of *Droit,* even if it means refusing to call "juridical" everything that is otherwise so-called [10], but that does not tally with the chosen definition. But such a definition would be of little interest, for it is impossible simply to dismiss teachings implicated in language and history. If something is—or has been—called "*Droit,*" it is more than likely that this has not been done by chance. But, on the other hand, it is materially impossible to bring together in a single definition everything that has been called "*Droit*" at any given moment and place: the content would be too disparate.

One must therefore look for a middle way. This way, moreover, can be none other than the one on which Plato already engaged, followed by his disciple Aristotle, and on which we were also able to meet quite recently one Max Weber. It is a matter of finding the "Idea" (Plato), the "Ideal type" (Max

---

1. [Theodor] Sternberg, *Allgemeine Rechtslehre,* vol. I (Leipzig: [G. J. Göschen,] 1904), 21.

Weber), the "Phenomenon" (Husserl), and so on, of the entity being studied by analyzing a concrete case that is particularly clear, typical, specific, pure.[2] In other words, one must discover the content which makes the given case a case of *droit,* for example, and not of religion or art, and so on. And having discovered it—i.e., having found the "essence" (*Wesen*) of the phenomenon—one must describe it in a correct and complete manner, this description of the essence being nothing other than the definition of the phenomenon in question.

Having obtained the definition, one must verify it. One must go through the different cases generally called "juridical" and see if the definition in question can be applied to them. This confrontation of the idea-essence with the various cases of its realization will probably bring about alterations and refinements of the definition. But if the latter is accurate, one will see it being applied to the vast majority of cases. It is more than likely, however, that one will find cases called "juridical" not conforming to the definition as well as cases that do conform that one does not generally call "juridical." In these cases one has the *droit* to correct the linguistic or historical usage. But in doing so one must show and explain every time the why of the mistake. In one case it will be necessary to pick out the traits which have allowed the given phenomenon to be confused with a juridical phenomenon. In the other case it will be a matter of indicating the traits which have concealed the juridical aspect of the phenomenon to the point of making it unrecognizable.

It is only after having gone through all the different types of human phenomena and having divided them into juridical and non-juridical (religious, political, moral, artistic, and so on), so that there no longer remains any unclassified type, [11] that one can be sure of having found a satisfying definition—that is, applicable to all the phenomena in question and to them only. And it would still be necessary to complete the phenomenological description by an analysis of the metaphysical (cosmological) and ontological substructure of the phenomenon being described in order to ward off the risk of the advent in the future of a new case, forcing the revision of the definition which was conforming to the cases realized in the present and the past.

It should be understood that I have not even tried to reach this ideal in the pages which are going to follow. On the one hand, I have deliberately avoided a metaphysical or ontological analysis. On the other hand, even the phenomenological description is probably far from being perfect, for its verification has not been pushed very far: I have only confronted very few cases called juridical with the definition that I propose of the phenomenon of "*Droit.*"

---

2. [Ed. See, for example, Plato, *Phaedo,* 75a–9a, 102a–15b, and *Republic,* 505a–9c; Max Weber, " 'Objectivity' in Social Science and Social Policy," in *The Methodology of the Social Sciences,* trans. Edward A. Shils and Henry A. Finch (New York: Free Press, 1949), 49–112; and Edmund Husserl, *Phenomenology and the Crisis of Philosophy,* trans. Quentin Lauer (New York: Harper and Row, 1965), and *The Crisis of European Sciences and Transcendental Phenomenology: An Introduction to Phenomenological Philosophy,* trans. David Carr (Evanston: Northwestern University Press, 1970).]

The description of the phenomenon of "*Droit*" that I give in *Part One*, there-fore, has a clearly provisional character (just like, moreover, the content of the other two Parts). But this being said, I will propose a definition of *Droit* which, in my opinion, takes into account the very essence of this phenomenon. This definition will allow the conditions of the realization of this essence to be set down. Finally, by knowing the essence of *Droit* and the mode of its realization, one will be able to close *Part One* with a comparison of juridical activity to other human activities, which will allow the specificity and autonomy of *Droit* to be demonstrated.

§ 2

For Plato, the essence of a phenomenon remained outside of time. In other words, an accurate definition was—according to him—everywhere and always valid. Since Hegel, one no longer generally thinks in this way. In any case, I accept that human phenomena (which are not just natural, animal [phenom-ena]) are born in time and "live" there—that is, are altered and disappear.

It is not enough, therefore, to define the phenomenon of *Droit* and to indi-cate the conditions of its realization. One must further show in the anthro-pogenic act, which generates man as such in time, the aspect which creates the juridical phenomenon in man. And one must see if this phenomenon, consti-tuted in time, does not undergo a temporal evolution in its very essence.

[12] It is *Part Two* which must give an answer—quite provisional—to these questions of origin and evolution. I there assume that the fundamental princi-ples of Hegelian philosophy are known and accepted, and I will try to apply them to the problem of *Droit*.

For the moment, I would only like to mention that the genetic analysis of essences does not necessarily imply a sociological or historical relativism. Of course, the isolated phenomenon, in its particular *hic et nunc* [here and now], is not "absolute": such a given *droit* is not *the Droit*, absolute and definitive; what has been "just" yesterday may no longer be so tomorrow. But if all that exists in time changes by this very fact, time as such does not change, nor the totality of temporal phenomena, which can therefore be called "absolute," if you will. Likewise, if all the particular juridical systems proposed in the course of history were organized into a systematic whole, which implies all juridical possibilities, this whole will no longer have anything "relative" about it. And in relation to this whole, the elements, while being "relative" in themselves, will also have an "absolute" value. In other words, the evolution of *Droit* can have a final goal and realize in this way an objective progress.

Moreover, the fact that *Droit* is constituted in time does not at all prove that a definitive juridical system is impossible. A system will be definitive, or indeed "absolute," if it implies all juridical possibilities, if all that is *Droit* can realize itself in this system without disrupting it. Or once again, the system will be "absolute" if it contains juridical norms making every act susceptible of alter-ing this system or overcoming it effectively impossible. However, in order for this to be the case, one must assume that the system perfectly understands itself [*s'est parfaitement compris lui-même*], that it has exhausted all the *theoretical* possibilities of *Droit,* either by implying them or by excluding them, and so rendering them innocuous. Thus, the "absolute" system must imply all the other [systems]: really or ideally. It must "understand" them in themselves and "understand itself." But it may understand them as superseded [*dépassés*] stages, and it may understand itself as a result of these stages, as their integration.

§ 3

An absolute juridical system will have a well defined structure, where all possible juridical phenomena will find [13] their place. But even a relative system, realized at any given moment in the historical evolution, will tend to take a "total" form by encompassing all juridical phenomena realized at this epoch. One can therefore study the Legal System even without supposing that it has reached the end of its evolution. However, one must acknowledge that such a system may be incomplete and that its structure may only be provisional.

It is in this sense that I will try to outline a Legal System in *Part Three* of this study. But I will confine myself to generalities and the analysis will remain fragmentary.

Part One

Droit As Such

§ 4

[17] LIKE EVERY REAL ENTITY, *Droit* 1) "shows" itself or "reveals" itself to man; 2) "exists" or enters into interaction with other entities (that it alters and co-determines while undergoing repercussions [itself]); and 3) "is" both in itself and in the totality of Being. A complete analysis of *Droit,* therefore, would have to take into account these three aspects, being not only "phenomenological" but also "metaphysical" and "ontological." But I will limit myself here to describing the "superficial" aspect of *Droit,* to analyzing it as a "phenomenon" given to the immediate consciousness of man, who "knows" what *Droit* is and distinguishes it from other things, while not being able to describe correctly this "immediate knowledge"—that is, to give a phenomenological definition of *Droit.*

It is such a definition that I will try to give in chapter 1 of Part One.

Afterwards, in chapter 2, it will be a matter of showing under what conditions *Droit* thus defined is real—that is, succeeds in remaining in existence despite the forces which tend to overcome it. There it will be a question of the relations between *Droit,* Society, and the State properly so-called.

Finally, it will be necessary to show in the last chapter that *Droit* is a *sui generis* [of its own kind or class] phenomenon, specific and autonomous. In other words, it will be necessary to compare *Droit* to other specifically human phenomena which are akin to it, such as Morality, Religion, and so on. One will then see that *Droit* cannot be reduced to any of these phenomena, nor to a combination of them, that it has its own specific "essence" [18] and an autonomous origin, namely the idea of Justice. It is in this way that the objective (or "behaviorist") definition of the first section will be completed by a subjective (or "introspective") definition, which will present *Droit* as a manifest realization or a realizing manifestation of Justice.

It is only then that one will be able to ask in *Part Two* the question concerning the origin of the idea of Justice and *Droit,* understood as the realizing process of this Justice.

Chapter 1

Definition of *Droit*

§ 5

[19] WHEN ONE DEALS with a human phenomenon, it is often useful not to begin by analyzing its "content," by asking introspection to reveal to us its "sense" or its "meaning," but first to study its external "form" by using the "behaviorist" method. Thus, in what concerns *Droit*, one can begin by wondering what are the externally perceptible acts which characterize a juridical situation as such and distinguish it from every other human situation.

To arrive at such a "behaviorist" definition of the juridical phenomenon, let us see how men act when they find themselves in a typical relation of *droit*. And let us ask ourselves if the very nature of these acts or their interdependence is enough to describe as juridical the relation which triggers them and the situation which implies them.

§ 6

First of all, one can divide all juridical situations into three groups. One is said to be in a *juridical situation* or in a *relation of* **droit:**

1) when one *has the* **droit;**
2) when one *does not have the* **droit;** and
3) when one *has the duty* (in the sense of juridical obligation) to do or to omit something.

In all these cases it is a matter of something other than the simple wish or desire of someone to act or to refrain [20] from an action: the concrete desire or the effective will can be totally lacking. And the juridical situation has nothing to do either with the material, physical possibility of doing or not doing something in a given case. For this situation to exist, it is enough that the action or omission is materially possible in a general way, in a typical case, and that man as such can want it or wish for it in certain cases. Only acts unrealizable in principle and not able to be the object of the will of any man are incapable of generating a juridical situation.

It is not enough, however, that an act is desirable and realizable for there to be a juridical situation. There are acts which only create juridically neutral situations, which do not give rise to relations of *droit*. For there to be a juridical situation, it is necessary (and sufficient) that there is added to the juridically neutral possibility of wanting and realizing an action or an omission either the

droit or the (juridical) *duty* to do it, or finally, the fact of *not having the* **droit** *to it.*

Before asking ourselves what this means, let us see if one may not reduce these three cases to a single type of juridical situation (or relations of *droit*).

It is easy to see that cases 2 and 3 can be immediately reduced to one another.

Indeed, not to have the *droit* to a given action is to have the (juridical) duty to refrain from it, and conversely. Likewise, not to have the *droit* to refrain from an action is to have the (juridical) duty to do it, and *vice versa*. One can therefore eliminate the second case and say that a juridical situation exists there, and there alone, when one has either the *droit* or the (juridical) duty to do or to omit something.

And one can take another step in this direction. Of course, "*droit*" and "juridical duty" are not one and the same thing; one can surely not reduce the *duty* to do or to omit something to the mere **droit** to do or to omit it. But the element of "*droit*" is necessarily implied in the (juridical) element of "duty." As soon as one has the *duty* to do or to omit something one has by the same token the **droit** to do or to omit it. Consequently, one can say that there is no juridical situation as long as the element of "having the *droit* to . . . " is missing, and that there is such a situation as soon as this element is present.

I will have to discuss further on the problem of juridical duty or obligation. It will then be necessary to ask whether the element of [21] "duty" is a *sui generis* juridical element, or if the situation which implies this element is juridical only because it also necessarily implies the element of "*droit*." For the moment it is enough to note that every juridical situation implies the latter element and that it is enough that a situation implies it for it to be juridical. It is enough, therefore, to consider only the phenomenon of "having the *droit*" in order to discover the *essence* of the phenomenon of "*Droit*" in general and thus to be able to say if such a situation is or is not juridical by indicating the reason for it.

One can therefore say:

> There is a *juridical situation* or a *relation of* **droit** everywhere—and there alone—where one *has the* **droit** to do or to omit something.

Let us now see if one can eliminate the distinction between action and omission in this formulation.

Of course, here again there is no essential identity: to act and to refrain from acting is not the same thing. But the fact that there can be a juridical situation in the two cases proves that this distinction does not have an essential juridical value. To have the *droit* to the action or the omission, to the abstention from acting, is to have the *droit* to the *effect* of this action or abstention, to the objective or external *result,* produced or noticeable from the outside. Now, the omission can effectively produce such an effect just as easily as an action properly so-called. In order to understand what a juridical situation is as such, in order to reveal its "essence," there is, then, no good reason to distinguish between actions and omissions. One can equally speak about, for example, a "behavior" to which one has the *droit,* this behavior being able to be both active and passive, consisting either in an action properly so-called or in an abstention from such an action.

In order to be able to be implicated in a juridical situation, the behavior must have an objective effect. It must either create or alter something outside of its subject, or create or alter something in the subject himself, but so that this is noticeable from outside. (Moreover, if this observation is an alteration produced by the behavior outside of its subject, one reverts, if you will, to the first case.) This is why, in order to bring out this condition, it is better to speak not of "behavior" simply, but of "*effective* behavior." Or once again, one can call "action" every "effective behavior" susceptible of being implicated in a juridical situation. But then one must not forget that [22] this "action" can be either "positive," when it is a matter of action in the proper sense of the term, or "negative," when it is a matter of a simple omission, of an abstention from acting.

Assuming this to be the case, one can ultimately say:

There is a *juridical situation* or a *relation of* **droit** everywhere—and there alone—where one has the **droit** to an effective behavior (or to an action either positive or negative).

§ 7

The essence of *Droit* is therefore revealed to us first of all in the phenomenon "to have the *droit* to. . . . " This phenomenon can only take place in the event of an "effective behavior." But this is of little importance for the moment. It is enough that there is "*droit*" or a "juridical situation," "relation of *droit,*" and so on, there and there alone where one is in the presence of the phenomenon "to have the *droit* to. . . . " To describe and define the phenomenon of "*Droit,*" therefore, is to describe and define the phenomenon "to have the *droit* to. . . . "

In order to arrive at such a descriptive definition (at first "behaviorist") of the phenomenon of "*Droit,*" let us consider some simple and typical situations in which one can say without ambiguity that one has the **droit** to a specific behavior.

Let us suppose that A wants to take a certain sum of money from B. Let us assume that the action (the behavior) of A provokes a reaction (a behavior) from B. This reaction from B can annul A's action, who will not have the money in question. Or again, A, being stronger than B for example, annuls the reaction of the latter and seizes the money by force. In neither of the two cases could one say with certitude that A had the **droit** to this money. But one could not do so either in the case when B spontaneously gives A the money which the latter asks of him. For if, in the first hypothesis, it can be a matter of an attempted robbery (successful or not), it can be a question of an act of charity in the other hypothesis: B can give A the money which the latter asks of him out of the kindness of his heart, without A having a **droit** to this money. The situation changes radically, by contrast, as soon as one alters the hypothesis in the following way: A acts with a view to obtaining the money; B reacts so as to keep it; but a third person C intervenes, annulling B's reaction so that A receives the money without having had to make an effort to get it, the reaction of B that A would have had to annul having been annulled by C's intervention. Let us add that A [23] and B are indifferent toward, or indeed unknown to, C and that C is not personally interested whether the money remains with B or goes to A. In this case one can say with certitude that A had the **droit** to B's money, that he had the **droit** to take it from him. One can suppose, for example, that A wanted to take back from B the money which he had deposited with him and that C was the court official who did the job [*l'huissier qui a fait l'opération*] on A's behalf, B not willing to make restitution spontaneously.

Let us take another case, when there is an absence of *droit* to a given behavior. Let us suppose that A is sitting on a bench in a park next to B; B casts his shadow on A; A undertakes an action with a view to dislodging B, who reacts. One will not say that A has the **droit** to his action (or, if you will, that he has the **droit** to the sun) as long as one does not know that he can have recourse to an (impartial and disinterested) third, in the person of the park warden, for example, who will annul B's reaction so that A obtains the desired result through him without making an effort.

This is what takes place in an analogous case. Let us suppose that B, A's neighbor, makes noise during the night. If A acts in order to put a stop to the noise, and B reacts in order to be able to prolong it, A will be able to have recourse to a disinterested and impartial third (the concierge or a police officer, for example), who will annul B's reaction, thus giving A's action the desired effect.

Let us now suppose that A is going for a walk along a river bank. B, who is the mother of a child who has just fallen into the water, acts with a view to inciting A to plunge into the water and save her child. A reacts so as to maintain his stance [*comportement*] as a mere bystander. As long as one does not notice that B can have recourse to a disinterested third, who will annul A's reaction, one cannot say that B has the **droit** to A's help. (It is understood [that] in the society where the event occurs and at the epoch when it occurs, this remark is valid for all the cases considered.) And if A can have recourse to a third who will annul the reactions of B provoked by his behavior, one will be able to say that he has the **droit** to remain a mere bystander.

Finally, let us suppose that A hits B, who reacts in order to put a stop to the blows. If A can resort to the intervention of a third, who is supposed to be capable of annulling B's reaction, so that A can hit him without experiencing resistance, one will say that A has the **droit** to hit B. One can suppose, for example, that B is the slave of Roman citizen A.

There is no use in extending this list of examples. The cases cited are enough to show that the phenomenon of "*Droit*" [24] (in the aspect "to have the *droit* to . . . ") exists every time that the intervention of a disinterested third takes place. As soon as this third annuls the reaction of B, provoked by an action of A, one will say that A has the **droit** to this action, [and] it is of little importance[1]

---

1. [Ed. Reading *peu importe* for *peut importe* as in the original manuscript.]

that this [action] appears normal and justified, or absurd, revolting, immoral, and so on. Conversely, in the absence of such an intervention, one will never be able to say with certainty that A has the **droit** to his action, even if this appears perfectly "natural."

One generally says that the disinterested third intervenes *because* A has the *droit* to his action (or to the result of the action). But this is not at all obvious *a priori*. It is possible that the relation is the opposite, that A's *droit* is not the *cause* but the *effect* of the intervention of the disinterested third. In other words, *Droit* could be considered an (oral or written) codification of cases when interventions of disinterested thirds had taken place, instead of being interpreted as the collection of principles provoking such interventions. And this is an important question which will be studied in *Part Two*, [which is] devoted to the study of the origin and evolution of *Droit*. For the moment it is enough to remark that one can discern the presence of *Droit* by basing it solely on the fact of the intervention of the third. And one can add, moreover, that it is enough to know that one is in the presence of a juridical situation in order to be forced to postulate (or to foresee) such an intervention (as possible, at the very least).

One must say, therefore, that *Droit* cannot be revealed to man without him noticing or postulating a disinterested intervention of a third. In other words, this intervention is a necessary or "essential" constitutive element of the phenomenon of "*Droit*." And it is thanks to this element that this phenomenon can be described or defined by a "behaviorist" method.

§ 8

On the basis of some of the examples considered in the previous section, one can formulate a: [25]

First "Behaviorist" Definition of Droit

Let us recall the relations between essence, existence, and the phenomenon with respect to the notion of *Droit*.

Droit as (empirical) *existence* realizes the *essence* of "*Droit*" in the material, spatio-temporal world, and the *phenomenon* of "*Droit*" reveals this essence (to man) through the medium [*l'intermédiaire*] of its realization.

This said, let us suppose that:

The essence of "*Droit*" is the entity (in the vague sense of a something {*Etwas*} which is not nothing {*Nichts*}—we will subsequently see that this entity is Justice or the "idea" of Justice) which is realized as the existence of "*Droit*" and is revealed as the phenomenon of "*Droit*" in the event of an interaction between two human beings, A and B, in and by the intervention of a third human being, C, impartial and disinterested, this intervention being necessarily provoked by the interaction in question and annulling B's reaction which responds to A's action.

Consequently:

> The phenomenon of "*Droit*" (in its "behaviorist" aspect) is the intervention of an impartial and disinterested human being, which is necessarily carried out at the time of an interaction between two human beings, A and B, and which annuls B's reaction to A's action.

This intervention is the specifically juridical element. It is this which confers a juridical character to the situation as a whole.

One can clarify the proposed definition of the phenomenon of "*Droit*" by elaborating upon it in the following manner:

1) Let us suppose that the interaction between two human beings, A and B, necessarily provokes the intervention of an impartial and disinterested third, C, this intervention annulling B's reaction to A's action.

2) In this case, and in this case alone, we will be able to say the following:

   a) A *has the* **droit** to act as he does; his action and the effect of this action constitute his *subjective right*,[2] and he himself is the *subject* of this *droit*, [and] therefore a *subject of* **droit** in general (or a *juridical person*, [26] either *physical* or *moral*); his action is a *juridical action* and his interaction with B a *relation of* **droit** (in the technical sense, the term "juridical action" designating the specific acts that A undertakes with a view to provoking C's intervention).

   b) A's action, or more exactly the effect or the goal of this action, is an *object of* **droit.**

   c) The element which necessarily links C's intervention to the interaction between A and B can be formulated in a proposition; this proposition (which allows one to foresee the intervention when one knows the interaction) is called a *legal rule* (which can either be thought alone, implicitly or explicitly, or expressed orally or in writing); the "legal rule" is the fundamental juridical element of the situation: every interaction which corresponds to a "legal rule" is a "relation of *droit*," every agent of such an interaction is a "subject of *droit*," and every object (or goal) of such an interaction is an "object of *droit*"; the "legal rule" constitutes *objective law*[3] as opposed to "subjective right,"[4] which the "subject of *droit*" corresponding to this "rule" possesses.

   d) Several "legal rules" can be logically connected to one another so as to form a systematic whole called a *juridical doctrine* [**théorie juridique**] (for example, the juridical doctrine of marriage or insurance); the total-

---

2. [Ed. In the original, the English word "right" follows the French phrase **droit subjectif** in parentheses.]

3. [Ed. In the original, the English word "law" follows the French phrase **droit objectif** in parentheses.]

4. [Ed. In the original, the English word "right" follows the French phrase *droit subjectif* in parentheses.]

ity of (real or possible) social actions which correspond to such a "juridical doctrine" (or which realize it) is called a *juridical institution* (for example, marriage as such, or the effective organization of insurance in a given society); the existence of a "juridical institution" creates a *juridical situation,* in which is found every "subject of *droit*" A susceptible of acting so that his interaction with B necessarily provokes the intervention of C, in conformity to a "legal rule" which is part of a "juridical doctrine" realized in the "juridical institution" in question (for example, every man capable of being married or effectively getting married is in a "juridical situation" determined by the "juridical institution" of marriage); (in what follows I [27] will not take into account the terminological distinction between "juridical situation" and "relation of *droit*"; I will use the expressions "juridical situation," "relation of *droit*," [and] "juridical relation" interchangeably, unless it is stated otherwise).

e) The totality of "legal rules" (or "juridical institutions") valid in a given society (during the whole length of its existence or at a given moment of its history) is called the *national* **droit** of this society (for example, Roman *droit* or French feudal *droit*); (a "legal rule" is "valid" when it corresponds to effective interventions—at least in principle—of a disinterested third, C, at the time of the interaction between A and B provided for by the "rule").

f) The totality of all the "legal rules" (or "juridical institutions") which have been valid (or which have been supposed to be able to be valid) in different societies in the course of universal history constitutes the *phenomenon of* **"Droit"** as such; it is this "phenomenon" which is studied in the present work: first of all (*Part One*) as such, i.e., in what there is in common between all the legal rules, whatever they are, namely from the point of view of their own content (the descriptive definition of chapter 1), of the conditions of their reality (chapter 2), and of their specific autonomy (chapter 3); then (*Part Two*) in its origin and general evolution; finally (*Part Three*), in its internal systematic structure, which reveals the existence of different types of "legal rules."

§ 9

The definitions a)–f) of the previous section are purely verbal and need no comment. Their real content has been put forth in the form of an "assumption." It is this [assumption] and this alone that will be commented upon subsequently; for the conditions indicated by this "assumption" are those which constitute the common element of the particular contents of all the (real or possible) "legal rules." It is by taking account of these conditions that one can state and resolve the [28] general problem of the reality of "legal rules." And it is the necessary presence of these conditions which allows one to notice the specific autonomy of these "rules"—that is, their essential difference from all other human phenomena.

Let us recall, therefore, that the essence of *Droit* is realized and revealed (or is manifested) in and by:

> The interaction between two human beings, A and B, which necessarily provokes the intervention of an impartial and disinterested third, C, whose intervention annuls the reaction of B opposed to the action of A.

This ("behaviorist") definition of the phenomenon of "*Droit*" implies three elements:

1) the interaction between two human beings;
2) the intervention of an impartial and disinterested third; and
3) the necessary relation between this intervention and the interaction and its consequence (that is, the annulment of B's reaction).

It is a matter of commenting upon all the terms of each of these three elements. It will be necessary to see what the following facts mean and imply:

a) that it is a question of *human beings,* A and B (§ 10),
b) who are *two* (§ 11), and
c) who are in *interaction* (constituted by an *action* and a *reaction*) (§ 12);
d) that there is an *intervention* (§ 13),
e) of a *third,* C (§ 14),
f) *impartial* and *disinterested* (§ 15);
g) that C's intervention, which is *necessarily provoked* by the interaction between A and B (§ 16),
h) *annuls* B's reaction (§ 17).

This analysis will allow one to clarify and complete, or indeed to alter, the first "behaviorist" definition of *Droit*—that is, to formulate a second one from it.

§ 10

a) There is no question of defining here the notion of a human being. Let us simply suppose that the human being differs essentially from both the animal and the inanimate thing. According to our definition, therefore, there are no juridical relations between things or animals.

For things, this is obvious. But among certain animals (in a horde of monkeys, for example) there are, it seems, [29] relations which could be called "juridical" in the sense that the interaction between two animals, A and B, provokes the intervention of a disinterested third (an adult separating two youths who are fighting, for example). Now, these relations are not juridical in the sense of our definition, precisely and solely because it is a matter of animals and not human beings. From the purely "behaviorist" point of view, this restriction may seem unjustified and the definition too narrow. It is only an "introspective" definition (which I will put forward at the end of this chapter) which will be able to justify our terminology by showing that relations between animals effectively have nothing to do with *Droit*. (This question will be discussed in Part Two, regarding the question of the origin of *Droit*.)

Of course, men have sometimes admitted the existence of juridical relations between animals (in myths, fables, and so on). But there it is a case of anthropomorphism. What is an animal for the author of myth is for us a human being in an animal's body. Thus, our definition also applies to these "poetic" juridical phenomena.[5]

---

5. On this occasion, one can make an important general remark. The "phenomenon" is the "revelation" of an entity (of an "essence") to a human consciousness. This "phenomenon" can be "adequate" or not depending on whether the consciousness reflects the entity (the "essence") correctly or distorts it. We assume that the essence is revealed in and by our consciousness as it is in reality. In other words, *we* are dealing with an *adequate* phenomenon, and it is this which is described in the definition that *we* propose. But other men have proposed other definitions which correspond to *inadequate* phenomena. A complete phenomenology of *Droit* must enumerate *all* juridical phenomena by contrasting the adequate phenomenon with inadequate phenomena, and by explaining the why of the latter. (One must also show how and why the "dialectic" of inadequate phenomena finally generates the adequate phenomenon, which allows one to explain them and which explains itself as their "dialectical" result.)

In the case of the "mythical" juridical phenomenon considered above, I assume that it is inadequate solely because it takes place in respect to relations between animals: one is mistaken in believing that the body of an animal can serve as support for a human behavior, in particular juridical. Here the "anthropomorphic" mistake is explicit, for the myth effectively attributes a human nature to the animal. But there are cases of an implicit mistake. One can believe, for example, that one sees the animal as it is in reality (i.e., as *we* see it), but what one says about it can imply (without one realizing it) elements incompatible with the nature of the animal. In cases of *unconscious* distortion (for example, anthropomorphism), the phenomenologist must, therefore, distinguish not only between the *essence* as it is *for us* (i.e., in reality) and as it is for the man in question (who distorts this essence in his consciousness), but also between the "psychological" phenomenon and [30] the "logical" phenomenon. In other words, the phenomenologist must: 1) reproduce the description (definition) that the corresponding consciousness gives of the inadequate phenomenon (this is the psychological phenomenon); 2) give a complete and correct description (definition) of this inadequate phenomenon ([this is] the logical phenomenon)—that is, make explicit everything that was unconsciously implied there by explaining the nature, reason, and significance of the unconsciousness; 3) indicate the nature, reason, and significance of the mistake of the inadequate phenomenon (in the complete and explicit form of # 2) by comparing it to the adequate phenomenon; [and] 4) describe (define) the adequate phenomenon (and justify it by the description of the "dialectic" of inadequate phenomena which leads to it). (Point 2 is nothing other than a "critique of ideologies.")

This is one part [of what the phenomenologist must do]. The other part is that he must distinguish between the "inadequate phenomenon" and the "terminological mistake." An inadequate phenomenon can be defined (described) in a certain manner (correct or not) by the man in question and the definition can be correctly applied. But it can also be applied in an erroneous manner, in which case the phenomenologist must reveal the mistake and not take into account cases to which the definition has only been applied by mistake.

[30] The question becomes more complicated when the interaction between animals or things provokes the intervention of a human being playing the role of the "disinterested third" of our definition. A man can intervene, for example, during a dog fight. According to our definition, the situation will have nothing juridical about it, and the intervention of the third will not turn the dog into a "subject of *droit*" having the **droit** to something, precisely because it is an animal and not a human being. Now, it does not seem that a juridical phenomenon effectively exists here such that our definition is too narrow (i.e., the phenomenon which corresponds to it [is] inadequate). By contrast, and in conformity with our definition, the [31] situation becomes juridical as soon as it is a matter not only of dogs fighting but also their owners. The action of going for a walk in the street with dog A can provoke a reaction of attack from dog B, which will be annulled by the intervention of a police officer C. This intervention realizes and reveals a juridical relation not between the dogs, A and B, but between their respective owners, A′ and B′. It is A′ who has the **droit** to go for a walk in the street with his dog A without incident; in particular, he has the **droit** that B′ does not bother him with his dog B. It is not the dog, B, but his owner, B′, who does not have the **droit** to bother the dog, A, of *owner* A′, who has the juridical *duty* to avoid cases where his dog, B, is going to do so.

It is the same when there is an interaction between a human being A and an animal B, with the intervention of C. If a police officer or a passer-by protects me against the attack of a dog, this still has nothing juridical about it, neither in fact nor according to our definition. By contrast—in fact and by definition—the intervention of the officer realizes and reveals a juridical relation between myself and the owner of the dog. As soon as there is an interaction between myself and another human being, I have **droits** in relation to this other, if there is—in principle—the intervention of the third. It is really the owner of the dog and not the dog who is juridically responsible.

This remark seems to be contradicted by the uncontestable juridical phe-

---

For example, one can suppose and say that juridical notions apply to animals and so apply them: the phenomenon will be "inadequate" (explicit [or] "logical," moreover) but there will not be a "terminological mistake." By contrast, there will be such a "mistake" if a traveller, who otherwise does not admit juridical relations between animals, notices relations of this kind between monkeys, which he takes for natives by mistake. In the Middle Ages, there were trials of animals, without there being conscious, mythical anthropomorphism (see below) or a "terminological mistake" (for one judged an animal while realizing that it was an animal). In this case there is good reason to distinguish between the "psychological phenomenon" (*droit* is only applied to men [and] animals are understood in the way which we understand them) and the "logical phenomenon" (in the action—i.e., in fact—although unconsciously, either *droit* is conceived so as to be able to be applied to animals or the animals are anthropomorphized). The phenomenologist will first describe the "psychological phenomenon" (which can be adequate, by chance); then construct the (inadequate) "logical phenomenon"; indicate the ("ideological") reasons for their discrepancy; and finally, he will compare these two phenomena with the adequate phenomenon—that is, with the way in which *Droit* and Animal are revealed to his own consciousness.

nomenon of "noxal surrender," where the responsibility seems to be able to pass from the owner to the "guilty" animal.[6] But if this is truly so, one is quite simply in the presence of a case of anthropomorphism (more or less conscious). Our definition therefore remains valid, provided that one supposes that in certain (inadequate) cases a human being can have the body of an animal for material support.[7]

The same remark, for example, [goes] for the trials of animals in the Middle Ages (already mentioned in the [previous] footnote). In these trials, the animal really does find itself in a juridical situation. There is then an inadequate juridical phenomenon—that is, not conforming to our definition. But one can see that one judges the animal (or the thing) only because one anthropomorphizes it (unconsciously, moreover, for one continues to [32] think that man differs *essentially* from animals and things). One cannot say, therefore, that our definition is too narrow and the phenomenon which corresponds to it inadequate: one simply reverts to the previous case, or that of "myth."[8]

A modern juridical phenomenon seems more disturbing. This is the law concerning the protection of animals. One could interpret it in this sense, that the animal has the **droit** not to be tortured by man, which is quite different from saying that man does not have the *droit* to do it, that he has the juridical duty to refrain from it. If this were really the case, our definition could not be applied: either it would be too narrow or the phenomenon implicated by the law would be inadequate. But this dilemma is only illusory. What is inadequate is only the interpretation (more or less consciously anthropomorphic) of the law and not the law itself. In its correct interpretation, it forbids not the ill-treatment of animals but infringing the "humanitarian" feelings of others by doing so. It is a law analogous to the law aiming at offenses against the public's sense of decency, and so on. It is a matter here, therefore, of an interaction between two human beings, the guilty and the public, which is carried out in respect to an animal, and not an interaction between the animal and man.

---

6. [Ed. Noxal surrender (*l'abandon noxal*) was the Roman practice whereby the father of a family, or the owner of a slave or animal, would surrender his son, daughter, slave, and/or animal to another person against whom the individual or animal did wrong. By so doing, the father or owner avoided making reparations himself to the injured party for the damage done by the individual or animal under his supervision and control.]

7. It seems, moreover, that originally animals played the role of a simple guarantee of security which, being abandoned, extinguished the obligation. It was only afterwards—and a lot later—that one imagined the anthropomorphic interpretation, which has generated an inadequate juridical phenomenon. (Cf. [A.-E.] Giffard, *Précis de droit romain*, [3rd ed.,] vol. II [Paris: Librairie Dalloz, 1938], 258n.1.)

8. In reality, the phenomenon in question is inadequate not only in relation to the animal (that one wrongly treats as a human being) but also in relation to *Droit* itself. The animal is judged because the judge is supposed to represent God, the divine upholder of justice [*justicier*], and because the relation between the animal creature and God is supposed to be similar to the relation between God and the human creature. There is, then, confusion between juridical, moral, and religious phenomena. But I do not insist on this point.

Interpreted in this way (and it is in this way, I think, that modern jurisprudence interprets it), this phenomenon therefore tallies perfectly with our definition.

Finally, there remains the juridical notion of property. It is commonly said that property is the ***droit*** to a thing, and it has often been thought that there is a juridical relation between the owner and the thing or animal possessed. Now this is contrary to our definition, which would thus be too narrow, given that it is impossible to deny the adequate juridical character of the notion of property.

In reality, only this interpretation of the notion of property is inadequate. The *droit* of property is not a *droit* in relation to the property (to the animal or thing). It is solely a *droit* in relation to other human beings, who are not owners of the thing or [33] animal in question. The ***droit*** of property is realized and revealed when there is an interaction not between the thing (or animal) and the owner but between the latter and other human beings.

For the Civil Code (article 544, for example) and Roman *droit,* the *droit* of property is the *droit* to use, enjoy, and dispose of a thing in an absolute, exclusive, and perpetual way.[9] Now, "absolute way" juridically means not that the owner can do what he wants with the thing or animal, but that he can do it *without giving an account to anyone* (which is not exact, moreover, since he does not have the *droit* to make use of it [in a way] prohibited by the general laws and he must, therefore, give an account to the State—but this is of little importance). "Exclusive way" means that the owner alone possesses such prerogatives on the thing and that he can oppose *another* who comes to dispute with him over them. Finally, "perpetual way" only means that the "absolute and exclusive way" is not limited in time, that the owner can exclude all others even by a posthumous will.[10] The possibility of "using and abusing" the thing possessed is a purely physical possibility; only the *exclusivity* of this possibility is juridical, the exclusivity in relation to other men. In the ***droit*** of property, it is therefore a question of an interaction (virtual or real) between two human beings, and consequently our definition applies perfectly to it. (It is in this way, moreover, that modern jurisprudence interprets the *droit* of property.[11] However, Durkheim[12] speaks of a direct juridical link between the owner and the thing which belongs to him.) Indeed, if my field does not let itself be plowed and if my horse resists me, there will not be an intervention of a "disinterested third" (the police, for example); or, if there was such an intervention, it would not create a juridical situation precisely because it is a thing or an animal which reacts to my action as an owner. But if this reaction comes from another man (who prevents me

---

9. [Ed. For this and all subsequent references to the French Civil Code, see *Code Civil,* ed. M. Henry Bourdeaux (Paris: Jurisprudence Générale Dalloz, 1938), or the English translation, *The French Civil Code,* trans. Henry Cachard, rev. ed. (Paris: The Lecram Press, 1930).]

10. Cf. [Henry] Solus, *Les Principes du Droit civil* [Paris: Librairie Armand Colin, 1933], 92.

11. Cf., for example, [Henri] Capitant, *Introduction à l'étude du droit civil,* 5th ed. [Paris: A. Pedone, 1929], 8.

12. Cf. [Émile Durkheim,] *De la division [du travail social,* 6th ed., (Paris: Librairie Félix Alcan, 1932), 84ff and] 123ff. [*The Division of Labor in Society,* trans. George Simpson (Glencoe: The Free Press, 1947), 115ff and 150ff.]

from plowing my field or from using a horse, by stealing it, for example), the "third" will necessarily intervene (in principle) and this intervention will then reveal and realize my **droit** to do what I am doing, i.e., my **droit** to property, precisely because there will be an interaction between two human beings.

In short, the exclusion of "natural" beings in the sense of [34] non-human—animals, plants, or things—from the definition of the phenomenon of "*Droit*" does not seem to make it too narrow: on this point, the phenomenon corresponding to the definition seems to be adequate. A phenomenon can, therefore, present all the appearances of a juridical phenomenon; [but] it will not be so as long as it does not imply an interaction between *human beings*. But an animal or even a thing can be likened to a human being. The expression "human beings" in the definition does not necessarily mean, therefore, beings of the species Homo sapiens. These are any beings at all who are supposed to be able to act and react as a being that we call human would do in their place.

b) Without trying to define the being which *we* call "human," let us also suppose that it does not differ essentially less from a *divine being* than from an animal or a thing. According to our definition, then, there are juridical relations neither between divine beings nor between divine and human beings. It remains to be seen if this definition is not too narrow.

The case of would-be juridical relations between divine beings is unimportant. One can assume that it is a case here of mythical anthropomorphism (conscious or not), in every respect similar to the [already] considered case of would-be juridical relations between animals.

But the case of would-be juridical relations between a divine being and a human being must be discussed.

The most general definition of a *divine being* can be stated as follows: A is *divine* in relation to B and for B (i.e., for the consciousness that B has of it) if A is supposed to be able to act upon B without B being able to react upon A.[13] There is, then, no inter-action possible between a divine being and a human being. In other words, seeing that our definition anticipates an *interaction* between two beings, A and B, it follows that a divine being cannot take the place of A or B. But this only changes the question to knowing if our definition is not too narrow.

In fact, there has always been the feeling that there are no properly juridical relations between man and a truly divine being—that is, omnipotent in relation to man. Thus, according to Roman *droit*, the Master (*pater familias* [head of the family]) is responsible for the wrongs [*délits*][14] committed by his Slave

---

13. For example, as long as men have believed that the stars acted upon them, but that they could not act upon the stars, the stars were considered divine; but as soon as physics revealed to us that the action of the stars upon us is exactly equal to our reaction upon them, they have been "secularized."

14. [Ed. In France, criminal offenses are divided into three groups in ascending order of severity: *contraventions, délits,* and *crimes*. In general, we will translate *contraventions* as "infractions," *délits* as "wrongs," and *crimes* as "crimes." The adjective *délictuelle* will be translated as "wrongful" or "in a wrongful way."]

(or in [35] general by an *alieni juris* [someone under the authority or control of another person] in his power) outside of the house; but when a wrong is committed by the Slave (or the *alieni juris*) against the Master himself, "it does not give rise to any (juridical) action," for a juridical obligation is not possible between the Master and the individuals subjected to his power.[15] There is, then, no juridical relation between A and B when A's action is not supposed to be able to provoke B's reaction, B being "subject to the power" of A. Now this is what takes places in the relations between man and his God (or his gods): without a reaction, no *inter*-action and consequently no intervention of a third (who would have no purpose)—that is, according to our definition, no specifically juridical element.

On the other hand, man often speaks of his relations with the divine in juridical terms, and he almost always attributes a divine character to *Droit*. Let us try, therefore, to explain this.

First of all, one must dismiss the very frequent cases of anthropomorphic theology. They are unimportant since with them we revert again to cases of anthropomorphic zoology, already discussed above. The phenomenon will then be adequate in its juridical aspect; only the theological aspect will be inadequate, the divine being [*étant*] falsely conceived as human. Our definition will thus be valid.[16]

---

15. Cf. [*The Institutes of*] Gaius, 4:78, quoted by Giffard, *Précis de droit romain*, vol. II, 257n.1. [Ed. Kojève adds the word "juridical" in parentheses to the quotation.]

16. *Magical* theology is always anthropomorphic. More exactly, Magic is by definition atheistic (being a Technique or an Art properly speaking) and has nothing to do with Religion. Indeed, the magician is supposed to be able to act upon the "divine." What is called "divine," therefore, is not divine *for us*. It is a human being, or more exactly, an anthropomorphic being, situated on the same plane as man and nature, and not *transcendent* in relation to them. The Religious [person] can only address prayers to his God, which do not exert any constraint upon God: the being to which one can only *pray* is therefore truly divine. The practice of magic, by contrast, acts necessarily; it *constrains* the being for whom it is intended. This being, therefore, is not divine in relation to the magician. On the plane of Magic, then, there can be juridical relations—in the sense of our definition—between man and what one wrongly calls the "divine" precisely because this pseudo-divine [being] does not differ essentially from the human. (Moreover, contrary to the goals of the Religious [person], which are essentially *transcendent,* the goals of the Magician are always *immanent* to the world. We will also see in chapter 3 that from this point of view magical relations can have a juridical character, in contrast to religious relations, which have nothing to do with *Droit*.) Now, every concrete Religion implies a lot of magical elements (or influences [*réminiscences*]), from whence comes the tendency for anthropomorphism and, consequently, for the *juridical* interpretation of relations between man and the divine (above all in "magical Religions" and "religious Magics." The former are *Religions* because the divine is correctly conceived, as omnipotent or transcendent in relation to the world and to man, but which are [36] *magical* to the extent that the goals of man remain immanent to the world—for example, the biblical Hebrew *prays* to God to send him food. The "religious Magics" are *Magics* because the ritual practices are supposed to act necessarily, but they are *religious* to the extent that the goal is transcendent—for example, the practices of yoga with a view to the salvation of the soul. A case of pure Magic [is] the infallible practice for compelling a "god" to make it rain; a case of pure Religion [is] to pray for the salvation of the soul.)

[36] There are cases when the theological phenomenon is adequate (omnipotence of God) and when one nevertheless speaks of juridical relations. According to our definition, then, the juridical phenomenon is inadequate. It is a matter of explaining the mistake and in this way justifying the proposed definition.

The analysis of concrete cases (Christianity, for example) shows that one begins by accepting a sort of bifurcation of the divine (of God): one distinguishes a celestial (transcendent) aspect or avatar B and a terrestrial (quasi-immanent) aspect or avatar C of God. Divine action is divided between B and C, and one assumes (more or less explicitly) that only the complete action is omnipotent, while the isolated action of B or C (or of the two) is not. One accepts, then, an *inter*-action between a human being A and the avatar B, for example, the avatar C playing the role of the "third" of our definition. It is in this way that one has the impression of being in the presence of a juridical situation (conforming to our definition).

In practice, the action of the immanent avatar C is delegated to a Church, which plays the role of arbiter between man and his God (in the transcendent avatar B). This Church can thus realize and reveal a "divine *Droit*." This is "canon *droit*" in the narrow and proper sense of the term, the "*droit*" being applied to sacrilege, heresy, and so on—that is, not to relations between human beings but to relations between men and God.

If such a "canon *droit*" is effectively a *Droit*, our definition is too narrow. But one can show that this would-be "*Droit*" is only an inadequate juridical phenomenon, and that it is so precisely because it implies a relation between a human being and a *divine being*.

Indeed, if the Church only represents God on earth, it is not distinct from him, it is not a "disinterested and impartial third" in relation to him. Now, no one will want to see a relation of *droit* when the injured party or the one vindicating a *droit* is at the same time juridical legislator, judge, and executor of the judgement. One reverts again to the [37] case of the relation between Master and Slave, which is not a juridical relation according to Roman *droit* or general juridical opinion [*sentiment*]. But if the Church differs essentially from God, it will be by definition powerless in relation to him, since he is omnipotent in relation to all that is not himself. The Church, therefore, will not be able to *intervene* in a conflict between man and his God: there will be neither arbitration nor enforcement—that is, there will be no observable juridical situation, there will be no juridical *phenomenon*. Of course, the Church will be able to act upon man, but here its intervention will be pointless, or indeed have no purpose, since the reaction of man is annulled as a matter of course, God being omnipotent in relation to him. Thus, when a human being A is in a relation with a divine being B, only two cases are possible: either there will be no intervention of a third, such that there will not even be the appearance of a juridical situation; or an efficacious third will be there, but he will only be in reality an emanation from B and not a *third* C properly so-called, such that there will only be an *illusion* of a juridical situation. And this is why the definition specifies that C's intervention must occur in the event of an interaction between two *human beings* for there to be an authentic juridical situation.

Practically speaking, the illusion of a "juridical" relation between man and his God appears when man wants to present something (to himself or to others) as a "*droit*" or a "juridical duty" without being able to give a juridical justification properly so-called for it (i.e., as we will see later on, without being able to deduce the would-be "*droit*" from the idea of justice accepted by him). Then one says that the "*droit*" or the "duty" in question are commandments of God, that to infringe upon this "*droit*," to fail in this "duty," is to offend God; to enter into a juridical relation with him; [and] to fall under the jurisdiction of "canonical *droit*." Now, *for us,* this is only an inadequate juridical phenomenon: if a juridical situation cannot be constituted in the event of a given interaction between two *human beings,* it cannot be constituted at all; in particular, one cannot create it by replacing one of these human beings by a divine being. And this is what our definition says.

Of course, sacrilege, for example, is (or has been) an incontestable juridical phenomenon. But it tallies with our definition provided that it is correctly interpreted, namely, one must interpret it as we have interpreted the [38] law protecting animals. Sacrilege committed by a human being is a *juridical* phenomenon not because it "offends God" but because it "offends" another human being, individual or collective (society as a whole, for example)—that is, because there is an interaction between two *human beings.* If sacrilege is punished solely because it offends God, the punishment has nothing truly juridical about it: there is only the illusory appearance of a "*Droit.*" By contrast, punishment will be authentically juridical if the sacrilege is punished because it offends the religious feelings of the community, for example, or really infringes upon its interests, putting it entirely in the grip of the divine wrath, provoked by the sacrilegious act.[17]

---

17. Let us take the case of incest. One can forbid it *juridically* only by assuming that it infringes upon some *human* interests. If this is denied, it can still be forbidden as "offending God"; but this ban will be moral or religious and not juridical. Compare [this to] modern French *droit,* which does not punish incest while recognizing its immoral (or indeed, "sacrilegious") character, but which refuses to recognize incestuous children, this being contrary to the interests of the family: incest, therefore, has a juridical existence only to the extent that it is related to human society, while *droit* ignores it to the extent that it is only related to God.

Primitive *droit* often limits itself to expelling the sacrilegious man in order that divine punishment only affects him alone and spares the social group to which he belongs. Here is the correct interpretation of it (which is not the one primitive *droit* itself gives). On the one hand, banishment is not a juridical sentence: the group simply is uninterested in the criminal by leaving to God the care of judging and punishing him; *droit,* therefore, is not applied to relations between the guilty and God. On the other hand, the banishment is a juridical punishment, but it is then motivated by the fact that the criminal has injured the group by bringing upon it the ire of God; (penal) *droit,* therefore, is applied to a relation between human beings.

In the Middle Ages, the State did not judge the heretic, limiting itself to handing him over to the Church. The Church did not punish the heretic (but only tried to correct him), limiting itself to handing over the incorrigible heretic to the State (which put him to

[39] Let us suppose, therefore, that there is no "divine *Droit*" in the sense of a juridical relation between a human being and a divine being (or between two divine beings). But one still speaks—and very often—of "divine *Droit*" when it is a matter of an interaction between two human beings. The divine being then plays the role of the "impartial third" C of our definition: he is either the Legislator who creates the legal rule, or the Judge who applies it to a given case, or finally, the power which enforces the judgement (or again, he combines his functions). Now, if it is contrary to our definition for A and B to be divine beings, it does not exclude the case when the divine being plays the role of C—on the contrary.

Indeed, we will see that C's intervention is supposed to be absolutely efficacious: C is, therefore, "omnipotent" in relation to A and B. In other words, he has a "divine" character in relation to the latter. Entirely unsurprising, therefore, that men have often divinized the "third" in question, and through this even *Droit* as such, which is realized and revealed precisely in and by the intervention of this third. *Droit* is often conceived as having its highest [*dernière*] source or guarantee in God, and God is generally understood as a supreme Legislator, Judge, or Upholder of Justice. As for the phenomenology of *Droit*, it does not solve the question of knowing if there are or not real "divine beings." It limits itself to noticing that in the case when an impartial and disinterested "divine being" was intervening in the event of an interaction between two human beings, A and B, by annulling B's reaction, one would be in the presence of an authentic juridical phenomenon.[18]

---

death). It seems that the (unconscious) reason is the following: the State admits that it embodies *Droit* properly so-called, but it realizes that heresy, being a relation between man and *God,* is not a juridical phenomenon. It is correct, therefore, to be juridically uninterested in heresy and to give up the heretic to the Church. But it is wrong to believe that the ecclesiastical action against the heretic is a court of law [*juridiction*]: a court of law *sui generis,* certainly, but a court of law all the same ("canon ***droit***"). The Church recognizes that the punishment is an authentically juridical phenomenon, while the ecclesiastical proceeding having to do with relations between man and God is not a genuine court of law. It is correct, therefore, [for the Church] not to punish the guilty itself and to think that all (juridical) punishment must be carried out by the State. But it is wrong to say (and the State admits this) that a non-juridical proceeding (based upon canon "*droit*") can and must generate a juridical punishment (based upon *Droit* properly so-called). To the extent that "canon *droit*" is applied to interactions [39] between human beings, it is an authentic *Droit.* (See the analysis in chapter 2 of "group *droit*"—that is, of "potential *droit*.")

18. We will see that in reality the "disinterested third" is Society or the State. Therefore, to divinize it [the third] is to divinize these latter. But one can accept with Hegel (and Durkheim) that the "divine" is never anything else but Society or the State "idealized" or "hypostatized"—that is, unconsciously projected into the beyond. Entirely unsurprising when man looks for the source and guarantee of *Droit* in God. [Ed. For Hegel's understanding of religion and the state, see, for example, *Phenomenology of Spirit,* trans. A. V. Miller (Oxford: Oxford University Press, 1977), 410–78; *Lectures on the Philosophy of Religion,* 3 vols., trans. Rev. E. B. Speirs, B.D., and J. Burdon Sanderson (New York: Humanities Press, 1968), I: 246–58, III: 138–51; and *Elements of the Philosophy of Right,* trans. H. B. Nisbet (Cambridge: Cambridge University Press, 1991), 290–304. For Durkheim's understanding of the same, see *Elementary Forms of the Religious Life: A Study in Religious Sociology,* trans. Joseph Ward Swain (London: George Allen & Unwin, 1976), 1–20, 205–14, and 415–47.]

[40] But the question of the "third" does not interest us for the moment. And the general problem of the relation between *Droit* and Religion will be discussed in chapter 3. For the moment, it suffices to note that, despite appearances, there is no adequate juridical phenomenon (i.e., conforming to our definition) either when a human being is interacting with an animal or a thing, or when he is in relation with a divine being—that is, omnipotent in relation to him. The *juridical* relation is necessarily a relation between *human beings.*

c) According to our definition, therefore, it is necessary to be a "human being" to be capable of being a "subject of *droit*." But does the term "human being" in this definition mean the same thing as "representative of the species *Homo sapiens?*"

We have seen that, in the case of anthropomorphism, "divinities," animals, or even things can be considered like "human beings," which only differ from man properly so-called by the fact of having another "support" than him, [but which] do not belong to the species Homo sapiens. We will now see that it is not enough to have for support the animal *Homo sapiens* in order to be a subject of *droit.*

First there is the case of slavery. The Slave is a Homo sapiens who, by definition, cannot be a juridical person, a subject of *droit.* If the interaction between two free persons, A and B, necessarily provokes the intervention of a "third" C, this same interaction will not provoke an intervention in the case where A or B (or A and B) are slaves. (Marriage, for example, is juridically recognized in Rome only between free persons.) There is, then, a juridical situation only in the first case, although in both cases it is a matter of representatives of the species Homo sapiens.

In no case can the Slave be a subject of *droit.* If A, or B, or A and B are slaves, C will never intervene and there will then be no juridical situation. There can be a juridical situation *regarding* a slave or *because* of him, but only if there is also an interaction between two free persons. The Slave is a [piece of] property, an animal or a thing, and everything that has been said above regarding property applies to him. But there are cases when even a free person cannot be a subject of *droit,* while capable of being one in other cases. A specific interaction between A and B, which necessarily provokes C's intervention [and] thus creates a juridical situation, may not provoke this intervention and consequently remain extrajuridical if A, [41] or B, or A and B are, for example, young children, or the insane, or women, or if they belong to a specific social class, and so on.

In fact, the "third" C (and the State) is "omnipotent" in relation to A and B only to the extent that it concerns the interaction in question; otherwise, A and B can *act* upon C. (For example, as long as the State remains what it is, it is an "omnipotent" judge of its nationals; but these can alter the State through a revolutionary action.) In other words, the "third," the State, and consequently *Droit* itself, are not really *divine.* They only have the appearance of the divine, which explains the fact that they are often divinized (consciously or not, but always wrongly). *Droit* may seem to be "*divine*" to the individual because he cannot alter *Droit* through his *direct* action. But it only *seems* to be so, because the same individual can alter *Droit indirectly,* for example, by forcing the State to alter *Droit* in the desired sense.

Thus, the taxing question concerning who is a subject of *droit* or a juridical person makes its appearance. I will have to discuss it, but later on. For the moment, the following remarks must suffice.

If there were not inadequate juridical phenomena, one would have been able to dismiss the question for the moment by reversing the situation. One could have said that A and B are subjects of *droit* every time that, and to the extent that, their interaction necessarily provokes C's intervention. The restrictive term "human beings" could then be eliminated from the definition. But we have seen that there are inadequate phenomena, illusory "juridical" situations. For example, whatever interaction between A and B provokes the intervention of C, the situation will not be juridical if A or B is an animal. And we have said that it is necessarily so as soon as A, or B, or A and B are animals, things, or divine beings. One must ask, therefore, if the phenomenon does not become inadequate from the sole fact that A or B belong to a special category of human beings (Homo sapiens). For the moment I will not ask why an interaction between representatives of one such category of human beings does not provoke C's intervention, thus remaining extra-juridical, while it does so if it takes place between representatives of another category. I neither ask, for example, why a human being is a Slave nor why a Slave cannot be a subject of *droit.* I only ask if there are categories of human beings which, like animals or God, cannot be subjects of *droit,* even if the interaction provokes, or at least seems to do so, the intervention in conformity with our definition—that is, even if they *seem* to be subjects of *droit.* In other words, can one consider a juridical phenomenon inadequate *solely* because the role of A or B (or A and B) is played by the representative of a special category of "human beings"— Homo sapiens?

It seems that the answer must be negative. If all the other conditions mentioned in our definition are fulfilled, it is sufficient that A and B are beings belonging to the species Homo sapiens for the juridical phenomenon to be adequate.

The historical evolution of juridical consciousness ends up at this conclusion. For modern European *droit* has [42] as a principle that "by the sole fact of his existence, a human being (read Homo sapiens) is a subject of *droit.*"[19] A Homo sapiens can be affected with "special incapacities" or even "general incapacity,"

---

19. Cf., for example, [Julien] Bonnecase, *Introduction à l'Étude du Droit* [3rd ed. (Paris: Librairie du Recueil Sirey, 1939)], 42.

This principle, moreover, is quite recent, since the Napoleonic Code still recognized "civil death," which was only abolished in France in 1854. [Ed. Civil death occurred when a person was sentenced to a penalty that deprived him or her of all civil rights, e.g., property rights, the right to vote, the right to inherit, and so on. Civil death was spelled out in articles 22–33 of the Civil Code.]

The term "existence" must be taken in a very broad sense, since the "subject" can exist both after the death of the corresponding Homo sapiens (the case of the child acknowledged [attribué] *post mortem* [after death: in other words, the child's paternity is recognized after the death of his or her father], article 315 of the Civil Code) and before his birth, or indeed before his conception (the case of "unborn children," article 1048 of the Civil Code).

as the jurists say, but his "incapacity" will never be absolute. In other words, from the modern point of view there will always be cases when an action of any Homo sapiens, arousing a reaction, will necessarily provoke the intervention anticipated by our definition, which will yield an authentic juridical situation, where the Homo sapiens in question will play the role of a subject of *droit.*

Of course, it is not enough to take note of the existence of this point of view in modern jurisprudence. One must also justify it phenomenologically by presenting the modern point of view (which is ours) as a necessary result (i.e., "comprehensible" or "deducible afterwards") of the "dialectical" evolution of the phenomenon of "*Droit.*" I will not be able to do this here. But I will try to justify this point of view in Part Two (chapter 1) by showing that the primordial anthropogenic act necessarily implies a juridical element. In other words, the act in and by which an animal Homo sapiens creates itself as an authentic human being is necessarily such that it makes him capable of entering into interaction with another human being created in the same manner so as to provoke the intervention of a similar third being, in conformity with our definition. In short, by constituting himself as a human being, the animal Homo sapiens by the same token constitutes himself as a subject of *droit,* who can be neither a non-humanized animal nor a god.

There remains, however, a difficulty that must be removed right here and now. The anthropogenic act is surely not carried out by an infant or a psychologically abnormal person, an idiot or an insane person. We say with modern *droit,* however, that they can be subjects of *droit* in an authentic juridical situation. And yet, they still do not effectively differ from an animal, and they are, moreover, treated as such (through the use of brute force, without the intervention [43] of language). At first glance, therefore, this would be an inadequate juridical phenomenon.

It seems that one can avoid this consequence only by assuming (which we will try to justify subsequently) that the juridical relation is in its very essence "eternal." Of course, it can only be realized and manifested in time, but it implies the *totality* of time and not only such a specific moment of time (present, past, or future). Thus, the subject of *droit* is not only the Homo sapiens as he is at a given moment of his existence, but as he is in the *totality* of this existence, presumed eternal (or at the very least, with whatever undefined limits). In our definition the infant is treated as a "human being" (subject of *droit*) because he is one day supposed to become one, and the insane person because he is supposed to have been or to be able to be one.[20] By contrast, a thing and an animal, as well as a divine being, are never supposed to be able to become authentic human beings. They cannot, therefore, be subjects of *droit,* while an already dead man can still be one, precisely because he has been a human being properly so-called.

Let us assume, therefore, that our definition would not become too broad if we replaced the term "human being" with that of "Homo sapiens." In other

---

20. Thus, the Civil Code (article 725, § 2) declares the "non-viable" child incapable of inheriting. As for the insane, modern jurisprudence does not seem to accept juridically the existence of cases of *incurable* congenital insanity.

words, all the other conditions of the definition being fulfilled, if A and B are representatives of the species Homo sapiens, whomever they are, the phenomenon will be authentically juridical.

But let us point out once again that it is not sufficient that A and B belong to the species Homo sapiens for there to be C's intervention—that is, a juridical situation. Not only can a lot of interactions between A and B be extra-juridical or juridically neutral, such that they do not necessarily provoke the intervention of the "third" C; [but also] one and the same interaction may or may not provoke this intervention—i.e., be juridical or not—depending on whether A and B are adults or children, men or women, sane or insane, or depending on whether or not they belong to a specific social class, or for still other reasons. I only say that *if* this intervention of C takes place, the situation will be authentically juridical, seeing that A and B belong to the species Homo sapiens, [44] and that it will not be so if A, or B, or A and B are things, animals, or gods.[21]

d) We have just admitted that our definition does not become too broad if we replace the term "human beings" with that of "Homo sapiens." In other words, we assert that every Homo sapiens is a "human being" in the sense that the definition has in mind. But the opposite is not true. And this is why one cannot substitute "Homo sapiens" for "human being": the definition would become too narrow. If the notion of "human being (as a subject of *droit*)" can authentically be applied to every Homo sapiens, the latter cannot be applied to the former.

Indeed, we have seen that gods, animals, and even things can be juridically anthropomorphized. We will not return to this, all the more so because these (juridically adequate) cases are inadequate in the sense that the beings in question are not taken for what they are in truth (i.e., for us). But there are cases when the being is taken such as it is for us (i.e., in truth) and when it is nevertheless an authentic subject of *droit* while not being a Homo sapiens properly so-called. These are cases when A or B, or A and B of our definition, are what the jurists call "moral persons."

One must briefly discuss these cases (assumed to be authentically juridical) in order to clarify definitively the sense of the term "human being," [which is] supposed to be applied in our definition both to "moral persons" and to "physical persons," as the jurists say.

For French jurisprudence, the notion of "physical person" coincides with that of Homo sapiens: every Homo sapiens is *eo ipso* a "physical person," and every "physical person" is a Homo sapiens, whatever his sex, age, and mental state.

In contrast to "physical persons" are "moral persons." These are either "associations (*lato sensu*) [in the broad sense]" or "institutions [*fondations*]."[22] All these "moral persons" are said to be "of private *droit*." As for "moral per-

---

21. Moreover, it is not only the *fact* of C's intervention but also its *nature* (or its mode) which is a function of the adherence of A or B to a specific category of human beings.

22. "Associations *lato sensu*" are either non-profit "associations *stricto sensu* [in the strict sense]"—"simple," "declared," or "state approved"—or profit-making "societies," which are either "societies of persons" or "societies of capital." But these purely technical distinctions do not interest us here.

sons [45] of public *droit*" (which are either "public administrative apparatuses [*administrations*]," i.e., the State, Departments, Districts, and Colonies, or[23] "public enterprises [*établissements*]"),[24] I will speak about them later on in this same section. "Associations" (*lato sensu*) are "moral persons who have at their base a group of physical persons, formed with a view to one or several specific goals"; therefore, these are "unions of physical persons," "physical persons grouped [together]," [or] "looked upon as associated." "Institutions," by contrast, are "independent of all grouping"; "they reduce to a charitable, intellectual, or benevolent undertaking, endowed with a material organization, and graced with a personality."[25]

In other words, when there is the action of an "association," there is always a group of wills and actions of normal adults of the species Homo sapiens. The action of the association is nothing other than the result of their actions, which is formed according to a specific but otherwise indifferent [*quelconque*] principle (unanimity, majority rule, and so on), and which can be called their "collective action or will." The association is born from such a "collective will" (which is a necessary if not sufficient condition), and the same will which has created it can also annihilate it.[26] In order to bring out this aspect of an "association," I propose to call it a "*collective moral person.*"

The "institution" is also born from a will or action of a normal and adult Homo sapiens, or a group of normal adults—that is, a "collective will." But once born, it can free itself from this will, which can no longer annihilate it. And the action of the "institution" can be quite independent of the action of the founder. This action, therefore, is autonomous. Of course, there is always an individual or collective action of Homo sapiens, the institution obviously being unable to act effectively itself. But the relation of the agent with the institution will be the same as the relation between the agent and the principal [*le mandataire et le mandant*].[27] From the juridical point of view, there will be an autonomous action of the institution, carried out through the intermediary [46] of the manager, and so on. When there is an action of the institution as such, there will then be no action of a Homo sapiens. One can also say that by creating an institution one abstracts from the action of the founder. This is why I propose to call institutions "*abstract moral persons.*"

Now, I think that a third type of moral person must be added to these two,

---

23. [Ed. Reading *soit* for *sont* as in the original manuscript.]
24. According to [Maurice] Hauriou. [Ed. This is perhaps a reference to *Précis élémentaire de droit administratif,* 5th ed. (Paris: Librairie du Recueil Sirey, 1943), 28, and/or *Précis de droit administratif et de droit public général,* 5th ed. (Paris: Librairie du Recueil Sirey, 1903), 191–2.]
25. Cf. Bonnecase, *Introduction,* 53.
26. If an association, a labor union for example, is imposed on its members, who can neither dissolve nor leave it, this can only be done ultimately by the State. The association will then be an "administrative apparatus," i.e., a moral person of public *droit,* even if its action is only the collective action of its members. I will speak about "administrative apparatuses" below.
27. [Ed. The *mandataire* (the agent) is someone who is given a mandate to do something by someone else; the *mandant* (the principal) is the person who gives someone that mandate.]

which I propose to call an *"individual* moral *person."*[28] It is only by taking account of this third type that one can correctly interpret the other two.

To arrive at the notion of this third type of moral person, one must recall that the notions "Homo sapiens" and "physical person" are not interchangeable; for the latter notion only has meaning if one admits that every "physical person" is by definition a *juridical* person—that is, a subject of *droit.* Now, it is enough to think about the notion of *Capitis deminutio* in Roman *droit* or about "civil death" in the Napoleonic Code in order to notice that a man can cease being a "physical person" without changing what he is as a Homo sapiens.[29] Consequently, and we have already taken note of it above, it is not enough to be a Homo sapiens in order to be a "physical person." Every Homo sapiens *may* be one without the juridical situation being unauthentic by this fact, but it is not *necessarily* so.[30] Every Homo sapiens *may* be a "physical person," but in order to be so effectively he must be recognized as such by the State.[31]

This remark allows one to see clearly in a long debate in respect to (collective and abstract) "moral persons." For certain [authors],[32] these "persons" are "fictions" because their mission presupposes the intervention of the law. For others,[33] they are "real" because the law is only made to recognize a fact without creating it: "following the example of physical persons, moral persons *impose* their mission [*consécration*] [47] on the public powers."[34] Now, we have just seen that the "physical person"—i.e., Homo sapiens here—just as little "imposes" his "enterprise" on the State as the "moral person." If everything that is created by the law is a "fiction," the "physical person"—i.e., the juridical person here—is just as "fictive" as the "moral person." On this point there can be no difference between the two.

However, a difference does exist.

According to our definition, A is a subject of *droit* or a juridical person when his action provokes a reaction from B, with the intervention of C, and so on. When this action from A is the effective action of an individual and real Homo sapiens who is none other than A himself, one can say that A is a *"physical*

---

28. In German, I would have called the three types *besondere* [particular], *allgemeine* [general], [and] *einzelne* [individual], respectively.

29. [Ed. *Capitis deminutio* (literally diminished capacity) was the loss, diminution, or curtailment of a person's legal status, with all the benefits (and burdens) that this status implied. This could occur through the loss of citizenship, becoming a slave, being convicted of a serious crime, and so on.]

30. I am not speaking in this context about the Slave, because according to certain theories (for example, that of Aristotle [*Politics,* 1253b23–1255b40]), slaves do not belong to the species Homo sapiens, being a distinctive, anthropomorphic species, but in fact [they] belong to the species of] animal.

31. It is of little importance for the moment why [this is so], and what this "recognition" means. This will be the question of chapter 2.

32. For example, for [Theophile] Ducrocq, *Cours de droit administratif* [*et de legislation française des finances avec introduction de droit constitutionnel et les principes du droit public*], 7th ed., vol. IV [(Paris: A. Fontemoing, 1897–1905)], 13.

33. For example, Bonnecase, *Introduction,* 61ff.

34. Bonnecase, *Introduction,* 64.

(juridical) person" (in the sense that he is the subject of right[35] determined by the fact and the nature of C's intervention). But when A's action is in reality either the *result* of several individuals of the species Homo sapiens, A not being any of them or a Homo sapiens in general (case of an association), or an "*ideal*" action which can only be realized in and by a *Homo sapiens* other than A, who is not one of them (case of an institution), then A is a "collective" or "abstract" "*moral* (juridical) person." Likewise, when A's action is "ideal" in the sense that it can only be realized (in fact or in principle) by a Homo sapiens other than A, A himself nevertheless being a Homo sapiens, A will be a "*moral* (juridical) person," but this time this moral person will be "*individual.*" For example, an infant A is incapable *in fact* of performing an act of a commercial nature. A minor, A, can be capable of doing it in fact, but he is incapable *in principle* (according to the law). In the two cases, therefore, A's action is "ideal," *necessarily* realized by another Homo sapiens A' (the guardian, for example). But in the two cases A is a Homo sapiens,[36] [and this is] the same situation for an insane person, or for a woman in certain cases, and so on. In other words, there is an "individual moral person" every time that, and to the extent that, a "physical person" [48] (in the ordinary sense) acts while being juridically "incapable" of doing so such that he is effectively obligated to act through another. It is enough to think about cases when A is an unborn child or an already dead man to realize that the "individual moral person" differs essentially from the "physical person" (in the sense that I attribute to this term). In these cases, the "individual moral person" does not differ a lot from the "abstract moral person" (institution): if you will, there is a sort of "institution" for the benefit of the Homo sapiens who is at the base of the individual moral person. But the existence of this Homo sapiens in the case of the "individual moral person" distinguishes it from the case of the "abstract moral person." In any case, the action of the guardian is comparable (juridically) to that of the manager of the institution or the representative of the will of the association. He is the only one effectively to act, but from the juridical point of view the action is not his but that of the person whom he represents.

For modern European *droit,* every living Homo sapiens, whatever his sex, age, mental state, race, class, and so on, is always capable himself of performing certain real acts such that he is also always a "physical person" (while being able to be an "individual moral person" for other acts, if he is struck with a general or special "incapacity"). But it was not always so. (For example, in ancient Roman *droit,* the newborn child was not so before his recognition by the father.) I have not discussed here the question of knowing in which cases and why a Homo sapiens can

---

35. [Ed. In the original, the English word "right" follows the French phrase *sujet du droit* in square brackets.]
36. The case of the normal adult acting through an agent is somewhere in between. One can say that he is a "physical person" (having the *droit* to act either himself or through the intermediary of another), but one can also say that this is an "individual moral person" (in the case where he acts through the agent). What is essential is that he can—in fact and in principle—act himself. Therefore, it is better to call him a "physical person" in all the cases.

act so as to provoke the intervention of C anticipated by our definition—that is, so as to be a subject of *droit*. I say only that *if* he can act in that fashion, he is an authentic juridical person: "physical" when he acts (or can act, in fact or in principle) in that fashion himself, and "individual moral" when he is incapable, in fact or in principle, of doing so, but nevertheless acts through the intermediary of another juridical person (physical or moral).[37]

[49] Of course, the notion of a "moral person" allows one to create juridical persons having for a [material] base a thing, an animal, or a god, just as the "individual moral person" has for a base some Homo sapiens (living, dead, or unborn). If the action of the "guardian" A′ of the animal A, and so on, arouses a reaction from B which is annulled by the intervention of C, one can say that there is a juridical relation and that A is a subject of *droit*—that is, a (*sui generis* "moral") juridical person. And this is what one sometimes does. But I say that in this case the phenomenon will be juridically inadequate, precisely and solely because A is an animal.[38]

The reason has already been indicated above (see *c*, page 52).

Droit is related to time. But it is not exclusively related to a given moment of time. It is related to the whole of time: to the past, present, and future. Now, in relation to a given moment, the unborn child and the minor *will be* (in principle) an adult and "normal" Homo sapiens, and the deceased has *been* one. For *Droit*, therefore, they *are* "normal" representatives of the species Homo sapiens, since they will be or have been one at some moment in time. The "fiction" of the individual moral person, which effectively allows them to be one at the considered moment, i.e., to act *as* if they were "normal," is therefore *juridically* justified.[39]

---

37. The same Homo sapiens can be a "physical person" in one case and an "individual moral person" in another case. For example, the infant A has the **droit** to life, since the third C annuls B's reaction (who desires to kill A) provoked by A's action, which consists in living, in breathing for example. Now the infant himself breathes. Likewise, the infant (or the insane) is a "physical person" when the law protects his property, since it is enough simply to be living in order to "exercise himself his *droit* to property." But the same infant is effectively incapable of performing acts of a commercial nature, for example. As a [49] subject of commercial *droits*, therefore, he is an "individual moral person."

38. One says that a testator can bequeath a sum to a horse, [or] more exactly for the maintenance of a horse. But one should not say this. One must not say that the horse has a *droit* to the bequeathed money, to be fed, and so on. The horse is only the object of an institution and not a subject of *droit*. The subject is the testator (or the institution), who has a *droit*, even being already deceased, to be fed—that is, to cause his horse to be fed. The deceased testator feeds his horse not in fact but in law [*en droit*], as an "individual moral person." The horse is fed in fact, but it does not have a **droit** to be fed.

39. In the case where *droit* assumes that the child will *never* be a "normal" adult, it can deny him individual moral personality. For example, the Civil Code does not allow a "non-viable" child to inherit. But one can wonder if this way of reasoning is juridically justifiable. But the State can, as we will see, deny a juridical personality to whom it sees fit.

The notion of "prescription" does not contradict our remark about the "eternity" of *Droit*—on the contrary. "Prescription" justly presupposes a "total" vision of time. *Droit* says in this case [that] such a *droit* exists up until the moment *t*, and it no longer exists after this moment—"until the end of time." The juridical situation (the existence of a *droit* plus the non-existence of this same *droit*) therefore encompasses the *totality* of time.

The case of the insane does not essentially differ from that of [50] the child. If *Droit* does not recognize the existence of incurable cases, it admits that the insane can become normal "one day." Therefore, they *are* [normal] juridically speaking, from whence comes the "fiction" of their individual moral personality.

Cases of sexual (a woman) and social (a slave, and so on) "incapacities" are more complicated.

Let us take the case of the Slave (and of incapacity for social reasons in general). If *Droit* admits (with Aristotle) that the Slave can never become a "normal" Homo sapiens and can never have been one, and if it denies him all juridical personality, it is juridically logical with itself. It can say that *every* Homo sapiens is a juridical person but that the Slave is not a Homo sapiens. But if in this hypothesis *Droit* assigns to the Slave an individual moral personality (as Roman *droit* did), the phenomenon is juridically inadequate. Conversely, if *Droit* admits that a "normal" (free) Homo sapiens can become a slave and that a slave can be emancipated (i.e., become a "normal" Homo sapiens), and if it denies an individual moral personality to the slave, it is in contradiction with itself. More exactly, it does not take into account the very essence of the notion of *Droit*, which is related to the *totality* of time. Now, every phenomenon tends to become adequate—that is, in particular, to overcome its internal contradiction. The *Droit* in question, therefore, will end up by seeing in the slave an individual moral person. Now this is to treat him as a "normal" Homo sapiens and not as a slave. In this case, then, there is a *juridical* cause for the abolition of slavery, independent of economic, religious, moral, and other causes.

Let us now take the case of women. No *Droit* has assumed that a woman has been or will be a man one day. If *Droit* does not admit any *juridical* difference between men and women, there is no difficulty; because *for us* the woman is no less a "normal" Homo sapiens than the man.[40] A situation conforming to our definition, when the role of A or B, or of A and B, is played by women, is therefore authentically juridical. [But there is] nothing to say either against the *droit* which denies women the quality of [being] a subject of *droit*, i.e., of both "physical" and "moral" persons, since, as we have seen, it is not at all necessary that *every* Homo sapiens is such a subject. A *droit* can deny the juridical personality [51] of everyone taller than six feet, for example, without this *droit* hence becoming juridically unauthentic. A difficulty only arises when *droit* denies the "physical personality" of the woman while attributing to her an "individual moral personality"—that is, when the woman is struck with a general or special, but not absolute, "incapacity." Indeed, the justification of the "moral personality" of the child, the deceased, and the insane is not applied to the case of the woman, seeing that she has never been and will never be a man. It seems, therefore, that she differs *essentially* from him, that she belongs to another *species*, that she is not a human being. Now, in this case, her "moral personality" would be just as juridically inadequate as that of an animal or a

---

40. A justification of this proposition would require a metaphysical analysis of the problem of the sexes, which there is no question of doing here.

god. Nevertheless, almost all legal systems in the past (and a good number of current legislation) have admitted cases when the woman cannot be a "physical person," when she must act through the intermediary of another—that is, when she is, just like the child, the deceased, or the insane, an "individual moral person."

It seems that the justification of this behavior must be looked for in the fact that a woman is necessarily the daughter of a man and that she can have male children. We will see, indeed, that inheritance [*hérédité*] seems to be justified juridically by the conception according to which the identity of the father (or the parents) is preserved in the children: the father and child, for example, are one and the same person.[41] Now, if this is the case, men and women are essentially identical. In a certain sense one can say that the woman has been or will be a man, if this is related to the *totality* of time (realized in and by the Family, for example). And one can express this identity of *essence* by saying that a woman "would have been able" to be a man—that is, a "normal" Homo sapiens. The guardian A' of a woman A, therefore, acts as this woman would have acted *if* she had been a man. Now she *could have been able* to be one. One can therefore consider the action of A' as an action of A. The fiction is therefore juridically justified and the cases when the woman has an "individual moral personality" are juridically authentic even from the point [52] of view of *droit*, which does not admit that a woman can effectively be or become a "normal" Homo sapiens.

Just as in the case of the Slave, therefore, there is it seems a purely *juridical* reason to treat the Woman as a subject of *droit*, independent of economic, religious, and other reasons. And it seems that this reason must be sought in the *droit* of succession [*successoral*].

But this is of little importance. What should be recalled from all that has been said so far is the fact that the "individual moral person" is justified juridically by the idea that the real support of this "person"—the unborn or young child, the minor, the insane, the deceased, the woman, and so on—has been, will be, or "could have been able to be," a "normal" Homo sapiens. If the action of the "guardian" A' is attributed to A, this is because A *could have been able* to act exactly as A' acts, either at another moment in time or in other (contingent, moreover) circumstances; for even the woman "could have been able" to be a man if the "circumstances" of her conception had been different. In any case, when A' acts in the name of A, he is supposed to ask himself what A would have done in the case being considered if he was a "normal" Homo sapiens; or, what amounts to the same thing, A' acts by assuming that he is in A's place, that the action he undertakes concerns A' and not A. Now these fictions are

---

41. The purely agnatic conception of inheritance among the Romans tallies well with the fact that Roman *droit* had the tendency to treat the woman as a perpetual minor. But logically one ought to deny in this case any juridical personality of the woman. However, even in the agnatic conception, the daughter is to a certain extent identified with the father. It is only the child who does not depend upon the mother, being directly connected to the father (the woman being only a receptacle of the seed of the father).

justified only if A "could have been able" to act like A'. This is what takes place if A belongs to the species Homo sapiens (or has belonged to this species while he was alive). By contrast, a thing, plant, animal, or a divine being are by definition (i.e., when they are understood such as they are in truth, that is, for us) *incapable* of acting in the way a "normal" Homo sapiens acts—that is, acting "humanly." In these cases, therefore, the fiction of the action of A' related to A is not justified: the action of A' has nothing to do with the action of A, [and] A' cannot "represent" A. In other words, every "individual moral person" who does not have for a "base" a representative of the species Homo sapiens is juridically unauthentic; but it is authentic whomever the representative of the species Homo sapiens is. The action of a Homo sapiens A or of his representative A' may not provoke B's reaction, and so on, [and] there will then be no juridical situation; but if it does [provoke B's reaction], the situation will be authentically juridical. Conversely, an action of a natural being (animal, plant, thing) or divine being A, or its representative A', can provoke a reaction anticipated by our definition. The situation will then be juridical but it will be unauthentic precisely and solely because A is not a Homo sapiens, [53] such that the human action of A' cannot be attributed to him. The natural or divine being cannot authentically be a "physical person" or an "individual moral person" because it is not a Homo sapiens.

Now a "*collective moral person*" is not an individual representative of the species Homo sapiens either. Nevertheless, this "person" is juridically authentic. And here is why.

The "reality" of "collective persons" has been discussed at length by speculating whether there is a "collective will" as such, distinct from the individual wills making up the collectivity. It really seems that the answer is yes. When two young newlyweds decide to go on a honeymoon, neither of them has the intention to travel alone. The decision to travel, therefore, is really a collective decision, which differs from the isolated wills. (One assumes that neither of them would have gone if one of them had had to take the other by force.) Of course, each of them has the intention to travel, but each one has it only to the extent that the other one does, i.e., to the extent that each one is part of the "collectivity": outside of the collectivity, the will to travel does not exist. Likewise, if one cannot say that the "collectivity" travels independently of its members, one must say that they only travel as a "collectivity." One can therefore say that the act of travelling is an action of the "collectivity" as such. Moreover, the collective will can be opposed to the will of all the members of the collectivity taken individually. Thus, if two persons make an appointment to see each other, they can go there even if they both changed their minds in the meantime and are no longer anxious to meet one another. Of course, the collectivity only acts in and through its members; but in each of them the "collective" will is opposed to the "isolated" will. Or once again, ten men decide to lift a beam weighing 1000 pounds. They can only do it all together, the weight exceeding the strength of the isolated members of the collectivity or even some part of them. Therefore, if the action of lifting the beam provokes a reaction, with an intervention of a third in conformity with our definition, i.e., if this action generates a juridical situation, one must really say that the collective action alone was able to do it. It is therefore the collectivity as such which is here the subject of *droit*; none of the members would have been able to be so taken individually. Let us now assume that two men join together in order to lift a beam which neither of them can lift alone. But they find a third [person], sufficiently strong to do it himself, and they hire him to do it. The action [54] will then be carried out by this third, but it will only realize the collective will of the other two. His action, therefore, should be related to the collectivity, exactly as if this third was only an animal or a machine used by the collectivity.

Collective action or will, therefore, is something other than individual will or action. There is no real individual of the species Homo sapiens having in fact this will or performing this action: he can only be the "guardian" or the "agent" of the collectivity to which the will and action in question belong. In other words, the collectivity as such is not a "physical person": it can only be a subject of *droit* as a "(collective) moral person." But one must then wonder if the juridical situation still remains authentic in the case when A, or B, or A and B of our definition are "collective moral persons." It should be understood that a collectivity A, just like a Homo sapiens A, is not *necessarily* a subject of *droit*: his action may very well not provoke C's intervention. The collectivity is only a "collective moral person," a Homo sapiens is a only "physical person," *if* his action provokes the intervention in question. In the case of the Homo sapiens, the situation will then be authentic. It is a matter of knowing if it will be the same in the case of a collectivity.

The answer is yes. But one can no longer say that the collectivity has been, will be, or could have been able to be, a "normal" Homo sapiens. One justifies the notion of "collective moral person" by the assumption that a "normal" Homo sapiens could have been able to have the same will, could have been able to perform the same action, as the collectivity. Thus, for example, a single man could have been able to have the intention of lifting the beam weighing 1000 pounds; but he is "incapable" of doing it and he hires ten men who do it for him. These ten men are then his "agent" (collective, but this is of little importance), whose role is quite similar to the role of the "guardian" of an "incapable" minor (an infant, for example). One therefore likens the action of the collectivity to the action of a "normal" Homo sapiens, because such a Homo sapiens is supposed to be able to will this action. And the collectivity is necessarily a moral and not a physical person when its action cannot be carried out by a single "normal" Homo sapiens. And a collectivity can be a moral person every time that its action or will is not in fact an individual action or will, while being able to be so in principle.

In other words, if the collective *will* (or *intention*) is not [55] in fact a will of a real Homo sapiens, it can be so in principle. Therefore, it does not differ from it essentially. As for the collective *action*, it can certainly be such that no "normal" Homo sapiens could perform it (lifting a weight of 1000 pounds, for example). But this action will be carried out by a group of individual Homo sapiens. Therefore, it differs quantitatively but not qualitatively from the action of a "normal" Homo sapiens. In other words, it will not differ essentially either. Collective will and action thus remain *human* and differ essentially from natural (animal) or divine action and will. And this is why the situation will be authentically juridical every time that a collective will or action will provoke C's intervention, conforming to our definition. In all these cases, the agent will be called a "collective moral person."[42]

Finally, let us go to the case of an "institution"—that is, of an "*abstract moral person*." Here again—and by definition—there is in fact no real Homo sapiens performing the action of the "institution," which provokes the intervention of the "third" [and] thus creates a juridical situation. This is nevertheless authentic, contrary to situations having an animal or divine being for a base.

One can justify the juridical authenticity of the "abstract moral person" in the same way one justifies the authenticity of the "collective moral person." The justification is then due to the fact that a "normal" Homo sapiens would have been able to have the same will as the "institution," and that the action of the "institution" is always performed by one or several "normal" representatives of the species Homo sapiens. But still, one could accept a direct justification. If the "institution" is created by the will of a "normal" Homo sapiens (or by a group of "normal" representatives of this species), it will be a human entity and its action could be likened to the (individual or collective) action of a "normal" Homo [56] sapiens: this action is supposed to realize the will of one or many founders, just like the effective action of a real Homo sapiens realizes his own will. Of course, the will of the institution is by definition detached from the will of the founder, but it prolongs it as it were and does not differ from it essentially. Being given that *Droit* is related to time in its entirety, the will which has been that of a "normal" Homo sapiens at a given moment (at the moment of the institution) is so "eternally"—that is, in its "essence." But if an institution arises from a natural (animal, for example) or divine action, it will not be an authentic subject of *droit,* even if its action provokes the intervention of the third anticipated by our definition.[43]

---

42. This reasoning assumes a general principle according to which an interaction between beings belonging to a certain ontological category can never transcend that category. Thus, whatever interaction [takes place] between natural beings (animals, for example) can never result in a human entity—for example, a work of art or a State. Consequently, a collectivity established by human beings will always be a human entity, and not animal or divine: this is why its action can be likened to the action of a "normal" Homo sapiens. But this general principle has a metaphysical character and cannot be discussed and justified here.

43. If the Church were instituted by God, it would not be an authentic "abstract moral person." In fact, it is one, but only because *for us* (i.e., in truth) it is a *human* institution. Moreover, one can wonder (just as in the case of the State) if it is an "institution" or an "association."

The direct justification is based upon a general principle according to which the effect differs from the cause, but does not differ *essentially* from it: the cause and the effect are always on the same ontological plane. Thus, everything that arises from man as man (and not as an animal) is human, and conversely. This principle requires a metaphysical analysis which cannot be done here.

To sum up, then, one can say this:

A situation will be authentically juridical 1) if it otherwise corresponds to our definition; and 2) if A, or B, or A and B are:

a) A real Homo sapiens who effectively performs the action in question himself or is supposed to be able to do it (A is a physical person).

b) A (present, past, or future) Homo sapiens incapable [57] of performing the action being considered himself or is only supposed to be incapable of it (individual moral person).

c) A group of representatives of the species Homo sapiens themselves carrying out in common the action in question or supposed to be able to do it (collective moral person).

d) An entity created by one or several representatives of the species Homo sapiens, this entity not being a Homo sapiens (and therefore incapable of acting itself) (abstract moral person).[44]

(A "collective moral person" can imply "individual moral persons" or can only be made up of such persons. An "abstract moral person" can be created both by a "physical person" and by an "individual moral person" or a "collective moral person.")

If one divides all the ontologically possible beings into 1) natural beings (animals, plants, and things); 2) human beings; and 3) divine beings, one can say that there is an authentic juridical situation every time that our definition is applied—that is, in particular, when A and B are "human beings," which means that they are neither "natural beings" nor "divine beings."[45]

But in order to draw attention to the phenomena discussed under d) in this

---

By definition, the State is not a "physical person" (nor an "individual moral person"). If a monarch justifiably says, "*l'État, c'est moi* [I am the State]," he is a private property owner and not a monarch, [and] there is no State. But it has been and is debated whether the State is an "association" or an "institution." One can say that it is *in principle* an "institution" but *in fact* an "association." Or once again, the State is an "association" which acts *as if* it were an "institution," which has a tendency to understand itself as an "institution." In other words, the will of the State is the result of the wills of the citizens, but these citizens have a tendency to detach themselves from their collective will. This detached collective will of the collectivity is the Constitution. Likewise, an Administrative Apparatus is an "institution" only in principle and not in fact. It is a pseudo-institution in which the founder (i.e., the State) is always alive and can do away with or alter it as it pleases.

44. We will see later on that there is no juridical relation between the individual and the State or between sovereign States. Nevertheless, the State is really a "moral person" such as we have defined it. As we will see, our definition cannot be applied to these relations because there is no "third" C; this "third" could only be the State itself, which already takes part in the interaction. Therefore, it is not the fact of being a "moral person" which here determines the unauthenticity of the phenomenon.

45. This trichotomy has a metaphysical character. Therefore, it cannot be analyzed and justified here, nor can the three terms be defined. The "human being" is for us here only an intuitive *phenomenon*. But I am not making a phenomenological analysis of it.

section, it is better to replace the expression "human beings" in our definition by that of:

"Physical or moral persons (individual, collective, or abstract)."

The term "person" indicates that it is not a matter of natural beings (animals, plants, or things), and the term "physical [58] or moral" means that the person in question is not divine. It is, therefore, really a question of human beings (real or ideal).[46]

§ 11

Our definition postulates that in every authentic juridical situation, there are necessarily *two* agents, A and B. That is to say:
a) neither more than two;
b) nor less than two.
[59] a) If an agent is simultaneously in relations of *droit* with B, B', B", and so on, one can always break up this complex relation into as many elementary relations as there are B's; for otherwise, it would be necessary to say that the B's

---

46. If one wants to introduce the term "person" into a *definition* of *Droit,* it is really necessary to state that a "person" is not *eo ipso* a *juridical* person, a subject *of **droit***. If not, the definition would be circular. A (physical or moral) "person" will be a "(physical or moral) *juridical* person" only if his action provokes an intervention of the "third" anticipated by the definition. Since "physical person" means nothing other than "Homo sapiens," it is obvious that there are "physical persons" who are not "(physical) juridical persons." But it is easy to see that it is the same for "moral persons." They can also exist outside of any juridical situation—that is, be and act without provoking the intervention of the "third" anticipated by our definition. If I ask my friends to meet every Sunday in a cafe for one year after my death, and they do it, there will clearly be an "institution" or a real "abstract moral person"; nevertheless, it will have nothing juridical about it (at least in France at the moment). Likewise, when four players simply meet to play cards, there is an "association" or a real "collective moral person," but it is not at all juridical. (It is in this way that a sovereign State can be a "collective moral person" without being a subject of *droit.*) Finally, there are non-juridical "individual moral persons." This is what takes place, for example, when the Church baptizes a newborn child. It is surely not the physiological "support," the *animal* Homo sapiens, which is baptized: it is the "normal," i.e., truly *human,* Homo sapiens. But he still does not exist in fact: he is only one in potentiality; however, he *will be* one in actuality some day. Likewise, when the Church prays for the deceased, it is not the cadaver that it has in mind, but the human being, who does not ([or] no longer) exists, however, as a Homo sapiens. In the two cases, therefore, there is a real "individual moral person." But it only exists on the religious plane of human reality, since the acts in question have nothing juridical in themselves, not provoking the intervention of a "third" in conformity with our definition. One would be wrong, then, to believe that the notion of "moral person" is a specifically juridical notion: religion, ethics, [and] politics, for example, are also familiar with it. A "moral person" can exist on the juridical plane of human reality alone, but it can also exist outside of this plane. And in this case, just as for the "physical person," i.e., a Homo sapiens, it may or may not be a "juridical person"—that is, a "subject of *droit*" in the sense of our definition.

are forming an "association." Now we admit that B (like A) can be a "collective moral person," being thought of as a single agent.

The assertion that there are *not more than two agents* in a relation of *droit*, therefore, is purely analytical. It needs no comment and presents but little interest.

b) More important, but also less obvious, is the assertion that there is *not less than two agents* in an authentic juridical situation.

This amounts to saying that one cannot have a *droit* in relation to oneself, that one does not have a juridical obligation (duty) toward oneself. One never speaks, as it were, of "*droits*" in relation to oneself. (Nevertheless, if one had *juridical* duties toward oneself, one would have by this very fact "*droits*," namely the "*droit*" to do one's "duty.") But one sometimes speaks of "duties" in relation to oneself. I suppose, therefore, that one is only able to do this by underlining that the term "duty" has a religious, moral, and so on, meaning, but not one of *juridical* obligation.

Truth to tell, the case of a single agent is out of the question from the sole fact that the definition requires the intervention of a *third* C: if C is a "third," it is necessary that there are "two," these two being precisely the *two* agents A and B. But if an agent C intervenes in the same (impartial and disinterested) manner that the "third" of our definition intervenes, one may have *the illusion* of a juridical situation even when this intervention is provoked not by an *interaction between two* agents, A *and* B, but by the action of A alone. If C annuls A's action, one will be able to say, if you will, that A has the "duty" to refrain from his action (or the "*droit*" to refrain from it). But *for us*, this "duty" (and this "*droit*") will have nothing *juridical* about them. If such a situation is considered juridical (C being, for example, a judge also judging cases truly juridical), we will then say that there is an *inadequate* juridical phenomenon. And this precisely and solely because A is the only agent [and] there is no B who reacts to A's action, such that there can be no *third*, the C in question therefore having only the illusory appearance of being one.

There are, however, authentically juridical cases which [60] do not seem to tally with our definition because, at first glance, there is only a single agent A.

Thus, for example, modern English *droit* punishes suicide (or more exactly attempted suicide); certain *droits* punish serious self-mutilations, such as castration; [and] all *droits* punish the self-mutilation of a draftee which makes him unfit for military service. Conversely, certain primitive *droits* prescribe self-mutilations, for example ritual tattooing. If in all these cases, it was effectively a matter of an "interaction" with oneself, the situation would not fit our definition and would therefore not be authentically juridical (while being able to be moral or something else). But in reality it is not only A who acts. There is also a B able to react, and it is only the presence of this B which makes C a "third" and the entire situation a relation of *droit*: this is why the situation is juridically authentic. Its interpretation alone is erroneous, and it is only in this sense that this juridical phenomenon is inadequate: one wrongly neglects, or abstracts from, B and his reaction to the action of A. This B is none other than

Society or the State, i.e., a "collective moral person," which is interacting with a "physical person" A[47] in the examples cited above, these examples thus conforming to our definition.

If I have the *juridical* obligation not to commit suicide, I do not have it toward myself, but solely toward the State. If there is a *right*[48] in this case, it is only the State which has it: the State has the **droit** to have my life at its disposal; it has the **droit**, therefore, [to see] that this life is not eliminated, in particular by myself. If the State A behaves ("acts") in a certain way toward my life, and if this behavior generates a reaction on my part (I = B) tending to annul this behavior, a "disinterested third" C (the Judge or Police) will necessarily intervene to annul my reaction. Thus, one encounters the situation anticipated by our definition. It is the same in the three other cases cited above. And its working is particularly apparent in the case of self-mutilation of a serviceman in time of war. If a civilian A enjoys himself in time of peace [and] cuts the forefinger of his right hand, the State B does not react, C does not intervene, and the situation has nothing juridical about it. Everything changes if this same citizen A is a soldier in time of war. Why?—solely because the State has an interest in this case to assert its *droits* upon the body of the citizen in question. There is, then, a juridical situation not because [61] citizen A is in "interaction" with his own forefinger, but because he is in interaction with an agent B—namely, the State.[49]

Contemporary jurisprudence has a tendency to interpret cases analogous to the cases cited above in the way I have just done. But it has not always been so. While being in the presence of a juridically authentic case, one used to interpret it as if there was only a single agent A by introducing the notion of a "duty" (in the sense of *juridical* obligation) toward oneself. Now this phenomenon is inadequate because *for us* (i.e., in truth) this "duty" (if it exists) has nothing juridical about it, precisely because it does not imply an interaction between *two* distinct agents. But this erroneous interpretation is relatively rare and rather recent. Generally, one introduces a second agent B, but one views it as a divine being. Suicide and mutilation, for example, are supposed to be *juridically* forbidden because these acts "offend God." Here as well, the phenomenon is inadequate since *for us* (i.e., in truth) relations of *droit* are not possible

---

47. [Ed. Reading *A* for *B*.]

48. [Ed. In the original, the English word "right" follows the French word **droit** in parentheses.]

49. We will see later on that there are no authentic relations of *droit* between a citizen and his State. And this is solely because in these cases C and B coincide. But I have only wanted to show that the juridical situation in the cases cited above presumes the existence of a second agent B. And my incorrect interpretation can show it. In order that the interpretation is truly correct, it would be necessary that B is an agent other than the State (of which A is a citizen): a "physical person," for example, or a "moral person" such as the Family, or Society, or any "association" at all, or anyone whomsoever, and so on, except the sovereign State. It is, moreover, easy to imagine or find such examples. One can assume, for example, that a *droit* punishes attempted suicide—or self-mutilation—on the part of A if A has concluded a labor contract with B. Here again, only the existence of B creates a *juridical* situation, the State then playing the role of C.

between a human being A and a divine being B. But if "God" is here only an (unconscious) projection into the beyond of a social, i.e., human, reality, the relation can be juridically authentic: only the interpretation will be erroneous. One will therefore have a *juridical,* but inadequate, phenomenon. By contrast, if C's intervention is truly justifiable only by A's relations with a divine being or with himself, this intervention will have nothing juridical about it: the situation, therefore, will be religious or moral, but will have nothing to do with a relation *of droit.* There will not be, then, a "juridical phenomenon" at all, but a simple "terminological mistake," [62] a misuse of language of which the phenomenologist does not have to take account in his definition.[50]

One can therefore keep the term "two" in our definition. At the very most, one can strengthen it by replacing the expression "two (human) beings" by:

"two distinct beings (of which each one can be either a physical person or an individual, collective, or abstract moral person)."

§ 12

Our definition further postulates that the "two distinct beings" in question must be in "*interaction*" with one another.

"Interaction" is a compound [*complexe*] entity which naturally breaks down into an "action" A and a "reaction" B. An action in general is called an "action" in the narrow sense when it is considered arising spontaneously. By contrast, an action is said to be a "reaction" if it is considered determined in its being and nature by another action, namely by the "action" in the narrow sense, which then forms with it an "interaction." In other words, [63] B's "reaction" would not exist such as it is were it not for A's "action."

---

50. The historical dialectic of the phenomena in question is generally the following: one begins by forbidding A's act for *religious* reasons, believing that this act offends a divinity; then, for whatever reasons, one no longer believes in the existence of this divinity, or again, one no longer admits that the act in question might offend it. If one does not drop the ban, one then tries to give a *moral* justification for it, by introducing the notion of duty toward oneself. If one realizes (or believes he realizes) that the act does not have in reality a (negative) *moral* value, and if one nevertheless wants to keep the ban, one presents it as a simple ban of "positive *droit*": the act is forbidden because it is forbidden (by the State). But this situation is untenable in the long run. Either the ban will be abolished sooner or later, or one will look for a *juridical justification* for the ban. Now one can only find such a justification provided that one introduces an agent B, distinct from A and not being divine (or "natural"). If one succeeds in introducing such a B, and if one finds the *juridical* justification of C's intervention (i.e., as we will see later on, if one succeeds in deducing it from the idea of Justice), one will say that the situation has always been authentically juridical, but that the phenomenon has been until now inadequate, or that the situation has been badly interpreted. If one fails, by contrast, one will say that the situation had nothing juridical about it. One will then do away with the ban, adding that it had been a simple misuse of language ("terminological mistake") when one spoke in juridical terms about it (both the juridical stage and the moral or religious stages).

When there is an "interaction" between two distinct agents, A and B, by definition we will call A the agent who "acts" (in the narrow sense of the word) and B the agent who "reacts" to A's "action." Therefore, it is always A who provokes the "reaction" and so generates the "interaction." As for his own "action," it is supposed to be "spontaneous."

We must now see what an "interaction" means as such (a juridical meaning being intended). To this end, one must analyze its two constitutive elements, namely:

a) A's *action;* and

b) B's *reaction.*

a) Generally speaking, human action (in the narrow or broad sense of the word) has three aspects or elements. First, there is the element of the "will." This aspect distinguishes a "voluntary" from an "involuntary" action: reflex, being forced, and so on. One can have a "will" to act without an effective action. But all effective action is characterized either by the presence or the absence of a will to carry it out. Secondly, there is this effective action itself, willed or not: this is the "act," or, if one prefers, the "object" of the action or will (if it exists). Finally, there is the "goal" of the action or the will, or, if you like, the "determining motive," or once again, the "intention." Here as well, the intention or goal can be detached from the act and will. But every voluntary act and will are characterized by their goal. An act can be carried out without a goal, since it can be involuntary. But a voluntary act necessarily has a goal, just like the simple will to act, even if it is not followed by the corresponding act.

[Take the following] example. 1) I decide to drink a glass of water. ([This is the] "*will*" to act. If I express it some way, [it is] the "*declaration of the will*" to act. If I spill a glass of water without wanting to, there will be an "involuntary" action—that is, the absence of the "will" to act.) 2) I take the glass and drink the water. ([This is the] act. The fact of drinking the water in this glass is the "*object*" of the action or will.) 3) I drink this water in this glass to quench my thirst, or swallow a tablet, and so on. ([This is the] "*goal*" of the action or will, or the "intention" or "motive.")[51]

[64] It is sometimes said that *Droit* differs from Morality in that it only takes into account the act by abstracting from the will and the goal. But this is fundamentally false. Of course, a *Droit* may not distinguish (in certain cases or in general) between voluntary and involuntary action without ceasing to be an authentic *Droit.* Thus, a lot of archaic or primitive *Droits* do not distinguish,

---

51. There is no question here of doing an ontological or metaphysical analysis of these three elements of an action, or of action itself. It would be necessary, by contrast, to give a phenomenological description of them. But [64] this would take me too far. I assume that the notions in question are known in an immediate, intuitive manner. And indeed, everyone knows very well how to distinguish in general voluntary from involuntary actions, and to contrast the act with its motive. But in a concrete case, it can be very difficult to know if the action is voluntary or not, and to disentangle the "true" motive from it. This is when a precise phenomenological analysis of the phenomena in question can be of great service, just like a metaphysical or even ontological analysis.

for example, between involuntary murder and premeditated assassination. But generally speaking, the juridical value of an action varies depending on whether it is supposed to be voluntary or not. Likewise for the goal or intention: *Droit* may not take account of them. But it can also do this without ceasing to be an authentic *Droit*, without becoming a Morality. Thus, in modern public and private *droit*, the notion of the goal plays a bigger and bigger role without one being able to say that this *Droit* is juridically less authentic than the *Droit* (still rather recent) which asserts that the goal or "cause" did not play any role in the formation of a civil obligation, for example.[52]

Generally speaking, therefore, one can distinguish two actions *juridically* not only according to their objects, i.e., according to their nature as "acts" properly so-called, but also according to their elements of "will," and "intention" or "goal." Thus, for example, one can distinguish an action which implies the "act" of killing from one which implies the act of stealing, and so on. One can distinguish the "acts" of killing according to the way in which the murder is carried out, or according to the person killed, and so on. But one can also distinguish between two actions, which imply exactly the same "acts," but of which one is "voluntary" and the other not. Likewise, one and the same voluntary action can have different "goals," and those actions which only differ by their goals or motives can also be distinguished juridically. For example, the voluntary murder of a given person [65] (carried out in a certain manner) can have a different juridical (and not only a moral) meaning depending on whether it is the action of a sadist, a wrongdoer killing in order to steal, or of someone who only wanted to cut short the sufferings of a dying man. Once again, an authentic *Droit* may not take account of these differences. But if it does, it does not cease by this to be authentic.

There is more. Just as *Droit* can abstract from the elements of "will" and "goal," it may not take account of the element of "act." There can be a juridical situation even when the action boils down to its element of "will" (which is necessarily accompanied by the element of "goal") or of "intention." Thus, for example, the French penal Code does not distinguish, as regards the sentence, between murder and attempted murder—that is, the "will" alone to commit it. And one can imagine a *Droit* which punishes the "intention" alone, even if it is not accompanied by the "will" to carry out the act conforming to this "intention." (For example, one could have punished a man who says that he wanted to kill the king, even if he has still not decided to attempt the act which could realize this goal.)

Nevertheless, there is truth in the assertion that *Droit* differs from (religious or "secular") Morality because it only takes account of the effective action, and not the intention or will. Thus, the penal Code only punishes "attempted mur-

---

52. Cf. [Léon] Duguit, *Les transformations générales du droit privé* [(Paris: Librairie Félix Alcan, 1912)], 52ff; cf. also Duguit, *Les Transformations du droit public*, [(Paris: Librairie Armand Colin, 1913)], 157ff, 206ff, 220, where the modern notions of "usurpation of power" and "abuse [*détournement*] of power" are analyzed, both of which are related precisely to the *goal* of administrative action.

der" if there is a beginning of an effective act. And, quite obviously, a *Droit* can only punish the "intention" if it manifests itself in some manner: God and the moral conscience alone can know what only exists in a man's "soul."

I believe that our definition solves the difficulty. According to it, A's action can have a *juridical* existence only by the fact that, and to the extent that, it provokes B's reaction. In other words, it must be *real,* objective; it must express or manifest itself by altering the world outside the agent (this alteration, moreover, can boil down to the sole fact that someone—B, for example—knows about this action of A). But *if* this action of A provokes a reaction from B, it can generate a juridical situation (assuming that the other conditions of the definition are fulfilled) even if it does not implicate all three constitutive elements. The action can boil down to the pure and simple "act." But it can also implicate only the element of "will" (plus the "goal") or boil down to the "goal" alone. It is enough that it be *objectively noticeable* to be able to provoke a [66] reaction. Now *if* A's action provokes B's reaction, followed by C's intervention, the situation will be authentically juridical, even if this action boils down to the "intention" or "will" alone to act.

Otherwise, A's action can be anything at all, and this in all its three elements. Any of A's acts whatsoever (voluntary or not) will generate a juridical situation if it provokes B's reaction followed by C's intervention, anticipated by our definition. And it is the same for the "goal," which can be economic, religious, moral, aesthetic, or something else: in every case A's action will generate a juridical situation as soon as there is B's reaction and C's intervention.[53]

Moreover, the term "action" must be taken in its broadest usage. This can just as easily be a "positive" as a "negative" action—that is, a simple abstention from acting. Truth to tell, as I have already remarked above, it is a matter of "behavior" in general, which can be "active" or "passive." It is only necessary, and sufficient, that A's "behavior" generates another "behavior," that of B, which is connected to it as the "reaction" is connected to the "action" in some "reaction." This "behavior," therefore, must *alter* the ambient environment in a certain manner. And this is why one can call it an "action" in the broad sense of this term.

b) Concerning B's "*reaction,*" one can first of all say everything that we have said about A's "action." It also implies three elements, since it is an "action" in the general sense of the term, or if you will, a human "behavior." And these elements can be split up and partly lacking.

Thus, for example, when A comes to collect a debt from his debtor B, and the latter "reacts" so as not to pay it, *Droit* may be uninterested in the question of knowing if he acts in this way because he does not want or is unable to pay (not having the money, for example): *Droit* therefore abstracts from the element of will, as it generally does in this case from the element of "goal." But C

---

53. It should be understood that it is possible that there are acts (or "intentions") which may not—in principle—have these consequences. But this is a question which does not concern us here. What is essential for us is that the nature of the act cannot by itself make the situation juridically unauthentic, if it is created in fact.

could intervene even if B's "reaction" boils down to the mere "will" to react or even to the mere "intention." A single condition must be fulfilled: since C's intervention [67] must annul B's reaction, the latter must be "capable of being annulled [*supprimable*]." In other words, just like the "action," it must alter the ambient environment through at least one of its elements.

To speak properly, all the examples discussed under a) are related not to A's action but to B's reaction; for as we will see, it is B's reaction which is "criminal" when it provokes C's intervention, which annuls it. But I simply wanted to show that *Droit* takes account not only of the "act" but also of the "will" and "goal." Of course, A can have the **droit** to a simple "will" to act, or to a "goal," independently of its active realization. But in practice, it is in B's reaction above all that the elements are separable.

Be that as it may, the sole difference between A's action and B's reaction is due to the fact that the former is considered "spontaneous" while B's reaction is determined in its being and nature by A's action. And it is only in this way that the two actions together form an "interaction." Now, for there to be an "interaction," it is not enough that the action A determines an action B. It is necessary that action B *react* upon action A. In physics, the reaction is equal and opposite to the action. In *Droit,* this equality is not necessary: the reaction can be weaker or stronger than the action. But the condition of being opposite must be maintained. In other words, B's reaction must tend to thwart A's action, and—at the limit —to overcome it completely. And this condition must be fulfilled in all three elements of the reaction. B's "will" constitutes a "reaction" only if it is a "will" to act so as to overcome A's action. B's "act" is a "reaction" only if it has for an object the suppression of A's action. Finally, B's "intention" (or "goal") is a "reaction" only if, and to the extent that, it implies the negation of A's action. In short, the third C only intervenes to the extent that the behavior (action) of B (will, act, or goal) tends to overcome the behavior (action) of A (will, act, or goal)—that is, to the extent that B's action is a genuine "reaction," i.e., to the extent that there is an "interaction" between A and B. It is only then that C tends to overcome B's reaction, which creates a *juridical* situation where A has the **droit** to his behavior. As long as there is no "interaction" between A and B, i.e., as long as B's action is not a "reaction," the intervention of a third C could not create an authentic juridical situation. [68] There would only be an illusion of *Droit,* a simple "terminological mistake" of which the Phenomenologist does not have to take account.[54]

At first glance, the juridical reality [*fait*] of Contract seems at odds with what I have just said. But this is not so. Indeed, one is right to say that Contract, as a juridical reality, differs from a simple convention without juridical significance solely because the Contract is "sanctioned," that its non-execution provokes C's intervention (of the Judge, and so on) that our definition has in mind. Now this

---

54. If the "reaction" exists in fact, but does not appear in the consciousness of those for whom the situation in question exists, it is juridically authentic, but the phenomenon is inadequate (since it does not, as a *phenomenon,* conform to our definition, while conforming to it *for us*—that is, in truth).

"sanction" only makes sense if the Contract is not executed in fact, or at the very least, may not be executed. Now in the case of the non-execution of the Contract by B, A will act against B with a view to forcing him to execute the Contract, and if B "reacts" so as overcome A's "action," C will intervene in order to annul B's "reaction." It is only then that one will be able to say that the situation is juridical and that A has the ***droit*** to his action. The Contract itself, therefore, is only a simple convention without juridical value. It is a (juridical) Contract only to the extent that it allows one (C) to ascertain that A has the ***droit*** to a certain action. It is a juridical reality only to the extent that A's behavior implies C's intervention should B react in order to annul it. If such a reaction from B was impossible *in principle,* or if A could not *in principle* act so as to provoke such a reaction from B, C would not intervene and the situation would have nothing juridical about it.

We can, therefore, keep the term "interaction" in our definition. But in order to bring out its meaning, one can replace it with the following expression:

"action of A, which provokes a reaction from B, [who] overcomes this action or tends to do so."[55]

§ 13

[69] It is not enough that there be an "interaction between two human beings"; there must also be an "intervention of an impartial and disinterested third." Let us first of all see what the term "*intervention*" means.

The "intervention" in question is a human action in the strong sense of the term.[56] Therefore, it implies the three constitutive elements of all human action: the "will," "act," and "goal." And for there to be a genuine "intervention," there must first of all be the element of "act." The "intention" alone (the conscious "goal") is not enough, even if it is accompanied by a "will" to act. An

---

55. It should be understood that B's "reaction" does not need to exist in fact. It is enough that it is possible in order that the situation could be authentically juridical. Of course, C effectively intervenes only if the reaction takes place (as will, act, or goal). But the situation will be juridical even if there is only a mere *possibility* of C's intervention. Now this possibility is there as soon as there is a *possibility* of a reaction on the part of B. It is the same, moreover, for A's action: it also may only be *possible.* A legal rule can have in mind actions which have never yet been carried out. It is enough that it is *possible* that there is an action from A, capable of provoking a reaction from B such that it necessarily leads [69] to an intervention of C, in order for there to be a legal rule—that is, a juridical situation, if not real, at least "ideal." Even A and B may only be "possible." One can, for example, establish the juridical status for a kind of association without such an association existing in reality. Finally, the legal rule itself may exist in the state of a simple proposal [*d'un simple projet*]. Our definition, therefore, applies both to real juridical situations (legal rules applied in fact) and to situations [that are] only *possible*—that is, "ideal" (legal rules not applied in fact or draft legal rules [*projets de règles de droit*]). (As long as a legal rule only exists as a juridical *draft* law [*projet de loi juridique*], C's intervention is only possible, "ideal," even if the interaction is real.) But all this is so obvious that it is pointless to indicate it in the very text of the definition.
56. I have said that in a lot of juridical phenomena the "third" is conceived as a divine being. But *for us,* i.e., in truth, it is, of course, a matter of a human being.

"intervention" alters the situation in which it occurs. And in order that an "intervention" might alter an "interaction," it must be an "action" in the sense of "*act.*" It must alter the ambient environment; it must be objectively operative, noticeable from the outside.

It should be understood that if any situation is purely "ideal," only possible or imagined and not real, the intervention is also "ideal." It remains so as long as the interaction in question remains "ideal," either because A does not act at all or because B does not react for whatever reason. But as soon as this reaction, and consequently the interaction, really exist, the intervention also exists, and it exists as an "act." Nevertheless, this "act" does not need to be material, as it were. If B does not react because he knows that there would be in this case an intervention of C, annulling his reaction (and this either by simple "fear" [70] of C—of the Judge, Police, and so on—or by "respect for the law" embodied in C and realized by his intervention), the intervention does not take place materially. But it has taken place "morally." It is this which has altered the interaction by overcoming the reaction. Therefore, it has had the value of a genuine "act," and of a *real* "act" (although "moral" and not "material" [or] "physical").

But for there to be an "intervention" in the proper sense of the term, the "act" which it implies must come from a "will" to act in the way in which one acts. The "intervention" must be a *voluntary* action—that is, conscious [*consciente*] and free. At first glance, it seems that the expression "voluntary" ought not appear in a "behaviorist" definition. But one can also give a "behaviorist" definition of it without having recourse to the "introspective" notions of "freedom" and "consciousness." *On the one hand,* "voluntary" means (and this is its "free" aspect) that the intervention is not "mechanically" generated by the interaction: if the intervention cannot take place without the interaction, the latter may very well not provoke the former. The intervention, therefore, has its own cause, other than that established by the interaction. And this is all that is meant by the term "voluntary" (in the sense of "free") in its "behaviorist" usage. In other words, there is nothing in a given interaction which might transform it into a juridical situation implying a legal rule. It gets this quality from outside; it is created by C's intervention, which can take place or not for reasons which are appropriate to him. Of course, if the intervention takes place, it will necessarily occur (as we will yet see) every time that the interaction in question is going to recur. But the situation could have occurred without there being an intervention. Or again, as it is said, all *Droit* is a "positive *Droit*": there are no legal rules "necessarily and universally valid." Any interaction whatsoever (conforming to our definition) can provoke an intervention of C (anticipated in this definition), realizing and revealing a corresponding legal rule. But the system which implies this rule is just as juridically authentic as that which does not recognize it.[57] It is enough that the rule *always* be applied in the corresponding cases, if it exists, and that it *never* be [71] applied,

---

57. A system can be authentically juridical while being incomplete or even contradictory. The sense of what has just been said will become clearer later on.

if it does not exist. Thus, *Droits* that punish parricide, for example, punish it every time the case arises. But the case can arise in other *Droits* without producing an intervention, for the simple reason that these *Droits* do not include a legal rule concerning parricide (as is the case in a lot of archaic or primitive *Droits*). *On the other hand,* "voluntary" means (and this is the "conscious" aspect) that the "intervention" is conditioned (without being determined) by the interaction to which it is related. It is not some spontaneous action. It only takes place if the interaction in question does, and *if* it takes place, it takes place every time that the interaction occurs. And the nature of the act that the intervention implies is also conditioned (without being determined) by the nature of the corresponding interaction. In other words, the same interaction can generate different legal rules in different legal systems, which can all be juridically authentic. Thus, the same crime can be punished differently by various juridical decrees. But in each of these systems, the legal rule is related in an univocal manner to a given interaction.[58]

It is in this "behaviorist" sense that one must take the term "voluntary" if one wants to introduce it into our definition. C's intervention is "voluntary" because the "act" that it implies 1) would not take place if a given interaction did not exist (in fact or simply hypothetical [*supposée*])—this is the "conscious" aspect of C's action; 2) would have been able not to take place even if the interaction did exist (in fact or hypothetically)—this is the "free" aspect of C's action.

Now if an action is "voluntary," it also necessarily has a conscious "goal"— that is, an "intention." C's intervention implies, therefore, not only the elements of "will" and "act" but also the element of "goal" or "intention."

The "intention" is an "introspective" notion that must not [72] be introduced into a "behaviorist" definition. We will see later on, while going through the "introspective" definition of *Droit,* that this "intention" of C, in an authentically juridical situation, is nothing other than the desire to realize and reveal the idea or ideal of Justice. But the "intention" also has a "behaviorist" aspect, and it is this aspect that the terms "impartial and disinterested" take into account. One could say, therefore, that C's intervention is an "impartial and disinterested voluntary act," even if it means defining the first two terms in "behaviorist" language, which seem at first glance purely "introspective" (as I will try [to show] in § 15). Thus, the three constitutive elements of C's act of intervention will be defined [as follows]: there will be 1) the "act"; 2) the "will" to act; and 3) an impartial and disinterested "intention" (or "goal").

But I prefer to connect the terms "impartial and disinterested" not to C's action, i.e., to the intervention as such, but to C's very person. I do not say,

---

58. In all the rules, it is a question of an "annulment" of B's reaction. But we will see that the modes of this annulment can vary, from whence comes the variety of legal rules relating to the same interaction. On the other hand, every *Droit* can interpret the situation in its [own] manner. Two interactions which are identical *for us* (i.e., in truth) may not be so for a "positive" *Droit* (authentic but inadequate). Thus, "barbarian *Droits*" distinguish between the murder of a free man and a serf, a man and a woman, a German and a Gallo-Roman, and so on. One must not confuse these two sources of differences between "positive" *Droits.*

therefore, an "impartial voluntary act" but a "voluntary act of an impartial C" (and I will explain the terms "impartial and disinterested" when speaking about C in § 14 and § 15). I do this for the following reason: if the legal rule (and therefore *Droit* in general) realizes and reveals the idea of Justice, and thus participates in the "essence" of the latter, the idea of Justice precedes its realization—that is, [the realization of] *Droit.* If Justice only really exists in and by *Droit,* or, if one prefers, as *Droit,* this *Droit* itself can exist and be born only because there is an idea of Justice. Consequently, given that the impartiality and disinterestedness of C's intervention is the "behaviorist" aspect of the realization and revelation of Justice by *Droit,* one must say that C's intervention can be impartial only because C himself is impartial, because he has been so before intervening (at the very least, in relation to the interaction which corresponds to his intervention). C is a Judge in the broadest sense of the term. Now if a man acting as a Judge is surely a "juridical man" (Homo juridicus?) in actuality, he can be and become a Judge only because he is a "juridical man" in himself, and not only a Homo sapiens, or Homo economicus, religiosus, and so on. Being by definition "impartial and disinterested," if he intervenes all the same, he has a *sui generis* "motive" (a "goal," an "intention"), which, as we will see, is nothing but the desire to realize Justice (for it is only in this case that the situation will be authentically *juridical*). [73] It is this desire which causes him to intervene, which makes his intervention impartial and disinterested. It is disinterested because C is disinterested. It is because C is supposed to be disinterested that his intervention has a *juridical* meaning, which implies among other things that it is itself disinterested.

All this can only be justified later on (notably in chapter 3 of Part One and in Part Two). For the moment I simply wanted to indicate the reason I connect the quality of impartiality and disinterestedness not to C's intervention (to which this quality equally belongs) but to C's person (as intervening in the interaction between A and B by a voluntary act). As for the intervention itself, it is enough to clarify that it implies an "act" and a "will," the latter being by definition inseparable from an "intention": for if the agent as agent is impartial and disinterested, his action (or more exactly, the element of "intention" or "goal" or "motive" of this action) will also necessarily be so. Therefore, instead of saying "intervention" simply, I will only say:

"an intervention—that is, a voluntary act."

§ 14

The intervention in question must be carried out by an "impartial and disinterested third"—that is, first of all by a "*third.*" And we will see later on that this condition has a capital importance, allowing one to recognize the *specificity* of the juridical situation as such—that is, of *Droit* in general.

If C is a "third" in relation to the interaction between A and B, it is because he neither is nor can be A or B. If A and C, or B and C, are but one, the situation has nothing juridical about it. This is obvious and has always been accepted: one cannot be judge and party at the same time. But there are cases when this absence of a genuine "third" is not apparent, and one then has supposedly "juridical" phenomena which are not so in truth—that is, *for us* or in agreement with our definition. If a man (or a collectivity) is the representative of a divinity's "interests" on earth, and if he intervenes in an "interaction" which is a relationship between a human being and this same divinity, he is not a genuine "third," and it is a matter of a simple "terminological mistake" if he is called [74] a Judge in the juridical sense of the word (without speaking of the fact that in truth there cannot be a genuine *interaction* between a human being and a divine being). And there is an inadequate juridical phenomenon if C is a genuine "third" and only *believes* himself to be a "representative" of God, or if the interaction is carried out in fact not between a man and a divinity but between human beings. Likewise, there is no genuine juridical situation if there is an interaction between a citizen and his State, that same State intervening as a "third." It is from this case above all that "inadequate juridical phenomena" and "terminological mistakes" are born. And we will have to deal with this later on (above all in chapter 2 and in Part Three, chapter 2, B).

For the moment, it will be enough to underline the importance of the fact that there is a "third" in any authentic juridical situation. As for the intrinsic nature of this "third," he can surely not be a "natural being," seeing that his intervention must be a *voluntary* act. Therefore, the "third" is human or divine. Now, I have already said that a divinity can play the role of this "third" C, obviously provided that he is neither A nor B, and that he intervenes by a voluntary act, being an impartial and disinterested agent. I have even said why one has a tendency to divinize the "third" in question. His intervention having to be, as we will see, "irresistible," it has in relation to the agents interacting the value of a divine intervention. And if *for us* the "third" is necessarily human, this is solely because there are no divine beings for us. But if God existed, he would have been able to play the role of Judge in human interactions. As for the real "third" (who is, as we will see, Society or the State), he is human because, as I have already said, the "irresistibility" of his intervention is only relative. If and when the "third" intervenes in order to overcome B's reaction, B is not supposed to be able (in principle) to oppose it, just as A cannot influence this intervention. But outside of their interaction, which has provoked C's intervention, A and B can act upon C and act so as either to alter the nature of his intervention or to overcome it completely. If C is the State and A and B its citizens, they can surely not act upon the official Judge as litigants. But they can act upon the State as citizens, and the State can alter or overcome the intervention of the Judge (by altering or overcoming the legal rule which corresponds to this intervention).

Therefore, for us, i.e., in truth, the voluntary act of the [75] impartial and disinterested third is always carried out by a human being, who can be either a "physical person" or a "moral person." All three agents (A, B, and C) of a juridical situation, therefore, are on the same ontological plane for us. But for this situation to be juridically authentic, there must be *three* distinct agents on this plane.

In other words, *Droit* is an essentially social phenomenon. *Tres faciunt collegium* [three individuals make a corporation], a Roman adage states, and this is profoundly true. Two human beings are just as little a Society (or a State, or indeed a Family) as is an isolated being. For there to be a Society, it is not enough that there be an interaction between two beings. It is necessary—and sufficient—that there also be an "intervention" of a third, it being of little importance whether he is, by this "intervention," a mediator, arbiter, goal, cause, or a mere bystander of the interaction, and so on. This is why there is no *Droit* without, outside of, or contrary to Society (as such), and perhaps no Society without *Droit.* I will have the opportunity to come back to this question later on and to try to justify what I have just said. For the moment, it is enough to have underlined the importance of the existence of the "third" in the juridical situation. But given that the qualifiers "impartial and disinterested" sufficiently indicate that C is a being *distinct* from B and A,[59] it is pointless to underline it expressly in the definition itself.

§ 15

It remains for us to clarify the nature of the third's intervention, to analyze his capacity [*qualité*] as a third [who is]:

a) *impartial;* and

b) *disinterested.*

a) At first glance, *impartiality* is a purely and exclusively "introspective" notion. C is said to be "impartial" in relation to A and B if he does have a "preference" for one of them, if he neither loves nor hates them, if he refers to their acts and not their persons, and so on. But it is very easy to express this notion of impartiality in "behaviorist" terms. Indeed, it is enough to say that C is "impartial" in relation to A and B if his intervention in their interaction will not and could not be altered by the sole fact of interchanging A and B, A playing the role of B, and B that of A. In principle, at the very least, one can then check the impartiality (the "justice") of a Judge in the same way one checks the accuracy [76] (the "precision" [*justesse*]) of a scale. In any case, for there to be an authentic juridical situation, A and B must be interchangeable in our definition. And this is what the definition means by saying that C is "impartial."

b) The term "*disinterested*" being a lot more important than the other, it is also more difficult to define, even using "introspective," i.e., "normal," language.

First of all, the expression "disinterested" must not be taken in too broad a sense. Indeed, one can say that all voluntary, i.e., conscious and free, action has a goal or motive, and one can call this motive the "interest" the agent has in his action. If one acts in a certain way, it is because one has an "interest" in so act-

---

59. [Ed. Reading *A* for *C.*]

ing. In this broad sense, therefore, C's intervention is not "disinterested" since it is voluntary. But the big question is knowing if the "interest" which prompts C to act is or is not a *sui generis* "interest," a "*juridical* interest." If so, we will say that his intervention is "disinterested" in the narrow sense of the word. And it is in this narrow sense that the expression is taken in our definition.

But one cannot introduce the notion of "*juridical* interest" into a first *definition* of *Droit* as such. We are supposed to know all possible and imaginable "interests" except the "juridical interest." The latter, therefore, can only be defined in a negative manner. If C intervenes without an "interest" that we know is moving him, we must assume that he has an unknown "interest" to do so, and this unknown "interest" will be called the "juridical motive": the intervention will then be said to be "disinterested."

Let us not forget, however, that our definition must be "behaviorist." Now, in "behaviorist" language, one can distinguish two types of action, and consequently two "goals," "motives," or if you will, "interests." On the one hand, there are actions which react upon the agent himself, who feels the repercussion of them, so to speak. The agent is (objectively) altered as a result of his action. (In everyday language, he profits from it or it harms him.) In these cases, the "interest" (in the broad sense) could be called "material" or "practical." On the other hand, there are actions which do not rebound upon the agent, who remains as he would have been if he had not acted: his action does not (objectively) affect him in any manner. In these cases, the "interest" which moves him to action will be said to be "moral" or "theoretical."

Let us now suppose that any action which rebounds upon the agent by objectively ("materially") altering him has an "interested" motive, goal, or intention: it is an "interested action." By contrast, any action which does not objectively [77] ("materially") alter the agent will have a "disinterested" goal or motive or intention: this will be a "disinterested action." Henceforth, then, "interest" will mean "material or practical interest." The action which arises from a "moral or theoretical interest" will be called "disinterested." C will have to intervene, therefore, in a "disinterested" way in the sense indicated. His intervention, while altering the interaction between A and B, i.e., while (objectively) altering A and B themselves, will not (objectively) alter the state of C.

In the context with which we are dealing, this is really the ordinary sense of the term "disinterested." A Judge or Arbiter, for example, is called "disinterested" when his judgement and its enforcement bring him nothing and do not at all harm him, thus leaving him "indifferent." It is of little importance to him that A acts or not, or that B reacts or not, or finally that he himself intervenes or not in order to annul B's reaction: his existence will be the same in every case. He has no "egoistic" motive for intervening. If he intervenes, it is for purely "moral" or "theoretical" reasons, in order to cause the reign of Justice, for example.

Nothing says, however, that his motive is necessarily juridical. At first glance, it can just as easily be ethical, aesthetic, religious, or something else, even if it means being "disinterested" in the sense indicated. But I will try to show later on (chapter 3) that it is not the case. Of course, a "disinterested" motive can be, generally speaking, both juridical and ethical, aesthetic, and so on. But if all the other conditions of our definition are fulfilled, and if C is "disinterested" in the sense indicated, his intervention cannot have another motive than the idea of Justice: therefore, it will be specifically and exclusively juridical.[60] For the moment this assertion must be accepted without proof. We simply assume that C's intervention is exclusively and specifically juridical when it is carried out with the other conditions anticipated by our definition, while being in addition "disinterested" in the sense indicated—that is, when it does not objectively alter the agent himself, namely C.

But if it is easy to give a verbal "behaviorist" definition of C's "disinterested" intervention, i.e., of an authentically juridical situation, one must say that this definition does not have any *real* value. In other words, it [78] cannot be applied to any concrete case. Indeed, C's intervention is by definition an "act"—that is, it objectively alters the ambient environment, the world where C lives. Now an alteration of the world always affects those who live there—that is, precisely what constitutes this world. In other words, an objective, real action, i.e., an "act," is never "disinterested" in the sense indicated; for it objectively alters the agent (as an integrated element of the world where the act is carried out), and he can realize it. This anticipated alteration, therefore, can determine the action itself; it will not necessarily be "disinterested" in the sense indicated. The Judge, therefore, is always "interested." Directly or indirectly, he always benefits from, or is injured by, his intervention. In fact, there is no "disinterested" Judge.

It is because one realizes this difficulty (more or less explicitly) that one has always wanted to see C as a *divine* being. Indeed, God alone is truly "disinterested" in the sense indicated; for he is outside of the world where the interaction and his intervention take place. This divine intervention really alters the world where it is carried out, but this world has no influence upon God himself. Only God, therefore, is a truly "disinterested" Judge, and *Droit* is only authentic if it implies in the final analysis a divine intervention in human interactions—that is, if the (juridical) Legislator, the Judge, or the executor of the Judge's decision (the Police) are divine. The old adage *Fiat justicia, pereat mundus* [let justice be done, though the world should perish] comes from the same difficulty. Its genuine sense is the following: Justice must be carried out, i.e., *Droit* must exist, even if the world should perish—the world and all that it implies, in particular the Judge who applies *Droit*. In other words, the Judge is truly "disinterested" only if he accepts his own ruin as a result of his intervention. And there is an authentic juridical situation only if this situation implies the intervention of such a Judge. The feeling that is the basis of this adage, then, conforms to our way of seeing things: C must be "disinterested." Now his

---

60. This will be so *for us*—that is, in truth. It should be understood that he himself can be mistaken about the nature of his own motive. There will then be an "inadequate phenomenon," but [a phenomenon] authentically juridical nevertheless.

intervention always reacts upon himself (to the point, if the case arises, of being able to destroy him). He must therefore abstract from this reaction, from the repercussion of his intervention. He must intervene [or] act *as if* he was a divine being, transcendent in relation to the world in which he acts.

Therefore, if C is a human being intervening in a human interaction, he is never necessarily [or] automatically "disinterested." Seeing that he always in fact feels [79] the repercussion of his intervention (and even A's action, as well as B's reaction), he can be "disinterested" only if he *abstracts* from this repercussion, only if he acts in the state of mind: "Come what may . . . ," [or] "But if the world perishes and myself with it . . . ," I will act as I have the intention of doing. The human Judge is never "disinterested" *in fact*. He is said to be "disinterested" when he intervenes *as if* he were not [human], when he *abstracts* from his "material or practical interest." Now the notion of intention does not have in itself a "behaviorist" sense: it is not objectively discernable, controllable from the outside. From the "behaviorist" point of view, the "as if" in question can only be defined in the following manner: C is "disinterested" if he can be anyone at all [*quelconque*]; C's intervention is "disinterested" if it remains the same when a given C is replaced by any other C. The idea is the following: C's intervention reacts upon C himself; if C' differs from C", the results of this reaction will be different; therefore, if C' and C", while being different, intervene in the same manner in a given case, it is because their intervention does not depend upon the repercussion that it has upon them. Therefore, it is "disinterested," [and] they intervene *as if* the intervention did not affect them— that is, *as if* C' and C" were not different, *as if* there were one and the same C who was intervening and who would thus be "disinterested" *in fact* (i.e., quasi-divine).

One starts with this idea when one selects judges by lot. By doing so, one takes "any" C and assumes that they will be "disinterested" just because they have been selected by lot—that is, because they are "anyone at all." And it is often said in this case that selecting by lot reveals a divine intention: from the mouth of the judges selected by lot the divinity itself speaks, [and] it is the divinity who intervenes in the interaction in question.

It should be understood that this reasoning is fallacious. If C is "any" man, he will be by definition a "disinterested" man; but he will remain a *man,* he will not become God. There will be a "disinterested" intervention, i.e., "just" [or] authentically juridical, but this *Droit,* this Justice, will nevertheless be *human;* for the quality of being "anyone at all" (selected by lot, for example) only eliminates the variations of human nature and not this nature itself. However, if there is nothing above man, if God does not exist, this *relative Droit,* since it is only human and not divine, will become *absolute:* it will be *Droit* simply. If there is nothing conscious beyond [80] man, it will be enough, then, that C is truly "anyone at all" in order for him to be "disinterested," in order that his intervention is authentically, specifically, and exclusively juridical.

Let us note in passing that the notion of "disinterested" implies that of "impartial" (without the opposite being true). If C is truly anyone at all, A and

B can have no influence on his intervention, and consequently can be inter-changeable. One can therefore do away with the term "impartial" in our defi-nition. It will be enough to say that C is "disinterested."[61]

But is there in fact a "disinterested" C—that is, truly anyone at all?

If C were truly anyone at all, there would only be a single intervention pos-sible in a given case. Whoever C is, he intervenes in the same way if a given A is in a given interaction with a given B. In other words, for every given case, there would only be a single legal rule on earth. Now, in fact, there is nothing of the sort. *Droit* varies according to epochs and peoples. In other words, one and the same interaction may or may not provoke an intervention depending upon whether C belongs to such and such a society, lives in such and such an historical epoch. Since dead men and the unborn cannot play the role of C, C can only be chosen among contemporaries: he is only "anyone at all" at a given moment in time. And practically speaking, he is not "anyone at all" even at this moment. One only chooses him from within a given society, and not among all the representatives of the human species. Now experience shows that C's intervention varies as a function of space and time. The state of the society within which C is supposed to be "anyone at all" co-determines in fact his intervention. If C is anyone at all within a [81] given society, this society itself is not so: it is unique in its kind and cannot be replaced by another identical to it. Thus, practically speaking, C has never been "anyone at all" on earth, and he cannot be so even in our day.

Now, if C's intervention is not a "constant," if it is a function of C's social membership, this is because C is not "disinterested" in the sense defined—that is, he does not act exclusively for specifically juridical reasons. Indeed, he is determined by the society to which he belongs. Now his intervention alters this society. And since society determines him, he himself will be altered by his alteration of society. He will feel the repercussion of his intervention, i.e., he will not be "disinterested," he will always be more or less a "party" and not a genuine "third," unless he abstracts from this repercussion by adopting the

---

61. If C cannot be a woman, if C is only any *man,* his "disinterestedness" is not guaranteed. If the (juridical) Laws are also applied to women, and if men alone make and apply them, the intervention of any (masculine) C might not be "disinterested." Indeed, the "Phryne case" occurs in various forms at every step even in our time, notably when C is supposed to be "anyone at all" because he was selected by lot among all the men (a masculine jury). I do not mean, however, that masculine justice is by this very fact juridically unauthentic; it can be authentic even if it is determined by a (sexual) "interest." I will explain why this is the case when I analyze more closely a little further below the notion of "anyone at all." For the time being, it is enough to say that this "anyone at all" can never be taken literally. Thus, C will never be an insane person, nor a young child. And one can clearly assume that C can-not be a woman either. [Ed. Phryne was a famous fourth-century B.C. Greek courtesan, and she was the inspiration and model for many Greek painters and sculptors. Accused of pro-faning the Eleusinian mysteries, she was defended in court by the orator (and her lover) Hyperides. When he saw that the case was going against her, Hyperides loosened her dress for the all-male Athenian jury, who were so taken with her beauty that she was immediately acquitted and carried off to the Temple of Aphrodite.]

attitude *fiat justicia, pereat mundus.* The "behaviorist" criterion of "anyone at all," therefore, is not sufficient.

If C's intervention is determined or co-determined by the society to which he belongs, it is because the motive which moves him to act in the way that he does is not purely juridical. As we will see, the purely juridical motive is the desire to realize and reveal the idea of Justice. The motive determined by his social membership can be called "reason of State"; for to be determined by a society in a given state is not to be able to deny it, or indeed to alter this society and its state, [but] to act so as to keep it in existence and in the state it is in. Now, to judge or legislate (juridically) with a concern not to alter the state of society and not to endanger its existence is precisely to be inspired by "reason of State."

A lot of theorists have wanted to reduce all *Droit* to what I call "reason of State"—or what is the same thing—to "social utility," the maintenance of "public order," and so on. For them, there is not and cannot be "any" C—that is, "disinterested" in the sense defined. But to accept this point of view is to deny the existence of *Droit* as a specific and autonomous phenomenon: *Droit* is only an element of social or political phenomenon. This is what the supporters of "natural *Droit*" would not accept in any form. And for them, this natural *Droit,* i.e., authentic *Droit* (truly "just" [and] specifically and exclusively juridical), is the *Droit* that *any* C "says," a "disinterested" C in the sense of [82] our definition. It is the *Droit* which is valid everywhere and always, which is independent of social conditions.

Our definition, therefore, is in agreement with the "rationalist" conception of *Droit.* But when it is a matter of finding the conditions of the *realization* of this definition, one must take into account the results acquired by the "historical" or sociological conception, which has shown that *in fact* there is not "any" C, that the real C (juridical Legislator or Judge) is always determined or co-determined by the society in which he lives, that he is never "disinterested" in the sense indicated.

I will have to deal with the conditions of the realization of *Droit* conforming to my definition in chapter 2. But it will be necessary to say a few words about it even here.

First of all, it is obvious that the "rationalists" are right in the sense that *Droit* does not boil down to "politics" alone, that there are specific juridical reasons essentially different from "reason of State," "public utility," and so on. Indeed, man has always protested against "reason of State" and has always known how to distinguish between the "just" and the "useful," even the politically or socially useful. One can accept a degree [*mesure*] of it if one considers it useful to society, or indeed indispensable for maintaining the State. But very often this same degree is considered *unjust* (in which case one would want to know that it is provisional; one looks for the means to change the social and political conditions so as to be able to do without it). Likewise, in criminal *Droit,* the specifically juridical element is undeniable. It is enough to read the theories of the "Italian school" to realize to what extent criminal *Droit* is something else than "social hygiene." To punish a "normal" and adult criminal is truly quite different from locking up a non-offending insane person. The idea of a "just punishment" cannot be discounted. One cannot definitively replace it by considerations of social utility, public hygiene, protection, preventative measures, and so on. And the same goes for all the spheres of *Droit:* everywhere the specifically juridical phenomenon is there. At the very most, it is concealed by political, ethical, religious, or other phenomena.

I will try to show this in chapter 3. Let us admit it for the moment as "obvious." The question, then, is to know how to resolve the difficulty which we have come up against. On the one hand, there is an authentic *Droit,* or at the very least an idea—and ideal—of such a *Droit.* And this *Droit* is only possible if C is "anyone at all," for this *Droit* is nothing but the one anticipated by our definition. But, on the other hand, [83] *in reality* there is not any [*quelconque*] C; C is always determined by society, by thus acting according to "reason of State."

This difficulty does not exist only *for us,* for the phenomenologist of *Droit.* The man who "lives" the *Droit* has realized this for a long time himself. And he has tried to *realize* the conditions necessary for the existence of "any" C anticipated by our definition. C would therefore be "disinterested" in the sense that he would not depend upon the social and political conditions in which he lives—and "intervenes" as a "third"—that he would not be inspired by "reason of State" but only by the ideal of Justice.

It is from such a desire of man that the idea of the "separation of powers" was born—that is, the separation of *Droit* and juridical life from the State embodied in its Government. One has assumed that by making the Judge (C) independent of the Government, by shielding him from its influence, one would make him independent of the State and Society—that is, of spatial and temporal conditions. In short, one believed that one could thus transform him into a "disinterested third," intervening in human interactions solely for juridical reasons—that is, according to the idea (presumed to be *universally* and *eternally* valid) of Justice. One believed that such a C would be "anyone at all," that the "separated" Judges "would intervene" everywhere and always in the same manner. In a word, one believed one could thus realize the necessary conditions for the *reality* of the phenomenon described in our definition.

The big question is to know if this is possible, if by "separating" C one makes him truly "anyone at all."

First of all, it is necessary to explain the idea of "separation" in its adequate form. I have said, and I will say again, that the "third" C is not only the Judge (or Arbiter) and enforcer of the Judge's sentence (judicial Police in the broad sense of the word); he is also, and even above all, the juridical Legislator. In order that the *application* of *Droit* be juridically authentic, it is first of all necessary that a juridically authentic *Droit exists.* Now it is the (juridical) Legislator who creates it. "To separate" C, therefore, is first and foremost "to separate" him as a Legislator, as intervening "for the first time" in a given interaction and thus *creating* the corresponding legal rule. Now, this truth has been generally misunderstood. One has only wanted "to separate" the Judge (and the Police), leaving the care of juridical *legislation* to the Government. In other words, one has tried to make C "anyone at all" in his capacity [84] as Judge and Police, and not as Legislator. Without a doubt, this has a certain value. And it can be said that one has truly succeeded in making the Judge and Police "anyone at all"—that is, "disinterested." When it is a matter of *applying* and *enforcing* a given juridical law, *all* Judges and all modern Police act in one and the same manner (as, among other things, the practice of "private international *Droit*" proves: a French judge, for example, applies German law just like a German judge does).[62] But all this is insufficient as long as the Law itself remains without a guarantee of its juridical authenticity. Now as long as juridical *legislation* is not "separated" from the Government, it is without this guarantee. And the fact of variations between national *Droits* sufficiently proves this.

I do not want to discuss the question of knowing if such a "separation" is possible. It really seems not, seeing the obvious difficulties of "separating" juridical from political legislation. I would only like to say that it would be of no use, even if it were possible.

The "rationalists" "reason" in the following manner: *Droit* implies the idea of Justice, a *sui generis* idea which has nothing to do with "social utility" or "reason of State"; these change with places and epochs; *therefore,* the idea of Justice is universally and eternally valid; if one isolates a man from Society and the State, he will find the idea of Justice in its pure state and will build upon it a *Droit* which will be the same for everyone and always. The "sociologists" make an opposite "argument": experience shows that the very idea of Justice varies according to places and epochs; "social utility" and "reason of State" do as well; *therefore,* the idea of Justice is not at all autonomous, it can be reduced to "social utility" or "reason of State."

It is easy to see that these two "arguments" are fallacious. In reality, the idea of Justice is a function of place [85] and time no less than social utility and reason of State; nevertheless, it is essentially something different from them.

I will try to show later on (Part Two) that the idea of Justice has three consecutive forms: the (thetic) Justice of equality of the Master, the (antithetic) Justice of equivalence of the Slave, and the synthetic Justice of the Citizen. The first two never exist in a pure state. All real [kinds of] Justice are synthetic. But they differ from one another, so to speak, according to the proportions of Mas-

---

62. It should be understood that I assume that the Judge is "ideal." I abstract from *mistakes* in the application of the given Law. In fact, these mistakes, or indeed variations, are always possible, from whence comes the institution of Appeal. This Appeal, moreover, is nothing other than one of the methods to make C "anyone at all": one replaces one C by another in order to see if C's intervention does not vary by this fact. Thus, if the appeals court [*l'instance d'appel*] sends the case back, it sends it to *another* court of the same degree. As for the supreme court [*l'instance définitive*], it is considered "anyone at all" by definition, which is obviously only a fiction. But these technical questions do not interest us. (Cf., moreover, the practice of giving a ruling "*en banc* [with all the judges of the court hearing the case rather than a quorum]" in important cases.)

tery and Servitude, of equality and equivalence. There is in principle, then, an infinity of synthetic Justices, one of which is characterized by the perfect equilibrium of its two constitutive elements and which can be called the "Justice of the Citizen" in the narrow and proper sense of the term.

We will see that each of these Justices is a function of time and space, that each shows solidarity with the Society or State where it is born and lives. More exactly, the idea of Justice and the *Droit* which follows from it, the social and political organization, the religious, moral, aesthetic, and so on, conception, are only various aspects of one and the same human phenomenon, which is born and evolves in time and is localized in space. Consequently, even if it were possible to isolate the juridical aspect from all the others, one would not obtain a single *Droit* but a plurality of Legal systems, varying according to places (i.e., Societies) and epochs. But this juridical aspect, while being variable, and even if it is inseparable in fact from the other aspects, is perfectly distinct from them and cannot be reduced to or deduced from them. One sees this because a given State or the given state of a Society, for example, can be considered *unjust* by the very men who realize or "live" in them. And if in the case when the State and Society are in agreement with the ideal of Justice which the men have who live there, the opposition between the social and political idea and the juridical idea being no longer apparent, their essential distinction is not, for all this, done away with.

If the existence of a "separated judicial power" were truly possible, this power would have elaborated a *Droit* independent of "social utility" or "reason of State," and one would then see if the social and political institutions are or are not in agreement with the principles of this *Droit*. But this *Droit* would not be universally and eternally valid. It would be the *Droit* of a given human group at a given moment, the various aspects of this group, such as the [86] juridical, social, and political aspects, for example, being capable of being in harmony or not.[63]

As soon as one takes into account the *reality* of *Droit*, i.e., as soon as one speaks about real or "positive" *Droit*, one cannot then introduce into the definition the (introspective) notion of "disinterestedness" (or its behaviorist equivalent, i.e., the notion of C [being] "anyone at all") without limiting the significance of this notion. In a given real *Droit*, C is not truly "anyone at all":

---

63. In this last case there would be conflict. Now, we will see that Justice (idea) becomes *Droit* (reality) only to the extent that it is applied by the State—that is, by the Government (by the legislative and executive power). In case of conflict, then, there will be no authentic *Droit*. The activity of the State will not be juridical because it will be at odds with the idea of Justice, and this idea will not be juridical because it will not be applied in fact (by the State). As Justice tends to be realized, i.e., to become *Droit*, and the State tends to be "justified," i.e., to become "legal," there will be a struggle between the "judicial power" (and the citizens taken as "juridical men" in general) and the governmental power (i.e., the citizens taken as "political men"). Authentic *Droit* will be determined by the outcome of this struggle, by its "result." All "positive" *Droit*, i.e., all real *Droit*, is such a "result." I will have the opportunity, moreover, to come back to this question.

he is only anyone at all inside of a given group at a given moment of its historical existence. In other words, C will be "disinterested" only from the point of view of this group and not in an absolute fashion. An observer situated outside of the group will see that he is determined by the group in question in its given historical state, that he is therefore "interested" in maintaining this group, in the preservation of this state of things, since his intervention, by altering the group, would alter himself, since he thus feels the repercussion of his "intervention." And he will be "interested" even in his capacity as C, i.e., as a "juridical man"; for he will want to *realize* his ideal of Justice. He will want, therefore, to intervene in an efficacious manner, i.e., by being supported by the State, by making the State act in his place, in conformity with his intention. But he has a "ready-made" notion of the State. He will necessarily intervene, therefore, so that the State, such as he conceives it, can support his intervention. In other words, he will intervene by taking account of "reason of State," such as he understands it. His "power" will not be "separated" in fact from that of the State.

Of course, one can introduce into the general definition of *Droit* the expression: "(a third C) disinterested, i.e., supposed to be able to be anyone at all." But one must then say that such a [87] *Droit* does not exist on earth and has never yet existed. If one wants to define real *Droit*, i.e., *a* given real or "positive" *Droit*, one must say: "disinterested, i.e., supposed to be able to be anyone at all *inside a given Society at a given moment of its historical existence.*"

But even this restriction is not enough to make our definition applicable to reality, i.e., to a given real or "positive" *Droit;* for it is obvious that C is never in fact "anyone at all" (i.e., disinterested), even inside the Society where he intervenes. Indeed, no Society will consent to take into account the "interventions" of an insane person or a young child. Ancient Societies excluded slaves, [and] even in our day, in France for example, a woman cannot play the role of C, although she can be subject to the effect of his intervention. And besides, juridical legislation and the exercise of justice in general often (if not always) represent in fact the ideas (and consequently the "interests") peculiar to some group within a Society, and not those of all the members of this group. This is above all when one speaks about "class justice"; this is when one realizes that the idea of Justice (meaning the idea of Justice being formed by a group which does not succeed in realizing this idea by the State) is at odds with "reason of State" or "social utility" (meaning as they [both of these reasons] are understood by the group which succeeds in having its ideas realized by the State).

All these facts are undeniable. And yet, it is quite obviously impossible to declare all positive *Droit* juridically unauthentic when the (juridical) Legislator and Judge are not truly anyone at all. A *Droit* forged and applied by free men to the exclusion of slaves, by men to the exclusion of women, by one "class" against the will of another "class," and so on, can very well be juridically authentic, can be a *Droit* in the proper sense of the term, and not simply force or violence.

Therefore, it is necessary to take account of this fact in our definition if we want it to be applicable to real or positive *Droit*. On the other hand, it is just as obvious that if one completely does away with the condition according to which C must be "disinterested," i.e., "anyone at all," one abolishes as a result the very notion of *Droit*. Therefore, one must look for a compromise.

Let us first recall that C has three distinct, but complimentary and equally indispensable, aspects: he is (juridical) Legislator [88] to the extent that he creates a legal rule; he is Judge to the extent that he applies a given rule to a concrete case; and he is the (judicial) Police to the extent that he enforces the given application of a given rule.[64] If a Legislator promulgates a legal rule that no one else would have promulgated if he were in his place; if he is alone in wanting to apply it to concrete cases; and finally, if no one other than himself wanted to enforce his judgement, one must quite obviously say that he is neither Legislator, Judge, nor Police: a juridical phenomenon does not exist at all, but a simple [act of] violence. Let us now assume that no one has legislated and judged like him but that *anyone* enforced his judgement (because it is a judgement and his judgement). It would then be necessary to say that one is in the presence of an authentic juridical phenomenon. It would be necessary to say that his will alone makes the law, that it is the one and only source of the *Droit* in question, but that this *Droit* is really a *Droit* and not an [act of] violence.[65] It will be the same if the Legislator is not "anyone at all" [but] the Judge who applies his law is "anyone at all" (the enforcer being so or not). If all the members of a society apply a legal rule, this rule is juridically authentic, even if none of these members would have promulgated it in the case when it would not exist. Finally, a legal rule that any member whatsoever of a society would have promulgated would not cease being a legal rule if no one wanted to apply or enforce it. It should be understood that all these cases are imaginary, for generally one does not refuse to apply a legal rule that everyone would have promulgated, and one does not enforce a rule that no one accepts as a rule. I only wanted to show that it is enough that C be "anyone at all" in one of his three aspects for the phenomenon to be authentically juridical.

But in practice C is never "anyone at all" in any of his aspects, and it is here that the difficulties begin. If the Legislator establishes a legal rule [89] that only a *part* of the members of the society accept as a rule, if only a *part* consent to apply it, and if only a *part* enforce this application—in short, if there is "class justice," is the phenomenon juridical or not?

In my opinion, there is only one way to answer.

In a Society or State, if a group (or "class") M, inside of which a given C is anyone at all, can *suppress* [*supprimer*] another group N (where a C of another

---

64. Sometimes the Judge decides a case without there being a law; but then he is in a single person Judge *and* Legislator. Likewise, the (winning) party can itself be charged with enforcing the judgement; but then it does so no longer in its capacity as a party but as the Police. In all the cases when there is *Droit*, then, there is a triple "intervention": that of the Legislator, Judge, and Police.

65. One can deny this only by contrasting this enforced judgement to a judgement based upon the idea of an eternally and universally valid justice—that is, upon "natural *Droit*." Now this "*Droit*" still does not exist.

type is also anyone at all), without the Society or State perishing, the C of group M can be called "anyone at all" simply (within this Society, of course): the legal rule which it sets forth, applies, and enforces will be authentically juridical. By contrast, in a Society where no group can play the role of group M, there will not be *Droit* in the proper sense of the term.

The term "suppress," moreover, can have two different meanings. One can take it literally. Group M can *suppress* group N (or all non-M groups) by killing them or by expelling all its members. In this case C will truly be *anyone at all* in the Society in question since it will then coincide with the former group M. But one can also take the term "suppress" in the sense of *exclude*. Indeed, it is enough not to take account of the members of non-M groups in the choice of C, while letting them remain within the Society, where they can play any role other than that of C—that is, any non-juridical role. Thus, for example, women are excluded in France from active juridical life; modern French *Droit*, therefore, is exclusively masculine; nevertheless, given that the French State exists, it is an authentic *Droit*.

It should be understood that the methods of "exclusion" can vary greatly. In a Parliament which is in the process of voting a juridical law, the C which votes for it is only anyone at all within the majority (group M), since a member of the minority (group N) would not have voted for it. Group N, therefore, can be "excluded" according to the principle of majority rule. But this method is far from being the only one possible. One can also, for example, draw lots or form an homogenous "elite" (e.g., the "elite" males excluding women, and so on). For there to be (positive) *Droit*, it is necessary and sufficient that C is anyone at all within a group which can remove from all the other groups the possibility of playing the role of C, without Society as such ceasing to exist because of this exclusion (which would mean, moreover, [90] the ruin of the group itself as the group of the Society in question).[66]

Let us call the "exclusive group" any group within a State or Society which can suppress or only exclude all the other groups without the Society or State perishing by this fact. If it is only a question of "exclusion," the State can have several "exclusive groups" in one and the same Society. It will be called "religious" when it is going to exclude possible participants from the (active or passive) religious life of the Society, [or] "aesthetic" when the exclusion only concerns aesthetic life, and so on. An "exclusive group," therefore, will be "juridical" when it can exclude without danger to the State all the candidates for the role of C who "would intervene," if the case arises, differently than a representative of this group would have done. C can then be called "anyone at

---

66. The "group" can reduce to a single individual in principle. But in fact, such a "group" will never be able to "suppress" the non-M group, formed of several individuals, since he will be weaker than it. If a single [individual] has *authority*, he can certainly be "stronger" than even a very numerous group. But this would be a misuse of language if one then wanted to speak about "exclusion" (or even of "force"); for those who submit to his authority form by this very fact a *group* with him. His will being their will, they will act (in principle) as he does: in the group formed by them and him, therefore, C could be anyone at all.

all" within a given Society if he is anyone at all inside of an "exclusive juridical group" of this Society. But since in a definition of *Droit* it can only be a matter of an exclusive *juridical* group, it is pointless to specify it.

Therefore, the expression "an impartial and disinterested third C" can be replaced by that of "a third C supposed to be able to be anyone at all within an exclusive group of a given Society at a given moment."[67]

Let us now go to the limit, as mathematicians say.

Let us suppose that the Society in question implies all of humanity, that it is a "*universal* State," if it is organized into a State. In this case, one could say: "a third C supposed to be able to be anyone at all within an exclusive group at a given moment." Let us now suppose that humanity (or the universal State) is *homogenous* (universal and homogenous State or "Empire") in the sense that no one has "private interests." [91] At a given moment, C could be truly "disinterested," i.e., "anyone at all," without restriction: generally speaking, if everyone can play the role of another, there is no reason at all to suppose that he will play a juridical role differently than another. Therefore, one could say: "a third C supposed to be able to be anyone at all at a given moment."[68] But if the State (or Society) is truly universal and homogenous, one does not see how it could perish or even change. Without external wars, without internal struggles, i.e., without revolutions, the State ought to remain indefinitely in identity with itself. The restriction "at a given moment," therefore, no longer makes sense if it is a matter of a universal and homogenous State or Society. Therefore, one could finally say: "a third C supposed to be able to be anyone at all"— that is, in "introspective" language, "a disinterested third C."

At the limit, then, we come back to our point of departure. We have eliminated the restrictions that we were required to introduce in order to take account of *reality*, a reality where Societies are multiple, where no Society is homogenous, and where all consequently change. As soon as the universal and homogenous State will be a *reality*, therefore, one will no longer need to introduce the restrictions in question into the general definition of *Droit*.

Now, without these restrictions, our definition is nothing other than the definition of "natural *Droit*" about which the "rationalist school" speaks. We have only introduced these restrictions in order to take into account the various "positive *Droits*." But "at the limit," positive *Droit* coincides with natural *Droit*; for the *Droit realized* in and by the universal and homogenous State is just as much one, just as *universally* and *eternally* (i.e., "necessarily") valid, as the would-be "natural *Droit*." We can say, therefore, that the "positive" *Droit*

---

67. If the Society is a State, this amounts to saying that all *Droit* recognized by this State is by this very fact authentic. (Moreover, this results from the fact, as we will see, that C "annuls" B's reaction in an *irresistible* way.) But I have wanted to use a more complicated and general terminology because the Society in question can be any at all—that is, it does not need to be a State in the proper sense.

68. It should be understood that it is a matter of an unreal limit case. A woman will never be a man, a child an adult, nor the insane sane. But homogeneity can be more or less near this limit.

of the universal and homogenous State realizes "natural" *Droit*, which is nothing other than *the Droit* as such—that is, the "essence" of *Droit*. In the universal and homogenous State, therefore, the "rationalist" theory of *Droit* coincides with the "historical or sociological" theory.

That is the very core [*le fond*] of Hegelianism, or, if one prefers, of the dialectical understanding of history.

The idea, the essence, the ideal, the universally and necessarily [92] (i.e., eternally) valid, the True, the Just in itself—it is of little importance how it is expressed—all this is not a beginning but a *result*, not a being but a *becoming*, and a becoming properly so-called—that is, a becoming *in time*, in history. Thus, "absolute *Droit*" does not exist from the beginning [and] it does not *yet* exist. But it does not follow that all *Droit* will *always* be "relative." The *Droit* of the universal and homogenous State will not be so: it will be "absolute" since it will be the only one and will not change. But it will be so only at the end of history, when the State in question will be a reality. For the moment, there is no absolute *Droit*, and all real *Droit* is effectively relative, both in relation to space and time.

As long as the Empire will not be realized, *Droit* will remain relative. And it is very possible that this Empire will never be realized; for historical evolution proceeds by negation—that is, freely, or in an unforeseeable way. But if this Empire is realized, one will be able to know what it is, one will see that it is universal and homogenous, and one will be able to conclude that it will no longer change. One will know, therefore, that its "positive" *Droit* is *the Droit*, the absolute, unique, and immutable *Droit*. And one will then be able to see that this *Droit* is synthetic, that it results from all the preceding relative *Droits*. In other words, one will be able to "deduce" it afterwards. In relation to it, all the other *Droits* will be able to be arranged in a system of dialectical triads, formed by a position, by the negation of this position, and by the result of their struggle. One will see that the absolute *Droit* is the final result of this dialectic of relative *Droits*, that it is their integration. It is not that this *Droit* is a simple sum (necessarily contradictory) of all the previous *Droits*. It will keep some of them and will only imply the others in the form of their negation. But it will take account of them all by explaining in what ways and why it keeps some and rejects others. And it is by understanding its past that it understands itself, that it will justify itself as the result of this past. Moreover, it is this perfect self-understanding by the understanding of its becoming that will allow it to understand itself as definitive. And this revelation of its absolute character will be the proof and evidence of the reality of this character. It will be absolute because it will know itself to be such, because it will be able to show that no other *Droit* is possible, seeing that it implies (positively or negatively) all the possibilities realized in the course of history—that is, *realizable* in general.

[93] This absolute *Droit* will be a **Droit**. And this is why one can give here and now a *formal* definition of it, which allows one to distinguish a *Droit* from all that is not juridical and to recognize as such all that is. But it would be futile to want to determine in advance its *content*. We only know that the absolute

Droit will be the positive *Droit* of the universal and homogenous State. But we cannot know in advance *what* this positive *Droit* will be. We cannot deduce it *a priori* from the relative *Droits* with which we are familiar. It is only afterwards that we will be able to understand it (i.e., to deduce it *a posteriori*) from these relative *Droits,* as the final result of their historical dialectic with which we will then be entirely familiar.

It is in this sense that our definition must be understood.

It gives no information about the *content* of *Droit,* whatever it is. It only allows one to see if a given content (a phenomenon) is or is not authentically juridical. And it allows one to do this whatever this content. This is why one can say that it is a *formal* definition (behaviorist, moreover) of the *essence* of *Droit.*

The *first* behaviorist definition, such as was given in § 9, i.e., without the restriction proposed in the present section, cannot be applied to the juridical *reality* with which we are familiar. But this is not so bad for the definition; this is too bad for reality. It is not the definition [but] reality which cannot hold out, so to speak; for real "positive" *Droits* are—as experience shows—*ephemeral* realities, limited in space and time. They *are* not, to speak properly: they are born and die; they *pass away.* Only their formal character remains the same, their essence; and this is what is described in the definition. The existence of *Droit* will only conform to this definition when it will truly conform to its essence, and it is only at this moment, as conforming to the definition, that it will be truly *real* or real *in truth*—that is, everywhere and always.

In order to take account of this ephemeral existence of the essence, of these partial and transitory realizations of *Droit* as such, one must replace in our definition the terms "impartial and disinterested"—or translated into behaviorist language—"anyone at all," by the expression:

"supposed to be able to be anyone at all (inside an exclusive group of a given Society at a given epoch)."

Our definition, therefore, does not apply to the case when there [94] would not be at a given moment an "exclusive group" in a given Society: according to our definition, then, there would be no authentic *Droit* at all in this Society at this moment. Now this is the way things effectively are; for a Society without an "exclusive group" is a Society in the midst of a revolution. The definition therefore implies the assertion that there is no revolutionary *Droit,* that on the contrary, revolution is an absolute negation of *Droit* (it being understood a given positive *Droit,* since revolutions only exist as long as there is no universal and homogenous State, and since there is no absolute *Droit* outside of this State). And indeed, when there is a genuine revolution, a given (positive) *Droit* dies in order to generate another, and one can say that every time that a *Droit* dies in order to generate another there is a genuine revolution. Revolution, therefore, is the *passage* from one *Droit* to another; it is very much an absence (which is a "potentiality" [*puissance*]), a (creative) negation of *Droit.* As long as *Droit* is recognized, the action is juridically legal, and a juridically legal action is not revolutionary. And revolutionary action has nothing juridical about it (other than the negative sense in which a political or ordinary *crime* is "juridical"), as long as the revolutionaries have not constituted an "exclusive group" in a new Society which they have created in and by their revolution.

But everywhere else, everywhere then where there is an exclusive group in whatever Society, organized or not into a State, there is a possibility of applying our definition, provided that one introduces the proposed restriction: there will be an authentic *Droit* if—all the other conditions of the definition being fulfilled—there is a third [who is] supposed to be able to be anyone at all inside the exclusive group in question.

If a Society is *homogenous*, one can eliminate the words, "of an exclusive group." If it is *universal*, one can eliminate the words, "of a given Society." If it is homogenous *and* universal, one can eliminate the whole parenthetical expression—that is, the whole restriction introduced in this section. The definition of the *essence* of *Droit* will also then be applied to the *existence* of *Droit*, precisely because existence and essence will be but one: the essence of *Droit* will be fully realized and the existence will be entirely penetrated by the fullness of the juridical essence. Justice will be fully realized in and by *Droit* because all human existence will be determined by Justice.

§ 16

[95] I have commented upon the condition of the interaction between A and B in § 10–12, [and] of C's intervention in § 13–15. It is now necessary to see (in § 16–17) how these two conditions must be linked to one another in a general (formal and behaviorist) definition of the phenomenon of "*Droit*."

I have said in the first definition that the interaction "necessarily provokes" the intervention. Therefore, it is necessary to see what the [following] terms mean:

a) *provoke;* and

b) *necessarily.*

a) A commentary upon the term "*provoke*" has already implicitly been given in what has preceded.

C's intervention is *in relation* with the interaction between A and B. The intervention is not some spontaneous act. It only takes place because the interaction in question takes place. But it would have been able not to take place despite the existence of this interaction. The interaction provokes the intervention, but the intervention is an act, which could exist [*être*] or not, and which can have such a nature or another: only its nature will always be in relation with the nature of the interaction which provokes it. In short, in ordinary (i.e., "introspective") language, C is free to intervene or not, and he can intervene as he sees fit, provided that he is always impartial and disinterested. His intervention, therefore, is not *determined* by the interaction; it does not result from it automatically; it cannot be foreseen starting from the interaction. But the intervention is always *in relation* with the interaction; for C intervenes or does not, and he intervenes in a certain manner according to the idea he has of the interaction in question (as well as according to a juridical principle which is his own—that is, according to the idea of Justice such as he conceives it). C intervenes for a "disinterested" motive, namely for a specifically juridical motive, which is nothing other than the desire to realize and reveal his idea or ideal of Justice. But he wants to realize it in the event of a concrete case, by applying it to this case, which is precisely the interaction in question between A and B. Or once again, taken individually, a given interaction contains nothing which could allow one to say why it generates (in a given Society) such a legal rule rather [96] than another; but every legal rule allows one (in principle) to distinguish concrete cases—that is, the interactions to which it is supposed to be applied.

These remarks apply to all juridical situations whatever they may be. But one can distinguish two types of juridical situations which differ precisely by the way in which C's intervention is "provoked."

I have said that the interaction between A and B anticipated by the definition can be anything as regards its nature, motive, and significance. In principle, therefore, it has nothing to do with C and his intervention: it can be such as it would have been if C did not exist or did not intervene. In other words, C can intervene spontaneously in this interaction in the sense that he intervenes because he really wants to, because it is him alone who decides to intervene—that is, to annul B's reaction. But there are cases when C's intervention is conditional. In this case, C only intervenes if A's action, directed against B, also implies an element oriented toward C, [or] in ordinary language, if A solicits C's intervention. When the interaction between A and B does not imply this element of solicitation, C does not intervene. If this element is there, C can still intervene or not; and if he intervenes, he does so as he sees fit. But if he intervenes, he does so because he has been solicited by A. In the first case, by contrast, C can also intervene or not, but he does so independently of any solicitation.[69] Finally, there are cases when C intervenes only if he is solicited by A and B simultaneously, although it should be understood that here also he can very well not intervene despite this dual solicitation, and if he intervenes he does so as he sees fit.

If C does not intervene, the situation is in no way juridical. But if he intervenes, the other conditions of the definition being fulfilled, the situation will be juridical in all three of the cases distinguished: every time there will be a *Droit*, an essentially and specifically juridical phenomenon. But there will be

---

69. It should be understood that B may also solicit C's intervention—that is, may want C to support his reaction by making it irresistible and to annul A's action. But to be able to apply our definition, we must then say that it is B who acts, A who reacts, and that C annuls A's reaction [opposed] to B's action. Now, we have agreed to call A the one who acts and B the one who reacts. By only anticipating A's solicitation alone, and not B's, our definition thus has a general significance: it is enough to change the terminology and nomenclature to apply it to the case when it is B alone who solicits C's intervention.

two, or if you will, three different types of *Droit*. [97] In the first type, C's intervention is "provoked" only by the interaction between A and B. In the second
type, it is "provoked" by this interaction only to the extent that it implies a
"Solicitation" on A's part. Finally, in the third type, this "Solicitation" must
come from A and B simultaneously.

It is easy to see that the first type of *Droit* is nothing other than *penal* (i.e.,
public) **Droit,** while the two other types form *civil* (or *private*) **Droit.** And one
can also say that in the two first cases it is a matter of (criminal or civil) *Judgement* properly so-called, while in the third case there is (civil) *Arbitration*.

If one wants to take into account these distinctions inside of the general
juridical phenomenon, one can introduce in the definition a parenthetical
expression. Instead of simply saying that the interaction between A and B "provokes . . . ," one can add (in parentheses): "by itself or through a solicitation
coming from A, with or without B's consent. . . . "

b) Our definition also says that the interaction between A and B "*necessarily* provokes" C's intervention.

Truth to tell, the expression "necessarily" is not a felicitous one because it
can make one believe that the interaction *automatically* produces the intervention. Now we have just said that it is nothing like this since the intervention may not take place even if the interaction occurs. However, this expression corresponds to a necessary element of the definition.

Generally speaking, the "necessary" is contrasted to the "contingent" or
"fortuitous." Now, it is obvious that there will be no *Droit* when C's intervention is "contingent," in the sense that C intervenes in a different manner in the
event of *identical* interactions between A and B.[70] One can therefore say, [98]
if you will, that the interaction "*necessarily* provokes" C's intervention, meaning by this that *identical* interactions provoke *identical* interventions. But we
have said, on the other hand, that a given interaction can "provoke" whatever
intervention, or not generate it at all. "Necessarily provokes," therefore, can
only mean this: if a given interaction does or does not provoke a specific inter-

---

70. One interaction can be identical to another even if the roles of A and B are played by
different persons: the murder of X by Y can be identical to the murder of M by N, for example, or of Y by X. But this is not always the case. According to "barbarian *Droit*," for example, the murder of a German X by a Gallo-Roman Y was punished differently than the murder of the Gallo-Roman Y by the German X. (At first glance, parenthetically, this fact seems
to be at odds with the requirement of C's "impartiality" that we have defined above as the
possibility of reversing A and B without this altering the nature of C's intervention. But in
fact this is not so; for in this case there is not—*for C*—an identity between the two interactions. Indeed, *for him,* the interaction is not the "murder of some A by some B," but the
"murder of some *German* A . . . ," or the "murder of some *Gallo-Roman* A. . . . " A and B
are only reversible provided that the interaction remains the same from C's point of view.
Thus, in the case of the "barbarian" Judge, one must say that his intervention would not be
altered if the [98] "German A" was—by some remote chance—the "Roman B" and the
"Roman B" the "German A," which precisely means that for him the "Roman" or the "German" can be anyone at all. And this is why one can say that he is "impartial.") Be that as it
may, as soon as C believes himself to be in the presence of two *identical* interactions, he must
intervene in the same manner for his intervention to have a juridical meaning.

vention, this intervention will recur or be lacking *every time* that an *identical* interaction to the given interaction occurs.

One can also say that the intervention is contingent in relation to the interaction but that it is not contingent in itself. In other words, one cannot foresee the intervention starting from the interaction taken individually. But one can *foresee* it if one knows the interaction, on the one hand, and C's idea of Justice, on the other hand. Now, that which is *foreseeable* can be called "necessary."

"Necessary" or "foreseeable" also means in this case that the intervention will be the same whomever C is. Now we have already assumed in the preceding section that C can be anyone at all. But this condition is not sufficient. Indeed, let us assume that the idea of Justice does not exist. No matter the extent to which C can be anyone at all, i.e., disinterested, he will have no reason to intervene rather than not to intervene, or to intervene in a certain way rather than another. In this case, therefore, the intervention will be contingent or unforeseeable; it will be the work of mere fate alone. Now, in these conditions, it will surely have nothing juridical about it. For there to be *Droit* (i.e., ultimately, the application of an idea of Justice), it is thus necessary not only that C is anyone at all but also that this C intervenes in the same way every time that the same interaction susceptible of provoking his intervention recurs. In other words, C must be "anyone at all" not only in relation to space but also in relation to time. Not only must all the candidates for the roles of C intervene in the same way in a given interaction, but they must not alter their intervention if the interaction in question recurred in the future.

[99] Now, as soon as one wants to apply the definition to historical reality, one meets with a difficulty which requires a new restriction. This is because in reality *Droit* evolves over time such that two interactions considered identical can provoke different interventions if they take place in different epochs. Thus, for example, one and the same act of poaching would have been punished with death in France in the Middle Ages and with a small fine at the present time. And yet, the fact that a *Droit* varies does not make it juridically unauthentic. Thus, Medieval French *Droit* is just as much an authentic *Droit* as modern *Droit*.

This is because all authentic *Droit*, while evolving in fact, is immutable or "eternal" in principle. Of course, men can acknowledge that their present *Droit* is going to change one day; but this is an extra-juridical conception. *Droit* as *Droit* does not recognize its temporal and temporary nature. A given legal rule is valid "for all time (to come)": *it* never changes. If *Droit* changes it is because a legal rule has been replaced by another one. But none of these rules can vary in itself: if it is applied to a case, it will be applied to all the cases identical to this one as long as it remains what it is—that is, a *legal* rule *in force* and not a *memory* of what had one day been a legal rule. This *memory* has nothing juridical about it just as the *evolution* of Droit has nothing juridical about it. *Past Droit* (a repealed law) is just as little a **Droit** as the *Droit to come* (a bill). And the *present Droit*, the *Droit* which has a real presence in the world, does not vary.

In short, a legal rule *is always supposed* to be applied—that is, *every time* that the interaction to which it is applied arises. But *in fact* it is applied *every time* only as long as it is not annulled or replaced by another one. In other words, it will very well be applied "every time," but only during a certain period, at a certain epoch (and, it should be understood, in a certain Society).

We therefore encounter the restriction introduced in the definition in respect to the term "anyone at all." This restriction already appeared there [and] it is pointless to repeat it. One can therefore say "every time" simply. The sense will be at any rate: "every time in a given Society at a given epoch."

When all is said and done, we can replace the expression "the interaction between A and B necessarily provokes C's intervention" by this other one:

[100] "provokes [C's intervention] every time that it [the interaction] recurs (by itself or through a solicitation coming from A, with or without B's consent."[71]

§ 17

C's intervention, provoked by the interaction between A and B, has for a motive and an effect to *annul* B's reaction to A's action. A can thus reach his goal without meeting with resistance—that is, without needing to make an effort. And this is precisely why one can say that A has a *droit* to his action.

It is now necessary to comment upon this notion of "*annulling.*"

First of all, let us note that the term "annul" ought to be taken in a strong sense. C annuls B's reaction without possible resistance on his part. It is enough that C decides to annul this reaction for it to be really annulled.[72]

---

71. It should be understood that there can be a juridical situation even if C's intervention does not take place *in fact* or "materially." It is enough that it *could* or *ought* to take place, that it takes place *in principle* or "ideally." I mean that the situation remains juridical and that A has a *droit* to act as he acts even in the case when by chance no Judge intervenes, either because he has not been informed, because he is mistaken about the genuine nature of the interaction in question, or because he is dishonest [*mauvaise foi*], and so on. The definition assumes an "ideal" case where C is who he ought to be. But this is so obvious that it is pointless to mention it in the very text of the definition. One must say, however, that C's intervention is never totally absent when there is an authentic juridical situation; for let us not forget that "C's intervention" can simply mean the "presence of a legal rule anticipating the interaction in question." What the interaction "provokes," then, is quite simply the application of the rule to a concrete case, of the rule as a rule and not as a judgement or enforcement of a judgement. Now, such an "application" is always there as soon as there is a rule established beforehand (this rule, moreover, is capable of being a simple "precedent," a judgement—enforced or not—made in the event of an identical case). Without the existence of this rule, i.e., without "C's intervention" at all, the situation would not be juridical. When there is neither an enforcement, an effective judgement, nor even an applicable legal rule, there is no *Droit* at all.

72. It should be understood that here as well the definition has in mind an ideal case: it abstracts from weaknesses in the Law, Justice, and the Police. Therefore, one could write: "the intervention is supposed to annul," or "annuls in principle," or "ought to annul," and so on. But this restriction is too obvious to be useful being expressed in the very text of the definition.

As I have already said, C can support B's reaction and annul A's action. But one will then be able to call B—A—and apply our definition without changing it.

This irresistible character of C's intervention is necessary [101] for there to be *Droit* or a juridical situation. And this is what one has in mind when one says that there is no *Droit* without a sanction, for this sanction is supposed to be irresistible. This is why, as I have already said, C is often conceived as a divine being: he acts upon A and B without them being able to react upon him (in the juridical situation in question). Practically speaking, it is *social* or *state* action which is (in principle) irresistible in relation to the isolated individuals. And this is why, when one says that *Droit* implies and presupposes a sanction, one has in mind a sanction coming from the State or Society as such. In other words, it is a matter of a sanction from which one cannot escape.

I will have to stress this point in the following chapter. For the moment, I simply want to point out that the "irresistibility" of C's intervention is linked to the fact that C is anyone at all; for to say that C's intervention is in the final analysis an intervention of the State or Society as such is to say that a lot of other members of this Society (and at the limit, everyone) would intervene in the same way C intervenes, since they help him to intervene—that is, to annul B's reaction. Now this is rightly [*justement*] to say that C is "anyone at all."

The annulment of B's reaction by C is irresistible or absolute in the sense that B cannot oppose it: B can neither annul nor alter C's action which annuls his reaction. Now this "reaction" of B is an "action" in the broad sense of the term, and like every action, it has or can have three constitutive elements: 1) the will to act; 2) the act itself; and 3) the motive which makes him act or the goal of the action, or again the intention. The annulment, therefore, can annul either all three of these elements, or only two or one of them, from whence comes several modes of annulment—that is, of C's intervention.

Let us see what these various modes are.

First of all, C can nip B's reaction in the bud, so to speak. In other words, he can annul in B the will to act. B does not react, therefore, solely because he knows that C would intervene in this case in order to annul his reaction. It is definitely C, therefore, who annuls B's reaction by annulling his will to act. C's "intervention," then, does exist. The will to act being annulled, B does not react and A reaches his goal without resistance—that is, without making an effort. He has, therefore, a *droit* to act as he does, and this whatever B's "motive," "goal," or "intention" is. It is enough, therefore, that C annuls the will to act. Since the act does not occur, it is "annulled" [102] by this very fact, and the action's "goal" is unimportant seeing that there has been no act, that the action has not been realized. Therefore, C does not need to annul the "motive" if he annuls the will, and he cannot annul the will without annulling by this very fact the act (it being assumed to be voluntary, of course).

Let us now assume that C has not annulled in B the will to act—or once again, let us assume that B's action is involuntary. In this case the annulment will have to concern the act itself. B goes into action, i.e., tries to annul through an effective reaction A's action; but C intervenes, interposes himself between B and A, and overcomes through his irresistible intervention the effect of B's action directed against A. Here as well, A does not meet with resistance; he acts without making an effort; [and] he therefore has the *droit* to do so. This time B's reaction is real; it is an act; but the act is without effect for A, it is for A as if it did not exist, thanks to C's intervention. It is of little importance, therefore, that C does or does not annul in B the will to act and the motive for his reaction. For there to be a juridical situation, it is enough that C annuls B's act.

But let us assume that B has had the time to realize his reaction (voluntary or not). He has, therefore, annulled A's action, who has not reached his goal while having had to make unsuccessful efforts to vanquish B's resistance—that is, to overcome his [B's] reaction to his [own, A's] action. It seems, therefore, that our definition does not apply; that A did not have the *droit* to act as he did; [and] that the situation has nothing juridical about it. And it would effectively be so if C did not succeed in annulling B's reaction. For there to be *Droit*, he must annul it in an irresistible manner. Now since he has not been able to annul the act or the will to act (if there was one, i.e., if the action was voluntary), he must (irresistibly) annul the third constitutive element of B's action—that is, of his reaction to A's action. C must annul what we have called the "goal," "motive," or the "intention."

Indeed, this is what takes place in all the cases when one speaks about A's "*droit*" to act, and when A nevertheless does not succeed in effectively acting. In all the cases where C—practically speaking as the juridical Legislator, Judge, or (juridical) Police—does not succeed in annulling a criminal or wrongful action (i.e., precisely what is supposed to have been annulled by C) as the will or act, i.e., in all the cases where the crime or wrong has been committed, C acts in three different ways. In the first place, C can annul the illicit action by reversing it, so to speak, by carrying it out [103] in reverse: for example, if Y has stolen X's horse, remove this same horse from Y and give it to X. Second, if such an operation is impossible for whatever reasons, C carries out (or has carried out against Y) an action comparable to restitution properly so-called, which is a simple reversal of the illicit action. For example, if X's horse has died between times, C requires Y to restore to X an equivalent horse or the price of the stolen horse. Finally, third, if no restitution, even symbolic, is possible, C punishes B, making him pay a penalty. It should be understood that C can combine these various modes of action. Restitution properly so-called can be accompanied by a "symbolic" restitution, which will then be called "compensatory damages." Thus, if Y steals X's work horse and only gives it to him a week later, he has in fact stolen the horse plus seven days of work; therefore, he will give back the horse plus the equivalent of those seven days, for example, a certain sum of money. Real or symbolic restitution, or the combination of the two, can be accompanied by a punishment. Thus Y, while having given back the horse and paid for the seven days, can also be sentenced to three months in prison, for example, or to pay a fine (collected by C or transmitted to X in certain cases, without this being confused with the "compensatory damages" paid to X—that is, with restitution. It is in this way that the thief in certain cases had to give back double to the victim according to Roman *Droit*).

When C intervenes in that fashion, one says that the situation is juridical and that A is the subject of a *droit*. Now, in the language of our definition, this means precisely that C has annulled the "goal," "motive," or "intention" of B's reaction.

Indeed, let us consider the case of restitution properly so-called. C has neither been able to annul the act (the theft of X's horse by Y, for example) nor the will to act (assuming that there has been one, the action having been voluntary). But he has really annulled the "goal," and so on; for Y wanted either to remove the horse from X, or to appropriate it, or both simultaneously. Now while having performed the act appropriate to this goal, he has not attained it, since the horse is again with X. Without touching the act (which cannot be annulled, seeing that it belongs to the past), C has therefore annulled the "goal" or "intention" with which this act has been committed. In this case, therefore, the annulment of the "intention" alone is enough for there to be *Droit*.

The same applies for "symbolic" restitution. Of course, the solution here is only approximate, but the principle is the same: while having acted, B has not realized his *goal*. But [104] let us change the example a little. If Y had the intention of causing X pain [*peine*] by removing and killing a horse that was dear to him, C is incapable of annulling *this* intention of B. Our definition, therefore, does not apply. But this "exception" only confirms the correctness [*justesse*] of the definition; for in *this* case, there is effectively no *juridical* situation. Indeed, X has a *droit* of property, but one cannot say that he has a **droit** not to be grieved. To the extent that Y's action strikes a blow at X's property, it is annulled (in its intention); but to the extent that it only grieves X, it has nothing illicit about it. And this is why it is not annulled as such (or more exactly, it is because it is not and cannot be annulled in *this* aspect that it is not illicit).

Let us admit, however, that an (imaginary) *Droit* condemns as criminal the act of causing grief to someone. In order that our definition remains valid, therefore, C must be capable of annulling Y's act—that is, the act of having killed a horse dear to X. The act having been performed, only the intention can be annulled. Now, in fact, C, who acts according to the *Droit* being considered, *will punish* Y (fine, prison, corporal punishment, death sentence, and so on). One must therefore say that punishment corresponds to the annulment of the guilty [person's] "intention," of the criminal action taken as "intention," "motive," or "goal." And this is effectively the way things are. Ultimately, Y wanted to obtain a *pleasure* by causing X grief. Now, by punishing him, C inflicts an evil on Y; he makes him *suffer;* he therefore *annuls* his pleasure (at least he is supposed to do it by punishing him), and by this very fact the "goal" or "motive" of his action. One can even add that X will have *pleasure* learning that Y is punished, and that this pleasure is going to attenuate the grief that Y wanted to cause him. Of course, one can assume that Y has acted "without a motive" in injuring X. In this case, the punishment would annul nothing, and our definition would therefore not be applied. But here as well the would-be "exception" confirms the correctness of the definition; for in the case when Y would have truly acted "without a motive," C would not punish him: Y would be declared an insane person, or in a state of moral irresponsibility, for to act "without a motive" in the strong sense of the term is to act as an animal and not as a human being. Likewise, there would be no annulment of the intention if the punishment did not cause any pain to Y. But here as well C would not have punished Y; for if a being cannot be disciplined [*peiné*] by any punishment, it is because he is "unconscious" (insane, idiot, and so on): he is not a truly human being and will therefore not be punished. As for X, he will not have any "*droit*" in these two cases, [105] according to our definition. And indeed, one cannot say that someone has a **droit** not to suffer from non-human, "natural" events: no one has the **droit,** for example, not to be struck by lightening, or not to get soaked by the rain, and so on. Now the act of an insane person or in general of a Homo sapiens who is not a human being properly so-called is comparable to the act of an animal or to the action of a thing. Finally, even the limit case of the death penalty can be interpreted juridically as an (irresistible) annulment of the intention, since by doing away with life one does away with the intention at the same time.[73]

When C, not being able to annul the act or the will, makes do with annulling the intention, and annuls it through *restitution,* properly so-called or "symbolic," one is in the presence of what Durkheim has called "restitutionary justice" (which just about overlaps with the *Droit* called "civil"). When the annulment of the intention takes on the form of a punishment, there is a case of Durkheim's "retributive justice" (which more or less corresponds to the *Droit* called "penal").[74] But as I have already said, C can combine these various modes of annulment of the intention. And he can even combine the annulment of the intention in its three modes with the annulment of the act or the will to act. Thus, for example, the French penal Code provides for the punishment of an attempted murder which has been prevented by the intervention of the Police. In this case, C annuls the act (in his capacity as Police) and the intention (in his capacity as Judge) in such a way that only the will to act escapes annulment.[75]

Therefore, it seems that our definition can be applied to all possible cases. However, if one wants to take into account the variety of cases, one must clar-

---

73. If one accepts the immortality of the soul, this conclusion is no longer necessary. The assassin can very well enjoy his crime after his death. But if one accepts immortality while wanting to retain the idea of *Droit*, one must postulate the existence of an immortal C having a hold over the soul after death. One must postulate a divine C. And to the extent that God plays the role of C, he acts in conformity with our definition. In our example, the divine Judge will replace the pleasure through a punishment of the criminal's soul. It seems, moreover, that it is impossible to accept the immortality of the soul without postulating the existence of a God.

74. [Ed. See Durkheim, *The Division of Labor,* 68ff. It should be noted, however, that while Durkheim speaks about restitutionary (*restitutive*) and repressive (*répressive*) law and justice, Kojève speaks about restitutionary and retributive (*rétributive*) law and justice.]

75. Preventative detention, measures taken to rehabilitate the guilty, and so on, can be interpreted juridically as annulments of the will to act alone, not followed by acts.

ify in the very definition the nature of the annulment. Thus, instead of just saying "annuls" simply, it will be necessary to clarify it by saying "annuls (B's reaction) as will, act, or goal."[76]

[106] If C's intervention annuls a reaction (of B), i.e., an action in the broad
sense of the word, it is because it is an action itself. C's annulment of B's reaction is an *action* of annulling. Therefore, it equally implies, or can imply, the
three constitutive elements that B's reaction implies. One can also therefore
distinguish three modes of annulment by relating them this time no longer to
B but to C.

In certain cases, C can only annul B's reaction by effectively intervening, by
a real "*act.*" This is the way the police intervene in a murder which is in the
process of being carried out. Generally speaking, C will have to intervene in
this way every time that B will be stopped in his reaction neither by a law which
forbids it nor even by a judgement which applies this law to him. If B refuses
to return to A what he is owed despite the legal rule (of the Law) which requires
him to, and in spite of the sentence of a judge who has said to him that the rule
really applied to his case and that he was to comply, then C will have recourse
to the police, to a court clerk, and so on, who will effectively have to act—that
is, perform an act in the proper sense of the term. In this case, therefore, C will
have to be not only the (juridical) Legislator and Judge, but also the (judicial)
Police (judicial [being understood] in the broadest sense of the term). And C
will intervene in his aspect as the "Police" every time that he will annul the
reaction by an "act" properly so-called.

But it is possible that the judgement is enough for B to renounce his reaction—that is, for it to be annulled. It is still C's intervention that annuls it, but
C only intervenes this time in his capacity as Judge. The capacity of Legislator
was not enough since B, while knowing the Law, was ready to act. But the
capacity of Police did not intervene because B renounced his reaction from the
moment the Judge reached a verdict. Now one can say that B has renounced
his reaction because he knew that the Judge's sentence would necessarily lead
to the Police's intervention if B himself did not comply with it. One can therefore say that the judgement corresponds to a "*will*" to act, that it is an intervention of C which annuls B's reaction while only being a simple will to act,
and not an act. But one can also say that the judgement, the Judge's sentence,
is a "will" to act in itself, and not only because B knows that it ends [107] in an
intervention of the Police. Indeed, it is this sentence which makes the Law *operative*, which *realizes* it by applying it to a real concrete case, which makes it go
from potentiality to actuality. In relation to the Law, therefore, the Sentence
plays the role that the will to act plays in relation to the motive which moves
one to action—that is, in relation to the intention or the goal. One can there-

---

76. The terms "will" (to act) and "goal" seem to be "introspective." But one could translate
them into "behaviorist" terms. Thus, [106] "will" can mean "the reaction of B which would
have taken place if C did not exist, but which has not taken place in fact." The "goal" (or
"intention") means "the behavior of B which would have followed his reaction to A's action
if C had not annulled this reaction."

fore say that in his capacity as Judge, C annuls B's reaction by his "*will*" to act alone.

As for the capacity of "juridical Legislator," we have just said that it corresponds to C's "*intention*," to his intervention which annuls B's reaction while only being a simple "intention," "motive," or "goal." Such an annulment takes place every time that B renounces his reaction, as soon as he realizes that there is a law which forbids it. He does not need to think about the Judge and Police. He can refrain through respect for the law alone and not through fear of the Judge and Police, who depend upon it. Now what is a juridical Law if not an "intention" [or] a "goal" that one gives oneself and which can be reached by a will to act and an appropriate act? The Legislator's intention is condensed in the Law; it serves the goal that he has posited; it reveals the motive of his activity. Thus, the Law which forbids and punishes murder has for a *goal* that there is no murder on earth; it has for a *motive* the desire that murder never occur; it expresses the *intention* of acting so that there are no more murders. If this *intention* alone is not enough to overcome or annul murders, one will go to the *will* to act; one will apply the Law to concrete cases; and if there is good reason one will carry out the *acts* which follow from this will. One can therefore say that when C annuls B's reaction by the sole fact of promulgating a juridical Law, i.e., when he annuls it by intervening in his capacity as juridical Legislator, he annuls it by his "intention" alone, by the element of "goal" or "motive" of his action which annuls B's reaction. And it is of little importance that it is a matter of a Legislator in flesh and bones or the simple result of the activity of this Legislator as Legislator—that is, of a juridical Law or a legal rule. If it annuls B's reaction, it "intervenes" in the interaction between A and B. It therefore plays the role of C: it is C. When we speak of C as a "legislator," therefore, we have just as much in mind C as the "Law." (It should be understood that the existence of the Law presupposes that of a Legislator. But the latter may no longer exist at the moment the Law still exists, and exists in the strong sense, existing as juridical Law—that is, intervening in the interaction between A and B and annulling B's reaction either by itself [108] or by the intermediary of the Judge, supported by the Police or not.)

This analysis shows us why C can have three distinct aspects: that of the Legislator or the Law, the Judge, and that of the Police. And it shows us what each of these three aspects means and what their mutual relations are. Therefore, one sees how and why C can be realized in three distinct persons, either individual or collective. But it is also possible that these three aspects are realized in one and the same person (individual or collective). Thus, for example, the Police can arrest an individual without a prior judgement and even for an action which is not foreseen by the law in force. In this case, the Police is at the same time the Legislator who sets forth the legal rule applicable to the action in question and the Judge who applies this rule to this action. Likewise, a Judge who gives a ruling on a case not foreseen by the law or in the absence of laws in general is at the same time Judge and Legislator. Conversely, a Legislator can be Judge, or Judge and Police, and a Judge can also be the Police, by enforcing his judgements himself.[77] C can be only the Legislator or the Law. He can also be only the Legislator (or the Law) and the Judge, either in one person alone or in two distinct persons. But he cannot be only the Police. If he is the Police, he is also necessarily Judge and Legislator (or the Law) in one or several persons. And if he is Judge, he is also Legislator. [109] This is obvious. And this is explained very well by our interpretation; for if an "intention" or a "goal" can exist without the act which realizes them and even without willing to act, just as our will may not be followed by the corresponding act, an act (voluntary being understood) cannot occur, i.e., exist, without the will to act, and the will to act implies and presupposes the intention.

Our definition, therefore, applies to all the modes of annulling B's reaction by C's intervention, and this both in relation to B and to C himself. C can act in his capacity as Legislator (or the Law), Judge, or Police, and he can annul B's reaction either by nipping it in the bud, preventing it from being realized, or finally by annulling it afterwards, and this both by a restitution properly so-called and by a symbolic restitution, or by the punishment of B—that is, by the annulment of the *consequences* of the reaction carried out by B. In all these cases, our definition will be applicable and there will then be *Droit* and a juridical situation.

But if one wants to bring out in the definition this entire variety of possible cases, one must not limit oneself to saying that C's intervention "annuls" B's reaction. One must say that this intervention:

"irresistibly annuls (by his will, act, or goal) B's reaction (as will, act, or goal)."

The word "irresistibly" is superfluous, the term "annul" not being equivocal. But the corresponding notion having a capital importance, it is better to underline it and recall that the term "annul" must be taken in its strong sense.

---

77. I have already mentioned the case where enforcement is entrusted to the winning party. But then the party is a party only to the extent that it benefits from the enforcement. To the extent that it carries out the enforcement it is not a party but the Police. Thus, in primitive societies where this practice is observed, one sees that a vengeance without judgement, for example, is clearly distinguished from a vengeance in enforcing a judgement which has allowed, or indeed prescribed, this vengeance. In the first case, the vengeance is a private act enforced at one's own risk and peril, and which is even an illicit and punishable act, while in the second case, the act will not be punished and will not be able to provoke a vengeance in response. This is because in the second case the party acts in the name of Society, in the capacity of the Police. Of course, this case is not "authentic" because in his capacity as Police C is not a genuine *third* in relation to A and B. And this is why these practices are disappearing with time. But they are conforming to the general schema of our definition, seeing that B's reaction is at least annulled from the outside, by another than B himself. By contrast, it does not make sense to say that B plays the role of Police in the case where he himself complies with it; for in this case there is no longer even the semblance of a *third* C. This self-enforcement has nothing juridical about it as such. Likewise, one cannot say that B is "his own Judge" when he refrains from reacting through respect for the Law which forbids him. If he is "Judge," this "Judge" has nothing juridical about him.

§ 18

If one introduces into our first behaviorist definition of *Droit* all the alterations mentioned in § 10–17, one can formulate a:

Second *"Behaviorist" Definition of* Droit

"One is in the presence of a *juridical situation* when the following conditions are fulfilled:

1) When there are two distinct beings, A and B, each of which can be either a physical person or a moral person [110] (individual, collective, or abstract), and when there is an interaction between these two beings—that is, when A's action generates B's reaction, suppressing this action or tending to do so;
2) When there is an intervention, i.e., a voluntary act, of a third C, [who is] supposed to be able to be anyone at all (inside an exclusive group of a given Society at a given epoch); and finally,
3) When the interaction between A and B provokes every time that it recurs (by itself or by a solicitation coming from A, with or without B's consent) C's intervention, who irresistibly annuls (by his will, act, or goal) B's reaction (as will, act, or goal).

In this juridical situation, A is said to be a *subject of **droit,*** having a specific *subjective right*[78] to act as he does. The proposition (mental or expressed, either orally or in writing) which defines (describes) this *droit* is a *legal rule* or an *objective law.*[79] The totality of valid legal rules (inside a given Society at a given epoch) constitutes *positive, domestic* [*interne*], or *national **Droit*** (of this Society at this epoch). The totality of all legal rules, both of rules being or having been valid somewhere and those rules which are only possible, constitutes *the **Droit*** as such. *Droit* or one of its constitutive elements, taken as the content of a human consciousness, is called the *juridical Phenomenon.* The description of juridical phenomena is called the *Phenomenology of **Droit.*** The description of all these phenomena in their entirety constitutes the *System of the Phenomenology of **Droit.***"

§ 19

In order to check this definition, it would be necessary to go through all the situations which are or have been called "juridical" and see if the definition applies. If one then finds that it applies as a rule but that there some exceptions,

---

78. [Ed. In the original, the English word "right" follows the French phrase ***droit subjectif*** in parentheses.]
79. [Ed. In the original, the English word "law" follows the French phrase ***droit objectif*** in parentheses.]

one must 1) show that these exceptional cases do not merit being called juridical; and 2) explain from where the mistake comes which made them be called such. It should be understood that one can group the situations by types and only check the definition's application to the types.

This enormous work cannot be carried out here. And I confess [111] to have never done it. It is nevertheless indispensable. The reader will be able to contribute by seeing in every concrete case that he meets with if it can be presented so that our definition is applicable.

For the moment, I will limit myself to giving a provisional justification of my definition by showing that, starting from it, one can arrive at the majority of fundamental juridical notions and their standard definitions. I will also indicate the fundamental notions which do not tally with my definition, and I will try to show that they effectively have nothing juridical about them. A part of this task, moreover, has already been accomplished in what preceded (such that I will only have to recall what I have already said above), and another part will be carried out in what follows, above all in Part Three (such that I will limit myself to referring the reader there).

First of all, let us note that the proposed definition does not contradict the classic definition of Jhering, according to which *Droit* is a "protected interest"; for if the definition speaks of an interaction between two persons, of A's action, this is because it acknowledges that A has an "interest" to act as he does.[80] And according to Jhering, "protected" means protected by the State or in general by a force "irresistible" in principle. Thus, if our "interaction between A and B" corresponds to Jhering's "interest," his "protection" corresponds to our "intervention of C." This is seen very well if one considers whatever one of the standard definitions of subjective right[81] based upon Jhering's conception. For example, take the one of Capitant: "Subjective *droit* is an interest of a material or moral order, protected by objective *droit,* which gives this effect to the one who is vested with it, [namely] the power to do the necessary acts in order to obtain the satisfaction of this interest."[82] The "interest," therefore, moves [him] to perform the "acts"— that is, to act. The "objective *Droit*" or legal rule "protects these interests or acts in the sense that it gives the power . . . "—that is, it allows agent A to perform his action without incident, without meeting with resistance on the part of a B. Now this is what our C does, who in our definition is not only the Police and Judge but also the Legislator or Law—that is, precisely the "legal rule" or "objective *droit.*"

I believe, however, that my definition is more precise than the standard definitions and that it is not pointless for this [112] reason; for it allows us to draw some important consequences from it.

---

80. [Ed. Rudolph von Jhering, *L'Esprit du droit Romain dans les diverses phases de son développement,* vol. IV, 2nd ed., trans. O. de Meulenaere (Paris: A. Marescq, 1880), 326. The book was originally published in German under the title *Geist des römischen Rechts auf den verschiedenen Stufen seiner Entwicklung,* vol. III (Leipzig: Breitkopf und Härtel, 1852–65), 339.]
81. [Ed. In the original, the English word "right" follows the French phrase *droit subjectif* in parentheses.]
82. Cf. Capitant, *Introduction à l'étude du droit civil,* 5th ed., 25.

But exactly [*justement*] because my definition is more precise than that of Jhering and others, it may be narrower than the latter's. There is, then, the danger that it is too narrow, not being applied to authentically juridical cases.[83]

Therefore, let us see if the proposed definition applies, on the one hand, to the large juridical categories such as those of "a *droit* to," "criminal act," and "duty to . . . "; and let us rapidly go through, on the other hand, the large traditional divisions of *Droit* in order to see if the proposed definition applies to the materials which are treated there by considering them all together.

Our definition applies very well to cases when A has a *droit* in relation to B (for example, a *droit* arising from monetary obligation [*un droit de créance*])—if A has a *droit* to something B gives him, or does something, or refrains from doing something. But there are cases when, at first glance, A has a *droit* to something without there being a B. For example, A can have the *droit* to move about freely, to go where he sees fit. Now, according to our definition, a B interacting with A is needed for there to be *Droit*. But I have already said that in reality as well there is always a B when A has the **droit** to something. Thus, in the example cited, one can say that A has the **droit** to move about solely because he can be prevented from it. Where an action is such that it can be annulled, it may be a question of a **droit** to this action. Thus, it makes no sense to say that a man has the **droit** to have an opinion deep within him. He has at the very most the *droit* to profess it, to express it, and so on—thus, to do the acts according to this opinion which can be annulled and which justly must not be. Now, if there is an obstacle, a possible annulment, there is also someone who can prevent and annul it. In our example, there are men who could annul A's freedom of movement. And A has the **droit** to move about in relation to these men, i.e., in relation to a B, such as is anticipated by our definition. And as this B can be a "moral person," A's *droit* can have a general, "impersonal" character: if B is the Society as such, to say that A has the *droit* to move about means that a reaction of Society (i.e., of whomever) tending to overcome A's action [113] (his free movement) will be (in principle) annulled by C's intervention (by the Police, for example, and so on).

When the "behaviorist" definition asserts that there is always a B when there is a legal rule setting down A's subjective *droit*, this means—in "introspective" or ordinary language—that C (i.e., ultimately, the Legislator) must follow a *social goal* when enacting the (objective) legal rule which sets down the subjective *droit* in question. If the Legislator only has in mind A himself, or the relation between A and C, or once again the relation between A and a nonhuman (natural or divine) being, I say that C is not a juridical Legislator, that there is neither A's **droit** nor a *legal* rule, but only a religious, moral, aesthetic, or another [kind of] rule.[84]

---

83. As for Jhering's definition, it is clearly too broad. Every "protected interest" is surely not juridical. Thus, in a civilized [*policé*] State, the "interest" the citizens have for their health is surely "protected" by the State. But if, with a view to this protection, the State undertakes works to drain swamps, there is nothing juridical about it.

84. If B exists in fact (and for us), but not in C's conscious intention, the Law will be authentically juridical, but the juridical phenomenon will be inadequate.

Now this is generally admitted. One commonly accepts Jhering's idea, which attributes a decisive role to the element of a "goal" in juridical phenomena (*der Zweck im Recht* [the goal in right]): for the Law to be juridical, the Legislator must pursue a *goal* when enacting it.[85] And one defines this goal as being the "common good" [*bien public*].[86] Of course, this notion of the "common good" is more than vague, and the most diverse interpretations are given to it. For "Liberalism," the "common good" boils down to individual happiness to the extent that it is compatible with the happiness of other individuals (the greatest happiness for the greatest number). For "Statism," the "common good" is everything that benefits the State as such (*Droit* is thus confused with "reason of State"). Others still (notably Duguit and the Socialism called democratic) subordinate the individual and the State to Society, the "common good" at which the juridical Legislator ought to aim being for them the "good" of this apolitical Society ("social *Droit*")—and so on.[87] But I do not have to discuss these variations, for I do not need to introduce the notion of the "common good" into my definition of *Droit*. I do not even say that the goal of the Legislator must necessarily be the maintenance of the State which realizes the *Droit* the Legislator enacts, since he can adopt the principle *Fiat justicia, pereat mundus.*[88] I say only that there must be a *goal* and that this goal is *social.* In other words, if the Legislator has in mind to assign to A [114] a subjective *droit* through a legal rule, he must consider A not in his relations with himself, nor in his relations with the Legislator, but in a (real or possible) interaction with another human person (individual or collective)—that is, with a B in the sense of the definition. Thus, *pereat mundus* only means that *this* Society must perish if it does not conform to *Droit.* But the Society that would conform to it, and that would therefore not have to perish, is also a Society in the proper sense of the word—that is, an interaction between at least three persons, A, C, and some B. Now everyone agrees that there cannot be *Droit* when there is a single human being, or only two. There must be a third in addition to the subject of *droit* and the Legislator. Now this third, indispensable to the existence of *Droit*, is precisely our B. To say that C must pursue a "social goal," therefore, simply means that the juridical Legislator must have in mind an interaction between at least two human beings—that is, between an A and a B as our definition says.

It seems, therefore, that this definition applies to all *positive* subjective *droit*—that is, A's *droit* to do or to refrain from doing something.

But there is still the notion of *negative droit*, of the juridically *illicit* act (infraction, wrong, crime), of what A *does not have the* **droit** to do, from what

---

85. [Ed. *Der Zweck im Recht* is also the title of a book by Jhering. It has been translated as *Law as a Means to an End,* trans. Isaac Husik (New York: The MacMillan Company, 1924).]
86. Cf., for example, Bonnecase, *Introduction,* 33: "The legal rule can be defined [as] a precept of conduct . . . imposed . . . with a view to the realization of social harmony. . . . "
87. [Ed. Perhaps a reference to Léon Duguit, *Le Droit social, le droit individuel, et la transformation de l'état,* 3rd. ed. (Paris: Librairie Félix Alcan, 1922).]
88. There is, however, a dialectic that I have already mentioned and that I will discuss in the following chapter.

A *does not have the* **droit** to refrain. And it seems that here the presence of a B is not necessary. Now, if one wants to apply our definition to an illicit act, to a negative *droit,* one can only do it by identifying this act to B's reaction. The fact that C irresistibly annuls this reaction means precisely that it is illicit [or] criminal, that B does not have the *droit* to carry it out. But B's illicit act is a *reaction,* which presupposes an action from A—that is, which presupposes A and his positive *droit.* Crime and illicit acts in general would therefore be the active negation of a **droit.**

Individualistic Liberalism asserts that all crime, that all negative *droit,* is effectively the negation of a positive *droit,* namely an individual *droit.* I do not have the *droit* to act so as to suppress an act or behavior to which another has a *droit.* But the "social" or "socialist" conception does not accept this interpretation: according to it, there can be an illicit act even if this act does not infringe upon any individual *droit.* This is possible; it is even certain. But I do not have to discuss this question; for my definition does not say that there is an infringement of an *individual droit* but of [115] *some* (positive) *droit* which can have for a subject Society as such (since A can be a "moral person"). Therefore, I say that an act is not juridically illicit, that it cannot be said that one does not have the *droit* to perform it, if it does not infringe upon any individual positive *droit* ("protected interest"), nor that of Society taken as a whole. Thus, an act which only injures a natural being (for example, an animal that is mistreated) or a divine being (blasphemy, for example, which is not supposed to harm Society or some particular person) can, of course, be forbidden, and provoke the annulling action of "some third," but this third's intervention will have nothing juridical about it and the act will not be able to be considered *juridically* illicit. Now this seems to be generally accepted. In every juridically illicit act, therefore, one can find the element of a reaction to a (real or possible) act to which a (physical or moral) person *has a* **droit,** and which this reaction tends to suppress. In other words, one can always define the illicit act as B's reaction to A's action, in conformity with our definition.[89]

It should be understood that this detour is often pointless. It is a lot simpler to say that A's act is juridically illicit when (and because) C intervenes to annul it. But I only wanted to show that one can always say that this "A" is in reality the B of our definition, who tries to suppress by his reaction the action of an A who has a *droit,* this A being able to be, moreover, some individual or collectivity, or indeed Society as a whole. I simply want to show that our definition seems able to be applied to all juridically authentic cases when it is a matter of an illicit act (infraction, wrong, or crime) or a negative *droit,* of the fact of not having the *droit* to act or behave in a certain manner, of doing or refraining from something.

---

89. The act will not be juridically illicit if it only suppresses a *droit* of the agent himself, if it only harms his own interest. The supposedly contrary cases are explained by the fact that agent B is taken as a member of Society: it is Society which is the A injured by B's act, and this is why it is illicit (the case of self-mutilation during war, or self-castration, and so on).

There remains the notion of juridical *duty* or juridical obligation (or, if you will, imperative *droit*). Now, as I have already remarked above, this notion can be reduced to that of an illicit act, a negative *droit*.[90] It is enough to recall [116] that an infraction, wrong, or crime does not necessarily consist in acts in the narrow sense of the word. They can just as easily consist in a "negative act"— that is, in an absence of an act, in an abstention. Now the juridical duty of doing something is nothing other than the expression of the fact that it is criminal (in the broad sense) not to do it. And the duty not to do something expresses the fact that it is criminal to do it. The notions of duty and crime are strictly equivalent, and the one adds nothing new to the other. If killing or stealing is a crime, I have the *juridical duty* not to do it. If paying municipal taxes is my juridical duty, it is because I *do not have the **droit*** to refrain from it. What this means [is that] the individual (A) has the *droit* to life and property (or Society {A} has the *droit* that its members remain alive and are not dispossessed); the district has the *droit* to take away from me such a sum of money (just like the depositor has the *droit* to take away his deposit from the depository). What this also means [is that] if the individual A acts so as to remain alive, and if B reacts so as to suppress this action by killing A, C will annul B's reaction; if the district acts so as to take away the sum owed by B, and if B reacts with a view to suppressing this action by not paying, C will annul B's reaction.

In short, our definition also seems able to be applied to all cases when it is a matter of the notion of juridical duty. But it should be understood that here as well it is often simpler and more natural not to use the language of the definition and to say that A has the *duty* to do or not to do something when his behavior, which would tend not to do or to do it, is annulled as a matter of course by C.

Our definition, therefore, seems to apply to the fundamental juridical notions of *positive **droit**, illicit act,* and *obligation*.

Let us now briefly go through the main traditional divisions of *Droit*. These are public international *Droit*, private international *Droit*, constitutional *Droit*, administrative *Droit*, procedural *Droit*, penal *Droit*, civil *Droit*, and commercial and industrial *Droit*.

Our definition does not apply to *public international **Droit***, for in the interactions between sovereign States, there is no C (no irresistible annulment). But everyone agrees that this *Droit* is an "imperfect" *droit* [117] precisely because it does not imply any sanction. On the other hand, I will take into account the juridical element in international relations by introducing in the following chapter the distinction between the actuality and potentiality of *Droit*. And we will see that our definition can be applied to international *Droit*, provided that one says that there is *Droit* to the extent that there is a C who *is supposed to* have

---

90. On the other hand, all duty is also a (positive) *droit:* I always have the [116] **droit** to do all that my juridical duty requires of me. The definition, at any rate, gives an account of the juridical nature of duty to the extent that it gives an account of the positive *droit* which is implied in it.

to annul irresistibly B's reaction to A's action, while not having in fact the possibility of intervening in an irresistible manner.

As for *private international **Droit,*** it is only a domestic *Droit,* either private or public.[91] There is no good reason, then, to speak about it especially.

Concerning *constitutional **Droit,** administrative **Droit,*** and (civil and criminal) *procedural **Droit,*** one can say that they form one and the same *Droit—public **Droit,*** in the narrow sense of the word, as distinguished from criminal *Droit.* Now, I have already said that there is no relation of *droit* between the citizen and his State, it being given that the State necessarily plays the role of C. The State, therefore, cannot also play the role of A or B. It would therefore seem that our definition does not apply to public *Droit.* But (as I will say in the following chapter and in chapter 2, B, of Part Three) one can speak about a public *Droit* and apply it to our definition by distinguishing between the State as such and its agents and representatives (taken either as civil servants or as private persons [*personnes privées*]). Then the State can play the role of C—that is, intervene as "some" third in the interaction between an (individual or collective) private person [*particulier*] A and an (individual or collective) agent B, or an agent A and a private person B, in order to annul irresistibly B's reaction to A's action, in conformity with our definition.

Let us now pass to *penal or criminal **Droit.***[92] Now I have already said that the notion of an illicit act (infraction, wrong, or crime) is in agreement with our definition, or in any case can be made to agree with it after an appropriate terminological revision. And I have already briefly indicated the juridical sense that this definition attributes to punishment (the annulment of B's reaction taken as goal or intention).[93]

[118] I nevertheless want to discuss briefly even here some fundamental types of crime anticipated by penal *Droit.*

Archaic and primitive *Droits* severely punished sacrilege by seeing it as a capital crime. Now, if sacrilege is only an interaction between a man and the divinity, C's intervention (the punishment of the guilty) has nothing juridical about it according to our definition, since B is not a "person"—that is, a human being. The banning of sacrilege, however, can be an authentic juridical phenomenon (i.e., conforming to our definition) if sacrilege also infringes upon "protected interests"—that is, the *droits* of the Society or a private person. Now one sees that *Droit* was implying laws against sacrilege only so long as one was believing that it was a "public danger," since it was bringing upon the community and its members the divine wrath. From the moment when one stopped believing this, sacrilege has gradually stopped being considered a crime in the juridical sense of the word. It seems, therefore, that unconsciously

---

91. Cf., for example, [Paul] Lerebours-Pigeonnière, *Précis de droit international privé,* [6th ed. (Paris: Librairie Dalloz, 1954)], 46.

92. Cf. Part Three, chapter 2, C.

93. This interpretation does not seem to be generally acknowledged. But I consider it as the only one which is truly juridical. To see this in more detail, see Part Three, chapter 2, C.

one has thought in conformity with the principles implied in our definition. At present, even a religious man will not attribute a *juridical* character to relations between man and God.

Another capital crime, punished by all positive *Droits,* is treason. Now what happens when there is treason? Let us assume, for example, that someone has sold to the enemy a military secret. We can describe the *juridical* situation in the following manner. The army (i.e., A) has the *droit* to act so that its secrets remain unknown by the enemy. Someone (i.e., B) reacts against it and overcomes the acts carried out at the base of this *droit,* since he acts so that the secrets are known by the enemy. Then the State (i.e., C) intervenes and irresistibly annuls B's reaction (in his goal, for example, by punishing B). The situation, therefore, conforms very well to our definition.

It is the same for another capital crime, universally punished: desertion. Here as well the army A has the *droit* to act so that B is where he has been assigned. If he reacts with a view to overcoming A's acts, which are supposed to lead him to this place, if he flees for example, the State (C) will intervene to annul irresistibly B's reaction.

As for murder (and crimes against a person in general) and theft (as well as all crimes against property), I have already spoken about them above. Without any doubt, it is a matter of infringing upon individual or collective *droits,* the subject of which is either a private person or Society as such.

[119] *Commercial and industrial* **Droit** is only a branch of civil *Droit,* and it has nothing specific in relation to the other branches of this *Droit.* Everything that is not civil *Droit* belongs either to penal *Droit* or to administrative *Droit* (or to private international *Droit*).[94] Therefore, it remains for us to speak about civil **Droit** in order to end this brief survey of the Legal system.

Civil *Droit* is divided into the *Droit* of persons (or familial *Droit*) and the *Droit* of inheritance [*patrimonie*] (or property [*biens*] *Droit*).[95]

In the final analysis, the *Droit* of persons defines the "status" or the juridical state of human beings. Now everyone agrees to see in "status" only the whole of subjective *droits* belonging to the person for whom one establishes the "status."[96] Now our definition applies to the notion of the subject of *droit,* holder of positive *droits.*

There remains the *Droit* of inheritance. It is generally subdivided into the *Droit* of property [*propriété*] and the *Droit* of obligations. Now I have already had the opportunity to show that the *Droit* of property is not the sanction of a relation between the property owner-man, and the thing or animal possessed. There is *droit* in property relations only to the extent that there is an effective or possible interaction between two persons regarding a thing possessed. And if the property is a juridical "status" of the person, it is only such to the extent

---

94. Cf., for example, [Leon] Julliot de la Morandière, [*Précis de*] *droit commercial,* [vol. 1, 2nd ed. (Paris: Librairie Dalloz, 1959–62)], 2–4.
95. Cf., for example, Capitant, *Introduction,* 5th ed., 41.
96. Cf., for example, Capitant, *Introduction,* 5th ed., 144.

that it is the totality of subjective *droits* relative to such interactions between A and B, where C intervenes in order to annul B's reaction. The *Droit* of property, therefore, seems to be in agreement with our definition.

There remains the *Droit* of obligations. This can be either contractual (or quasi-contractual) or delictual (or quasi-delictual).[97]

Let us first speak of contracts and quasi-contracts. I have already had the opportunity to recall that a juridical contract only differs from a simple convention without juridical significance by the fact that it is "sanctioned" by judicial legislation, courts, and the police—that is, by C in our terminology. Now the "sanction" has no reason to exist except if one of the contracting parties does not keep his commitments. But then one reverts to the case anticipated by our definition. The contract creates in A a subjective positive *droit,* which is infringed by B, [and] which provokes C's intervention. The contract is juridical [120] only to the extent that it allows A to act so that B's reaction, which tends to overcome A's action, is irresistibly annulled by C's intervention. And it is the same for quasi-contracts. Let us take the gift, for example. It is only juridical to the extent that there is a subjective positive *droit* either of the donor or the one who receives the gift. When A makes a gift, he performs an action which is such that all attempts by a B to overcome it provoke C's intervention, which annuls this attempt. And the *droit* of the donee is nothing other than the possibility of acting with a view to appropriating the gift without needing to make an effort, C being charged with annulling all possible reactions from a B.

Finally, let us pass to obligations coming from delicts and quasi-delicts. The delict or quasi-delict is juridical only to the extent that it generates an obligation sanctioned by the law—that is, by C. In other words, B's delict or quasi-delict (an involuntary act, for example) has a juridical character only if some A (an individual, collectivity, or indeed Society as such) can act against B in a certain manner (to take from him a sum of money, for example) without fearing a reaction on his part, this reaction having to be annulled by C if the case arises. Moreover, A can act in that fashion toward B (ask for compensatory damages, for example) because B has reacted so as to overcome an action to which A had the *droit*—that is, precisely an action of which the suppression by a B had to lead to C's intervention, annulling B's reaction. Thus, for example,

---

97. [Ed. In civil law, the general field of obligations includes two main branches: contract and delict. These branches correspond roughly—but only roughly—to the common law areas of contract and tort. However, in the civil law of obligations, both contract and quasi-contract are included, the latter including those obligations that arise from unilateral promises (which are protected, to a limited extent, in the common law through doctrines such as promissory estoppel). Obligations also include delict and quasi-delict. Here, the distinction corresponds roughly to the distinction in the common law of tort between intentional torts such as battery, defamation, and so on (delict) and negligence (quasi-delict). Thus, delict can refer to the general branch of obligations including both delict and quasi-delict or the narrower sense of something like an intentional tort. The French word for delict is *délit,* which can also mean, in the general sense, a wrong or (in the context of penal or regulatory offenses) a misdemeanor. In these final paragraphs of chapter 1, Kojève clearly uses *délit* to refer to delict.

if B throws a rock and breaks his neighbor A's window (intentionally or by chance), B owes him compensation because A had the *droit* to act so that a window is there where it was and where it had been struck by the rock thrown by B. B has reacted to A's action (the act of placing a window in a given spot), and this reaction has overcome A's action (the window no longer being in its place), from whence comes C's intervention, which annuls B's reaction (in its motive or goal, i.e., in its consequences). And it is this intervention which transforms every situation into a juridical situation and conforms to our definition.

When all is said and done, therefore, it seems that our definition can be applied to all the cases when there is an authentic *Droit.* We can therefore abandon it and no longer use its "behaviorist" language, which is heavy, complicated, and even incomprehensible when it is not explained. Seeing that the fundamental juridical notions can be translated into its language and are [121] conforming to our definition, we can use them such as they are expressed in an "introspective" language—that is, ordinary [language]. Henceforth, we can speak of positive subjective *droit,* illicit act or crime, duty or juridical obligation, property, contract, and so on, without always retranslating these clear and simple terms into a language conforming to our definition.

It is by using ordinary "introspective" language that we will study in the following chapter the question of knowing what are the conditions which must exist in the world in order that *Droit* can be *realized,* in order for there to be a valid positive *Droit* in this world— that is, in order for there to be effective interventions of real C's in real interactions between real A's and B's. But, while speaking this language, we will not lose sight of our "behaviorist" definition, which will allow us to analyze better these conditions and to resolve certain difficulties.

Chapter 2

The Reality of *Droit: Droit,* Society, State

§ 20

[122] WE HAVE SEEN THAT *Droit,* whatever kind it may be, can only exist when there are at least three persons: two "subjects of *droit*" (of which one has a positive subjective *droit* and the other a negative subjective *droit;* the one the *droit* to act [and] the other the duty not to oppose him, for example) and a "legal rule," and consequently a person distinct from the other two, who either creates this rule (the Legislator), applies it (the Judge), or enforces it (the Police). Now one can say that three persons (distinct from one another) already constitute a Society, whereas an isolated person, or even two persons interacting, still have nothing social about them. Therefore, one can also say that *Droit* can only exist within a *Society.*[1]

[123] In order that *Droit* effectively exists within a Society, there must be (in fact or in principle, in potentiality, [or] as a simple possibility) *interactions* between its members. These interactions, moreover, can be anything at all, provided that they take place between two members of this Society and that they provoke the (irresistible) intervention of a disinterested third, of a Legislator as well as a Judge, backed up by the Police.

Therefore, the content, diversity, [and] complexity of the real *Droit* of a Society depends, on the one hand, upon the content and richness of the social interactions; for every social interaction (real or possible) can generate a legal rule, and every legal rule corresponds to a social interaction (real or possible). But on the other hand, the content of *Droit* also depends upon the will of the juridical Legislator; for we have seen that a social interaction does not *automatically* generate a legal rule, since the disinterested third may or may not intervene, and intervene as he sees fit.

---

1. One can also say the opposite: a Society can only exist (in the strong sense of the term, i.e., last indefinitely, last as long as an *external* cause does not destroy it) if there is a real *Droit* in it. Indeed, let us assume in order to simplify matters that an isolated Society is made up of only three persons. It is truly a Society, i.e., a unity, only if its members are united among themselves—that is, if they are interacting. Now, when there is interaction, there is necessarily action and reaction, and the latter can annul the action or tend to do so. In other words, there can be conflicts within a Society. Of course, as long as there is no conflict the Society can exist without *Droit.* But when conflicts are *impossible,* there will be no Society (unless its members associate in order to enter into interaction with the outside, with another Society, for example; but we are assuming that the Society being studied is *isolated*). Indeed, conflict is *impossible* when the individuals have nothing to ask of one another; but then they are independent of one another, and there is no reason that they unite—that is, enter into interaction. As soon as they do so it is because they need one another—that is, they do not have the same means, the same goals. But as a result, [123] they *may* oppose one another's means and goals, and a conflict between them becomes *possible* by this very fact. Now one can define the possible (cf. Aristotle [*Metaphysics,* 1019b22–20a6, 1047a21–6,

Thus, one and the same social interaction can constitute a juridical situation in a given Society at a given moment, and not have a juridical character in another Society or at another historical epoch in the same Society. One notices, for example, that civil obligations (delicts and above all quasi-delicts) become more and more numerous as the Society evolves. [124] By contrast, everything that has to do with Religion, ritual, vestment, and so on, gradually loses its juridical character. Finally, a given interaction generates legal rules which vary according to places and epochs. Of course, when there is a legal rule, it anticipates the annulment of the reaction contrary to the action to which one has the *droit*. But this annulment can have different modes. Let us take the interaction in which a member of the Society maims the body of another member of this Society. The act, judged criminal, can be annulled either according to the principle of lex talionis or according to that of simple compensation (*Wergild*),[2] or once again by a punishment of the guilty, which can vary from capital punishment to a simple public reprobation (coming from the part of the disinterested third).

I do not mean by this that the Legislator's intervention is purely arbitrary. To the contrary, we will see that it is determined by the idea that he has of Justice. But the fact nonetheless remains that real *Droit* is a function just as much of social interactions as of the will to resolve them through an "arbitration"— that is, precisely to transform them into juridical situations, to create legal rules which correspond to them. In principle, therefore, a Society relatively poor in social interactions can have a relatively rich *Droit*, and conversely. But in reality, the two evolutions go hand in hand: the more complex [*complique*] a Soci-

---

1047b4–30; *De Interpretatione,* 22a14–3a26] and the precise formulation of Diodorus Cronos, cited by [Federigo] Enriques, *Causalité et déterminisme* [*dans la philosophie et l'histoire des sciences* (Paris: Hermann & Co., 1941)], 11) as that which is not (yet) real but which will realize itself one day. A Society, therefore, where conflicts are *possible* cannot exist indefinitely, i.e., cannot be truly real, without the conflicts one day becoming *real* in it. Let us assume, then, that there is a conflict between two members of our Society. If the conflict is "serious" (and all conflict is in principle "serious," i.e., it can become so), it ends in the elimination of one of the members (at least as an agent of a given interaction), i.e., in the destruction of the Society (at least in its aspect represented by the interaction in question), since there remains only two members. For Society to continue to exist, then, there must be compromise, i.e, none of the members of the interaction ought to act only as a party; each one also ought to take into consideration the interest of the other, in other words, look at things from the point of view of a disinterested third in relation to the members in conflict. Consequently, compromise is always comparable to the intervention of a third. Now, for Society to continue to exist, it is *necessary* that this intervention takes place. It is, therefore, an "irresistible" intervention. In short, there is a juridical situation. Society, therefore, can be truly real, i.e., last indefinitely, only if there is a real—that is, valid, i.e., applied in fact— *Droit* in it.

2. [Ed. Lex talionis is the law of retribution, whereby the same act is inflicted upon the criminal as he inflicted upon the victim (e.g., an eye for and an eye, a tooth for a tooth). *Wergild* means the price of homicide, or any other grave and serious crime (e.g., compensation would have to be paid by the criminal to family members for the loss of their father; to a lord for the loss of his vassal; and/or to the king for the loss of his subject).]

ety becomes socially, the richer its *Droit* becomes; for *Droit,* like all human phenomena (and even all phenomena in general), tends not only to achieve real existence and to remain there indefinitely, but also to propagate itself as much as possible, to expand itself in space so as to reach its "natural frontiers." Seeing that in a given Society there is a real juridical will in the person of a (juridical) Legislator (of the Society taken as collective Legislator), this will is going to aim at encompassing everything that is susceptible of being a juridical situation. This is why an increase in social interactions always brings about (seen on a large scale) an increase in the number of Legal rules—that is, an enrichment of real *Droit.*[3]

[125] But it is necessary to distinguish here between two types of real *Droit,* which are the *Droit* called *public* and the *Droit* called *private. Droit* is public if the Judge (assisted by the Police) intervenes as soon as an interaction occurs belonging to the type anticipated by a legal rule (public *droit* being understood). By contrast, the legal rule belongs to private *Droit* if the Judge (and the Police) only intervene at the request of one of the two persons interacting (anticipated by this rule) or the two simultaneously. There is, of course, an important difference, but *Droit* is *real* or "valid" in both cases; for *if* the intervention takes place, it is effective in both cases, or indeed, irresistible. In the case of private *Droit,* however, it may or may not take place, while in a case of public *Droit* it necessarily takes place (in principle being understood—that is, it *ought* to take place everywhere and always).

One must say, however, that this difference has a verbal character. Indeed, one can say that the *Droit* called "private" is equally a "public" *Droit*—that is, a *Droit* according to which the intervention of the Judge (and Police) is *necessary* and not optional. To this end, it is enough to change the terminology and to define differently the interaction which corresponds to the legal rule. There is public *Droit* properly so-called when a given social interaction is supposed to provoke necessarily a specific intervention of the Judge. There is private *Droit* when this intervention is optional. But this can be expressed differently. One can say that a given interaction not provoking the intervention of the Judge is not a juridical situation. But this same interaction, if it implies recourse to the Judge by one (or both) of the agents, is a juridical situation necessarily provoking the intervention of the Judge.

One can therefore say that all real *Droit* is a public *Droit.*[4] But the fact nonetheless remains that in certain Societies, ("public") *Droit* is only concerned with an interaction if it implies recourse from the interested parties [*intéressés*] to the Judge, while in another Society, ("public") *Droit* is con-

---

3. At first, there is even a tendency to exceed the "natural frontiers," to formulate pseudo-legal rules in respect to events which have nothing juridical about them even in potentiality, not being *social* interactions properly so-called—that is, interactions between members of the given Society. It is only by becoming conscious of itself, i.e., by becoming "philosophic," that *Droit* itself limits the [125] sphere of its application to cases which can be authentic juridical situations.

4. As Durkheim does; cf. *Division du travail,* 71. [*The Division of Labor,* 102–3.]

cerned even without this recourse. And this difference of attitude is very significant and important. This is why there is a point in keeping the traditional distinction, even if it means recalling that private *Droit* is no less real than public *Droit*.

Practically speaking, in contrast to public *Droit,* the real existence of private *Droit* presupposes not only the existence [126] of social interactions and the will of the Legislator to make Legal rules correspond to them and to apply them, but also the desire of the litigants to submit to them spontaneously. In other words, private *Droit* can only really exist if the Legislator (the State or Government, for example) enjoys the juridical confidence of the members of the Society (i.e., only if he has a juridical Authority). Only public *Droit* can be imposed by force. And this is why one sees that private *Droit* can cease to exist in fact in a State when the citizens do not have juridical confidence in the Government (i.e., in either the Legislator, Judge, or Police). It is in this way that the merchants in the U.S.S.R. avoided the Soviet Tribunals (of private *droit*) during the period of the N.E.P.[5]

The extension of private *Droit,* therefore, is to a certain extent an index of a harmony between Society taken as a whole and its members taken individually. But one must not believe that private *Droit* shrinks (relatively, i.e., in relation to the corresponding public *Droit*) only during revolutionary periods. It does so every time that the collective interest is opposed to private interests: in time of war, for example, or during serious crises, and so on. This is why the "liberal" conception, according to which juridical evolution (and progress) consists in the shrinking of public *Droit* and the enlargement of private *Droit,* is false.[6] Certainly archaic or primitive *Droits* do not know, so to speak, private legal rules, which hold an enormous place in Roman *Droit* and modern *Droits.* But we are at present witnessing an opposite process: private legal rules more and more have a tendency to be replaced by public legal rules. And this fact can just as well be the index of a "period of crisis" as the expression of a revolutionary change of the very notion of *Droit*—that is, the idea of Justice which forms its base.

Be that as it may, *Droit* can only be real in a real Society, when there are real or possible interactions between the members, and when some Legislator creates legal rules applicable to these interactions. As for the effective application

---

5. [Ed. Vladimir Lenin's New Economic Plan (1921–8) was a partial and temporary retreat from "true" socialist economic principles. Faced with the near total collapse of the Soviet economy, Lenin advocated returning agriculture, small business, and light industry to private ownership while still maintaining state control of banking, trade, transportation, and heavy industry. Kojève himself escaped from the former Soviet Union in 1920 and lived the first half of the decade in Germany. See Auffret, *Alexandre Kojève,* 39–83.]

6. This is the conception according to which the *Droit* of "statuses" gradually gives precedence to the *Droit* of contracts. Cf., for example, [Henry] Sumner Maine, *Ancient Law: [Its Connection with the Early History of Society and its Relation to Modern Ideas,* (Boston: Beacon Press, 1963)], 165, cited by [Henri] Decugis, *Les Étapes du Droit* [(Paris: Librairie du Recueil Sirey, 1942)], 93.

of these rules by the Judge (supported by the Police), it can be either sponta-neous or solicited by the agents interacting.

§ 21

[127] In certain conditions, *Droit* can be *real*. Now, generally speaking, an entity can be real either *in potentiality* (*dynamei on*) or *in actuality* (*energeia on*) (cf. Aristotle).[7] One must not confuse the *real* in potentiality with the possible, which is *ideal*. The possible does not exist *in reality*, neither in actuality nor in potentiality. But it *can really* exist, i.e., ought to be realized at some moment in time (assumed to be infinite), as opposed to the impossible ideal, which will never be realized. Thus, the relation between pure ("abstract") numbers such as $2 + 2 = 4$ is possible (since even at this moment two apples plus two apples are four apples), while the relation $2 + 2 = 5$ is not possible. Nevertheless, it subsists just as much as the first, as an *ideal* entity: for I understand *the mean-ing* of the two relations, and I know that the second is false just as I know that the first is true (or can be true, if the truth is the coincidence of the ideal with the real). Or once again, the plane of the 18th century was only *possible*, i.e., ideal (it was possible because it is real in this day and age), but not at all real. But a *real* entity can be real in potentiality or in actuality. Thus, the egg is not less real ("material") than the chicken. But if one says that the chicken is real *in actuality*, it is necessary to say that the egg is only real in potentiality: it is the potentiality of the chicken. In other words, *all* the chicken's constitutive ele-ments are already in the egg (in the form of "genes," for the sake of argument), and they are real there, but none of them is there *in actuality*, for none can accomplish the *actuality* which is appropriate to it, and thus alter or annul an actual external reality. The beak is there, for example, but it can still not peck [and] crush grain. The chicken, therefore, really exists in the egg, but it cannot *act* there (as a *chicken*). Or once again, its actuality is still in the process of com-pletion: the beak as a "gene" is transforming itself into the chicken's beak which is going to crush grain. The entity in potentiality, therefore, *really* exists, but its reality is the reality of a *becoming* [*devenir*]. The reality in potentiality is a reality on the way to becoming, while the reality in actuality is the reality "having become" [*devenue*], the result or integration of its becoming.

This being recalled, can one distinguish a (real) **Droit** *in actuality* from a (real) **Droit** *in potentiality*?

To answer this question, let us take a simplified case. [128] Let us assume that a Society is made up of three persons, X, Y, and Z. This Society anticipates the possibility of a conflict (of a given type) between its members and resolves it in advance, i.e., the three members agree on the following point: if this con-flict occurs between X and Y, Z ought to intervene in a certain manner. Each of the members, therefore, can play the role of X, Y, or Z. There is, then, in this

---

7. [Ed. Aristotle, *Metaphysics*, 1019a15–20a6 and 1045b27–52a11. The terms *en puissance* and *en acte* will be translated as "in potentiality" and "in actuality," respectively.]

Society a legal rule, a *Droit*, a juridical Law, it being of little importance that it is only thought by its members, or determined orally, or finally drawn up in writing. Let us now assume that the conflict between X and Y, purely possible (ideal) at first, is realized. Let us assume that X acts "legally" and that it is Y who reacts in an "illicit" way. What has happened? As coauthor of the legal rule, i.e., as a "juridical man," Y condemns his way of acting just as he would have done if he were in Z's place. The true conflict, therefore, is not between X and Y, or between X and Z and Y, but between X, Y, and Z taken as "juridical men" and Y taken as a "non-juridical" man. The motive which causes Y to act in an "illicit" way can be anything at all: religious, aesthetic, economic, sexual, and so on. To simplify matters, we assume that this motive is purely biological: Y acts as an animal would have acted in his place. In this case, X, Y, and Z act as juridical men against Y as an animal. But in reality, i.e., in actuality, Y acts as an animal: his juridical action is replaced by animal action, which alters the actual surrounding reality and is thus real in actuality. *Droit*, therefore, is real in actuality only to the extent that X's and Z's action is real in actuality. In order to be real juridically in actuality, the action must overcome the actual reality of Y's animal action (which is real in actuality). In principle, two animals are stronger than a single animal of the same type. X's and Z's intervention, therefore, will overcome Y's animal action and will realize in its place their juridical action. And since the animal action was real in actuality, the (juridical) action which overcomes it is equally real in actuality. Consequently, the legal rule, i.e., *Droit* in general, has become real in actuality in this Society because the interaction between its three members has resulted in the overcoming of a real action in actuality, namely Y's animal action. This action has been overcome by Z's juridical action (supported by X: Z is the Judge, X is the Police). The juridical action, therefore, has been real in actuality. And one sees very well that real *Droit* is a social reality presupposing the existence of at least three members interacting. Without X, there [129] would be no cause of the conflict; without Y, no conflict [and] therefore no intervention of Z, without whom there would be no juridical action. The latter is real in actuality only because it overcomes (or can overcome) a non-juridical real action in actuality. In other words, the "criminal" Y must be present in Society, and he must be overcome as a "criminal" *inside* this Society for the *Droit* of this Society to exist really and in actuality.

It is *enough* that Y remains within Society for *Droit* to be actualized there; for we have said that in principle two members are stronger than one alone. But this strength would be of no use if Y was able to leave Society. Then his actual animal action would not be overcome, and the juridical action would therefore not become actual as such. Society, therefore, must be *isolated* (without external relations) for *Droit* to be necessarily actualized there under the assumed conditions. Now to be isolated from the outside is not to be interacting with the outside, and in particular not to be subject to any disruptive action coming from without. One can therefore say that an isolated Society is an *autonomous* Society: it only exists as a function of the internal interactions between its members.

(An unisolated Society is not autonomous; for there is an "outside" for it, [and] Y can escape there. Now his escape alters the state of the Society; therefore, this alteration is a function of the "outside," since without this "outside," Y would have not been able to escape.) *Droit*, therefore, is necessarily actualized (in principle being understood, for the actualization in fact can always be prevented by causes due to "chance") only in [such] a Society.

The "outside" exists for the Society as Society only to the extent that this "outside" is social, by being itself a Society, another Society. Indeed, let us assume that our Society implies the whole of humanity. Y can certainly escape into the "jungle," but he does not cease by this [action] from being part of humanity—that is, of our Society. He eludes juridical action in fact, "by chance" as it were, but not in principle. And the social Police can in principle reach him everywhere he can go. The Society which implies all humanity, therefore, is truly autonomous, and *Droit* is necessarily *actualized* there as soon as it exists in reality. It will be the same for a Society truly *isolated* from the rest of humanity. This will be the case, for example, if our X, Y, and Z are castaways on a desert island, without hope of return. But practically speaking, a Society is never isolated, or in other words, it is never truly autonomous; for even if there is no effective interaction between it and [130] the neighboring Societies, these always exercise an action upon it by the sole fact of their existence. In our case in particular, Y will always be able to elude the combined action of X and Z by taking refuge in another Society. And the *Droit* in our Society, therefore, will never pass into actuality. Indeed, nothing says that the new Society where Y is going to live will apply to Y the legal rule accepted in the previous Society. Let us assume that it does not do so. In order to actualize its *Droit*, therefore, the previous Society will have to go to look for Y in the new Society. Now, by definition (since Y is supposed to be accepted by the new Society as a member) the new Society will defend Y against his previous Society (if not, the two Societies will only be a single Society in relation to the legal rule in question). Now nothing says that X and Z will be stronger than Y supported by his new Society. At any rate, this question could only be decided by a struggle (actual [*effective*] or only possible: the new Society can submit without combat, through fear). If X and Z succeed in punishing Y despite the support of the new Society, *Droit* will be actualized in the previous Society formed by X, Y, and Z. But if the new Society efficaciously opposes the action of X and Z, the *Droit* of the previous Society will not be actualized.

One cannot say, however, that this *Droit* does not exist, that it is not real. It is incontestably so since it has caused Z to act and has even reacted upon Y, by requiring him to escape. But it has not succeeded in annulling Y's animal action. The juridical action, therefore, was not on the same ontological plane as the latter. Now this was a real action in actuality. The juridical action, and consequently the corresponding *Droit*, is therefore real without being so *in actuality*. And this is what one calls being real *in potentiality*. Indeed, all the constitutive elements were there, and they were really there: the legal rule, X's legal action, Y's illicit reaction, Z's intervention. But just as the chicken in the egg cannot crush actual grain, so the *Droit* in question has not been able to annul Y's actual action.

Droit in potentiality has been and remains real in the Society X-Y-Z (reduced to X and Z). It will therefore tend to be actualized (for the reality in potentiality is nothing other than a "tendency" to actuality). To this end, X and Z will try either to reintegrate and punish the Y in question, or to prevent the possibility of escape of a new member Y', who has come to replace Y. In the first case, they may, for example, conclude a treaty of extradition with the Society where Y took refuge. [131] In the second case, they may issue (with Y') a new legal rule banning, for example, the carrying out of all acts making possible the passage to another Society. In the two cases, the original *Droit* (that we have assumed to contain only a single legal rule) will have to be completed—that is, altered. It has therefore been altered because, being real, it has not been able to be actualized. And this is precisely why it is said to be real in potentiality: it must be *altered* to be actualized, its reality is the reality of a *becoming*.

These considerations allow one to tackle the famous question of the "*Droit* of bandits."

Let us assume that a group of Frenchmen form in France a Society of wrong-doers. This Society can have a *Droit* which is appropriate to it: legal rules, real conflicts judged in conformity to these rules by "disinterested thirds" (taken from within the Society), and enforcement of these judgements by a sort of internal Police. This *Droit* will therefore be real. And this is why sociologists are correct to speak of a "*Droit* of bandits." But this Society is not isolated; it is not autonomous: for every member is also a French citizen. Now as such he can elude, if he wants to, the *Droit* in question. It is enough for him to go and see the French Police in order for them to protect him efficaciously (at least in principle) against the "judicial" action of the members of the Society (while perhaps punishing him because of his previous membership in this Society— but this is another question). This is because the "*Droit* of bandits," while being a *Droit* and a real *Droit*, is only real in potentiality. All the constitutive elements of *Droit* really exist there, but they are in principle ineffectual; for the Society itself only exists "by chance." "In principle," the French police should have eliminated it.

Now, it is obvious that public international *Droit* does not differ essentially from the "*Droit* of bandits" as regards its reality: this reality is only in potentiality, for this *Droit* is purely optional. When two States submit to the arbitration of a third (or—which is the same thing—to the arbitration of an international Tribunal, a League of Nations, or even of "world opinion"), there is a *real* juridical situation, since all the elements (the Judge and the Parties) are real. But seeing that this arbitration is optional, this real *Droit* only exists in potentiality. The two States-parties and the State-arbiter very much form a "Society" that implies a real *Droit*. But every member can leave this Society and form a Society "from without." [132] The real *Droit* of this Society, therefore, is not *necessarily* actualized. It is a real *Droit* in potentiality. And this is why contemporary international *Droit* must be *altered* in order to become real in actuality.

Therefore, *Droit* is only necessarily actualized in an autonomous Society, i.e., in a Society which—among other things—removes from its members the possibility of leaving it (for by leaving it and joining another Society, they would at the same time make the first Society dependent upon the other, if only on the will of the other to hand over or not the fugitive). In a voluntary [*facultative*] Society, *Droit* is only real in potentiality.

At first glance, there are exceptions to this rule: for example, canon *Droit.* But in fact, this is not so; for this *Droit* has been real in actuality only in epochs when a member of the Church was not able (in principle) to leave it. However, it is not the Church which prevented him from doing so but the State: it is the State which pursued in actuality the "fugitive." This is why it is necessary to say that canon *Droit* has never been a *Droit* in actuality as the *Droit* of the Church. It was only so to the extent that the State made it its own. Therefore, it is the *Droit* of the State which was real in actuality. And it is of little importance that this *Droit* of the State implied legal rules worked out by the Church, and that it [the State] had ecclesiastical Judges apply these rules. Seeing that the judgements of these Judges were automatically sanctioned by the State (acting as Police), they were the State's Judges, differing not at all from other state-sanctioned [*étatiques*] magistrates. And seeing that the State accepted the legal rules of canon *Droit,* these rules became an integral part of the State's *Droit.* One can therefore say that *Droit,* which was real in potentiality as canon *Droit,* was real in actuality as the *Droit* of an autonomous State.

The same applies to familial [and] corporate *Droit,* and so on. Either this *Droit* is only real in potentiality, or, if it is real in actuality, it is sanctioned by the State, and it is then the State's *Droit* in the same way as all state-sanctioned *Droit* properly so-called. It is of little importance that the State gives a free hand to the father to judge his children. Seeing that the State will bring back to the father his runaway child, thus effectively allowing him to punish this child, it is the State, and not the Family, which actualizes familial *Droit.* This *Droit,* as actual, is a state-sanctioned *Droit.* The *autonomous* Society is here the State and not the Family, or the Corporation, and so on, and it is only within the State that the *Droit* in question is realized *in actuality.* If the Family, for example, is practically "isolated," i.e., [133] "autonomous" (in relation to familial *Droit*), it is not because it is closed in upon itself, isolated from the outside. It is the State which encloses it, which reintegrates its fugitive members. Therefore, it is the State which actualizes its *Droit.* The same *Droit,* which is only real in potentiality as familial *Droit,* is real in actuality to the extent that the State's *Droit* implies this familial *Droit.* And it is of little importance that it has borrowed it from the Family or not, and that it entrusts or not its enforcement to the head of the family. Familial *Droit* only exists in actuality if the Family is an autonomous Society—that is, isolated from the rest of the world. But practically speaking, such isolated "Families" have never existed on earth.

The results of what has preceded is that the *Droit* of a Society (organized into a State or not) can only be real in potentiality if this Society does not encompass the whole of humanity. In particular, all "positive" or "domestic," "national," *Droit* is a (real) *Droit* in potentiality. And one must say that experience confirms this way of seeing things; for it shows that all national *Droits* evolve with time. Now this proves that they are not real in actuality, but at the very most are going from potentiality to actuality. At this moment in time, then, *Droit* as such only exists in potentiality, being only the totality of national *Droits,* all non-actual. And one effectively has to assume everywhere that real *Droit,* i.e., realized so far on earth, will continue to evolve.

As I have already said, only the universal and homogenous State is no longer supposed to vary, seeing that it will no longer have, by definition, either external wars or internal revolutions. Its *Droit,* therefore, will not vary at all. Now this State implies all of humanity. It is, therefore, a truly "isolated" or autonomous Society. Its *Droit,* therefore, will be a *Droit* in actuality. And this is why it will no longer vary. This real *Droit* in actuality will be one and unique, and it will be the result of all previous *Droits;* for the universal and homogenous State will result from the interactions of national States (warlike or pacific)—that is, also from the interaction of national *Droits.* The evolution of *Droit,* therefore, will be a becoming of the *Droit* of the universal and homogenous State. The history of *Droit,* therefore, is the passage of *Droit* from potentiality to actuality. Consequently, one can say that *Droit* exists in this day and age only as a becoming of the actual *Droit* of the future Empire.

One must say, however, that a part of *Droit* already exists in actuality to a certain extent. I have in mind the fact that certain criminals are handed over by all "civilized" States to the State which is in charge of punishing them. In relation to these legal rules, [134] therefore, humanity constitutes this very day a single and unique (juridical) Society. Nevertheless, one must say that this actualization is not absolute, and not because certain States still do not hand over criminals, nor because there is still a part of humanity not organized into States; for one can say that these are only anachronisms which are disappearing before one's very eyes. *Droit* is not truly actual because the adherence of States to extradition treaties remains optional, because every State can annul it without one being able to compel it not to do so. The *juridical* unification of humanity, therefore, is not enough for *Droit* truly to exist in actuality, for the juridical Society thus formed depends upon States and is not therefore autonomous. Juridical unification, therefore, must be backed up by a *political* unification. Once again, *Droit* will only be real in actuality in the universal and homogenous State.[8]

---

8. Let us note that if one hands over in principle common criminals, political criminals are generally not handed over, and not only in fact: the *principle* that they ought not to be is generally accepted. Now this is important; for to accept this principle is to say that political criminals will *never* be handed over. But to say this is to say that "political" *Droit* will *never* be realized in actuality. Now, what will *never* be realized in actuality is not even real in potentiality. Political crimes and the rules which define them, therefore, do not form a real *Droit.*

§ 22

Droit can be real *in potentiality* in any Society whatsoever. But it is only real *in actuality* in an isolated or autonomous Society. In this day and age, and in the civilized world, autonomous Societies (practically "autonomous," i.e., [135] more or less so) are always organized into States. It is only in a Society organized into a State that the members of the Society cannot leave it as and when they like. (In principle, the State must give its consent for its citizen to be able to change nationality. But practically speaking, the citizen can very well do without it.) One can therefore say that at present, in the civilized world, all real *Droit* in actuality is a *Droit* of the State, sanctioned by the State, a *state-sanctioned* **Droit**.

Therefore, one must see what are the relations between *Droit* and the State as such.

A lot of Legal theorists think that there is no other *Droit* than state-sanctioned *Droit*.[9] For them, *Droit* is always a Law promulgated by the State.

It should be understood that the term "Law" must be taken in a very broad sense. In this day and age, it is generally a matter of a Law properly so-called—that is, drawn up in writing and officially promulgated by an appropriate organ. But state-sanctioned Law can just as well be an oral "custom" that the State tacitly makes its own by the sole fact that it applies it in its courts. Finally, the "Law" may exist only in a mental state, not expressed orally or in writing. Thus, in English jurisprudence for example, a "Law" can exist solely as implied in a concrete judgement. As general Law, it has existed only in the spirit of the judge, who has applied it to the concrete case in question, and who has never expressed it as such.

But this is not the question. It is a matter of knowing if *Droit* is truly real only as state-sanctioned Law.

The answer is already given in what has preceded. If one assumes: 1) that real *Droit* is real *in actuality;* and 2) that the autonomous Society is a State, one can effectively say that *Droit* is nothing other than the Law. But we have seen

---

One can therefore say that humanity ("public opinion") denies the existence of a "political" *Droit,* of a *Droit* that would have the State punish its citizens for their acts directed against the State as such. Of course, one does not explicitly, consciously, deny this. But the practice of the "*droit* of exile" shows that one denies it in fact. It remains to be seen if one is correct to do so. (Or once again, this "political" *Droit,* if it is not real, neither in actuality nor in potentiality, it is at least ideal, i.e., only possible, before being realized one day.) I believe I can answer affirmatively. There is no authentic **Droit** according to which the State punishes political crimes, for the relations between the citizen and his State have nothing *juridical* about them. This does not mean that I condemn the fact that political crimes are punished—far from it. But I believe that one can explain, or indeed justify, these acts of the State only by specifically political, and not juridical, reasons. Indeed, what is this "*Droit*" when the party which believes itself injured is at the same time the juridical legislator, judge, and executor of the judgement? I will have the opportunity, moreover, to return to this question.
9. Notably in Germany, [Hans] Kelsen for example; cf. Joseph Barthélemy, *Précis de droit public* [(Paris: Dalloz, 1937)], 10.

that *Droit* can be real while only being in potentiality, and that this *Droit* in potentiality can exist even within a non-autonomous Society—that is, with optional participation. Now as such Societies exist even within a State, one can speak of a non-state-sanctioned, real potential *Droit*. Thus, for example, the rules applied in a sports association are clearly legal rules; there is then a (potential) real *Droit* in this association, which has, however, nothing to do with the State as such, nor with the state-sanctioned Law [136] (cf. also what will be said in § 24). On the other hand, it is not correct that every autonomous Society is necessarily organized into a State. Of course, it is only a question here of a definition, and one can call a "State" any Society whatsoever, provided that it is (practically) autonomous. But one can define the State in a more precise manner, even if it means not calling a "State" certain archaic or primitive Societies. And then one will no longer be able to say that there is no *Droit* in actuality outside the State. A real *Droit in actuality* exists in every *autonomous* Society, even if it is not a State in the proper sense of the term. And at any rate, the sphere of real *Droit* as such is more extensive than that of state-sanctioned *Droit*, for real *Droit* in potentiality is not state-sanctioned while being an authentic *Droit* and a real *Droit*.

Practically speaking, in the contemporary civilized world, real *Droit* in actuality is confused with state-sanctioned Law: real *Droit* in actuality is the totality of juridical laws applied by the State; it is the "Code" of laws in force. But one is wrong, I believe, to reverse this proposition and say that all state-sanctioned Law is a juridical Law, a *Droit;* for, in my opinion, there are a lot of state-sanctioned Laws which are political or other Laws, without juridical significance. If all *Droit* in actuality is a Law, all Law is not a *Droit.*

When the Persian government decides to call this country "Iran," or when the Weimar State proclaims that the national German flag will henceforth be made up of the colors black, red, and gold, without any doubt it is a matter of state-sanctioned Laws. But I do not think that these Laws have anything to do with any sort of *Droit.* These are state-sanctioned Laws which are not juridical. And a lot of state-sanctioned Laws are of this character. Of course, if a German citizen displays the new flag and his neighbor tries to prevent him from doing so, the former will be able to resort to the Police, or indeed, the Judge. This is because he has *the **droit*** to display this flag. But what is juridical is not the Law concerning the national colors; it is the (explicit or implicit) Law which says that every citizen has the ***droit*** to display the new colors. Now it is not at all necessary that this second Law accompanies the first. And even if this is the case, it is nevertheless necessary to distinguish between the non-juridical state-sanctioned Law and the juridical state-sanctioned Law.

A juridical character is generally attributed to all state-sanctioned Law because all state-sanctioned Law anticipates a sanction, even if it does not explicitly mention it. Indeed, all action contrary to the Law (whatever it may be) will in principle be [137] annulled. And as this "annulment" is generally carried out by the same organs (Judge and Police) who "annul" the illicit acts from the juridical point of view, one has the impression that the "annulment" in question also has a juridical nature, and consequently that the Law also has it. And the illusion is all the stronger because the organ of the State which enacts non-juridical Laws also enacts juridical Laws. But the big question is knowing if the two "annulments" in question are truly juridical.

I will discuss this question in the following section. But for now I once again repeat that the sanction of a non-juridical Law cannot make it juridical, for this sanction itself has nothing juridical about it. In the examples cited, the Law rules on something which interests the State as such: its name, its emblem. Therefore, the State is a party. Now if a party performs the act it has the intention to do by using force, this does not at all mean that it has the *droit* to do so. Let us assume that two castaways live on a desert island. The one decides that the other must serve him, or call him "Mister," and so on, and he forces the other to behave accordingly. No one would want to say that there is a *Droit* on this island. Now the island is comparable to a sovereign State; one of the inhabitants to the Government; the other, to the governed. It seems, therefore, that there are non-juridical state-sanctioned Laws which remain such despite the fact that the acts which are contrary to them are in principle annulled in an irresistible way by a state-sanctioned action.

We will see (chapter 3) that a rule of conduct is a *legal* rule only to the extent that it is an application of the principle of Justice (however so conceived) to a case which admits such an application. Now it is obvious that there are Laws which regulate conduct without any relation to the principle of Justice. For example, what relation does Justice have (whatever it may be) to the flag or the name of a country? There are, then, non-juridical state-sanctioned Laws. When the principle of Justice is applied to a concrete case which lends itself to it (to a social interaction susceptible of being just or unjust), there is a legal rule or *Droit* in general. But if this application is carried out inside of a State, the *Droit* will only be real *in actuality* if it is the State itself which makes the application in question, and which—consequently—"annuls" the corresponding illicit acts. And in this case, the real *Droit* in actuality will be a state-sanctioned Law.

One can therefore say, on the one hand, that all state-sanctioned Laws are not juridical Laws. But one must add, on the other [138] hand, that the totality of state-sanctioned Laws must also necessarily imply juridical Laws. In other words, there cannot be a State without state-sanctioned *Droit,* just as *Droit* cannot exist in actuality in a State except by being state-sanctioned.

Indeed, let us assume that several Societies, autonomous and consequently equipped with real *Droits* in actuality, conglomerate in order to establish a single Society organized into a State. By this very fact, these partial Societies stop being autonomous: their members can either freely leave them or are forced to belong to them by the State (and no longer by the Societies themselves). Consequently, their *Droits* stop being real in actuality. Therefore, if the State does not adopt these *Droits,* or does not replace them by a *Droit* which is appropriate to it, the global Society (organized into a State) will be a Society without *Droit* existing in actuality. Now we have seen that any Society whatsoever cannot really exist, i.e., last indefinitely without disintegrating as a result of internal processes, without possessing an actual *Droit* which is appropriate to it. The global Society, therefore, must possess a real *Droit* in actuality. But as it is organized into a State, this *Droit* can only be a state-sanctioned *Droit*. One therefore sees that any State whatsoever must count among its Laws juridical Laws.

One can explain this reasoning, moreover, in a somewhat different form.

The integration of an autonomous Society into a State does not completely destroy the *Droit* of this Society. It only makes it go from actuality to potentiality. Now every potentiality tends to be actualized. The *Droit* of the Society integrated by the State, therefore, will have a tendency to become a state-sanctioned *Droit*. If the State accepts as its own the *Droit* of the Society that it absorbs, there will be no difficulties. But if it refuses, if it does not make its own the *Droit* in question, and above all if it replaces it with another (state-sanctioned) *Droit*, there will necessarily be a (juridical) conflict between the State and the Society that it has absorbed. In order to keep the *Droit* of the latter in a state of mere potentiality, the State will have to exercise a continuous pressure (for naturally potentiality tends to be actualized, the reverse process thus being "against nature"). Now to exercise a pressure is to be in conflict, and all internal conflict tends to dislocate the whole, i.e., to overcome the union of elements in conflict; for all conflict, being a *contradiction,* tends to overcome itself. Now to overcome the conflict is to overcome the interaction of the members of the conflict to the extent that there is nothing other than the conflict itself. And [139] one overcomes the interaction either by breaking off contact or by overcoming both or one of the two members. In our case, then, there will be either a tendency of the integrated Society to separatism or an attempt on its part to monopolize the State, to substitute itself for it. If the State wants to keep and preserve its integrity, it will therefore have to overcome this Society to the extent that it [the Society] serves as support for the *Droit* (in potentiality) that it [the State] does not want to make its own (that it does not want to actualize by making it its own). Thus, the State that does not want to make canon *Droit* its own always has a more or less marked tendency to overcome the Church as a *sui generis* Society, which continues to exist within the State. Conversely, the State which wants to keep within its bosom a specific Society must actualize the *Droit* appropriate to this Society by making it its own, by decreeing it through a juridical Law. Thus, for example, if the State wants to preserve the Family formed by marriage, it must make its own the fundamental principles of familial *Droit*: the banning of divorce, the punishment of adultery, the inequality between natural and legitimate children, and so on. Unfortunately, the State is not always conscious of this necessity. It does not always see that it must necessarily choose, in the end, between the suppression of the particular Society included within it and the adoption of the *Droit* appropriate to this Society.

§ 23

At first glance, there is a contradiction when one says, on the one hand, that all *Droit* in actuality is state-sanctioned, i.e., a Law, and on the other hand, that the relations between the State and its citizens have nothing juridical about them. But the contradiction is only apparent. This has given rise, however, to many misunderstandings and to inconclusive polemics between statist theoreticians like Kelsen, partisans of "natural *droit,*" and sectarians [*sectateurs*] of "social *droit,*" such as Duguit.[10] In order to resolve the question, it is necessary to see what are the State and the citizen about which one speaks when one discusses the juridical nature of relations between State and citizen.

Of course, I cannot study here the nature and structure of the State as such; but it will be necessary to say a few words about it: for one contrasts the "individual" to the State, [and] one speaks of their relations without sufficiently clarifying in which aspect one is considering them. This is because in reality the State and the "individual" are very complex entities, and it is important to know which aspect [140] of the "individual" is related or contrasted to the State, and in which aspect this State itself is taken.

a) First, let us consider the "*individual.*"

Hegel and a lot of modern sociologists agree in saying that man is a truly human being only to the extent that he is social. The anthropogenic act, which turns the animal of the species Homo sapiens into a human being (having this animal for support) is an interaction between *two* human beings (struggle for recognition, which generates the humanity of the two).[11] A Homo sapiens who by definition is not in any social relations at all is therefore only an animal. A truly "isolated" "individual," i.e., absolutely "asocial," is therefore not a human being but the animal support of a human being, deprived of his human suprastructure. But in all human beings this support continues to subsist: in every man there is an animal. One can therefore consider all human "individuals" in their animal aspect.

Now the State is as much in relation with the Homo sapiens who is only an animal as with a human individual taken as an animal. Thus, measures concerning public health often have the animal in man in mind. On the other hand, the State is even in relation with a mentally incompetent, who has nothing human about him: it [the State] forbids him from being killed, for example, or orders him confined to an asylum, and so on.

But generally speaking, the "individual" is not only an animal; he is also a human being properly so-called—that is, he is a member of a Society, he is in social interactions. Now the human being can be human in various

---

10. [Ed. Perhaps a reference to Hans Kelsen, *Pure Theory of Law,* trans. Max Knight (Berkeley: University of California Press, 1967).]

11. Two do not yet constitute a Society in the proper sense of the word. But in fact there is always a "bystander," a "third." A struggles with B 1) in order that B recognize him; and 2) in order that C know that he is recognized by B. It is the triad A-B-C which forms a Society, and it is such a Society which is organized into a State when a relation of governor to the governed between B and C is established—that is, when B or C recognize the (political) Authority of C or B, and when the group A-B-C is exclusive in relation to all the other groups, D, E, . . . , and so on.

ways: as a religious, moral, aesthetic, economic, political man, and so on. In other words, the social interaction which humanizes the Homo sapiens can be moral, religious, economic, political, and so on. Or once again, the "individual" can be a member of a Society either religious or economic or political, and so on. Therefore, it is not only as a citizen, i.e., as a member of a political Society that we call the State, that the "individual" is more than an animal. [141] He is also one, for example, as a member of a religious Society called the Church. He can simultaneously be an animal, believer, and citizen—and so on.

Let us call "Society" in the narrow sense the totality of all social unities other than the Family, the State, and Humanity. And let us distinguish between trans-political [*trans-étatiques*] and sub-political [*cis-étatiques*] Societies— that is, Societies which extend beyond the State or which are set up inside the State (the Family is therefore a sub-political Society in the modern State; Humanity is a trans-political Society in relation to all national States). We can then say that in the vast majority of cases an "individual" is simultaneously an animal (i.e., an individual taken as isolated), a member of a Family, a citizen, a member of various sub- or trans-political Societies, and finally an integral element of Humanity.[12] Now the State can be in relation with the "individual" in all his aspects. One cannot, therefore, speak of the relation between the State and the "individual" without clarifying the aspect of the latter to which the State is supposed to be related. Generally, one opposes to the State the individual taken as a member of a "Society," of economic Society, for example. But one forgets to specify this, speaking of the "individual" simply. And one forgets that the opposition or conflict between the State and the individual taken as a member of a "Society" (economic, for example) reproduces itself inside the individual himself: the citizen can enter into conflict in himself with himself as "Homo economicus," the former showing solidarity with the State against the latter—and so on.

But there is more. A member of a Society (in the broad sense) [142] can act (and to act is *to be*) as a "particular" or as a "universal"—that is, being a mem-

---

12. All human beings are part of Humanity, taken as a general or abstract notion: "the human *race*." But in this day and age, Humanity is also a *real* entity, seeing that there are real "world-wide" *interactions*. And real Humanity exists in several aspects. Thus, the Catholic Church is in principle a universal Church, just as the communist State is a universal State. This Church [and] this State therefore claim to be Humanity in its religious or political aspect. Of course, this Catholic or communist Humanity still does not exist in actuality. But it exists in potentiality (as a sketch); it is *real* in potentiality. It is not enough, therefore, to say that a Catholic or communist are members of trans-political Societies. One must say that they exist as members of Humanity realized (in potentiality) in its religious or political aspect. And this is precisely what complicates the relations between a Catholic or communist, and the national State of which he is a citizen. If the national State can still (perhaps) be uninterested in the religious aspect of human existence, it cannot ignore the political aspect, since it is itself a political entity. A national State, if it wants to remain national, ought not to tolerate, therefore, the existence of communists among its nationals.

ber of a Society, I can act ([at least] while acting as a member of this Society) either in my own interest, for my own account (taking myself always as a member of this Society), or in the interest of this Society as such.[13] Thus, for example, the member of a Family can either act in the interest of this Family taken as a whole, or act according to interests that he has within this family in occupying the place that he occupies. For example, to the extent that a son can influence his father who is making a will, he can either try to have a greater part than his brother ("particularistic" attitude) or to see to it that the familial patrimony remains intact ("universalistic" attitude). And the two attitudes are possible in all Societies for each of its members.

Consequently, it is not enough to say that the State is in relation with an "individual" taken as a member of a family, for example, or a guild. It is still necessary to specify if this member acts in a "universal" or "particular" way while acting in his capacity as a member of the Societies in question; for the attitude of the State can vary according to the attitude the individual takes toward his Society. For example, if the State wants to overcome a Society, it could support the "particular" actions of the members of this Society and fight the "universal" actions.

And this is not all. Societies (in the broad sense) are multiple, and often they intersect or fit into one another: a Society A can encompass a Society B and be encompassed in its turn by a Society C. In other words, the same "individual" can be a member of several juxtaposed or interlocking Societies. In particular, the State deals with "individuals" who are members of both sub- [143] and trans-political Societies, which already complicates things very much. Now, in each of these Societies, the individual can take either a "particular" or "universal" attitude. If he only participates in two Societies, A and B, we already have four cases: he is either "particular" or "universal" in both, or "particular" in one and "universal" in the other. And as soon as the individual participates in several Societies, the complexity becomes enormous.

It is important to know how the individual behaves in the various Societies to which he belongs. And as these Societies can enter into conflict with one another, it is also important to know which one the individual will opt for in the end. Thus, for example, the national State can tolerate the membership of its citizen in a trans-political Society (a union, a Church, and so on) provided that [the State] can assume that the individual will act as a loyal citizen in the

---

13. It is only at the two limits that this distinction between the "particular" and the "universal" disappears. At the lower limit, the animal realizes the goals of the species by pursuing its own goals, and conversely. (One can say that every animal "individual" is an *integral element* of its "species"; but it is better not to say that it is a *member* of it, precisely to bring out that in this case there is no difference between the "particular" and the "universal"—that is, no possible conflict between the whole and the member parts.) At the upper limit, the citizen of the universal and homogenous State realizes his "particular" ends by acting with a view to the "universal" good of the State, and he realizes this good by acting in his own interest. But this is only a limit case, which assumes an absolute homogeneity.

case of a conflict between the State and the trans-political Society (as was the case for the socialist party, the S.F.I.O.).[14]

One sees, therefore, that the problem of relations between the State and the "individual" is much too complex, as regards the "individual," to be set down and resolved globally. Of course, a real action (in actuality) is always, in the end, the action of an "individual" (or a sum of such individual actions). But the "individual" can act either as an animal, or as a member of a Family or a sub-political Society, or as a citizen, or finally as a member of a trans-political Society. He can act, moreover, in several ways simultaneously. And every time he can be either "particular" or "universal." Thus, although it is true that the State is always in real interaction (in actuality) with "individuals" and with them only, as long as one has not clarified who the "individual" is with whom the State is interacting, one has not said a whole lot. In particular, in order to know what the *juridical* relation is between the State and the "individual," one must take into account the complex nature of the latter.

b) This suffices for the "individual." Let us now see what the *State* is as such.

For there to be a State, the following two principal conditions must be fulfilled: 1) there must be a Society, of which all the members are "friends," and which treats as an "enemy" all non-members, whoever they are; 2) inside this Society a group of "governors" must be clearly distinguished from the other members, who constitute the group of the "governed." Each of the two conditions is necessary; but taken individually neither is sufficient. [144] There is a State, then, only if both [of these conditions] are fulfilled.[15] "Friend" and "enemy" mean "*political* friend" and "*political* enemy." Ultimately, the "friend" is the "brother in arms," and the "enemy" the military enemy, who must yield or die; and if he does not yield and is not killed, one must die oneself. But I assume as known these two fundamental, specifically political, categories.[16] And I am not at all wondering (in this place) how these existential categories are born or how real Societies of "friends" are formed. As for the "governors," this is nothing other than the "exclusive group" of which I spoke about above (cf. § 15). It is a group within a Society which can substitute itself for the totality of the members of this Society, i.e., remove Society from the influence of all the members of Society and use it as they like, without it per-

---

14. [Ed. The Section Française de l'Internationale Ouvrière (SFIO) was a socialist party that formed in 1905 and that briefly held power in a coalition government under the leadership of Léon Blum from 1936–7. After suffering several electoral defeats in the 1960s, the old SFIO dissolved and was more or less replaced by the Parti Socialiste (PS). Although it is unclear to what event Kojève is specifically referring, it may be to the fact that in World War I French workers fought for the French state rather than supporting international socialism and communism.]

15. The first condition determines an "autonomous political Society," not organized into a State properly so-called. If the second condition alone is fulfilled, the Society will be "organized," but it will not be "political"; it will not be, therefore, organized into a *State*. This is the case of the Church, for example.

16. Cf. Carl Schmitt, *Der Begriff des Politischen*. [*The Concept of the Political*, trans. George Schwab (New Brunswick: Rutgers University Press, 1976).]

ishing because of this and without the "excluded" members leaving the Society in order to form another. It is in this way that the "excluded" also form a group within the Society, which is subordinated to the "exclusive group." When the Society is *political,* i.e., when it is formed by "friends" who oppose themselves as a whole to the "enemies," the "exclusive group" and "excluded group" are *political* groups: one then calls them the "governing group" and the "governed group" ("ruling class," "political elite," "aristocracy," and so on). The "governors" have the State at their disposal, they govern it, and they impose it, just as they have constituted it and as they govern it for the governed.[17]

[145] Assuming this to be the case, what does one understand by the "State" when one opposes it to the "individual," or when one speaks of the juridical or other relation between the "individual" and the "State"?

The State is a "moral person." Those who create a State generally claim that this State is an "abstract moral person," i.e., an Institution, having a status (the "Constitution") which can no longer be changed by the will of those who live in this State. But in fact it is a matter of a "collective moral person," i.e., an Association, which is a result of the wills of those who constitute the Association in fact at a given moment (this result also being the result of the relations between the governors and the governed). Being a "moral person," the State cannot act itself. One or several "physical persons," i.e., one or several "individuals," must act for it, [must] act in its name. Practically speaking, there are always several persons acting in the name of the State; for even an absolute monarch delegates his power to other persons, in order to be able to govern the State in fact. The totality of persons (chosen by the governing group) who act in the name of the State can be called the "Government" (in the broad

---

17. The governing group provides candidates for support of [its] political Authority (by choosing those of its members who have a political Authority within the group). The governed accept the candidates proposed by the governing group because they recognize the political Authority of this group. This is the ideal case when the "aristocracy" bases its power upon Authority. [A] worse case [is when] the governing group nominates candidates who have Authority within the group but this group does not have Authority among the governed: the candidates must then be imposed upon the governed by force (case of "class dictatorship"). [A] mixed case, [and] generally [one] of transition [is when] the group does not have Authority, but a candidate of the group can have a personal Authority among the governed (the group will disappear sooner or later). Another case [is when] the group has Authority, but a candidate is imposed on the group by force, either by having or not having Authority among the governed—and so on.

If you will, one can say that the relation between governors and the governed [145] is a projection inside the political Society of the fundamental political relation of friend and enemy. The governed, therefore, will be the "internal enemies" of the governors, who form a group of "internal friends." This would tally very well with the theory of [Ludwig] Gumplowicz [*Outlines of Sociology,* ed. Irving Louis Horowitz (New Brunswick, NJ: Transaction Books, 1980), 192–237] and several modern sociologists (above all Anglo-Saxon), according to whom all States properly so-called would be the result of a conquest, the victorious friends becoming the governors and the vanquished enemies the governed, who recognize the Authority of the victors. But I do not want to discuss here this theory. It is literally true only at the limit—that is, when the governed are *slaves* of the governors.

sense).[18] To the extent that the State acts, and in particular is in relation with "individuals," it is nothing other than the Government. The relations, juridical or otherwise, between the individual and the State are therefore always in fact relations between the individual and the Government.

Now the members of the Government are themselves "individuals." To the extent that they represent the State, they [146] are citizens, and when they act in the name of the State they act as citizens. But in fact they are not only citizens. On the one hand, they are also animals; and on the other hand, [they are] members of Families as well as of various sub- and trans-political Societies.[19]

It is necessary, therefore, to pay close attention when one speaks of relations between the "individual" and the "State." In all cases it is a matter of relations with the Government—that is, ultimately, with its members, with the individuals who make it up. But when it is a matter of relations with the State properly so-called, these "administrative" or governmental "individuals" must be taken as citizens. By contrast, when an "administered" individual (and I call "administered" every citizen not being part of the Government, whether or not he belongs to the "governing group"; thus, an adult male student in France is "administered" but he is—legally—a "governor," while a female student is "administered" and "governed") is in relations with members of the Government taken as non-citizens (as animals or members of Families or Societies), he is not in relation with the State. In this case there is simply a relation between "individuals," every "individual" being able to act in some one of his aspects, except that the "administrator" does not act by definition in his aspect as a citizen. And the same applies for the relations between governors and the governed. There is a relation with a governor only to the extent that the member of the governing group with which one is in relation acts as a citizen. But, even in this case, the relation with the State is only indirect. By being in relation with a governor taken as such, i.e., as a citizen, one is indirectly in relation with the State to the extent that the governor can make the Government act in his place (in the person of a member of the Government).[20]

---

18. In a "bourgeois" Democracy, the legal governing group is constituted by all the normal and adult men, or by all the adult and normal citizens of both sexes. The Government, by contrast, formed by the totality of the various representatives [*députés*] and civil servants [*fonctionnaires*], is always relatively restricted. In the socialist State (the U.S.S.R.), by contrast, almost all the citizens are civil servants and thus are—legally—part of the Government in the broad sense. But one must distinguish between the legal Government (and governing group) and the effective Government (and group).

19. Plato [*Republic,* 449a ff] wished that in the ideal State the Government, and even the governing group as a whole, would be made up of individuals who are only citizens, from whence comes his "communism," the abolition of the family, absolute isolation in relation to the outside, and so on. But the Platonic ideal has still never been fully realized.

20. One must distinguish, moreover, between the legal situation and the real, effective situation. Often the Government is made up of straw men, the real Government being outside of the legal Government. Likewise, the real governing group may not be recognized as such legally. Thus, in a truly absolute monarchy, the legal governing group boils down to the person of the monarch alone. But in fact there is always a governing group more or less extensive.

[147] c) Let us now see what can be, from the juridical point of view, *the relations between the "individual" and the "State."*

First of all, the "individual" can be a "friend" or an "enemy" of the State. Now there is no relation between "friends" and "enemies" except that of mutual exclusion (which is—when it is completely actualized—war to the death, called the war of extermination)—that is, the elimination of interaction. One can therefore say that there is no interaction properly so-called between "friends," on the one hand, and their "enemies," on the other.[21] The State tends to overcome, or indeed to absorb, all its "enemies" (wars of extermination or conquest), and if it does not succeed, it tries to isolate itself politically from them as much as possible (the ideal of autarchy).[22] This tendency to isolation is translated into the juridical sphere through the fact that (national) state-sanctioned *Droit* is only applied to nationals. Foreigners, supposedly enemies, are by definition "outside the law." One generally says that one has the "*droit*" to do anything to an enemy: to kill him, rob him, and so on. But in reality there is not any "*droit*" here, but simply the absence of *Droit*: the foreigner is not a subject of *droit*; *Droit* does not apply to relations between foreigners or with nationals. Seeing that there is no genuine interaction between A and B if A, or A and B, are foreigners, there is no juridical situation at all. And this is what one observes in archaic or primitive societies—at Rome, for example, during the archaic period.

One can explain this situation a little differently. If A is a citizen and B a foreigner, i.e., an enemy, the State puts itself in all cases on the side of A. It is therefore neither impartial nor disinterested; it is not a Judge but a party, and the situation is therefore political but not at all juridical. When A and B are both friends, the situation is, by contrast, necessarily juridical; for if the State takes A and B in their political aspects as "friends," they are equal in the sense that both of them are friends and not enemies. [148] They are thus interchangeable—that is, the State is *impartial*. And it is also "*disinterested*" in the sense that its representative, i.e., the government in its capacity as Judge, can be *anyone at all*. Indeed, any compatriot is a friend for any other compatriot: any Judge will therefore treat him as a friend. All interactions between political *friends* can therefore generate an actual juridical situation in the sense that the State *can* play the role of an impartial and disinterested Judge. One can there-

---

21. I assume, in order to simplify matters, that the State does not have allies—that is, foreign political "friends."

22. Cf. the Platonic ideal [*Republic,* 369a–74e, 422a–3e], as well as that of Fichte ["Der geschlossene Handelsstaat" ("The Closed Commercial State") in *Fichtes Werke,* vol. 3, ed. Immanuel Hermann Fichte (Berlin: Walter de Gruyter & Co., 1971), 389–513] and so on. In fact, a national State never succeeds either in absorbing all its enemies or in completely isolating itself from them. The limit is only attained by the universal State or Empire. But then there are no longer "enemies"—that is, no longer a *political* sphere. The Empire, by completely *actualizing* the fundamental political relation of friends-enemies, exhausts the political "*potential.*" Now actuality annuls itself as soon as it exhausts its potential. The Empire, therefore, is no longer a *political* entity in the proper sense of the word: it does not have a political *history.*

fore say that the possibility of juridical relations is the expression in the sphere of *Droit* of the political fact of "friendship," while the political relation of friend to enemy is juridically expressed by the impossibility of an actual juridical situation. But for there truly to be a juridical situation between "friends," the State-Judge must still be disinterested in the sense that it is not at the same time a party, an element of the interaction that it judges. Now if it takes A and B in their capacity as citizens, the State is by this very fact in political interaction with them. It is always therefore a party and cannot be Judge in the proper sense of the term. For there to be a juridical situation, then, it is necessary 1) that the State is related to political friends, that A and B, who are interacting, are citizens; and 2) that A and B are in a non-*political* interaction between them, so that the State can be disinterested in the nature of their interaction and not be a party when it is supposed to be Judge.

Originally, then, there was *Droit* in actuality, i.e., state-sanctioned *Droit*, only between friends—that is, between the citizens of the State in question. But for there truly to be a *Droit* in this State, the State must be related to these citizens by taking them in their non-political aspects—that is, as members of Families or any other Society at all. But, in principle, the Family, and above all the Society, can be both sub-political and trans-political. Now, seeing that the State, in its capacity as Judge, abstracts from the fact that it is dealing with its citizens, it can take one step further and even judge foreigners in their non-political interactions both between themselves and with its nationals. And this is what one actually observes. In more evolved Societies, little by little *Droit* extends beyond national borders. It is in this way that Roman *droit* adds to national *jus civile* [the law binding on Roman citizens] a *jus gentium* [a law binding on all nations], which is also applied to non-citizens. Of course, it is only a matter there of "Roman subjects," of inhabitants of the Roman Empire. But in principle, one can apply it to anyone whomever (cf. the Roman idea of *jus naturale* [natural law or right], common to the human race), and it is in this way that one applies it in modern States. But the distinction [149] between *jus civile* and *jus gentium,* that the Romans kept until the end, shows that originally *Droit* in actuality, i.e., state-sanctioned *Droit,* was only applied to nationals.

At any rate, if the State judges a foreigner, it is because it likens him, on the juridical plane, to "friends"—that is, to nationals. More exactly, it abstracts from the political difference between friend and enemy, and takes the litigants in their non-political aspect—that is, if you will, politically "neutral."[23] Practically speaking, this is only possible as long as the *political* relation remains in potentiality—that is, as long as peace reigns. In time of war, enemy citizens again become political "enemies" and thus stop being subjects of *droit.* They are again "outside the law." Of course, in civilized countries, enemy citizens

---

23. In *politics,* there are no neutrals: the non-friend is by definition an enemy and conversely. To treat a man or a Society, or indeed a State, as a "neutral," is simply not to have *political* relations with them; it is only to have economic, cultural, [and] religious relations, and so on.

are not handed over to their fate. They have a status. But this status no longer has anything juridical about it; it is purely political. In any case, valid *Droit* for nationals stops being applied automatically to enemies. In short, as soon as the political relation of friend-enemy is actualized, the juridical relation disappears, or passes to a state of potentiality, no longer being applied by the State.

Therefore, the State applies its *Droit* to foreigners only if it takes them in their non-political aspect, if it does not treat them as "enemies." In other words, it is the *Droit* called civil that is applied to them, and not the *Droit* called public (which is not, moreover, a *Droit* properly so-called). The State considers them as members of the Society formed by the totality of Families, or as members of the Society constituted by the totality of economic relations, and so on. It is in this way that at Rome, foreigners enjoyed the *droit* of *conubium* [marriage] and *commercium* [commerce or trade], but not the *droit* of the city. And this is the way things always are. No State will punish a foreigner because he has been a deserter in his country, or a traitor, and so on, and it will not be worried about his "*droit*" to vote, and so on: for it treats him not as a *citizen* of a foreign State but as a "private person [*personne privée*]," a non-citizen, a member of a family, a merchant, and so on.[24] [150] Let us take economic Society. If this is an autonomous Society, it actualizes on its own its *Droit,* and if it is organized into a State, it applies it to "friends" while abstracting from this fact in the application itself. But it is possible that the members of this Society are divided between several independent States. The Society itself, therefore, is no longer a State; it is no longer even an autonomous Society. *Droit,* therefore, can only exist there in actuality provided that it is applied by the States which share the members of the Society in question. But since this *Droit* is applied to the citizens not as citizens but as members of the economic Society, which extends beyond each of these States, every State can actualize the *Droit* by applying it to whichever member of economic Society, it being of little importance whether he is a national or a foreigner.

Things are complicated if economic *Droit* varies from State to State. But the general situation remains the same: economic *Droit* is actualized by its application by States, and States apply this *droit* to the members of the economic Society taken as such, and not as citizens. However, there are now two possible alternatives: that of the *Droit* called "territorial" and that of the *Droit* called "personal." In the first case, the State applies its own *Droit* to all the members

---

24. Private international *Droit* deals with the nationality of foreigners—that is, with their political status as citizens. But it does so only in order to know if the person in question is or is not a foreigner. Thus, there is simply [150] a relation between the aforementioned person and the State, which is consequently a party and not a Judge. The State can, of course, apply the law of the country of origin in order to determine the nationality of the expatriate [*ressortissant*]. But this application has nothing juridical about it (as the law applied, moreover, has nothing juridical about it). To say that the son of an Englishman born in France is English or French is no more juridical than annexing a part of England or ceding a part of France and declaring afterwards that the inhabitants are French or English. These are purely political decisions or laws—that is, non-juridical.

of the economic Society, nationals or foreigners. In the second case, while continuing to exercise in fact justice on its own territory, the State applies its *Droit* only to its nationals, while applying to foreigners the *Droits* of their respective States (which generates "private international *Droit*" properly so-called). But the situation remains the same in principle; for in doing this, the State continues to be related to the litigants as members of the economic Society, and not as citizens. State A does not worry about the way in which a citizen of State B is treated as a citizen of this State; it only wonders how State B treats a member of the economic Society as a member of [151] this Society if he is its citizen. In other words, if the economic Society is not homogenous as regards its juridical structure, it remains an economic Society, i.e., non-political, and its members are treated by all the States that it involves as "private persons," as non-citizens.

When all is said and done, then, one can say the following.

When a society is organized into a State, *Droit* can only be actualized there[25] by a state-sanctioned application.

When the State deals with political "friends" (individuals or collectives), it can and ought to apply a *Droit* to them; for the application of *Droit* is nothing other than the juridical translation of the political relation of the State with its "friends"—that is, with its citizens.[26] If the State intervenes in the capacity of a Judge in an interaction between A and B, this is because it does not treat them as political enemies. Now, in politics, the non-enemy is a friend. To judge, therefore, is to treat them as friends—that is, the State treats politically as friends those whom it judges, but it does not judge them in their capacity as friends. By contrast, when the State refuses to intervene as Judge in an interaction between A and B, this is because A and B, or A, or B, are political enemies—that is, foreigners.

But for there to be *Droit*, it is necessary that the State-Judge not be a party—that is, a co-agent in the interaction. In other words, it must not take A and B in their relations with itself—that is, as citizens (nationals or foreigners). This is why it can also judge A and B when they are foreigners; but politically, the foreigner is an enemy—that is, by definition he cannot be a litigant. In order to be able to judge foreigners, therefore, the State must treat them as "neutrals"—that is, not having *political* relations with them. And this is only possible in time of peace, when the political element is not actualized. Even in time of peace, the foreigner remains a political enemy (since we assume that the State does not have allies). But the State can act in its non-political capacity as Judge, and in this politically "neutral" attitude it will be able to judge foreigners. In time of war, by contrast, the State is a political entity in actuality. All its relations are therefore political, and it is related to the foreigner as an enemy. Therefore, it can no longer see him as a subject of (its) *droit*. As for the national,

---

25. [Ed. Reading *ne peut que s'y actualiser* for *ne peut s'y actualiser*.]
26. I repeat that I have assumed, in order to simplify matters, that the State does not have foreign *allies*.

he is also treated by it politically, but he is treated as a political friend. [152] Now the State can always judge friends. The citizen, therefore, remains a subject of *droit* even in time of war.[27]

Let us now see what the political distinction between governors and the governed yields in the juridical sphere.

The governors, i.e., the "exclusive political group," puts out [*sécrète*] the Government, which actualizes the State as such by acting in its name. The rest of the population, i.e., the governed (or "the excluded political Group"), is subjected to governmental action without being able to put up resistance (at the very least in principle).[28] In particular, in a society organized into a State, only the Government can actualize *Droit* by applying it effectively; for only the Government can make *Droit* truly efficacious by preventing the litigants from eluding juridical action by leaving the society where it is supposed to take place. The State as Judge (in the broad sense, i.e., the State taken in its juridical aspect in general) is in the final analysis, therefore, nothing other than the Government.

This does not mean that the Government creates *Droit* from start to finish, that there is no *Droit* without government. For there to be *Droit*, it is enough that there be persons interacting, i.e., a Society (in the broad sense), and an idea of Justice applicable to these interactions. However, if there is a State, i.e., a Government, *Droit* exists *in actuality* only to the extent that it is applied by this Government. The interactions to which *Droit* is [153] applied are obviously "given" to the Government: it finds them outside of itself. As for the idea of Justice, which determines the fact and nature of its juridical intervention, it can be either the Government's own or it can equally be borrowed from without, as a "given." Thus, a Government can apply (actualize) a preexisting juridical "custom" or one independently created by the Government properly so-called. It is also possible that the Government applies a *Droit* of which it disapproves, that it believes is unjust or pernicious. But then one must distinguish two cases.

---

27. It should be understood that the State can apply to its nationals in time of war a "private" *Droit* other than that which it applies to them in time of peace. (It can declare a moratorium, for example.) But there will always be an domestic "private" **Droit**, and the citizen will remain a subject of *droit*. As for public "*Droit*," it is a *Droit* neither in time of war nor in time of peace.

28. It should be understood that the governed may recognize the (political) Authority of the governors. The latter, therefore, are not at all always required to employ force, but they are supposed to be able to and must employ it if the necessity arises.

At the limit, the governing group stops being "exclusive" by encompassing the totality of citizens. This is the case of the homogenous State. Now I have said that there is a State properly so-called only when there is a distinction between governors and the governed. As in the friend-enemy case, the total actualization is also here equivalent to the annulment. The State is only "absolute," i.e., indefinitely lasting and immutable, provided that it is perfectly homogenous. But the homogenous State is no longer a State properly so-called. The universal and homogenous State, or Empire, is therefore neither a State nor a political entity in general. But this is only a limit case, for in fact homogeneity is never absolute: there are differences of age, sex, "character," and so on, and consequently sub-political groupings.

In the first, the Government as such shows solidarity with the *Droit* it applies, but the members of the Government, taken as "private persons" (members of Families or of sub- or trans-political Societies), do not recognize its juridical authority. But this case does not interest us, for we are speaking of the Government and not of private persons. In the other case, the Government is opposed as such to the *Droit* it nevertheless applies. It does it, therefore, under pressure from extra-governmental forces. Consequently, it is not a genuine Government: it is a matter of a transitional period, when the State, deprived of Government, does not exist in actuality. But in the "normal" case, the Government shows solidarity (as such and in the person of its members) with the *Droit* that it actualizes by applying it. And therefore, it draws the principles of this *Droit* from the idea of Justice which is its own. Now, seeing that the Government is put out by the exclusive political group, i.e., by the governors, the idea of Justice of the Government is nothing other than the idea of this group. The latter, therefore, is also the "exclusive juridical group" mentioned in our general definition of *Droit*.

The "normal" case is therefore the following. Within a society an exclusive juridical group is set up. In other words, this group can exclude from active juridical life (creator of *Droit*) all those who do not accept the ideal of Justice accepted by the group, without the society perishing from this. This group is at the same time an exclusive political group. It therefore puts out a Government, and this Government actualizes the *Droit* of the group by making it the state-sanctioned *Droit* of the society (organized into a State). All the "administered" without exception, therefore, are subject to this *Droit* without being able to oppose it. But the governors are subject to it by recognizing its authority, while the governed submit to it because the Government forces them to do so. But there are cases when the exclusive juridical group does not coincide with the exclusive political group, [154] or cases when the Government as Judge is not a product of the emission of the governors. And these "abnormal" cases will be discussed in the following section.

For the moment, let us remember that the Government is alone in actualizing the State, both as political entity and as Judge. To be related juridically to the State, therefore, is ultimately to be related to its Government; for however much one tries to "separate" the juridical power, the enforcement of the judgement (the Police) is ultimately always incumbent upon the Government, and it enforces it only if it makes it its own (for otherwise it would be the juridical power which would act as the Government and there would no longer be a "separation" either). As soon as there is a State, therefore, all justice in actuality is necessarily state-sanctioned, i.e., governmental, it being of little importance that it is so explicitly (as in France, where the juridical laws are the work of Parliament) or only in an implicit manner (as in England, where juridical legislation is the work of judges). The "administered," i.e., the "individual" (and of course the member of the Government taken as a private person, who is "administered" like anyone else), only has the choice between two possibilities: either he freely recognizes the juridical authority of the Government, or the Government forcibly compels him to submit to the governmental juridical action. But as the Judgement is enforced (in principle) in both cases, there is always a *Droit* in actuality.

Let us now draw the consequences of the preceding.

The Government actualizes the State both in its political aspect and in its juridical aspect. As soon as there is a State and as soon as there is a *political* interaction in this State, the State represented by its Government cannot be Judge of this interaction, since it is by definition a party. By contrast, when it is a matter of non-political interactions (familial, economic, and so on), the Government can play the role of a third. Only *non-political* interactions, therefore, can generate an authentically juridical situation in a State.

The situation is particularly clear in the case of private or civil *Droit* properly so-called (as it will be defined in greater detail in Part Three). In these cases, the juridical intervention of the Government is optional: it is only carried out at the request of the interested parties. This behavior of the Government shows that the interaction in question does not affect it as such; or, more exactly, the Government thinks—wrongly or rightly—that this intervention [155] does not affect it. From the point of view of the modern State, for example, one can be a good citizen while not paying one's private debts. If B owes A money, the State believes it can have no interest in the question of knowing if B will give back this money to A or will keep it himself. This is why the Government does not intervene if A does not react to the non-payment of B's debt. What interests the Government as a political agent in this case is that there are no fights between *citizens* for private reasons. This is why it forbids A from acting spontaneously against B, and requires him to go and seek governmental arbitration. But this requirement has nothing juridical about it in itself: it is neither a "*droit*" nor a "duty" in the *juridical* sense of these terms. It is a *political* requirement which forbids "civil war" in all its forms. And this requirement does not at all determine the *nature* of the governmental juridical intervention. In its political aspect, the Government decides to suppress certain conflicts between its citizens by imposing on them a governmental juridical arbitration. But it is in its juridical aspect that the Government sets down the mode of its intervention. And it does so by drawing inspiration from its idea of Justice, by applying it to the interaction in question.[29] It is this application by the Government of the governmental idea (i.e., accepted by the Government) of Justice to a non-political interaction which constitutes *Droit* in actuality.

Generally speaking, the Government can play the role of a Judge, i.e., an "impartial and disinterested third" who intervenes according to his idea of Justice, everywhere it is a matter of an interaction between members of Families, or of sub- or trans-political Societies, these members acting as members of

---

29. For the moment, I am not discussing the question of knowing if the idea of Justice is an autonomous phenomenon, or if this idea is a result of the economic "interests" of the Government (or indeed, of the governors), or of its political, moral, or other ideas. It is enough for me that these non-juridical "interests" or ideas go through the idea of Justice before being applied to the interactions submitted to the juridical arbitration of the Government.

these Families or Societies, and not as members of the State—that is, as citizens. As a political entity, the State does not have an interest in these interactions, and this is why its intervention is optional. But, if it intervenes, it does so according to juridical principles which are appropriate to it. The Government decides the way in which the conflict submitted to its arbitration will be resolved, and one cannot say that the "individual" has a *droit* in respect to the Government. He has a *droit* in respect to [156] another "individual," and this *droit* is set down by a governmental decision. That is all. Of course, the interaction can take place not only between individuals properly so-called, but also between "collective persons" or between individuals and societies (in the broad sense). But this changes nothing in the general situation: the individual acts in his capacity as a non-citizen and the society is something other than the State. When these individuals and these societies are interacting, the Government can play the role of a *third,* for it is a matter of an interaction between these individuals and these societies, and not of their interactions with the State.[30]

One cannot say, therefore, that the individual (or a non-political society) has the **droit** to be judged by the Government, nor that the latter has the juridical *duty* to judge him. One cannot say, consequently, that the individual has the **droit** to be judged in one way rather than another. It is only because the individual is judged by the Government, and judged in a certain way, that he has juridical **droits** and *duties,* and he has them in relation not to the Government but toward other individuals or non-political societies.

The situation is less clear when it is a matter of penal *Droit*—that is, cases when the juridical intervention of the State is no longer optional. If the Government intervenes spontaneously, even if it is not solicited by the interested parties, this is because it is "interested" itself, it is because it is or believes itself injured by the interaction in question. Therefore, it can no longer be Judge; it is already a party. It seems, therefore, that penal *Droit* is not an authentic *droit.* But this solution is clearly paradoxical, [and] it is all the more so because the boundaries [157] between civil *Droit* and penal *Droit* vary according to epochs

---

30. If the "social *droit*" which Duguit speaks about, for example, regulates the relations between the members of an economic-cultural Society and this Society as such, taken as a whole, it is a matter of a private *Droit.* The State, therefore, is just as little required to make its own the interests of this Society as it is to show solidarity with the interest of one of the members of the aforementioned Society. If not, one must say that the so-called "Government" is the administrative organ of this non-political Society: it is then no longer the Government of a State, there is no longer a State, [and] there is no longer the friend-enemy relation. Indeed, Duguit always reasons by forgetting that there are wars; for one cannot truly say that the State sees to the "happiness" or "well-being" of its citizens if it kills them in order to remain in existence as a State. In the case of war, the Government subjects non-political interests to political interests: "social *droit*," therefore, must be subordinated to purely political demands. "Social *droit*," therefore, is only possible when the Society can subsist without being a political entity, a State—that is, when there are no wars. Duguit's "social *droit,*" therefore, only makes sense in the universal State that Marx had in mind: one cannot admit this "*droit*" while retaining the ideal of a *nation* organized into a State.

and places. Now one cannot truly say that the banning of murder, for example, has stopped being juridical in modern States from the sole fact that the Government spontaneously punishes murder, while in archaic States the Government only intervened at the request of the interested parties. Now this paradox allows one to resolve the problem.

If cases of penal *Droit* have been able to be cases of civil *Droit,* and cases of civil *Droit* cases of penal *Droit,* this is because there is a "civil" element in penal *Droit.* In other words, it is a matter of interactions between "private persons [*particuliers*]," when the Government intervenes or can intervene in the capacity of a *third.* The only difference with the case of civil or private *Droit* resides in the fact that the government intervenes spontaneously. Still, one must distinguish the two cases. In the first, the Government intervenes because it assumes that the interested party should have solicited it "normally," that he did not do it "by chance," so to speak. It is in this way that the Government can intervene "spontaneously" when one infringes upon the interests of a child. But this case is unimportant, for it does not differ essentially from cases of civil *Droit* properly so-called. The Government defends the interest of the litigant, taken as a private person [*personne privée*], and not its own. In the other case, by contrast, the State intervenes because the action that it judges infringes upon its own interests. Thus, the murderer not only deprives the Family and the Society of its member, but he also removes a citizen from the State. In this case, then, there is good reason to distinguish between a juridical intervention and a political intervention of the Government. The Government intervenes juridically, i.e., in its capacity as juridical Legislator, Judge, or judicial Police, when it punishes the murderer of an isolated individual (of an animal Homo sapiens), of a member of a Family, or a sub- or trans-political Society. But it intervenes politically when it punishes the same murderer for having removed a citizen from the State. And the latter punishment, then, has nothing juridical about it.

This distinction can appear very subtle. But it is phenomenologically justified. And we will see later (Part Three) that it allows one to resolve certain difficulties about the theory of the penal [*peine*]. One sometimes sees that a penal measure of a political character (for example, the forfeiture of civic "*droits*") comes to graft itself on a juridical sentence (for example, imprisonment or corporal punishment). This is because there has been a dual intervention of the Government: a juridical intervention of penal *Droit,* and a non-juridical political intervention. [158] Without a doubt, the Government decides in both cases the nature of the sentence and the necessity of applying it. But in the first, its decision creates a juridical situation, while in the second there is only a purely political relation between a citizen and his Government.

Generally speaking, there is penal *Droit* properly so-called when the Government intervenes spontaneously, but in the event of interactions which take place between "private persons [*particuliers*]," and not between citizens taken as such. And the Government only acts juridically to the extent that it abstracts from the fact that the interactions in question also infringe upon its own political interests. Without a doubt, it can defend its own interests while defending those of private persons taken as private persons. But then it will no longer act as Judge but as a party, and its action will have nothing juridical about it. What one generally understands by "penal *Droit*," therefore, is in reality a hybrid entity, where authentic juridical elements are combined with political elements.

One can explain the situation in the following manner. The Government sets down the status of the citizen, which says not only at what age he becomes a voter, for example, and so on, but also that a citizen cannot be a bigamist, or an assassin, and so on. The Government sets down this status as it sees fit, and this status has nothing juridical about it. The law which determines it is no different from the law which determines the national colors, for example: it is a political and not a juridical law. If an individual behaves as a citizen, he is supposed to live and act in conformity with his status. If he acts otherwise, it is because he acts as a non-citizen, a private person [*personne privée*], a member of a Family or a Society. In this case, there is a conflict in him between himself taken as a citizen and as a private person. The State then intervenes and supports, as it were, the citizen against the private person by forcing the latter to act as a citizen—that is, in conformity with his status. The State is here a party and the situation has nothing juridical about it. But it is possible that by acting contrary to his status as a citizen, the individual also infringes upon the interests of another private person or of a non-political Society. Thus, for example, the assassin infringes upon the interests of an isolated individual; the bigamist, those of the (monogamous) Family. In this case, the Government intervenes not only politically, in order to enforce the status of the citizen that it has set down, but also juridically, in order to apply its idea of Justice to the case of an interaction between two private persons, individual [159] or collective, physical or moral. And "penal *Droit*" is a *Droit* only to the extent that it implies such legal rules applicable to interactions between non-citizens.

By contrast, when it is a matter of "public *Droit*" in the narrow sense, i.e., of constitutional and administrative "*Droit*"—that is, when it is a matter of relations [or] interactions with the State itself—there is no juridical element at all. The State being party, it cannot be at the same time Judge. *Droit*, if there is *Droit*, cannot then be *actualized*.

Moreover, if the citizen acts as a citizen, he cannot—by definition—enter into conflict with the State. If not, it is a matter of a revolutionary action, which quite obviously has nothing to do with *Droit*. It is illegal politically, and at odds with the acknowledged status of the citizen. But it is absurd to say that it is juridically illegal. It simply denies the *Droit* in force; it occurs outside of the *Droit* in actuality. But just as one cannot say that one has a "*droit*" to *Droit*, one cannot say that it is *juridically* "criminal" to deny the *Droit* in force. Be that as it may, if the citizen is not revolutionary and if he nevertheless acts against his status as a citizen and thus enters into conflict with the State, it is because he acts against the State as a non-citizen, a private person, a member of a Family or a Society. The State then defends itself against an external force, as it were, and it is very well a party and not the Judge in this conflict. As for conflicts between citizens, they are also impossible when the citizens act as citizens, i.e., in conformity with their statuses; for the State can exist indefinitely, it is truly politically viable, only if its structure is in harmony with the status of the citizens, and if this status itself is such that the citizens who are conforming to it cannot enter into conflict between themselves. The State, therefore, never deals with conflicts between citizens as such, nor with conflicts between these citizens and the State. It makes do with setting down its own status as well as that of the citizens, and making them respected by non-citizens, it being of little importance that the non-citizen is an integral element of the concrete person of the citizen or a "subject" of the State, or once again a foreigner. In all these cases, there is no juridical situation and the intervention of the State can be likened to a case of war: the State overcomes by force the non-citizen or forces him to respect the status of the citizen.

Why does one speak, however, of "constitutional guarantees," of constitutional and administrative "public *Droit*"? It is because the members of the Government are—generally [160] speaking—not only citizens, i.e., precisely members of the Government, but also private persons, members of Families and of non-political Societies. Now what I have just said applies only to relations with the Government as such, i.e., with its members taken as citizens, and not to relations with these very members, taken as private persons. If an individual or a society enters into conflict with a member of Government (or the totality of these members) taken as a private person, i.e., as an isolated individual or member of a Family or a Society, there is an interaction between private persons. In any case, there is no interaction with the State. The State, i.e., the Government as such—that is, its members taken as citizens—can therefore intervene as a *third* in this interaction. It can be Judge. It can therefore have a legal rule, a juridical situation. And "public *Droit*" is a *Droit* only to the extent that it implies such legal rules, regulating the relations between the administered and their administrators, the latter being taken as private persons.

It is not at all a matter, therefore, of doing away with public *Droit*, of denying "constitutional guarantees." It is simply necessary to interpret them correctly. To the extent that the Constitution sets down the status of the State and its citizens, it has nothing juridical about it. This is a purely political law that the State, i.e., the Government, creates as it wants and that it can change when it wants. It makes no sense to have recourse to the Constitution against the State, represented by its Government; but only the State can change the Constitution. In other words, the Government must act as a Government: its members must act as citizens and not as members of Societies other than the State. And this is what the origin of our modern Constitutions very clearly shows. They were imposed on kings and they aimed at preventing the king from confusing the interests of the State with those of his dynasty—that is, of his Family or with his other private interests. The Constitution annulled the king's action when he acted as a private person in the name of the State. The Constitution was therefore a legal rule being applied to interactions between individuals and a *private person* (implicated in the concrete person of the king). By setting forth this rule, the State therefore acted as a *juridical* Legislator; and it is as a Judge that it applied it; it is as the judicial Police that it enforced its judgement. Now what is true for the monarchical Constitution [161] is true for all Constitutions in the broad sense—that is, also for all state-sanctioned Administrative Apparatuses.

One has always distinguished between the act of a member of the Government (king, minister, or civil servant) acting as a citizen, i.e., in the name of the Government, as a member of the Government, and his private act, when he acts as an isolated individual, or member of a Family, or of a Society other than the State. And in the latter case, one applied to him the common *Droit*—justifiably, without any doubt. In this case the State dealt with a private person [*particulier*] entering into interaction with other privates persons. The State, therefore, had only to apply its civil or penal *Droit.* But one must not forget that there is still a third case. The member of the Government can act in the name of the State and nevertheless pursue his private, non-political interest. And this interest does not need to be his strictly personal interest. It can also be that of his Family, or his "class," in general of a Society of which he is a member and which is not the State itself, being sub- or trans-political. Here as well there is an action of a private person [*personne privée*] such that the State can intervene in the capacity of a third and thus apply a *legal* rule. But this *Droit* will no longer be the common criminal or civil *Droit,* for the private person here acts in the name of the State while pretending or believing [himself] to act as a citizen, as a member of the Government representing the State as such. The legal rule which is applied to such cases will therefore be a part of a *sui generis Droit,* and this *Droit* is none other than the *Droit* called public, constitutional or administrative.

In sum, the Constitution (and "administrative *Droit*") is only a "guarantee" to the extent that it allows one to distinguish the cases when the members of the Government act[31] as such, i.e., as citizens, from cases when they act as private persons in the name of the State. In the first case, their acts are "constitutional"; in the second, they are "unconstitutional." And the Constitution is *juridical* only to the extent that it annuls the "unconstitutional" acts or when it provides for sanctions against the members of the Government acting in the name of the State as private persons (these sanctions generally—but wrongly—being inferred, not explicitly formulated). When a minister commits an unconstitutional act, he is supposed to have acted according to interests other than those of the State (consciously or not): he has acted in the name of the State, but it is not the citizen, i.e., the minister as such, who has acted in him. He has acted [162] (consciously or not) as a private person, and the State intervenes (by applying the juridical aspect of its Constitution) in order to annul this private action. As for the aspect of the Constitution which sets down the status of the State (and the citizens), it has nothing juridical about it. The

---

31. [Ed. Reading *agissent* for *agissant*.]

Constitution is created by the State and the State can change it when it wants and how it wants. No Constitution, moreover, presents itself as immutable, since it generally provides for the method that one must follow to amend it. But it is only the State itself which can change the Constitution. In other words, the Government which changes the Constitution must act as the Government: its members must act in their aspect as citizens, as members of the Government (in the broad sense, the Parliament being a Government, for example), and not as private persons, whomever they may be. And the method of change that the Constitution provides for aims at guaranteeing this condition: the formalities are supposed to be such that only men acting in their aspect as citizens can succeed in changing the Constitution. Of course, these guarantees are never sufficient in fact, and no Constitution has prevented a State from being a "class" State, where the Government acts in the name of the State in order to serve not the State as such but a sub- or trans-political Society, an economic or religious Society, for example. But it is such a guarantee that Constitutions have in mind. And they are juridical only to the extent that they allow the State to intervene in the cases when private persons want to act in the name of the State. It is against these private persons that the State intervenes as a Judge. Now, as long as the Constitution is not changed in a "constitutional" way, i.e., by citizens acting as citizens, any person whomever acting in a way contrary to the Constitution is assumed to be acting as a private person, even if he acts in the name of the State, being a member of its Government.

To have recourse to the Constitution regarding a governmental act, therefore, is to assert that the Government (or its member) acts in this case not as a citizen but as a private person; and this is [supposed] to incite the State, i.e., the Government taken as such, to act as a state-sanctioned Judge—that is, as a third against itself taken as a private person. And this action will be effectively juridical, for the State (by its Government) will judge an interaction with a private person other than itself, even if this person is its Government; for if this Government acted contrary to the [163] Constitution in its capacity as the Government, i.e., as the State itself, it would have been able to change the Constitution so as to render its action "constitutional." If the Government cannot [do] so, it is because it does not act as the Government, it is because it is not the State itself in its action. And then the State is a third in relation to it and its action against it can be that of a Judge.

It is in this sense and this sense only that there is a constitutional and administrative *Droit;* for it makes no sense to say that there is a *droit* toward the State as such. The Constitution (in the broad sense, i.e., the totality of laws regulating the structure of the State, its administrative apparatuses, and the status of its citizens taken as citizens) is applied by the State, and if one invoked it against the State, it would simultaneously be party and Judge, which is juridically absurd. Moreover, it is the State which creates its Constitution and it is only valid as long as the State applies it. When the State acts against the Constitution as a State, it repeals it purely and simply, and no one can have any complaint about that. But as long as the State keeps it, it has two very distinct functions. On the one hand, it describes the structure that the State gives itself at the epoch when the Constitution is valid; and it is useful to know what is right [*au juste*] in a given State, although this knowledge has nothing to do with *Droit,* being a purely political knowledge. On the other hand, the Constitution allows one to distinguish between acts of State and private acts wrongly performed in the name of the State, in which case the State can intervene in its capacity as Judge in order to annul these acts to the extent that they generate conflicts with the "administered." In its juridical aspect, the Constitution and "public *Droit*" in general only affect private acts made to appear as state-sanctioned actions. As for truly state-sanctioned acts, they have nothing juridical about them: since they are performed by the State as such, they cannot be judged by this State, and since there is no *Droit* (in actuality) in a State other than that which this State itself applies.[32]

§ 24

[164] Inside a State, state-sanctioned *Droit* is the only *Droit* existing in actuality. All *Droit* is a "positive" *Droit*. *Droit* is the juridical Law enacted by the Government. And it makes no sense to oppose a "natural *Droit*" or "Custom"

---

32. One often says that the parliamentary monarchical Constitution (English, for example) limits royal power. This is false. It only prevents the king from acting as a private person in the name of the State, from seeing that the State serves his private interests, for example, [his] dynastic [interests]; for if the king acts as a citizen, i.e., as king, as the Government, he is supposed to be in accord (according to the Constitution) with the other citizens (represented by the Parliament). And indeed, if he is in accord with the citizens (i.e., if he has the assent of Parliament), he can "do what he wants." His truly *political* power, therefore, is not at all limited. The Constitution limits, or indeed annuls, the power of the king when he is at odds with the Parliament. [164] But this is because, according to this Constitution, the king in this case did not act as a king, i.e., as the Government embodying the State, but as a private person. And what is true for the king is true for whatever Government: a Constitution only limits governmental action in the case when the Government would like to act not as a Government but as a private person, representing interests other than those of the State—that is, of its citizens *taken as citizens.* But this is only true in principle. In fact (in a non-homogenous State) the Constitution does not "guarantee" the political interests of all the citizens, but only those of the governors, of the exclusive political group. Now, practically speaking, this group is also a non-political Society, first and foremost economic, a "class."

If the "individual" does not have any **droit** in respect to the State, he does not have a *juridical duty* toward it either; for there is nothing juridical when there is no *third.* Now, in *droit* as in duty in respect to the State, the State is by definition a party and therefore cannot be a third. And as there is not in the State another *Droit* in actuality than state-sanctioned *Droit,* there is nothing juridical in the (positive or negative) relations with the State. But it does not follow from this that there is a risk of the arbitrary from both sides. The individuals (and Societies, Families) have without any doubt duties in respect to the State and the State has duties in respect to them. But these duties are *political* and not juridical. Just as one distinguishes *moral* or *religious* duties from *juridical* duty, one must also distinguish from the latter *political* duties. And [one does so] for the same reason: in none of these cases is there the intervention of a *third.* In the moral duty, I myself am my "Judge"; in the religious duty, God is simultaneously "Judge" and party; and it is the same in the political duty, when it is the State which is both the "Judge" and the party. Now, when there is no Judge distinct from the parties, there is nothing juridical about it.

to it; for one does not oppose a simple potentiality to actuality. There is no *Droit* opposable to the State; no one has a *droit* in respect to the Government taken as such: for all *droits* exist only inside of state-sanctioned *Droit*, and this *Droit* is nothing other than the totality of the State's juridical prescriptions. It is the Government which creates the actual *Droit*, and it can alter it when and how it wants.

This is the way a Kelsen sees things nowadays. This is the way a Hobbes, a Bentham, and an Austin saw them.[33] But this point of view has always been criticized. It has been objected that there is an idea or ideal of Justice, independent of state-sanctioned or governmental positive *Droit*, and opposable to [165] this *Droit*. It is undeniable that one distinguishes between a "just *Droit*" and an "unjust *Droit*" when one speaks of a positive *Droit*. And the "statists [*étatistes*]" are certainly wrong to respond that the category of Justice opposed to positive *Droit* is a purely moral, not juridical, category. When one describes a positive *Droit* as "unjust," one opposes to it not a morality or a religion, but a (just) **Droit**. Nevertheless, the statists are correct to say that it makes no sense to oppose a "just *Droit*" to the positive *Droit*; for there is no *Droit* without a sanction and the State alone is capable of sanctioning a *Droit*. There is then no *Droit* outside of the *Droit* sanctioned by the State—that is, outside of positive *Droit*. The State, i.e., the Government, has at its sovereign disposal the content of *Droit*.

I think that one cannot put an end to this debate without resorting to the distinction between *Droit* in actuality and *Droit* in potentiality. The idea or ideal of Justice is truly a juridical idea, and not moral or religious. It is even the "principle" of *Droit* as such, of all *Droit* and consequently of all "positive" *Droit*. Without this idea, *Droit* can neither be born nor remain in existence. But in the first place, Justice is only the "principle" or the source of *Droit*: it is still not *Droit*. Justice becomes *Droit*, i.e., a juridical entity in the full sense of the word, only if it is applied to whatever social interactions (allowing such an application). One cannot, therefore, oppose to a *Droit* Justice as such. One can only oppose to it another **Droit**, i.e., another application of Justice, or an application of another Justice, to social interactions; for, second, the idea of Justice is not given once and for all. It also evolves in time. One cannot, therefore, oppose to a positive *Droit* a natural *Droit*, valid everywhere and always. Absolute *Droit* will only exist at the end of history, being the correct application of the idea of Justice worked out in the universal and homogenous State for social interactions existing in this State. Up until then, to speak of an "unjust" positive *Droit* can only mean two things. Either one means by it that the "unjust" positive *Droit* is not correctly applying the idea of Justice which is at its base; or one is asserting that this very idea is false or insufficient. In that

---

33. [Ed. Perhaps references to Thomas Hobbes, *Leviathan*, ed. Edwin Curley (Indianapolis: Hackett Publishing Co., 1994), 89, 172–6; Jeremy Bentham, *An Introduction to the Principles of Morals and Legislation*, ed. J. H. Burns and H. L. A. Hart (London: The Athlone Press, 1970); and John Austin, *The Province of Jurisprudence Determined* (London: Weidenfeld and Nicolson, 1954).]

case one opposes to the positive *Droit* in question another *Droit,* based upon another idea of Justice (cf. Part Two). Finally, third, one must not forget that one and the same idea of Justice, realized in and by a *Droit,* can exist either in actuality or [166] in potentiality. In the two cases, there will be a *Droit,* and this *Droit* will be real. But when a real *Droit* in actuality is opposed to a real *Droit* in potentiality, the latter will have to recede [*s'effacer*] as all reality in potentiality recedes before a reality in actuality, as the egg recedes from the chicken that is hatched from it.

Sumner Maine[34] has objected to Austin that a lot of Governments, even "despotic," i.e., fully and absolutely "sovereign," have never enacted juridical laws and have not meddled in the juridical life of their subjects. And he has stressed the fact that *Droit* is born before States, that there are non-state-sanctioned, "customary" *Droits.* Without any doubt, these remarks are correct. But one can also prove Austin (and Kelsen) correct if one distinguishes *Droit* in actuality from *Droit* in potentiality.

As long as Society was not organized into a State, but was nevertheless a (practically) "autonomous" society, there was a *Droit* in it, and this *Droit* was real in actuality. But as soon as this Society organizes itself into a State, it stops being autonomous as a non-state-sanctioned Society: it is only autonomous as a State. As a result, its *Droit* only exists in potentiality to the extent that it has not become state-sanctioned. It is the *Droit* accepted and sanctioned, or created, by the State which alone exists in actuality. That which is not accepted by the State becomes a simple "custom." This is without any doubt a *Droit,* but it no longer exists except in potentiality. And it makes no sense to oppose this potentiality to the actuality of state-sanctioned *Droit.* To do so would be to want to actualize or re-actualize the potentiality, the "custom," and this is equivalent to the desire to overcome the actuality of state-sanctioned *Droit.* In other words, one either wants to turn the custom into state-sanctioned *Droit,* by imposing it on the Government, or one wants to overcome the Government and thus to return to a pre-state-sanctioned State. In neither of the two cases, therefore, does one oppose a *Droit* in potentiality to a *Droit* in actuality. And one cannot effectively do so. One simply wants to replace a *Droit* in actuality by another *Droit* in actuality, which will be a governmental or "positive," state-sanctioned *Droit,* every time that the Society where this substitution is carried out will continue to be a State. However, one must not think that the Government (the "sovereign") ought necessarily to abolish the old *Droit* or create its *Droit* from start to finish. The Government of a Society organized into a State may very well limit itself to making its own the *Droit* which reigned in this Society before it became a State. [167] And in this case there will not even be a passage from potentiality to actuality, since the old non-state-sanctioned *Droit* was actual as long as there was no State. It stopped being so only when the State

---

34. Cf. *Historie des institutions primitives,* chapters XII-XIII [Henry Sumner Maine, *Lectures on the Early History of Institutions,* 7th ed. (Port Washington, NY: Kennikat Press, 1966), 342–400].

was born. But if this State makes it its own, it once again becomes actual. One can therefore say that it has never stopped being so, that the transformation of the Society into the State has not affected the juridical aspect of its existence. The non-state-sanctioned ("customary") *Droit* was actual as long as there was no State, and it remained actual without having changed its content in the State by the fact that it became state-sanctioned. But if it had not become state-sanctioned, it would have passed from actuality to potentiality, and one could not then oppose it to the actual *Droit* of the State; for in the State, *Droit* is only actual through governmental sanction, and one cannot oppose to actuality what only exists in potentiality.

Sumner Maine is therefore wrong to criticize the principle which is at the base of the arguments of a Bentham and an Austin, namely the principle according to which "the Sovereign prescribes all that he does not forbid." Indeed, the Government sanctions a "custom," i.e., a *Droit* which was originally non-state-sanctioned, by the sole fact that it does not repeal it and allows its application; for *Droit* stops existing as *Droit* (and once again becomes a pure and simple ideal of Justice) as soon as it is not sanctioned, as soon as the Judge no longer has at his disposal an irresistible force (in principle) to enforce his judgements. Now this force does not exist where the litigant can escape judgement by fleeing, by leaving the Society where the *Droit* is supposed to be valid. But as soon as this Society is organized into a State, it is only the Government which can prevent him from doing this, since it is the Government which represents the Society in its relations with the outside, which draws the (in principle) impassable limit which separates friends from enemies. The State, therefore, always sanctions in the final analysis the *Droit* which is supposed to be valid, and it is only thanks to this state or governmental sanction that *Droit* exists in actuality. All *Droit* openly exercised in a State, i.e., with the explicit or tacit approval of the Government, is therefore a state-sanctioned *Droit*. And in this State one cannot oppose to it any other *Droit*. Of course, if the new State makes do with sanctioning (tacitly, for example) the old, non-state-sanctioned *Droit*, one can say with Sumner Maine that it has changed nothing from the juridical point of view. But one must add with Austin that by this sanction it has turned a non-state-sanctioned *Droit* (existing in actuality) into a state-sanctioned *Droit* (existing in actuality), and that henceforth [168] only the state-sanctioned *Droit* can have an actual existence. Everything that the State did not want to sanction in the old *Droit* stops existing in actuality, and everything that the State will subsequently reject will also fall again into a state of potentiality, which will make no sense to oppose to the actuality of state-sanctioned *Droit*, it being of little importance that it be an old "custom" sanctioned by the Government, or a new *Droit*, created from start to finish by this Government and perhaps contrary to the old *Droit*. As long as the "customary" *Droit* is not in conflict with the state-sanctioned *Droit*, one cannot say—as Sumner Maine does—that the "custom" is only an actual *Droit* thanks to the sanction of the State, as Austin says. But as soon as the State removes its sanction, i.e., alters or repeals the custom, one sees immediately that it falls back into a state of simple potentiality which it would be futile to want to oppose to the actual state-sanctioned *Droit*—unless one wanted to impose it by force on the Government (which is equivalent to a violent change of Government) or to try to overcome the latter as such. But in this case it would be a matter of a political revolution (carried out or attempted for juridical reasons), which no longer has anything juridical in itself. It is not the juridical entity of the old *Droit* that one then opposes to the state-sanctioned *Droit*: it is a political action that one opposes to the political reality of the State, [which is] supposed to result in either a violent change of its nature or its total suppression.

Inside a Society organized into a State, therefore, only state-sanctioned or governmental *Droit* exists in actuality: *Droit* in actuality is what the Government decrees to be such. This does not mean, however, that the Government has the power and the possibility to give any content whatsoever to the actual or "positive" *Droit*. And Sumner Maine is perfectly correct to remark that it is ridiculous to assert that the British Government, for example, can introduce polygamy into England or authorize murder. One only means that all that the Government has *effectively* been able to promulgate in fact as juridical laws is juridically valid. It does not make sense to oppose to *effective* state-sanctioned *Droit* either a would-be universal "natural *Droit*" or a particular "custom"; for all *Droit* other than the actual state-sanctioned *Droit* exists and can exist in the State only as a *Droit* in potentiality.

But the existence of a *Droit* in potentiality next to a *Droit* in actuality is not at all without importance. And it is very important to know if this *Droit* in potentiality agrees with or not [169] the actual *Droit* promulgated by the Government. And it is these relations between state-sanctioned *Droit* in actuality and the *Droit* or *Droits* in potentiality that we must now study.

Droit can only exist in actuality provided that [it] has at its disposal a force (in principle irresistible) which sanctions it and makes it respected, as one says. Now in a Society organized into a State, only the Government can provide this force. And this is why state-sanctioned *Droit* alone is an actual *Droit* there. But in any human reality whatsoever, force is never but a substitute for Authority. Force can and must be applied when Authority is lacking. But Authority ought to be lacking as little as possible; it always ought to replace force as much as possible, making it useless. And it is not otherwise in the juridical sphere. Here as well the legal rule must be valid (as much as possible) because of its Authority, and not on the grounds of the force that is connected to it.

Now it is the Government or the State which has at its disposal the force in a Society organized into a State. The "customary" *Droit*, i.e., non-state-sanctioned, not accepted and sanctioned by the Government, does not have force at its disposal, and this is precisely why it is said to exist only in potentiality. If it exists all the same, i.e., if it is *real* while only being in potentiality, it is because it enjoys an Authority. State-sanctioned *Droit*, by contrast, can only exist in actuality thanks to the use of force. But if the State is content to sanction and make its own a *Droit* which has existed, or which is supposed to be able to exist, without state sanction, i.e., without the use of force, one can admit that this state-sanctioned *Droit* also enjoys an Authority in the Society in question.

It is in this sense that "anti-state" theoreticians like Sumner Maine oppose "custom" to (juridical) "law." One says that a state-sanctioned or "legal" *Droit* can have Authority only when it adopts a "custom," being content with clarifying and developing it, and that it becomes "tyrannical," having to resort to brute force, every time that it is at odds with the "customary" *Droit*. Moreover, [since] force is never able to replace completely (and in the long run) Authority, the Government cannot even practically assert a *Droit* which would be completely at odds with the valid "custom." It is in this way that the British government cannot introduce polygamy in England or authorize murder. Even if it succeeded in enacting corresponding juridical laws, they would not be obeyed, unless the government tried to impose them [170] by force alone. But in this case it would sooner or later fail, and it would either have to repeal its laws or perish with them.

Without any doubt, *Droit* in general, and state-sanctioned or "legal" *Droit* in particular, must rest as much as possible on Authority. But it is not true that the State must always accept custom, that it cannot change it without becoming "despotic," without having to support its anti-customary *Droit* through brute force alone.

And first of all, of which "custom" is it a question?

Without any doubt at all, in the vast majority of cases, it is not a question of unanimity. Even in the least extensive and heterogenous Society, one will always find individuals or groups which do not recognize the Authority of such legal rules or even of state-sanctioned *Droit* as a whole. The "custom" in question is nothing other than the *Droit* whose Authority is recognized by an "exclusive juridical group." It is the *Droit* which correctly applies to social interactions the ideal of Justice accepted in this group. This group then constitutes a kind of juridical "Parliament," a "standing Assembly," which reveals the Authority which the positive *Droit* has at its disposal. If the actual state-sanctioned *Droit* is in agreement with the *Droit* in potentiality that is valid in the group in question, one can say that it has a recognized Authority. If not, it will have to be said to rest upon brute force alone. In this case, one will be in the presence of an "unjust" positive *Droit*. In the other case, the actual state-sanctioned *Droit* will be simultaneously a "positive" and "just" *Droit*.

Let us assume that the "exclusive juridical group" is at the same time the "exclusive political group" in the State, which is, moreover, the "normal" case. The "just" *Droit* will then be the *Droit* whose Authority is recognized by the governors (administered or administrators). In this case, the Government put out by the governors will automatically adopt, so to speak, the "customary" *Droit* of the exclusive political and juridical group. The state-sanctioned or "legal" *Droit*, therefore, will rest upon Authority. The actual *Droit* will then actualize a *Droit* which also exists in potentiality. The actuality, therefore, will not be separated from, [or] deprived of, its potentiality. This will therefore be a "potent" actuality, i.e., efficacious or robust: it will be able to keep itself indefinitely in existence while remaining identical to itself.

But experience shows the juridical group does not coincide everywhere and always with the political group. In this case, the Government can decree the *Droit* appropriate to [171] the governing group, and this *Droit* can be at odds with the *Droit* recognized by the juridical group. In this case, the positive *Droit* will be called "unjust," and it will rest—generally speaking—upon force, and not upon Authority. Now a *human* reality resting upon brute force (i.e., animal, "inhuman") cannot be efficacious in the long run. It will not be able to exist indefinitely by remaining what it is. And the same applies for *Droit*. If the state-sanctioned *Droit* is at odds with the "customary" *Droit*, it is because the *Droit* exists in actuality (as "law") without also existing in potentiality (as the "custom" recognized by the juridical group). This will be, therefore, an actuality separated from and deprived of its potentiality: an actuality without potentiality, an impotent actuality.

One can wonder how an entity without potentiality succeeds in existing in actuality, or even simply in being real. This is because the actuality without potentiality is the actuality which has exhausted its potentiality by actualizing it completely. There was a time when this entity was supported by the potentiality which it was in the process of actualizing. It is this potentiality which has carried it to existence, to reality, and it is as the actualization of this potentiality that it has existed and exists in actuality. But if this actuality has exhausted the potentiality by actualizing it *completely*, the entity will not be able to keep itself indefinitely in the present [*l'actualité*], nor even in any reality whatsoever: it will entirely pass into—sooner or later—the ideality of the past. And this general ontological law also applies to our case. The "unjust" *Droit* can exist in actuality because it has once been "just," because it has actualized a customary *Droit* accepted by the exclusive juridical group of the epoch by making it state-sanctioned. But it has completely exhausted this "custom" by totally realizing it in actuality, and it is in this way that it has become "impotent," or indeed perishable, or indeed "unjust"; for the exhausted potentiality, actualized, has in the meantime been replaced by another, which is no longer actualized by the actual *Droit* in question and which is still not actualized by an actual *Droit* which is appropriate to it. Thus, it tends toward actuality, and it tries to overcome the actuality of the old potentiality. The actual state-sanctioned *Droit* can only oppose to it force alone: the cadaver or mummy of its old Authority. As for the new "customary" *Droit*, it can only oppose to the force of the state-sanctioned *Droit* the Authority of the custom. But Authority ends by defeating force, because a potentiality tending to actuality is more potent than the actuality which has become impotent by exhausting, i.e., actualizing, its potentiality. The old *Droit* is worn out because it has been efficacious: [172] it is no longer efficacious because it has been so. It will sooner or later yield, therefore, its place to the new state-sanctioned *Droit*, which will actualize the new juridical potentiality, until it exhausts it in its turn. And this game will continue until the juridical group will have stopped being *exclusive*, by encompassing humanity as a whole. But this will take place only in the universal and homogenous State—that is, at the end of (historical) time.[35]

Be that as it may, when state-sanctioned *Droit* or the juridical "Law" (oral or written) does not actualize the "custom" (oral or written), there is a conflict of *Droits*, a juridical conflict. Now, the one who says conflict says contradiction, and every contradiction tends to overcome itself; for contradiction is the expression of nothingness: to actualize it is therefore to "actualize" nothingness—that is, to annihilate [it]. And everything that is—and the contradiction also exists—tends to existence in actuality: the contradiction, therefore, tends to its own annihilation.

But there are various ways to annihilate a contradiction—that is, to resolve a conflict. There are then various ways to resolve the conflict between Law and Custom, to overcome the unjust *Droit* or the injustice of the *Droit*.

The juridical group can throw out the old political group and put itself in its place. Its *Droit* will then become a state-sanctioned *Droit*, which will be "just" or based upon Authority. In this case there will be a *political revolution,* a change of the governing group, this revolution having had a juridical cause, a need to change *Droit* and the ideal of Justice. One changes the governing group, one alters the State, in order to replace an unjust *Droit* by a just *Droit*.

But the juridical group may not succeed in making itself a political group. The State and the Government will therefore remain in the hands of the old group. But the juridical group can "educate" the political group and induce it [173] to accept the *Droit* appropriate to the juridical group. Now, the state sanctioned *Droit* will still be "just," but the change will be carried out without a revolution. There will be a *political evolution,* a peaceful transformation of the ideas of the governing group. And this political evolution will also have had juridical causes, a need for just *Droit*.

Or once again, the juridical group will be able neither to replace nor to alter the political group. In these conditions the conflict will be able to be resolved only by the annihilation of the governing group. Two cases then arise. In the first, the ruin of the governing group will have as a consequence not only the fall of the State but the annihilation of the Society as an autonomous Society. And in this case there will no longer be actual *Droit* at all. In the second case, the ruin of the governing group, i.e., the State, will not bring about the disap-

---

35. At first glance, this schema is Aristotelian; but in reality it is Hegelian—that is, dialectical or historical (human) and not biological (natural). For Aristotle, the new potentiality is the *potentiality* of the actuality which has actualized the old potentiality: the chicken, born from the egg, lays a new egg, and so on infinitely. For Hegel, by contrast, the new potentiality is the impotence of the actuality, which therefore disappears without returning: the new potentiality is actualized in and by an actuality which is essentially other than the preceding actuality. Because for Hegel, the new potentiality is the *negation* of the actuality: the antithesis of the thesis which only maintains itself in this way as a synthesis. The Christian Middle Ages is born from Antiquity, but it has "laid" [i.e., the egg of] Modernity, which is, if you will, a "Rebirth [*Renaissance*]" of pagan Antiquity, i.e., its synthesis with Christianity, but not a simple return to paganism.

pearance of the autonomous Society. This will then exist as an autonomous apolitical or politically "neutral" Society, and it will be able to have an actual just *Droit*. But an apolitical or politically "neutral" Society is not supposed to have "enemies." Now, in fact, all limited Societies have "enemies" (and this is why it must organize itself into a State or be divided between [several] States). It will not, therefore, be able to maintain itself indefinitely: either it will have to defend itself against its "enemies," and then it will be organized into a State (we revert, therefore, to the first case of a political revolution) or it will stop being autonomous and will then no longer have a *Droit* in actuality. An apolitical Society, therefore, will only be able to have an actual, permanent *Droit* provided that it is universal, encompassing all of humanity. But if the Society is universal, the juridical group coincides with the political group such that all conflict between state-sanctioned *Droit* and customary *Droit* is impossible. In this limit Society, *Droit* is "just" by definition and it will no longer ever change.

One can therefore say that the conflict between an unjust state-sanctioned *Droit* and a just customary *Droit* can only be resolved by a political revolution or evolution, but never by the simple suppression of the political sphere—that is, of the State. And when, at the limit, the State and politics will be overcome in the universal Society (i.e., without "enemies"), there will no longer be conflict over *Droit*—that is, no longer political revolutions or evolutions for juridical causes.

So far, we have assumed that the State keeps an outdated *Droit,* having lost its Authority [and] becoming unjust. But it [174] is possible that the terms of the conflict be reversed. The State, i.e., the Government and the governing group, can actualize the new *Droit* while the exclusive juridical group can retain in potentiality the old state-sanctioned *Droit.* The new state-sanctioned *Droit* will still be "unjust" because at odds with the *Droit* adopted by the juridical group: it will rest upon force and not upon Authority. But now the conflict will be resolved differently.[36]

The governing group will be able to replace the juridical group, making itself a juridical group in its place. State-sanctioned *Droit* will then become a

---

36. According to the Hegelian dialectic, which proceeds by negation and ends in synthesis, a return is not possible. It can have a momentary stop and even a total destruction again, but never a return backwards. In principle, history can at every instant lose itself in anarchy. But if history continues, it will either be stationary or there will always be something new. Thus, as soon as a new *Droit* appears, all return backwards becomes impossible: for to negate this new *Droit* is not to come back to the old as it existed before the appearance of the new; to negate it is to create yet a new *Droit,* a synthesis of the old and the new that one has negated. But if one does not negate a given *Droit,* it can maintain itself indefinitely. Each new stage is the *negation* of the given stage; it is therefore an act of *freedom,* which means precisely that it would have been able never to take place (being "impossible"). All new *Droit,* therefore, is an optional negation of a given *Droit.* And as soon as this negation has taken place, one can no longer come back to the negated *Droit;* for to negate the new *Droit* is to negate the negation of the old. And in dialectical or historical reality, the not-not-A is not A but C, [which], being the synthesis of the thesis A and the antithesis not-A (= B), is other than A and not-A.

just *Droit*. And it can be said that one has carried out a *juridical revolution*. And this juridical revolution will be generated by a political revolution; for the governing stratum [*couche*] could have introduced a new "unjust" *Droit*, i.e., not accepted by the juridical group, only because it is a new stratum, established by a revolution.

But it is also possible that the governing group does not replace the old juridical group. Then the conflict will only be able to be resolved provided that the governing group succeeds in altering the ideology of the juridical group. If it succeeds, its *Droit* will become just, and there will have been a *juridical evolution*. This has been generated by a political evolution, since it is the political group which will have changed the *Droit* that the juridical group would have wanted to retain intact.

Or once again, the governing group may overcome the conflict only by overcoming the juridical group as such. But then there will no longer be a *Droit* based upon Authority. The state-sanctioned *Droit* will rest upon brute force and it will therefore perish sooner [175] or later: and the State itself will perish in this juridical anarchy unless the State can do without *Droit*. But this is only possible if there are no conflicts between its citizens, which can only take place (in principle) when the State is perfectly homogenous. Now, in the limit case of the homogenous State, there is no distinction between the juridical group and the political group. Therefore, if the State was able to exist without *droit*, it would not have within it juridical conflicts, the *Droit* being "just" by definition.

In other words, either there will not be juridical conflict between two *Droits*, or it will not be able to be resolved by the simple suppression of the juridical sphere. The new unjust *Droit* will have to become a just *Droit*, and it will only be able to become so following a juridical revolution or evolution.

In this way, therefore, a conflict between an unjust (state-sanctioned) *Droit* and a just (customary) *Droit* is always either the consequence or the cause of a political revolution, which—at the limit—can look like an "evolution." And *Droit* and the State are going to "evolve" or be transformed by "revolutions" as long as the definitive just *Droit* will not be realized in and by the universal and homogenous State.

Now if it happens that a juridical evolution or revolution provokes a political evolution or revolution, one can wonder from where this evolution or revolution comes—that is, how and why a new *Droit* is born which shows the old *Droit* as an "unjust" *droit*.

I will endeavor to show in Part Two that *Droit* changes as a result of change in the idea or ideal of Justice.[37] But I would like to point out even here that the transformation of *Droit* is a phenomenon a lot more complex than the change of the idea of Justice.

---

37. The appearance of new social interactions can force a given *Droit* to develop, but not to be abandoned, as long as the ideal of Justice remains intact, such that even if the change of social relations changes the *Droit*, it does so only through a change in the ideal of Justice.

"Just" *Droit* is a *Droit* based upon Authority, and a *Droit* stops being "just," becoming "unjust," as soon as it loses its Authority. Now the specific juridical Authority is of the "Judge" type (cf. my analysis of the Notion of Authority).[38] A man or collectivity have this Authority when they are deemed to be "impartial" or "equitable"—that is, when they embody Justice, so to speak. Now, since *Droit* is nothing other than a realization or embodiment of Justice, the Authority which is appropriate to it is clearly of the "Judge" type. [176] To say that a given *Droit* enjoys an Authority J is to say that it is a "just" *Droit*.

But the three other types of Authority, i.e., the Authorities of the "Father," "Master," and "Leader" [*Chef*], can equally be met with in the juridical sphere, just as they are met with in the political sphere. Thus, a *Droit* can have Authority not because it is "just" (Authority J) but because it is "traditional," being applied for a very long time (Authority F). Or once again, it will have a rational [and] fitting Authority, easily applicable to new or complicated interactions, and so on (Authority L). Or finally, it can have Authority simply because it is working and efficacious, because it is a *Droit* in force, existing in actuality (Authority M). And it should be understood that all these juridical Authorities can be combined between them, the combinations also differing by the relative weight of their various elements. Of course, *Droit* is authentically "just" only if it enjoys the Authority J. But it is also possible that a *Droit* may be considered unjust solely because it is missing Authority F, and so on.

Therefore, one sees the complexity of possible juridical conflicts, particularly of those between a state-sanctioned *Droit* and a customary *Droit*. But this is not all.

We have seen, and we will yet see (§ 25), that *Droit* is inseparable from the Society or the State where it is realized. If a State or Society cannot exist without *Droit*, neither can *Droit* exist in actuality without a State or an autonomous Society. And state-sanctioned *Droit* is nothing other than the realization and manifestation of this interdependence between the State and *Droit*. At any rate, *Droit* will always endeavor to support the State which applies it, just as the State will endeavor to keep the *Droit* which is appropriate to it. It will then be possible that a *Droit* will have Authority not because it is a *Droit* of a given juridical character (corresponding to a given idea of Justice) but because it is the *Droit* of such and such a State. Of course, the Authority of *Droit* in this case will not be authentically juridical: it will be a political Authority being exercised (wrongly) in the sphere of *Droit*. But in fact, even the *Droit* enjoying a political Authority will be considered "just" and opposed to the *Droit* which will be called "unjust" solely because the State does not recognize it as its own.

The State (or Society) acts not only politically but also juridically, in its aspect as juridical Legislator, Judge, and judicial Police. And it is in [177] this

---

38. [Ed. This analysis on the notion of authority is a separate manuscript of over 100 handwritten pages that was apparently completed around the same time as the *Outline* itself (1942). The original manuscript is among Kojève's personal papers and remains unpublished to date.]

aspect above all that it enjoys the Authority of the type J. Now it is possible that a *Droit* (state-sanctioned, for example) is said to be "just" solely because it is created or applied by the juridical aspect of a State enjoying Authority J (in this aspect). Of course, to recognize the authority of a judgement because it is pronounced by a judge that one believes to be "just" (or by a representative of the State that one knows to be "just") is quite different from recognizing this same judgement because one sees that it is conforming to the idea of Justice that one accepts. And it is only in this second case that the Authority of the judgement (and therefore of the legal rule which is at its base) will be authentically juridical. But even in the first case one is, as it were, not too far removed from authenticity. By contrast, one is farther removed from it if one connects to a *Droit* a political Authority other than that of type J; for it is also possible that one recognizes the Authority of a state-sanctioned *Droit* solely because, for example, one recognizes the Authority F of a State. In other words, one can voluntarily submit to a *Droit* not because it is conforming to an ideal of justice, nor even because it is traditional itself, but only because it is promulgated by a State having a venerable past. Or again, one can authorize [*faire passer sur*] *Droit* through the political Authority of the M or L type—and so forth. And it is obvious that not only *Droit* can enjoy all possible combinations of political Authorities, but that this political Authority of *Droit* can be combined with any juridical Authority at all.

One thus sees the almost infinite complexity of possible relations between a "just" *Droit* and an "unjust" *Droit*, and of the very notion of a "just" *Droit*, i.e., accepted on the grounds of its (juridical or political) Authority and not imposed by force: one sees that one and the same *Droit* can be "just" from a certain point of view (juridical or political) and "unjust" from the other. But one must not forget that a *Droit* is *authentically* "just" only if it enjoys the *juridical* Authority of type J—that is, if it is supposed to realize correctly the ideal of Justice accepted by the exclusive juridical group of a given Society (organized or not into a State).

I do not have the intention to pursue the analysis of the complex problem I have just pointed out. But I would still like to say a few words about the general dialectical relation which exists between *Droit*, and the Society or State which realizes it.

§ 25

[178] Every entity, whatever it may be, if it is still ideal and not real, tends to go from ideality to reality: every "possibility" tends to be realized and is realized one day, if the time is sufficiently long, for otherwise it would be "impossible." And every non-actual real entity tends to go from potentiality to actuality. Now this passage has a dual aspect. On the one hand, the real entity tends to maintain itself indefinitely in existence by remaining identical to itself: it tends to *preserve* itself. On the other hand, it tends to *propagate*, to expand itself as much as possible, to absorb the totality of real being, to be assimilated to it

entirely and completely. Now in these two aspects the tendency to actuality comes up against an external resistance which also tends to "propagate" by absorbing, i.e., by annulling, the entity in question. There is then a contradiction inside reality as such: there is a conflict and a struggle. And this contradiction, inherent in reality itself, is encountered in all that is real. It is in this way that the two complementary aspects of the tendency to actuality enter into conflict with one another and mutually "contradict" each other.

This conflict, immanent in the real entity in the process of being actualized, is particularly obvious when the entity in question is a biological reality, a living being, an animal for example. Every animal tends to preserve itself and to propagate: there is always an instinct of self-preservation (defense and food) and an instinct of propagation (sexuality). Now these two instincts are contradictory. And one often sees that the animal must die in order to generate, in order to propagate. But on the plane of "natural" reality (i.e., non-human or non-historical) this immanent contradiction is not dialectical: it does not end in a synthesis; it remains in identity and resolves itself by identity; and this is why it does not lead to a creative evolution, to a progress, to an *historical* process. The not-not-A is here equal to A. If the individual producer is sacrificed to reproduction (propagation), the negation of this, i.e., the fixation of the reproductive process in and by the product, leads back to the point of departure, to the individual: the individual product is identical to the individual producer, and this is why the process is repeated indefinitely. This is because the negated entity is negated absolutely and not dialectically: it is annihilated in and by the negation and is not preserved [179] as negated—that is, as altered or "evolved." If the animal dies in order to propagate, it disappears completely while leaving the place free. And it is in this way that it can be repeated by what is born from the negation of the negation: the animal which is born, and which stops, which thus negates the process of *propagation,* since the newborn is *preserved,* can be *identical* to the animal which died in order to generate it, which has been negated as preserving in order to exist as propagating.[39]

---

39. One speaks of a biological "evolution" that one likens to the historical evolution. But this is anthropomorphism. Biological evolution exists for us, for man, and not in Nature, for the animal which "evolves." And this is why the animal does not evolve in reality but remains *identical* to itself, or perishes completely. The ancestor of the horse was not a horse, and the horse is not its ancestor. One notices that one species *replaces* the other, but one cannot say that one species *becomes* another—turning into, evolving, progressing. Moreover, modern biology rejects Lamarckism. The animal is impermeable to external influences; it does not transmit them to its descendants. If it changes, it changes through spontaneous "mutations." But a "mutation" is not an evolution, nor even a change properly so-called. A "mutation" is equivalent to a simple replacement of one species by another. [Ed. Based on the evolutionary theories of Jean-Baptiste de Monet, chevalier de Lamarck (1744–1829), Lamarckism basically states that animals will develop certain characteristics necessary for survival, and that they can pass on these acquired characteristics to their offspring. Although Lamarckism was largely abandoned in the twentieth century, it did hold great sway in the former U.S.S.R. during the 1930s, and ultimately stunted Soviet genetics research.]

Among man, by contrast, on the plane of human or historical reality, the contradiction between the actualization by preservation and that by indefinite propagation is dialectical. It is resolved not in and by an identity, a repetition, a return backwards, but in and by a totality, a synthesis, an evolution, a progress. For the negation is here dialectical: it preserves what is negated, but preserves it as negated—that is, altered and evolved. The not-A is not zero but B. The negation of pagan Antiquity is not the ruin of humanity but its "evolved" existence—the Christian Middle Ages. Now, if the negated is preserved while changing, it does not leave its place free. The not-A is B and this B has taken the place of A. The not-not-A can therefore be neither B nor A: it is a new, evolved entity—it is C. And just as B, being not-A, is still A, C, being not-B, i.e., not-not-A, is still B and therefore A. A has become C after having been B: from being the thesis [*thétique*] that it was, it has become synthetic after having been antithetic. And as synthetic, it has a *history*. The negation of the Christian Middle Ages is not a return to pagan Antiquity but an historical evolution or progress, leading to the synthesis of Modernity, beginning with a Renaissance of Antiquity.

If a human reality obstinately persists in *preserving* itself, in maintaining itself in identity with itself, it may succeed in doing so. But [180] then it will not succeed in *propagating* itself, in expanding itself indefinitely. It will have to negate itself as identical, it will have to change, evolve, or progress, to be subject to an historical process, if it wants to continue to expand itself. And if it is in the process of expansion, it will still have to change if it wants to maintain itself in existence by preserving its identity. Thus, Greek civilization had to change and become Hellenistic in order to be able to propagate itself indefinitely. And the French Revolution had to change (after Napoleon) in order to be able to maintain itself in France (as the Third Republic, for example).

What applies to human existence in general also applies to the existence of *Droit* in particular. On the one hand, a given *Droit* also tends to maintain itself indefinitely in actual existence by remaining identical to itself: it has, therefore, an "instinct" of self-preservation. But on the other hand, it tends to propagate itself as much as possible: it likewise has an "instinct" of reproduction or propagation, and this not only qualitatively but also quantitatively. *Droit* tries to be complete in the sense that it wants to be applied to all possible and imaginable types of social interactions (allowing an application of *Droit*). And it also tries to be complete by being effectively applied to all the concrete interactions of a given type. All *Droit*, therefore, tends in principle 1) to be applied to the whole of humanity; and 2) to embrace the whole life of humanity. But this tendency to propagation generally enters into conflict with the tendency to preservation. A given *Droit* only succeeds in expanding itself by altering itself, and it can stop its evolution only by limiting the sphere of its application. And this is why it changes continually, evolves or progresses. *Droit* is subject to an historical evolution which leads it toward the point where the two tendencies coincide: in the limit State, universal and homogenous, *Droit* is applied to the whole social existence of humanity and nevertheless remains identical to itself.

What I have just said about *Droit* can also be said about the State. It also tends simultaneously to preserve and propagate itself. And it also can only succeed provided that it changes, [that it] evolves historically or progresses until the point where it becomes the universal and homogenous State.

In the two cases, then, there will be an historical evolution. But experience shows that these evolutions do not always coincide. There are often discrepancies. The *Droit* of a State can tend to propagation when the State tends to preservation, and be limited as a consequence, just as the State can try to expand beyond its limits and alter itself [181] in order to be able to do so, while its *Droit* does everything to preserve itself while remaining identical to itself, and is ready to limit the sphere of its application. It seems, therefore, that it is a matter of two independent processes.

But we have seen (§ 24) that the evolution of *Droit* provokes a political evolution and *vice-versa*. The two evolutions, therefore, are not absolutely independent, while not being identical. *Droit* and the State are moving, as it were, on two parallel lines. But they can move at different speeds and sometimes even in opposite directions. Of course, there is nothing here to surprise us. Specifically human phenomena all show unity with one another from the very fact that they are human. And this is why a Fustel de Coulanges happens to "explain" political institutions by religious ideas, just as easily as a Marxist "explains" politics and religion by the economy.[40] Seeing that man evolves, so to speak, as a whole, seeing that he radically and completely changes, he changes in all his behaviors and in all his ideas. Thus, political evolution is always accompanied by an economic and ideological evolution, and conversely. But the fact nevertheless remains that the connection between *Droit* and the State seems to be more intimate than that between the State and the other aspects of human existence.

Let us see, therefore, if this is truly the case.

Justice as such is an idea or ideal (that we assume to be "possible"—that is, supposed to be realized one day). It is an ideal entity which tends—as all ideal entities—to be realized, to pass onto the plane of real existence—that is, spatial and temporal. Now the *reality* of Justice is *Droit*, and *Droit* is nothing other than the application of the idea of Justice to social interactions. Justice, therefore, can be realized only by becoming a *Droit* (or the *Droit*). To want to realize and actualize Justice is therefore to want to realize and actualize a *Droit*. Consequently, it is also to want to realize and actualize social interactions; for without the actuality of these interactions, there would be no *Droit* in actuality and consequently no real Justice, existing in actuality. And seeing that there is *Droit* only when *three* persons are in relation—the two parties and the Judge—the actual realization of Justice implies and presupposes the actual reality of a Society in the proper sense of the term. One cannot want Justice without wanting *Droit*, nor want *Droit* without wanting Society.

---

40. [Ed. Fustel de Coulanges, *The Ancient City: A Study on the Religion, Laws, and Institutions of Greece and Rome* (Garden City, NY: Doubleday Anchor Books, 1956).]

Conversely, one cannot want Society without wanting [182] *Droit,* and consequently Justice. Of course, in the limit case of a perfectly homogenous Society, when all conflict between its members is excluded by definition, one could do without *Droit.* But one can wonder if a homogenous Society will still be a Society, if it will maintain itself as a Society; for in Societies with which we are familiar, the social bond is conditioned by the diversity of the members, the one giving to the other what the other does not have. (This point has been very well brought to light by Durkheim, in his book on the *Division of Labor.*) But this is of little importance, for the real Societies with which we are familiar are never homogenous. Now social heterogeneity is a social conflict in potentiality, which will necessarily be actualized one day. Society, therefore, must be able to exist despite its internal conflicts. Now the method which allows one to maintain social unity despite the conflicts which form there is nothing other than *Droit.* And *Droit* can exercise this social function only because it has a principle other than those which are at the base of the conflicts that it is called upon to "calm," this specific juridical principle being the idea of Justice. To want to maintain a Society in existence, therefore, is truly to want to maintain in existence an appropriate *Droit,* and—consequently—to realize a certain idea of Justice.

Society and *Droit,* therefore, mutually presuppose one another. Of course, one can say this of any human phenomenon whatsoever, since there is nothing human outside of Society, since man becomes a human being only by becoming a social being, and conversely. Therefore, it is correct to say—with Hegel and the modern Sociologists—that there is outside of Society neither morality, nor religion, nor any culture at all. But when it is a matter of phenomena other than *Droit,* their relation with social phenomenon only exists *for us* (i.e., in truth), for the phenomenologist or sociologist. In any case, it may not exist for these phenomena themselves. A religious person, a moralist, a scholar, and so on, can very well not realize the social nature of their activity. Thus, for example, a Religion can be antisocial without contradicting itself. A religious person can preach celibacy while perfectly realizing the fact that his complete success would mean the annihilation of Society as such; for his goal (the salvation of the soul) is transcendent in relation to Society and can therefore be realized even if it perishes. But to want to realize a *Droit* which would have as a consequence the ruin of Society is contradictory or "absurd"; for the *Droit* which destroys [183] Society destroys itself, seeing that it is nothing other than the application of the idea of Justice to *social* interactions. As well, no one has yet consciously imagined a Justice or a *Droit* incompatible by definition with the existence of Society as such, just as no one has consciously wanted a Society unjust by definition and fundamentally anti-juridical.

Let us now assume (without discussing here the validity of this assumption) that a Society can only subsist in the given circumstances provided that it is organized into a State of a given type. In this Society, then, to want to realize Justice, i.e., to want *Droit,* is equivalent to wanting the State in question. If the *Droit* wants to maintain itself in existence, it must want to maintain this State in existence. Likewise, if it wants to propagate indefinitely, it must want the indefinite propagation of the State. Now generally speaking, we have seen that the tendency of preservation enters into conflict with the tendency of propagation, and this just as much in the political sphere as in the juridical sphere, from whence comes a specific dialectic of the evolution of *Droit*. If *Droit* simply wants to maintain itself, it will try to maintain the State in its identity with itself, and it will therefore enter into conflict with the latter if it tends to expansion at this moment and changes accordingly. Conversely, if *Droit* changes in order to be able to propagate, it will also have to want to expand the State and consequently to change it. It will therefore enter into conflict with the State if it [the State] tries at this moment to preserve its identity with itself. Now in principle, *Droit* would like to avoid all conflict with the State, since the State is the necessary condition of its existence. The conflict is therefore immanent to *Droit*: it is an internal or dialectical conflict. And it is this internal conflict which determines the evolution of *Droit*. Thus, *Droit* may not want to change either because it does not want to change itself or because it does not want to change the State, or because it does not want to enter into conflict with the State, which does not want to change—and so on.[41]

[184] On the one hand, therefore, *Droit* necessarily wants to create or maintain in actual existence a given Society or State. In other words, the man who has juridical "interests" necessarily has, and by this very fact, social or political "interests"—and this not only because "juridical man" is also at the same time a "social or political man." He is so, without any doubt, and he acts simultaneously in both capacities. But this is another question. He also acts politically in his capacity as a "juridical man" just as he also acts juridically in his capacity as a "political man." Social or political utility, therefore, is not imposed on *Droit* from the outside: it is pursued by *Droit* itself, and to the extent that this *Droit* has in mind its own juridical interest, to the extent that it pursues what is useful for *Droit* as *Droit*. It is not only the State which introduces "reason of State" into juridical life. *Droit* necessarily does so itself. Likewise, it is not only *Droit* [but] it is also the State itself which introduces a juridical element into social and political life. And this is why it is futile to want to separate the "judicial power" from supposedly specifically political "powers."[42]

---

41. Duguit and the anti-statists assert that *Droit* can be uninterested in the State, from whence comes the idea of a non-state-sanctioned "social *Droit*." Without a doubt, the idea of a Society where there is a *Droit* in actuality and which is not a State has nothing absurd about it. The big question is knowing if a Society can effectively exist without being a State— that is, while not being a political Society. Experience has shown that the historical evolution has made states of all Societies. And it is obvious that a Society can exist without being a State, i.e., a *political* Society, only provided that it does not have [184] political "enemies." Now, practically speaking, this is only possible if the Society becomes universal, by implying the whole of humanity, so that there are no longer any political Societies—that is, States. Thus, whether Duguit wants it or not, the ideal of "social *Droit*" implies Marxist internationalism.
42. I do not mean by this that it is always useless to give to the judicial power a basis independent from those of the other powers. But by doing so, one must not believe that one obtains a non-state-sanctioned justice. Even "separated," the judicial power is just as political or

But on the other hand, there is the old saying "*Fiat justicia, pereat mundus*"; and a very useful political measure can nevertheless be considered unjust (and then is either rejected or accepted all the same, for a "reason of State"). Conversely, the State can take politically useless, or indeed harmful, measures with the sole goal of [185] safe-guarding *Droit*. It seems, therefore, that Justice and *Droit* are quite different from the State, that juridical life has nothing to do with political life.

Now, in reality, this apparent paradox is resolved in a truism. A given *Droit* supports that State which is conforming to it, which applies it, which thus realizes in actuality the idea of Justice appropriate to this *Droit*. In the "reason of State" that *Droit* invokes as *Droit*, the State is supposed to be a "just" and juridically "legal" State. Conversely, the State is concerned with the *Droit* which is conforming to it and which is ready to support it. When "juridical man" says "*pereat mundus*," he has in mind an "unjust" world, a State or Society at odds with what are for him *Droit* and Justice. And when "political man" says "*fiat justicia*," he has in mind a Justice and *Droit* compatible with the existence of what he believes the State ought to be. And every time that a *Droit* makes a State perish, it replaces it by another (or accepts that which has come in its place), just as a State which destroys a *Droit* hastens to create another in its place or to accept the new *Droit* which has replaced the old.

However, in reality, the fit between *Droit* (and the ideal of Justice) and the State is never complete nor perfect. In fact, the equilibrium between the juridical and the political is the result of a compromise, when *Droit* spontaneously distorts itself for "reasons of State" and the State mutilates itself for juridical reasons; for *Droit* risks perishing itself by annihilating the unjust or "illegal" State, just as the State risks its ruin by overcoming the *Droit* which bothers it. As well, the conflict only breaks out when all compromise has become impossible.

Now there is conflict only when there is no fundamental identity. And there is no compromise when there is not any mutual dependence. One must therefore say, since there is conflict and compromise between *Droit* and the State, that these are neither identical nor independent of one another. And this is what one effectively notices.

Droit is the *realization* of *Justice* by its application to actual social interactions, of which the State is the necessary condition (as we have assumed). In its "reality" aspect, therefore, *Droit* is necessarily state-sanctioned and statist [*étatique et étatiste*]: it is state-sanctioned and statist as soon as one wants to *real-*

---

state-sanctioned as the legislative or executive power. Moreover, as long as the legislative power also enacts juridical laws, the separation is illusory. In England, the separation exists (more or less) even in the sphere of legislation, since juridical laws are elaborated by the courts instead of being voted on by Parliament. But it must be understood that there has simply been here a division of "Parliament," the Parliament properly so-called dealing with non-juridical legislation, while this [juridical legislation] has been entrusted to the "Parliament" formed by the totality of English judges. But these Parliaments are both political or state-sanctioned: it is their totality which constitutes the Government.

ize Justice. But this Justice itself, the "justice" aspect of *Droit,* is independent of the State as such. Justice, i.e., the fundamental juridical category or the "principle" of *Droit,* has nothing to do with the fundamental political category [186] of Friends-Enemies, nor with the properly state-sanctioned category of Governors-Governed. And this is why one can say that if there is never a *real* separation between the judicial power and the political powers, there is always an *ideal* separation between them. It is this ideal separation which generates, while being actualized, the conflicts between *Droit* and the State, while the real union of the powers works out the compromises. When the ideal separation is actualized in the form of a conflict between *Droit* and the State, their real union intervenes to safeguard the real existence of the two. The actualized separation can be expressed by the birth of a new *Droit* in a State which does not change. And the real union will then try to change the State to put it again in agreement with *Droit,* while altering this new *Droit* in order to make the joining easier. Conversely, the ideal separation can maintain the identity of *Droit* despite the change of the State. And it is still the real union which will reestablish the harmony, by working out a compromise between the new State and the *Droit* in force: it "will legalize" the State, but it also "will modernize" *Droit.*

In sum, then, one can say the following.

Droit (which is the realization of Justice) can be realized as soon as there is a Society of at least three members, and it can be real only in such a "Society." *Droit,* therefore, will never be antisocial. But in order to exist in actuality, *Droit* must be efficacious: the Legislator must be backed up by a Judge, supported by a judicial Police, who enforces his judgements with a force irresistible in principle. Now for this truly to be the case, the members of the Society must not be able to leave the Society without its consent. In other words, the Society must be autonomous, or—if you will—sovereign. By its tendency to actuality, *Droit* will therefore try to transform the Society where it is applied into an autonomous Society, and it will endeavor to maintain the Society which is already there—provided, however, that the autonomous Society consents to resolve its internal conflicts in conformity with the *Droit* in question. If the Society departs from the *Droit* and becomes juridically "illegal," *Droit* will try to lead it back to juridical "legality." Conversely, if *Droit* evolves for whatever reasons, it will endeavor to alter Society so as to make it conform to it. But in both cases, *Droit* will try to safeguard both the autonomy of Society (i.e., its own actuality) and the social reality as such (i.e., its own), from whence come compromise and "reasons of State." And what applies to relations between *Droit* [187] and a non-political autonomous Society, i.e., not organized into a State properly so-called, also applies to relations between *Droit* and the State. Not that *Droit* has an innate tendency to make a state of the Society: the autonomy of the latter is enough for *Droit* as such, since it is enough to actualize it. But if the Society can only be autonomous provided that it is or becomes a State, *Droit* will be state-sanctioned. And as soon as the Society is organized into a State, *Droit* can only exist in actuality as a state-sanctioned *Droit.* But alongside an actual state-sanctioned *droit,* a "customary" *droit* can exist in potentiality. If the "legal" state-sanctioned *droit* actualizes this potentiality, there is no juridical conflict and the situation can remain indefinitely stationary. But if the "customary" *Droit* changes spontaneously, or if the State alters (for political reasons) the "legal" *Droit*, there will be a conflict between the two *Droits*, and consequently, synthesis or compromise and historical evolution— that is, progress.

The occurrence of a juridical evolution is undeniable, nor can one deny a progress of *Droit*, as one cannot contest its progressive universalization, as well as its increasing unification or homogenization. One can therefore assert that *Droit* tends to propagate more and more while maintaining itself more and more in identity with itself—that is, while preserving itself. In a word, *Droit* tends toward the absolute *Droit* of the universal and homogenous State.

But one can wonder if this juridical evolution or this progress are spontaneous, i.e., specific and autonomous, or if it is a matter of a simple consequence of other processes. I have just said that the idea of Justice is independent of the political idea and that it can, consequently, evolve spontaneously. But it would be necessary to come back to this question. Furthermore, even if the idea of Justice is autonomous in relation to the political, it can be dependent upon other human phenomena, such as morality, religion, economics, and so forth. Before wondering what is the spontaneous evolution of the idea of Justice, and consequently of *Droit* in its properly juridical element (what I propose to do in Part Two), it is necessary, therefore, to see if *Droit* has a truly specific and autonomous principle, irreducible to other human phenomena. In other words, one must discuss the question of the specificity and autonomy of the idea of Justice.

Chapter 3

The Specificity and Autonomy of *Droit*

§ 26

[188] EVERYTHING IS HELD TOGETHER in human existence precisely because man remains identical to himself while negating himself—that is, while becoming other than he is. It is one and the same human being who acts and thinks sometimes as a political man [and] sometimes as a juridical, religious, moral, or an aesthetic man, and so on. It would be just as futile to isolate these different "men" as it is impossible to separate the "faculties of the soul" or to oppose the "soul" to the body. Of course, the fact remains that human existence has complementary and inseparable, but nevertheless distinct, aspects. For example, to act and think economically is surely something different from acting and thinking religiously, and the man who eats and digests is quite different from this same man solving a mathematical problem or praying to God. It is correct, therefore, to distinguish several types of existential attitudes, all the more so because these attitudes can enter into conflict with one another, and they sometimes do inside one and the same concrete existence, in one and the same individual person. On the other hand, their fundamental unity as *human* attitudes is not only guaranteed by their coexistence in a single person, [but] they remain united even when they are distributed among different persons; for even when they exist separately within a Society, they mutually condition each other. As well, when one of them happens to change, the others always feel the effects of it sooner or later.

While accepting the fundamental unity of human existence, there is, then, good reason to distinguish those typical and permanent aspects [189] within it that can be individually described. But if one must not mix what is distinct, then one must not separate what is in reality unitary. One must isolate only what is truly irreducible to something else, and in describing every autonomous type, one must indicate all that belongs to it, all that depends upon and can be deduced from it. And the principle task of the Phenomenology of human existence consists in the search for a complete description of all its truly autonomous aspects—that is, the ones that are irreducible to others or qualitatively specific. Now, the criterion of specificity or autonomy is in the final analysis mutual negation. Two aspects are autonomous in respect to one another when there is the possibility of negation of one by the other—that is, of a "conflict" between them. But this conflict must not automatically follow from their nature, for in this case there would still be mutual dependence, albeit negative. In other words, the possibility of a conflict must coexist with that of a harmonious alliance, or indeed a compromise. It is then and only then that the autonomous and specifically different aspects will form an essentially synthetic unity: an identity of difference, a differentiation of the identical, a union in and by separation and opposition.

I have said, and it seems beyond doubt, that a State [which is] politically justifiable and justified by its success can be considered juridically unjust: the juridical aspect of human existence, therefore, can enter into conflict with its political aspect. But on the other hand, the idea of a politically valid, i.e., efficacious, State that is nevertheless juridically just is perfectly conceivable, even if it is still not fully realized: the juridical aspect can, therefore, be in harmony with the political aspect. And one can conclude from these two observations that the juridical and political attitudes are two autonomous aspects of one and the same human existence. But one must still ask whether these two attitudes, irreducible to one another, cannot be deduced from other human attitudes.

The present chapter will be devoted to the question of knowing whether the phenomenon of "*Droit*" is truly an autonomous and specific phenomenon—that is, irreducible to other human phenomena.

Now it is obvious that this problem cannot be resolved by itself. Indeed, in order to really solve this problem, it would be necessary to have a complete list of autonomous phenomena and to demonstrate that the phenomenon of "*Droit*" is not reducible [190] to any of them. And there can be no question of undertaking this task in the present study. Here, it is only a matter of offering an incomplete, and consequently quite provisional, solution.

In the first place, I will leave aside all the phenomena that are—at first glance at least—so different from the phenomenon of "*Droit*" that a reduction of "*Droit*" to them would appear without question to be impossible. The aesthetic phenomenon is such an example. But I realize that here as elsewhere the "evidence" can be deceiving, all the more so because for the ancient Greeks, for example, a reduction of the Just to the Beautiful or the Beautiful to the Just did not seem to be absurd. Second, when comparing *Droit* to certain other phenomena in order to distinguish it from them, I will assume them to be specific and autonomous without having demonstrated their autonomy. Now, here as well, it is dangerous to trust the "evidence," which is not at all, moreover, overarching [*générale*]. Finally, third, the comparisons themselves that I am going to make will not be complete. And I will not discuss the many attempts to reduce the phenomena that I will try to separate to other phenomena.

Practically speaking, I will limit myself to taking up the traditional subjects of discussion relating to the problem of the autonomy of *Droit* which interest us here. The relations between *Droit* and Morality (§ 31) and the relation between *Droit* and Religion (§ 30) are subjects of this kind. I will also discuss (§ 29) the opinion of the "statists" and "utilitarians"—those who would like to reduce *Droit* either to "reason of State" or to "social utility"—by referring above all to what I have said in the preceding chapter. It will also be necessary to see what the validity and significance is of the Marxist attempt to reduce *Droit*—like all other human phenomena—to the economic phenomenon (§ 28). Finally (§ 32), I will say a few words about the relation between the juridical attitude and what are generally called the egoistic and altruistic tendencies of human existence.

But I will begin by making a general remark that suggests the idea that *Droit* is effectively a specific and autonomous phenomenon, [an idea] which I will try to prove (or make plausible) by the discussions in this chapter. In other respects, [however,] the autonomy of *Droit* depends upon the autonomy of its "principle"—that is, the idea of Justice. The present chapter, therefore, is only a kind of introduction to Part Two, where this idea will be analyzed. And it is there above all that I will try to establish the autonomy of this idea, and consequently of *Droit* itself.

§ 27

[191] Generally speaking, in studying a phenomenon and comparing it to other phenomena in order to reveal its specificity and to demonstrate its autonomy, one must take it in its concrete totality [*intégrité*]; study, as well, all its constitutive elements; and situate it in the whole of human existence.

Now, when one speaks about *Droit* or its autonomy, one has a tendency to become too exclusively attached to the "litigants," so to speak. One looks for the motives of those who passively *submit to* the *Droit*. One wonders what the motives are of a man acting in conformity to a legal rule or what the motives are of the criminal acting contrary to this rule. And one notices that these motives can be the most diverse: one emphasizes reasons of a biological nature [*ordre*] (notably with criminals), economic or social "interest," for example, or morality, and so on. In short, one risks not finding any specifically juridical motive.

But in reality the existence of the "litigants" is still not enough for there to be *Droit*. An "impartial and disinterested" third must be present, and one can even say that the specificity of *Droit* lies precisely in the presence of this third. One or another interaction becomes a juridical situation solely because it provokes the intervention of a third. As well, in order to understand the juridical phenomenon, one must analyze the character [*la personne*] of this third. In any case, one must not neglect it.

Of course, no one denies that the existence of *Droit* implies and presupposes the existence of this "third." But when speaking about *Droit*, one often forgets this and speaks only about those to whom *Droit* is applied instead of those who apply it; or again, one takes the "third" above all in his aspect as a juridical Legislator or judicial Police. One wonders what are the goals or the motives of his legislation, [and] one asks the whys and the hows of judicial constraint. And as the Law-making and Police [powers] are in the vast majority of cases in the hands of the State, of the Government, one wonders why the State enacts such and such juridical laws and makes them respected by using force. Nothing surprising, therefore, in referring to "reason of State" first and foremost, and even exclusively, when [192] trying to reduce the phenomenon of "*Droit*" in its entirety to the principle of social or political *utility*.

Now, in fact, the third is not only Legislator and Police; he is also, and even above all, Judge or Arbiter. Indeed, the Police only enforce the decisions of the Judge, and the Legislator enacts his juridical laws with a view to their application by this same Judge. Therefore, if a situation is juridical only because it implies an "impartial and disinterested" third, this third himself is a specifically juridical entity only to the extent that he implies an aspect of the Judge and Arbiter. And it is above all as Judge that he is supposed to be truly a "third"—that is, "impartial and disinterested."

Therefore, in order to understand what *Droit* is, in order to see whether or not it is an autonomous phenomenon, one must first of all ask why, for what motives, man becomes a Judge or Arbiter. First of all, we will see that one can act as a Judge even if there is no juridical Law, or in any event a legal rule, which would allow the case to be judged. And one can even be a Judge if one knows that the judgement will not necessarily be enforced—that is, without having at one's disposal an irresistible force. Moreover, one can "judge" even when one knows that the "judgement" will not have any real significance and will in no way change the situation. Of course, this will not be a case of *Droit*, for *all* the constitutive elements of this phenomenon will not be present; but I only mean that one of its essential elements can exist without certain other ones, such as the element of constraint. Next, we will see that the judgement (even if it is enforced) can have a juridical value only if the Judge has been "impartial and disinterested." In other words, the Judge is only supposed to have acted for the sole motive of wanting to have been Judge or Arbiter. Of course, all action presupposes a goal, i.e., an "interest"; but the "interest" of the Judge is supposed to boil down to the desire to realize Justice, to apply to a given case the idea of Justice. All "utilitarian" motives are therefore excluded by definition. The "ideal" Judge is not "interested" in the judgement that he issues: this judgement neither brings him anything personally nor is it harmful to him. And he does not even think about "public" utility in the case when he knows that his judgement will not be enforced. If he judges all the same, it is because he has a *sui generis* "interest," immanent to the very act of judgement. He has a "juridical interest," which is determined by the idea of Justice.

Introspection and the study of human behavior[1] [193] confirms this way of seeing things. Man is spontaneously inclined to serve as Judge or Arbiter. Everywhere and always one finds men ready to intervene as "disinterested thirds," to serve as Judge or Arbiter. And everyone can see in himself a "tendency" to judge, one that becomes an imperious need as soon as one is in the presence of some "injustice." For example, in seeing a powerful man assault a weak invalid, everyone will rush forward to defend the latter. This is so because, in the blink of an eye, one will have formulated a "law" that forbids this action, applied this "law" to the given case, and attempted to enforce this "judgement." Now obviously one is not injured by this event, and one will not

---

1. [Ed. In the original, the English word "behavior" follows the French word *comportement* in parentheses.]

benefit from the intervention—on the contrary. And it would be truly artificial to say that one intervenes thinking about "Society," about the fact that in a Society or a State the weak should be protected against the strong, and so on. Moreover, one can notice that intervening in the capacity as Judge or Arbiter provokes a keen pleasure independent of the "moral" character of the case that is judged or arbitrated. For example, a dispute during a sports competition spontaneously generates a mass of benevolent Arbiters. This is because one takes pleasure in arbitrating and this pleasure is truly "disinterested." It is a *sui generis* pleasure, just as specific as sexual or aesthetic pleasure, for example. Now this is a pleasure that one gets from the fact of being able to be "disinterested and impartial"—that is, [of being able to be] "just." Therefore, it is a specifically juridical pleasure, [one that is] incomprehensible if one denies the existence of an autonomous juridical attitude based upon the idea of Justice. Thus, in the case of the invalid, it is the sole occurrence of "injustice" (i.e., of inequality here) that moves one to intervene. One does not even ask if the strong person is right to beat the weak person, nor does one ask who the one and the other are, what the one who is beaten has done to the one who beats him. It is only the disproportion of forces, i.e., "injustice" in its pure state, that makes one act. And it is possible that afterwards, having learned the motives of the strong person, one approves of them and helps the strong person to mistreat the weak person.

Among certain primitive peoples, fathers teach their sons that there are only two imperative "moral" duties: to be brave and to render justice, to judge fellow citizens as impartial and disinterested thirds.[2] One speaks about "morality," but in reality it is a matter of a political "virtue" and a juridical "virtue." One must be brave toward [194] "enemies" and one must act as Judge (when the occasion arises) among "friends." Of course, to render Justice is to do a socially and politically *useful* deed, just as it is *useful* to Society and the State that its citizens are brave. But it would be truly artificial to say that one is brave for "reasons of State" or considerations of public utility; and it is absurd to look for an "interest" in the act of bravery that brings about the death of the brave person. Likewise, if it is socially useful to be Judge, it is not this utility which moves one to do it. The primitive person in question will say to his son that it is a "duty." The Phenomenologist will say that here there is a *sui generis* motive, which he will call "juridical" and whose "principle" he will say is Justice. One loves to be Judge or Arbiter because one possesses an idea or an ideal of Justice, and because one tends to realize all one's ideas. Now the idea of Justice is realized by its application to human interactions—that is, in and by the *Droit* that is concretized in and by the action of the Judge. The specific (and specifically human) pleasure that one experiences being Arbiter testifies to the existence in man of a *sui generis* idea that he tends to realize. And this idea we call the idea of Justice, while its realization is called *Droit*.

---

2. Cf. [Maurice Rea] Davie, *La Guerre dans les sociétés primitives,* 363. [*The Evolution of War: A Study of its Role in Early Societies* (New Haven: Yale University Press, 1929), 241–2.]

This way of seeing things is corroborated by the phenomenological analysis of Authority (cf. my Note on *Authority*).[3] I have tried to show that there is a pure *sui generis* Authority of the "Judge" type. Indeed, in a lot of cases, one obeys a man solely because one believes him to be "just," "impartial," "disinterested," "objective," "equitable," and so on, without being concerned with his other qualities. In particular, when one wants to submit a lawsuit to the judgement of a third, of an Arbiter, one goes and seeks those who enjoy the Authority of the "Judge" type. However intelligent, energetic, provident, handsome, or anything else a man is, one will not choose him if he is presumed to be "partial" or "interested" (or if he is "unjust" in general) in the case that one would like to submit to him. Conversely, if one knows him to be "just," one can close one's eyes to all his faults. Of course, one will choose a "virtuous" or "moral" man; but this is because one assumes that "virtue" or "morality" necessarily imply the "virtue" of "justice." And if one prefers to choose a "religious," "pious" man, it is still because one presumes him to be "just" or "equitable," and not because he has specifically religious "virtues," such as having obtained the salvation of his soul, for example.

[195] There is, then, a *sui generis* Authority which qualifies the Judge as such. This specific quality is nothing other than his "justice" or his "equity"—that is, an active incarnation of the idea of Justice that one should consequently consider as a specific and autonomous idea. And it would be of no use to say that the "just" man, whom one chooses to Arbitrate decisions to which one voluntarily submits, is "just" because his behavior conforms to a (juridical) law. This would only shift the problem or simply change its terms; for this law itself has a *sui generis* Authority, the same as that of the Judge. And it often happens that a law has Authority solely because it has been decreed by a legislator who enjoys the Authority of a Judge, being considered "just" or "impartial and disinterested," at the very least in the case aimed at by his law.

It is enough, therefore, to introduce into the study of the juridical phenomenon the essential constitutive element of the "disinterested third" in order to be aware that this phenomenon does not admit of "utilitarian" interpretations. There is a *sui generis* "interest" that moves man to act juridically, at the very least as Judge. And this "interest" has nothing to do with biological or economic or social or political interests, nor even with the specifically religious "interest," which is the salvation of the soul; for if an iniquitous judgement is a "sin," nothing says that being judge is a religious "duty." It is not for any of these "egoistic" reasons that man becomes Judge or Arbiter in a case that does not at all "interest" him, except this of it being a case to which the idea of Justice or equity can be applied.

What remains to be discussed are "altruistic" motives as well as Morality in general. But before tackling the often discussed problem of the relations between *Droit* and Morality, one must critically examine more deeply the

---

3. [Ed. See Part One, chapter 2, note 38 above.]

"utilitarian" theories of *Droit*—and this is only because of the immense credence given them.

§ 28

It is pointless to discuss the biological "theories" of *Droit*. It is too obvious that *Droit* is a specifically human phenomenon that is not found in non-human nature. If the human interactions to which *Droit* is applied can be likened in certain cases to [196] animal interactions, the intervention of the third, who "judges" them as an impartial and disinterested third, has no equivalent in the animal world. One cannot, therefore, explain it biologically (cf. Part Two).

But when the "Utilitarians" speak about "interest," they do not only have in mind vital, biological interests. There are also specifically human interests other than those of *Droit,* and it is a matter of knowing whether *Droit* can be reduced to one of them or to a combination of them.

Nowadays, it is above all *economic interest* that is privileged. For the Marxists, for example, and for a lot of economists in general, *Droit* is only an epiphenomenon of the economic life of humanity.[4]

First of all, let us note that economic life is quite different from biological life. Homo economicus is not only the *animal* homo sapiens: he is also and even above all a being truly and specifically human. The human economy is based upon work and exchange, which do not have equivalents in the animal world (cf. my Note on *Work*).[5] Therefore, to explain man by the economy is quite different from explaining him by biology. The "economic materialism" of Marxists is materialism in name only. If one wants to oppose "spiritualism" to biologism or materialism, one must say that the Marxist reduction of man to the act of work is clearly of "spiritualistic" inspiration, one which comes, moreover, directly from Hegel. Authentic Marxism is an "anthropological" theory that discovers in man a specifically human act which one finds nowhere else, namely the act of work, and that tries to explain all that is human in man according to this anthropogenic act.

Now, in doing this, Marx was wrong to simplify and truncate the Hegelian conception. For Hegel, the act of work presupposes another act, that of the fight for pure prestige, whose true value Marx does not appreciate. Now there is no doubt that economic man is always coupled with a "man of vanity," whose interests can collide with his economic interests. It is enough to be convinced of this by thinking about the Eskimo, who trades the furs of his residence for European trinkets and who suffers from the cold in order to satisfy his vanity. It is therefore impossible to reduce [197] the whole of human existence to economic activity—that is, to Work and Exchange.

---

4. Cf. also [Rudolf] Stammler, *Wirtschaft und Recht nach der materialistischen Geschichtsauffassung* ([Leipzig: Verlag von Veit & Comp.], 1896).
5. [Ed. The location of this "note" on work remains a mystery, although it, like the analysis on authority (see Part One, chapter 2, note 38 above), may be among Kojève's personal papers.]

But could one not at least reduce *Droit* to it?

The economy is constituted by Work and Exchange. But it is obvious that Work as such cannot be a source of *Droit*. Work sets man against Nature. Now the relations between man and Nature have nothing juridical about them; for no human being can play the role of the "impartial and disinterested third" in this case. No one would seriously want to defend the interests of Nature against those of man, and in the case of a conflict between them, everyone will automatically side with man against Nature. As for the social relations generated by work, and notably the one between employer and employee, they have nothing fundamentally economic about them; and for the moment, then, we do not have the space to take them into account.

By contrast, the Exchange element of the economic phenomenon is closely connected to the juridical phenomenon. In the vast majority of cases, the legal rules of modern *Droit* have in mind exchanges of an economic nature, and one can say that almost all our *Droit* is a commercial *Droit,* in the broad sense of the term. The development of economic life, and notably of commerce, has always provoked a blossoming of juridical life, an expansion of *Droit,* and an intensification of jurisprudence. Finally, the ideology of the merchant always has a character more or less juridical: it advocates the rule of *Droit* on earth, [and] it aspires to a *Droit* that is universally valid and always respected.

This affinity between *Droit* and the commercial or exchangist aspect of economic life is easily seen. When a merchant works out an exchange that he is about to make, he must not only take into account his own interest but also that of his partner. In other words, he must look at things from the point of view of an "impartial and disinterested third." Therefore, he will have nothing against the intervention of such a third in his commercial interactions with others. On the contrary, he will voluntarily have recourse to the good offices of this third. The merchant is naturally inclined to regulate his commercial activity by Judges or Arbiters—that is, by juridical legislation ultimately.

On the other hand, all exchange has as its base the principle of equivalence. Now we will see (in Part Two) that equivalence constitutes the second fundamental type of the idea of Justice (the first being equality). And we [198] will see that this second type can be called "slavish" or "bourgeois," in contrast to the first, which is essentially "aristocratic," being originally the Justice of the Master. The Bourgeois (metamorphosed from the Slave), who is above all a Merchant (in contrast to the Slave properly so-called, who is above all a Worker or producer), is naturally prone to adopt the ideal of a Justice of equivalence and to make it triumph wherever this is possible. This is why he will have, generally speaking, a "juridical" ideology: he will consider all human existence from the point of view of *Droit,* it being understood that this *Droit* is based upon the idea of the Justice of equivalence and not on the idea of the Justice of equality. The Bourgeois-merchant does not want to be equal, even economically speaking, with his "customer," nor even with his "competitor." And if he does want this, it is not in his capacity as homo economicus, as a merchant. As a merchant, it is enough for him that the profit of his "customer" is *equivalent* to his own and that his "competitor" is placed in conditions *equivalent* to his own. By contrast, all offenses against the principle of equivalence will be considered an "injustice": in the eyes of the merchant there will be either an "illicit rise in prices" or "unfair competition."

But can one truly say that the idea or ideal of the Justice of equivalence, and consequently the *Droit* which realizes it, are a simple epiphenomenon of economic, or indeed commercial, activity? I do not think so, and not only because it is quite obvious that the sphere where this Justice and its corresponding *Droit* are applied extends far beyond the properly economic sphere. Here, it could be a matter of the phenomenon of "transference": the specifically economic idea could be applied to a sphere which is in principle foreign to it.

I think that the economic theory of Justice and of *Droit* is insufficient because it does not explain the possibility of the existence of the "third," without whom there would be no *Droit*. Of course, in practice, the Judge or Arbiter is paid in one way or another. One can say that they also "exchange" their juridical "work" for economic gain. But if the Judge were truly nothing other than a merchant acting as homo economicus pure and simple, one would need a super-judge to arbitrate the possible conflicts between him and his customers in order to set down the "equivalence" in question—and so on infinitely. In order that this infinite progression be stopped, i.e., in order that the reality of *Droit* become possible, a truly "disinterested" Judge (or Legislator) must be reached, [199] one who will judge without any economic interest on his part. Otherwise, there would perhaps be economic exchanges complicated by the "commercial" exchanges between Judges and litigants, but there would be no commercial **Droit** properly so-called—that is, the *Droit* based upon the idea of Justice. The law of supply and demand certainly operates when it is a matter of setting down the remuneration of Judges, the costs of justice. But for there to be *Droit*, this law must not influence the content of the juridical sentence. If the Judge is automatically on the side of the one who pays the most, he is no longer a Judge but a party, and the entire situation has nothing juridical about it.

Therefore, the judge must be "disinterested" in the ordinary sense of the word. But if he is so, this is because his judgement is no longer made according to his economic interest, because he no longer judges as homo economicus. We can therefore say that he judges as homo juridicus, without clarifying for the moment what this juridical man is. It is enough for us to know that he is something other than economic man, and we will call the principle which determines his way of acting the idea of Justice.

In a "bourgeois" society (i.e., non-aristocratic and non-civic), where economic activity in its commercial aspect predominates (exchange and not production), the idea of Justice will be (more or less) conforming to the principle of equivalence, and the *Droit* in force will realize Justice in this form. [This is so] because, on the one hand, commercial interactions lend themselves to the application of the principle of equivalence and not of equality, and *Droit* is nothing other than the application of the idea of Justice to given social interactions, which are here commercial. On the other hand, [this is so] because the juridical Legislator, as well as the Judge, are themselves members of this society—that is, of the Bourgeoisie for whom the "just" is first and above all the "equivalent." But if the Justice of equivalence corresponds to commercial activity, one cannot say what the outcome is. The Judge and the Legislator are economically "disinterested" (in principle, at the very least) and they nevertheless can distinguish the just from the unjust. [They can do this] because the idea of Justice and the *Droit* which realizes it have a source other than commercial activity: these are autonomous phenomena in relation to the economy.

Justice (even that of equivalence) and *Droit* cannot be obtained starting from the economy by a simple process of abstraction or "deduction," or indeed, [by a simple process] of "analysis." One can be a merchant and reason *as* a merchant, and one can also be a "scholar" and reason *about* commerce, [200] analyzing or describing it, deriving its laws or principles by a process of abstraction, and deducing the consequences of these principles. It is in this way that economic science proceeds. But if this science can lead to abstract or general "laws," such as the law of supply and demand, it will never arrive at the idea of Justice and it will never be able to found a *Droit*, even commercial [*Droit*]. Thus, for example, the price is determined for the merchant as it is for the theorist of commerce, by the law of supply and demand; and this has been known for a long time, [or] in any case since the Middle Ages. This has not prevented this same Middle Ages from elaborating a theory of the "just price" (cf. Saint Thomas, for example).[6] Therefore, it is neither as a merchant nor as an economist that medieval man elaborated this theory. He did it as a jurist, starting from the idea of Justice (which was for him an ideal of equivalence). And he consciously set the juridical notion of the "just price" against the economic notion of the price determined by supply and demand.

In sum, therefore, one can say the following.

Droit is the application of a certain idea of Justice to given social interactions. Now economic exchanges, i.e., commercial interactions, are particularly fit to serve as points of application for the Justice of equivalence. There is, then, an affinity between this form of Justice and commercial activity. This is why, on the one hand, the *Droit* based upon this Justice has above all a commercial content (in a broad sense), being directed at the cases of exchange of economic values; and this why, on the other hand, (commercial) economic activity stimulates juridical life and causes everything related to the idea of the Justice of equivalence to flourish. Generally speaking, to the extent that *Droit* is determined by the interactions to which the idea of Justice that is at its base is being applied, it will be broadly determined by the economic, notably commercial, state of the Society where it is in force. Therefore, it is not at all futile to speak of a "class justice" along with the Marxists. But one must not forget that *Droit* is also something different from the economic interactions governed by *Droit*. It is an application to these interactions of a certain idea of Justice. And this

---

6. [Ed. *Summa Theologica*, Pt. II-II, Q. 77, Art. 1.]

idea, while generally being in harmony with the economic conditions, is autonomous in relation to them. This idea adds something different to them, and this is because it adds something that it creates alongside economic situations from juridical situations, which can be contrasted to them in certain cases. Anyway, it is still possible [201] (cf. Part Two) that one could speak here of a "class justice." But the "class" which elaborates a given form of the idea of Justice is something other than an economic "class." It is possible for this "class" to confuse the just with the "useful"—but then it is a matter of a "utility" other than economic utility.

§ 29

Legal Utilitarianism, by identifying the "just" or the juridically "legal" with the useful, does not always have in mind purely economic utility. One often speaks of "social utility" and "reason of State" when maintaining that the Society and State have specific interests other than economic or commercial interests. *Droit* would therefore be a function of these specifically "social" or "political" interests.

One must say, however, that the nature of these interests is generally left unclear. Therefore, it is a matter of clarifying it [the nature of these interests] and of seeing whether *Droit* and consequently the idea of Justice can effectively be deduced from social (in the narrow sense of the word) and political (in the proper sense) phenomena.

For classical Utilitarianism social utility is equivalent to the greatest amount of happiness for the greatest number of persons. But it is false that man pursues happiness first and foremost, that this pursuit for happiness determines social life. Hegel has shown that man longs for the satisfaction (*Befriedigung*) given by universal recognition (*Anerkennen*) of his personal worth. One can say that every man, ultimately, would like to be "unique in the world and universally worthy." One wants to be distinguished from others as much as possible; one wants to be "original"; one is "individualistic"; [and] one seeks to highlight one's "personality," which is supposed to be one of a kind. What everyone else does, what everyone else has, what everyone else is—all this is without genuine worth. Man pursues novelty and would like to be "novel"; this is what the Individualism of Modernity (starting from the Renaissance) has brought out very well. But the "individualists" forget to add that "novelty" only has worth to the extent that it is "recognized" by society and—at the limit— by all. No one would like to be worse than everyone else, whether the ugliest, the laziest, [or] the most stupid person in the world. Therefore, man certainly longs for universal recognition of his distinctive personality in [202] the final analysis. It is this recognition that gives man satisfaction, and he is ready to sacrifice his happiness for this satisfaction if he cannot do otherwise. It is not only for being beautiful that one must suffer.

We will see (in Part Two) that the desire for satisfaction by recognition is intimately linked to the idea of Justice. But we do not have to speak about this here, for all of this has nothing to do with Utilitarianism. To seek "Hegelian" satisfaction is quite different from pursuing the "useful" in the ordinary sense of the word—that is, all that is necessary for "happiness" or "material well-being." If Society arises from the desire for recognition, its supreme goal is the satisfaction of its members and not their happiness. This is certainly not to say that satisfaction is incompatible with happiness: on the contrary, at the limit, in the ideal State, the socially satisfied man is also (in principle) individually happy. But when it is necessary to choose, it is satisfaction which wins outs, and it is the desire for satisfaction, not the need for happiness, which determines social life as a whole. If this were not true, one could not succeed in explaining, nor indeed "justifying," the phenomenon of war. Now experience shows that a healthy Society never turns away from war when it is forced upon it by circumstances. And these "circumstances" imply the need for recognition—that is, the feeling of honor, as it is called. It is for the sake of this need that Society makes war, and war is surely a sacrifice of happiness, even if it is not a sacrifice of life.[7]

Be that as it may, it is futile to want to deduce Justice and *Droit* from the sole need for happiness (which coincides, moreover, to an enormous extent with economic interest, according to the Utilitarians themselves). It is enough to show this by resorting to the common notion of "unjust happiness." Even the happy person himself can realize the fact that he is "unjustly" happy. And all things being equal, a "just" happiness, i.e., universally recognized, is worth more than an [203] "unjust" happiness, i.e, purely subjective [or] personal. Furthermore, when an "impartial and disinterested third" intervenes in the capacity as Judge in a social interaction, he is surely not thinking about the happiness of the agents interacting, and it is not the idea of happiness which determines the nature of his judgement. And he is not even pursuing his own happiness when he intervenes.

Can one say that the "third" intervenes for a "reason of State"? In other words, can one reduce the idea of Justice and the *Droit* which realizes it to the political phenomenon?

To the extent that the political existence of man is determined by his desire for recognition, it is intimately linked to his juridical life, as we will see (in Part Two). But it would be just as wrong to want to reduce the juridical to the political as it would be to deduce the political (in the proper sense) from the juridical. The idea of Justice, which is at the base of *Droit* as such, is a specifically juridical category, [or] in any case a category irreducible to specifically political categories.

---

7. The consistent Utilitarians are radical pacifists. And they are right from their point of view, for to pursue happiness is effectively to repudiate war in every case. But since real (and healthy) Societies do not reject war, it is because they are living according to other principles than those of the Utilitarians, because they are not pursuing happiness *at any price*. I am speaking about "*healthy* Societies"; for in current conditions, a Society which turns away from war is sooner or later absorbed by those which do not do so. This Society thus dies, and this is why one can say that it is "ill" when it rejects war in all cases.

These fundamental political categories are those of Friend-Enemy and Governor-Governed.

It is obvious that the political category of Enemy has nothing to do with Droit nor with Justice. Neither the ideal of Justice nor the occurrence of Droit implies the existence of political enemies of the Society where Droit is valid. Therefore, it is impossible to deduce the political from the juridical. Conversely, political relations with the enemy have nothing to do with Droit, being rather the negation of juridical relations. In fact, there is no "disinterested third," nor a Judge or Arbiter, when it is a matter of an interaction between an autonomous State and its enemies.

As for the political category of Friend, we have seen that it is linked to juridical categories. But seeing that the political category of Friend is determined (negatively) by the political category of Enemy, it has a specific character, irreducible to juridical categories. As "non-Enemy," the Friend has nothing to do with Justice nor with Droit. Political friends, however, are linked together by bonds which are also juridical. As friends are equal or "equivalent" as friends, their interactions lend themselves to the intervention of an "impartial and disinterested" third (friend), being capable of generating juridical situations. But it is not as political friends that they are in this juridical situation. First, in principle, friends are not supposed to have lawsuits. And then, for [204] the third, who creates the situation as juridical, the fact that they are friends is unimportant since both of them are the same to him [juridically]. For there to be the possibility of Droit, it is enough that the litigants (or one of them) are not enemies. Politically, this means that they are friends (since there are no neutrals in politics). But juridically, all this means is that they are not enemies. For the Judge, they are politically neutral—that is, he does not treat them politically, [and] he does not see them as political men. Far from arising from the political, therefore, Droit can only be developed in political neutrality, in a sphere shielded from the political. In fact, this "neutrality" is purely fictitious and this fiction can only be maintained among political friends. But for Droit, this is only a contingency and in principle Droit can do without the political opposition of Friend-Enemy. This is why, far from overcoming Droit, the suppression of Enemies in and by the universal State actually realizes Droit in its fullness.

Of course, the State, as a Society of Friends opposed to Enemies, cannot do without Droit (inside [of Society] at the very least). But Droit can very well do without a State which is opposed to Enemies. It can flourish when there are not or no longer (external) enemies at all. Therefore, the idea of Justice is autonomous in relation to the fundamental political category Friend-Enemy. And this is why it can oppose this category in certain cases by generating (at least in potentiality) an international Droit, which precisely denies the politically irreducible opposition between friends and enemies by seeing everywhere only litigants, equal or equivalent by definition "before the Law." As well, humanity, in its juridical aspect, is familiar with the notion of an "unjust war," something which makes no sense politically speaking.

There remains the other fundamental political category—that is, of Governor-Governed.

Of course, in practice and in Societies organized into a State, the Judges and Legislators are always (more or less) the Governors and the litigants the Governed. And since the intervention of the Judge must be irresistible in order that *Droit* exists in actuality, the actual reality of *Droit* and therefore of Justice presupposes the existence of a relation of Governor to the Governed. But in potentiality *Droit* can exist even when this relation is not found; for arbitration is an authentically juridical phenomenon based upon an idea of Justice, and yet the Arbiter is not necessarily a Governor in relation to his litigants. Indeed, the specifically juridical Authority [205] of a Judge has nothing to do with the specifically political Authority of a Master or a Leader, appropriate to the Governor as such.

In its tendency to actuality, therefore, *Droit* stimulates the creation of a political relation of Governor to the Governed, and it is completely natural that the Governors serve as Judges in respect to the Governed. For the Governors as such, the Governed are supposed to be equal or equivalent in their capacity as Governed: the Governors are therefore capable of playing the role of an impartial third in the interactions of the Governed among themselves. And they are supposed to be "impartial" in respect to these interactions precisely because they are the Governors, who are not dependent on the Governed. Conversely, the Governors have an interest in making *Droit* and Justice reign among the Governed, for it is only in this way that they can support them as a society of political friends of which they are the Governors. To support *Droit* is both to support the governed Society and to be supported as Governors. But this affinity between juridical life and domestic political life does not at all mean the identity of the two spheres. One cannot govern a Society or a State without making reign some sort of *Droit* which realizes a certain idea of Justice; and one cannot realize in actuality the idea of Justice by a *Droit* in a Society which was ungovernable. But the idea of Justice can generate a *Droit* in potentiality independent of every Government properly so-called, and this *Droit* can be opposed to a given political Government. It is in this way that the juridical notion of an "unjust or (juridically) illegal Government" appears, [a notion] that makes no sense politically, the political as such not knowing the opposition between "*de facto*" and "*de jure.*"

When one calls to mind "social utility" or "reason of State" in speaking about *Droit,* one has in mind the fact that, on the one hand, *Droit* is "useful" to Society and the State, and that, on the other hand, Society and the State are "useful" to *Droit.* Thus, the State would elaborate *Droit* while pursing its own goals in such a way that *Droit* in fact defends first and foremost all these social and political interests as such.

I have already said (in chapter 2) what one must think about this.

It is altogether correct that the State as State pursues specifically political goals and only upholds *Droit* to the extent that this is indispensable for the realization of its goals. It is also true that *Droit* cannot exist without Society and that it cannot be actualized in a State without [206] being a state-sanctioned *Droit.* Therefore, *Droit* must make its own the interests of Society and the State. It cannot be that the very existence of Society and the State is impossible from this fact. One cannot say, therefore, that Society and the State impose their own ends on *Droit. Droit* itself, by tending to actual existence, is constituted in such a way that Society and the State are able to exist.

But this *harmony,* "pre-established" as it were between *Droit* and the State, does not prove their fundamental *identity;* for this harmony can be transformed into an acute conflict, as historical experience shows. This is because if Society and the State need *Droit* in order to exist, they do not put up with any *Droit* whatsoever. Likewise, if *Droit* needs a Society or a State, it does not put up with any Society or State whatsoever. In certain cases Society can consider a given *Droit* as being "anti-social," and the State can find a *Droit* politically harmful. Conversely, a given *Droit* can describe as "unjust" a certain Society or State. And in these cases, the tendency to actualize *Droit* will enter into conflict with the tendency to support the Society and State in existence: at the limit, *Droit* can adopt the principle *Fiat justicia, pereat mundus.* Thus, if the State only upholds the politically or "socially" useful *Droit, Droit* only upholds a juridically "just" or "legal" State, just as it will only embrace the goals of a Society which conforms to it. Now, all this clearly shows that the juridical and political spheres are autonomous in respect to one another. The fact that in "normal" cases *Droit* is state-sanctioned and the State legal does not prove that *Droit* and the State are one and the same thing; for if they were, they would never be able to enter into conflict with one another.[8]

---

8. One could object that a political (or juridical, and so on) idea which enters into conflict with another political idea is nevertheless an idea just as political (or juridical, and so on) as the other. Conflict would then seem to be compatible with fundamental identity. This is correct, and this is the very principle of dialectic. Even in this case, however, there is an "independence": the conflict, being the expression of a negation, cannot be "deduced" *a priori.* The new idea does not "result" from the previously negated idea: it negates it spontaneously in and by act of freedom, [and] it is therefore independent or autonomous in relation to it. But being determined in its content by the content of the negated idea, it remains fundamentally "identical" to it: the negation of the previous idea generates a new idea as a synthesis of the negated idea and the negating idea. But in the case of a conflict between two different entities, there is no negation properly so-called of one by the other, and consequently there is no synthesis, when the difference of the two entities would be overcome. The conflict actualizes the incompatibility, i.e., [207] precisely the difference or autonomy of the two entities, and this incompatibility provokes an immanent transformation of these entities. But, while changing, each remains what it is—that is, remains different from the other. And this is what takes place at the time of a conflict between *Droit* and the State. *Droit* does not negate the State, [and] it does not want to be put in its place, just as the State does not want to overcome *Droit* as such. *Droit* only wants to overcome a certain form of the State, and the State wants to overcome a certain form of *Droit.* The conflict thus ends up at a transformation of the State or of *Droit,* or the two simultaneously. But even after the conflict, the State remains a State and *Droit* remains *Droit.* On the contrary, when two political (or juridical, and so on) ideas enter into conflict, the one wants to replace the other. It therefore wants to negate the other as such and to be asserted in its place. And this is possible only because it is a matter of one and the same entity. As well, the conflict is

§ 30

[207] Legal Utilitarianism often takes a religious, or more exactly, a theological form. It is said that *Droit* and Justice are divine institutions, and that one must obey juridical laws and conform to the ideal of Justice because this is "useful" for the salvation of the soul. Of course, in this case, one does not speak about "Utilitarianism." But this religious "Utilitarianism" can be likened to Utilitarianism properly so-called, for in both cases *Droit* is related to values other than properly juridical values whose ultimate ground is the idea of Justice. One institutes *Droit* here not so much [208] to realize Justice but in order to obtain the salvation of one's soul. Likewise, in Utilitarianism properly so-called, *Droit* is supposed to assure "public salvation," the prosperity of the State, of Society and its members, understood now not as "souls" but as concrete human beings.

But is it really true that the juridical phenomenon can be reduced to the religious phenomenon?

In order to answer this question one must first of all distinguish between the authentic religious phenomenon, properly so-called, and pseudo-religious phenomena. Thus, one must not conflate Religion with Theology. Just as an authentic Religion (for example, primitive Buddhism) can be strictly atheistic, a Theology (such as that of Aristotle, for example) may be perfectly areligious. To speak about God when speaking about *Droit*, therefore, is not necessarily to transform the juridical phenomenon into religious phenomenon. The idea of God can be introduced into a juridical conception without it thereby ceasing to be authentically juridical.

Let us assume that a situation conforms to our general definition of the juridical situation, except that the role of the "impartial and disinterested third" is played by a divine being. In this case, God will be considered, in the

---

resolved without the entities in conflict transcending the sphere which is proper to them. But when *Droit* enters into conflict with the State, for example, the conflict cannot be resolved if *Droit* remains *Droit*, if one does not go beyond the juridical sphere. *Droit* can juridically condemn a State which is "unjust" or "illegal" from its point of view; but in order to enforce this judgement it must act politically, by carrying out a political revolution, for example. Therefore, the alteration of the State remains a specifically political event, even if this alteration has been incited by a transformation of *Droit*. Likewise, if the State alters a *Droit*, it is not acting politically but juridically. (In this case, however, the difference is less apparent.) Even by changing in respect to one another, *Droit* and the State still remain autonomous in relation to one another. And it is precisely the fact that they cannot mutually overcome each other even when they are in conflict which proves that they are autonomous respectively; for if they were one and the same thing, and if they were unable mutually to overcome each other, there would never be a conflict between them, just as no conflict is possible between political (or juridical, and so on) ideas that have no tendency to put themselves in the place of another. In this case there is simply different but compatible, or indeed complimentary, aspects of one and the same thing. By contrast, when *Droit* and the State are compatible and complimentary, they are nevertheless different; for they can enter into conflict while being unable mutually to overcome each other.

first place, a juridical Legislator. One will then say that the content of *Droit* is decreed by God, that it is constituted by the totality of divine commandments. Second, God can be considered acting as Judge. One will then say that legal disputes between men are definitively resolved by divine judgments, declared either directly (trial by ordeal, judicial duels, and so on) or through the intermediation of the representatives of God on earth (Church, State, and so on). Finally, third, the divinity can be supposed to act as the judicial Police. One will then say that the judgments are ultimately enforced by God himself, either on earth [*ici-bas*] or in heaven [*au-delà*], such that the intervention of the "third" is always efficacious, or indeed irresistible. And it should be understood that one can believe that the divinity performs all these various juridical functions.

In this theological conception, *Droit* is supposed to be realized even if the litigants are opposed to it. *Droit* is realized through the omnipotence of God, even contrary to the will of men. But this also goes for the atheistic conception, which is our own. Here also, the "third" is endowed (in principle) with an irresistible power, and he is able to use constraint in order to realize *Droit* without the situation [209] ceasing to be authentically juridical. The authenticity of the phenomenon does not depend upon the nature of constraint that is used.

Now let us assume that the litigants voluntarily conform to *Droit*. The theologian will generally say that this is necessary for reasons of "religious utility." The litigants remain Law-abiding [*en accord avec le Droit*] because they "fear God," because they know this is a necessary (if not always sufficient) condition for the "salvation of their souls." But theologians also sometimes say that the religious person subject to law [*le justiciable croyant*] remains law-abiding [*dans la légalité juridique*] for "disinterested" motives: through respect for the divinity or the love of God. Now this same dualism is to be found in the atheistic interpretation. On the one hand, it is said that men act in conformity with *Droit* for purely utilitarian reasons: either from fear of sanctions or because "honesty is the best policy,"[9] or finally, because they want to keep in existence the Society or State to which they belong. On the other hand, it is asserted that *Droit* can enjoy a *sui generis* Authority, that it is possible to conform to *Droit* quite simply out of "respect for the *Droit*" (cf. Kant's "*Achtung fürs Gesetz*" [respect or reverence for the law]),[10] because one wants the Justice that *Droit* realizes. Therefore, the authenticity of the juridical situation does not at all depend upon the recorded motives of the litigants. It is of little importance whether they are for or against the *Droit*. And it is of little importance, if they are for it, whether it is for some "utilitarian" motives, religious or secular, or in a "disinterested" way. And it is of little importance, in the latter case, whether they act out of respect for the *Droit* as such and for its principle, i.e, for Justice, or out of respect for the character [*la personne*] of the one or of those who promulgate the *Droit*, this character being able to be,

---

9. [Ed. In the original, this phrase is in English.]
10. [Ed. *Groundwork of the Metaphysics of Morals*, trans. H. J. Paton (New York: Harper Torchbooks, 1964), 68.]

moreover, either human or abstract (such as the State, for example) or, lastly, divine.

When we assert the autonomy of *Droit*, we are not thinking of the motives of the litigants, but rather of those "disinterested thirds," the Legislator, Judge, or the Police. And we assert that this "third" acts juridically according to an irreducible *sui generis* idea, which is that of Justice. Now when the theologians assign the role of this "third" to God, they also say that God acts in his capacity as Judge or as juridical Legislator, as well as enforcer of his judgments, according to the idea of Justice. And this idea corresponds to a specific and autonomous aspect of the divine character, according to the theologians themselves; for [210] not only do they distinguish Justice from other divine attributes, but they sometimes oppose it to them, by admitting a kind of conflict between the Justice of God and his goodness or his power, for example.[11]

While admitting the existence of God and in attributing to him the phenomenon of *Droit*, the theologians therefore recognize the specificity and autonomy of this phenomenon, since they base it upon a *sui generis* idea of Justice, irreducible to other divine ideas. The sole difference with our atheistic interpretation resides in the fact that the source of the autonomous idea of Justice is placed in God—that is, beyond the world, and not in man himself.

For the atheist, this transposition of the idea of Justice onto God (who consequently becomes the source and guarantor of *Droit*) is nothing other than a projection into the beyond of a juridically human phenomenon. Thus, this is why for Hegel, and after and according to him for Feuerbach, as well as later still for Durkheim and the modern sociologists, all theology is constituted by such projections of the immanent onto the transcendent.[12] For reasons that are possible to discover, theological man describes in an inadequate way authentic human phenomena by introducing elements of transcendence into relations that are in reality (and for us) purely immanent to man. Thus, in respect to juridical phenomenon, transcendence is introduced in order to give an account of certain authentic aspects of *Droit*. One says that *Droit* is a divine commandment in order to account, however obscurely, for the fact that *Droit* and Justice cannot be derived from biological phenomena and are radically opposed to them, being their negation (with no substitution possible). One speaks of judgments of God because one senses that the Judge should be absolutely impartial and disinterested. And one imagines a divine enforcement

---

11. Thus, before the destruction of Sodom, Abraham will reproach God (in very forceful terms) for the *injustice* of the intended action, seeing that the innocent could also be harmed. And it is to God's justice, and not his goodness, to which he has recourse against the almighty [Genesis 18:16–33].

12. [Ed. See, for example, Hegel, *Phenomenology of Spirit*, 410–78; *Lectures on the Philosophy of Religion*, 3 vols., I: 246–58, III: 138–51; and *Elements of the Philosophy of Right*, 290–304; Durkheim, *Elementary Forms of the Religious Life*, 1–20, 205–14, 415–47; and Ludwig Feuerbach, *The Essence of Christianity*, trans. George Eliot (New York: Harper Torchbooks, 1957), 1–32, and *Lectures on the Essence of Religion*, trans. Ralph Manheim (New York: Harper & Row, 1967), 17–24.]

of judgments based upon the idea of Justice because one understands that this enforcement should be carried out in principle in an irresistible way. Finally, one has recourse to God because one has the correct feeling that ideally *Droit* should be realized according to his authority, and not solely through the use of constraint.[13]

[211] When one makes God intervene in interactions between human beings by attributing to him the role of an "impartial and disinterested third," judging the interaction in question starting from a certain idea of Justice, the juridical nature of the situation is not distorted and its specificity and autonomy are implicitly recognized. But if God only intervenes in order to settle human controversies and to make Justice and *Droit* reign *on earth*, there is nothing specifically *religious* about the situation: it is authentically juridical but it is not authentically religious. In order for a situation to be specifically religious, man must be in a relation with the beyond and not only with the world or his fellow man. A man is truly religious only if he pursues a *transcendent* goal in relation to the world in which he lives, only if he seeks "salvation," as is said. Two litigants may be judged by God or submit to a divine *Droit*, but their situation will be juridical, and not religious, as long as they do not understand themselves, beyond their relationship with one another, in direct relation with God (taken in his capacity as Judge, or otherwise). Each of them would have to know that the action that relates him to his neighbor also relates him to God himself, and it is only to the extent that he knows this that he is also (subjectively) in a situation that we can call religious.[14]

Now the relations of man with God have nothing at all to do with *Droit*, and to the extent that a situation becomes authentically religious, it ceases to be juridical (and conversely). First of all, in a religious situation, man is isolated and remains alone with his God. Of course, he continues to interact with the world and his fellow man. But all these "worldly" interactions taken together are but one of the terms of his relation with God, and God is related exclusively to these "worldly" interactions of man taken together. It is true that God judges man according to these worldly interactions; for example, he will condemn the assassin or the thief. But in this religious "judgment" the person killed or robbed does not intervene as [212] such. It is not to avenge the murder victim nor to protect or compensate the victim of the theft that God will punish the guilty person. He only does it with a view to the guilty person himself, to whom he connects, so to speak, the threads of his acts, cutting away the connection of these acts to others: thus, it is this guilty person isolated from the rest of the world who will be "judged" religiously. This is why, from the religious point of view, intention

---

13. I abstract from the aspect of the question which was so predominant in the time of Voltaire. But it is an undeniable fact that one has, above all [211] in the past, often attributed to God the origin of juridical laws which the litigants would [otherwise] refuse to obey without this theological sanction.

14. For a theist, man can find himself (objectively) in a religious situation, i.e., in relation to God, even with knowing it. But if God does not exist, there is a religious situation only when man *believes himself* to be in relation to the beyond or God.

alone is equivalent to the completed [*effectif*] act. If, in the case of murder, one is concerned only with the murderer and not with the murder victim, it is of little importance indeed whether the murder is reduced to the criminal intention or the effectively accomplished act. And this is why the divine commandments can have an asocial or even anti-social character, prescribing celibacy for example. This is because man can find himself in a religious situation even on a desert island, and when he is in a religious situation he is always as if in a desert, even if he lives amongst men. For the religious person as such is essentially and radically "egoistic." His religious goal is the salvation of the soul. Now he can only save his own soul, and he is the only one who can do so. He therefore isolates himself from the world in relating himself to God, and it is to this isolated man that God is related. Thus, in the religious situation, unlike the juridical situation, there are not two human beings interacting, but a single being withdrawn into himself. This being acts, and is therefore interacting with, the external world. But what counts religiously is only the action itself and the effects it produces on the agent, while its effects on the external world are not taken into account.[15] In the authentic religious situation, God is therefore not—as in the juridical situation—an "impartial and disinterested *third*," for the simple reason that aside from God, only *one* person is implicated: the religious man isolated from the world and in a direct and exclusive relation with God.

Now when there are only two beings in relation, these beings are "parties" and there is no "disinterested third"—that is, no Arbiter or Judge in the juridical sense of the word. And this is also how the Religious person himself views the situation. For him, to commit an "injustice" is not so much "to offend" men but rather to offend God. Conversely, the Religious person is "just" first and foremost because he "loves God" and wants to "please him," and not in order to be "just" toward his [213] neighbor. For even if he loves this neighbor and acts toward him accordingly, he only loves him with a derivative love: he loves him through, in, and by his love for God and as a function of his love. (Cf. "The three-fold way" of St. Bonaventure, for example).[16] Therefore, God is not at all a "disinterested third" for the Religious person: he is a "party," and the Religious person believes himself to be interacting with *God* and not with his fellow man. But it is obvious that a "party" cannot be Judge or Arbiter in the juridical sense of these terms. And this is why one must say that an authentically religious situation has nothing to do with a juridical situation.

One can also express this observation by saying that *Droit* has as its goal the realization of justice on earth, in and by a purely human society, while Religion has an essentially transcendent goal. Legal rules regulate an interaction between two human beings on the very plane on which it occurs. The divine command-

---

15. For many theologians, the external effect of an imputed act is not even the work of the agent himself, but rather of God. And the state of the world and of society depends not on the acts of the men who live there, but on divine providence.

16. [Ed. *The Works of Bonaventure*, trans. Jose de Vinck, vol. I (Paterson, NJ: St. Anthony Guild Press, 1960), 76–7.]

ment, by contrast, has in mind the fate of man in the beyond. Thus, when a Religious person acts in conformity with what for him constitutes Justice (prescribed by God), he does not do so for the sake of his neighbors, nor even for his own sake as one living in the world among his neighbors, but solely for his soul, isolated from the rest of the universe and considered as part of a "world" situated in the beyond and exclusively in relation with this beyond, whether personified or not.

In these conditions, it makes no sense to apply juridical categories to specifically religious situations. In particular, one should avoid speaking in juridical terms of relations between man and his God.

Nevertheless, confusions between the religious and juridical spheres occur very frequently and are, so to speak, inevitable; and the preceding analysis has explained the reason for this.

On the one hand, we have seen that *Droit* has the tendency to theologize itself by divinizing the character of the "third." Now, to the extent that Religion is theistic, there is necessarily a confusion between God taken as a religious entity and this same God acting as Judge, Legislator, or Police in the juridical life of men.

On the other hand, Religion itself has a tendency to cloak itself in juridical forms; for in realizing itself, Religion socializes itself in the form of a Church (in the broad sense). Now every society requires a *Droit* for its existence, and this *Droit* is connected to the relation between Governors and the Governed. Now within the Church, the Governor is ultimately God himself. It is therefore entirely natural that he is supposed to serve as Judge in [214] the proper sense of the term (from whence comes the idea of "canon *Droit*"). But it is easy to see that in this case the situation ceases to be authentically religious. Religion does not take an interest in *Droit* properly so-called except to the extent that it socializes itself by becoming the Church—that is, by realizing itself in the world. But a worldly reality is no longer a religious entity. It is a social or political entity like any other. Therefore, it is not surprising that one encounters [in such an entity] authentically juridical phenomena. The fact that these phenomena are theologized proves only that, for entirely comprehensible reasons, the authentic phenomenon is here not adequate in the sense that it is wrongly interpreted by those who experience it.

When all is said and done, one can therefore say that not only can the juridical phenomenon not be reduced to the religious phenomenon, but that these two phenomena are mutually exclusive as soon as they are authentic and adequate. For us, i.e., in truth, *Droit* has nothing to do with Religion because *Droit* is a relation between three members, while Religion is a relation between only two of them.

§ 31

There is no Religion without transcendence, and man is not truly religious except to the extent that he subordinates all this-worldly values to values situated in the beyond, where all life on earth is but a means for him to obtain satisfaction (or happiness) after his death—in any case, in a world other than the material spatio-temporal world. And this is why *religious* life in the world and in Society is completely lacking in juridical character. The religious relation is only a relation between two terms, one of which is necessarily transcendent in relation to the other, regardless, moreover, of whether this transcendent term is personified, or indeed anthropomorphized (theistic Religions), or impersonal (atheistic Religions, such as primitive Buddhism)—an "other world," a "beyond" in general.

But it is not enough to suppress the element of transcendence in order that the man who was living in a religious situation finds himself right away in a juridical situation. In the religious situation, the man was disinterested, as it were, in his relations with others (and he was even able—at the limit—to suppress these relations completely, [e.g.,] the case with hermetic Religion). These relations were only of interest to him [the religious person] to the [215] extent that they were determining his own being, the (religious) value of his own personality, in thus setting down the nature of his relations with God, who takes account of these relations when he (religiously) "judges" him—that is, "saves" him or "damns" him. The Religious person behaves in a certain way in the world and in society in order to realize a positive (religious) value in his own being, this value being understood to be recognized and rewarded (religiously) by God or in general in the beyond. Now this isolation, this religious "egoism" (egotism), individualism, or solipsism can be maintained even after the transcendent term (personified or not) of the religious relation has been suppressed, such that the man remains alone with himself. Thus, by ceasing to be religious, the situation becomes *moral* or *ethical* in the proper sense of the term.[17]

Just like the Religious person, the Moralist (as Moralist) only enters into interaction with the natural world and the Society of his fellow man in order to "perfect" his personality. Another person is never an end in himself for him, but only a means to attaining or maintaining his own "perfection."[18] The Reli-

---

17. Morality is therefore by definition areligious, or indeed atheistic. Of course, the moral man may be, *in other respects,* religious, just as he can be a citizen, an aesthete, a juridical man, and so on. But to the extent that man finds himself in an authentic moral situation, he is in complete isolation: he is alone in the world and is related only to himself. Therefore, he is not in a religious situation: he separates himself from the beyond to the same extent that he separates himself from the empirical world. And he is an atheist in the sense that the existence of God plays no role in his attitude: if he is "moral," it is from love of morality itself, but not from love of God. And this is precisely what distinguishes him from the religious man, who conforms to divine commandments, which may, moreover, have the same content as the "commandments" of Morality.

18. This seems to contradict what Kant says: "Man must never treat another man simply as a means." But the contradiction is only apparent; for according to Kant, one must not treat a man as a means because if one does so one does not realize one's own moral perfection. To treat another as an "end in himself" is therefore a *means* of being moral oneself. It is not for the sake of the moral perfection of my neighbor that I should treat him as an "end in himself" but in order to perfect myself. This is why it is intention alone that counts. [Ed. *Groundwork of the Metaphysics of Morals,* 95ff.]

gious person, however, seeks this (religious) "perfection" in order to please God, whereas the Moralist seeks (moral) "perfection" in order to please himself. Furthermore, the Religious person expects his perfection (sanctioned by God) only in the beyond, [or] in any case in radical opposition to the empirical world, while the [216] Moralist enjoys it down here, in continuing to live within the natural and social world. Through his religious perfection, the Religious person essentially differs from his "profane" fellow man, while the perfect Moralist is only "morally" superior to others, without being radically different from them. (As well, it is only religious conversion that constitutes a "second birth," the ascension of a "new man" replacing the "old Adam." A moral "conversion," by contrast, is only an improvement: in perfecting oneself morally, one remains the man that one always was and everyone else is, from whence comes the absence of all ritual or cultish symbols in Morality).

The Moralist therefore differs from the Religious person and is similar to the juridical man by the fact that he lives entirely in this world, without relating his being and his acts to some transcendent entity in relation to him. It is not in order to leave the world or society that one is "moral" or "just" (law-abiding [*juridiquement légal*]), and it is in this world that one "benefits." But whereas the "just" person wants to realize a value in the world, outside of himself, the "moral" person only has in mind a purely internal realization: the "just" person wants to realize Justice (through *Droit*) so that the world (the Society) becomes (juridically) perfect, while the moralist realizes Morality only so as to become (morally) perfect himself. And it is this fundamental difference between *Droit* and Morality that controls and explains all the others.

We have seen that the juridical situation necessarily implies *three* terms: the two "litigants" interacting and the "third" who judges them. Of course, if the "litigants" are spontaneously "just" they can dispense with the Judge. But in this case the Judge remains virtually present because each of the "litigants" is then not only a "party" but also an "impartial and disinterested third." He takes account of his co-agent, places himself on the same plane as the other, and applies to the interaction the idea of Justice (egalitarian or of equivalence); for this idea implies and presupposes an interaction between (at least) *two* human beings, and it loses all its sense if one eliminates one of the two. To realize Justice is to apply a legal rule, and this rule is directed not at a single isolated person, but always to (at least) two persons interacting.

The religious situation, by contrast, implicates only *two* terms which count: the "litigant" (religiously speaking) and the (divine) "Judge," or in any case the "beyond" [217] to which the "litigant" is related. As for the other person who is interacting with the "litigant," he is outside the religious situation, and the "Judge" does not take him into account in his (religious) "judgment." As well, when the "litigant" himself acts as Judge, he thinks only of his own relation with the beyond by abstracting from his co-agent. And this is why he can "judge" himself (religiously) and can be "judged" by God even if he is no longer interacting with another person, even if he is alone on earth.

Finally, in the moral situation, there is but *a single* term: the "litigant" (morally speaking) himself. Just like in the religious situation, he abstracts from the other term of the interaction. But because for him there is no longer God nor a beyond, there is no Judge but himself. He gives the (moral) Law to himself, it is he that applies it (through his moral "conscience"), and it is also he who "executes" his (moral) "judgement," either by forcing himself to execute the Law or by punishing himself for having transgressed it ("bad conscience," "repentance," and so on). He measures himself against his ideal of moral perfection. But this ideal is not outside of him: it is in him as an ideal, it is still in him as a (moral) duty, and it is also in him because it is supposed to exist once it is realized.

When, in a moral situation, man "judges" himself morally, this has nothing at all to do with the attitude of a Judge in the proper or juridical sense of the word; for he is not at all "impartial and disinterested" toward himself, [and] he does not at all put himself on the same plane as the other with whom he is interacting. He is only (morally) interested in himself, and he is (morally) uninterested toward the other. He judges *himself* in his interaction with the other: he judges neither the other nor the interaction with the other as such. And this is why the Moralist has no need of a (human) Judge properly so-called, of an "impartial and disinterested" *third,* of a man truly other than himself. The juridical man is able to do without an effective Judge. But he himself then plays the role of this Judge, and every juridical situation accepts the presence of an effective Judge, of a "disinterested *third*": when a man judges himself juridically, he does it exactly as another would have done it in his place, and the other can always judge him as he judges himself. But this is no longer the case when it is a matter of a moral "judgment." The third, i.e., the juridical Judge, addresses the litigant in his interaction with another—that is, considers only that which is externalized or externalizable in him, [218] that which is objective or objectifiable. The moral "Judge," by contrast, isolates the "litigant" and considers in his interaction with the other only what is internalized or internalizable in him, only what is subjective or subjectivizable: he is only worried about the *intention.* Now intention as such is not accessible to a (human) Judge who is other than the agent. Man, therefore, cannot be "judged" morally by another. Generally speaking, the other will "judge" him differently than he "judges" himself, for the other does not have the same data at his disposal. Of course, the Moralist may take into account moral "judgments" that others make on his account. But he can only accept them after verification, for they can always be false. But if he notices that they are true, he has in fact "judged" himself, and the "judgments" of others will no longer be of any interest to him. At the very most, they serve to bring to his attention certain aspects of his acts: they have a value only as stimulants of his own "judgment," and not as definitive "judgments" themselves.

Unlike the juridical man, therefore, the Moralist will never have recourse to an "impartial and disinterested *third*"; he has no need of a Judge or Arbiter in the juridical sense of these words. Conversely, as a Moralist, he will never serve as Judge himself in relation to others. And [this is] not only because he knows that he cannot do it, since he lacks the essential data, i.e., the intentions of the "litigant"; he will not [act as a Judge] because he has no reason to do so. As a Moralist, he is only interested in his own moral perfection, and that of others leaves him indifferent. Therefore, he does not "judge" it. And this is why Morality generally prohibits its disciples from judging their neighbors.[19] On the contrary, the idea of Justice invites man to judge his fellow man, and "justice denied" is always considered the most serious judicial wrong; for to realize Justice is to actualize *Droit*—that is, to apply as Judge (Legislator or Police) the principle of Justice to given interactions. Now to be a Judge is to be a "disinterested third": it is therefore to "have an interest" in something else besides oneself, to "have an interest" in others.

The juridical man is therefore characterized by the fact that he [219] is able to resort to a Judge other than himself and that he should not refuse to intervene in the capacity of Judge or Arbiter as soon as others resort to him. The moral man, by contrast, is not able to submit himself to the (moral) "judgment" of another and must refrain from "judging" others (morally).[20] But the moral man may "judge" himself (morally) while the juridical man is not able to judge himself (juridically). On the one hand, he is able to "judge" pure intentions which do not generate any interaction with others and which therefore exist only for himself. On the other hand, he can "judge" acts and behaviors (even purely theoretical) that do not imply the existence of other men; for since it is only a matter of his own perfection, he can in principle realize Morality even if he is alone in the world. Thus, one can imagine moral duties toward Nature: animals, plants, or indeed even inanimate beings (which means that one can attain moral perfection only to the extent that one behaves in a certain manner toward these natural beings). And one can even prescribe moral duties toward oneself: even in complete isolation, one must behave in a certain manner if one wishes to be morally perfect. But all these duties have no juridical significance, and this is why they are not found in *authentic* Legal systems;[21] for *Droit* only exists when there is an application of the idea of Justice. Now, this idea (both as egalitarian Justice and the Justice of equivalence) implies the notion of an interaction between (at least) *two human* beings, who are supposed to be equal or equivalent. One cannot be "just" or "unjust" toward

---

19. The *religious* sense of this evangelical formula is as follows: judge not your neighbor, because it is for God and not for you to judge him ("morally" in the "religious" sense). But the *moral* sense is: mind your own business. The theoretical interpretation of this would be: do not judge others because you are unable to do so.

20. It should be understood that the man who is a "moral man" can very well juridically judge others in his capacity as a "juridical man." Thus, the Gospel forbids religious (or moral) "judgement" of others but not *Droit* as such.

21. In fact, one finds this in written or customary codes. But if it is not a matter of simple mistakes, these juridical duties toward Nature and oneself are always ultimately duties toward other human beings, individual or collective. I have already spoken of this, and I will speak about this again a little later.

Nature or toward oneself, if one takes the words "just" and "unjust" in their proper sense—that is, in their juridical sense.

To realize Justice is to apply its principles to interactions between human beings. *Droit*, which realizes Justice, can therefore never want to suppress these interactions, can never (consciously) become anti-social. By contrast, Morality can be realized in and by isolated human beings. [220] One can therefore imagine that some Moralities entail the more or less complete isolation of the individual for (moral) perfection. And this is why there are Moralities that are more or less anti-social, just as there are anti-social Religions. Duties toward oneself may absorb all moral duties, such that there will no longer be moral duties toward others, unless there exists a moral duty to deny those others (actively or only in theory). It is in this way that Morality may lead to a strict solipsism, even more strict than religious solipsism, which always implies a dualism between [life in] this world, and thus the empirical I, and the world beyond (cf. Max Stirner's morality).[22]

All this clearly shows us that Morality is quite different from *Droit*. *Droit* is dominated by a social interest, by the will to realize a value (Justice) in Society, and its application presupposes (on the part of the Judge) an essentially "impersonal" attitude. By contrast, Morality isolates the individual from Society, being the will to realize a value (moral perfection) in every individual considered separately (the moral perfection of the Society being only the sum of the perfections of its members), and its application (by the moral "Judge") is strictly "personal." Therefore, it is obviously impossible to reduce *Droit* to Morality, and conversely: the moral situation excludes the "third" without whom there can be no juridical situation, and the latter does not take into account the isolated personality, removed from their "deep" or "intimate" interactions, in which all moral values are supposed to be realized.

Why have we, therefore, so often conflated those two spheres and why is their concrete delimitation so difficult?

Generally speaking, this is because there is no means of distinguishing by its content a rule of behavior that is a legal rule from one that constitutes a purely moral rule. Of course, there are moral prescriptions which have nothing juridical about them (those concerning animals, for example), and there are legal rules that have truly nothing to do with morality. But the vast majority of legal rules lend themselves to a moral interpretation, just as the majority of moral prescriptions can be transformed into authentic legal rules.

Thus, a Morality can state, for example, that achieving (moral) perfection is impossible if one does not conform to a given *Droit*. At that point, if you will, this *Droit* will be [221] a moral duty. But even in this case, Morality and *Droit* will remain essentially distinct, while having one and the same content; for the "disinterested third," i.e., the juridical Judge, will continue to be able to judge only interactions, while the moral "Judge" will be content to assess the intra-

---

22. [Ed. Max Stirner, *The Ego and His Own*, trans. Steven T. Byington (New York: Boni and Liveright, 1918).]

subjective projections of these objective relations, and therefore could only be the one interested himself. And if the juridical man develops and applies this *Droit* to realize Justice in Society, the Moralist will obey his moral rules identical to this *Droit* only in order to realize a value deep within himself.

Conversely, almost any moral rule can be transformed into a legal rule. To this end, it is enough to assume an appropriate interaction giving rise to a (juridical) judgment by a "disinterested third." Thus, Society or the State can decree that the application of a certain Morality is necessary for its existence. At that point, this Morality becomes a *Droit*. But here as well, *Droit* and Morality will remain distinct while having one and the same content; for the Moralist will continue thinking only about his own perfection and will have no need for an external Judge, while the juridical man will have in mind Society or the State and will only take into account objective interactions, contrary to or in conformity with the principles of Morality established as legal rules: he will remain indifferent to all of Morality's content which is not translated or can not be translated into an interaction.

It should be understood that for *Droit* to be authentic, it must be a realization of the idea of Justice in one form or another. A moral situation which does not imply any interaction to which one may apply the principle of Justice cannot therefore be transformed into an authentic juridical situation. Now certain *Droits,* above all archaic or primitive *Droits,* sometimes imply under a false juridical guise rules [which are] specifically moral, which the Phenomenologist does not have to take into account and which the juridical Legislator should have eliminated. Moreover, these pseudo-legal rules tend to disappear from modern juridical legislation more and more. But the majority of moral rules can receive an authentic juridical interpretation and thus be transformed into genuine Legal rules. For this, it is enough that the moral rule which has in mind the behavior of a single human being is transformed into a rule aiming at the interaction between two beings to whom the idea of Justice may be applied. It is in this way, for example, that many moral duties [222] toward oneself can be interpreted. Morality may forbid suicide, and this ban has nothing juridical in itself. But suicide can be interpreted as an interaction between the suicidal person and Society, and this interaction can become the object of a legal rule forbidding suicide, for one can say that it is "unjust" that a member of Society should voluntarily escape from obligations incumbent upon the other members. But the moral ban of the simple desire to commit suicide cannot become a legal rule since an unrealized desire, i.e., [a desire that is] not externalized in any manner, is not an interaction and therefore does not give rise to the principle of Justice.

Conversely, Morality can appropriate a *Droit* by transforming its juridical rules into moral rules only by accepting as a moral principle the idea of Justice which is at the base of the *Droit* in question. Thus, a purely egoistic or solipsist morality, for example, will never assimilate any *Droit* whatsoever; in this case, therefore, the opposition between *Droit* and Morality will be explicit and apparent. But as current modern Moralities always have a more or less "social" character and recognize the moral value of the principle of Justice, stating that one can only be morally perfect provided that one is also just, they can incorporate the major part of the valid *Droit* in the Society where they exist. And this is why it becomes difficult to determine the respective spheres of *Droit* and Morality. To do so, it is necessary to refer not to the content of juridical and moral rules, which may be identical, but to the attitude man adopts toward these rules, to the motive which makes him act in conformity to them. When the attitude renders impossible the intervention of a "disinterested third," and when only the "perfection" of an isolated agent is concerned, detached from the result of his acts, there will be Morality but not *Droit*. By contrast, when there will be an intervention of a "third," and when it is a matter of the fate of at least two distinct persons who are linked by an interaction, there will be *Droit*, but no Morality properly so-called.

It is generally said that the idea of Justice is a *moral* category. And we have just seen that one can say this provided that one clarifies that Justice is—for Morality—*one* of the *means* of becoming morally perfect, whereas for *Droit* the realization of Justice is an *end* in itself and its *only* end: by prescribing Justice, Morality wants to realize certain (moral) values in every man *individually*, whereas the *Droit* which realizes Justice wants to organize [223] in a certain manner the *relations* between men, irrespective of who these men are. It is therefore better to distinguish terminologically Justice as the sole *principle* of *Droit* from "Justice" as *one* of the *means* of Morality, and to say that the idea of Justice properly so-called is a juridical and not moral category. Of course, one can say that the idea of Justice can have an interpretation and a realization both moral and juridical. But if there are no *Droits* which are not based upon some form of the idea of Justice, there are Moralities, or at the very least moral rules, which have nothing to do with this idea and which are even contrary to it.[23] Furthermore, *Droit* realizes Justice in a direct and necessary manner: it only exists to realize Justice and it realizes it as soon as it exists. Morality, by contrast, only realizes Justice indirectly and in a sort of optional manner: it is there to make men morally perfect, and it realizes Justice only because men become perfect, and to the extent that they become so. If a Legal rule has been applied to a given interaction, such an interaction has become "just" by this very fact—or there has been no juridical application at all. By contrast, Morality is already realized if only one of the interacting agents is morally perfect. But if the other is not, the interaction may remain "unjust." Morality can therefore (partially) realize itself in a Society which remains unjust, while *Droit* necessarily makes Society just when this *Droit* is realized. And, once again, it is entirely possible that an authentic Morality would simply deny any idea of Justice.

---

23. Therefore, to give alms for moral motives, for example, has nothing to do with Justice, for the act morally benefits only the one who gives and not at all the one who receives. And almost all specifically moral acts are "unjust" from the juridical point of view, for these are "duties" to which no "*droits*" correspond.

Let us therefore say that the idea of Justice may be used for moral ends, but that its authentic realization generates not a Morality but a *Droit*. And this *Droit* as such no longer has anything to do with Morality properly so-called, for it can realize Justice even among profoundly amoral, or indeed immoral, men, which is, of course, of no interest at all to Morality; for Morality has no need of a Justice even perfectly realized by a *Droit*, if this realization does not imply the "internal" perfection of the men who act in conformity to this *Droit*. Now, since Justice tends to realize itself in and by [224] a phenomenon which is called *Droit* and which has nothing to do with Morality, one can say that it is a *sui generis* juridical idea, essentially distinct from specifically moral ideas.

One could even say that if—by some remote chance—one were able to separate the moral man from the juridical man, the first would never have introduced in his Morality rules based upon the idea of Justice, an idea which he would not even have. Conversely, the exclusively juridical man would never have thought that Justice also creates a strictly personal value that one can realize deep down within oneself in addition to and independently of the value that one realizes in and by, or better still, as an interaction with others: he would not know that he has to be "just" himself in order to realize Justice and that in realizing Justice one realizes it not only in Society, but also in every individual taken separately. And truth to tell, this moral, personal "Justice" has nothing to do with the juridical ideal of Justice, which is the idea or ideal of a relation, an interaction—that is, an externalization. It would therefore be better to designate this virtue or moral perfection by another word: by love, charity, or goodness, for example, or simply altruism.

But in fact, the concrete man is always a moral and juridical man at the same time (and many other things as well). And this is why his Morality generally implies rules inspired by the idea of Justice, while his *Droit* presents itself to him also in the form of moral "duties." But the Phenomenologist must be able to distinguish these two different phenomena, while expecting that the man who experiences them will learn to do it himself.

It is necessary to say, moreover, that *Droit* and Morality have always been felt to constitute two distinct phenomena, even if one has not always succeeded in formulating their difference correctly.

One generally says that *Droit* differs from Morality in that it does not take account of *intentions* and accepts the application of *constraint*. As it stands, this assertion is not correct. For on the one hand, *Droit* is well and truly concerned with "intentions," seeing that it can distinguish a voluntary from an involuntary wrong and can punish a straightforward attempted murder, for example. Likewise, according to modern *Droit*, the judge who reaches a decision concerning a contract should take account of the intentions of the contracting parties, and so forth. On the other hand, Morality does not at all exclude constraint. One can very well use violence for morally pedagogical reasons. [225] And a Society which wants to be morally perfect can very well constrain its members to conform to the moral ideal adopted by the Society. Of course, constraint alone does not realize Morality, but it can very well contribute to its realization: another person can help me to forcefully vanquish myself in order to make me conform to a moral ideal.

But the commonly accepted definition, well interpreted, can be kept by the Phenomenologist; for if *Droit* can be interested in the "intention," it does so only to the extent that this intention externalizes or objectifies itself in some manner—that is, manifests itself outside, being in this way in interaction with the outside. *Droit* always relates the intention not to the one who has it but to another, to his external object; for *Droit* is related to the interaction and not to the agents taken individually. Thus, it is not the intention to murder as such that is punished by *Droit,* but solely the intention *to kill another.* By contrast, Morality can forbid the simple desire to kill another without the will to kill him. As for constraint, its function in *Droit* is also different from the role it plays in Morality. Constraint may by itself fully and perfectly realize *Droit* (i.e., Justice). It is of little importance for *Droit* that its rules are voluntarily applied or under the pressure of constraint (physical or moral), for *Droit* is interested in the interaction as such and not in the characters [*aux personnes*] of the agents. Morality, by contrast, can only use constraint as a preliminary measure, purely pedagogical moreover. Action that is violently imposed on a man does not realize moral perfection in him. It can only help him to realize it; for man is only morally perfect to the extent that he does violence to himself, or in any case, develops solidarity with the violence done to him.[24]

§ 32

[226] Actions which relate man to his neighbor are generally divided into *egoistic actions* and *altruistic actions.* At first glance, these two categories are easy to define. An action is said to be "egoistic" when it is determined exclusively by the agent's own interest, by his desire for happiness or satisfaction, whatever it may be: it is not necessarily harmful to others, but it may be so, for it does not take any account of the interests and desires of others. By contrast, the "altruistic" action is determined, in part at the very least, by the interests and desires of others: thus, in certain cases, it can even be harmful to the agent himself and be in opposition to his own desire for happiness or satisfaction. But upon closer examination one becomes aware that the application of these definitions to concrete human actions is far from easy.

---

24. In a religious situation, violence is equally admissible and it can realize by itself a religious value in the assaulted man: the religious rite can be efficacious even if it works against the will of the interested party. But this constraint has, however, nothing juridical about it because it does not work to realize the idea of Justice in an interaction of the interested party with others. It is only done in the interest of the one to whom it is applied and—perhaps—in the interest of the divinity, while juridical constraint has in mind the interest of *another* than the one who is constrained, this other being situated on the same existential plane as him: it has, therefore, a social goal; it wants to realize Justice in an interaction between human beings.

Of course, there are very clear cases of egoistic actions. The sadist who kills for the pleasure of killing [and] with no intention of revealing his crime to anyone surely acts as an egoist. But can one say this of someone who harms someone solely in order to please another? Now the vast majority of human actions belong to this category, and one always experiences difficulties when it is a matter of qualifying "morally" the classic case of the mother stealing in order to feed her children. Furthermore, can an action performed for the sake of the desire for recognition (*Anerkennen*) be truly categorized as egoistic? Of course, one can say that in these cases, the agent is pursuing his own interest without taking into account that of others. But his "interest" consists in nothing other than the desire to provoke a certain state of mind in others than himself, this state of mind being, it is true, the recognition of his own value. And the difficulties further increase when one tackles the problem from the other angle by trying to define altruistic actions. Moralists have long observed that any action whatsoever, even those that appear most altruistic, can be brought back to the egoistic type of action by applying the following reasoning: if I please another, it is because pleasing others pleases me personally.

To reason in this manner, i.e., asserting that all human actions are "egoistic," is simply to deny the opposition "egoism-altruism," to suppress these [227] two categories. Now this is clearly impossible; for if it is difficult to grasp in a rational definition egoism and altruism, one cannot deny the existence of these two phenomena nor their immediate intuitive distinction. It is obvious that the would-be "egoist," who draws his pleasure from the pleasure (real or imagined) of others, differs essentially from the "egoist" properly so-called, who is completely uninterested in the pleasure or displeasure of others.

Concrete actions may generally be of a mixed character. Thus, the stealing mother is surely egoistic in relation to the one she robs, but she is also no doubt altruistic in relation to her children. We must, therefore, distinguish in principle in any human action an egoistic *aspect* and an altruistic *aspect,* leaving aside provisionally the question of knowing if there are *concrete* actions which present only one of these aspects. In the altruistic aspect of his concrete action, the agent will act for the sake of what he believes (rightly or wrongly) the interest of the one other than himself to be, the word "interest" being taken in its broadest sense. By contrast, in the egoistic aspect of the action, the agent will act for the sake of his own interest only, without taking account of what could be according to him the interest of the other in the case in question.

Assuming this to be the case, one can ask how the opposition "egoism-altruism" relates to juridical action as such.

One should notice first of all that a *concrete* action is never purely and exclusively juridical, *Droit* and Justice never being in fact the only motivations of the real agent. But just as one can artificially form the "abstract" notion of homo juridicus (akin to that of the homo economicus, religiosus, politicus, and so on), one can isolate artificially the specifically juridical element of the concrete action. And it is concerning this "abstract" element that one will ask if it should be categorized as egoistic or altruistic.

Now we have seen that a juridical situation necessarily implies *three* elements: the two interacting agents, i.e., the litigants, and the Judge (or Legislator or Police). And we have seen that the interaction of the agents could be anything, as well as the motives which make them act and react. Thus, although the existence of both agents is indispensable for there to be *Droit,* it is in the "third" that the essence of the juridical phenomenon is condensed. It is in the action of this "third," acting as juridical Legislator, Judge, or [228] judicial Police, that one finds the specifically and exclusively juridical element which is of interest to us.[25] The opposition "egoism-altruism" must therefore be related to the action of the "third" acting as a "third."

Now, in his three avatars as Legislator, the Judge or Arbiter, and Police, this "third" is characterized as a "third" by the fact of being "impartial and disinterested." One can therefore say that "impartiality" and "disinterestedness" characterize all specifically juridical action, that an action could not be said to be "juridical" if it does not present these two qualities.

Now, by definition, a "disinterested" action cannot be said to be "egoistic." And indeed, it is enough to observe that the action of the Legislator, of the Judge, or of the Police presents an egoistic aspect when it is carried out for the sake of his own interest, such that the juridical value of this action becomes suspect. Generally speaking, no one will want to say that the desire to pass law juridically, to judge, or to enforce judgments, testifies to an egoistic attitude. Of course, man may have an egoistic interest in being Judge, and so on: he may want to be one in order to earn a living or to occupy a certain social rank, and so on. But when he is a Legislator, Judge, or Police, and when he acts juridically as such, it is surely not for egoistic motives that he does so. When he formulates, applies, or enforces a legal rule, he is not supposed to draw any benefit from his act. In any case, he is supposed to abstract from his own interest in the matter.

Therefore, the juridical action as such is surely not egoistic. Let us now see if it can be called altruistic.

One can say that any altruistic action is carried out in an attitude of "love" (in the broadest sense of the word): to act for the sake of another's interests, to draw pleasure or satisfaction from his pleasure or from the advantages that he draws from the action, this is to "love" this other in some manner. And to love is to give a positive value to the very being of the one we love, to the simple fact that he exists, independently of his acts, [and] in particular independently of his acts toward the one who loves him, independently of his behavior toward him. (Cf. Goethe: "We love someone for who he *is,* and not for what he *does.*") Now the "third" who interests us [229] must not only be "disinterested" but also "impartial." Therefore, he must not act out of love for one of the two litigants, and if he loves one of them, he must abstract from this love in his juridi-

---

25. It should be understood that if the agents conform voluntarily to *Droit,* their action will imply a juridical element. But then each of them will act or think also as an "impartial and disinterested third," and it is as this third that he will act juridically.

cal action. This means that if he loved both, he would have to abstract from this dual love if he wanted to intervene juridically. And indeed, the interests of the litigants being by definition contrary, the love of the Judge for one would neutralize his love for the other, and he could judge them as if he did not love them at all. Juridical action, therefore, has nothing to do with individualized love. But it does not have anything to do either with generalized love for man as such, with the so-called "christian" love of the altruist properly speaking; for the Judge is interested in the *acts,* and not in the *being,* of his litigants. Detached from their interaction they are nothing for him. On the contrary, he detaches from them their interaction and he judges it without taking into account the agents individually. The legal rule that the "third" formulates, applies, or enforces in his juridical action is related to abstract interactions, so to speak, and not to concrete persons. If he pursues an "interest," it is not his own, nor that of others; he acts solely in the interest of Justice, as one says. It is in this way that he can forbid murder and punish the murderer without worrying about whether the victim was consenting or not, without asking whether the murder was in his interests or not (as in the case of the murder of someone terminally ill who is suffering). Thus, the idea of a judgment going against the desire and interest of both litigants is not at all absurd. And the adage *Fiat justicia, pereat mundus* shows very well that the juridical action can only be said to be "altruistic" if one calls "altruistic" any action which is not egoistic.

Now, in reality, the juridical action is neither egoistic nor altruistic: it is absolutely neutral in relation to this opposition. It arises neither from the interest of the one who acts nor from his love for others: it is impartial and disinterested in the strongest sense of these terms. And this absolute *neutrality* of the juridical action as such is an important argument in favor of the thesis of the specificity and autonomy of *Droit.*

If the juridical action arises neither from the agent's own interest nor from the idea he has of the interests of others, it is because it results from a *sui generis* "interest," and this "interest" is nothing other than man's desire to realize his idea of Justice. It is in the diaphanous and glacial atmosphere of [230] absolute *neutrality,* of perfect "impartiality" and of total "disinterestedness," that the realization of the idea of Justice is carried out in and by *Droit,* or better still as *Droit.* And it is in this same atmosphere that this idea as such is born and develops, the *sui generis* idea which is the base and the foundation of any *Droit* whatsoever.

We must now see what is the autonomous origin and development of the specifically juridical idea or ideal of Justice.

Part Two

The Origin and Evolution of *Droit*

§ 34[1]

[233] *DROIT* IS THE application of a certain idea of Justice to given social interactions. Its content is therefore determined both by the character of the idea of Justice which is at its base and by the nature of the interactions to which this idea is applied. Thus, to study the genesis and evolution of *Droit* is to study the genesis and evolution of social interactions as such—that is, to study the birth of history and the historical process as a whole. Moreover, like all human phenomena, *Droit* is intimately linked to all the other historical phenomena, such as Religion, Morality, Politics, and so on. In other words, the content of a given *Droit* will be co-determined by the religious, moral, political, and so on, ideas of the epoch. From this point of view as well the genesis and evolution of *Droit* cannot be studied in isolation: it is the totality of culture that must be studied by situating the *Droit* in question there.

One can, however, isolate from the given "positive" *Droit* its specifically juridical elements by eliminating from it all there is of religion, morality, politics, and so on. And one can still abstract from its concrete content in the sense that one can refer not to the social interactions to which the idea of Justice is applied which is at its [*Droit's*] base but to this idea itself. In other words, one can study the idea of Justice as realized in and by *Droit* by isolating it from all the other not specifically juridical ideas.

Now experience shows that the idea of Justice, even taken [234] in isolation in its autonomous juridical specificity, is subject to an evolution in time. The very principle of Justice, which is at the base of any *Droit* whatsoever, is not everywhere and always the same. One and the same social interaction can generate, at different epochs or among different peoples, different legal rules solely because one applies to it principles of Justice which are not the same.

One can therefore study the *evolution* of the idea of Justice as such. One can also consider the problem of the *origin* of this idea. Finally, one can speculate on what the Justice of the future will be—"absolute" Justice in the sense that it will be universally and eternally valid, being accepted for all time by the whole of humanity.

This is what I intend to try to do in Part Two. As for *Droit* properly so-called, I will not speak about it. In order to go from the study of the idea of Justice to that of *Droit*, one must study, on the one hand, the social relations

---

1. [Ed. Although Part 1, chapter 3 ended with § 32, the first section in Part 2 begins with § 34. Although it is possible (albeit extremely unlikely) that there is a missing section (i.e., § 33), we have decided to begin Part 2 with the Gallimard section number in order to avoid confusion with the French edition.]

to which the idea of Justice is applied originally and during its evolution, and on the other hand, take into account influences that this application is subject to from other historical phenomena such as Religion, Morality, Politics, and so on. Now such a study would take me too far. Moreover, it is the idea of Justice which constitutes the specific and autonomous juridical element of *Droit*. The specific and autonomous juridical evolution of humanity, therefore, is in the final analysis nothing other than the evolution of its idea of Justice.

To say that the idea of Justice is a *sui generis* idea, specific and autonomous, is to say that it is contemporaneous with man himself, being directly rooted in the human being as such, independently of other phenomena which arise from this being. To study the *origin* of the idea of Justice, therefore, is to show why and how it is generated by the anthropogenic act itself—that is, by the act in and by which the human being creates himself from the animal homo sapiens, which always serves him as [material] support. And to study the *evolution* of the idea of Justice is to show how and why this idea transforms itself according to alterations that the anthropogenic act is subject to during time, i.e., during history; for man creates himself in time and he creates himself as a temporal being. The anthropogenic act, therefore, is itself essentially temporal: it is realized in the form of successive stages, the totality of these stages forming the historical evolution of humanity. And just as "integral," "perfect," or "absolute" man [235] is nothing other than the result or totality of this historical process, absolute Justice is the result or integration of its evolution.

The analysis of the anthropogenic act is taken up in Hegel's *Phenomenology of Spirit*. And I assume familiarity with it (cf. my "Autonomy and Dependence of Self-consciousness" in *Mesures*).[2] It will quite simply be a matter of connecting to this analysis that of the juridical phenomenon. The present Part, therefore, is nothing other than an application of Hegel's fundamental principles of phenomenological anthropology to the phenomenon of *Droit*, [or] more exactly, to the idea of Justice which constitutes its base. I will endeavor, consequently, to be as brief as possible.

In my *first chapter*, I will endeavor to show how the anthropogenic desire for Recognition (*Anerkennen*) can be the source of the idea of Justice in general, and as a result, of all that is authentically a *Droit*. In the *second chapter*, it will be necessary to show how and why the idea of Justice (and therefore *Droit*) is born under a dual, or indeed oppositional [*antithétique*] form, as an "aristocratic" Justice of the Master and a "bourgeois" Justice of the Slave;

---

2. [Ed. Hegel, *Phenomenology of Spirit*, 104–19. Kojève's translation of and commentary upon this section was first published as "Autonomie et dépendance de la Conscience-de-soi: Maîtrise et Servitude," *Mesures*, January 14, 1939. It was subsequently republished as "En guise d'introduction," in Kojève's *Introduction à la lecture de Hegel*, ed. Raymond Queneau, 2nd ed. (Paris: Gallimard, 1947), 9–34. The English translation is by James H. Nichols Jr., "In Place of an Introduction," *Introduction to the Reading of Hegel*, ed. Allan Bloom (Ithaca: Cornell University Press, 1980), 3–30.]

and it will be necessary to analyze these two Justices as bases of two types of *Droit*. Finally, in the *third chapter,* one will have to show that these two oppositional Justices tend to mutually complete one another in order to form the synthetic Justice of the Citizen—this synthesis, which is carried out in time, being nothing other than the historical evolution of Justice and *Droit* properly so-called. All concrete or "positive" *Droit* has for a base a *synthetic* idea of Justice, and these ideas only vary by the range of the proportion in which the two oppositional Justices are found. All real *Droit* is a *Droit* of the citizen, and it is only in a relative sense that one can contrast a (more or less) aristocratic *Droit* to a (more or less) bourgeois *Droit*. And it is also this synthetic *Droit* of the citizen that will be the "absolute" *Droit* of the future, this definitive *Droit* being characterized by the absolute equilibrium or perfect neutralization of its two oppositional constitutive elements.

Chapter 1

The Source of *Droit:*
The Anthropogenic Desire for Recognition as the Source of the Idea of Justice

§ 35

[237] THE SPECIFICALLY HUMAN BEING creates himself from the animal Homo sapiens in and by the act (by definition free) which satisfies a desire (*Begierde*) about another desire taken as desire. Better still, man creates himself as this act, and his specifically human being is nothing other than this very act: the genuine *being* of man is his *action*.

The desire which is about another desire can therefore be called *anthropogenic desire*. As soon as such a desire appears (and we admit that it can only appear in a representative of the animal species Homo sapiens), man exists in potentiality. This desire *is* man in potentiality, and it is the potentiality of man; for man in actuality is nothing other than the realization or satisfaction (*Befriedigung*) of this desire, this realization or satisfaction being carried out in and by the action which is generated by this desire. It is therefore this desire which creates man, and it is also this which causes him to live and evolve as a human being by the action that it generates with a view to being satisfied.

All animal or "natural" desires are about a real entity, [which is] supposed to be present in the space-time outside of the desiring being, but absent in this very being. Desire, therefore, is the real presence of an absence; it is an emptiness which maintains itself in fullness and which nihilates [*néantit*]¹ there by tending to disappear as an emptiness—that is, to be filled by the action which realizes or satisfies the desire. Consequently, to desire a desire is to desire an absence, an unreal entity, an emptiness in space-time filled by (material) reality. And to realize or satisfy [238] this desire, i.e., to realize oneself by satisfying it, is to "fill" an emptiness by another emptiness, an absence by another absence. Therefore, if the genuine being of the human being is action, in and by which the desire for a desire is satisfied or realized, this being is only an emptiness in the natural world—that is, in the space-time filled by material reality, he is himself the presence of an absence. One can say, if you will, that the emptiness created in the natural world by the anthropogenic desire is filled by the human or historical world. But one must not forget that man as such is only an emptiness in the natural world, a something where nature does not exist. One must say, of

---

1. [Ed. Kojève here makes up a new French word, *néantir*, which is translated as "nihilate" throughout. *Néantir* would seem to be the verbal form of the noun *néant*, which means "nothingness."]

course, that man is present in nature. But one must add that he is only the presence of an absence, of the absence in him of nature in general, and in particular, of the animal Homo sapiens that he would be if he was not constituted as a human being by the satisfaction of his desire for desire. It is in this way that man is essentially and radically something other than nature, than the animal which serves him as support: being their absence, their nothingness, their negation, he is independent in respect to them; he is autonomous or free. And this is why I have said that the act which satisfies the desire for a desire is by definition free.

The animal satisfies its desire for natural or material reality by assimilating itself to it through its activity. If you will, its being is also then its action. But by realizing its desire it annihilates it as desire: it fills its emptiness, it replaces the absence by a presence. It *is,* therefore, the being that it desires, i.e., a natural or material reality, and it *is* nothing else: its desire, which is the absence of this reality, is born only to disappear, to become a presence of this very reality. The animal is hungry; it eats in order to satisfy its desire; and it *is* what it eats: "*er ist was er isst.*"[2] Now man as man "feeds" on desires (thus, for example, he not only mates as an animal with the woman; he also wants—as a human being—to be loved by her). And if he also "*is* what he eats," he is and remains desire as such— that is, the *absence* of reality properly so-called, of materialized space-time. Desire, being absence and not presence, *is* not in the strong sense of the word, but *nihilates* in real Being. But animal desire *annihilates* itself by nihilating [*s'anéantit en néantissant*], and yields the place to the *being* of Being, for its tendency to satisfaction, i.e., its "actualization," its passage to actuality or action, overcomes it [desire] as such. Human desire, by contrast, being the desire for a desire, remains what [239] it is in its very actualization, for it is satisfied by what it is itself, by a desire, by an absence which nihilates. The nihilation of human desire in real Being, therefore, is not an annihilation but a permanence (*Bestehen*): it is a *Being* which *exists* and not a Nothingness which disappears. But being the b̓eing [*étant l'être*] of a desire, this Being is the negation or absence of *real* Being: it is an unreal or *ideal* Being, which *exists* in real Being in the sense that it *nihilates* there without *annihilating* itself, because its annihilation is its very existence. It is this ideal Being which is the human being—[the] absence of real or natural Being. And it is the existence of this Being which is human or historical, or indeed free, existence—permanent nihilation in the natural world which, being the no [*le non*] of the world, maintains itself in this world only by its negation. As *being* [*être*] or permanent existence in the world, man *is* in this world as things are, and he is this world. Therefore, he negates himself by negating it: he *is* not, therefore, but *nihilates.* However, this nihilation is his very being: he *is* what he is—a *human* being—by negating himself through the negation of the world. Man negates the world by satisfying through action his desire for desire, and he negates himself by doing it. But this self-*negation* is precisely his specifically human *existence.*

---

2. [Ed. Cf. Ludwig Feuerbach, "Das Geheimniss des Opfers, oder Der Mensch ist, was er isst," in *Sämtliche Werke,* vol. 10, ed. Wilhelm Bolin and Friedrich Jodl, 2nd ed. (Stuttgart-Bad Cannstatt: Frommann Verlag, 1959–60), 41–67.]

Now what is this anthropogenic desire, this desire for desire?

All desire tends to be satisfied by an action which *assimilates* the desired object. It is a matter of negating it as external, of internalizing it; or once again, of overcoming it as other, to make it one's own. The desired object is supposed to become an integral part of the subject who desires it: from the object that it was, it must become subject. It is in this way that the food absorbed by the animal is assimilated and becomes (in part at the very least) an element of this animal itself.

This sketch also applies to the desire for desire. To desire a desire is to want to be assimilated to it, to make it one's own, to overcome it as external or objective while preserving it as desire. In other words, it is to want to become oneself the object of the desired desire. I will be fully satisfied when the being of which I desire the desire will have no other desire than the desire for me. His desire will then remain a desire, but it will no longer be external to me, by being the desire for me: it will be an integral part of my very being while being another's desire. By wanting me, he wants all that I want; he identifies himself to me and becomes me, while remaining himself.

One can say that to desire a desire is to want to be loved. But this term is either too vague or too narrow. Generally [240] speaking, the one who desires another's desire wants to play for this other the role of an absolute value, to which all other values are subordinated, and in particular the one that this other represents in and for himself. Let us say, therefore, that to desire a desire is to want to be "recognized" (*anerkannt*). The desire for desire, i.e., the anthropogenic desire, is the desire for "recognition" (*Anerkennen*). Consequently, if man is the act by which he satisfies his desire for desire, he exists as a human being only to the extent that he is *recognized*: recognition of a man by another is his very being. (As Hegel says: "*Der Mensch ist Anerkennen* [Man is Recognition].")

Now man is also an animal (of the species Homo sapiens). To exist as man, he must therefore exist as a man in the same way that he exists as an animal: he must be realized in his capacity as a man on the same ontological plane upon which he exists in his capacity as an animal. Now two entities are on the same ontological plane when they enter into interaction—that is, at the limit, when one can annul the other. The man who is recognition must therefore be able to be annulled as an animal: his desire for desire must be able to annul his animal or natural desire. Natural desire being in the final analysis the "instinct of self-preservation"—the desire to preserve his animal life—anthropogenic desire must be able annul this "instinct." In other words, in order to be *realized* as a human being, man must be able to risk his life for recognition. It is this risk of life (*Wagen des Lebens*) which is the genuine birth of man, if it is carried out as a result of the desire for recognition alone.

Now this desire necessarily gives occasion for such a risk; for man can only desire the desire of another man. But this other, being a man, also desires for himself the desire of the one who desires his desire. He also desires to be recognized, and he is ready to risk his life in order to be so. It is in this way that the desire for desire can only be realized in and by a struggle to the death (*Kampf auf Leben und Tod*) for the sake of recognition. If the risk realizes man, it is because he can only be realized by a struggle that implies such a risk.

If the anthropogenic desire is the same among the two, the struggle for recognition can only end in death, either of both adversaries or one of them. And then there is no recognition, and consequently, no man who would really exist. In order for man to be realized, the struggle must therefore end in a unilateral recognition of the victor by the vanquished. But for this to be possible, the anthropogenic desire [241] must not be the same among the two adversaries. That of the future victor must be stronger than his natural desire; that of the future vanquished, weaker. In order to yield by renouncing the struggle, the vanquished must have been afraid. His desire for recognition must therefore be subordinate to his natural desire for self-preservation. The man in him is and is revealed as weaker than the animal which serves him as support: his humanity remains in a state of potentiality and is not actualized, not reaching the plane of reality determined by his animal life. The victor, by contrast, has been able to subordinate his animal instinct of self-preservation to his human desire for recognition. He has therefore actualized his humanity, and he is a man just as truly [*réellement*] as he is an animal. And this is what unilateral recognition reveals—or more exactly—realizes. The vanquished recognizes the human reality (or value, dignity) of the victor that effectively exists; the victor does not recognize the human reality (or value, dignity) of the vanquished, and this does not exist in fact. And it is just as true to say that human reality is recognized or not depending upon whether it exists or not, as to assert that it exists or does not exist depending upon whether it is or is not recognized.

The victor who is recognized by the vanquished without recognizing the other in his turn is called the Master (*Herr*); the non-recognized vanquished who recognizes the victor, the Slave (*Knecht*). And one sees that man can only create himself in this antithesis of Master and Slave—that is, as a man existing in actuality and a man existing in potentiality, the latter tending to be actualized and the former to maintain himself in actual existence.

But by looking more closely at it, one sees that the actuality of the Master is a pure illusion. Of course, he does not exist *in potentiality* because he does not at all have a tendency to change, to become other than he is, to be what he is not: for the opposite [*l'autre*] of the Master is the Slave, and a Master does not at all want to become a Slave. But he does not exist in actuality either; for the actuality of man is recognition. Now the Master is not recognized. He is "recognized" by the Slave, but the Slave is an animal since he has refused the anthropogenic risk, having opted for his animal life. "Recognition" by the Slave, therefore, does not actualize the humanity of the Master. The latter is not at all satisfied by the fact of being recognized by a Slave, whom he does not recognize as a man properly so-called. And, being Master, he cannot recognize the Slave, just as he cannot stop being Master either. The situation is therefore inconclusive. He never obtains the satisfaction of his [242] desire for recognition. His anthropogenic desire, therefore, is not satisfied or realized. In other words, he has not been *realized* as a human being. And as he is not one either *in potentiality,* he is not one at all. Therefore, he does not really *exist* as a truly human being, which means that one can only *die* as a Master (in a struggle for recognition) but one cannot *live* mastery. Or once again, the Master appears in history only in order to disappear. He is only there for there to be a Slave.

For the Slave, who is only human in potentiality, can and wants to change, and he can maintain himself in human existence in and by this change. He is human to the extent that he recognizes the human reality and dignity (the value) of the Master: there is the *idea* of the human in him. But he *is* not human in actuality because he is not *recognized* as such. He has a tendency, therefore, to make himself recognized, to become other than he is. If the Master cannot want to become Slave, the Slave can want to become Master, |can| want to be recognized as the Master is recognized. But in fact, even if he succeeds (by resuming the struggle, i.e., by accepting the risk), he does not become Master; for the Master does not recognize the one who recognizes him, while the Slave starts from the recognition of the other: he will recognize, therefore, the one whom he will require (by the struggle) to recognize him. He will become and will be, therefore, not the Master but—let us say—the Citizen.

It is the Citizen, and him only, who will be fully and definitely satisfied (*befriedigt*); for he alone will be recognized by one whom he himself recognizes and he will recognize the one who recognizes him. Therefore, it is only he who will be truly realized in actuality as a human being. And this is why one can say that the Master is only there for there to be a Slave; for the Slave is only the potentiality of the Citizen, who is the actuality of human reality.

Consequently, if man is only born in the opposition of Master and Slave, he is only fully and actually realized in the synthesis of the Citizen, who is a Master to the extent that he is recognized by others and a Slave to the extent that he himself recognizes them. This means that he is neither one nor the other: neither actuality without potentiality, nor potentiality without actuality, but actualized potentiality.[3]

[243] Man is therefore *real* only to the extent that he is a Citizen: the Master and Slave are only logical "principles," which do not exist in fact in a pure state. But the Citizen is a synthesis of mastery and servitude, and this synthesis is a passage from potentiality to actuality—that is, an evolution. This evolution, which is nothing but the history of humanity, leads to a perfect neutralization—to a definitive equilibrium of mastery and servitude—by passing through intermediary stages, where one or the other of these two constitutive elements predominates. And according to this predominance, one can speak either of (relative) aristocratic mastery or (relative) bourgeois servitude.

---

3. The actuality which realizes its potentiality exhausts it and is consequently annulled. This is why man is a finite being, even taken as such. Humanity can realize in actuality human reality, but it cannot be eternal. If there is an end of history, marked by the perfection of [243] man, there is also an end of historical humanity, marked by its complete disappearance.

Now this dialectic of universal history is also—among other things—the dialectic of *Droit* and the idea of Justice. Just as mastery fuses with servitude in citizenship, (more or less) aristocratic Justice will one day fuse with (more or less) bourgeois Justice in the synthetic Justice of the Citizen properly so-called, of the citizen of the universal and homogenous State.

§ 36

Human or historical reality is actualized in and by the active negation of natural or animal reality, in and by the risk of life during the struggle for recognition. Thus, these two realities are on the same ontological plane. For it is not only the animal which can annul in man his specifically human being; this being can also annul the animal by pushing the struggle to the very end—that is, until death. If man cannot exist outside of the animal Homo sapiens, being nothing other than the active or actualized negation of the latter, he is nevertheless essentially something other than it, being its negation, and he is no less real or actual being active negation, or indeed [negation] in actuality. And man does not exist less "objectively" than the animal in him and the world outside of him; for the human being is the act of recognizing and of being recognized. Man is always at least two, and he can only exist in actuality as two, in and by a relation of recognition. Therefore, man only exists in reality or in truth [244] as recognized by another, and it is only in and by recognition of this other that he also exists in and for himself, that he knows [*connaît*] and recognizes [*reconnaît*] himself. He is only a "subject" to the extent that he is an "object": his being only exists as an *objective* being.

The human being, therefore, is just as *real* and *objective* as the natural being. And he is just as *actual* (or active) as the latter. One cannot say, however, that there is a dualism here in the ordinary sense of the word: man is not a *substance* opposed to natural substance. For man is only the *negation* of Nature: he is *Negativity,* and not *Identity* or Substantiality. If the Universe is a ring, and if Nature *is* like the metal of which this ring is made, Man *is* only like the hole of this ring. For the Universe to be a ring and not something else, there must be a hole in the same way as the metal which surrounds it. But the metal can exist without the hole, and the Universe would be something without being a ring. The hole, by contrast, would be nothing without the metal, and there is no Universe that would only be a hole. Thus, Nature can exist without Man, and a purely natural Universe is perfectly conceivable (although its conception in actuality presupposes in fact the existence of man who conceives it and who this Universe includes). A purely human Universe, by contrast, is inconceivable, for without Nature, Man is nothingness pure and simple.

In other words, it is not enough for man to be kept in identity with himself in order to exist really and actually. To be actualized, to exist, to be kept in identity with himself, i.e., to be man, man must be the negation of Nature; he must negate it really and actively. As well, he can only exist at the expense of Nature: he presupposes it, both in his birth and in his existence, for he is born and exists only to the extent that he negates it. And this is why the death of the animal in man is the death of this man himself.

The negation of Nature which realizes Man is realized in potentiality and is revealed as potentiality in and by the risk and death, or as risk and death, of the Master in the Struggle. But this reality is actualized and is actually revealed only in and by the Work of the Slave (and the Citizen). This is why one can say that Man only exists to the extent that he works, that Work is the very essence, as well as the existence, of man. It is by Work that man puts in place of the natural world, which is hostile to him and which he negates (in this very Work), a technological [*technique*] [245] or cultural (historical) world, where he can live as man.

Therefore, the anthropogenic desire and act necessarily create, by creating the field of human existence or the historical world (within the natural world), an economic sphere, based upon Work and stemming from it. This economic sphere is specifically human (or historical), for it is the actual *negation* of purely animal existence. And it is just as real and objective as the natural world, precisely because it is the *actualized* negation of it, existing in actuality in the negated itself, this negated only being able to exist by effectively being altered as a result of its negation. One can say that the economic sphere is just as objective and actual as the natural world. But if one calls the latter "real," it will be necessary to call the economic sphere "ideal" in order to show that the one is the *negation* of the other. Or again, if one calls the two "real," it will be necessary to distinguish the "natural or material reality" of the natural world from the "historical or ideal reality" of the economic sphere, as from the human world in general.

One can therefore speak of a (dynamic) "dualism" without assuming the (static) existence of two separable or separated "substances." The anthropogenic act creates a *sui generis* autonomous human existence, without one being able to say that there is a human being (a "soul") outside of the natural being (the "body"). And what holds for man as such holds for all that is human. Human phenomena are specific and autonomous in respect to natural phenomena. But they do not exist outside of the latter, and are in a pure or isolated state of nothingness. They only exist in and by their *opposition* to natural phenomena, for they are nothing other than their *negation* in actuality or in potentiality, and consequently presuppose them.

The ultimate origin of all human, cultural, or historical phenomena is anthropogenic desire and the act which realizes or satisfies it—this act being, on the one hand, the Risk of the Master in the struggle, and on the other hand, the Work of the Slave which results from it. In other words, all human phenomena have as their basis War and Economics, based upon Work. It is economics and war which constitute the *actuality* of human reality, of the historical existence of humanity. But the dynamic dualism of Man and Nature can be manifested in still other forms, which are like the by-products of the production of Man (starting from Nature) by the Struggle (war) and Work (economics)—specific and autonomous by-products, irreducible [246] neither to one another, nor to a final product, nor to the agents of production.

Thus, Man creates himself as Warrior (Master) and Worker (Slave). But in the fullness of his actuality (as Citizen), he is neither one nor the other, being one and the other simultaneously. And if he is Man, and not Animal, as Warrior, Worker, or Citizen, it is not only as such that he is so. He is just as human as a "religious subject," or a "moral subject," and so on, or finally as a "subject of *droit.*"

As soon as man has constituted himself as a human being opposed to the animal which is in him and which he also is himself, he opposes inside himself the specifically human to the purely natural or animal; for the opposition exists not only objectively, in reality or in truth, and for us, i.e., for the Phenomenologist, but also subjectively for man himself. This is because the anthropogenic act is also the act which generates self-consciousness (*Selbstbewusstsein*, starting from animal sentiment of self, from *Selbstgefühl*)—the recognition by others also being recognition by oneself, the self-knowledge or awareness of oneself by oneself. Thus, among other things, man can be opposed to the animal that he also is by considering himself as a *subject of droit*. Of course, Man can only be a subject of *droit* because he is—or has been—a Warrior or Worker. And it is because he is a subject of *droit* that he will one day be an integral Man or Citizen. But to be a subject of *droit* is nevertheless something other than being a Warrior, Worker, or Citizen.

The real or actual opposition, created by the Struggle and Work, between Man and Nature in general, and the nature or animal in Man in particular, allows Man to oppose the human entity that he calls "subject of *droit*" to the animal which serves him as [material] support, and of which it [the human entity] is the "substantialized" negation. On the one hand, not all anthropomorphic, Homo sapiens animals will be called everywhere and always a "subject of *droit*": one will see limits drawn by age, sex, physical or psychic health, race, or by social characteristics—that is, specifically human ones (economic, religious, and so on). These restrictions are juridical "mistakes," juridically inadequate phenomena. But they are possible only because the human being is effectively *something other* than natural being in general, and the animal which serves him as support in particular. Seeing that the animal Homo sapiens is not [247] by himself, or so to speak automatically, a human being, one can assert of any given representative of this species that he is not humanized, and consequently that he is not a subject of *droit.*[4] On the other hand, this same real opposition between Man and animal allows one to detach the human entity called "subject of *droit*" from his natural support. First, there are juridically unauthentic cases when the subject of *droit* is supposed to have a support other than the animal Homo sapiens, being another animal, for example, or a thing, or a divinity, when there is thus only an illusion of humanity. But there

---

4. The Warrior, Worker, and the Citizen are human by definition. It is therefore false to say that they are not subjects of *droit:* this is a juridical inadequacy. But these mistakes are rather frequent. Notably, aristocratic (i.e., warrior) Society tends not to recognize the Worker (or the Slave, the non-warrior, and the woman) as a subject of *droit.*

are also authentic cases when the subject of *droit* is an individual, collective, or abstract "moral person." Seeing that the specifically human action is something other than the purely animal action, being its negation, one can assume that the former still exists when the latter no longer does, and one thus obtains the notion of the "Institution," of the "abstract moral person." Likewise, one can allow that there is human action when its animal support does not exist as a real individual being, and one thus ends up with the notion of "Society" or the "collective moral person." Finally, one can say that the human action subsists even when the corresponding animal is not, is not yet, or is no longer capable of really carrying it out himself, and one then has the notion of the "incapable person" (who can also be dead or not yet born)—that is, of the "individual moral person."

The real and actual opposition between man and the animal in man justifies the notion of "subject of *droit*" in general, and that of "moral person" in particular. And it is to this opposition (stemming from anthropogenic desire) that all "realist" theory of the moral person must resort in the end. But "fictionalized" theory can draw on the fact that man does not exist outside of the animal which serves him as support. In other words, the ideal reality of the "moral person" must always be brought back in the end to a human reality effectively opposed to a concrete animal Homo sapiens serving him as support in the past, present, or future; for being a specifically human reality, the moral person can only get his existence [248] from a real anthropogenic act. However, this act being a *negation* of animality, the juridical moral personality is essentially something other than physical individuality. And this is why one can detach it from the latter, or indeed oppose them. The subject of *droit* is not a "substance," an entity existing *per se,* separable from the natural world. But if he only exists inside of this world, the subject of *droit* can be opposed to all that is purely natural; for if the "not-A" is pure nothingness if "A" does not exist, he is, as soon as he is something, not "A" but "B."

Man can be opposed to the animal as being and as action, and this opposition allows man to distinguish between what is and what *should* be, between what is done and what *ought* to be done. In the anthropogenic act of the Struggle for recognition, the Risk goes against the animal instinct for self-preservation: the man who creates himself wants the opposite of what the animal wants, which risks death in and by him. The animal *is* and it wants to remain in existence. But according to man, he *ought* not to do so and he *ought* not to be if he only wants to be what he is—an animal which refuses the risk. As for man, he still *is* not. But if he opposes himself to the animal which is, this is because he *ought* to be and attain existence. In short, human reality creates itself by the anthropogenic act not only as *reality,* and reality conscious of itself or "reflective," but also as a positive *value* or as a *duty* to be and do. Man not only risks his life; he also knows that he *ought* to do so. And he does not content himself with working; he knows that work is a *duty.* But it makes no sense to say that man struggles or works *because* it is (for him) his duty. On the contrary, he has a notion of duty only because he struggles and works; for it is this struggle and this work which create him as a human being *opposed* to natural being. And the notion of *duty* is nothing other than the manifestation of this opposition: it is the very *being* of man who is a *duty-being*, and the notion of duty only isolates in and by self-consciousness the "duty" aspect of the specific human being.[5]

The real opposition between man and the animal in man, [249] therefore, allows man to oppose what is (and all that is) to what *ought* or *should* be. Only specifically human reality stemming from the anthropogenic act of the struggle for recognition and of work, which appears following this struggle, *is* and at the same time *ought to be*. As for animality, it certainly *is;* but to the extent that it is *opposed* to humanity, it *should* not be, it being of little importance that it *is* in fact or not.

The word "duty" is taken here in the broadest sense. It simply means that man can be opposed—both by his acts and in his judgement of value—to all that is, either in him or outside of him, just as he can notice that that which is does not give rise to such an opposition. In the first case, man will say that the given reality is not as it *should* be; in the second, that it is what it *ought* to be. And generally speaking, he will try to transform reality so that what *is* is what it *ought* to be.

In particular, man will be able to and should distinguish between reality and *Justice:* he will speak of an unreal Justice and an unjust reality, as well as of a realized Justice, or a just or justified reality. It remains to know to what "duty," i.e., to what aspect of human "duty-being," stemming from anthropogenic desire, the juridical notion of Justice corresponds.

§ 37

Man creates himself in and by the anthropogenic Struggle for recognition, when he risks his life for the sake of a desire for desire. This risk negates the animal in man, for he goes against his instinct of self-preservation at any price. The existence of the risk, therefore, is not only a *being*, but also a *duty-being:* man *ought* to risk his life in certain circumstances to be truly human, to be a "man." Moreover, the existence of this risk is a lot less "being" than "duty"; for it is a pure negation of the animal being, which "*actualizes itself*" as nothingness—that is, in death. Therefore, this is not a *being* properly so-called: this is the *potentiality* of an ideal being which is actualized by the active negation of material being. The risk as such—being a potentiality which is actualized by the negation of what is—is a "duty" properly speaking: it is the *duty* [250] to be human, the *being* [*être*] of man being [*étant*] this very *duty* of the being [*être*]—or if you will—the being [*être*] of this duty.

---

5. The "duty-being" is in the end the "duty-to-be-recognized," which is only an awareness of "wanting-to-be-recognized"—that is, an anthropogenic desire. The "duty" aspect simply reveals the fact that the anthropogenic desire or want necessarily implies a *negation* of the natural or animal given, which is at the base of the existence of the one who so desires.

Now by definition the anthropogenic risk is carried out in a struggle for recognition. There must be two [beings], then, capable of risking their animal life so as to generate a human existence. The one who risks his life by this very fact imperils the life of the other, and his is imperiled only because the other has risked his life. There is, then, absolute reciprocity, and the situation is strictly symmetrical. In other respects, the risk of the one is provoked, but not determined, by the risk of the other; for each risks his life freely, i.e., voluntarily and consciously, being very well capable of not doing so. Or, more exactly, freedom, i.e., the conscious will and the acting consciousness, is nothing other than this risk itself, the risk which appears for the sake of a desire for desire— that is, the desire for recognition. And it is this aspect of the situation which is the ultimate source of the *idea of Justice.*[6]

One of the two adversaries, by imperilling the life of the other in and by the Struggle, injures the "vital" or natural interests of the other. But he does it, as it were, with the other's consent (tacitly expressed by the acceptance of the struggle). Likewise, it is with his own consent that the other imperils his life. And this is why one can say that the one injures the interests of the other without acting in an *unjust* manner toward him. It is the *mutual consent* of the parties which excludes *injustice* from the situation, this consent preceding the Struggle—that is, all use of force, all "pressure" of one upon the other.

Of course, the absence of Injustice is still not in itself Justice, and one cannot say that the situation is *just* from the sole fact of it not being *unjust;* it can be neutral from the point of view of Justice. But obviously there cannot be Justice when there is Injustice. Thus, the mutual consent which excludes Injustice, leaves the field free, so to speak, to Justice, which may or may not be established there. This notion of *consent* is very important juridically; for if there is not [251] necessarily justice when there has been consent, there is surely no injustice. One cannot deduce the *content* of the idea of Justice from the sole fact of consent, since consent can generate a juridically neutral situation—that is, neither just nor unjust. But consent is the sign of the *possibility* of Justice, since it overcomes the injustice that excludes Justice—provided that it is free, i.e., conscious and voluntary. This does not mean that consent is a *necessary* condition of Justice; for a situation can be just even without implying a consent. But it cannot be unjust if it implies it: a treatment cannot be unjust toward the one who consents to undergo it. The duty-being man, which is the very being of man, is surely then not *unjust* from the juridical point of view, since it implies and presupposes consent. In other words, the anthropogenic act *may* be just, and the man who creates himself in and by this act is therefore suscep-

---

6. Of course, the anthropogenic Struggle is a theoretical "construction," an unobservable hypothetical phenomenon. But the phenomenon of Duelling has preserved traces of it. Therefore, it is by analyzing this phenomenon of Duelling that we can describe the juridical aspect of the anthropogenic Struggle. However, the Duels familiar to us always presuppose the idea of Justice, and even its realization in *Droit,* while the anthropogenic Struggle, being the source of human existence in general, is the source of the idea of Justice as such.

tible of being just, of maintaining juridically just interactions with his fellow man.

But there is not only *consent* in the anthropogenic act of the Struggle for recognition: there is also *mutual* consent. And this is also juridically impor- tant, for we have here the ultimate source of all that will later be juridical *con- tract*. Of course, the Struggle is still not a "contract" in the proper or juridical sense of the term; for contract presupposes the existence of a "third," of an arbiter, and in the Struggle there are only the "parties," the two adversaries, present. And it is not a "convention" properly so-called either, for this implies the idea of an *exchange,* while the Struggle is the expression of a will of mutual *exclusion*—that is, at the limit, the annihilation of one by the other. The one wants to subordinate entirely the other, i.e., to take everything from him with- out giving him anything in exchange, and the other does not at all consent to being treated in that fashion. He himself wants to treat his adversary in this way, without worrying about his consent to this treatment. There is then no "convention." But there are two independent wills, two consents to action, which make the interaction possible. There is a mutual consent to the risk, which is *for us* (or in truth)—if not for the participants themselves—the meaning [*raison d'être*] of the entire interaction. Therefore, it is—*for us*—the result of a kind of "convention" or "contract," without being one for the agents interacting. And this is why *we* can say [252] right here and now that the man who creates himself in such a situation is *capable* of concluding "con- ventions" with his fellow man and of giving to his interactions with them the form of a juridical "contract." Just as the presence of *consent* in the anthro- pogenic Struggle makes possible the realization of Justice in the human or his- torical world, the *mutuality* of this *consent* makes possible the existence of contracts in this world.

Let us leave aside contracts. They presuppose reciprocal, and not unilateral, recognition. Therefore, they will only appear later; because for the moment— in the Struggle—it is only a matter of mutual exclusion, the one seeking to be recognized by the other without wanting to recognize him in return. But let us deal with *Justice;* for if it is an autonomous and specifically human phenome- non, it is in the anthropogenic act that one must seek its source. And since con- sent is the sign of its possibility, let us analyze the conditions of this consent in order to find the content of the idea of Justice.

First of all, the consent of the one presupposes that of the other. By defi- nition, each one engages in the struggle only for recognition by the other. Now the other is fit to recognize only to the extent that he is also ready to struggle for recognition with him; and it is because there are *two* consents that the Struggle is not unjust and may be just. If the adversaries attacked without there being consent on both sides, the situation would be juridically neutral; for in this case there would be nothing human or anthropogenic about it: it would be a thing due to chance or a struggle between animals. And if the one voluntarily attacked the other without the consent of the latter to struggle, the situation would be unjust or neutral, for it would not be anthropogenic either: the one who refuses the struggle has already recognized the one who offers it (unjust attack), or is in general incapable of doing so, still being only an animal.

One of the adversaries, therefore, consents to struggle only because he assumes that the other equally consents to do so. But this is not enough. He still assumes that the other effectively risks his life in the same way that he does so himself. If he thought that the other engages in a struggle against him without risk to himself, he would not have consented to engage in it. One can therefore say that he gives his consent to the struggle only because he assumes that the other's consent has *the same* nature as his own, the two consents consciously implying *the same* risk of life. And it is this element of *equality* in [253] the interaction which constitutes the aspect which is revealed to human consciousness as the idea of Justice.

The anthropogenic Struggle, therefore, is *just* because it is by definition *equal*, because it is engaged under *the same* conditions by the two adversaries. This equality is expressed in the consciousness of a third by the *mutuality* of the consent, and it exists in the consciousness of the participant as *consent*. It is in this way that the consent, and its mutuality, are the signs of Justice. It is as *equal* that the Struggle is *just* for the participants, and it is because it is also *equal* for the third—and for us, i.e., in truth—that it is objectively just. It is just because—in principle—each of the two adversaries would have engaged in it even if he was in the place of the other. And one can say that it is because this is the case, because the Struggle is just, that it is engaged in with a mutual consent. As well, this mutual consent allows a third to notice that the Struggle is just. Now, by extension, every interaction with mutual consent will be called *just* to the extent that it will imply the *equality* of the participants. And all that is *equal* in social relations will be called *just,* even if there is no consent; for consent is only the subjective sign of Justice, Justice as such being the objectively observable Equality.[7]

The idea of Justice, therefore, appears at the very moment of the anthropogenic Struggle, and it only discloses its *egalitarian* aspect. To say that it is *just*

---

7. The situation of the anthropogenic Struggle still recurs today in wars between States. A war by free, mutual consent will never be juridically unjust. By contrast, every "unprovoked" attack will be called unjust, precisely because it excludes the consent of the one attacked. On the other hand, one describes as unjust the attack of a weak [state] by the strong [one]. This is because the struggle is then objectively *unequal,* because—at the limit—the risk is only *from one* side. But practically speaking, the weak will never voluntarily attack the strong. Therefore, one will also have the subjective sign of the absence of mutual consent.

The principle of the absolute *equality* of the adversaries' situation is also at the base of (private or judicial) Duelling. And one speaks of an assassination only when there is not an *equality* of situation, and—consequently—of mutual consent.

As for the case of murder with the consent of the victim, it is complex and complicated.

Let us also note that if war is neither a contract nor a genuine convention, it generates contracts (or more exactly conventions, since there is no arbiter)—namely, peace treaties. But it only leads to conventions if there is a mutual consent to wage war.

is to assert that the adversaries [254] engage in it under strictly *equal* conditions: objectively and subjectively.[8] And if man can realize Justice in and by his social interactions, it is because he is born from an anthropogenic Struggle, *just* by definition, since it is essentially *equal.* By being born by and in equality, and from equality, he can only be fully realized in social equality. And this is why it is said that he can be truly human only by being just.

But if man is born in the equality (or Justice) of the anthropogenic Struggle (which has nothing to do, let me say in passing, with physiological or natural equality, it only being an equality of human conditions), and if he is only fully realized in the equality of peaceful existence (in the universal and homogenous State), it is not always as equal that he exists in his historical becoming. And this is why Justice is still something else than equality.

Indeed, if the anthropogenic Struggle begins in equality, it ends up in injustice. Now if the beginning of the Struggle is the potentiality of man, it is only its culmination which actualizes the latter. And the Struggle ends up in unilateral recognition of the victorious-Master by the vanquished-Slave. There is then a total inequality of the participants at the conclusion of the Struggle. But seeing that the Struggle has been just, its result must also be so. There is then a just inequality. And inequality is *just* to the extent that it results from primordial *equality.*

Let us see what is this Justice of inequality which is the result of egalitarian Justice.

Inequality (unilateral recognition) arises from the fact that one of the two adversaries abandons the struggle and surrenders to the other through the fear of death that the other could overcome to the very end. This abandonment of the Struggle (this surrender) is supposed to be just as free, i.e., conscious and voluntary, as his engagement: if not, there would not be "recognition," and therefore no creation of an actual human reality. And the freely offered surrender is accepted just as freely. There is still then mutual consent. And this is why the situation does not become [255] unjust and can therefore be just, while henceforth being unequal. But here as well, consent is only[9] the sign of the possibility of Justice. It is necessary to analyze again the conditions of consent in order to find the content of the new idea of Justice that it reveals.

Here as well there is mutuality of consent. The one offers his submission because he believes that it will be freely accepted, and the other accepts it

---

8. In principle, objective equality coincides with subjective equality, i.e., with consent, the latter supposedly being *conscious* and voluntary—that is, corresponding to the reality. But it happens that the adversaries (or in general, the parties) *believe* themselves in equal conditions without really being in them, or are really in them without being aware of it, from whence comes a casuistry of Justice (the principle, "You asked for it, George Dandin"). [Ed. See Molière's play "George Dandin, ou Le Mari Confondu," in *Oeuvres Complètes,* ed. Maurice Rat, vol. II (Paris: Bibliothèque de la Pléiade, 1956), Act I, scene 7, pg. 312. Dandin was a rich but proud farmer who decided to marry into the nobility. He was subsequently punished for his action by the infidelity of his wife. Dandin speaks these lines to himself, and they could literally be translated as "You asked for it, Buddy."]

9. [Ed. Reading *le consentement n'est que l'indice* for *le consentement n'est pas l'indice.*]

because he assumes that it is freely put forward. And this is why the situation *may* be just; and here is why it effectively is so. The vanquished freely offers his recognition in exchange for his life; the victor freely gives life in exchange for recognition. One can therefore say that in the eyes of the Slave security in servitude or (by derivation) servitude in security has *the same* value that mastery in risk or (by derivation) risk in mastery has for the Master. There is, then, an analogy with the original equality (explicable by the fact that the new situation results from the egalitarian situation in the beginning). But there is no longer equality properly so-called, neither objectively (the recognition being unilateral) nor subjectively; for the one put in the place of the other would no longer have acted like him: the Master in the place of the Slave would not have surrendered, and the Slave in the place of the Master would not have continued the struggle to the very end. And the Slave knows just as well as the Master that there is no equality between Master and Slave, between the stance [*attitude*] of the one and that of the other. But if there is no longer *equality* of condition and stance, there is *equivalence*. The benefit [*avantage*] that security presents in the eyes of the Slave is *equivalent* to that of mastery. Conversely, in the eyes of the Master, the benefit of mastery is *equivalent* to that which security presents. Or once again, for the Master the burden [*désavantage*] of the risk *is compensated* for by the benefit of mastery, while for the Slave the benefit of security *compensates* for the burden of servitude. And the situation is called *just*, on the one hand, because the conditions of the participants are *equivalent*, and on the other hand, because in each condition the burden is strictly *compensated* for by the benefit (or conversely), so that in each case one can also speak of an *equivalence* of benefit and burden. It is this *equivalence* that constitutes the content of the new idea of Justice. And it is this Justice of *equivalence*, which manifests itself in and by the mutual consent, that puts an end to the Struggle engaged in by a mutual consent, which manifested the Justice of *equality*. Thus, a *Justice of equivalence* has just been added to the primordial *egalitarian Justice*.

[256] It is this Justice of equivalence and compensation which is going to generate the notion of juridical contract. But the relation between Master and Slave is still not a contract; for this relation is by definition unilateral and not reciprocal. The Master does not recognize the Slave, i.e., he considers and treats him as an animal: the Slave is an animal both for the Master and for the Slave himself. The Master alone is recognized as a human being, and he alone is a human being both in his own eyes and in those of his Slave. Of course, *for us* or in truth, the Slave is not an animal pure and simple. He has engaged in the anthropogenic Struggle for the sake of a desire for desire. He is therefore a human being in potentiality. But not having gone to the very end of this struggle, he has not actualized his potentiality: in actuality, he is effectively the animal which he is for the Master and in his own eyes. But seeing that he is a human being, if only in potentiality, there is—*for us* or in truth—a possibility of a juridical relation between him and his Master. However, this relation is not that of contract, which presupposes a reciprocal recognition—that is, an actual humanity of the two participants. The juridical relation is here one of

property: the Slave is juridically the property of the Master, and a property justly acquired (as the mutual consent from which it results reveals).[10] If one wants to call "contract" every relation between human beings stemming from a free, mutual consent, one must call "contract" the relation between the Master and his Slave. But this is a *sui generis* "contract," when one of the "contracting" parties only has *droits* without duties or obligations, and the other only obligations or duties without any *droit*. Now such a "contract" is nothing other than the relation which unites the (juridically legitimate) owner to his property.

Be that as it may, the juridical analysis of the anthropogenic struggle shows that the idea of Justice springs up in the dual form of a Justice of equality and a Justice of equivalence. Just as man creates himself simultaneously as Master and Slave in their oppositional relation, it is in an oppositional form that he becomes aware, in a [257] dual idea of Justice, of the juridical aspect of his own origin. And we will see that these two Justices are effectively opposed as a Justice of the Master to a Justice of the Slave. But being born from a single act (dual, but reciprocal), man can be completely actualized only in its unity, by the synthesis of mastery and servitude in the Citizen. Likewise, absolute Justice, i.e., universally and definitively valid, can only be one, being a synthesis of the two original Justices. And the whole history of Justice, the whole of its historical evolution, is nothing other than this synthesis being carried out gradually in time. And just as every real man is to a certain extent a Citizen, every effectively accepted Justice is, if not a synthesis, at least a certain compromise between the *aristocratic Justice of equality* and the *bourgeois Justice of Equivalence:* it is a *Justice of equity*.

§ 38

It remains for us to see how the idea of Justice, whatever one it may be, generates the phenomenon of **Droit** which realizes it.

We have seen that the juridical situation properly so-called necessarily includes *three* parts. One can also say that the *Droit* which realizes Justice is embodied in the person of the "impartial and disinterested third," in his three avatars as the juridical Legislator, Arbiter or Judge, and the judicial Police. It is he who applies the idea of Justice to a given social interaction, transforming it by this application into a juridical situation, into a relation of *droit* between two subjects of *droit*. And *Droit,* as the effective application of the idea of Justice to real interactions, is the realization of this idea. Therefore, if the idea of Justice is born in and from the anthropogenic Struggle between *two* adversaries, it is realized and exists as actual reality thanks to its application to bipar-

---

10. I will speak below about property in the modern sense of the word—that is, about the property of an animal or a thing.

The possession of a human being is the only case when one can speak of a *juridical* relation between the propertied and the possessed. In all other cases, the juridical relation of property is a relation not between the possessor and the possessed but between possessors and other persons—that is, the non-possessors.

tite interactions by a *third* who—by his impartial and disinterested intervention—makes the interactions in question conform to the idea or ideal of Justice, or at the very least, notices their conformity or non-conformity to this ideal. As for this ideal itself, it can be based upon either the aristocratic principle of equality or the bourgeois principle of equivalence, or finally upon a certain synthesis of these two primordial principles carried out by the Citizen, and that one could call the principle of equity.

Let us suppose as given the existence of a human third, i.e., [258] already humanized, in addition to the two adversaries humanized in and by the anthropogenic Struggle for recognition; and let us assume that this third becomes aware (already being a human being, i.e., endowed with a consciousness of the world and himself) of this primordial Struggle as a whole. His consciousness will include, among other things, the fact of the *equality* of the conditions of the adversaries at the beginning of the struggle, and their *equivalence* at the end. Now, we have seen that the Struggle as a whole is not only a being but also a *duty-being* or a *duty;* for it implies an active *negation* of the real given, this given being considered as natural or animal, while its negation is human in the sense that it creates a reality other than the negated natural reality. The negated has a negative value in relation to the negation, and therefore to what results from this negation: the natural is a non-value for man, while the human is a positive value for him as such. And one can say that to realize the human by an active negation of the natural is a *duty* for man, who therefore *realizes* himself as man by fulfilling his duty. In other words, to the extent that man is human, he will endeavor to realize the value that is for him human reality by the active negation of the non-value of natural reality (in him or outside of him). And man is or becomes human only to the extent that he endeavors to realize this value in this way—that is, to the extent that he fulfills his *duty,* the "duty" being precisely the realization of a value by the active negation of the corresponding non-value. Thus, the third who becomes aware of the anthropogenic Struggle becomes aware of the fact that there is a *duty,* a duty to realize the human by the negation of the natural, i.e., of the non-human (the human being [*étant*] the non-natural); for the active negation of the given for the creation of a new reality is nothing other than the fulfillment of a "duty." As well, the third does not limit himself to noting that the Struggle presents an aspect of equality at its beginning and an aspect of equivalence at its end or in its result. These two aspects are for him aspects of a *duty.* Equality (or equivalence) not only *is,* but also *ought* to be. In other words, one must realize equality (or equivalence) by the active negation of inequality (or non-equivalence). And since equality (or equivalence) is a value to realize by the negation of a non-value, i.e., a duty, only because it is the condition *sine qua non* of the *anthropogenic* Struggle, i.e., of the creation or realization of the human being as such, the value of [259] equality (or equivalence) can be detached from the fact of the Struggle. Equality (or equivalence) will have to be realized by the active negation of inequality (or non-equivalence) *everywhere* it will be a matter of *human* or humanizing interactions, [and] *every time* that one will want to create or assert a human value and reality in and by an interaction between two human or humanizable beings. Generally speaking, equality (or equivalence) will be opposed to inequality (or to non-equivalence) as the "human" is opposed to the "inhuman" or to the simply "natural," or indeed the "bestial."

To the extent that the third is human and becomes aware of the fact of the anthropogenic Struggle, he will therefore have an idea or ideal of Justice (equality or equivalence). Equality ([or] equivalence) will appear to him as a necessary condition of humanity or humanization, and consequently, as a duty-being, as a value to realize by the negation of the corresponding non-value; and it is this value that he will call the idea or ideal of Justice, the equal (or equivalent) being for him the just to assert, and the unequal (or non-equivalent) the unjust to overcome. To the extent that the third is human, he will not limit himself to having an idea or ideal of Justice. He will endeavor to *realize* this Idea by the active negation of its opposite, for this idea exists in his consciousness in the form of a *duty*. Or once again, the third will be humanized and will be human only to the extent that he has an idea of Justice in the form of a duty and endeavors to fulfill this duty by realizing Justice by the active negation of its opposite. Be that as it may, as soon as he will notice an inequality (or non-equivalence) in an interaction supposed to be human, he will try— to the extent that he is human himself—to overcome it and to put in its place an equality (or equivalence). He will actively intervene, therefore, in this interaction with the sole concern to make it "human"—that is, conforming to his idea of Justice. He will therefore act according to the duty he has to realize this idea by the negation of its opposite; and this is to say that he will intervene and act juridically as Legislator, Judge, or Police.[11]

[260] Therefore, it is enough that the consciousness of the third includes an idea of Justice for him to apply it right away to the social interactions that will be presented to him, trying to make them conform to it. Now such an application is nothing other than *Droit*. One can therefore say that the phenomenon of Justice is spontaneously transformed into the phenomenon of *Droit* as soon as it is constituted in the consciousness of a *third*; for there to be *Droit*, it is enough that there are two human beings interacting and a third conscious of the idea or ideal of Justice. Of course, this idea already exists in the consciousnesses of the two adversaries of the anthropogenic Struggle. And it is even in these consciousnesses that it appears for the first time on earth, since it is generated in and by this very Struggle. This is why this Struggle is "just" not only "objectively," i.e., for *us* and for the external observer in general, but also "subjectively," i.e., for the participants themselves. Therefore, it realizes, if you will, Justice. But as long as there is no *third*, this realization cannot be

---

11. Indeed, one can say that there is *Droit* if a third intervenes in a social interaction *with the sole concern* to make it conform to an ideal of Justice. This is the "introspective" equivalent of the expression "impartial and disinterested" in the "behaviorist" definition of *Droit*. If the third is "impartial and disinterested," and if he intervenes all the same, it is because he acts according to his ideal of justice conceived as the *duty* to realize it by making given social interactions conform to it.

called *juridical.* The anthropogenic Struggle is the source of the idea of Justice and *Droit,* and it realizes *Justice* to the extent that it is just. But it still does not realize **Droit***;* it is still not a relation of *droit;* [and] its agents are still not subjects of *droit,* as long as there is no Arbiter—that is, a third intervening with the sole concern to make Justice reign.[12] But as soon as the idea of Justice will exist in the consciousness of a *third,* this one will apply it to social interactions that will present themselves to him. And in and by this application, the phenomenon of Justice will become a phenomenon of *Droit.*

The question of the source of *Droit,* i.e., of its formation starting from the idea of Justice, therefore boils down to the question of knowing how a human third appears and how the idea of Justice penetrates into his consciousness. The ultimate source of the *idea of Justice* is the anthropogenic desire for desire, which is realized in and by the Struggle for recognition. And this idea is created in and by the consciousnesses of the two adversaries who confront each other in this Struggle. As for the ultimate source of **Droit,** it is the penetration of this idea of Justice into the consciousness of a third, i.e., of a man other than the two adversaries in question; for there [261] will only be *Droit* when this third intervenes in an interaction (in a Struggle for recognition, for example) in order to make it conform to the ideal of Justice. And he will intervene as soon as he has an ideal of Justice. It is a matter, therefore, of knowing from where this third comes and how the idea of Justice penetrates into his consciousness.

As the third has to be human, and as man is only realized in the anthropogenic Struggle, we must still turn to this Struggle to find the origin of the third in question. Let us assume, therefore, that we have two simultaneous Struggles—that is, two pairs of adversaries, A-B and A'-B'. A and B, [and] A' and B' are "enemies" in the political sense of this word. They do not struggle for reasons of *personal* animosity but in order to make themselves recognized by *any given* human being (who they do not want to recognize in return). Therefore, A could have just as easily struggled against B' than against B, and A' could have just as easily struggled against B. We can therefore assume that during the two simultaneous struggles A and A' exchange their adversaries, A struggling with B' and A' with B: the significance of the Struggle, i.e., its anthropogenic value, will not be changed because of this. Now one can say that from here on out B and B' are the enemies both of A and A'. A and A' have common enemies. And one can express this fact by saying that A and A' are "friends" in the political sense of the term. Finally, by adding a third pair A"-B", one can constitute a group of "friends" formed by A, A', and A", i.e., having *three* members, to which is opposed as an "enemy" group another group of *three* members, formed by B, B', and B", who are equally "friends" among themselves.

---

12. Thus, a war can be just or unjust, but it has nothing juridical about it in the narrow sense of the word. The relations between enemies are not relations **of droit,** but they always conform or are contrary to a certain ideal of Justice.

None of the six can play the role of an impartial and disinterested "*third*," i.e., moved by the sole idea of Justice, in the Struggle itself, i.e., in the interaction between "enemies"; for he is a "*party*" in this Struggle, wanting first and foremost to make himself recognized, and not to realize Justice alone. If he realizes Justice in and by his behavior, it is to be able to struggle so as to make himself recognized. One cannot say that he struggles to realize Justice. There will not be, then, relations of *droit* between the enemies, and even the multiple Struggle will not be a juridical situation. Such a situation will only be able to be constituted inside a group of friends. And it will be constituted if A, for example, intervenes in an interaction between A' and A" with the sole goal of making it conform to his idea of Justice, an idea which will be formed in him (as in all six adversaries) in and by the anthropogenic Struggle.

[262] Therefore, let us see what are the relations of the "friends" among themselves.

Each of the three "friends" is not only a *participant* in the Struggle, but also a *witness* of the Struggle of the two others. As a participant, he realizes his own humanity. As a witness, he becomes aware of the act by which the two others realize their humanity. One can therefore say that he becomes aware not only of his own humanity, but also that of his friends; for he has changed places with them during the Struggle, and consequently he knows that they have done what he has done himself, and that they are therefore humanized and human in the same way as him. Therefore, they are for him his equals, and they are equal among themselves.

At first glance, therefore, it seems that the friends mutually "recognize" one another in the technical sense of the term. If the Master is not satisfied by his recognition from the Slave, who is not for him a truly human being, his desire for recognition seems to be fully satisfied by his recognition by the friend, who he himself recognizes in return. But in fact, it is nothing like this; for man desires to be "recognized" in his strictly personal reality—that is, in his *particularity*, unique in the world and exclusively his own. The friend, by contrast, only "recognizes" the man (or the Master) in him in *general*, the *universal* aspect of his human being. Political friendship results from the interchangeability of the combatants, and it is therefore the Combatant in general, and not such and such an individual, who is recognized by the friend. The friends only "recognize" what they have in common: the aptitude for risk and mastery. If you will, they recognize Mastery in the individuals but not the individuals themselves. Being recognized by friends, man is *a* Man in general, but not a particular human being. And this is why this recognition does not fully satisfy man, just as his recognition by the Slave does not satisfy him. The relation between Master and Slave, it is true, is particularized to the highest degree: the Master has such or such a Slave, and the Slave has such or such a Master, the property relation being strictly exclusive—that is, individualizing. But this particularism does not imply recognition: the Slave is not at all recognized by the Master, and the Master is not satisfied by the recognition of the Slave, whom he does not recognize. As for the recognition between friends, it is certainly a recognition in the sense that it is mutual, but it does not satisfy man either because it excludes individuality. And this is why [263] man does not stop at the "aristocratic" stage of the possession of Slaves and the political friendship between Masters, but continues to search for authentic recognition by a Struggle between enemies.[13]

But this is of little importance for the moment. Let us only recall the simple observation that the anthropogenic Struggle can generate in the witness a "recognition" of the humanity of the combatant.[14] Now this humanity is only recognized in its universality: the ones recognized are interchangeable for the one who recognizes them; he recognizes one in the same way as the other; they are equal for him. And this is to say that he is *impartial* toward them, which makes him fit to be their Arbiter, as soon as he will not be *interested* in their interactions. Now they will only be in conflict by acting as particulars, for their universality opposes them in common to the enemy and therefore makes them show solidarity with one another. Therefore, it is only as particulars that they will need an Arbiter. And this Arbiter can very well be *disinterested* in their conflicts, since in their particularity they are quite different from him. He will only be "interested" in the assertion of their (universal) humanity by the negation of their (particular) animality. And this is to say that he will act according to his idea of Justice by intervening as Arbiter, or indeed as Legislator, Judge, or Police, in their conflicts; for in their humanity (as Masters) they are *equal* for him, such that to assert their humanity (or mastery) is equivalent in his eyes [264] to asserting their *equality* by the negation of their natural inequality. The Arbiter will therefore intervene in the interactions of his political friends in an impartial and disinterested manner, with the sole goal of making them conform to the principle of equality—that is, to the ideal of Justice that he accepts just as they themselves accept it. His intervention will therefore transform their interactions into juridical situations, into relations of *droit*.[15]

---

13. If the Master is only *recognized* in his universality, it is because he also *exists* only as a universal: he is a Master or a Warrior, completely similar as Master or Warrior to others. For his humanity has only been realized by the *global* negation of animal reality in the risk: it is therefore global or universal itself. As for the Slave, he humanizes himself by Work, which is a differential negation of nature and which thus particularizes him by humanizing him. The recognized universality of the Master, therefore, must be synthesized with the non-recognized particularity of the Slave to give the total and absolute recognition of the Citizen—where universality fuses with the particularity of mutual recognition, thus giving a definitive satisfaction to the anthropogenic desire for recognition.

14. In a lot of primitive or archaic aristocratic societies (among the Aztecs, for example), a young man was recognized as a citizen (i.e., Master) only after having captured a prisoner of war (i.e., Slave). And "rites of passage" are nothing other than a symbol of the Struggle, the young man having to negate his animal nature (overcoming grief and the fear of death) for the sake of his desire to be "recognized" as a citizen (i.e., Master). But given the "exhibition [*spectacle*]" of the Struggle, the young man is only recognized as *a* citizen (i.e., Master), completely similar to all the others, and not in his individuality, unique in the world.

15. That one of the "friends" who will act toward others solely according to his recognition of their universal humanity, i.e., the one who will effectively treat them as interchangeable equals, will enjoy an Authority of the Judge. It is he that will be chosen for Arbiter. It is his legislation, his judgements, and his police activity that will create "positive" *Droit*.

Such is the source and genesis of *Droit*—or more exactly, of *a Droit*, of the aristocratic *Droit* based upon the egalitarian Justice of the Master; for we have assumed in our deduction that the group of friends emerge victorious from the Struggle, that this is a group of Masters, of brothers in arms. But the vanquished group, the group of Slaves, also has been a group of brothers in arms in the Struggle. Therefore, it is also a group of friends—even [if they were] vanquished. And in such a group there is a place, as we have seen, for an impartial and disinterested "third" to intervene in the interactions between friends in order to make them conform to the ideal of Justice. Here as well, then, there is a possibility of *Droit*.

Of course, the vanquished combatant, the Slave who has renounced the Struggle, is only human in potentiality, not being actualized in and by the risk. But in potentiality the situation here remains the same that it is in actuality in the group of Masters. The Slaves mutually recognize each other as Slaves, and a Slave can be a "third" in the interaction between two other Slaves, creating by his impartial and disinterested intervention a juridical situation. There will then be *Droit*. However, this *Droit* will only exist in potentiality, seeing that humanity is not actualized in this social group. And indeed, the arbitration of the Slave will not have the force of law as long as the Slaves remain Slaves; for their law is the law of the Master: it is he who will resolve their differences as he sees fit. Slavish *Droit*, therefore, will only be a virtual application of the slavish idea of Justice to social interactions, which will only be able to be actualized at the moment the Slave will cease to be a Slave (the moment at which his Justice will cease to be a slavish Justice, without becoming by this a Justice of the Master). But this *Droit* in potentiality will nevertheless be a *Droit*.

[265] And this slavish or bourgeois *Droit* will be other than aristocratic *Droit*. Mastery is created in the *equality* of the Struggle, and this is why the Justice which forms the base of aristocratic *Droit* is egalitarian. Servitude, by contrast, arises from renouncing the Struggle, and this is why the Justice which generates bourgeois *Droit* is a Justice of equivalence, motivated by the principle of the *equivalence* of conditions. And this same difference is manifested in the behavior of the respective Arbiters. The Masters are equal and interchangeable, and the Arbiter will treat them as such. The Slaves, by contrast, are not interchangeable. If B is A's Slave, he is not the Slave of A' or A", and A's Slave is B, and not B' or B". But if the Slaves are not interchangeable, they are equivalent in the sense that the value of one can be compared to the value of another or measured by it (the Slave has a price). Therefore, if the Arbiter-Master is impartial by treating Masters as interchangeable equals, the Arbiter-Slave will be so by treating Slaves as equivalent persons. And if the two are disinterested to the extent that they will intervene solely to realize the ideal of Justice, their ideal will not be the same, the one wanting to realize equality in social interactions, and the other equivalence.

Droit appears, therefore, in the dual (and oppositional) form of aristocratic *Droit* and bourgeois *Droit*. In the beginning, only the first exists in actuality, the other only being a *Droit* in potentiality. Now all potentiality tends to be actualized. The Slave will therefore endeavor to realize his ideal of Justice in and by a *Droit* existing in actuality. But he will be able to do so only by making it a state *Droit* [*étatisant*]—that is, by seizing power and thus ceasing to be a Slave. His *Droit*, by being actualized, will therefore cease being a purely slavish *droit*. Just as the Slave can only free himself by synthesizing mastery with his servitude, his *Droit* can only be actualized by being synthesized with the *Droit* of the Master. And just as the freed Slave (by a resumption of the Struggle and an acceptance of the risk) is neither Master nor Slave, but Citizen, actualized slavish *Droit* is neither slavish nor aristocratic: it is the synthetic *Droit* of the Citizen based upon the Justice of equity.

The evolution of *Droit* (i.e., the juridical evolution of humanity, or the juridical aspect of his historical evolution) therefore reflects the evolution of man as such: it reflects the dialectic of Master and Slave, which is nothing other than the progressive self-creation of the Citizen in time. In truth, i.e., *for us*, man is always [266] a Citizen—that is, simultaneously Master *and* Slave (and therefore neither Master nor Slave). However, in the beginning, the Master alone is actualized, the Slave (as a human being) only existing in potentiality. At the end, by contrast, the two are fully actualized in and by, or better still, as the Citizen. And the same applies to *Droit*. From its origins, *Droit* is dual: an aristocratic *Droit* is opposed to a bourgeois *Droit*, as egalitarian Justice is opposed to the Justice of equivalence.[16] But in the beginning aristocratic *Droit* alone exists in actuality, the other *Droit* being pure potentiality. But little by little bourgeois *Droit* is itself also actualized. And one can say that this progressive actualization of bourgeois *Droit* is its synthesis with aristocratic *Droit*— this synthesis, which is carried out in time, being nothing other than the historical becoming of the *Droit* of the Citizen, based upon the idea of the Justice of equity, upon the synthesis of the Justices of equality and equivalence.

It is this antithetical character of *Droit* in its nascent state, and the becoming of its final synthetic state, i.e., its evolution, that we must now study.

---

16. [Ed. Reading *Justice de l'équivalence* for *Justice de l'équité*.]

Chapter 2

The Birth of *Droit:*
The Antithetical Justices
of the Master and Slave

§ 39

[267] WE HAVE SEEN HOW a "third" can appear in inter-human or social inter-actions; how he can have an idea or ideal of Justice; and how he can intervene in these interactions, having as sole motive the will to make these interactions con-form to his ideal of Justice. In other words, we have seen how *Droit* can appear on earth; for *Droit* is nothing other than the application of an ideal of Justice to given social interactions, this application being done by an impartial and disin-terested third—that is, acting solely according to his ideal of Justice.

This third can be either a Master or a Slave. Of course, in an aristocratic soci-ety—and Society is aristocratic in its nascent state, arising from the anthro-pogenic Struggle—it is only in the first case that *Droit* will exist *in actuality;* for it is only by being a Master that the Third will be able to be a part of the exclu-sive political group, and thus to become a Government, having the possibility of imposing its intervention (its judgement) in an *irresistible* way (in princi-ple). The intervention of a Third-Slave will always be (in principle) *optional,* and the *Droit* created by this intervention will therefore only exist *in potential-ity,* the Slave being by definition excluded from the exclusive political group, and therefore never able to be a Governor capable of imposing his decisions by an irresistible force. But this is of little importance for the moment, for in the two cases there will be *Droit:* in actuality or in potentiality. The Third-Master will *actually* apply his ideal of Justice to given interactions, while the Third-Slave [268] will only do so *virtually.* But the two will intervene solely accord-ing to their ideas of Justice and will therefore create by their impartial and dis-interested interventions authentic juridical situations.

What is important is that the third can apply to given social interactions *two* different Justices, based upon *two* distinct principles: that of *equality* or that of *equivalence.* Consequently, *Droit* is born in a dual form. It is born as *aristocratic* **Droit** when the Third applies the Master's *aristocratic Justice* of equality, and it is born as *bourgeois* **Droit** when the Third applies the Slave's *bourgeois Justice* of equivalence. But in its nascent state, *Droit* is only *actualized* in its aristocratic form, bourgeois *Droit* existing only *in potentiality* in the beginning.

Now we know (cf. Part One) that there is *Droit* in general (in potentiality or in actuality) only if the Third is *impartial* and *disinterested* in his intervention. First, [let us speak about being] *impartial.* And "impartial" means that the non-juridical quality of the litigants does not influence the nature of the judgement, that the litigants are interchangeable as non-juridical persons. In other words,

— 233 —

the litigants are equal before the judicial Law—certainly not in the modern sense of this expression, which means that *all human beings* are by definition a subject of *droit* or a juridical person, and that all juridical persons have the same *droits.* Juridical equality in the general sense of the term only means that all human beings *recognized* by *Droit* as juridical persons having the same *droits* are equal before the Law—that is, interchangeable, independently of their personal nature. And it is *this* "juridical equality" which is the condition *sine qua non* of *Droit.* Thus, one and the same *Droit* will be applied to Masters and Slaves *if*— and to the extent that—mastery and servitude are not juridical qualities, if Masters and Slaves are all juridical persons, having the same *droits* or not. In this case, aristocratic *Droit* will also be applied to Slaves, and bourgeois *Droit* to Masters.

Of course, where the exclusive political group and the exclusive juridical group are formed by the Masters, i.e., in a truly aristocratic Society, the (aristocratic) *Droit* in force will refuse to consider the Slaves as subjects of *droit.* This *Droit,* therefore, will not be applied to Slaves at all. But to the extent that an aristocratic *Droit* recognizes some *droits* for Slaves, i.e., treats them [269] as juridical persons (if only as "incompetent" persons), it is as aristocratic *Droit* that it will be applied: it is according to the principle of equality that not only the interactions between Masters will be treated, but also those between Masters and Slaves, or only between Slaves. Now the categories Master-Slave are not juridical categories right away. These are "social" categories in the narrow sense of the word, which only become juridical to the extent that they are recognized by the *Droit* in force. And nothing in *Droit,* even aristocratic, absolutely requires this recognition. In fact, it is the State as political Government which establishes the status of the governed, by deciding who will be a juridical person and who not, and by setting down the *droits* of the various categories of persons. And this status only becomes juridical to the extent that an impartial and disinterested third intervenes to annul acts contrary to the status in question (to the extent that this status conforms to the idea of Justice). Now the State may well ascribe certain *droits* to Slaves, and nothing prevents an aristocratic *Droit* from sanctioning those *droits* if they do not contradict the principle of egalitarian Justice which is at its base. Of course, the State which admits the positive status of the Slave will not be purely aristocratic; but this is of little importance for us. What is important is that aristocratic *Droit* can very well be applied to interactions between Slaves, or between Masters and Slaves, while remaining purely aristocratic—that is, by being inspired solely by egalitarian Justice. In other words, the exclusive juridical group of a society can be purely aristocratic even if its exclusive political group is no longer so. In this case *Droit* will be strictly aristocratic, but it will be applied—generally speaking—both to Masters and Slaves (which does not mean, moreover, that Masters and Slaves, being subjects of *droit,* will necessarily have *the same droits*).[1]

---

1. Moreover, it is *aristocratic Droit* which tends to apply the principle of juridical equality in the modern sense, for it is the one which is based upon the principle of equality, and not bourgeois *Droit.* I will speak about this below.

Just like aristocratic *Droit*, bourgeois *Droit* can also be applied equally to Slaves and Masters. Of course, in the beginning, this *Droit* only exists in potentiality. But this virtual *Droit* has from the outset a tendency to universalism in the sense that it tends to be applied to Masters in the same way that it is applied to Slaves; for if [270] the Master does not recognize the human personality of the Slave, the latter recognizes from the beginning that of the Master. Therefore, bourgeois *Droit* right away has a tendency to treat Masters as subjects of *droit*. But one must underline that the involvement of Masters in bourgeois *Droit* is just as extra-juridical as the involvement of Slaves in aristocratic *Droit*. It is as a Slave and not as a Third that the Third "recognizes" the Master, and it is as a Master and not as a Third that he refuses to "recognize" the Slave. To the extent that the Third is a Third, i.e., to the extent that he acts according to his ideal of Justice, he *may* (without being required to) apply this ideal both to Masters and Slaves, and this both in the case when his ideal is egalitarian and when it is based upon the principle of equivalence. In principle, therefore, *Droit* can be applied to *all* social interactions, whatever they may be, it being of little importance that this *Droit* is either aristocratic or bourgeois. And without this *universalism, Droit* would not be what it is— that is, a **Droit**, a *juridical* phenomenon.

Therefore, *Droit* is not aristocratic or bourgeois because it is applied to Masters or Slaves: all *Droit* can be applied to both of them. Nor is it aristocratic or bourgeois because it is applied by Masters or Slaves: a Master can just as easily apply and make his own bourgeois *Droit* as a Slave can make his own and apply aristocratic *Droit*. Indeed, *Droit* is *Droit* only because it is applied by the Third; and this Third must not only be impartial but also *disinterested*—that is, he must abstract in his juridical activity from his interests of a non-juridical character, just as he abstracts from the non-juridical character of his litigants. Now to the extent that mastery and servitude are "social" and not *primarily* juridical phenomena, the Third as Third may well abstract from the fact that he is a Master or a Slave. A Master, therefore, can apply the principles of the bourgeois Justice of equivalence (to any given interactions), just as a Slave can apply the principles of the aristocratic Justice of equality, such that Masters can realize bourgeois *Droit* and Slaves aristocratic *Droit*. Generally speaking, of course, the Master will have a tendency to apply aristocratic Justice. Thus, in a given Society having an exclusive aristocratic political group, the exclusive juridical group will generally be aristocratic as well. But this situation is not [271] juridically necessary, and it is possible that the aristocratic political group comes to coexist with a bourgeois juridical group. Conversely, the aristocratic juridical group can extend beyond the aristocratic political group and involve Slaves in it. Thus, the theory of aristocratic *Droit* has sometimes been made by Slaves, and often bourgeois *Droit* is actualized because the ideal of the Justice of equivalence which is at its base has penetrated into the environment of the Masters, who have then made it state *Droit* [*étatisé*]. Of course, the social and political dialectic of Mastery and Servitude, which ends in Citizenship, broadly coincides with the juridical dialectic of aristocratic *Droit* and bourgeois *Droit*, which leads to the synthetic *Droit* of the Citizen. But these two dialectics do not absolutely coincide, precisely because of the autonomy of the juridical phenomenon—that is, if you will, because of the impartiality and disinterestedness of the Third who creates *Droit*. As well, in certain cases, the more extensive application of the Justice of equivalence, i.e., the progress of bourgeois *Droit*, can precede the progress of the social and political emancipation of the Slaves, or be behind them.

Droit is not, therefore, aristocratic or bourgeois because it is applied to or by Masters or Slaves. These *Droits* differ solely because the one exclusively realizes egalitarian Justice and the other that of equivalence. Now we have seen that these two Justices have two distinct, albeit interconnected, sources. The one reflects the aspect of the Struggle realized by the Master, the aspect of the equality of the risk—that is, of the condition of the adversaries in the Struggle. The other manifests the aspect realized by the Slave, the aspect of the equivalence of conditions when the Struggle has finished. And this is why egalitarian Justice can be called "aristocratic" while the Justice of equivalence deserves the name of "slavish" or "bourgeois" Justice.

Now it is easy to see that these two sources of Justice and *Droit* are strictly independent of one another. The two adversaries can adopt once and for all the point of view of the (future) Master and confine themselves to the principle of equality alone. The Struggle will then finish in death. Or again, one of the adversaries adopts the point of view of the Slave and subjects his conduct to the principle of equivalence alone. The Struggle then ends in servitude.[2] Nothing forces man, therefore, [272] to go from the egalitarian point of view to that of equivalence; and if he accepts equivalence, he negates equality. This is to say, therefore, that these two principles are independent of one another. But they are nevertheless compatible, since their simultaneous preservation by the Master and Slave generates the dialectical, but not contradictory or impossible, relation of mastery and servitude. However, in fact, the Slave renounces equality by accepting equivalence, and the Master does not take into account equivalence by preserving equality: for he is ready to go to his death, which is equivalent to nothing (or is equivalent to the nothing), being pure nothingness.

And what is true of the principles which are at the base of the two Justices is also true of the Justices themselves, as well as the *Droits* which are based upon them. Having independent sources, these Justices and these *Droits* are independent of one another. In other words, one can realize an egalitarian *Droit* without taking account of the Justice of equivalence, and one can realize a *Droit* of equivalence while neglecting the Justice of equality; for indeed, one can neither deduce equality from equivalence nor the latter from equality. Thus,

---

2. The two cannot right away adopt the slavish point of view, i.e., the principle of equivalence, for the humanity of man is [272] constituted only in and by the risk—that is, the Struggle and the *equality* of its conditions. Therefore, equivalence *presupposes* equality without necessarily following from it; and it presupposes it as negation presupposes the negated.

nowadays, we still call "just" a share of *equal* parts, which does not take any account of what the distributed parts mean (or "are worth") for those who receive them. But we also call "just" *progressive* taxes, without concerning ourselves with the inequality that it creates and without letting ourselves be impressed by the equality of a simply proportional tax. By accepting equality in the first case, therefore, we do not go to equivalence, just as we do not go to equality in the second case by accepting equivalence. Originally, then, there are *two* independent *Droits*. But these *Droits* are not incompatible, and we will see that, on the contrary, the absolute *Droit* can only be a perfect synthesis of the two. But, being independent, they *may* enter into conflict with one another, and it is to the extent that they may do so that they are *oppositional:* for aristocratic *Droit*, being independent of the principle of equivalence, can imply legal rules which contradict this principle; and bourgeois *Droit* can be in contradiction with the principle of equality, being independent of this principle. Now in these cases, there will be a conflict between these *Droits*. Aristocratic *Droit* will fight against bourgeois *Droit* to the extent that the latter [273] will sanction inequalities, and bourgeois *Droit* will fight against aristocratic *Droit* which will sanction no equivalences: and this all the more so because the two *Droits*, being authentic *Droits*, will seek application to *all* social interactions, whatever they may be, by trying to apply to them the principle of Justice which is appropriate to them, by negating that which is opposed to them.

This conflict of *Droits*, this juridical dialectic, will necessarily lead to a synthesis, to the synthetic *Droit* of the Citizen, based upon the Justice of equity, which unites the principle of equality with that of equivalence; for these two principles are perfectly compatible, just as Mastery and Servitude are compatible. In order to be resolved, therefore, the conflict will limit itself to eliminating the inequality of bourgeois *Droit* and the non-equivalence of aristocratic *Droit*. Thus, little by little, these two *Droits* will make but one, by ceasing to be what they are in and by their opposition: an aristocratic *Droit* without equivalence and a bourgeois *Droit* without equality.

As I have already said several times, the real *Droit* in force is never aristocratic or bourgeois in the proper sense of these terms. By definition, there are neither slavish Societies nor Governments. Bourgeois *Droit*, therefore, can only be actualized by being made state *Droit* by those who are no longer fully Slaves. Therefore, it will have possibilities to include aristocratic elements while going from potentiality to actuality. On the other hand, man is never only a Master (for he always works more or less, thus implying a slavish element in his being). In any case, he cannot be a Governed, and therefore a Governor, if he were only that (for the Governed must submit). As actual, i.e., as state *Droit* or accepted by the Governors, aristocratic *Droit* also has possibilities to commandeer elements of bourgeois *Droit*. All *Droit* in force, therefore, is more or less synthetic: a *Droit* of the Citizen, in a state of becoming.

But the fact nonetheless remains that this real *Droit* of the Citizen is a *synthesis* of two autonomous elements, and a synthesis which is only *progressively* carried out. This is to say that *Droit in its nascent state* is *dual* and that its *unity* only appears at the end, as a *result*. In other words, the nature of *Droit* is dialectical, its evolution going from antithetical opposition to synthetic unity. Thus, even if the pure antithesis of the birth of *Droit* is only a theoretical construction, there is a point in doing this. By opposing their pure, and theoretical, states—aristocratic *Droit* to bourgeois *Droit*—one better understands their entanglement [274] in the real *Droit* in evolution, as well as the sense of this evolution. And this is why I will try a summary construction of aristocratic and bourgeois *Droits* taken in their pure ([and] moreover purely theoretical) states by beginning with the first.

A: The Justice of Equality and Aristocratic *Droit*

§ 40

The human being creates himself from animal being in and by the negation of the latter, i.e., in and by the risk of life for the sake of the desire for desire, which is the desire for recognition by one who is ready, as the other is, to risk his life for this same recognition. The human being, therefore, creates himself in and by an interaction between two *equal,* or indeed interchangeable, agents—that is, placed in the same conditions in relation to the Struggle and Risk. And the human existence which is thus realized is the existence of the Master. By looking at things from the aristocratic point of view, i.e., by admitting that truly human existence is that of the Master and it alone, one must therefore admit that human existence presupposes *equality,* namely the equality of risk [of life in the struggle]. The human being can only be constituted in and by an interaction between two human beings (who are humanized in and by this very interaction) placed in strictly *equal* conditions as regards the risk that they run. Without this primordial equality there would be no human being: humanity creates itself in equality.

The risk of life is *actualized* as death. One can therefore say that man is truly, fully, and definitively a Master only to the extent that he *dies* on the field of honor during a Struggle for pure prestige. Now, death being a global negation of existence as such, all are strictly *equal* in front of death: death is the same for all, independently of the particular conditions of the life of each one. In other words, mastery ends in equality (in death) just as much as it presupposes it (in the risk). Masters are just as equal in their nascent state, when they still exist only in potentiality, as they are in the fullness of their "being," in [275] their fully actualized "existence" (as death or in and by death). And this is why their real existences properly so-called, i.e., the actualizations of their potentialities, are also strictly *equal:* Masters, taken as Masters, are everywhere and always *equal.* Indeed, Mastery consists in the risk of life for recognition, for honor pure and simple. Now this risk, being total, negates the given, whatever it may be, in an identical way. The result of the negation does not depend here on the nature of the negated. The human is here the global negation of the natural, of the animal. He is a human being in general, who does not depend upon his origin. If one can live in various ways, there is only a single manner of dying on the field of honor and of risking one's life. There is only a single way of being a Master, of realizing Mastery by and in his existence.

Thus, by supposing that being a man is being a Master, and by assuming that being a man is not only a fact but also a "duty," one must recognize that *equality* is a "duty" as well. And this equality, understood as a duty-being, is Justice in the aristocratic sense of this word. An interaction can only be human if it is generated in the equality of the participants: there are human interactions only between equals. And since the interactions *ought* to be human, since one *ought* to humanize them, it is necessary to create equal conditions for all (it being understood for all *human* beings, which here means for all *Masters*). The interaction will only be "just" if it is generated in the equality of conditions. Likewise, a truly human interaction ought to end up in equality. It is, therefore, such as it *ought* to be; and it is only by being such that it will be "just." Now having to arise from and end in equality, the truly human interaction ought to be developed and exist in this same equality. The interaction, therefore, will only be "just" provided that it maintains and reasserts in its outcome the equality from which it springs. If to be a man is to be a Master, and if to be a Master is to be equal to others (and to risk his life for this equality, to prefer death to inequality, to submission), humanity can only be created and maintained in equality. As well, equality, as the condition *sine qua non* of humanity, is "just" by definition. And aristocratic Justice is nothing other than the *equality* of human conditions, the equality in mastery.

From this point of view, a social interaction can be perfectly "just," i.e., truly human or [276] humanizing, only if it arises from the equality of the agents interacting (at the very least in relation to the interaction itself); maintains their equality in and by its development; and ends in their equality, i.e., reasserts it, in its final result. Conversely, all interactions which are generated, developed, and end up in the inequality of the co-agents will be absolutely "unjust." But complex [*mixtes*] cases can be opposed to these straightforward cases, which gives rise in all to a casuistry of the aristocratic Justice of equality. An interaction can still be called "just" if it is carried out in inequality in order to overcome a preexisting inequality of conditions. And an interaction which ends in inequality can be called "unjust" even if it is part of a preexisting equality and is developed in the equality of conditions—and so on.

I have not developed here this casuistry. It is enough to indicate that from the aristocratic point of view, Justice is a function of equality alone. In complex cases the situation or interaction will be called "just" or "unjust" depending upon whether the elements of equality or inequality predominate. Equality and inequality can, moreover, be either static or dynamic. In the first case, it will be a matter not of interaction or action but of an inactive behavior, of a given situation. This situation will be "just" if the participants in the situation are in equal conditions, i.e., if they are equal in relation to the situation, from the point of view from which one considers this situation. In the second case, it will be a matter of an interaction, and this will be "just" if the participants are placed in the same conditions in relation to this interaction. In short, in the two cases there is "justice" if the participants are interchangeable in the sense that the situation or interaction does not change from the sole fact of a permutation carried out among the participants. Finally, by implication, a state of things can be called "just" even if there is only a single person at issue. In this case "justice" will mean that the aforementioned person can be kept in equality with himself. The static or dynamic conditions in which a person finds himself are "just" if they do not force him to become other than he is, to cease being equal to himself. And here as well there are complex cases, for example the case when "unjust" circumstances in themselves (i.e., generating an essential change) are called "just" because they overcome preexisting "unjust" circumstances—and so on. Now, here as well, it is the relation of equality and inequality which will determine the "juridical" nature of the phenomenon.

[277] There is no need to insist upon all this, for aristocratic judgements of value are to a large extent still our own (to the extent that our synthetic Justice of the Citizen implies aristocratic elements). Thus, in relation to social reality, the words "equality" and "justice" are still to a large extent synonymous. A share is called "just" if each of those who share has received an *equal* part to those of the others. And when one speaks of "social injustice," one has in mind above all the *inequality* of the distribution of the goods, situations, conditions, and possibilities of existence. Finally, when one says, for example, that it is "unjust" that an epidemic takes away a vigorous young man or that an honest merchant goes bankrupt (for reasons beyond his control), one has the feeling that a situation which could have kept indefinitely the same identity should not be altered so that the one involved experiences a radical change of state and does not remain equal to what it was.

If one studies societies with an aristocratic air, one is aware that they always generate egalitarian practices [*faits*] or ideologies. From the political point of view, the aristocrat will only call "just" institutions which guarantee his *equality* with his fellow man (i.e., with other aristocrats, the commoners not being truly human for him). It is in this way that the Spartans were calling themselves "equal" and that the feudal King was a "*primus inter pares* [first among equals]." Universal suffrage (of aristocrats), equality of votes in the (aristocratic) assembly, and—at the limit—the *droit* of absolute veto of each one (as formerly in Poland) are aristocratic political notions and claims. Socially, the aristocrat fiercely defends his equality with others, refusing any submission, any attempt to humiliate him in some way [and] not to treat him on an equal footing. Finally, economically, the Justice of equality ends up, at the limit, in the complete communism that one finds in a lot of (mythological or "scientific") utopias of aristocratic origin. And to the extent that one comes up against a primitive "communism," one notices an aristocratic structure of the society in question. Finally, communitarian tendencies become clear in the army, and above all on the field of battle, which is precisely the place where the Master truly lives as Master. In short, to be "just" for a Master is to treat Masters as Masters—that is, as equals.

Of course, a truly aristocratic society, a group of [278] Masters, is never egalitarian in the modern sense of the word, since this [society] always implies

Slaves. But there is no contradiction here, because for the Master the Slave is not a human being and his relation with the Slave has nothing to do with Justice. It is in this way that among us domestic animals are not on an equal footing with ourselves, without this being considered "unjust," even from the point of view of egalitarian Justice. The contradiction only appears when the Slave is considered as a human being, human in the same way as the Master himself; or once again, when the *Droit* in force treats the Slave (if only negatively) as a subject of *droit,* as a juridical person (that it punishes, for example). In this case, from the point of view of aristocratic Justice, all injustice between Master and Slave will be considered unjust.

Now one observes in effect that aristocrats who no longer treat their Slaves as simple animals are ready to recognize (at least in principle) their absolute *equality* with them (cf. the idea of "natural *droit*" in Greece and Rome). And often egalitarian revolutions have been started by these very nobles against whom the revolutions were directed. But this will only be true provided that the aristocrat preserves the aristocratic ideal of Justice. Now the Master who recognizes the humanity of his Slave is no longer a complete Master. He implies a slavish element in his consciousness (since he can look at things from the point of view of the Slave). He synthesizes, therefore, his mastery with servitude and is thus (more or less) a citizen. He can therefore easily adopt the bourgeois ideal of Justice. Now this Justice of equivalence does not at all require equality. Therefore, one can very well recognize the humanity of the Slave without asserting his equality with the Master (provided that their equivalence is required). And it is in this way that egalitarian revolutions, inspired by aristocratic Justice, end up by becoming bourgeois—that is, by accepting the bourgeois Justice of equivalence, in an equivalence of political, social, and economic conditions, which imply a fundamental inequality (that of property, for example). At the beginning of the revolution, the given inequality is considered unjust because the revolutionaries apply the ideal of aristocratic Justice. But if, while imposing themselves, they also impose their bourgeois Justice, this same inequality can cease being considered unjust after the revolutions.

The Master does not "recognize" the Slave because he [279] refuses to risk his life in a Struggle for recognition. But if the Slave rises up against his Master, if he resumes the Struggle by accepting the risk, he ceases to be a Slave (in order to become a Citizen—in potentiality). By struggling against him, the Master will implicitly recognize him (by his risk), and the situation will be "just" from the aristocratic point of view, for the conditions (of the risk) will again be equal. And if Society or the State supports the Master in his struggle against the insurgent Slave, the State only does what it does when it supports a "friend" (i.e., its citizen) against an "enemy" (a foreigner) in a war, for example (cf. the episode of Spartacus). The situation is then political and not juridical. And, once again, it is "just" from the aristocratic point of view, for there is equality of conditions (of risk). But as long as the Slave does not rise up, he remains a Slave—an animal in human form. As well, the relation of the Master with his Slave is as little juridical, as little "just" or "unjust," as his relations with things and animals. Of course, the State can help the Master to master or punish his Slave. But this will be a simple intervention of the police, comparable to the intervention of the State in relations between men and beasts. In this instance, there will be no relation of **droit** between the Master and his Slave, and their interaction will not give rise to *Droit*—that is, to an application of the ideal of egalitarian Justice. (Thus, Roman *Droit* did not punish the Slave for wrongs committed in the *domus* [home], as it did not punish the dog who killed its master.) But since the Slave is an animal of the species Homo sapiens, which also serves as the base for the Master, a confusion easily occurs. *Droit* can be applied to interactions between the Master and his Slave, by punishing the latter, for example (not at the request of the Master, which would be a simple, non-juridical Police action, but by decision of a Court). In this case, the Slave becomes a juridical person in the same way as the Master, and then from two things [comes] one: either *Droit* remains based upon aristocratic Justice, in which case there will be a tendency to grant the Slave *the same droits* as his Master; or, by being applied to Slaves, *Droit* will (also) be inspired by the bourgeois ideal of Justice, in which case it will be able to keep the fundamental inequality between Master and Slave, even if it means asserting their equivalence.

Be that as it may, the existence of Slavery is compatible with the aristocratic ideal of egalitarian Justice, provided that the Slave is not recognized as a human being. [280] By contrast, all inequality between human beings will be considered unjust from the aristocratic point of view, and only this *inequality* will be considered an injustice.

One could object that aristocratic societies are hierarchical, implying inequalities other than those between Master and Slave. However much the feudal King happens to be *primus* among *pares,* he is *primus* all the same, and there is not, then, absolute equality. And even in war, the leader receives a greater part of the booty than the simple solider, and so on.

This is undeniable. But this is because we are not familiar with purely aristocratic Societies; for there to be a State, there must be citizens. Now all citizens are also—more or less—Citizens in the sense that we give to this term: a synthesis of Master and Slave. Nothing surprising, then, in the State putting up with—more or less—a certain inequality, notably between Governors and the Governed (who are often, moreover, the vanquished—that is, quasi-Slaves). And if they do not consider these inequalities unjust, it is because they judge them according to the bourgeois ideal of the Justice of equivalence, such that their Justice is synthetic like themselves: a Justice of equity appropriate to the Citizen, a Justice which brings together the principle of equality with that of equivalence, if not in a synthesis, at least in a compromise (more or less happy, i.e., more or less in tension—that is, more or less stable and viable).

But it is of little importance that all ideals of Justice effectively applied are always more or less synthetic. What counts is that a situation can be called "just" solely because it is conforming to the principle of equality, without regard for that of equivalence; and that, nevertheless, a situation can realize these two principles simultaneously, thus being "just" both from the point of view of egalitarian Justice and from the Justice of equivalence, in which case it will be just from the point of view of the Justice of equity.

There is then—at least in theory—a purely and exclusively aristocratic Justice, where the "just" is synonymous with the "equal" (in human interactions). It remains to see what the application of this Justice will be by a Third to given social interactions—that is, aristocratic *Droit*.

§ 41

[281] Man constitutes himself (starting from the animal) in and by the Struggle for recognition, which makes [of him]—at its conclusion—the Master of a Slave. Having renounced risk, the Slave surrenders to the mercy of the Master and no longer offers him any resistance, in exchange for which he has his life saved. Henceforth, the Master can obtain all that he wants from his Slave without needing to make an effort, since he no longer encounters resistance on his part. The situation, therefore, is similar to a juridical situation: one could say that the Master has "*droits*" in respect to the Slave, since he does not encounter resistance on his part while doing what he does (just as the creditor does not encounter resistance while recovering his loan from the debtor). And the situation is "just" from the point of view of aristocratic Justice, for it arose from an absolute equality of conditions (i.e., of risk). Of course, it is fundamentally unequal; but having refused the risk, the Slave has renounced his humanity. There is no longer, then, a term of comparison between him and his Master, such that their "inequality" has nothing human about it—that is, nothing "just" or "unjust." But this is precisely why the relation between the Master and his Slave is not a relation of *droit*. And indeed, the absence of resistance on the part of the Slave, i.e., the absence of effort on the part of the Master, is not due to the intervention of an impartial and disinterested *third*. There is, then, only a *quasi*-juridical situation, and not a juridical situation in the proper sense of this term. The situation is "just" since it conforms to the ideal of Justice, or in any case, is not contrary to it. But seeing that there has not been an application of the principle of Justice by a *third*, one cannot say that there is *Droit* or juridical legality properly so-called.

Therefore, the Master only has quasi-*droits* in respect to the Slave. But he has them all, without any restriction; for the Slave is not supposed to resist in any of his acts. By contrast, he does not have any (juridical) duty toward the Slave, being able to resist any act of the latter. If Mastery is therefore determined in its relations with Servitude, one must say that being Master is being able to do everything without encountering resistance, and being able to oppose anything that the others do. Now Mastery is constituted as a "just" situation from the point of view of the aristocratic Justice of equality. [282] *Droit*, therefore, may want to sanction it juridically—that is, to recognize in the person of a third that it is conforming to the ideal of Justice which is at its base. Aristocratic *Droit* will then have to say that the Master, as a subject of *droit* or juridical person, embodies *all* subjective rights[3] and no juridical duty or obligation. The Third will therefore have to intervene—in principle—every time that one will react against the actions of the Master in order to annul these reactions, just as he will annul all the actions against which the Master reacts.

However, the application of this legal rule generates a dialectic. Seeing that every Master (as Master) possesses the *plenitude* of *droits* without having any duty, all Masters are *equal* from the juridical point of view and have the *same droits:* the maximum excludes the distinctions. Seeing that Mastery is determined by its relations with servitude, and that there is only one kind of relation between Master and Slave, all Masters are equal in their Mastery. By admitting the *plenitude* of the *Droits* of the Master and the absence in him of all duty, *Droit* should therefore admit the juridical equality of all the Masters. And it does so all the more voluntarily because this equality is conforming to the principle which constitutes the Justice which is at its base.

Aristocratic *Droit*, therefore, admits the following fundamental rule. Every juridical person, i.e., every human being—every Master or "aristocrat" (for only the human being is a juridical person, and only the Master is a human being properly so-called)—is endowed with the plenitude of subjective *droits,* and he can exercise them as he intends—provided that by his acts he does not infringe upon his fundamental juridical equality with other juridical persons. Or once again, each can exercise his *droits* provided that he does not infringe upon those of others, which are, moreover, strictly equal to his own. Or finally, a Master has the **droit** to act as Master to the extent that he treats other Masters as Masters—that is, respects their equality with him. In the contrary case, the third will intervene to reestablish equality and to overcome the action or reaction which infringes upon this equality and which is thus a juridical *wrong*. Every Master has the **droit** to do all that is compatible with the others' equality with him, and he has the **droit** to oppose all that is incompatible with his equality with others. He has the **droit**— that is, the third will act in his place if the case arises and will annul the reactions.

This fundamental principle of the aristocratic Master is clear, [283] but its application is difficult, or indeed impossible. In fact, the vast majority of social interactions presuppose or imply an inequality or lead to one. The ideal of aristocratic *Droit* is therefore the absence of all interaction between Masters. However, *Droit* only exists to the extent that it applies—by the Third—its ideal of Justice to social interactions—here, that is, to interactions between Masters. One can therefore say that the ideal of aristocratic *Droit* is not to exist in actuality, not to be applied. Now there is nothing paradoxical about this; for aristocratic *Droit* will first and foremost be called upon to overcome actions or reactions which infringe upon equality. Therefore, it will be above all a *criminal Droit*. Now the ideal of criminal *Droit* is obviously to be applied in actuality as little as possible; for if it is good to annul wrongful actions, it is better still that these actions not occur at all and that criminal *Droit* not be practiced.

---

3. [Ed. In the original, the English word "rights" follows the French phrase *droits subjectifs* in parentheses.]

Aristocratic *Droit* has a tendency to be confused with criminal *Droit* because all interactions are basically criminal for it, being always more or less an infraction of equality. Contrary to bourgeois *Droit,* which is based upon the principle of equivalence (and therefore of contract); which admits the juridical validity of a practically infinite mass of social interactions; and which is thus above all a civil *Droit,* aristocratic *Droit,* based upon equality (and therefore on static status), is only acquainted with very few juridically valid interactions, thus being above all a criminal *Droit* which suppresses interactions instead of sanctioning them. And historical experience shows that archaic or primitive *Droit* is first and foremost *criminal* and not *civil.* Now this *Droit* always presents a very pronounced aristocratic aspect. In "primitive" Societies, i.e., truly "aristocratic" (without being by this fact a group of Masters properly so-called), social interactions are above all criminal: the people—being economically and socially equal—live there while being isolated, having no need of one another, and they enter into interaction above all to mutually injure one another. Thus, robbery or abduction are more frequent than commercial exchange, and murder is more frequent than contractual collaboration.

Nevertheless, a Society can never—by definition—do without all social interaction. Now, if in these interactions the Master must limit his *droits* so as to respect those of others, it is because he also has juridical *duties* or *obligations.* And this is contrary to his status as a Master, which is juridically determined by the plenitude of *droits* [284] and the absence of duties. The Master and his *Droit* react against this by limiting the number of juridically lawful interactions (by forbidding the sale of land, for example). But they do not succeed in suppressing them completely. And to the extent that they accept them, they also accept the *duties* which result from them. However, they try to attenuate the contradiction with the fundamental principle of the absence of all duty by acknowledging only purely *negative* duties: juridical obligations to *refrain* from certain acts and not to *do* certain things. The Master continues, therefore, not to have any *positive* juridical duty (contrary to the Slave, who has above all positive quasi-duties). And he has all the positive *droits* which are not in contradiction with the negative duty not to infringe upon his equality with others.[4]

Be that as it may, the existence of even negative duties is in contradiction with the fundamental principle of strict aristocratic *Droit.* And indeed, the Master who enters into *peaceful* interactions (with other Masters) is not a Master properly so-called: it is not in his capacity as Master that he does so. Of course, he can—while doing so—preserve his aristocratic ideal of egalitarian Justice. And this is why he will only consent to limit his *droits* according to the ideal of equality. But no longer being an authentic Master, he will be prone to synthesize his aristocratic *Droit* with bourgeois *Droit,* based upon the ideal of

---

4. Our *Droit* of the citizen (still not perfect, moreover) still feels the effects of its aristocratic origins. Our juridical obligations are also above all *negative* in nature. Thus, if I have the duty to respect the life of another, I do not have the duty to help him to live: my neighbor can harm himself in front of me, [and] I do not have any juridical obligation to save his life.

equivalence. And it is in this way that the civil *Droit* of (more or less) aristocratic societies generally presents a bourgeois character. It even sanctions interactions contrary to the principle of equality, if these interactions correspond to the principle of equivalence. And so, the notion of juridical person no longer coinciding with that of Master, *Droit* will even be able to acknowledge the existence of *positive* juridical duties, of obligations *to do* something.

In his relation with the Slave, the Master has on his side all the *droits* (or quasi-*droits*, since this relation is not properly speaking juridical), and he does not have any duty (even negative). And his *droits* are here *exclusive* in the sense that it is alone in being able to exercise them, the Slave being *his* Slave and his only: no one else has *droits* over his Slave. Indeed, [285] to have *droits* over his Slave is to limit his *droits* to himself, and these are unlimited by definition.

The relation between Master and Slave being "just," aristocratic *Droit* can sanction it. And it does so by saying that the Master has a **droit** *of property* over his Slave. This *droit* of the owner over his property is *absolute* and *exclusive* in the sense that it is neither limited by the property itself (which only has, so to speak, negative and positive "duties" toward its owner and not any "*droit*") nor by other persons, who also do not have any *droit* over the property of the owner, such that he does not have any duty in respect to them as regards his property. Now this exclusive relation with others is a social interaction, a relation between two juridical persons. Seen from this angle, the *droit* of property is therefore a genuine *droit*. And by extension, it can be applied to all that is in the same relation with the Master as his Slave: an animal or a thing which are absolutely and exclusively "his own," as his Slave is "his own," will be said to be his *property*, sanctioned by *Droit*, which will annul all the actions which infringe upon it, limiting the *droits* of the owner.

The *droit* of property is therefore an essentially aristocratic *droit*, and aristocratic *Droit*, to the extent that it is a civil *Droit*, is first and foremost a **Droit** *of property* (while civil bourgeois *Droit* is above all a *Droit* of contract and obligations in general). Of course, the aristocratic ideal of Justice requires an economic equality (of Masters or "aristocrats"), from whence comes a tendency to the *communitarian* conception of property; for if each one possesses the same thing as others, nothing is opposed to the permutation of properties (which is something else than commercial exchange, where the things exchanged are by definition different), and nothing requires a separation of the parts of each one. As well, aristocratic property is often collective: familial, tribal, communal, and so on. But this "communitarian" property has nothing to do with "communism," and it is well and truly an absolute and exclusive property; for it is of little importance to have a separated property, or one part to oneself, in a collective property.[5] No

---

5. Communism denies property as such. The Russian collective farmer only draws his income from his work, and he is just as little owner of the land that he works as the factory worker is of "his" factory. If he did not work, he would not be fed, even if "his" land was very profitable, and he is paid in proportion to his work and not to the income from the land that he works. By contrast, the communitarian owner enjoys [286] (in proportion to his share) the benefits which come from the nature of his land, even if these benefits are independent of work.

one can encroach [286] upon the contribution [*participation*] of another, all the contributions having to be equal, and this from the sole fact of the *existence* of the contributors and independently of their actions (of their work in particular). Now seeing that juridical reasons do not determine the share, economic reasons can be opposed to them. What is important is that aristocratic property (i.e., property as *droit*, "property" in the strong and proper sense of the term) is not the *equivalent* of an action (of work, for example) but belongs to the *being* of the owner, who is owner because he *is* and not on the grounds of what he *does* (from whence comes the juridical possibility of sharecropping, and so on).

Of course, practically speaking, aristocratic *Droit* finds itself in the presence of economic inequalities, contrary to its ideal of Justice. But if it accepts them—through a compromise with itself or by allowing the bourgeois ideal of equivalence—it will endeavor to maintain them; for the Master has the *droit* to remain in equality with himself, and all action which infringes upon this equality is illicit. (For in theory aristocratic *Droit* assumes that the Masters are equal, so that to maintain the equality of each one with himself is equivalent to maintaining the equality between everyone.) Therefore, it will be illicit to decrease or increase property, from whence comes the ban not only against theft, but also against selling and buying. To the extent that property is part of Mastery, it must be maintained in identity with itself. And if the equality of properties is only an ideal, at the very least it will be forbidden for one to increase his property by decreasing that of another, it being of little importance if he does it with or without the other's consent. These acts will be forbidden because if ideal equality were realized, these acts could only abolish it, just as they cannot increase it if it already exists.[6]

Now property is effectively an integral element of Mastery, and the Struggle for recognition can also be interpreted as a struggle for property, for the absolute and exclusive *droit* to a thing (which can also be an animal, even of the species Homo sapiens: the Slave). Animals [287] struggle among themselves for the possession of a thing. Men also struggle in order that a thing is *recognized* as exclusively theirs by another (even if this thing has no value in itself), and it is only to the extent that this is the case that the Struggle is human and anthropogenic. As well, the Struggle for recognition can be engaged around a thing (which can be a woman, for example). However, if the adversary renounces the risk, he not only recognizes that the thing is the exclusive property of the other; he also recognizes himself as such property by becoming the Slave, i.e., the "thing," of the other. And this is why there are no relations of *droit* relative to property (of the Slave or something else) between the Master and his Slave. But every non-owner, even if he is not the Slave of the owner, even if he is also a Master, is in the same situation as the Slave in respect

---

6. The casuistry of aristocratic *Droit* accepts alterations aiming at economic equalization. But practically speaking, only the State can do it, for the one who has more will not want to spontaneously give [it] away to one who has less. Now a state-sanctioned action has nothing juridical about it. In this case, however, it is not contrary to the principle of the *Droit* in question, since it is in agreement with the ideal of Justice.

to the property of others: he has no *droit* over it (while having the negative duty to respect it). One can therefore say that from the juridical point of view, every Master is comparable to the Slave when it is a matter of relations with the property of others. However, he is Master in other respects, and this is why his relations with the owner relative to the property of the latter are a relation of *droit*, the owner having kept a **droit** to his property. Now the similarity of juridical situations is here explained by the similarity of their origin. The Slave is Slave because he has refused every sort of risk. By contrast, the non-property owning Master does not reject a Struggle for recognition in general. He only refuses to risk his life in a Struggle for the recognition of the exclusive property of a given thing. It is by this refusal that he recognizes the property of the other, who is ready to risk his life for the thing, and it is this recognition, by the refusal of the risk, that sanctions aristocratic *Droit*. As soon as there is no war for a possession (in which case the relation ceases to be juridical), the possession uncontested by force of arms is a property in the juridical sense of the term: it is the Third who undertakes to defend it against "pacific" injuries (for example, by a thief or buyer). But one must really say that even partial, unilateral "recognition" (by the refusal of risk) always has the character of Servitude. And this is why one can say, by playing with words, that all property implies a "servitude" on the properties of others:[7] each one must henceforth use his property in such a way that the other can use his own; [288] each one must therefore limit his *droits* of property in order to allow others to exercise theirs. Now all juridical obligation, even purely negative, is contrary to the fundamental principle of aristocratic *Droit*, according to which the juridical subject is a subject with unlimited *droits* without any duty. This is why aristocratic *Droit* is opposed to economic exchanges, i.e., to interactions between properties or between Masters taken as owners; for it is only when properties are strictly isolated from one another that the "servitudes" that they mutually impose practically boil down to zero: these "servitudes"—and Servitude—grow with the growth of interactions between properties (with commerce in particular). Now the Master who does not limit himself to the interaction of the Struggle (of war), but who enters into interaction with his peers in the capacity of owner (becoming a "merchant" in the broad sense of the word), is no longer exclusively a Master, but a Citizen implying as well an element (more or less extensive) of Servitude. He will therefore be prone to apply to these economic interactions the principles of bourgeois *Droit*, which, being based upon equivalence and not equality, accepts the existence of economic "servitudes"— that is, of even positive juridical obligations.

I have said that aristocratic *Droit* is first and foremost a *Droit* of *statuses* and not of *contracts* (like bourgeois *Droit*). Now, at first glance, the anthropogenic Struggle and the relation of Master to Slave seems to be comparable to a con-

---

7. [Ed. Kojève plays on the dual meaning of the word *servitude:* its obvious and ordinary meaning of "servitude," and the technical and civil law meaning of an "easement," i.e., a legal right of way over someone else's property.]

tract, seeing that it is a matter of a free, mutual consent—that is, conscious and voluntary. However, the pseudo-contract of Servitude annuls the juridical personality of the Slave. Therefore, it is not a contract in the juridical sense of the word, but at the very most a convention (even though a convention supposes a *bilateral* recognition). Of course, there is no Mastery without Servitude, and the Master is Master only to the extent that he has a Slave who recognizes himself as such. But seeing that humanity is conflated with Mastery, only the Master can be a subject of *droit,* and a juridical situation only exists when there is an interaction between two Masters (of which each juridically unites with his Slave, the juridical person being "Master plus Slave"). Now Mastery does not arise from an interaction between Masters, and it is therefore not the result of a contract. Mastery is a *status* of the juridical person, which is universally recognized as a status. The other Masters limit themselves to noticing [289] the risk accepted by a given Master, without this risk resulting in a Struggle between them and him. Thus, they limit themselves to noticing a *state* which does not depend upon them, and it is this observation that sanctions *droit* in the *status* of the Master—that is, of the juridical person. In other words, *Droit* requires that Masters treat Masters as Masters, and the Third annuls all action contrary to this legal rule. But to treat a Master as Master is in the final analysis to let him act as he pleases, without entering into interaction with him, without reacting against his acts. In order for this to be the case (more or less so, it should be understood, for in fact there are no pure masters, and the ideal of aristocratic *Droit* is never fully realized), there must be, if you will, a "social contract," where each promises to treat the others as they treat himself—that is, as Master. But this (tacit) convention is not a contract in the juridical sense of the word, for it excludes interactions far more than it presupposes them. It is simply a coexistence of wills (or "interests") in static equilibrium or in "preestablished harmony," without this equilibrium being dynamic even at its origin—that is, without it resting on an interaction and a contract.[8] Aristocratic Society is fundamentally *static:* It rests upon the *status* of its members, which in principle excludes their interactions—that is, precisely all contractual relation between them. When one is Master, one is it in order to remain so, and one remains Master by "doing nothing" in time of peace, among his peers or his political friends, the sole activity worthy of a Master being war (which has nothing juridical about it, seeing that there is no possibility of a Third). All contract, moreover, presupposes inequality of conditions; for if two persons are strictly equal, they have nothing to exchange, to give one another. Therefore, contract can only be justified juridically if *Droit* is based upon the Justice of equivalence. And this is why aristocratic *Droit,* which is only familiar with

---

8. It is here that the mistake of "social *contract*" theory appears. In aristocratic Society (which is the "first" human Society), social equilibrium rests upon a static coexistence, i.e., upon a status, and upon a convention that implies and presupposes interactions (as is the case in bourgeois Societies). Moreover, even when there is a social "convention," one cannot speak of *juridical* "contract," since this convention creates *Droit,* which does not exist before it.

the ideal of equality, is hostile to contracts, whatever they may be. Thus, for example, the merchant is always more or less likened to the thief by this *Droit,* and the status of the Master [290] generally excludes the possibility of engaging in commerce.[9]

Be that as it may, the status of the Master, i.e., of the juridical person of aristocratic *Droit,* is based upon the principle of equality: with oneself or with others. As well, this *Droit* will call juridically illicit all action tending to overcome this equality. And punishment, whose aim is always to annul the illicit action, will always imply the restitution of the equality overcome in and by crime. If crime is nothing other than the creation of an inequality (where one was not existing, let us say), punishment will be above all a restoration of equality.

This punishment (pronounced and enforced by the Third) will be accepted by the Master because it does not contradict the principle of Mastery—that is, of absolute autonomy. Indeed, if the Master acts as Master, he will not enter into interaction with his peers, his political friends, and he will not therefore be able to injure them by destroying their equality with him. If he does so, it is because he acts as a non-Master, i.e., as a Slave, or indeed as an animal. Now Mastery consists precisely in self-mastery—that is, in the negation in oneself of the animal and the servile. By undergoing the punishment that restores equality, the Master therefore restores his own Mastery injured by his crime. And this is why, as Master, he accepts the punishment imposed by aristocratic *Droit*—that is, the punishment based upon the ideal of equality.

Being based upon the principle of equality (and not upon that of equivalence), the aristocratic theory of punishment will be that of *lex talionis.* To reestablish equality, the Third will inflict on the criminal exactly the same treatment that he has inflicted on the victim of the crime: if he made him one-armed, he will be one-armed himself. And since the injury has been "objective," the punishment will be so also. What is criminal is the introduction of an inequality, and it is of little importance that it has been voluntary, premeditated, or accidental. It is a matter of objectively restoring the equality by applying the principle of lex talionis. Therefore, one will apply it without regard for the motives of the crime, without thinking about the *equivalence* between the crime *of the criminal* and the punishment undergone by him. It is enough that the punishment be *equal* to what is objectively [291] the crime. Now, if this is the case, it is of little importance even if it is truly the criminal who is punished. It is enough that an injury of equality is compensated for by another in the opposite sense: if *one* has made someone one-armed, it is necessary that *there* is another one. From this comes the "collective" and "substitutive" character of aristocratic punishment (supported as well by the presumed *equality* of the

---

9. The sole "contract" accepted is that of marriage. But this question is too complicated to be discussed here. At any rate, there is here a *difference* of the sexes, which makes the contract possible and that aristocratic ideology cannot deny. Still, one must point out that the woman is not—at first—a juridical person in the same way as the man. It is possible that the ban against incest and endogamy in general is the principal source of the penetration of the idea of contract into aristocratic *Droit.*

Masters—one arrives at the same result by acting on whomever among them): one can spread out the sentence of the crime committed by one alone among several [persons], and one can punish another in the place of the criminal. Now historical experience shows that aristocratic *Droit* (i.e., archaic or primitive) often acts in that fashion.[10]

B: The Justice of Equivalence and Bourgeois *Droit*

§ 42

Just like aristocratic Justice, bourgeois Justice reflects the anthropogenic Struggle. This time, however, this Struggle is reflected not in the consciousness of the Master but in that of the Slave. If aristocratic Justice corresponds to the point of view of the Master, bourgeois Justice reflects the Struggle from the point of view of the Slave. Now Mastery is constituted in and by the risk, i.e., in and by the Struggle as such, while Servitude is the result of this Struggle, determined by the negation of the risk and the Struggle, by the refusal to continue it (until death). As well, aristocratic Justice corresponds to the Struggle properly so-called, while bourgeois Justice corresponds to its conclusion, to its result. Now if the Struggle takes place in the absolute *equality* of conditions (i.e., of risk), the result is a total negation of this equality, the Slave being what [292] the Master is not, and conversely. At the conclusion of the Struggle, humanity excludes equality, since it implies the clear-cut difference between Mastery and Servitude: for the Master, it is true, the Slave is not human, and this is why he can keep his ideal of equality, seeing in equality the necessary condition of humanity. But if humanity is considered from the point of view of the Slave, it implies the *two* elements of Mastery *and* Servitude, and it thus necessarily implies *inequality*. The Slave who consciously and voluntarily renounces equality with the Master cannot see in equality a condition *sine qua non* of humanity. Therefore, equality is not for him a "duty-being," it is not in his eyes "just" as such. In any case, the Justice seen by the Slave does not presuppose equality, and the unequal is not "unjust" from the sole fact of being unequal. An inequality can be "just," as the inequality of the Master and Slave is "just" (for the Slave, because for the Master it is neither just nor unjust, the Slave not being a human being comparable to the Master in any relation at all).

The Slave "justifies" the inequality between himself and the Master by the fact that it has been freely accepted—that is, voluntarily and consciously. The

---

10. [Paul] Fauconnet, *La Responsabilité:* [*étude de sociologie,* 2nd ed. (Paris: Librairie Félix Alcan, 1928), 330–84] shows that *Droit* evolves from the objectivity and collectivism of the sentence to its subjectivity and individuality more and more strictly.

[Jean] Piaget, *Le Jugement moral chez l'enfant* [*The Moral Judgement of the Child,* trans. Marjorie Gabain (Glencoe: The Free Press, 1948), 195–325] shows that the child passes from the justice of equality to that of equity (i.e., of equivalence). The child therefore seems to remake the historical evolution of *Droit,* which also begins by the application of the aristocratic Justice of Equality, in order to continue it little by little with the bourgeois Justice of equivalence in the synthesis of the Justice of the equity of the Citizen.

Slave has renounced the risk of the Struggle and has submitted to the Master because in his eyes the troubles of the Struggle are *equivalent* to those of Servitude, because the benefits of security *compensate* for the burdens [*désavantages*] of Servitude. Or once again, Servitude is "just" because in it the benefits and burdens [*inconvénients*] mutually *balance off one another*. Servitude arose from this judgement of equivalence, which is its condition *sine qua non* (and that of Mastery, at least from the point of view of the Slave, since there is no Mastery without Servitude). Now for the Slave, Servitude is a form of humanity (if only as the condition *sine qua non* of Mastery), even if this form only realizes humanity in potentiality, virtually, and not in actuality. Indeed, the Slave is what he is, i.e., a Slave, only to the extent that he *recognizes* himself as such, if he "consents" to be so (by the free act of surrender).[11] He adopts the point of view of his Master and recognizes that he is only an animal, "the thing" of his owner. But [293] the very fact that he *recognizes* [*reconnaît*] it, that he *knows* himself [*se connaît*] as an animal, distinguishes him essentially from an animal properly so-called, which does not *know* that it is an animal, which has not *become* it by an act of its freedom. In other words, the Slave is an animal *for himself* but not *for us*, i.e., in truth, and he is not an animal, he is a human being *for us* precisely because he is an animal *for himself*, and not only *in itself*, in fact: because he *knows* that he is an animal—that is, because he *believes* he is. But if he is only a human being *for us*, i.e., *in itself* and not *for himself*, if he does not *believe* in his humanity and does not *know* himself to be a man, it is because he is one—for us or in truth—only *in potentiality*: he is one "in itself," i.e., virtually, and not "for itself" or in actuality. He *is* human because he has risked his life by first accepting the Struggle (or at the very least, if he refused the Struggle from the beginning, he called to mind the idea of risk and death for recognition). But not having gone to the very end, having refused to prolong the risk and to actualize it in and by death (on the field of honor), he has not actualized his humanity. And this is why he is only a human being in potentiality, which means that he must *change* in order to be actualized, that he must cease being a Slave (and become a Citizen) in order to exist in actuality as a human being—and this not only *for us* but also for himself, to the extent that he becomes aware of his humanity. For him, the human being is just as much a "*duty*-being" as for the Master; but while the latter fulfills this "duty" by remaining what he is, a Master—by keeping himself in identity or equality with himself—the Slave fulfills the duty-being man, such as he understands it, by changing, by becoming different. However, he can become different only by negating what he is, only by negating himself as a Slave. His actual (Citizen's) humanity presupposes his virtual Slave's humanity; and the latter implies inequality and presupposes equivalence: for the Slave, therefore,

---

11. A man made prisoner without his knowing it, without a struggle (in his sleep, for example), and deprived of the possibility of suicide, is not a Slave in his existence. Servitude, as a specific existential attitude, implies the will to be a Slave by abandoning the Struggle or the refusal of the risk.

"duty-being" is based upon equivalence and not upon equality. And his idea or ideal of Justice is thus based upon the principle of equivalence, which allows for inequality (without necessarily requiring it). The equal is not the "just" and the unequal is not the "unjust." The "just" is equivalent and the equivalent is "just," even if there is inequality. And the non-equivalent is "unjust" whether it is unequal or not; for the Slave, humanity or humanization is not possible without prior *equivalence* (for without this equivalence, there is no surrender, and without surrender there is only death: at the very least, this is how the Slave thinks, [294] who does not believe in his victory—that is, in the death of the other). Equivalence is therefore a "duty-being," and "duty-being" as equivalence is "just" even if it implies inequality. The bourgeois Justice of the Slave is a Justice of equivalence.

It is from the point of view of this Justice of equivalence that the Slave judges and justifies his own condition. He accepts it as just because in it the benefit of security is equivalent to the burden of the servile condition (first and foremost of working for others). And it is from the same point of view that he judges and justifies the condition of the Master. It is also "just" because in it the benefit of Mastery is equivalent to the burden of the risk, of the perpetual danger of death. However, the Slave knows very well that there is no *equality* between him and his Master, nor between Mastery and Servitude in general. Nevertheless, he "justifies" them because he considers them *equivalent*. The Slave knows that *for the Master* security does not compensate for servitude, since the Master, who is ready to go to the very end in the Struggle, prefers death to servitude. And he knows that *for him* mastery does not compensate for the risk of life, since by abandoning the Struggle and submitting he proves that he prefers slavery to death. Therefore, if the Slave "justifies" both Mastery and Servitude, if he "justifies" them in their coexistence and in their mutual relations, it is because he notices the *internal* equivalence or equilibrium of the two conditions. It is "just" that *the Master* is Master, because *for him* mastery offsets the risk, just as it is "just" that *the Slave* is Slave, because *for him* security offsets servitude. One can therefore say that the two conditions, while not being *equal* between them, are *equivalent:* Mastery is *for the Master* what Servitude is *for the Slave.* Two human conditions (equal or not), as well as their mutual relations, are "just," i.e., equivalent, if in each of them there is an equivalence of constitutive elements, of benefits and burdens, from the point of view of the one who is in the condition in question.

From the sole fact that it replaces equality with equivalence, bourgeois Justice therefore ceases to be objective and absolute, as was aristocratic Justice, in order to become subjective and relative. If the "just" is the *equal,* one can objectively notice it, without taking account of the point of view of the persons in question. But if the "just" is the *equivalent,* one can only notice it by taking account of the point of view of the interested parties (unless one assumes their fundamental *equality,* [295] which is not at all required by the ideal of bourgeois Justice, while being compatible with it): what is equivalent, i.e., "just," for one may not be so for the other. Of course, to the extent that the differences between persons are objectively noticeable by a third, one can in principle objectively work out the equivalences for each of them. But in fact and in the last resort, the interested party is the sole judge of what is equivalent in relation to him: the equivalent *in relation to him* is what is equivalent *for him;* for if it is necessary to judge from the point of view of the interested party, it is difficult to neglect his own point of view on the question to be resolved. As well, contrary to aristocratic Justice, bourgeois Justice always has a tendency to call "just" what the interested parties themselves consider as such. And if it is possible to require people to be equal, it is practically impossible to force them to consider as equivalent what in their eyes is not so. Now without this consent there is no equivalence, since the equivalent is equivalent not in general and among everyone, but solely in relation to those who are supposed to realize in themselves the conditions of this equivalence, their recognition of equivalence being one of these conditions.[12]

The bourgeois or servile ideal of the Justice of equivalence, which accepts inequality, still lives nowadays in our more or less synthetic Justice of equity, where it coexists (with more or less harmony) with the ideal of egalitarian, aristocratic Justice. And there are cases when the bourgeois ideal of equivalence appears in its pure state by being opposed to the aristocratic ideal of equality.

If it is a matter of sharing food for dinner between two persons, one of whom had lunch and the other not, we will say that the share will be just if the latter receives more. And we will say that it is just to give a child a slice of cake that is larger than the slices of the adults. It is also just that the weak carry less than the strong, and it is from an ideal of Justice that the practice of the handicap was born. From all of this, one need only go one step further in order to assert that it would be just to give a thing to the one who desires it the most. And one commonly says that it is just to give it to the one who needs it the most (cf. the principle of "communist" Society: to each according to his needs). Or once again, one will say that it is just to give the thing to [296] the one who has made the most effort to have it (cf. the principle of "socialist" Society: to each according to his merits)—and so on.

In all these cases, a Master would be struck by the injustice of inequality from the start. Thus, a poor but proud man will hide the fact that he has not had lunch in order to see the Justice of equality alone applied. And a weak person may through pride or amour-propre (the Bourgeois will say vanity) carry the same weight as the strong. Likewise, a child may be upset by a bigger share for himself if he wants to be treated "like an adult" first and foremost. And there are athletes who prefer to forfeit a match when the Justice of equivalence requires that others be handicapped. In short, the Master can require equality without taking account of equivalence, of the compensation of his inequality with others. By contrast, the Bourgeois or the Slave will be satisfied by the equivalence of conditions, without taking account of their inequalities. When

---

12. Thus, one sees the link which connects the bourgeois ideal of Justice with the principle of "Democracy."

the Master will say that the share is unjust because it is unequal, the Bourgeois will consider it just because it is equivalent.

Now history hands down to us social and juridical systems expressly based upon the principle of equivalence, coexisting with the fact of a recognized and justified inequality. Such is the Christian system of one St. Thomas Aquinas.[13] According to this theory, social and juridical Justice consists in the possibility of each one living *"according to his rank."* And the difference of "ranks" is accepted and justified by the equivalence of conditions, which follows from the fact that in every condition the costs are equivalent to the benefits. Thus, the idleness of the nobles is "justified," i.e., compensated for, by their obligation to make war and defend the commoners, among whom security compensates for, i.e., "justifies," work (and poverty!).

Now our contemporary world is to an enormous extent based upon the ideal of the bourgeois Justice of equivalence, and if it accepts inequality (economic, for example) it is by equivalence that it tries to justify it. Thus, the salary of a factory manager is supposed to be equivalent (although very unequal) to the salary of a worker, either because it requires [297] more effort (intellectual or moral effort being understood—[i.e.,] "responsibility") or because it has a greater return (from the point of view of the owner's benefits). And even the Thomistic idea of "rank" is far from being dead (cf. "entertainment allowances," and so on).

It is also from the ideal of equivalence that the idea of progressive income taxes arose. It appears just that the one who earns more than others pays more than them, not only speaking absolutely but relatively: 20% in taxes among one is equivalent to 10% in taxes among the other. And the same Bourgeois, who recognizes that this system of taxes is just, absolutely refuses to admit that it would be just to equalize wealth [*fortunes*] by rejecting the very proposal of a tax on capital.

It should be understood that the Justice of equivalence does not exclude equality and is compatible with it, just as the Justice of equality is compatible with equivalence. And in fact, the accepted idea of Justice always implies the two principles simultaneously (in varying proportions), being a Justice of equity, a Justice of the Citizen (more or less actualized). And it is as such

---

13. According to Hegel, the Slave goes through Christianity before becoming Bourgeois. Christianity equalizes the Slave with his Master. However, it only equalizes them in *servitude* (cf. the Rule of St. Benedict: "We are all equal in servitude.") By becoming Christian, the Slave does not become a Master (Citizen), [and] he does not free himself: but the Master ceases to be Master. Now the Bourgeois is precisely a Slave without a Master, or—which is the same thing—a Master without a Slave, from whence comes the search for an imaginary Master: God and Capital. [Ed. *The Rule of Saint Benedict*, ed. and trans. Abbot Justin McCann (Westminster, MD: The Newman Press, 1952), 19. The actual quotation reads as follows: "Let not a freeborn monk be put before one that was a slave, unless there be some other reasonable ground for it. But if the abbot, for just reason, think fit so to do, let him fix anyone's order as he will; otherwise let them keep their due places; because, whether slaves or freeman, we are all one in Christ, and have to serve alike in the army of the same Lord."]

that it evolves in time. But the previous analysis shows that it is a matter of a genuine *synthesis,* i.e., the fusing of two independent, if not contradictory, elements in themselves; for pure equality is realized without there being equivalence, and equivalence without there being equality. Therefore, it is not by developing the Justice of equality that one reaches the Justice of equivalence, and conversely. One reaches the Justice of equity by simultaneously adopting the two Justices, which are born separately and independently of one another, and which we have analyzed as separated and independent.

But before dealing with this synthetic Justice of the Citizen, let us see how the Justice of equivalence is realized in and by bourgeois *Droit,* through being applied by an impartial and disinterested Third to given social interactions, these interactions being, moreover, co-determined by this very Justice, [and] taking place in the Society where the *Droit* in question is valid.

§ 43

Properly speaking, aristocratic *Droit* is not applied in the relation between Master and Slave, seeing that the latter is not considered as a juridical person. But if [298] one wants to speak of this relation in juridical terms, one must say that the Master enjoys the plenitude of (quasi-) *droits* without having a single duty, while the Slave only has (quasi-) duties without any *droit.* But this is true only from the point of view of the Master. From the point of view of the Slave, his relation with the Master presents another aspect. If the Slave fulfills his (quasi-juridical) duty or obligation toward the Master, if he carries out his order, for example by working for him, and if someone tries to prevent him from doing so, he will not need (in principle) to react himself. The impartial and disinterested Third will intervene in his triple capacity as Legislator, Judge, and Police in order to remove the obstacle, which will therefore be criminal. In other words, there will be a juridical situation, a relation of *droit.* Of course, from the point of view of the Master (and of aristocratic *Droit*), this relation will only exist between Masters, between the Master who owns the Slave and the Master who does not, and not between a Master and the Slave. In the case being considered, the Slave is not a subject of *droit;* for the Law does not protect the Slave as such. It only protects him as the Master's property: to prevent him from working for his Master is to injure his Master, and it is only this injury of the Master which is annulled by the Third. But things appear otherwise from the point of view of the Slave. He notices that if his action (the work for the Master, for example) provokes a reaction which thwarts it, a Third comes to annul this reaction. He can therefore say that he has *the **droit*** to do what he does. It should be understood that he knows that the Third will only intervene in cases when his actions are done by order of his Master. In other words, the Third only intervenes if the Slave carries out his obligations toward his Master, if he fulfills his duty in respect to him. Therefore, the Slave has a ***droit*** only to the extent that he has a *duty.* If he considers his obligation toward the Master as his juridical *duty,* he can say that this *duty* is also his *right.*[14]

Of course, if the Slave recognizes that he has *duties* (toward his Master) in the juridical sense of the word, he already considers himself as a juridical person, as a subject of *droit,* in the same way as the Master. By this very fact, he recognizes himself as human just like the Master (without having the *same* humanity as the latter, the *same* "*droits*" as him). Properly speaking, therefore, he is no longer a Slave, for a Slave is treated as an animal, as a simple thing of his Master, who alone is supposed to be human and have "*droits.*" The Slave who recognizes himself as a juridical person is already—more or [299] less—a Citizen. This is why, generally speaking, he will have a tendency to develop a synthetic *Droit* by combining the principle of equivalence with that of equality. But this means, quite simply, that bourgeois *Droit* is a *Droit* in potentiality—that is, a *Droit* which must *change* in order to be actualized, which must become *other* than it is. Now the *Droit other* than bourgeois *Droit* is aristocratic *Droit.* Therefore, while being actualized or in order to be actualized, bourgeois *Droit* will tend to transform itself into aristocratic *Droit.* But in this process of transformation or actualization, it will be bourgeois and aristocratic simultaneously. Therefore, it will be neither one nor the other: it will be a synthetic *Droit* of the Citizen, and it is as such that it will finally be actual. At first, however, in its nascent state, as pure potentiality, this *Droit* will still not be synthetic, it will still not imply aristocratic elements based upon the principle of equality; or, if you will, equality will still not be real in actuality: it will be ideal, abstract, "formal." The Slave will be the "equal" of the Master only to the extent that the two will be subjects of *droit,* juridical persons; but their *droits* will not be equal. And there is still more. Among the Master, the primordial, juridical given is his *positive right.*[15] Among the Slave, by contrast, this first and irreducible given is his *duty:* if he has (positive) **droits,** it is solely because he has *duties* or obligations, and his *droits* are exactly the same extent as his duties. The Slave has the *droit* to do his duty—that is all.

From the outset, therefore, bourgeois *Droit* recognizes a strict equality between the duties of the Slave (toward his Master) and his *droits* (in respect to others, whomever they may be). Or more exactly, since the relations of the Slave with his Master are nonetheless *something different* from his relations with others, it is better to say that from the beginning, bourgeois *Droit* recognizes a strict *equivalence* between duties and *droits.* Therefore, every duty is equivalent to a *droit.* Now if A is equivalent to B, B is equivalent to A. One can therefore say that all *droit* is equivalent to a duty. In other words, if the duties of the Slave are compensated by his *droits,* the *droits* of the Master must be

---

14. [Ed. In the original, the English word "right" follows the French word **droit** in parentheses.]
15. [Ed. In the original, the English word "right" follows the French word **droit** in parentheses.]

compensated by his duties. Thus, for example, if the Slave has the *droit* (and the duty) to work, the Master has the duty (and the *droit*) to make war.[16]

[300] Of course, by complementing the equivalence of duties and *droits* with that of *droits* and duties, bourgeois *Droit* takes one step forward in the juridical equalization of the Master and Slave. But we have already seen that this *Droit* is transformed into the *Droit* of the citizen by being actualized (i.e., by evolving), [and] this *Droit* implies the aristocratic principle of equality. But this equalization remains abstract or formal: it is purely legal [*juridique*], as they say. Furthermore, even in the juridical sphere, there is no equality; for if the Slave only has *droits* because he has duties, the Master only has duties because he has *droits*. Furthermore, the *droits* of the Master are not at all *equal* to those of the Slave, just as their respective duties are not *equal*.

The fundamental principle of bourgeois *Droit* is the *equivalence of **droits** and duties* in every juridical person. All subjects of *droit* have *droits* which are strictly equivalent to their duties, or—what practically amounts to the same thing—duties strictly equivalent to their *droits*. *Droits* and duties can be anything at all, and they can vary as one wants from one person to another. Nevertheless, all the conditions will be juridically *equivalent,* since in each of them *droits are equivalent* to duties, and conversely.

One thus sees the entire difference which separates bourgeois *Droit* from aristocratic *Droit*. The latter attributes to every juridical person the plenitude of *droits* without any duty, from whence comes the consequence that all juridical persons have exactly the same *droits*. Bourgeois *Droit,* by contrast, is not familiar with *droits* without duties (nor duties without *droits*), and it requires a strict equivalence between the two; this is perfectly compatible with the fact that various categories of juridical persons have different *droits* (and duties).

If one applies the bourgeois juridical principle to the phenomenon of property, one ends up with a "functional" interpretation of the latter. Property is no longer only a *droit;* it is also a duty, and a duty equivalent to the *droit* itself. Now it is easy to see that property thus conceived is no longer property in the proper (i.e., aristocratic) sense [301] of the term: it is no longer an exclusive and absolute *droit*. For if the *droit* of property ultimately boils down to the exclusion of this property from all the non-owners, the "equivalent" duty can only be an obligation toward the latter relative to this very property: the fact of having a property imposes upon me duties toward the society which recognizes me as owner. But to say this is to say that I am not an exclusive owner: at the very most, I am a co-owner, or better still, Society is the owner.[17]

---

16. It is upon this principle that the relation between the lord and his serfs in the Middle Ages is supposed to be based. And they tell us that this relation began [300] to be considered unjust from the moment that the nobles no longer had the opportunity to fulfill their duty toward the serfs by defending them with weapons in hand. This is so because there was no longer an *equivalence* between the *droits* and duties of the nobility, while this equivalence continued to exist among the serfs.

17. The *droit* of property is no longer even "absolute." Of course, there is no juridical relation between the owner and his property, and he therefore has no *droit* or duty toward it.

Contrary to aristocratic *Droit*, therefore, one notices that bourgeois *Droit* is in principle hostile to property (in the proper and strong sense of the term, just as aristocratic *Droit* is in principle hostile to contract). The ideal realization of the *exclusive droit* of property is the absence of all interaction between the owners; it is their strict isolation. Now the *duties* of the owner can only be realized by an interaction of his property with those of others. And we have seen that all interaction between properties imposes "servitudes" upon them, which are precisely the duties coming to graft themselves on the *droits* of property. Therefore, if these duties are strictly equivalent to the *droits,* there no longer remains, so to speak, anything of the original notion of property. From being static, it becomes dynamic: it becomes a perpetual *exchange.* Contrary to the aristocratic principle, therefore, property is not kept in its *equality* or identity with itself. At the very most, it remains *equivalent* to itself while changing its nature. And one can also say that from the point of view of bourgeois *Droit,* property is no longer an eternal and immutable "status" but a simple "function."[18]

But if his property must also be of use to others, the owner must act toward it accordingly: he cannot do "what he wants" with it. Thus, bourgeois *Droit* can require the owner of land to work it. This will be a duty toward Society. But one can say, if you will, that this is a quasi-duty toward the land itself. In this sense, the *droit* of property ceases to be "absolute" by ceasing to be "exclusive."

18. One could also say that bourgeois *Droit* tends to replace property by *work,* or by effort in general, property being juridically valid (or "just") only as a function of this effort. First of all, if the Master creates his humanity through the Struggle, the Slave only generates his through Work. Noticing that the human being is a result or a "function" of Work, the Slave conceives the latter as a "duty-being," and he considers all human value as the result of [302] Work or effort (negating the given) in general (except that of the Struggle, where it is not effort but the risk alone which counts). In particular, it is by Work that he "justifies" property. But there is more. The Equivalence of *droits* and duties must take place not only between different subjects but also inside every subject taken individually. The condition (or "status") of a subject is said to be "just" if the *droits* that it implies are equivalent to the duties which are appropriate to it. Ultimately, and at the prejuridical stage of Justice, this equivalence is nothing other than the equivalence of (objective and subjective) benefits and (objective and subjective) burdens. Now the joy of a thing that one possesses, and what the *droit* of property sanctions, is a benefit. If one wants to compensate for it inside the very subject, one must connect to it a burden, one uniting it with the benefit. Now this is what takes place when the thing possessed is a product of the negating effort of the one who possesses it, from his Work first of all. A possession, therefore, will only be called "just" if it results from a (negating) effort, made with a view to obtaining it. In particular, it will be "just" that the producer of a thing is also the owner of it, and the idle owner will always be suspect. The fundamental category in the system of bourgeois Justice, therefore, will not be property but work, or effort in general. Property will be a simple result, or indeed a "function," of effort and Work, which is annulled with the annulment of the latter and varies with it. However, there is no relation *of droit* inside one and the same person. As well, the relation between property, and the work or effort of the owner, can be called "just" or "unjust," but it has nothing *juridical* about it; for there to be *Droit,* there must be an interaction between two different persons. Therefore, in our case, it is necessary that the effort (or work) is provided by A, for example, and that the thing which is supposed to be possessed according to the work by B. In this case, there will be an *exchange* between the work of A and a property of

[302] Generally speaking, bourgeois *Droit* tends to replace the aristocratic notion of "status" with that of [303] "function." This is why this *droit* is first and foremost a *Droit* of *contract*.

The juridical contract sanctions (in the person of the Third) *exchanges* of properties or services. And exchange presupposes inequality—that is, the fact that some do not have or make what others have and make. Now if aristocratic *Droit* condemns all inequality, bourgeois *Droit* recognizes it without difficulty. It is not, therefore, hostile to contracts on principle. Furthermore, the principle which governs contracts is that of the equivalence of the exchanged things and acts, and this principle is the very one which at the base of bourgeois *Droit*. On the other hand, we have seen that the equivalence of benefits and burdens—i.e., juridically speaking, of *droits*, and duties or obligations—can only be established relatively—i.e., in relation to the subject of *droit* in question— and that this implies the fact that the interested subject freely recognizes it as such—that is, voluntarily and with full knowledge of the facts. Therefore, this element of personal assessment and free consent comes into play [*intervient*], which is also at the base of all genuine contract.

From this bourgeois point of view, even the relation between Master and Slave can be interpreted as resulting from a contract and thus being a contract. The Slave freely exchanges his freedom for security because he believes that the two things are equivalent, and he assumes that the Master gives him security in exchange for servitude because he acknowledges the equivalence of these things. Thus, the "statuses" of the Master and Slave arise from a contract and are only the static side of the latter.[19] Status is juridically justified here by contract, while in aristocratic *Droit* status rules out contract.

Now to justify status by contract is ultimately to deny it as a status properly so-called—that is, as a static state of things, as immutable and eternal. Status is now

---

B, which becomes the property of A, while B enjoys the effort produced by the work of A. Now an exchange is juridically sanctioned in the form of a contract, called a labor contract or salary (in the broadest sense). The property of A will therefore be a function of his work and the result of a *contract*. Now the property of B, in order to be juridically valid, must also be a function of his work and result from a contract. Ultimately, all exchange of property will boil down to an exchange of work. The *Droit* of property will therefore be replaced by a *Droit* of contract, which will regulate the exchanges of work or effort. Property therefore ceases to be a "status" in order to become a simple term of *contract*. And we will see right away that the substitution of the notion of contract for the aristocratic notion of status characterizes bourgeois *Droit* in general. I have spoken of Work; but it is a matter of effort in general—that is, the negating act which negates the natural given. Now, by extension (phenomenologically inadequate, moreover) one can apply the notion of effort to the Struggle, to the risk of the Master, to his "warlike effort" or "military work." It is in this way that bourgeois *Droit* justifies the property which arises from war: booty. Here as well, property is supposed to be "*functional*." And it is still conceived as the result of a *contract* of exchange between the labor of the worker exempt from military service and the "effort" of the noble who devotes himself to being a "solider." (It is this conception which is at the base of the notion of fief.)

19. It is this point of view which is at the base of the Theory of "social contract." One therefore sees that it is a deeply "bourgeois" theory.

juridically valid only if there is an equivalence between the *droits* and duties that it implies. And this equivalence can only be observed from the point of view of the interested party. But then the *droits* and duties of B can appear non-equivalent from the point of view of A, even if they appear to be such to B himself—and conversely. The sole objective means of verification is an interaction between A [304] and B, having the type of interaction between the Master and Slave. If B's duties are A's *droits*, and B's *droits* A's duties, and if A recognizes the equivalence of his own *droits* and duties, he can no longer deny the equivalence of B's duties and *droits*. Now if this is the way things are, it is because there is an exchange between A and B—that is, contractual relations, or at the very least relations which can be drawn up in a juridical contract. But if the statuses of A and B are justified by this contract, they are juridically valid only as long as the latter remains valid. Now if A's condition changes, it is possible—for him—that his *droits* are no longer equivalent to his duties, [and] consequently neither the *droits* and duties of B, even if B's condition remains the same. In order for B's status to remain valid, it will therefore be necessary to change it according to the change of A's status,[20] conditioned by the change of his condition. And to say this is to say that there is not in reality an eternal and immutable status, that there is only a contract which is by definition variable since it is based upon an exchange—that is, upon a change. In other words, statuses mutually condition and depend upon one another: every status is, if you will, a function of a "social contract," for it is the totality of contracts existing within a given Society which sets down the statuses of its members.

By replacing the principle of status with that of contract, bourgeois *Droit* declares itself hostile to the principle of the right of inheritance [*l'hérédité juridique*]. And in this as well it is opposed to aristocratic *Droit*. This *Droit*, being based upon the ideal of equality, tends to preserve the equality of the juridical person with himself at any price, from whence comes the idea of an immutable status, which remains identical to itself even despite the *death* of the interested party. By denying all change, aristocratic *Droit* would even like to deny biological changes—in the first place, the one introduced by death. Therefore, aristocratic status (which implies the *droit* of property) is supposed to be continuous, and it is so to the extent that the heir inherits from the deceased without this inheritance altering the status at all. For bourgeois *Droit*, by contrast, it is the equivalence of conditions alone which counts. Now equivalence does not imply equality, and it therefore accepts change. Therefore, nothing requires *Droit* to preserve a status after the death of the person who enjoyed it. On the contrary, it will have a tendency to suppress it as a result of this death; for if A's status is a function of a contract with B, he must be able to change if this contract changes, and [305] the con-

---

20. [Ed. Reading *du statut de A* for *du statut de B.*]
21. Thus, the "contract" between the lord and his serfs changed from the sole fact that the latter no longer needed to be protected militarily. The "status" of the lord has been altered according to this change of the state of the serfs. And it is of little importance that the lord continued to be ready to defend them if the case arose.

tract must change even if it is only B's condition which is altered.[21] Now, by definition, the dead person cannot change, and he can change nothing. The idea of a contract concluded with someone after his death being absurd, the status of a dead person is also a juridical non-sequitur from the point of view of bourgeois *Droit*. Now an inherited status is nothing other than a status of a dead person.

The principle of equivalence is also at the base of bourgeois *penal* **Droit**.

Crime is now no longer the negation of equality but that of the equivalence of conditions. Consequently, to annul the crime is to reestablish the equivalence which was infringed. And if this annulment is carried out by punishment, it is still the principle of equivalence which is going to determine the latter.

Now equivalence is always subjective and relative. The crime infringes upon the equivalence of conditions between the criminal and the victim because it overcomes the equivalence of *droits* or benefits, and duties or burdens, both among the victim and the criminal. It is not enough, therefore, to reestablish this equivalence in the person of the victim. One must also reestablish it in the person of the criminal. In other words, the sentence must "fit" the crime: the burdens of the punishment must offset the benefits that the crime was supposed to produce.

Since it is no longer a question of restoring equality, the principle of lex talionis no longer makes sense. In relation to the victim, mere equivalent compensation ("*Wergild*") is enough to satisfy *Droit*. And in relation to the criminal, it is the equivalence of his own *droits* and duties which must be reestablished. But nothing says that his *droits* and duties must remain the same. After his crime, he may have other *droits* and duties than before. What is important is that these new *droits* and duties are equivalent between them. And this is assured by the proportionality between the crime and the punishment.

Now it is obvious that this penal principle is incompatible with the objective and collective character of aristocratic criminal *Droit*. On the one hand, in order to be able to make the punishment fit the crime, one must take into account the *intention* of the criminal, [306] the *subjective* aspect of the crime. On the other hand, one must take into account the *individuality* of the criminal; for one can obviously not establish an equivalence between the sentence and the crime by punishing someone who has not committed it and who therefore has not profited from it.

Chapter 3

The Evolution of *Droit:*
The Synthetic Justice of the Citizen
(The Justice of Equity)

§ 44

[307] WE HAVE SEEN THAT Justice and *Droit* are born in two autonomous forms: as the Justice of equality and the Justice of equivalence. These two Justices are born simultaneously from the same source, which is the anthropogenic Struggle, ending up in the relation between Master and Slave. The aristocratic Justice and *Droit* of equality reflect this Struggle and its result from the point of view of the Master, while the bourgeois Justice and *Droit* of equivalence reflect them from the point of view of the Slave. Or once again, bourgeois *Droit* corresponds to the *equivalence* of conditions at the conclusion of the Struggle, while aristocratic *Droit* corresponds to the *equality* of risk in the Struggle itself. One can therefore say that the primordial juridical dualism is an aspect of the dualism of the human being himself in his nascent state: just as man at his origin is Master *and* Slave, nascent *Droit* is aristocratic *and* bourgeois. And one can conclude from this that juridical evolution will be an aspect of the evolution of the human being as such. If this evolution goes from duality to unity, it will be the same for juridical evolution. Just as the existences of the Master and Slave are synthesized little by little into the single existence of the Citizen, aristocratic and bourgeois *Droits* are progressively going to fuse into a single *Droit* of the citizen. And just as the real existence of man is nothing other than the becoming of the Citizen (this becoming being the History of humanity), real *Droit* will be nothing other than the *Droit* of the Citizen in the process of becoming (this becoming being the history of *Droit* as such). It is now a matter of seeing what is the general sense [308] of this evolution of *Droit* and the idea of Justice that it realizes.

From the beginning of the juridical life of humanity, the two Justices are autonomous or independent of one another in the sense that one can try to realize equality without taking the principle of equivalence into account, just as it is possible to assert this principle without thinking about equality. But one cannot say that these two Justices contradict each other in the sense that they are mutually exclusive; for equality puts up very well with equivalence, and equivalence is not at all opposed to equality. One can only say that for there to be Justice and *Droit,* whichever one they may be, one must either acknowledge at least the principle of equivalence (if one denies that of equality by accepting inequalities between subjects of *droit*) or postulate equality (if one does not want to take into account equivalence). But one can very well acknowledge

both principles at the same time without contradicting oneself. And this is
what the Citizen does in his Justice of equity and in the *Droit* which realizes it.

Truth to tell, perfect equality implies equivalence. If two different situations
can be equivalent, strictly equal situations *are* equivalent by definition. Therefore, one cannot say that one *passes* from equality to equity. There is only a *passage* to equity starting from equivalence; for equivalence can be *completed* little by little by equality, which it may lack originally. Therefore, the *evolution* of
Droit in general begins with bourgeois *Droit*, and it is, if you will, only an evolution of the latter.

One can also say that aristocratic *Droit* right away attains its perfection; for
originally (purely theoretical, moreover), *Droit* only considers man inasmuch as
he is Master: the notions "Master" and "juridical person" coincide. Now all Masters are effectively equal as Masters. There is, then, no internal contradiction in
Droit at all—that is, no imperfection at all, no cause for any change, any evolution, any progress at all. If one only considers juridical persons those who are
effectively equal, juridical persons will be equal—that is, conforming to the fundamental principle of Justice. However, all human beings cannot be Masters:
[this is true not only] by definition, since there is no Mastery without Servitude,
such that aristocratic Society must imply Slaves; [but it is also true] for biological reasons, since this Society—in order to last—must imply women and children incapable of the Struggle—[309] that is, of Mastery.[1] Of course, the aristocratic jurist may simply not recognize them as subjects of *droit*, and then there
will not be any evolution of *Droit*. But if he recognizes them, he must postulate
their equality with the Masters. The evolution of aristocratic *Droit*, therefore, can
only consist in a progressive expansion of equality. However, a Master who "recognizes" a non-Master, who thus "recognizes" without a Struggle, is no longer a
genuine Master and does not act as a Master by doing so. There is, then, no reason at all that he apply aristocratic *Droit* to this "recognition." Generally speaking, he will apply bourgeois *Droit* and will only acknowledge the juridical *equivalence* of Masters with non-Masters, and not their equality. He will recognize
their **droits,** but he will not acknowledge the equality of their *droits* with his own,
limiting himself to postulating their equivalence. And then there will not be an
evolution of aristocratic *Droit*, but a passage to bourgeois *Droit* (or indeed, to the
Droit of the Citizen, to the extent that the newly accepted bourgeois *Droit* forms
a more or less coherent whole with the old aristocratic *Droit*).

But one must underline that there is not any *juridical* reason to complete
aristocratic *Droit* with bourgeois *Droit;* for there are no *juridical* reasons to recognize as a subject of *droit* all animals of the species Homo sapiens. Recognition of new juridical persons will have to be made for extra-juridical reasons,
and *Droit* will limit itself to applying its principle of equality to all the subjects

---

1. In fact, a Society of Masters (for example, a gang of "bandits") can be exclusively masculine, and a *purely* aristocratic Society must even be so: for intra-familial relations have
nothing to do with Mastery. But in fact, Masters get married. The taxing problem of the
Family, moreover, will have to be treated separately.

of *droit*. *Droit* recognizes the juridical equality of all juridical persons, which means—from the point of view of *Droit*—all the beings recognized as human. But it does not belong to *Droit* to determine which real being (of the species Homo sapiens) will be recognized as human or not; nor are there any extra-juridical reasons why the Master should recognize the humanity of a non-Master (Slave, woman, or child). The non-Master is—for the Master—the Slave (or the slain adversary, if you will), and he has no desire at all to be a Slave. Not wanting *to be* a non-Master *really*, he will not want to be one either *ideally*, i.e., in his consciousness, by looking at things from the "point of view" of the non-Master, by *mentally* putting himself "in his [310] place." As there is no reason for the genuine Master *really* to become a non-Master (since he prefers *to die*), there will be no reason either for him to accept the point of view of the non-Master, and in particular his bourgeois *Droit*. And this is why there is not any reason for aristocratic *Droit* to *evolve* in any way whatever: neither by expansion of its own egalitarian principle nor by a synthesis with the principle of equivalence of bourgeois *Droit*. One can therefore say, if you will, that it is "perfect" right away.

Entirely different is the situation of the Slave and his bourgeois *Droit*. From the beginning, the Slave recognizes the humanity of the Master. If, therefore, in considering himself a juridical person, i.e., a human being, he promulgates a *Droit*, he cannot but recognize the Master as a juridical person. And this is why, by acknowledging his inequality with the Master, he can only create a *Droit* by basing it upon the principle of equivalence. Now if the Slave claims to be a juridical person, i.e., a human being, it is because he is no longer truly or solely a Slave. He is also a non-Slave, i.e., a Master, to the extent that he does this. He looks at things from the point of view of a Master; he mentally puts himself in his place. Therefore, it is natural that he also accepts the fundamental principle of aristocratic Justice and *Droit*. There will then be an *evolution* of bourgeois *Droit*, not only by an expansion of its own principle of equivalence (which is here natural, since the Slave "recognizes" the other before and rather than himself), but also by a synthesis with the principle of aristocratic *Droit*.

Now there is an immanent *juridical* reason for this evolution of bourgeois *Droit*; for by recognizing the juridical equivalence of two beings, he necessarily recognizes them both as subjects of *droit*. He therefore recognizes their *equality* as juridical persons: the two are equal in the sense that they are both subjects of *droit*. Of course, this equality is purely "formal" or "abstract": the "content," i.e., the respective "*droits*" of these subjects, may be different. But seeing that every "form" tends to "mold [*former*]" its content in order to assimilate to it, one can say that all "formal" equality tends to transform itself into an equality of content. In other words, the Justice and *Droit* of equivalence have an immanent tendency to become a Justice and *Droit* of equality—and this all the more so because the Slave is also moved toward equality by extra-juridical ("social") reasons. For if the Master has no desire at all [311] to become a Slave, the Slave always wants to become Master (to the extent that he is not a pure Slave; but he is no longer one if he works out a *Droit* by recognizing himself as a juridical person). For both "social" and specifically juridical reasons, therefore, the Slave will not want to realize his bourgeois *Droit* in a pure state, but will tend to fuse it with aristocratic *Droit* in a *Droit* of equity.

Therefore, it is not the evolution of aristocratic *Droit* which generates the *Droit* of the citizen. This *Droit* results from the evolution of bourgeois *Droit*. Of course, for this *Droit* to evolve, for it to adopt the aristocratic principle of equality, the Slave must aspire to equality with the Master, he must want to become Master. He must therefore cease—at least in potentiality—being a Slave (who is fully satisfied by equivalence alone). He must therefore be a Revolutionary. But the Slave who ceases to be a Slave does not become a Master. Revolution is something other than Mastery, and the Slave who frees himself in and by a revolutionary struggle for "recognition" becomes something other than a Master. The "Master" who has *become* "Master" is quite different from the genuine Master, who is born as such (or who constitutes himself as such starting from an animal): he is a Citizen. Therefore, if the evolution of bourgeois *Droit* implies and presupposes (or indeed generates) an egalitarian Revolution, it does not end in the aristocratic *Droit* of simple equality. The *Droit* which *becomes* egalitarian differs from that which has been so *from the beginning:* it is a *Droit* of the citizen, where equality fuses with equivalence into equity.

Bourgeois *Droit* does not exist *in actuality,* and this is why it *evolves.* In order to *actualize* his bourgeois *Droit,* the Slave must make it state *Droit* [*étatiser*]. He must therefore become a Governor and cease being a Slave. But one *becomes* a Governor (without having been one from the beginning) only by being a *Citizen. His Droit,* therefore, will no longer be the bourgeois *Droit* of the Slave, but that of the Citizen. As soon as the Slave will be able to actualize his *Droit,* he will no longer be a Slave and *his Droit* will be a *Droit* of the citizen. One can therefore say that bourgeois *Droit* is actualized as the *Droit* of the citizen. The juridical evolution is neither an evolution of bourgeois *Droit* properly so-called nor a return to aristocratic *Droit* starting from a bourgeois *Droit.*

As for aristocratic *Droit,* it is actualized from the beginning (and this is why it does not evolve, or is "perfect"). Change therefore means for it to be annulled, to disappear. One can therefore say that on the plane of actual existence, the *Droit* of the citizen *replaces* aristocratic *Droit.* But the *Droit* of the [312] citizen is a synthesis of bourgeois *Droit* and aristocratic *Droit.* The latter is also therefore *preserved* (*aufgehoben*) as the *Droit* of the citizen. Or once again, one can say that the *Droit* of the citizen is an actualization of bourgeois *Droit,* since the latter only exists in actuality inside the former. But in reality, the *Droit* of the citizen is neither bourgeois nor aristocratic. Being the synthesis of aristocratic *Droit* and bourgeois *Droit,* it is neither one nor the other. And this synthesis exists from the beginning, for from the beginning aristocratic *Droit* in actuality coexists with bourgeois *Droit* in potentiality. From the outset, therefore, *Droit* is a *Droit* of the citizen, and its evolution is nothing but the progressive actualization of its integral bourgeois element, this actualization being at the same time a progressive fusion with the always actual aristocratic element. By evolving, the *Droit* of the Citizen, i.e., *Droit* as such, thus remains what it is: a *Droit* based upon the Justice of equity—that is, upon a synthesis (more or less complete) of the bourgeois principle of equivalence with the aristocratic principle of equality.

A phenomenon only evolves to the extent that it implies an immanent contradiction. And the same applies to *Droit*, as well as to the idea of Justice that it realizes.

Now if one takes *Droit* as a whole, it implies from the beginning two juridical principles: that of equality (in actuality) and that of equivalence (in potentiality). And as coexisting in one and the same juridical system, these principles are contradictory. Or more exactly, they make this system contradictory. Of course, equality and equivalence are perfectly compatible. But a system based upon equivalence can accept inequality. And if it does so, it is in contradiction with the principle of equality, i.e., with itself, if it also implies this principle. Likewise, *Droit* finds that equality may take no account of equivalence as such. If one therefore applies the single principle of juridical equality to subjects who are recognized in fact as unequal by the *Droit* of equivalence, one can enter into conflict with the principle which is at the base of the latter. Thus, there will again be an internal conflict, and consequently, an evolution, the evolution being nothing other than the progressive elimination of the internal contradiction.

Now, at least originally, the simultaneous application of aristocratic *Droit* and bourgeois *Droit*, i.e., the first realization of the *Droit* of the citizen, is necessarily contradictory in the sense indicated. Bourgeois *Droit* has no reason at all not to recognize the juridical personality of persons [313] whose human ("social") conditions are unequal. And to the extent that this *Droit* is applied by the Slave (or the ex-Slave), he necessarily recognizes unequal subjects, and he juridically gives an account of this recognized inequality of persons by assigning them different *droits* and duties. Now, by doing this, he enters into conflict with aristocratic *Droit*, which, on the other hand, must be maintained in the same way as bourgeois *Droit*. Put in the presence of unequal persons recognized as subjects of *droit*, aristocratic *Droit* will, on its side, apply to them its principle of juridical equality. Now the same "*droits*" do not have the same value when one relates them to different subjects: being equal from a formal point of view, they may not be equivalent in fact, from whence comes a conflict with bourgeois *Droit*, which is supposed to be equally valid. This *Droit* will therefore alter the formal equality to make it conform to effective equivalence, [and] this will not be recognized by aristocratic *Droit*, which will want to eliminate the juridical inequalities thus introduced: and so forth.

This permanent conflict of aristocratic and bourgeois tendencies within *Droit* will result in the gradual elimination of the non-equivalences introduced by the first of these tendencies as well as the inequalities introduced by the second. And it is this reciprocal and complementary elimination which constitutes the historical evolution of *Droit*, which is—once again—the evolution of the synthetic *Droit* of the citizen.

By definition, this evolution will not be indefinite. It will only last the time that an internal conflict in the *Droit* in force subsists—that is, as long as the bourgeois tendency will not have eliminated from *Droit* all non-equivalences, and the aristocratic tendency all inequalities. And moreover, truly absolute and universal equality coincides with equivalence, just as truly strict and objective equivalence (i.e., verified by the interactions, by the matching of *droits* with duties) ends up in equality. Once this stage is reached, i.e., all conflict eliminated, the evolution of *Droit* stops. And one can say that in its final form the *Droit* (of the citizen) is an *absolute Droit*. Being the only one and no longer changing, it is universally and definitively valid: it is "perfect," for it can no longer be improved, no longer being able to change.

Now this absolute *Droit*, where the equivalence of the *droits* and duties of each is coupled with an equality of *droits* and duties for all, can only be actual when all are equal [314] and equivalent not only juridically, "before the law," but also politically and "socially"—that is, in fact. In other words, the absolute *Droit* can only exist in the universal and homogenous State. Conversely, the *Droit* of this State will be an absolute *Droit;* for as the State—by definition—can neither change nor perish (external and civil wars being ruled out), its *Droit* will not change either: it will be eternally and universally valid. And it will be egalitarian and equivalent at the same time, being the sanction of the political and social equality and equivalence of its litigants.

Thus, while acknowledging that Justice appears on earth in a dual form, and that it is impossible to say that equality is more "just" than equivalence, or conversely; [and] while noticing that *Droit* necessarily evolves, one does not end up with juridical relativism. One can retain the idea of a single *Droit* and Justice, universally and eternally valid. However, this *Droit* and this Justice are not given from the beginning; they are not *a priori,* outside of time and history. On the contrary, it is in and by history that they are constituted. The absolute *Droit* is the *result* of the juridical evolution, or—which is the same thing—the integration of this evolution—that is, the synthesis of all the constitutive juridical elements, which are so many stages of the historical evolution of *Droit,* taken as a whole.

Of course, this evolution is still not finished, and therefore absolute *Droit* is still not known to us as regards its positive content. But we can know the general sense of the evolution which leads there and the character of the synthesis which constitutes it. Now as we have just indicated the general sense of the juridical evolution of humanity, it remains for us to analyze briefly the global (and formal) character of the synthetic Justice of equity (§ 45) and of the synthetic *Droit* of the citizen (§ 46), which realizes it by applying it through an impartial and disinterested Third to given social interactions.

§ 45

There is not a lot to say about the Justice of equity, which includes the two fundamental principles of equality and equivalence—except that these two oppositional principles mutually stimulate each other to the extent that they contradict and oppose one another, and that they thus tend to fuse [315] into a single synthetic whole, where one is realized only to the extent that the other is. In the interaction of the two principles, that of equivalence eliminates all the non-equivalences introduced by the application of the principle of equality, while the latter overcomes the inequalities that the realization of the principle of equivalence generates. Thus, the synthesis of the two principles overcomes all that is unilateral—that is, particular and restricted [about them]. It therefore realizes them in their plenitude and in what they have universally—that is, [what they have that is] truly essential. Now in their plenitude, in the complete and perfect realization of their essences, they coincide with each other; for if there is a perfect *equivalence* of benefits and burdens within each, in every particular condition, it remains identical or *equal* to itself, just as conversely, an immutable *equality* with itself generates the *equivalence* of positive and negative aspects of existence. Thus, the *equivalence* of all conditions, which results from their internal equivalences, is nothing but their *equality*, resulting from their equalities with themselves.

Let us take up again the example of sharing food for dinner. The principle of equality will require a share of equal portions between those having *droit*, and it will no longer be concerned about anything else. But the principle of equivalence will ask if the equal portions are truly equivalent. If one observes that some are more hungry than others, one will see [to it] that this is not so. One will then share the food differently, making the portions proportional to the hunger of each one. The principle thus being satisfied, one will leave matters there. But the other principle will be offended by the inequality of shares, and it will try to eliminate it. However, in order not to offend the principle of equivalence, it will be necessary to eliminate the inequality of the participants. One will therefore ask why some are more hungry than others. And if one observes that this difference results from the fact that some have had lunch and others not, one will see to it such that from now on all might have lunch. The principle of equivalence will therefore have incited that of equality to realize itself more perfectly. And by becoming perfect, equality coincides with equivalence; for if those having *droit* are truly equal, the equality of their parts no longer differs from their equivalence; their equivalence is nothing but their equality.

Let us assume in a general way that the Justice of equity is applied within a given Society which is still not absolutely conforming to the ideal of this Justice. And let us assume [316] that at a given moment a being acting in a certain way is considered a human being: a warrior for example, idle in time of peace. By relying on the principle of equality, one will consider human all the beings who act in the same way, and them only. But by relying on the principle of equivalence, one could observe that an action different from the action in question can be equivalent to it, and that there will then be good reason to consider human the being who carries it out. Thus, for example, the fact of working for Society can be equivalent, from the social and political point of view, to the fact of defending Society with weapons in hand, and the act of providing children to

Society, i.e., future citizens, can be equivalent to the act of working or waging war. One will therefore recognize workers and women as human beings in the same way as warriors. But by taking into account the difference of their actions, one will assign different "statuses" to them. But placed in the midst of recognized human beings, one will, in accepting the principle of equality, try to equalize them—that is, to equalize their actions. One will require, for example, that warriors work in time of peace and that workers take part in wars. But in the case of women, one comes up against an irreducible difference: men cannot have children. One is thus forced to keep the principle of equivalence while trying to overcome as much as possible the human ("social") consequences of irreducible biological differences. Practically speaking, one will try to establish a perfect equivalence between maternity and military service, while putting men and women on an equal footing everywhere else.

Let us take another example. The principle of equivalence allows one to consider human those beings who will act humanly only in the future, i.e., young children; for if an action at moment *t-1* is not equal to an action at moment *t-2*, it can be equivalent to it. The principle of equality will then assign the same *droits* to children and adults. But this formal equality will be unacceptable from the point of view of equivalence; for example, the *droit* to conclude contracts and to act personally in legal proceedings will be valueless for the child. To establish equivalence, one will assign tutors to children. But then there will no longer be equality between the free action of an adult and the supervised action of the child. Not being able to overcome supervision of children's action, one will therefore introduce a supervision of adult action. However, if one assigned private tutors [317] to adults, one would again change the principle of equivalence, from whence comes a tendency to submit both to an equivalent system, for example, by introducing a supervision of all activity by the State (the command economy). Now this supervision will sooner or later end up (in the socialist Society) in an equalization of the situations of children and adults, [with] the adults, in a Society without private property, ceasing to exercise the majority of *droits* that the children are incapable of exercising themselves.

And so forth.

Generally speaking, the Justice of equity will only be satisfied when the greatest possible *equality* reigns. But the realization of equality will not overcome *equivalence*. A condition will be called "just" not only because it is *equal* to all the other conditions, and not only because it is "*equal*" to itself, i.e., because it can last indefinitely without needing to change from the sole fact that it lasts (as, for example, the state of health of an malnourished man must change), but also because there is in it an *equivalence* between benefits and burdens (in particular, between those which are juridically set down in the form of *droits* and duties). Any condition whatsoever will be considered "unjust" from the sole fact that the benefits are not offset by the burdens, or conversely—which does not make any sense from the point of view of egalitarian Justice alone. However, as I have already said, internal equivalence will only be able to be objectively observed and established, i.e., will only be able to be truly real, if there is a matching of benefits with burdens, if the burdens of some are the benefits of others. Now, in this case, the evolution will necessarily go toward an equalization; for the matching of interests stimulates exchanges, and exchanges which are truly equivalent establish equality.

But, once again, the equality of all is only a limit idea; for irreducible biological differences (such as the differences between the sane and insane, man and woman, adult and child) will always render necessary the application of the principle of equivalence alongside that of equality. But as long as the limit imposed by the natural or animal given is not attained, there will be a social or historical evolution according to the ideal of the Justice of equity, and consequently an evolution of this Justice itself, which merely reflects the historical evolution; for every triumph [318] of equivalence will provoke an expansion of equality, and *vice versa*.

At every stage of its evolution, the idea of Justice is characterized, on the one hand, by the expansion of its two principles, and on the other hand, by their mutual relation. On the one hand, Justice is going to evolve because one will gradually discover the injustice of *all* the inequalities or non-equivalences which *can* be equal and equivalent. Thus, for example, after having discovered the injustice of the political inequality of men, one discovered the injustice of the political inequality between men and women; and after having discovered the injustice of political inequality, one discovers that of social or economic inequality. On the other hand, Justice will evolve because equality will not go hand in hand with equivalence. Thus, for example, after having discovered that it is unjust to deprive workers of vacations granted to others, one understood that it is just to grant them tickets at reduced prices. As long as equality and equivalence will not be expanded to *all* spheres which can be equal or equivalent, their equilibrium will not be stable; for the one will be able to expand itself beyond the other, and thus generate a disequilibrium. And this disequilibrium will be corrected by a corresponding expansion of the other. But for its part, it will be able to go beyond the limits of the first, thereby creating a new disequilibrium—and so on.

At a given moment, the Justice of equity will simply be able to reflect the equalities and equivalences realized within the Society which adopts this Justice. But one will also be able to notice discrepancies: for example, the Society could be more or less egalitarian than its Justice. Here as well, the disequilibrium between Justice and the social reality will only be temporary. But in the first case, it is the idea of Justice which is going to evolve according to the social reality, and there will be, if the case arises, a juridical revolution; while in the second case, it is the reality which will evolve according to the idea of Justice, and there will be, if the case arises, a political or social revolution.[2]

---

2. Generally speaking, one will have the following sequence. If the political-social evolution introduces a new equality, this is going to penetrate within the idea of Justice. There, it will generate a demand for an appropriate equivalence. And this equivalence, conceived as just, will be introduced sooner or later into the social reality. Or again, the social evolution introduces a new equivalence, which is complemented in Justice by equality, the latter being introduced into the social reality.

Be that as it may, if Justice does not already reflect a real state of things, it will tend to make itself conform to it. And at any [319] rate, it will not want there to be interactions contrary to its principles—that is, implying inequalities or non-equivalences where it does not admit them, at the given stage of its evolution. Now the application of the idea of Justice to given social interactions is nothing other than *Droit*. Therefore, the Justice of equity will also be realized as a *Droit*. And the content of this *Droit* of the Citizen will be determined at every stage by the content of the idea of Justice that it realizes. Generally speaking, at a given epoch *Droit* will be in agreement with the idea of Justice of this same epoch. But here as well, one can encounter discrepancies and stimulations either of Justice by *Droit* or of *Droit* by Justice. And in all the cases, *Droit* will be an intermediary between the idea of Justice and its evolution, and the evolution of the social reality, for *Droit* applies this idea to this reality.

Let us therefore see what are the general characteristics of the *Droit* of the citizen, which realizes the Justice of equity.

§ 46

In its pure state (purely theoretical, moreover), aristocratic *Droit* is characterized by the fact that the juridical person possesses the plenitude of *droits* without having any duties, from whence comes the equality of all juridical persons and their *droits*. Bourgeois *Droit*, by contrast, lays down in its pure state (just as theoretical) the principle of the equivalence of *droits* and duties in relation to every juridical person, which is perfectly compatible with the inequality of these persons—that is, with differences between the *droits* and duties of one person and those of another.

Now the *Droit* of the citizen (i.e., all real *Droit* in general), being based upon the Justice of equity, which synthesizes equality and equivalence, must be by definition a synthesis of aristocratic and bourgeois *Droits*. In its pure state (not yet realized, moreover), this *Droit* must therefore combine in a perfect equilibrium the equality of *droits* and duties of all juridical persons with the equivalence of *droits* and duties in each of these persons. Contrary to aristocratic *Droit*, the *Droit* of the citizen will not accept the existence of *droits* not compensated for by duties, nor duties without corresponding *droits*. But in agreement with aristocratic *Droit*, this *Droit* is going to postulate the equality of all *droits*, and consequently, of all juridical duties—from whence comes a community of *droits* and duties, the *droits* [320] and duties of one also being the *droits* and duties of all, and conversely, the *droits* and duties of the community also being the *droits* and duties of each of its members. In this way, to the *droits* of someone are going to correspond not only his own duties but also those of others, and conversely: there will be a matching of *droits* with duties.

Here as well, then, there will be a synthesis of the universalism (or collectivism) of aristocratic *Droit* and the particularism (or individualism) of bourgeois *Droit*. Just like the Master, the Citizen will have *universal droits* (and duties). The *droits* of all being equal, they will follow from the membership of each one to the whole, to Society as such or to the State. And the duties will be duties toward all—that is, toward the Society taken as a whole or toward the State. But seeing that the State is universal and Society homogenous, the *droits* and duties will belong not only to groups but to each one taken individually. It is not as a citizen of such and such a national State, or as a member of such and such a family (aristocratic, for example), or of such and such a social group (class) that a man will have *droits* and duties, but as an individual. Pushed to their respective maximums, juridical individualism and universalism are going to coincide: the most personal *droits* and duties, which can only be exercised by the individual in question, will be the most universal *droits* and duties—that is, those of the citizen taken as a citizen, or those of all and of each.

Be that as it may, the *Droit* of the citizen will sanction all social interactions compatible with the principles of equality and equivalence. In other words, if a citizen acts so as to upset neither the equilibrium between his *droits* and duties nor the equality of his *droits* and duties with those of others, and if he nevertheless encounters resistances on the part of others, these will be annulled by the disinterested intervention of an impartial Third, such that the citizen in question will have no need to make efforts himself to overcome these resistances. Conversely, this same Third will annul all actions tending to imbalance [*déséquilibrer*] a given relation of *droits* and duties, or the equality between *droits* or duties.

Juridical *liberty*, therefore, will consist in the possibility of each one doing everything that he wants, provided that he remains in agreement with the equality of *droits* and duties, and their respective equivalence. And juridical *equality* will be guaranteed [321] by the fact that the juridical value of an interaction will not be altered if one changes the places of the members interacting.

Seeing that the *Droit* of the citizen recognizes the matching of *droits* with duties, which makes the *droits* of some the duties of others and conversely, this *Droit* must accept social interactions: it is in and by these interactions that one exercises his *droits* and fulfills his duties. In this the *Droit* of the citizen therefore conforms to bourgeois *Droit* and is contrary to aristocratic *Droit*, which accepts status and excludes contract. Just like bourgeois *Droit*, the *Droit* of the citizen accepts contract as a fundamental juridical category. But being synthetic, it conceives of contract, which is the fundamental bourgeois juridical category, as aristocratic *Droit* conceives its own fundamental category—that is, status. What characterizes "status" is that it is supposed to be able to be realized in isolation, without interaction with others, and that it remains indefinitely identical to itself, not being a function of variable circumstances. Now the contract of the citizen realizes this second essential character of aristocratic status. Being based upon equality and equivalence, contracts will not alter the conditions of the contracting parties, and they will therefore remain stationary themselves. Practically speaking, it will be a matter of contracts with Society as such or the State, and these will be collective contracts. One will therefore be able to say of them that they set down the "status" of juridical persons. But this status of the citizen will differ from aristocratic status in that it will be the result or expression (set down juridically) of social *interactions*. Status will therefore be a contract, and contract a status. And it is in this way that there will no longer be either statuses in the aristocratic sense of the term nor contracts in the bourgeois sense.[3]

If one considers relations of the individual with the State, one can say that the evolution of the *Droit* of the citizen reveals a growing supremacy of the bourgeois principle of contract over the aristocratic principle of status. Indeed, the State juridically recognizes less and less the existence of eternal and immutable statuses. On the one hand, statuses cease to be [322] inherited. On the other hand, they are no longer even set down for life: one can change jobs, social class, family, and even nationality as one likes. And every membership is a function of a conscious and voluntary *activity*, of an *interaction* with the State or Society, i.e., with its members: one is what one does; the activity is not set down by one's being. But if one considers the relations of individuals among themselves, one can say that the evolution of the *Droit* of the citizen consists in the progressive replacement of bourgeois contracts by aristocratic statuses; for the freedom of contract decreases more and more. The State imposes types of contract that the individual has only to accept or reject. And contracts between private persons [*particuliers*] must be in agreement with the statuses of these private persons set down by the State (by its collective contracts). Thus, for example, contracts that workers can conclude are decided by their status.

This same dialectic recurs in the evolution of the juridical notion of *property*.

In its bourgeois aspect, the *Droit* of the citizen adopts the "functional" conception of property. It is the juridically determined result and expression of a given [*fourni*] effort, first and foremost of a work carried out for the sake of its obtention. Therefore, it always has for its ultimate source an interaction, i.e., a contract; for one creates nothing from nothingness, but one only transforms a given, a "raw material." Now if these are "raw," it is because they have not been made by anyone. They therefore belong to no one—that is, to no one in particular, but to all, to Society as such or the State. All property therefore presupposes an interaction with the State, juridically determined in the form of a contract.

But in its aristocratic aspect, the *Droit* of the citizen postulates the equality of property. In the final analysis, therefore, property is supposed to be a function of the very being of man: one has property because one is a human being, and one has the same property as others because one is human in the same way as them. The Citizen, therefore, has property because he is a man and citizen, and he only has it to the extent that he is so, just as the Master possesses his property because he is Master or as he is Master. Property, therefore, is part of

---

3. According to [Henry] Sumner Maine (*Ancient Law*, 10th ed. [Boston: Beacon Press, 1963], 164–5), the evolution and progress of *Droit* consists in the progressive replacement of statuses by contracts. It can be objected that one is nowadays witnessing an opposite movement, with contracts tending to become statuses. In reality, there is a passage from aristocratic (or properly so-called) status to properly so-called (or bourgeois) contract, and from there to the status-contract or contract-status of the synthetic *Droit* of the citizen.

the *status* of the Citizen, just as it was part of the status of Mastery. However, the status of Citizenship is just as much a status as a *contract*. And the same therefore applies for juridical property in the *Droit* of citizen.

[323] And what is true of the *droit* of property also holds for the principle of *inheritance* as such; for these two principles are effectively in solidarity with one another. If there is no genuine property without inheritance, neither is there any inheritance which matters if it is not accompanied with (inherited) property.

Now the *Droit* of the citizen, on the one hand, is similar to bourgeois *Droit* in the sense that it is hostile to inheritance. This *Droit* limits or denies the hereditary transfer of property and the hereditary determination of functions and activities of individuals. But on the other hand, by seeing to the equality of all, the *Droit* of the citizen asserts, if you will, the permanent, i.e., hereditary, character of the human condition: this condition is handed down from father to son, remaining always equal to itself. The son of the Citizen is a Citizen, and he is the same Citizen as his father, just as the son of a Master is a Master and the same Master. One can therefore say that the *Droit* of the citizen asserts the principle of inheritance just as much as it denies it; this is because it denies the inheritance of the particular, of individual or personal "acquired characteristics," but asserts the eternal inheritance of the universal, of generic characteristics common to all.

*The criminal **Droit*** of the citizen is just as synthetic as its civil *Droit* and public *Droit* properly so-called. If public *Droit* is just as much a *Droit* of status as a *Droit* of contract, and if civil *Droit* is a *Droit* of property in the same way as a *Droit* of work (contractual), or effort in general, penal *Droit* also brings together the fundamental principles of aristocratic and bourgeois criminal *Droits*.

Aristocratic penal justice tends to overcome all the acts which overcome the equality of juridical persons, and it tries to reestablish this equality in and by punishment. As for bourgeois criminal justice, it proscribes departures from the equivalence of *droits* and duties, as well as from that of juridical persons among themselves, and it tends to restore this equivalence in and by the sentence. The criminal *Droit* of the citizen, which combines (more or less perfectly) these two principles, will therefore see a crime or a wrong in all action which destroys either the equality of juridical persons or the equivalence of *droits* and duties, or the two things at the same time. And punishment will have to follow a dual purpose. On the one hand, it will have to equalize the criminal with the other citizens and his victim by reestablishing (to the extent possible) the *status quo ante,* or at the very least to reestablish their equivalence. On the other hand, punishment will have to restore the equivalence between *droits* and duties, or indeed between the benefits [324] and burdens of the very person of the criminal, this equivalence having been destroyed by the crime.

Now we have seen that the exclusive application of the aristocratic penal principle ends in the theory of lex talionis and an objectivist and collectivist conception of the sentence. As for the exclusive application of the bourgeois penal principle, it leads to a theory of compensation and the subjective and individualistic conception of punishment. The criminal *Droit* of the citizen must therefore combine, or more exactly synthesize, these two theories and these two oppositional conceptions. It is a matter of simultaneously asserting what they have essentially in them while overcoming their particularities— that is, all this by which they mutually contradict and exclude one another.

Concerning lex talionis and compensation, their radical difference disappears as the conditions of existence are equalized, and as these conditions are functions more than states. Lex talionis requires that one does to the criminal *the same thing* that he did to his victim, while the principle of compensation limits itself to the mere equivalence between the criminal act and the punishment undergone. Now if the state is nothing but a function, to injure the state of the victim (and that is the content of the crime) is nothing other than to prevent him from normally exercising his function. Therefore, if the punishment, conforming to the principle of compensation alone, does not strike at the state of the criminal and only touches his function, it will nevertheless make the criminal undergo the same thing that he inflicted on the victim, which will conform to the principle of lex talionis.

Furthermore, the penal justice of the citizen will have to combine objectivism with subjectivism. One will therefore take into account the intention, the motives of the crime, and so on. But one will try at the same time to overcome the objective causes of criminal motives. By justifying the criminal, one does not therefore justify the crime, and one will treat the latter just as objectively as aristocratic penal justice would have done.

Now to overcome the causes of crimes is to carry out social reforms, which touch just as much non-criminals as criminals. There will then be, if you will, a "collective responsibility," just as in the former aristocratic *Droit*. But just like in bourgeois *Droit*, the *individual* repercussion of the crime will only be able to touch the person of the criminal himself and not that of another.[4]

---

4. It is Fauconnet who has insisted on the collectivist character of modern criminal *Droit*, notably on *Droit* such as it appears in the theories of the Italian school (cf. *La Responsabilité*, 339ff).

Part Three

The Legal System

§ 47

[327] THE JURIDICAL EVOLUTION of humanity having not yet been completed, it would be futile to try to establish a perfect Legal System—that is, complete and definitive. But one can acknowledge that this evolution has progressed sufficiently to allow the *framing principles* [**cadres**] of the definitive System to be set down right here and now. In other words, we know all the main types or possible genres of social interactions (many of which are no longer or not yet realized) and all the modes of applying the idea of Justice to these interactions, as well as all the possible variations of this idea. But if we are able to construct right here and now, and—if you will—*a priori*, these variations and modes; and if we already know all the *types* or *genres* of social interactions, we do not know all the possible concrete interactions, nor even all their kinds [*espèces*]. Now a legal rule is first and foremost the application of a certain idea of Justice to a concrete interaction, or to a concrete kind of these interactions. Therefore, we do not know all possible legal rules. And this is why we are not yet able to *fill* the framing principles constructed from the Legal System with a juridical content.[1]

[328] In Part Two, I indicated the three main variations of the idea of Justice, pointing out that the third (and the only real) variation allows for an infinity of degrees, as it were. One could therefore construct the (purely theoretical) framing principles of a pure, aristocratic Legal System, as well as those of a pure System of bourgeois *Droit*. And one could construct the framing principles of the principal Legal Systems of the citizen, these Systems corresponding to the formative [*marquantes*] stages of the historical evolution of this *Droit*.

On the other hand, one can determine the various modes of applying a given idea of Justice to social interactions. One can distinguish, for example, the application in actuality from the application in potentiality. And these various modes of application will give us an initial division of the Legal System that we will consider.

Finally, one can divide all the known social interactions (at the epoch when the System in which we are interested is valid) into various types or genres. And

---

1. It should be understood that an *a priori* construction is only possible afterwards. If we can construct the variations of the idea of Justice and the modes of its application, as well as the main types of social interactions, it is solely because all these variations, all these applications, and all these types have already been realized in the course of history, or at the very least have become realizable. Furthermore, one can only *construct* a *Droit* in potentiality, since the *Droit* in actuality is the *Droit* effectively applied. Therefore, one can only *observe* the actual *Droit*.

one can then divide all the possible legal rules into these types—that is, all the possible applications of the idea of Justice to given social interactions. One thus obtains a new division of the Legal System, which is going, moreover, to intersect with the first one.

Having thus obtained a complete, rational System of the *Droit* in question, i.e., the System of all possible applications of a certain idea of Justice to a given whole of social interactions, one can compare it to the System accepted in the society where this *Droit* is in force. On the one hand, one will see if the latter System is rational from the point of view of its form—that is, if the accepted division of legal rules into the categories [*rubriques*] of the System is well done, and if these categories themselves are well chosen. On the other hand, one will be able to realize the perfection of the system as regards its content—that is, to see if the existing rules exhaust or not all the juridical possibilities of the *Droit* in question, and if they are correct or not.[2]

In chapter 1, I will briefly determine the main categories of the rational Legal System, adapted to the highest point actually reached by the political, social, and juridical evolution of humanity. By assuming that a [329] certain variation of the idea of Justice (of the citizen) is applied to a given whole of social interactions, I will ask how—broadly speaking—the legal rules which form this application ought to be classified.

In chapter 2, I will briefly analyze the character of the content of each of the main categories of the System. It will not be a matter of formulating legal rules. I will limit myself to indicating the traits common to the rules grouped under a single category, which distinguish them from rules grouped under other categories.

The exposition, moreover, will be incomplete and fragmentary: incomplete in the sense that it will end with the main categories and will ignore their subdivisions; and fragmentary, because I will only stress certain aspects of the content of these main categories, treating some less completely than others.

---

2. If an accepted, so-called legal rule does not correspond to the general definition of the legal rule, it will have to be excluded from the rational System as juridically unauthentic. If an accepted rule arises from the application of an idea of Justice other than the one which is at the base of the System, it will have to be excluded from it as juridically inadequate.

Chapter 1

Classification of Juridical Phenomena

§ 48

[331] AFTER HAVING INTRODUCED the notion of Justice into the analysis of *Droit*, it is useless to revert to the behaviorist definition of this phenomenon, formulated in Part One. It can be replaced by an

Introspective Definition of **Droit:**

"Positive *Droit*," or the "System" of a given *Droit*, is the totality of all "legal rules," i.e., of the rules which determine the behavior of a third intervening in the event of given interactions between "physical" or "moral" persons (individual, collective, or abstract); this intervention has for its sole goal or motive either simply to observe the conformity between the interactions and a certain ideal of Justice (existing only in the consciousness of the third or also set down objectively, orally or in writing), or to make the interactions conform to this ideal if they do not do so right away; [and] this intervention may be irresistible or not, and in the two cases it can be carried out either spontaneously or at the request of at least one of the agents interacting.[1]

[332] Any *Droit* whatsoever can only contain legal rules that conform to this definition. If a given society passes off as legal rules phenomena that are at odds with our definition, the phenomenologist of *Droit* does not have to take them into account, and he must exclude them from the Legal System in question as having nothing to do with *Droit* in general.

On the other hand, one must only include in a System the rules that correspond to the application of one and the same ideal of Justice. To every given ideal, therefore, a single System or a single positive *Droit* corresponds. It is possible that, in fact, the *Droit* in force is not homogenous, in the sense that it implies rules which presuppose two or more different ideas of Justice. The phenomenologist will then have to separate these rules into two or more different Systems, even if it means completing each of these Systems so that each contains all the possible rules. But practically speaking, the *Droit* that is even slightly stabilized and stable is never contradictory in this sense. The contradictions between the various legal rules in force only manifest themselves in transitional epochs, when one System is in the process of giving way to

---

1. The ideal of Justice is rarely given in an explicit form; it is generally given implicitly, in some legal rules of axiomatic validity, that the other rules must not contradict. In other words, the application of new rules must never lead to situations incompatible with those to which the application of the axiomatic rules leads.

another. Moreover, the simultaneous presence of rules that conform to the Justice of equality and the Justice of equivalence does not at all mean that the *Droit* is contradictory. This presence only proves that we are dealing with a *Droit* of the citizen. But in order that this *Droit* not be contradictory, it is necessary that the proportion adopted between equality and equivalence be the same in all the rules of this *Droit*. This is, moreover, easier to express as a general principle than to verify for every rule in particular. Practically speaking, it is enough that the application of a given rule never introduces equalities or equivalences incompatible with those which result from the application of the other rules as a whole.

If the (rational) System excludes all that is not juridical, as well as all the rules incompatible with the idea of Justice which is at its base, it implies, by contrast, *all* the rules resulting from the application of this idea to social interactions. A rule can be stipulated in a code, for example, and never be applied because the interactions at which it aims do not take place. Or again, an interaction can occur and a third can intervene without there being beforehand an appropriate rule: the third will then create it *ad hoc*. Or once again, a possible rule will not be stipulated and the interaction which corresponds to it will not be carried out. Finally, [333] stipulated rules will be applied to corresponding real interactions. Now the phenomenologist who establishes a legal System does not have to take account of these differences. In other words, the "System" or "positive *Droit*" implies all these cases at the same time: both the effectively stipulated rules, applied or not, and the not yet stipulated rules, but [which are nevertheless] compatible with the given ideal of Justice and are being applied to possible social interactions. Indeed, if one only takes into account stipulated or effectively applied rules, one will have to say that a "positive *Droit*" is always in the process of evolution; for the number of legal rules increases without end. And one can say that the new rules, stipulated or applied, are drawn from the reservoir of "possible" rules—that is, compatible with the ideal of Justice which is at the base of the positive *Droit* in question. The complete and stable System of this *Droit* therefore implies both effective rules, and rules that are not yet expressed, but possible.

It remains to see how the totality of rules forming a given System can be rationally subdivided.

If the rules are part of the System only by virtue of conforming to the definition which has just been given, it is in this definition that one must look for the principle of classification for the legal rules—that is, the divisions of the System which imply them. Now this definition admits of the following varieties of legal rules that conform to it:

1) One can distinguish legal rules which give rise to an *irresistible* intervention of the third from those which only provoke a possibly ineffective intervention—that is, an intervention from which the litigants are able to opt out [*se soustraire*] (§ 49);

2) One can distinguish rules which correspond to *spontaneous* interventions

of the third from rules according to which the third is only supposed to intervene at the express request of at least one of the litigants (§ 50);

3) One can distinguish legal rules according to the character of the *personages* [**personnes**] of the litigants (§ 51);

4) One can distinguish legal rules according to the nature of the *interactions* to which the rules are applied (§ 51).

As for the distinction between cases where the third limits himself to noticing the juridically legal character of an interaction from those where he alters the interaction in order to make it conform to the juridical law, it yields nothing for the classification of the legal rules themselves; for in the two cases it is a matter [334] of one and the same legal rule. In the first case, the third notices that the given interaction is conforming to the legal rule that he has in mind. In the second case, he notices the non-conformity of the interaction with this same rule and alters it in order to make the former conform to the latter.

We must therefore see (§ 49–51) what the four types of possible distinctions between legal rules mean. On this basis, it will be necessary to deduce the structure of the rational Legal System from them—that is, to determine the main categories into which one must divide the totality of rules which constitute a given "positive *Droit*" (§ 52).

§ 49

Let us first examine the meaning of the distinction between legal rules corresponding to an *irresistible* intervention of the third and those corresponding to an intervention not having this character of absolute necessity in relation to the litigants—that is, to the agents interacting.

First of all, the intervention may be called "irresistible" even in cases when the judgment has not taken place for some reason, as well as in cases where the judgement has not (by chance) been enforced. These are empirical contingencies that do not yield any rational subdivision between legal rules. For the third's intervention to be irresistible, it is enough that *in principle* every interaction not conforming to the legal rule in question be made to conform to this rule by the intervention of a third, without the agents interacting being able to oppose it. By contrast, the intervention will not be irresistible, it will be "optional," if, the judgment having taken place, its enforcement depends upon the consent of the litigants, who can opt out if they see fit. This is the case in arbitration properly so-called, where the impartial and disinterested third, playing the role of arbiter, has no means to *impose* his award on the will of the interested parties. At the other extreme is the case of a judgment against a wrongdoer who is already in custody and who has no means at all of resisting the enforcement of the judgment.

Between these two extreme cases, there is situated an intermediate case: the judgment takes place within some sort of society, of which both the litigants are members. If they want to remain members of this society, they must uphold the judgment that concerns them. But they can opt out of it, provided that they definitely leave the society, [335] which is not able to oppose their leaving. Now in this case, we will still say that the intervention is not irresistible, that it is "optional"; for if it is irresistible within the given society, it is not absolutely so, seeing that the litigants can opt out. Here as well, therefore, enforcement depends upon the good will of the litigants.[2]

When the enforcement of the third's judgment is *irresistible,* we will say that the legal rule exists *in actuality.* In the case where enforcement is *optional,* the rule will only exist *in potentiality. Droit* in actuality is the totality of rules of the first type; *Droit* in potentiality is the totality of rules of the second type. In both cases, it is a matter of *Droit,* for there is the intervention of a third who only intervenes in order to apply a given ideal of Justice to given social interactions. But in the second case, *Droit* will not exist *in actuality* because the interaction will not necessarily be made to conform to the ideal of Justice. It may forever remain juridically illegitimate or illegal: it will be a non-juridical reality. And even if the interaction comes to conform, or is conforming to, the ideal of Justice, it is due to the will of the parties, and not that of the third. Its *actual reality,* therefore, is always non-juridical, it being of little importance that it is illegal or legal. In this last case, of course, the third observes the agreement of the‹ interaction with the ideal of Justice. But the interaction is not what it is by virtue of this observation; for it remains (or may remain) what it is even if this observation does not take place, if the third observes a disagreement between the interaction and the ideal of Justice.

This distinction between *Droit* in actuality and *Droit* in potentiality should not be confused with the distinction between cases where the intervention of the third is spontaneous and those where it occurs at the request of at least one of the litigants. Indeed, an intervention can be "spontaneous" while being "optional." Thus, for example, a society may not tolerate certain interactions between its members, and thus intervene spontaneously to suppress them; but at the same time, it may be incapable of preventing the interacting agents from ceasing to be members of the aforementioned Society and from persisting in their "illicit" interaction. On the other hand, a "provoked" intervention may be "irresistible": the interested parties, [336] who requested the intervention of the third, are no longer able to stop it and must submit to it to the very end, without being able to offer any resistance to it at all. In other words, the intervention of the third can be "spontaneous" or "provoked," both in *Droit* in actuality and in *Droit* in potentiality.

When a society is organized into a State, only state-sanctioned *Droit* exists in actuality. This *droit* is then formed by the totality of rules that correspond to judgments whose enforcement is guaranteed by the State. Indeed, only the

---

2. One must not confuse this case with one when the judge gives the convict a choice between exile and punishment within the society; for in this case, exile is also an enforcement of the judgment, which is thus irresistible. In the other case, by contrast, exile (which is voluntary) is a means of making enforcement impossible.

State can forbid its citizens from ceasing to be citizens without its consent. Therefore, a citizen cannot—in principle—opt out of the application of state-sanctioned *Droit*. The intervention of the third, therefore, is in this case irresistible.

In state-sanctioned *Droit* the third represents the State: he is a "Governor" in the broad sense of the word, or a "Civil Servant." He can be so in all three of his avatars as juridical Legislator, Judge, and judicial Police. But it is also possible that in one of the two former aspects, or even both of them simultaneously, the third would be a "private person [*personne privée*]." *Droit* will be state-sanctioned and will therefore exist in actuality as soon as the third is a "Civil Servant" in his capacity as judicial Police, charged with enforcing Judgements conforming to the juridical Laws. One can say in this case that the third legislates and judges by delegation, the State automatically enforcing the judgments of its deputy. Now even in his capacity as Police, the third can be a "Civil Servant" in the very broad sense of the word; for here as well there can be delegation by the State. The enforcement can be carried out by a "private person," the State only intervening in the case of a resistance that the deputy cannot overcome. But seeing that the resistance will end up being overcome (in principle), one can say that *Droit* exists in actuality—that is, that the intervention of the third is "irresistible."

Droit will still exist "in actuality" if it is applied within a group which enjoys juridical autonomy inside the State, provided that this autonomy is sanctioned by the State. In other words, the State must forbid the members of the group from leaving it, [or] at the very least from leaving it in order to elude [*se soustraire*] the enforcement of a judgment made within the group conforming to the juridical law which is in force. Thus, for example, if the State makes it obligatory for certain of its citizens to belong to a professional "union," the *Droit* that this union will apply to its members will be a *Droit* in actuality. And this *Droit* will be, in the final analysis, state-sanctioned, since the State (tacitly) makes it its own, seeing that it guarantees its enforcement, i.e., its actual reality, [337] by preventing [*s'opposant*] the litigants of this *Droit* from escaping its action. (Membership in the union is part of the citizen's status, in the same way as nationality.) And this *Droit* will exist in actuality only to the extent that it is state-sanctioned.

Droit in potentiality, therefore, can only be a *Droit* that is applied in Societies that are not organized into a State, i.e., trans- or sub political, in which membership is purely optional. In the second case, the members of the Society are all citizens of one and the same State. In the first, the Society is made up of citizens from different States. But in no case is membership in the Society in question obligatory: it is not part of the citizen's status set down by his State. The member of the Society can cease to be its member without this changing in any way his situation as a citizen of his State. In any case, the fact of eluding a judgement of the Society (by leaving it) does not alter at all his capacity as citizen. His State will therefore do nothing to impose the enforcement of the judgement. And since, on the other hand, the State will defend its citizen against all attempts to alter the state [*état*] of the latter, if this state remained the same in the eyes of the State (i.e., if the latter has done nothing incompatible with his status as citizen), it will oppose, in fact, the enforcement of Society's judgment—at the very least, if the citizen has recourse to the State in order to elude this enforcement. Enforcement will therefore depend upon the willingness of the litigant (since by definition the Society cannot enforce its judgment against the will of the State, which in this case is in solidarity with the will of the litigant). In other words, the *Droit* of the sub- or trans-political Society will only exist in potentiality. It is in this way that the "canon *Droit*" of a State religion exists in actuality, while the "canon *Droit*" of a Church "separated" from the State is only a *Droit* in potentiality.

Of course, the citizens of a State can dissociate themselves from the state-sanctioned *Droit* in force, by seeing it as an "unjust *Droit*." In this case, they can oppose another *Droit*—the "just *Droit*"—to this state-sanctioned *Droit*, which will only exist in potentiality as long as the State does not make it its own (by abandoning its "unjust *Droit*"). But this *Droit* in potentiality will be *another Droit* than the *Droit* in actuality, since it will have for a base another ideal of Justice. In this case, there will be an opposition between *two* Systems—one of which will want to actualize itself at the expense of the other—and not an opposition or distinction inside one and the same Legal System. If one wants to divide a [338] given Legal System, i.e., a "positive *Droit*," into two parts, one of which contains *Droit* in actuality and the other *Droit* in potentiality, these two *Droits* must have for their base *the same* ideal of Justice. In other words, the State may lose interest in enforcing judgments issued by sub- or trans-political Societies, but it should not consider them as juridically "illegitimate"—that is, ultimately as "unjust." If it loses interest in, or opposes, their enforcement, it is solely because it considers that a certain degree of "injustice" is compatible with the state of the citizen, namely the "injustice" that results from the non-conformity of interactions between its citizens and the valid legal rules in the sub- or trans-political Societies in question. Conversely, if these Societies can "lose interest in" certain interactions, abandoning their judgments to the State, they should not consider these judgments "unjust," i.e., incompatible with their own judgments, relative to other interactions.

Now if one can keep the actual aspects of a reality while ignoring its virtual aspects, one cannot keep what exists only in potentiality while ignoring what exists in actuality, since actuality only actualizes potentiality, such that to deny actuality is to deny potentiality itself. As well, seeing that state-sanctioned *Droit* actualizes the same ideal of Justice that exists in potentiality in the *Droits* of sub- and trans-political Societies, they cannot lose interest in state-sanctioned *Droit* as the State can lose interest in their *Droits*. They cannot say that one can be "unjust" as a citizen and nevertheless remain "just" in one's capacity as a member of the Society. If the Society cedes certain judgments to the State, it must nevertheless show solidarity with them. In other words, Societies must see in state-sanctioned *Droit* an actualization of their own *Droits* and behave accordingly. They must reserve only the non-state-sanctioned part of their

Droits, and it is precisely this part that is *Droit* in potentiality. If not, there will be two different *Droits:* on the one hand, the state-sanctioned *Droit* existing in actuality; and on the other, another *Droit,* which exists—in potentiality—within the Societies in question and which will want to be actualized at the expense of state-sanctioned *Droit*—from whence comes an inevitable conflict between these two *Droits.*

Generally speaking, an essence is determined by its actualization, and potentiality is only determined as potentiality by its actuality. It is therefore state-sanctioned *Droit* which determines the unity of a Legal System, which sets down the character [339] of a given "positive *Droit.*" This state-sanctioned *Droit* constitutes the part of the System that is called "*Droit* in actuality." As for the other part, called "*Droit* in potentiality," it is constituted by the totality of legal rules valid in different sub- or trans-political Societies, provided that these rules are based upon the same ideal of Justice as the rules of state-sanctioned *Droit.* These Societies realize in potentiality the same Justice, and consequently the same *Droit,* as the State, which realizes them in actuality; from whence it follows that the boundaries between these two *Droits* are always in flux, a legal rule being able to pass from one sphere to the other.

In other respects, the two parts of the System will have the same subdivisions. We have already seen that in both cases the intervention can be either "spontaneous" or "provoked." Furthermore, one can divide both *Droits* according to the persons implicated. And finally, one can subdivide them according to the interactions at which the legal rules aim. For if *Droit* in actuality only actualizes *Droit* in potentiality, every actualized legal rule has been able to exist or will be able to exist in a state of mere potentiality, just as every rule in potentiality can be actualized or come from an actual rule.

Practically speaking, *Droit* in potentiality is only of interest nowadays in the case where the persons in question are States (i.e., "collective moral persons") and the interactions are interactions where these States intervene as States—that is, "political" interactions governed by the political categories of Friend (or "ally") and Enemy.[3] In other words, *Droit* in potentiality is truly interesting only to the extent that it is "public international *Droit*" (the trans-political Society in question being Humanity, the League of Nations, the European League, the civilized World, Christendom, or something else of the same genre).

I will analyze the idea of this "international *Droit*" later on (chapter 2, A). For the moment, it suffices to say that it is far from being the only *Droit* existing in potentiality, even nowadays. One could locate it in the same part of the System not only as "canon *Droit*" (Catholic, for example), or the *Droit* that governs the inner life of the Free Masons, the Pen-Club, and so on, but also innumerable other *Droits* [340] of sub-political Societies, such as "pri-

---

3. There are also interactions where two States do not treat each other as States. This is when they mutually recognize each other as "neutrals." But then these two States (or at the very least one of them) still have other interactions, which are "political." If not, there would be no State at all—that is, no "public international *Droit.*"

vate," national sporting or professional associations, for example. It is only the persons in question and the intended interactions that distinguish these various types of *Droit* in potentiality (assuming that they all correspond to one and the same ideal of Justice). Therefore, if jurists limit themselves to treating public international *Droit* (and sometimes also canon *Droit*), leaving to the sociologists the responsibility for studying the other virtual *Droits,* it is for purely practical reasons that they do so—for reasons of social and political interest—and not for reasons of legal theory. In contemporary legal Encyclopedias, the Part of the System entitled "*Droit* in potentiality" is dropped as a whole, except for the two categories which correspond to "public international *Droit*" and "canon *Droit.*" But in fact, there exist a great number of other *Droits* in potentiality, and the phenomenologist should take them into account if he wants to establish a complete Legal System, formulating and classifying as well all the legal rules (possible or real) that only exist in potentiality (at a given moment in the evolution of the *Droit* that one is systematizing). But I must limit myself to pointing out this problem while indicating the framing principle where all these virtual *Droits* have come to rest.[4]

§ 50

One commonly distinguishes "civil *Droit,*" which does not imply the idea of penalty or punishment properly so-called, from "criminal or penal *Droit,*" which is based upon this idea of punishment. Otherwise, as "private *Droit,*" "civil *Droit*" is contrasted to "public *Droit,*" which implies "criminal *Droit*" alongside of "constitutional *Droit*" and "administrative *Droit,*" these last two forming "public *Droit*" in the narrow sense of the word. We must see what the relation is [341] of these two common distinctions with our distinction between "spontaneous" and "provoked" interventions of the Third.

Let us first discuss the *case of **Droit** in actuality*—that is, state-sanctioned *Droit* where the Third is a representative of the State. The subsequent application [of this analysis] to *Droit* in potentiality will be easy.

At the outset it is clear that legal rules with *spontaneous* interventions of the Third yield rules of *criminal Droit,* [while] rules with *provoked* interventions yield rules of *civil Droit,* when the Third effectively intervenes only at the

---

4. Let us note that one cannot divide "public *Droit*" into "public international *Droit*" and "domestic public *Droit,*" and contrast these two *Droits* as a whole to "private *Droit.*" On the contrary, it is "domestic public *Droit*" which is joined with "private *Droit*"; for these two are only types of the *Droit* that I have called "*Droit* in actuality." It is therefore necessary to contrast "domestic *Droit*" (i.e., state-sanctioned *Droit* or *Droit* in actuality) to "international *Droit.*" But one must not forget that one cannot align [*coordonner*] them; for if "domestic *Droit*" is a whole, the totality of *Droit* in actuality, "international *Droit*" is only a (minute) part of *Droit* in potentiality. It is therefore necessary to contrast domestic or state-sanctioned or actual *Droit* to *Droit* in potentiality or virtual, which implies—among other things—"public international *Droit.*"

request of at least one of the litigants—that is, of the two agents in the interaction to which the legal rule is supposed to be applied.

But it is necessary to begin by clearing up a possible misunderstanding. One must not think that in civil *Droit* the Third tolerates an "unjust" or juridically illegal interaction, and only tries to make it conform to the ideal of Justice in the case when one of the agents encourages him. In reality, the situation is wholly different. The interaction is such that it becomes "unjust" by the very fact of (at least) one of the agents having recourse to the Third. This recourse, which "provokes" the Third's intervention, reveals the fact that one of the agents does not accept the way of acting of the other. And it is only because of this disagreement that the intervention is "unjust" or can be such. If the same interaction were carried out with the mutual agreement of the agents, it would have nothing unjust about it, and the Third would therefore have no reason at all to intervene. Thus, for example, the non-payment of a debt has nothing in itself unjust or juridically illegal about it, as long as the creditor does not protest: a loan has simply been transformed into a gift.[5] The interaction is only unjust if the debtor does not pay back the debt when *required* to by the creditor. Now in this case, the latter is supposed to have recourse to the Third. Thus, the latter only intervenes, if you will, if he is "provoked." But as long as he is not, there is not any juridical reason to intervene, seeing that the interaction has nothing illegal or unjust about it.[6]

Practically speaking, this situation is encountered above all when it is a matter of applying the principle of equivalence; for as I have already said, one must take into account the point of view of the subject in order to establish the equivalence of his benefits (*droits*) and burdens (duties). One can therefore assume that there is equivalence [342] as long as the subject does not protest, that any interaction where the agents are in agreement is "just" from the point of view of the Justice of equivalence. This is why civil *Droit* is above all a "bourgeois" phenomenon, and this is also why it is first and foremost a *Droit* of equivalence or of "contract" (in the broadest sense of the term—or if one prefers, of "obligations").[7]

---

5. [Ed. In common law this is certainly not true. For example, forbearance by the creditor of his or her right to sue on the debt does not discharge the debt, or even less convert it into a gift.]
6. The situation, moreover, is conforming to our behaviorist definition: *Droit* only exists when B reacts or can react in such a way as to annul A's action, the Third annulling this reaction from B. As long as A and B are in agreement, therefore, the Third does not have to intervene. The situation is only juridical to the extent that there *can* be a disagreement between A and B.
7. When it is a matter of *equality*, the intervention of the Third can be "spontaneous," for equality is objectively noticeable. Thus, for example, a contract can be annulled by the Third despite mutual consent, i.e., in spite of its conformity with the principle of equivalence, simply because it is not *equal* to other contracts of the same genre. This is what takes place when the State sets a minimum wage, and the contract provides for a lower wage (even freely entered into). But in this case, there is an interaction not between the two contracting parties, but between them and the whole of economic Society. As well, the intervention of the Third may lead not only to the rectification of the contract, but also to a punishment of the contracting parties. There will then be criminal *Droit*, and no longer civil *Droit* (see below).

Be that as it may, the Third (who is in principle omniscient) does not intervene as long as there is no injustice. In the cases being considered, this means: as long as one does not have recourse to him, this recourse being the supposed sign of disagreement, [there is no] injustice (or its possibility). But as soon as there is recourse, i.e., as soon as there is injustice, the Third necessarily intervenes. One can therefore say that wherever there is *Droit*, the Third always intervenes "*spontaneously*" as soon as he finds himself in the presence of an interaction that does not conform to the ideal of Justice, or is supposedly not so (and—in principle—none of these interactions escape him). It therefore seems that there are no "provoked" interventions.

It seems, however, that there are cases of "spontaneous" intervention that differ radically from cases when the intervention appears to be "provoked." These are cases when the Third intervenes not only without waiting for recourse by the litigants, but also in spite of the opposition that the litigants make to his intervention. And in these cases of spontaneous intervention, this generally leads to a punishment of one or both litigants, which does not take place in cases of a provoked intervention.

Let us take some concrete examples.

First of all, the case of theft. Of course, theft implies the non-consent of the victim, for otherwise it would be a gift and not a theft. And since non-consent is equivalent to having recourse to the Third, one can say that here as well the intervention of the latter is "provoked." But there is nevertheless an essential difference [343] with the case of the non-payment of a debt, for example, when the intervention is "provoked" in the proper sense of the term. On the one hand, if I report [*dénonce*] the non-payment of a debt, the judicial apparatus will not be set into motion as long as the creditor himself does not lodge a complaint [*plainte*].[8] By contrast, if I report a theft, the State will intervene even if it has not received any complaint from the victim. One could say, it is true, that the victim is supposed to have recourse to the Third as soon as he becomes aware of the fact, such that the Third is "provoked" (in advance).[9] But it is possible that for some reason the victim does not want the Third to intervene and annul the "unjust" act. The Third will nevertheless do so. And on the other hand, in the case of the debt, the intervention of the Third will only result in

---

8. [Ed. The French make a distinction between the individual who actually reports a crime: if that individual is the victim himself, then he lodges a *plainte*, or "complaint"; if that individual is a neutral, third party, then he will *dénonce*, or "report," the crime to the proper authorities. Whenever possible, these words and their cognates will be translated as they are above (e.g., *dénonciation* will be translated as "report"). The word *dénonciateur*, however, will be translated as "informant" or "informing," rather than the awkward and perhaps misleading word "reporter."]

9. In the case of theft, the non-equivalence of the interaction seems to be able to be objectively noticed, seeing that the thief takes without giving anything in return. But even here this is not always true. Let us assume that someone steals my dog, one which I would like to get rid of, but which I do not have the courage to kill or which I cannot find someone to give it to. Subjectively, it would therefore be a matter of a gift. Nevertheless, the State can punish the thief.

the restitution of the thing owed (with simple compensatory damages if the case arises), while in the case of theft, there will be, in addition to the restitution of the stolen item, punishment of the thief.

The case of rape can be compared to that of theft. Of course, in reporting a rape as rape, the *resistance* of the victim is revealed by this very fact. But the Third will intervene here as well even if the victim does not desire his intervention. And there will be punishment of the guilty, independently of compensatory damages (required or not).

The case of murder with the consent of the victim is clearer still. The Third intervenes even with the knowledge that the "victim" was in agreement with the murderer. One cannot therefore say that the murder is forbidden because in every murder there would have been recourse to the third by the victim, if he had not been prevented from doing so. And the murderer can be punished even in the case when the "victim" who escaped death would be denied some sort of compensation by the murderer.

Finally, in the case when the Third punishes homosexuality, for example, he intervenes not only against the will of the interested parties, but also with the knowledge that the interaction was in conformity with the principle of equivalence (of pleasure, for example). There is more than a simple *assumption* of equivalence, based upon the fact that the interested parties did not have recourse to the Third. And nevertheless, there is an intervention followed by a punishment.

Now the analysis of the latter case allows one to solve the problem. [344] Quite obviously, there is nothing "unjust" in homosexual interaction freely consented to, neither from the point of view of equality nor that of equivalence. The Third, therefore, does not have any juridical reason to intervene. If he intervenes juridically, it is on account of another interaction, which is not conforming to the given ideal of Justice. It is a matter of an interaction between the participants in the homosexual act, on the one hand, and the whole of Society, on the other hand, which claims to be injured by this action. When the Third intervenes to annul the homosexual act, this simply means that Society has the **droit** to suppress homosexuality among its members, that it may do so without encountering resistance, the latter being annulled by the Third. Of course, for the intervention of the Third to be juridical, the interaction in question between the homosexuals and Society must imply an element of injustice, which will be suppressed through the suppression of the homosexual action. But it is easy to indicate several ways of finding an injustice in the case in question. One can give a "magical" interpretation of it, by assuming that the homosexual act will bring down a "celestial" punishment that will affect all of Society. In this case, it is unjust that some experience pleasure at the expense of others, that some have benefits while others only have burdens from this event. Or again, one can propose a "rationalistic" interpretation: it is unjust that some experience only pleasure when others also have the burdens connected to paternity; it is unjust for young women to have "unfair competition"; and so on. At any rate, the Third punishes homosexuality just as he punishes "bes-

tiality," for example, or as he could have been able in principle to punish mas-
turbation, when the only *inter*-action is between the guilty and Society.

The same goes for murder with the consent of the victim. Here as well, the
injustice only appears at the moment when one relates the act of the murderer
not to his victim, but to Society taken as a whole; for one can say in this case
that it is unjust that one gives up on life while others bear it to the very end—
and in this case one will also punish the victim, as one punishes suicide; or once
again, that it is unjust to deprive Society of one of its members without giving
it anything in return—and so on.

The same observations for rape. If it is punished without taking account of
the will of the victim, this is because one acknowledges that it injures the entire
Society. It is punished as one punishes the "corruption of minors," when the
consent of the [345] "victim" does not prevent either the intervention of the
Third or the punishment of the guilty. And by accepting a certain conception
of family life, *Droit* might punish sexual relations (consensual or not) with a
young woman in the same way that it could punish adultery.

Finally, in the case of theft, there is still an interaction between the thief and
the Society in question taken as a whole. It is to *this* interaction that the idea of
Justice is applied, which justifies the "spontaneous" intervention of the Third
and the punishment of the guilty, even if the "victim" is in agreement with the
criminal. And it is also in this way that a contract, freely entered into, can be
annulled by the Third (and the contracting parties punished) if one relates it
not only to the contracting parties but also to the entire Society.

Practically speaking, modern *Droit* only accepts as subjects of *droit* two
Societies: economic Society (the *Bürgerliche Gesellschaft* of the old German
writers) and familial Society. Thus, theft and murder will be related to the first,
while rape and homosexuality will be related to the second. But as there are still
many other sub-political Societies, the State can in principle intervene in many
other cases. Thus, for a long time the State transformed certain actions into
interactions between the participants of these actions and religious Society. Be
that as it may, in all these cases the Third intervenes solely because the Society
in question believes itself to be injured by the action at issue, and—in some
way or other—has recourse to the intervention of the Third. The latter therefore intervenes in order to alter an interaction that does not conform to a given
ideal of Justice, and he does so because he is "provoked." Thus, for example,
the Third would not intervene if Society (familial or other) did not object to
homosexuality among its members; for if there had not been this objection,
which is realized and revealed by having recourse to the Third, there would be
nothing unjust in the fact that certain members of the Society are homosexuals. And one also understands why the Third is "provoked" in these cases by a
"report" coming from a "disinterested" witness: it is because this informing
witness is not disinterested. He is a member of the Society that believes itself
injured by the action which he is reporting; he is therefore injured himself. One
can therefore say that this is a case of *pars pro toto* [one for all, or the part acting on behalf of the whole]: it is Society injured in its entirety that has recourse

to the Third through the mouth of the informant. A witness may very well not be directly injured by the theft or the rape which he reports; he is injured as a "bourgeois-owner" or "father of the family," for example, and [346] this is enough to provoke the intervention of the Third who recognizes as subjects of *droit* economic and familial Societies of the given type.

Seen from this angle, therefore, all juridical intervention of the Third seems to be "*provoked.*"[10] On the other hand, as we have seen, all intervention can be called "*spontaneous,*" seeing that it takes place every time that there is injustice (the latter being revealed to the Third by having recourse to his intervention).

Nevertheless, the distinction between spontaneous intervention and provoked intervention has a juridical meaning, all the more so because the former is accompanied by the application of a penalty, which does not occur in the other intervention. Thus, there is a point in maintaining this distinction within the rational Legal System.

One can only say that there is a "*spontaneous* intervention" when one and the same action is part of two distinct interactions. If the action of member A (individual or collective) of a Society puts him in interaction not only with another member B (individual or collective) but also with Society S^{11} in its entirety, such that intervention in one of these interactions implies intervention in the other, the Third can intervene in the interaction between A and B without being "provoked" by them, and even against their will (provided that he is "provoked" by S to intervene in the interaction between A and S). Thus, for example, if A steals something from B, he also injures by his act private property as such—that is, the entire economic Society S based upon this property. This is why any member whatsoever of this Society can have recourse to the Third. This is why he will intervene (as a result of the recourse by S), even if B does not have recourse to him and does not believe himself injured for whatever reasons. And, finally, this is why, in addition to the (eventual) compensation of B (restitution plus compensatory damages, for example), there will still be the compensation of S, and it is the latter which will be called "punishment" or "penalty." In the case of debt, by contrast, when A does not pay back B, Society S believes itself to be unaffected. This is why there is only an interaction between A and B, such that the Third does not intervene as long as neither A nor B "provoke" him, and this is why there is nothing to add to the simple compensation of B by A. Now, seeing [347] that the act in question has not been an interaction between A and S, the relations between them cannot be altered by the mere fact of an interaction between A and B. Therefore, these relations must not be altered either by the result of this interaction, i.e., by the compensation of B by A: this compensation should reestablish justice in the relations between A and B, without having altered the relations of A and B with

---

10. [This is] in conformity with our behaviorist definition of *Droit* in general, which acknowledges that "B's reaction" automatically provokes A's recourse to the Third, [who is] supposed to annul this reaction.

11. [Ed. Reading *Société S* for *Société B.*]

S. Now this is precisely what characterizes the "civil" (or "provoked") intervention of the Third in contrast to his "penal" (or "spontaneous") intervention.[12]

One can therefore say that the distinction between civil *Droit*, [characterized by] provoked intervention and without punishment, and criminal *Droit*, [characterized by] spontaneous intervention and with penalties, rests upon a difference between the juridical *persons* who are implicated. There is criminal or penal *Droit* when some part of a Society is in a (possibly) unjust interaction with this Society as a whole. There is civil *Droit*, by contrast, when the (possibly) unjust interaction only takes place between any two parts of this Society. But it should be understood that for there to be *Droit*, in both cases there must be a *Third*; and for this *Droit* to exist in actuality (in a Society organized into a State), this Third must represent the State. In other words, the State must recognize as subjects of *droit* or litigants both the Society as such and its various parts, these being in the final analysis individuals.

Now the history of *Droit* seems to confirm this way of seeing things. Let us take, for example, the case of murder (not consented to). It is agreed that the penalty (and the corresponding legal rule [348]) arose from the vendetta. Now the vendetta has nothing to do with *Droit*, since there is no Third present.[13] If the State (whatever one it may be) consents to play the role of this Third (disinterested and impartial, i.e., acting solely with a view to realizing the ideal of Justice, by overcoming—in this case—the injustice of murder), the non-juridical vendetta is replaced by a juridical process—that is, by a *Droit*. Now in the beginning the Third does not deal with individuals but with families, one of which belongs to the victim and the other to the murderer. As for other families, they are uninterested in the matter. One can therefore say either that the Society (made up of the totality of families) does not feel itself injured by the murder of one of its members (who is not, moreover, directly its member, being the member of a family which is itself a member of the Society) or that

---

12. I am only here speaking about the *framing principles* of the legal System, while abstracting from their content. I do not therefore ask why a given Society considers itself injured in certain cases and not in others. (At any rate, it is only a question here of *juridical* reasons, i.e., deduced from the ideal of Justice, which varies from Society to Society and according to epochs.) Now if it is difficult to visualize an economic Society that would not believe itself injured by theft, one can very well imagine an economic Society that would believe itself injured by the non-payment of debts. In this case, the non-payment could result in an alteration of the relation of the guilty with Society as such: there would then be a penalty—for example, imprisonment. Moreover, prison for debts should only be abolished in the Society that recognizes the freedom of movement of its members (if this Society does not believe itself injured by the non-payment of debts). A Society that does not recognize this freedom may very well accept the imprisonment of insolvent debtors, even if it considers that in this case the creditor alone is injured. In this case, the imprisonment would not be a penalty but a mere compensation of the interested party. There would then be civil *Droit* and not criminal *Droit*.

13. At the very most, there is a *Droit* in potentiality, that does not differ at all from our public international *Droit*.

this Society does not yet exist as such. At any rate, then, there is no interaction between a part and a whole, from whence comes the "civil" character of the *Droit* in question: a "provoked" intervention (the State only intervenes if the family of the victim has recourse to it) and the absence of punishment properly so-called (the process ending in the mere compensation of the victim, or more exactly, of his family—from whence comes the practice of *Wergild*). Now there comes a time when the family of the criminal dissociates itself from him.[14] The family of the victim, by contrast, continues to show solidarity with him. But there is more: even the family of the guilty shows solidarity with the family of the victim (or, more exactly, with the victim taken individually). Why does it do this? It is because in the meantime, the families are participating in an interfamilial economic life and thus become members of an economic Society, which has for members not only (and not particularly) families but also (and above all) their members—that is, individuals. Now economic Society is injured as a whole by the murder of one of its members. It therefore shows solidarity with the victim against the criminal. And to the extent that the family of the latter is a member of economic Society, it does the same. As a result, then, there is not [349] only an interaction between the criminal (or his family) and the victim (or his family), but also an interaction between the criminal (taken individually) and the totality of other members (individuals or families) of economic Society (of which the victim and murderer are equally members). Thus, there is an interaction between the part of a whole and this whole itself, from whence comes the penal or criminal character of the new *Droit*: spontaneous intervention (even if the victim does not object and if his family wants to bury the matter) and penalty or punishment in addition to compensation (of the victim or his family).[15]

Droit is therefore penal or criminal when the Third intervenes in order to make an interaction between Society as such (economic, familial, and so on) and some one of its parts conform to the ideal of Justice, the injustice having been introduced by the action of the latter. Now the injustice only exists to the extent that Society believes itself injured. In this case it is supposed to have recourse to the Third. But Society as such cannot act: it can neither declare itself injured nor "provoke" the intervention of the Third. Of course, one of its members can do so, as we have seen: the Third intervenes if the crime is "reported." But this expedient is only a last resort; for the Third never knows if the informant is truly acting as a member of the Society—that is, in its name, as its representative or agent. This is why it was decided to promulgate juridical *laws* (and to set them down

---

14. One can say that the family practices "noxal surrender": in handing over the guilty it escapes punishment and [the payment of] compensation. However—and this is the difference with noxal surrender properly so-called—the surrender is not to the injured family, but to the State (which represents here—as Third—the interests of the totality of families—that is, those of familial Society as such).

15. In the case of *Wergild*, the penal surplus [i.e., the amount in excess of that required to compensate the victim or his family] is collected by the Third, i.e., the State, which acts, as it were, as the representative of the Society in question.

definitively in a Code). These laws set down once and for all the reactions of Society. If an action is contrary to these laws, it is because Society feels itself injured by it. Non-conformity with the law is the equivalent of having recourse to the third by Society: it therefore "provokes" the intervention of the former,[16] from whence comes the principle *Nulla poena sine lege.*[17] For if the action is not contrary to a law, the Third accepts that it does not injure Society, which therefore does not "provoke" the Third, who consequently does not have to intervene.

One can also say that the juridical Laws set down the "status" [350] of sub-political Societies (economic, familial, and so on). Now Society being a collective person, its status also contains the statuses of its constitutive elements—that is, ultimately, the statuses of individuals as well, taken as members of the Society in question. If an individual action conforms to the status of the individual, it also automatically conforms to the status of the Society: there is then no injury to Society, [and] therefore no "provocation" of the Third nor intervention on his part—in short, no "injustice." On the contrary, any departure from the individual's status is equivalent to a "provocation" that brings about an intervention of the Third, who overcomes the injustice in question. Thus, to the extent that the individual's status is determined by the status of the Society, such that any departure from this status is equivalent to a conflict between the individual and Society, this status is conferred by the totality of penal or criminal Laws. But the status of Society leaves a certain margin with respect to the statuses of individuals: to a certain extent, individuals can differ, i.e., enter into interactions, without entering into conflict with Society. And this sphere of individual activity (i.e., the activity of all who are some one *part* of the Society), which is not set down by the status of Society as such, is governed by the civil Law. Here the action of an individual does not, by definition, injure Society. This action can only be unjust, therefore, if it injures another individual. The Third will only intervene, therefore, if he is provoked by the latter. And his intervention, by restoring justice in the relations between these two individuals, should leave their relations with Society as a whole intact.[18]

---

16. The existence of the Law does not prevent there being a "public accuser," a "[public] prosecutor." This one represents Society. And one can say that the Third, i.e., the Judge, intervenes (during the trial) in the interaction between the accused and the prosecutor (who represents the other party, i.e., the Society) in order to say if the latter has the ***droit*** to act with the guilty as he intents to do. I will speak about Trials in chapter 2.

17. [Ed. "No punishment without law." The obvious meaning is that the accused shall not be subject to criminal penalty where his or her act has not violated a previously promulgated provision of the written law.]

18. Dealing only with framing principles, I have not asked why such and such a Society has such and such a status, and why this status leaves the individual such a margin and not another. I will only say that this juridical status does not differ from the political status of the State and citizen, set down in the Constitution. However, since actions of the State and citizen, acting as a citizen, are very limited in number, the political status is above all positive: it indicates what the State and citizen may or must do. By contrast, individual acts that injure Society are much less numerous than acts that do not affect the latter, from whence comes the negative character of the status of this Society: this status indicates above all what the Society and its members must not do.

If a Society (economic, for example, or familial, and so on) sets down its status itself, this act has nothing juridical about it (just as there is nothing juridical in the act by which the State sets down its own status, i.e., the Constitution, which also implies the status of the citizens). But once this status is set down, and once the margin for free individual actions is established, [351] Society can play the role of Third with respect to individual interactions that occur within the margin. By contrast, when it is a matter of an individual action not conforming to the status of Society, i.e., injuring the latter, Society can certainly intervene, but then it will be a party and not a Third: there will then be no *Droit*. In other words, the *Droit* of an autonomous Society can only be what we have called "civil." What we have called "criminal *Droit*" would not be a *Droit* in this case. Now if this Society ceases to be autonomous by becoming an integral part of a State (by becoming a sub-political Society), a variety of juridical possibilities can be realized. The State may lose interest in the interactions between members of the Society that occur outside the margin of the status of the latter. The Society will then continue to act as Third: it will keep its own "civil *Droit*." But this *Droit* will no longer be but a *Droit* in potentiality. Or again, the State may appropriate this *Droit* and act as Third itself (it being of little importance whether this Third is a civil servant of the State in the narrow sense of the term, or the Society now judging by delegation in the name of the State). Civil *Droit* will then become a state-sanctioned *Droit*—that is, a *Droit* in actuality. But the State can be "impartial and disinterested" not only with respect to individual interactions between members of the Society, but also in relation to this Society itself—that is, also in relation to interactions between the latter and its parts. If the State intervenes in the capacity of such a Third in these interactions, there will be state-sanctioned *Droit*—that is, actual, penal, or criminal. The reactions of Society, which beforehand had nothing juridical about them, will now fully possess the character of **droit**, since a third will henceforth respond in its place: the non-juridical principles of action thus become legal rules—penal *Droit*.

Penal *Droit*, therefore, can only exist when a Society S1 is enclosed in a Society S2, which intervenes as Third in interactions between S1 and the members of S1. As long as S1 alone exists, its *Droit* can only be civil. If the global Society is organized into a State, S2 must be the State itself for penal *Droit* to exist in actuality. As for the civil *Droit* of S1, it will only exist in potentiality as long as S2, i.e., the State, does not make it its own. In other words, for there to be a civil *Droit* and a penal *Droit* in actuality, the State must be related not only to S1, but also directly to the members of S1, considering as its litigants [352] not only Society S1 as such, but also the members of this Society, taken independently of their interactions with this Society. The State must consent to apply a given idea of Justice both to the interactions of the parts of the Society in question with each other and to the interactions between these parts and the Society itself. But the State may limit itself to making the civil *Droit* of Society its own and transforming into penal *Droit* the non-juridical rules that determine the reaction of the Society to certain actions of its members, just as it can set down a new status of the Society with different margins for individual activity. For there to be (civil and criminal) **Droit**, it is enough that the State be an impartial and disinterested Third both in respect to Society and in respect to its members: in other words, it is enough that the State intervenes with the sole concern of applying a certain idea of Justice to interactions between individuals themselves and with the Society.[19]

---

19. The State can incorporate a part of the status of Society into its own status, and therefore into that of the citizen. One can say, for example, that a thief, a murderer, a homosexual, or a bigamist not only injures economic and familial Societies, but also the State itself, such that one cannot be a thief or bigamist, and a citizen, at the same time. But in this case, the State will be a party and not a Third, and it will then no longer be a matter of penal *Droit*, since there will be no *Droit* at all, but only a non-juridical political or social action of the State. One often says that the State intervenes when there is a murder, for example, because it is injured itself, having lost a citizen. If this were the case, its intervention would have nothing juridical about it. In fact, there is (penal) **Droit** because the State intervenes as a *disinterested* third. Indeed, if the (common) murderer also eliminates a citizen, it is not as a citizen that he kills him, but as a member of economic (assassination for theft) or familial (crime of passion) Society, for example. If the State only considers this aspect of the action, it can be the Third. But if the murderer targets the citizen as citizen, as is the case with a political or "terrorist" murder, the State is necessarily a party, and there is no longer the application of (penal) **Droit**. Indeed, one has the feeling that in these cases the ordinary courts are incompetent and the penal Code inapplicable. There are also countries which do not allow the death penalty for common crimes, but which do apply it to political crimes. One can find extra-juridical reasons for the juridical activity of the State, just as one can say that someone becomes a judge in order to make money. But the Judge is not a judge to the extent that he makes money; he is only one to the extent that he makes money by applying the law, i.e., a certain ideal of Justice, to inter-actions in respect to which he is impartial and disinterested. And it is the same for the State. It may very well be possible that the State functions as judge in order to make domestic peace reign. What counts is that in doing so, it makes peace reign through the realization of a certain ideal of Justice. Being a human entity, moreover, the State is spontaneously inclined to serve as Judge or Arbiter; for, as I have tried to show, the "need" to realize Justice has its source in the anthropogenic act [353] itself, such that every man experiences it to the extent that he is human. Therefore, every State also acts as Judge for purely juridical motives—that is, as a result of its will to realize its ideal of Justice. And the activity of the State is only juridical to the extent that it is a function of this will to Justice. As I am only dealing with framing principles, I have not asked why the State accepts or not an individual or a Society as litigants, and why, if it does so, it applies to them one *Droit* rather than another. The choice of litigants is arbitrary (and it makes no sense to say that one has the **droit** to be a litigant, or that one has the **droit** to have a given *Droit* applied) and it can have extra-juridical motives. But if the State recognizes a person as its litigant, it only proceeds juridically toward him provided that it acts as a *disinterested* Third—that is, with the sole motive to apply to him the given ideal of Justice. Once the persons and interactions subject to law [*justiciables*] have been chosen, the content of *Droit* therefore results from the application of the ideal of Justice accepted by the State to these interactions between these persons. An example will show the possible variations. The State can include the status of familial Society, consisting of monogamous families, in its own political status, by declaring, for example, that a bigamist cannot be a citizen. If it acts against bigamy, it will then act according to a political rule, which will not be a *legal* rule, nor consequently a penal or civil legal rule. But the State can also "lose interest" in this status, in the sense that it accepts that a bigamist can be a citizen. At the same time it can make "its own" the status of the Society, in the sense that it recognizes that bigamy injures this

[353] Let us now examine the meaning of the distinction between civil *Droit* understood as "*private **Droit***" and "*public **Droit**,*" [354] which is supposed to include among other things penal or criminal *Droit*.

I have said and I will say again (cf. chapter 2, B) that the interactions between the State and its citizens have nothing juridical about them, seeing that the State cannot be a party and Third at the same time. Now it is necessarily a party here. Thus, there is no Third, nor consequently *Droit* in general.

Society as a whole. If it recognizes this Society as its litigant, it will intervene as a disinterested third in order to suppress bigamy. It will then act in conformity with a *legal* rule, namely *penal droit*. But if the State does not recognize the Society in question, it will "lose interest" in bigamy, in the sense that it will not intervene to suppress it. This will not be a crime, then, in the juridical sense of the word, and if the Society proscribes it, this proscription will have nothing juridical about it (the State being able, moreover, to oppose it). Now the State may take yet another attitude. It can accept bigamy as such (not believing that the Society of monogamous families should be maintained as such), but it may require that the two wives must be in agreement in order to have the same husband. In other words, the State will be interested not in the relation between the bigamous family and the Society of (monogamous) families, but in the relation of the members of the bigamous family. Or once again, the State will establish a status of familial Society according to which the families which make it up can be both monogamous and bigamous, provided that there is consent among the interested parties. In this case there will again be *legal* rules relative to bigamy, but it will be a matter of *civil* legal rules. Finally, it is possible that the State completely loses interest in the question and does not intervene, for example, even if the first wife objects to the second marriage of her husband. In this case the civil legal rule in question will no longer exist *in actuality*. But if the Society itself (of monogamous and bigamous families) applies this rule (without being able to do so in an "irresistible" way, it should be understood), the civil *Droit* relative to bigamy will exist, but only *in potentiality*. Now one cannot say that monogamous Society, for example, has the ***droit*** to be recognized as such by the State. But *if* it is recognized, it has the ***droit*** to monogamy, since the state-sanctioned Third [354] will intervene in this case in order to suppress bigamy (i.e., the negation of monogamy). Likewise, if the State recognizes a familial Society, it does not at all follow that the latter must be recognized by it as monogamous. It is possible, however, that the State gives a polygamous status to familial Society, while it believes that a monogamous status is "just." In this case one cannot say that Society has the ***droit*** to monogamy. There is, quite simply, a conflict between two *Droits*, the one monogamous and the other polygamous, of which neither has the ***droit*** to supplant the other. The Society may struggle in order to make the *Droit* that is appropriate to it accepted by the State, and that only exists in potentiality as long as the State does not make it its own. But this struggle for *Droit* itself has nothing juridical about it: it is a social or political struggle. Society has just as little ***droit*** to apply its virtual, monogamous *Droit* as the State has the ***droit*** to apply its actual, polygamous *Droit* to it. It is a simple question of *fact*. But whatever *droit* is applied, its application will always mean the application of a certain ideal of Justice. And the difference may come either from the fact that the Society is applying another ideal than the State, or from the fact that the same ideal is applied to different persons or interactions: for example, in one case to the family, in the other to the individual; or again, in one case to the simple fact of sexual relations between one man and two women, in the other to the mental attitudes of those who participate have in respect to this fact. (For example, one can condemn bigamy from the point of view of egalitarian Justice: if certain [persons] have two wives, others will have none at all. But one can justify it from the point of view of the Justice of equivalence: it is just for one who has succeeded in seducing two women to benefit from it, as it is just for one who has seduced no one at all to remain single.)

The State sets down its status (which implies that of its citizens) by a political act which has nothing juridical about it. Therefore, the Constitution as such (and in the broadest sense of the word, it also implies the notion of Administrative Apparatus) has nothing to do with any *Droit* whatsoever: from the fact of a Constitution, the citizens do not have any **droit** in respect to the State, just as it does not have any **droit** in respect to the citizens; their relations are purely *political,* and it is only in the *political* sense that they can be legal or illegal. Therefore, if the so-called public "*Droit*" (constitutional and administrative) sets down relations between citizens taken as citizens and the State as such, it is not a *Droit* at all—just as penal *Droit* would not be a *Droit* if it proscribed acts injuring the State itself as a State. Now we have seen that the latter *Droit* aims at interactions between sub-political Societies and their members, when the State can intervene by way of a Third. Thus interpreted, criminal *Droit* is therefore effectively a [355] *Droit.* And by interpreting public *Droit* (constitutional and administrative) along similar lines, one can equally consider that this is also a matter of *Droit.*

The State is unable to act itself. It acts in and by the persons of its Civil Servants (in the broadest sense of the word), who, by acting in the name of the State, act as citizens, [or] more especially, as Civil Servants. And as long as this is the case, there is nothing juridical in their acts. But a Civil Servant is still something more than a Civil Servant or citizen: he is an animal Homo sapiens, on the one hand, and a member of various sub- and trans-political Societies, on the other; and he can act as such while being a citizen and civil servant. In this case, one will say that he is acting as a "private person." By acting in this fashion, he can enter into conflict either with other individuals or with some Society. The State will then apply to him the ordinary criminal or civil *Droit*—that is, "private *Droit*." If, for example, a civil servant does not pay his private debt or steals from another individual, he will be judged not as a civil servant but like any other private person. But it is also possible that the civil servant acts as a private person while believing and giving the impression that he is acting as a civil servant—that is, in the name of the State. By so acting, if he enters into conflict with Societies or members of Societies, the State will be able to intervene by way of a Third, since it is a matter of an interaction between "private persons." There will then be *Droit.* But this will be a very special case, since one of the agents claims to act in the name of the State. Owing to the practical importance of these cases, they have been grouped together as a special *Droit.* And this *Droit* is precisely "public *Droit*," constitutional or administrative.

Therefore, public *Droit* is, if you will, a "*Droit* of imposture [*de l'imposture*]*.*" Of course, if someone commits wrongs by passing himself off as a civil servant when he is not, the State will apply to *this* impostor private *Droit* (civil or criminal, depending on the case). But if the offender is effectively a civil servant and gives the impression that he is acting as such (even possibly believing this himself), while in reality he is acting as a private person, i.e., not in the name of the State, but in his own name, then the State will apply to this "impostor" public *Droit* (constitutional or administrative, depending on the case). A prefect, for example, will act as such an "impostor" if he appoints someone to a position not because he meets the requirements set by the State, but because he is a member of the prefect's family, or because he [356] gains a personal economic benefit from this appointment ("bribery"). And it is public (administrative) *Droit* that will then be applied.

But how is it possible to know whether a civil servant is acting as a civil servant or an "impostor"? To act as a civil servant is to act in the name of the State; it is the State which is acting through the civil servant when he acts as a civil servant. Therefore, if the State repudiates the act of the civil servant, it is because he did not act in the name of State but as a "private person"—that is, as an "impostor." It is enough, therefore, for the State to repudiate its civil servant in order that it may apply to him a **Droit**, namely public *Droit;* for to repudiate the civil servant is to notice that he acted as a private person (toward other private persons), and to be able, therefore, to apply *Droit* by intervening by way of a Third. Now the State is able, as it were, to repudiate in advance its civil servants. It can stipulate the cases in which one can be certain that the civil servant has not acted in the name of the State, but as an "impostor." These are cases when the civil servant acts contrary to the Law (this Law setting down either the status of the State and its Administrative Apparatuses, or that of the civil servants, or finally, the functioning of the State, Administrative Apparatuses, and the civil servants.) This Law is set down in the administrative and constitutional "Code" (which can be "customary").[20] This "Code" therefore allows one to know when the State can intervene *as Third* in the event of actions of its civil servants—that is, when it can apply *Droit,* namely public *Droit.* In this sense, this "Code" is therefore part of this *Droit,* or is, if you will, this *Droit.*[21]

Therefore, public *Droit* itself contains the criterion of its own applicability. If the action of a civil servant is contrary to the rules of this *Droit,* the State repudiates him and intervenes as a disinterested Third—that is, [it] applies this public *Droit.* In other words, if a "private person" (which can also be a Society recognized by the State as a litigant) is injured by this action of the civil servant and "reacts" against it, the State will overcome the resistance of the civil servant. One can therefore say that the person in question had the **droit** to react against the action of the civil servant. And it is in this sense, but only in this sense, that one may say that there is a public **Droit,** that "private persons" have **droits** in respect to [357] "public persons"—not in respect to the State, of course, nor its Administrative Apparatuses and their Civil Servants acting as such, but in respect to Civil Servants who act as private persons, while believing and giving the impression that they are acting in the name of the State.

---

20. [Ed. What Kojève means here by "customary" is unwritten norms or conventions, which play a very large role in Anglo-Canadian administrative and constitutional law as it applies to the functioning of the state (the role of the Crown, the Prime Minister, and so on).]

21. Therefore, it is not a matter of dispensing with public *Droit.* It can be left intact, but it must be interpreted differently than one is accustomed. But the new interpretation may result in an alteration of the very content of public *Droit,* notably the form in which its legal rules are expressed.

Generally speaking, it is enough to annul the illicit act—that is, the action of the "impostor" civil servant. But one may also make him personally liable in respect to the injured person. And this will also be (public) *Droit*. By contrast, when the State wants to punish the civil servant because he infringed upon the interests of the State by acting in that fashion, this will no longer have anything juridical about it, the State then being a party and no longer a Third. Likewise, the injured person does not have any **droit** to ask for compensation from the State, for here as well the State is a party.[22] Of course, the State may grant it (and even without repudiating the civil servant), but this act will have nothing juridical about it. It will only be juridical to the extent that it allows one to ascertain if the civil servant in charge of enforcement—of compensating the interested party—acts as a civil servant or as an "impostor." The interested party does not have a **droit** to indemnity from the fact of being injured; but he has a **droit** to the indemnity *granted* by the State (the act itself of granting having nothing juridical about it).

Be that as it may, public **Droit** only exists when a civil servant acts as an "impostor"—that is, as a "private person" and not a citizen. If this civil servant acts in the name of the State, it is the State which acts through him, and the action therefore has nothing juridical about it, since in this case there is no longer a Third. Now by acting as a civil servant in the name of the State, the civil servant is not acting as a "private person" but as a citizen. And to act as a citizen is to be related to other citizens taken as such, and not as "private persons" (as animals or members of some Society other than the State). The civil servant who acts as citizen is therefore either in relation with the State or it is the State that is in a relation—through him—with the citizens as such. Now in neither of these cases is there any *Droit* whatsoever. Of course, by acting as a citizen the civil servant can injure the State, or indeed, enter into a conscious and voluntary conflict with it. There will then be a *political* conflict or crime, which will have nothing juridical about it; for the State will then react as a party, and not as a Third. This is the case, for example, if the prefect makes illegal appointments in order to prepare a *coup d'État*. As soon as the civil servant acts as a citizen, or—which is the same thing—as soon as he is related in his acts to citizens taken as citizens, the State will always be [358] a *party:* either the State will develop solidarity with the civil servant, will itself act through him, or it will enter into a (political) conflict with this civil servant. There will then be no Third—that is, no *Droit,* and in particular no public *Droit.*[23]

---

22. [Ed. The situation here described by Kojève has given rise to institutions such as that of the ombudsperson, which are intended as disinterested thirds mediating between the individual and the state. While in theory these thirds are impartial and disinterested, they have no means available to overcome the resistance of the state to their judgment.]

23. If someone enters into conflict with the State while acting as citizen, i.e., while being related either to the State as such or to citizens as citizens, he always acts politically and more or less as a revolutionary. And this is precisely why his action is *politically* criminal, but not in the *juridical* sense of the term. Indeed, the revolutionary wants to transform the *Droit* in force by his action, at least in the sense that the new *Droit* justifies his revolutionary act. It

For there to be public *Droit,* the civil servant must therefore act as a "private person"; thus (which is the same thing), he must be related in his act to a "private person" as such. It is therefore a matter of an interaction between "private persons," and one thus reverts to the case of "private *Droit,*" except that one of the agents is an "impostor" believing or claiming to act in the name of the State. Consequently, one will be able to distinguish within public *Droit* the same two cases that we have distinguished in private *Droit.* The interaction between the civil servant (acting as a member of a Society) and his "victim" (also taken as a member of the same Society) may not injure the Society (to which both belong). If the State recognizes the members of this Society as its litigants, even if the Society itself is unaffected, i.e., if the State is directly related to them in its juridical aspect, it will apply *civil Droit*—that is, in this case, *public* civil *Droit.* But the interaction being considered may also be an interaction between the civil servant and the Society in question taken as a whole, which will be injured as such. If the State recognizes him [359] as its litigant, it will then apply *penal Droit*—that is, in this case, *public* penal *Droit.* In the first case, the State will only intervene if it is "provoked" by the person who claims to have been injured by the act of the civil servant (in our example, by a candidate for a position who would have, or, at the very least, might have been appointed instead of the one who was illegally appointed). And there will be no penalty, the intervention of the State being limited practically to annulling the act of the civil servant and reestablishing the *status quo ante.* In the second case, the State will intervene "spontaneously" (or again, in response to a "report" made by some member of the injured Society, even if he is not directly affected by the incriminating act). And in principle there could be a punishment inflicted on the guilty, in addition to measures which must satisfy the one who has been directly injured.[24]

The division between public and private *Droit,* therefore, intersects with that between civil and criminal *Droit.* One can either divide (actual) *Droit* into

---

is therefore a matter of a conflict between two *Droits* (or two conceptions of Justice in its concrete application). Now, as there is not a third *Droit* that encompasses them both, this conflict of *Droits* itself has nothing juridical about it. The revolutionary act that replaces one *Droit* with another is political or social, but not juridical: juridically speaking, it is neither illegal nor legal (while being *politically* illegal). The act of a common criminal, by contrast, leaves the *Droit* in force intact, which condemns this act. It therefore remains inside the given *Droit,* and this is why his act is criminal in the juridical sense of the word. The "successful" revolutionary is neither politically nor juridically a criminal. If he "fails," he is a political criminal, but he has not committed a crime in the juridical sense of the word. The common wrongdoer, by contrast, is always juridically a criminal, even he "succeeds"; for to "succeed" only means for him "to avoid being apprehended." Now the criminal is a criminal even if the law [*la justice*] has not been able to catch him, and even if—by chance—the law is unaware of the very crime.

24. Practically speaking, these cases are rare; for it is difficult to act against the status of a Society recognized by the State while believing that one is acting in the name of the State or giving the impression that one is. This is why public *Droit* is, generally speaking, a *civil Droit,* and not *penal.*

private *Droit* and public *Droit,* and subdivide *each* of these *Droits* into criminal and civil, or first divide them into civil and criminal, and then subdivide
each of these divisions into public *Droit* and private *Droit.* And since public
Droit only deals with very special cases, namely those when one of the agents
interacting is a civil servant—an "impostor"—it would be more logical to
accept this second division. But the practical importance of public *Droit* speaks
in favor of the first. Be that as it may, one cannot group within public *Droit*
constitutional and administrative *Droit* (i.e., "public *Droit*" in the narrow
sense) and criminal *Droit,* while contrasting to it civil *Droit* as private *Droit.*

Let us finally see how the preceding analysis can be applied to **Droit** *in
potentiality,* and in particular to the *Droit* called "public international *Droit.*"

Generally speaking, there is *penal Droit* when a Society S2, which encompasses another Society S1, intervenes in the capacity of Third in the interactions between S1 and some one of the parts of S1. Now it is very possible that
the intervention of S2 is not "irresistible" (if, for example, S2 is also a sub-political Society, the *Droit* of which the State has not made its own). There can thus
be a penal *Droit* in potentiality. By contrast, when a Society intervenes [360]
by way of a Third in interactions between its parts, there will be *civil Droit.* And
it is obvious that a *civil Droit* can only really exist in potentiality if the intervention of the Society in question is not "irresistible."

Droit in potentiality, therefore, can be both civil, and penal or criminal. But
concerning "public international *Droit,*" it is quite obviously a civil *Droit,* and
not penal; for the interactions between autonomous States can only be
"judged" by the "Society" formed by these States—that is, by the "League of
Nations" which implies—in principle—all of humanity. Therefore, if the
action of a State (in its interaction with another State) injures the entire Society, and if this Society reacts, it will be a party and there will be no Third possible. In other words, there will no longer be *Droit;* the reaction will not be
juridical. And this is why the intervention of the Third can only be "provoked"
here. And this is also why there is no punishment or penalty here exceeding the
mere compensation of the State injured in the interaction submitted to the
judgment of the Third.

On the other hand, it is clear that *Droit* in potentiality can itself also be either
private or public (by taking this term in a broad sense). It will be *public* if a
Society intervenes in the capacity of Third in the event of an interaction
between two of its parts, one of them being qualified to act in the name of the
Society as such and claiming to do so, but acting in fact as a "private person."
In all other cases, *Droit* in potentiality will be *private.* And it is easy to see that
the two *Droits* in potentiality can be both civil and penal.

As for "public international *Droit,*" it is in fact much more a private *Droit*
than a public *Droit.* Of course, a State often claims to act in the name of humanity or the "League of Nations," while only pursuing in fact its "private" interests. If humanity had thus given it a mandate to act in its name, it would be a
case of public *Droit* (civil, moreover, and in potentiality). But in fact these man-
dates do not exist. The State which claims to act according to such a mandate is

therefore similar to the impostor who passes himself off as a civil servant while not be so in reality. Now this is a case of private *Droit*. And it is clearly a matter of this same private *Droit* when States openly act to defend their "national" interests—that is, particular or private. In fact, to the extent that "public international *Droit*" is a *Droit*, it is a matter of "*private* international *Droit* (civil, and only existing in potentiality). It would therefore be better to call it simply "international *Droit*" (all the more so because [361] everyone agrees that the *Droit* that is called "private international *Droit*" is in fact a *domestic* and not an international *Droit*—that is, existing in actuality and not in potentiality).

§ 51

We have seen that the distinction of legal rules according to the mode of the Third's intervention, which can be either "provoked" or "spontaneous," in the end boils down to a distinction according to the *persons* interacting—that is, to a distinction between the litigants. Therefore, it depends upon the persons in question whether *Droit* is "civil," or "criminal" or "penal": the intervention of the Third is the same in both cases. Likewise, the distinction between "private *Droit*" and "public *Droit*" is also due to a distinction of persons, or—if you will—a difference in the nature of the interactions at issue. But here as well the intervention of the Third remains the same in both cases. And it is obvious that it will be the same for all the subdivisions that will ultimately be introduced into the main divisions already established.

Now we know that the essence of the juridical phenomenon is implied in the Third and in his intervention in certain interactions between given persons. The specifically juridical distinctions of *Droit*, therefore, can only be of two kinds. The one is due to differences between the ideas of Justice that the Third applies in and by his intervention, and which determine the latter. This is the distinction between the various legal Systems or various "positive *Droits*." The other distinction, which occurs inside each given System, is determined by the fact that in certain cases the intervention of the Third is irresistible, and in the others not (the Third applying in both cases one and the same idea of Justice). It is in this way that all legal Systems imply a "*Droit* in actuality" and a "*Droit* in potentiality." All the other distinctions within a given System have nothing more to do with the intervention of the Third, which always remains the same (as well as the idea of Justice, which determines this intervention, remains the same). The legal rules only differ, therefore, as a result of the *persons* and *interactions* at issue. The Third can apply in the same manner one and the same idea of Justice to different persons and interactions. If the persons at issue remain the same, the legal rules are going to be distinguished from one another [362] depending upon the difference that the interactions have in mind. And if the intended interaction remains the same, it is the difference between the persons at issue that will vary the legal rules.

If you will, these are still *juridical* distinctions, since *Droit* is the application of an idea of Justice to given interactions between certain human persons, these interactions in themselves having nothing juridical about them. But these distinctions do not come from the very idea of Justice, in which the juridical essence of the phenomenon of "*Droit*" is situated. They come exclusively from the non-juridical element of this phenomenon. They are determined by the social and political reality to which the given idea of Justice is applied in and by *Droit*—or better still, as *Droit,* the "positive *Droit*" in question or the "legal System" being understood. It is this reality that will determine the internal structure of the System, to the extent, it should be understood, that this reality penetrates into the System—that is, to the extent the given idea of Justice is applied to it.

Let us see, therefore, what is given to the structure of the System by these differences between *persons* and *interactions* that the legal rules which constitute this System have in mind.

We have seen that if one of the two persons interacting is part of a whole, this whole being the other person, the corresponding legal rule is part of criminal *Droit*. By contrast, if the two persons are parts of one and the same whole, the legal rule belongs to civil *Droit*.[25] Now this distinction, based upon the "formal" or "quantitative" difference [363] of the persons at issue, is itself a "formal" difference having to do with the form of the legal rules and not their content. But the persons also differ from one another "materially" or "qualitatively," and this difference yields a distinction of rules according to their content. Thus, we have seen that one can group together all the rules that are applied to interactions when one of the two agents is an civil servant-"impostor" in the sense indicated above. But this is a very special qualitative difference. Now there are differences that are a lot more general, which are nevertheless qualitative and not formal.[26]

---

25. There is no interaction between parts belonging to different totalities. If A, in his interaction with B, is related to B as a member of economic or familial Society, for example, he himself acts as a member of economic or familial Society. Likewise, for example, economic Society can enter into interaction with the Society called familial only if both are parts of a more immense Society that encompasses them. And then they will act as members of this comprehensive [*intégrale*] Society, and not as familial Society and economic Society. Practically speaking, the comprehensive Society is the State. As well, the State becomes indispensable as soon as there is a necessity for interaction between two "qualitatively" distinct Societies: familial Society and economic Society, for example. A familial Society that is self-sufficient can do without the State and does not need to be state-sanctioned. But if its members are at the same time members of an economic Society, for example, interactions between these two Societies and between their members become inevitable. It is then that the State appears. A member of familial Society enters into interaction with a member of economic Society to the extent that both are citizens; and the two Societies enter into interaction to the extent that both are sub-political Societies. [363] At that point, the *Droit* of familial Society and the *Droit* of economic Society only exist in actuality to the extent they are applied by the State. Actual state-sanctioned *Droit* therefore has two parts: family *Droit* and economic *Droit*. It is the juridical coherence of these two parts that is the juridical basis for interactions between the two Societies and between their respective members.

26. One could say, moreover, that the civil servant-"impostor" is a "part" who is supposed to be a "whole" (or to act in the name of this whole, as this whole), but who in fact remains

The persons (in the interaction in which the Third intervenes) can be distinguished depending upon the Societies to which they belong or that the Societies are. And this distinction, clearly "qualitative" and nevertheless very general, will yield the main "qualitative" or "material" categories of the legal System. In each of these categories, the persons aimed at by the legal rules will belong to one and the same Society, the latter itself being, moreover, a person to which the legal rules of the category in question can be applied.

I do not have to enumerate here all the Societies capable of being thought of as juridical persons, or at the very least as including such persons in the capacity of members. In principle, there is not any limitation here. In order for some Society or its members to be juridical persons, it is necessary and sufficient that the State intervenes by way of the Third in the interaction when the Society in question or its member is one of the agents. And this holds both for sub-political Societies and for trans-political Societies. However, in the latter case, the State will only intervene to the extent that the Society and its members find themselves on national territory, or are [364] subject in one way or another to the power of the State.[27]

I have also not asked which Societies at a given moment coexist with a State, either remaining within it or extending beyond it. The totality of these Societies constitute what one might call "civil Society" (the *bürgerliche Gesellschaft* of the old German writers). And this civil Society inserts itself between the State and the individual, taken as the animal Homo sapiens; for man is not only this animal, and he is not only a citizen. He is still a member of various sub- and trans-political Societies, which constitute as a whole "civil Society."

Now all these various Societies included in civil Society, as well as the members of these Societies, are not recognized by the State as juridical persons. Without asking why a State at a given moment recognizes such a Society rather than another, I will limit myself to pointing out that at the present moment States (let us say "civilized" States) only recognize in practice as subjects of *droit* two, or possibly three, Societies that are part of civil Society. First, there is familial Society; then economic Society; and finally, Society simply, Society properly so-called, [or] "social Society," so to speak, that for lack of a better term, I will call "worldly [*mondaine*] Society." (But there was a time when all States recognized as well religious Society as a juridical person of state-sanctioned *Droit*; and certain States still do so.)

---

a "part" (or acts in the name of a part, or as this part). Seen from this angle, the difference between public *Droit* and private *Droit* (where the "part" is supposed to be a "part" and effectively acts as such) would also be "formal" and not "qualitative."

27. It is in this way, for example, that "private international *Droit*" is applied to members of trans-political economic Society; however, in this case, the national State does not apply the (international) *Droit* of this Society itself, for this *Droit* does not exist. It applies the various national *Droits* relative to this Society, the latter being divided between various States, each of which applies to the part of the Society that is subject to it the appropriate *Droit*. Thus, State A can apply the law of State B, if the litigant—a member of the trans-political economic Society—is a citizen of B. This is why questions of nationality, which determine the application of such a *Droit* or another, are part of "private international *Droit*."

Familial Society is made up of the totality of families. It is thus the family, and not the individual, that is its specific unit. The individual is in direct relation with his own family, and it is only through the intermediation of the latter that he is in relation with familial Society as such. As for the State, it can recognize as juridical persons either familial Society itself alone; or the latter and its constitutive units, i.e., families; [365] or finally, both of these, and in addition every member of every family taken individually (but it should be understood [that every individual is taken] as a member of familial Society, and not as an animal, citizen, or member of some other Society). It is the last possibility that is realized in the modern State. The State can therefore intervene in the capacity of Third in the following familial interactions: a) between familial Society and the families; b) between familial Society and the members of families; c) between the families; d) between the families and their members; e) between the members of the families; and, of course, f) between familial Society and other Societies. (As for interactions between familial Society and the State, they have nothing juridical about them.)

Economic Society has for its specific unit the individual (taken as Homo economicus). But these individuals are able to form various economic associations ("joint stock Companies," for example, or others). And the Society can be interacting both with individuals and with these associations. Now, here as well, the State is in the presence of various juridical possibilities: for example, to recognize as juridical persons certain associations (and not others), without recognizing their members as such, and so on. But the modern State here takes the same attitude as in the case of familial Society. It recognizes as litigants both the Society and its members, both various associations and their members.

As for "worldly Society," it is more difficult to define and analyze. It is constituted by social classes and by the individuals occupying a certain place in the social hierarchy. It will be enough to say here that this Society includes all that is social, while being neither familial nor economic (which is, certainly, too broad a definition); for the State in general, and above all the modern State, intervenes but rarely by way of a Third in interactions that are neither familial nor economic. Practically speaking, then, there is no point in subdividing legal rules that have to do with these interactions by distinguishing various types of persons, i.e., non-economic or non-familial Societies, all the more so because traditional Codes do not even group these rules in a category aligned with categories that contain rules relating to the interactions of economic and familial persons.[28]

---

28. However, these rules do exist: for example, the rules of civil *Droit* relative to non-profit "Associations"; or the rules of criminal *Droit* [366] relative to defamation (which are a residue of former rules relative to the protection of the "social rank" of the nobility, for example), and so on. One could also place here rules that are relative to intellectual and artistic property (banning plagiarism, for example) to the extent that this is not an economic value, or is not supposed to be. Rules of this group are often classified among the rules of public *Droit* (the "*droits* of personality"). Codes also do not distinguish rules relative to interactions in which figure the animal Homo sapiens as such (attacks and injuries, murder, and so on). But the animal serves as a common support for all juridical persons, so that

[366] Be that as it may, the classic division of *droits* into "*droits* of inheritance [*patrimoine*]" and "familial *droits*" rests upon a qualitative difference between the persons who are the subjects of these *droits*—that is, the persons in the event of interactions in which the State intervenes by way of a Third. This distinction between "familial *Droit* and "economic *Droit*" generally occurs within civil *Droit*.[29] But it can be made as well within penal *Droit*. Thus, for example, the penal rules relative to bigamy, adultery, incest, homosexuality, and so on, will be classed in familial criminal *Droit*, while the rules relative to theft, for example, will be part of economic criminal *Droit*. Finally, this very distinction could equally be made in public *Droit*, although in practice the category of public familial *Droit* (civil or criminal) will remain blank. And it is self-evident that all these distinctions can be found in the sphere of *Droit* in potentiality.

I will not press any further the qualitative analysis of the different juridical persons [that are] possible. And I will not deal with either the distinctions between legal rules that come from differences between interactions in which one and the same person is able to participate. I will limit myself to repeating that all the subdivisions of the legal System are a function of the differences between the persons at issue and the interactions in question. But I would like to say a few words concerning a "formal" subdivision of the legal System, which comes from the distinction between the "person" and the "interaction" as such.

To the notion of "person" there corresponds the juridical notion of "*status*," to which one can contrast the notion of "*function*," which would then correspond to the "interactions" between the persons. There would thus be within the System a "***Droit** of status*" and a "***Droit** of function.*"[30]

[367] The person is juridically defined by his juridical status, which is nothing other than the totality of his subjective rights.[31] Now these *droits* can only

---

in injuring the animal one injures them all (notably when the injury leads to death). One can therefore place these rules in any category whatsoever. But a rational System should perhaps group them together and separately.

29. Cf., for example, Capitant, *Introduction*, 5th ed., 107–9ff.

30. [Ed. The difference between "status" and "function" will probably be familiar to those acquainted with Max Weber's discussion of law in *Wirtschaft und Gesellschaft* (which Kojève himself might have had in mind). Traditionally, law expressed the fixed status of persons within a society, which was a set of legal entitlements and duties attached to one's social position, or to an office or institution—e.g., lord, serf, professor, son, lawyer, and of course, a citizen. Weber argued, however, that in the West, law was losing this status-based character and becoming functionally or transactionally oriented, providing a basis for the facilitation of freely willed, mainly economic interactions between individuals. Legal entitlements were increasingly becoming based upon contract rather than status. In general, we have translated *statut* as "status," *statuts* as "statuses," and *fonction* as "function." In French, however, *statut* is also the word for "statute," and it can also signify the entire constitution, or the whole of public law that ultimately defines the status of the citizen and the state.]

31. [Ed. In the original, the English word "rights" follows the French phrase *droits subjectifs* in parentheses.]

be defined in relation to interactions, when the person behaves, i.e., "functions," in a certain manner. "Function" and "status" are thus, strictly speaking, inseparable. But it is nevertheless useful to distinguish them; for if status only makes sense in relation to function, and if it is only actualized in and by the latter, it nevertheless has a juridical existence even when the function has not taken place in fact: it is enough that it be possible. In this sense one can say that the person has *droits* "independently" of his interactions with other persons—meaning, he has them even if the (possible) interactions have not taken place in fact. On the other hand, there are these interactions themselves, when two *statuses* necessarily figure at the same time, and when they are considered in their mutual relations. Thus, for example, the juridical possibility for A to conclude a contract of a given type is part of his "status" ("juridical capacity"), while the fact of concluding a contract of this type with B and not performing it, for example, is part of A's (and B's) "function." Now an act can be legal or illegal solely because it is conforming or not to the status of the one who performs it. Thus, the contract concluded with an "incompetent [person]" is void even if it is correctly performed. But it is also possible that an act that is legal in the sense of conforming to the status [of the agent] is illegal as an act—for example, if a legal contract is not performed. Therefore, the illegality here no longer comes from the status of the interested parties, but from their functioning, i.e., their interactions.

Now this formal distinction between the *Droit* of status and *Droit* of function yields an interesting division of economic *Droit;* for status implies here the notion of property. Indeed, the owner is owner of the thing even if he does not "function," even if he does not enter into interactions with others: it is enough that these interactions be possible. Therefore, property is clearly a "status" in the indicated sense of the word. An obligation,[32] by contrast, and in particular a contract, is nothing other than effective interactions—that is, "functions."[33] The classic division [368] of *Droits* of inheritance into "real [*réels*] *Droits*" and "*Droits* arising from monetary obligation [*"Droits de créance" (obligation)*]"[34] is therefore practically equivalent to a distinction—in this sphere—between the *Droit* of status and the *Droit* of function. (However, the first also implies the "*Droit* of persons," to the extent that it treats the person as a member of economic Society, by setting down his "capacity," for example.)

---

32. [Ed. Obligations denotes a field in civil law that encompasses contractual and (unilateral promissory) quasi-contractual duties. It also includes both delict (which roughly corresponds to the Anglo-American common law field of tort) and quasi-delict (which is roughly equivalent to nonvoluntary tortious wrongs such as negligence and strict products liability).]

33. It should be understood that the *ability* [**faculté**] to conclude contracts is part of status. But practically speaking, it is a matter of "juridical capacity" in general, and not of the "capacity" to conclude such and such a contract. The *Droit* of status will therefore be subdivided into a *Droit* of capacity and a *Droit* of property. But the *Droit* of contract or of obligations will be a *Droit* of function.

34. [Ed. The distinction here is between entitlement in inheritance to specific real property as opposed to a claim on the monetary value of the estate.]

An analogous distinction could also be made in familial *Droit* (as well as in "social *Droit*"—which corresponds to "worldly Society," if one distinguishes it from the other two). And it holds not only for private *Droit,* but also for public *Droit.* Thus, if the distinction between constitutional *Droit* and administrative *Droit* has a precise meaning, it can only be so if the former is contrasted to the latter as a *Droit* of status to a *Droit* of function. "Constitutional *Droit*" will then imply the statuses not only of the State properly so-called, but also of Administrative Apparatuses and Citizens as such. By contrast, administrative *Droit* will be related to the "functioning" of the State *stricto sensu,* as well as of Administrative Apparatuses and Citizens.

On the other hand, the distinction in question is not limited to civil *Droit.* It can also be made within penal or criminal *Droit;* for the action of an individual (or, in general, of a part of a Society) can injure either the status of the corresponding Society taken as a whole, or its legitimate functioning—just as a "civil" action can be incompatible either with the status of the agent or with the legitimate functioning of the agents interacting.

Finally, it is self-evident that the distinction between *Droit* of status and *Droit* of function remains valid for *Droit* in potentiality.

§ 52

To classify juridical phenomena is ultimately to classify legal rules, i.e., to subdivide the legal System formed by the totality of these rules; for a human phenomenon is only juridical if it implies the intervention of an impartial and disinterested Third, who intervenes in a social interaction in order to make it conform to a certain ideal of Justice. In all juridical phenomena, therefore, the Third applies an idea or a principle of Justice to a given social interaction. Now this application can always be expressed in the form of a legal rule. And one can [369] say that the intervention of the Third, i.e., the juridical phenomenon itself, is determined by this legal rule. The Third only acts in order to make the given reality conform to a legal rule, and the juridical phenomenon is nothing other than the Third bringing the rule and the reality into correspondence.

Now we have seen that legal rules can be classified according to various principles and that these various classifications intersect with one another. One does not therefore arrive at a univocal rational structure for the legal System. Thus, for example, one can *begin* by distinguishing a *Droit* in actuality from a *Droit* in potentiality, and then introduce into these two main categories subdivisions (which will be, moreover, the same for both *Droits*). But one can also first subdivide *Droit* as such, with asking the question of its existence, and subdivide each of the *latter* categories thus obtained in two parts, the one including rules existing in actuality, the other those that only exist in potentiality. And the same goes for the other subdivisions that we have discussed in the proceeding sections. One can determine as one wants the *order* of the divisions into penal and civil *Droit,* into public and private *Droit,* into familial, social, and economic *Droit,* and so on, and into *Droit* of status and *Droit* of function. And it is impossible to choose *a priori* between these various possibilities of classification.

Truth to tell, it is impossible to establish a rational classification without taking into account the *content* of the rules to be classified, which is determined by the concrete interactions to which these rules are supposed to be applied. Now these interactions are extra-juridical, [i.e.,] social or political, givens. They are fixed in their nature and relative importance by the general historical state of the society in which they take place. Consequently, the rational structure of the legal System must vary according to epochs and places; for it must take into account the fact that the importance of the rules contained in a given category is not everywhere and always the same. Thus, for example, a given historical *Droit* can be almost exclusively a *Droit* of status, while in another the rules relative to statuses may have about the same importance (qualitatively and quantitatively) as those relative to function. And the same thing can go for the relative importance of civil and criminal rules, and so on. Of course, there is a privileged rational division of the System, which can be called "rational" in the proper sense of the word. This is the division imposed by the content [370] of the absolute Legal System—that is, universal and definitive. But this *Droit* of the universal and homogenous State at the end of history does not yet exist. We are therefore unable to know what the rational structure of its System will be.

In classifying juridical phenomena, i.e., by subdividing the legal System, it must be adapted to the requirements of the *Droit* that one has in mind. One will classify a primitive or archaic *Droit* differently than a modern *Droit,* for example. And the classification that I am proposing here only has in mind the modern *Droit* of western States.

This classification does not, in fact, differ very much from the traditional and today generally accepted divisions in the juridical codes—hardly surprising, moreover, since my classification wants to take into account the concrete content of *Droit,* just as the traditional classification does. But it nevertheless departs from it; for the current classification draws a lot of inspiration from considerations [*exigences*] of utility, of legal practice, while my classification does not take this into account at all, only being concerned with the problem logically. The Code brings together above all everything that the judge or lawyer would like to see grouped together. As for me, I would only want to group together what is logically similar. This is why it is not at all a matter of wanting to introduce the proposed classification into the codes. Moreover, I will limit myself to indicating the main categories, without filling them with a concrete content. I will thus leave to one side all the thorny questions concerning the divvying up of the various, given legal rules between the indicated categories of the System. I will only say that this question is very important; for the place that one assigns to a rule in the System should determine the manner in which this rule is formulated, interpreted, and applied.

This being said, here is what I propose as the

Structure of the Legal System:

"Positive *Droit*," i.e., the totality of legal rules in and by which one applies a certain ideal of Justice to a given whole of social interactions, is first divided into a

Droit *in potentiality* and a **Droit** *in actuality,*

the latter being state-sanctioned *Droit,* realized by a Third who is an agent of the State or its civil servant.

Droit in potentiality will have the same structure as *Droit* in actuality, which will be subdivided as follows:

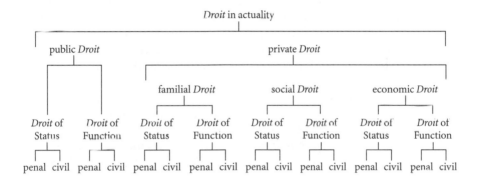

[371] One could have subdivided public *Droit* as one subdivided private *Droit*—that is, also to introduce there a distinction between rules with a familial, social, and economic content. But this is of little interest, seeing that almost all of the Legal rules will have an economic content. Furthermore, this *Droit* has a special character. It has above all as its purpose to set down in advance the cases when the civil servant (whoever that may be) does not act in the name of the State. And to do so, this *Droit* sets down the fundamental character of the status and functioning of the State (in the broad sense) as well as that of the Citizen. It should be understood that this "status" of the State and the Citizen has nothing juridical about it in itself. It has a juridical value and intervenes into public **Droit** only to the extent that the civil servant (who the State repudiates) enters into interaction with private persons, who belong to familial, "worldly," economic, and so on, Societies. One could therefore classify the rules of public *Droit* according to these Societies. But, in fact, it is not the private person as agent of the interaction who counts here, but the (repudiated) civil servant as agent. His "status" therefore matters more than that of the private agent. Now this "status" is set down by the "status" of the State and the

Citizen. It is therefore better to classify the rules of public *Droit* by relating them to the State, without taking account of those distinctions brought about by the interaction of the civil servant with various categories of private persons. It is in this way that this *Droit* will not have subdivisions of the "first order," contrary to private *Droit*. And this is why it is better to put it in line with the latter, instead of first dividing *Droit* into familial, and so on, and then subdividing every division (at whatever level) into "public" and "private." As for the division of public *Droit* into *Droit* of status and *Droit* of function, it corresponds *grosso modo* to the distinction between constitutional *Droit* and administrative *Droit*. Procedural *Droit*, [372] which according to everyone is part of public *Droit* (to the extent that it allows one to know when the Third does not act as an agent of the State, which takes place precisely when the Third does not conform to procedural *Droit*) should itself also be divided into *Droit* of status and *Droit* of function, the one having to do with the structure of the judicial apparatus, the other with its functioning.

In the sphere of private *Droit* (which also includes "private international *Droit*"), familial *Droit* and social *Droit* roughly correspond to the "*Droit* of persons" in our codes, while economic *Droit* corresponds to the "*Droit* of inheritance." Inside economic *Droit*, the *Droit* of status deals above all with "real *Droits*"—that is, first and foremost with Property. As for the *Droit* of function, it here corresponds *grosso modo* to the traditional "*Droit* of obligations," thus including the *Droit* of contracts.

I made the distinction between penal (or criminal) *Droit* and civil *Droit* as the *final* main division of the System, because from the strictly juridical point of view this distinction has only a minor [*faible*] importance. As well, the limits between these two *Droits* have varied a lot according to places and epochs. But it is self-evident that judicial *practice* requires a clear-cut distinction between the civil *Code* and the penal *Code*. By contrast, nothing seems to justify the joining of penal *Droit* to public *Droit*, in contrast to civil *Droit*, which is supposed to coincide with private *Droit*.

Chapter 2

Basic Study of Some Types
of Juridical Phenomena

§ 53

[373] THIS CHAPTER IS CONCERNED with analyzing some fundamental types of juridical phenomena. A complete Phenomenology of *Droit* would have to contain an analysis of all the possible juridical types, and this from the point of view of all the possible ideas of Justice. But there is no question of doing this here.

My exposition will be, on the one hand, fragmentary; for I will only discuss the questions upon which I believe I have something new to say. On the other hand, the exposition will be very basic. And at any rate, it will not concern concrete juridical phenomena, having a determined content. Thus, for example, I will not analyze such and such penal *Droit*, but penal *Droit* as such: it will be a matter of seeing what all criminal *Droits* have in common, whatever they may be, and what distinguishes them from all other juridical forms.

In these conditions, the order of the exposition is of little importance. Here is what I have adopted.

I will first speak about "public international *Droit*" and its relations with domestic *Droit,* as well as the fact that there are several coexisting domestic *Droits* (A). Then I will study the main divisions of domestic *Droit*. I will begin with "public *Droit*" in the narrow sense of the word, i.e., "constitutional *Droit*" and "administrative *Droit*," and I will say a few words about "procedural *Droit*" (B). Then I will speak about "penal *Droit*" and the notion of punishment (C). And I will conclude with a study of "private *Droit*" in its two principal branches, which are the "private *Droit* of [374] familial Society" (D, a) and the "private *Droit* of economic Society" (D, b). It is in speaking about the latter that I will analyze the juridical notions of property and obligation (first and foremost of contract).

A. International *Droit,* Domestic *Droit,*
and the Plurality of National Juridical Systems

§ 54

For "public international *Droit*" to be a *Droit,* our definition must be capable of being applied to it. In other words, there must be, on the one hand, an interaction between two human beings or two "persons"; on the other hand, there must be an intervention of an "impartial and disinterested third," annulling B's reaction to A's action. It is in this case only that one will be able to say that A had the **droit** to act as he did.

In the case in question, the two persons interacting are sovereign States— that is, "collective moral persons." And nothing prevents one from likening the State to an individual human agent [*agissant*]. From this point of view, there- fore, the idea of a public international *Droit* is not at all absurd. State A can act and State B can react exactly as individuals act and react in social inter-actions. But the person of the Third is here less well defined. Should this Third also be a sovereign State, or can it be an individual or some collectivity? And, in this case, what are its relations to the litigant States? Up to the present day, the Third in public international *Droit* has always been a mere Arbiter, chosen *ad hoc*, for a given arbitration. This was often a god (an "oracle"); in the Middle Ages, there were papal arbitrations; [and] it was generally a sovereign, i.e., a State, which arbitrated cases of international *Droit*. But private persons have written treatises on international *Droit;* and there is a juridical "world opin- ion," which is still something different from the points of view of different States. And for the future, either a council [*aréopage*] on which States them- selves would sit, or an inter-state tribunal made up of "private" judges, have been proposed. In short, it is not very [375] clear who the Third of interna- tional *Droit* would be, the day that this *Droit* would be actualized, the Third becoming a well defined and permanent institution.

It is often said that in relation to international *Droit*, the situation is analo- gous to that which must have prevailed at the dawn of history relative to *Droit* in general, to the juridical ordering of interactions between individuals. There as well it must have been a matter of arbitrations without genuine sanctions and without a permanent Third. And this is certainly true to a certain extent: actual sovereign States are comparable to individuals who are not yet citizens of a juridically organized State. But the analogy, however, is only correct to a certain extent. Pre-political man could have been totally unaware of *Droit*, and *Droit* would have created itself in and by the first interactions arbitrated by the Third. A state, by contrast, cannot exist as a State without realizing in its bosom a certain juridical organization. It is therefore necessarily in possession not only of a certain ideal of Justice, but also of a certain legal system, which applies this ideal to intra-state social interactions. Dealing with individuals-States, international *Droit* therefore deals with a preexisting (domestic) *Droit* domi- nated by a given ideal of Justice. The international *Droit* which creates itself must therefore be in accord with this ideal. This can be nothing other than an extension of (domestic) *Droit* to interactions between States, which governs social interactions inside the States in question. The Third, without whom there would be no *Droit* in general and who creates international *Droit*, does not then make it up from scratch. He starts from a juridical given, which is domestic *Droit*.

It is therefore necessary to distinguish two points of view when one studies international *Droit*. On the one hand, one must ask how this *Droit* creates itself starting from non-juridical interactions between sovereign States: one must see how and why the simple *fact* of acting in a certain way becomes for the State a **droit** to act in that way (meaning, in respect to another State). On the other hand, one must ask how and why given principles of domestic *Droit* begin to get applied to interactions between sovereign States. In other words, one can ask, on the one hand, to what extent international *Droit* could have constituted itself even if there were no other (domestic) *Droit* on earth; and on the other hand, one can seek to define the necessary conditions for the application of domestic *Droit* to inter-state interactions.

[376] Be that as it may, one thing is very certain. Up until the present day, international *Droit* has never been a *Droit in actuality*. By definition, this *Droit* is related to interactions between *sovereign* States. Now the very notion of sovereignty excludes the possibility of an irresistible constraint coming from the outside. Therefore, the Third in international *Droit* does not have any means to *impose* his intervention on the litigants, who can always opt out. If international *Droit* is a *Droit*, it can therefore only be a *Droit in potentiality*.

Now all potentiality tends to actuality. If international *Droit* is a *Droit*, therefore, it necessarily wants to actualize itself as such. In other words, there will be a tendency to render the intervention of the Third irresistible. But it is possible that this is incompatible with the sovereignty of the States subject to this *Droit*—that is, with the "international" character of the latter. It is therefore possible that by actualizing itself international *Droit* ceases to be that which it is as a *Droit* in potentiality.

In any case, one must ask two questions when one studies international *Droit*. In the first place, one must ask what this *Droit* is as a *Droit* in potentiality: is it truly a *Droit*, and if so, what are its relations with other juridical phenomena? Second, one must see how this *Droit* can actualize itself, and if it remains a *sui generis* juridical phenomenon once realized in actuality.

Now in our times, at least, *Droit* in actuality is nothing other than state-sanctioned or "domestic" *Droit*. To discuss the actualization of international *Droit*, therefore, is to study its relations to domestic *Droit*. I have already said that even while existing in potentiality, international *Droit* presupposes the actual existence of domestic *Droit*: without domestic *Droit*, [there would be] no State, and without States, no international *Droit*. And it is possible that the latter cannot actualize itself without ceasing to be "international." It will then be a matter of knowing if it must become a "domestic" *Droit* in the proper sense of the word.

Now I have already pointed out that these days domestic *Droit* itself is not perfectly actualized. There is in fact a plurality of national *Droits*. The individual, therefore, [and] even the citizen, is not forced in an absolute manner to submit to the intervention of the Third, understood as a given Third, linked to a particular domestic *Droit*. He can change nationality and thus escape the imposition of the *Droit* that is not agreeable to him. To a certain extent, therefore, all domestic *Droit* is only a *Droit* in potentiality; and as such, it has a tendency to actualize itself, to perfect its actuality. But actualizing itself means [377] eliminating the plurality of domestic *Droits*: it is, if you will, to "internationalize" itself. The actualization of domestic *Droit* can therefore only be done in and by a juridical interaction between sovereign States, having as their goal the unification of their respective domestic *Droits*. Therefore, if international *Droit* seems unable to actualize itself except by ceasing to be "international" and by becoming a sort of "domestic" *Droit*, domestic *Droit* seems unable to perfect its actuality except by becoming "international," by ceasing to be "domestic" in the proper sense of the word.

All this clearly shows that one can only study international *Droit* in its relations to domestic *Droit*, and that one must, in doing so, take account of the fact that the latter exists as a plurality of national *Droits*.

§ 55

Let us assume—by some remote chance—that there is not yet *Droit* on earth, but that there are nevertheless sovereign States and specifically political interactions between them (i.e., by definition, essentially human). Can one deduce from these interactions a public international *Droit*? In other words, can these interactions take on a juridical meaning in addition to their purely political meaning?

The State is constituted by a group of political friends having a common political enemy. And they are only friends because they have a common enemy. The result is that, by definition, every foreign State is the political enemy of a given State. The interactions between States taken as States, i.e., political interactions, are therefore actualized in the form of war. A Society organizes itself into a State because it is at war or may be at war. The *political* existence of the State in peacetime is only a preparation for war. One can also say that when the State behaves as a State, i.e., politically, it behaves as a Master does. For the State, it is of matter of winning or perishing. And winning means subjecting the enemy State, i.e., annulling it as a State—that is, assimilating it politically, making it "recognize" [the victorious State] without it being "recognized" in return.[1]

[378] Now war is not, properly speaking, an inter-action, since it is a relation of mutual *exclusion*, and ends in principle by the suppression of one of the two agents. In war, and in relation to war, there is then no *Third* possible. The war being over, the Third would be the second [agent] and as such the enemy—that is, a party and no longer third. Given that every entity tends to keep itself in identity with itself, the Third has a tendency to remain a Third—that is, to safeguard the duality of the agents to whom it is related. But war tends to do away with one of these agents. The Third must then deny war as

---

1. Primitive or archaic States, i.e., truly aristocratic or warrior-like, are not familiar with peace as a permanent political institution. [378] The Greeks, as well, were not familiar with *peace* treaties but only armistices or cease-fires. The Romans, by contrast, liked to sign treaties of "perpetual peace." But it is they who developed *bourgeois* civil *Droit*.

There is a political dialectic analogous to that of Mastery. It leads to "Empire," i.e., to "Federation," where the victor "recognizes" the vanquished who "recognizes" him: the two fuse into a higher union, so that there is neither victor nor vanquished in the proper sense of the words.

such, and war will not be able to generate or tolerate a third. In other words, there is no *Droit* that can recognize war as a *juridical* situation, and no war can generate a *Droit* by turning itself into a juridical situation. War is therefore an essentially a-juridical phenomenon, since there is no *Droit* without a Third.[2]

However, specifically political interactions can lead to the existence of a political Third, who has certain similarities to the juridical third. And this situation can generate a pseudo-*droit*.

Just like individuals (Masters), States can have a common State-enemy, and by this fact be States-friends or *Allies*. In order to simplify things, let us suppose that two States ally themselves against a third. The enemy is then a third in relation to the interactions between the two friends or allies. The allies do not want to destroy each other: they therefore maintain the Third as third. And the latter does not want that one of the allies overcomes the other: it therefore maintains itself as third. And this Third is certainly "impartial": the allies—its enemies—are for it interchangeable in their mutual relations; it does not have any preference for one over the other, seeing that both are its enemies, and this in the same way. But is it also "disinterested" as the juridical Third is disinterested? In a certain sense yes, for the domestic affairs [379] of its enemies are "none of its business": it does not benefit from them personally, seeing that it is excluded from the domestic life of the allies, being their enemy. But in another sense, it is not disinterested in them, because it is "interested" in discord among the allies, in the elimination of their alliance, and—consequently—of its own situation as third. And this is what distinguishes the political Third from the juridical Third; for the latter does not suffer from agreement between its litigants, just as it does not suffer from their disagreement.[3] But to want disagreement between the allies is first and foremost to want to avoid their complete union—that is, the absorption of one by the other as well. The Third therefore wants to maintain the *status quo;* he wants to maintain each of the two allies in its identity with itself and in the same relation with the other. One can therefore say that the Third is interested in the *equality* of the two allies, in a situation such that any one of the two cannot absorb the other. In short, the political Third has an interest making an egalitarian or aristocratic Justice and *Droit* reign among its allied enemies. Now,

---

2. This is why one cannot say that war is a *crime* in the juridical sense of the word. It is simply *outside* of *Droit.*

3. When, in domestic *Droit,* the State plays the role of the Third in respect to its citizens, it is interested in their agreement, and not their disagreement. This is why it consents to be a *juridical* Third: as Judge, it applies the *Droit* that helps its citizens reach an agreement. Now it is interested as a State; it therefore has a *political* interest in also acting *juridically* as a State—that is, to make *Droit* state-sanctioned. But in its *juridical* aspect, i.e., as Third-Judge, the State is interested neither in the agreement nor disagreement of the litigants: it is not because it wants them to reach an agreement that it applies *Droit* to them; it is because it applies *Droit* to them that they reach an agreement. As for the political Third, it does not want to apply any *Droit* whatsoever; for all *Droit* by definition helps reach an agreement, while the political Third cares about the disagreement of the other two.

given that States behave politically as Masters, this attitude of the Third is conforming to their ideal of Justice. And one thus has the illusion of a political
Droit, of a public international **Droit,** regulating the relations of States with
one another, [or] at the very least, *allied* States, which are by definition *at peace*
with one another.

But this is only an illusion, due to the mere coincidence of two essentially
different attitudes: the political attitude and the juridical attitude. Without a
doubt, if the stronger of the two "allies" attacks the weaker, the "enemy" Third
can intervene to support actively the weak against the strong. And it may be
that the possibility alone of such an intervention by the Third could stop war
between "allies": the conflict can be submitted to the arbitration of the third.
It may thus seem that there is a juridical situation, an application of public
international **Droit;** but in reality the Third intervenes for purely political reasons (moreover [380] "egoistic"), in conformity with the principle "*divide et
impera* [divide and conquer]," and not at all as a result of some Legal rule or
an ideal of Justice. It is, so to speak, by chance that the political intervention
coincides here with a juridical intervention, based upon the principle of equality and the upholding of status. This is a case of applying *political* law and not
juridical law. Now in the sphere of political interactions between States, the
interventions of a Third, or arbitrations, are generally of the type indicated: in
arbitrating, the Third pursues its own political interest, it acts and arbitrates as
an *enemy* (actual or eventual) of its "litigants"; for it is only the political conduct of the enemy that coincides with the juridical behavior of a Third (while
being essentially something else). The political behavior of the friend or ally
does not give rise to quasi-juridical conduct. Indeed, if there are three allies,
for example, and if one of them attacks another in order to absorb it, the third
will not have any *political* reason to intervene; for it is interested that its allies
be the strongest possible. Now two separate States are less strong as two than
these same States joined as one alone. But to admit that one of the agents interacting can overcome the other is precisely to renounce any intervention—that
is, to recognize the situation as not juridical.

Of course, there are treaties of alliance between allies that regulate their
mutual interactions. But a political alliance is always concluded against an
enemy (effective or eventual), and the relations between allies are a function of
their relations with the enemy. Even a peace treaty concluded with the former
enemy at the end of a war (or without war) is ultimately an alliance against a
new common enemy. Political relations between States, therefore, are always
projected onto a third, which is the common enemy of the States in question.
And it is this relation with the Third, this "intervention" of the third, that gives
to "peaceful" political inter-actions between States the appearance of juridical
relations (conforming to the aristocratic ideal of egalitarian Justice). But this
is only an appearance, because the Third is by definition an *enemy* (eventual at
the very least), who is *interested* in the interactions in question. It is precisely
because the alliance (and the interactions that it implies) are directed against
it that it has a political interest that the alliance does not become a genuine

union, but maintains itself as a pact [*contract*] between independent States. The "third" is therefore in reality a party. There is no genuine third in the *political* interactions [381] between States. And this is why these interactions have nothing juridical about them.

A third [*troisième*] ally does not have any political reason to play the role of a Third toward its allies. As for the *enemy* Third, it is prompted politically to play this role. But this is precisely why it is not a genuine Third in the juridical sense of the word. The ally does not intervene, and the intervention of the enemy has nothing juridical about it. For political interactions to have a juridical character, therefore, they must be related to a politically *neutral* third. But "politically neutral" means just as easily apolitical. One therefore sees that public international **Droit** cannot arise from *political* interactions between States. Even if *Droit* can be applied to the political, it is not the political which can generate it: it must penetrate the political sphere from the outside.[4]

Let us see what a *neutral* State is. One must not confuse neutrality with "non-belligerence." The non-belligerent, not being a friend or ally, is by definition an enemy. But it is an eventual enemy, an enemy in potentiality, in contrast to the effective enemies in actuality. This is enough, however, for there not to be a truly "disinterested," i.e., juridical, Third. As for the neutral State, which can play this role, it is never supposed to be able to actualize itself as an enemy. Now strictly speaking, this is only true for States without possible interaction. It is in this way that America was "neutral" in relation to the old world before its "discovery" by Columbus. And practically speaking, it is in this way that China has been "neutral" in relation to Europe in the Middle Ages. But then the neutral cannot play the role of Third; for to be able to do so, it must be in interaction with the "litigants." However, this interaction must not be political in the proper sense of the word—that is, it must not be able to actualize itself in the form [382] of a war. Now this is only possible if the neutral third is not a State properly so-called.

The neutral "Third" must therefore belong to the same non-political, religious, cultural, economic, or other Society as its "litigants." The members of this Society are divided between different States: at the same time, they are members of the Society and citizens of a given State. But the neutral "State" is not a genuine State. In other words, its "citizens" are nothing more than members of the Society in question. If we symbolize the non-political Society by a sheet of paper, and political Society by a superimposed sheet of paper, the neu-

---

4. We have derived Justice and *Droit* from the dialectic of Mastery (cf. Part Two). Now the political dialectic of interactions between States is analogous to that of Mastery. It would therefore seem that one can derive a *sui generis* political *Droit* from it. But this is not so, because there is a difference between the two dialectics. The Master *creates* himself as a human being in and by the Struggle for recognition. As for the State, it already *is* human to the extent that it exists (its humanity resulting from that of its citizens). Its interactions with other States (its struggles or wars for recognition), therefore, do not have an anthropogenic value, and this is why one cannot derive an ideal of Justice from them, nor consequently a notion of *Droit*.

tral "State" will be symbolized by a hole in this second sheet of paper. This "State" only has the aspect of a State because it has political *boundaries,* because the remaining mass of the non-political Society is state-sanctioned. But in reality, the neutral is not a State: it is a fragment of the non-political Society remaining in its pure state. It is in this way that the Catholic Church is neutral (at the very least, in principle) in relation to Catholic States. Or once again, it is in this sense that one can speak about the "neutrality" of the market (and merchants in general) in Medieval Europe. And it is still in the same sense that one must interpret the "neutrality" of the great religious festivals recognized by the Greek States.

To relate a political interaction to a Neutral, therefore, is to locate it in some non-political Society of which both the Neutral and the agents interacting are part. The States interacting are then likened to (collective) members of the Society in question, to sub-groups of this Society. And it is completely natural for the Neutral to play the role of the Third, seeing that it represents the non-political Society in its pure state, while the States interacting are not only members of this Society but also something else, namely States—that is, political entities. In relation to the neutral Third, i.e., from the juridical point of view, the States in political interaction are considered as members of the non-political Society. They are therefore subject to the *Droit* which reigns within this Society, and their political actions are juridically valid only to the extent that they are conforming to this *Droit,* which is embodied in the person of the neutral Third, intervening in the name of the Society in question. It is in this way that the "*droit* of nations" in the Middle Ages was embodied in the Church, and political arbitration was often entrusted to the Pope.

There is not then an autonomous genesis of public international *Droit.* [383] This *Droit* (to the extent that it is a *Droit,* and not only an aspect of *political* interactions) is the application to States interacting of a *Droit* appropriate to some non-political Society, of which these States are part. And it is applied by a qualified representative of this Society as such. It is therefore a matter of a "domestic" *Droit* of a Society: it is *Droit* such as we have studied it so far. One can therefore say of it all that we have said of *Droit* in general.

Now, if this is the way things are, the Third, which applies and embodies international *Droit,* and without which this *Droit* would not exist as *Droit,* has no interest at all to keep States as autonomous political entities—that is, as States properly so-called. It has an interest to make the *Droit* of the non-political Society state-sanctioned (cf. the analysis of the relations between *Droit* and the State in chapter 2 of Part One)—that is, to organize this Society into a State, which means the elimination of the States which are its members, their transformation into sub-political groups. For if the Society has for members autonomous States and is not itself a State, it cannot prevent its members from leaving it. Its *Droit,* therefore, only exists in potentiality. Now all *Droit* has a tendency to be actualized. And in our case the actualization of international *Droit* means the elimination of States to which it is applied—that is, its elimination as *international Droit,* its transformation into *domestic Droit. Interna-*

tional Droit, therefore, can only be a *Droit* to the extent that it exists in potentiality. It is the virtual, domestic *Droit* of a non-political Society applied to its members organized into autonomous States.

Now if "public international *Droit*" is the *Droit* of a non-political Society, it is not necessarily aristocratic. It would only be so if it arose from specifically political interactions, which always have an aristocratic character. "International *Droit,*" therefore, can in principle take on a bourgeois character, being based not upon egalitarian Justice but upon the Justice of equivalence. However, it would then immediately enter into conflict with the States to which it is supposed to be applied, which necessarily adopt, as States, the aristocratic point of view. This *Droit* can only really exist, therefore, as a *Droit* of the citizen, which synthesizes the two oppositional Justices. And this confirms the idea that this *Droit* has nothing specific about it, since we have seen that all real *Droit* is always—more or less perfectly—a *Droit* of the citizen.

§ 56

[384] Let us assume the existence of a non-political, economic, cultural, religious, or other Society, where a given *Droit* reigns—that is, where a certain ideal of Justice determines the intervention of a Third in certain inter-actions between members of the Society. And let us assume that this Society is divided between several autonomous States, such that every member of the Society is at the same time a citizen of one of these States. Let us finally assume that originally the States themselves did not apply this *Droit* to their citizens. The *Droit* in question will only then exist in potentiality. In other words, the intervention of the Third will not be irresistible. The litigants will always be able to opt out of its judgement by ceasing to be members of the Society and by limiting themselves to being citizens of their respective States.

Now all *Droit* existing in potentiality tends to actualize itself. Under the acknowledged conditions, the *Droit* in question can only actualize itself provided that it is adopted by the States between which is divided the Society being considered. A State itself may apply the *Droit* by intervening by way of a Third. Or again, it may entrust this application to the Society, the Third being a qualified representative of the latter. But in this case the State must sanction the intervention of the Third, or—which is the same thing—the Third must act in the name of the State. In other words, to opt out of the judgement of the Third must not only mean ceasing to be a member of the Society, but also ceasing to be a citizen of one of the States. Now the State removes from the citizen the possibility of ceasing to be a citizen (without the consent of the State). In these conditions, therefore, the intervention of the Third becomes "irresistible" and the *Droit* in question exists in actuality: it exists in the form of a plurality of domestic state-sanctioned *Droits.*

Let us now assume that for some reason the different States apply the *Droit* in question (let us say economic *Droit,* for the sake of argument) in different forms. It is possible, for example, that one and the same ideal of Justice is applied to different totalities of social interactions according to the different States. But it is also possible that all the States do not apply the same ideal of Justice: some can apply the ideal accepted by the exclusive juridical group of the Society in question, others the idea or ideas accepted by the excluded juridical groups. [385] In all these cases there will be a conflict between "territorial *Droit*" and "personal *Droit.*" One State A will be able to apply to a citizen of State B either its own *Droit* or B's *Droit.*

If the Society in question has nothing territorial about it itself, i.e., if the fact of belonging to it does not geographically determine the one who belongs to it, it is natural to apply "personal *Droit.*" If, for a given member of the Society, a citizen of State A, the *Droit* of the Society is actualized in the form of the domestic *Droit* of State A, it is this *Droit* which ought to be applied to him everywhere and always. And if a State B applies (on its territory) the *Droit* of State A to a citizen of this State, it is only a case of the domestic *Droit* of State A, the latter only making itself represented by State B. Here, so to speak, State B acts as a civil servant of State A. Or once again, the juridical territory of A exceeds its political territory and extends over all the territory occupied by the Society in question—that is, by the totality of States between which are divided its members. It should be understood that this extension of "juridical territory" is only possible when the States at issue juridically recognize the Society in question—that is, treat their citizens not only as citizens but also as members of this Society. In the contrary case, the foreigner would not be a subject of *droit,* a juridical person, in the eyes of the State. But seeing that all the States apply the *Droit* of the Society to all its members, this *Droit* exists in actuality, even if a given State applies the *Droit* in question (such as it understands it) to its citizens outside of its political territory—that is, by the intermediary of another State.

But the question gets complicated if State A has to resolve (on its territory) a controversy between a citizen of State B, and its own citizen or a citizen of a State C. As it is A who decides the way it is going to act, one can say that this time it is a case of A's domestic *Droit,* and not B's or C's. If one calls "private international *Droit*" the foreign *Droit* which is applied by a State to foreigners (on its territory), one must say at any rate that this is a *domestic Droit*—that is, either the *Droit* of the State which applies the *Droit* or the *Droit* of the State whose *Droit* is applied. It is therefore a *Droit* in actuality, which actualizes the *Droit* of the Society in question, being applied in an "irresistible" way to all its members by the States between which this Society is divided. Thanks to "private international *Droit,*" a member of the Society will never be able to escape its *Droit*: this *Droit* will always be applied to him [386] in an irresistible manner in one of the forms that it takes in the member States of the Society.

Now we have seen that *Droit* can only exist in a Society provided that it is exclusive [*un et unique*]. In other words, the Third must always belong to the exclusive juridical group. The States which actualize Society's *Droit* must therefore accept one and the same ideal of Justice. And indeed, a State A only applies (on its territory) the *Droit* of a State B if this *Droit* is not in contradiction with the fundamental principles of its own *Droit*. In other words, the differences between domestic *Droits* are only justified juridically by the territorial differences of the social interactions to which the *Droit* in question is applied. But since in principle a legal system implies all possible cases, one can say that all the States must apply one and the same *Droit*, which is nothing other than the *Droit* accepted by the exclusive juridical group of the Society in question. A given Society, therefore, will always seek to unify the *Droits* of the States between which its members are divided. And this means that from the *juridical* point of view of this Society, the existence in its bosom of a plurality of autonomous States is not at all justified. Of course, if all these States apply one and the same *Droit*, namely the *Droit* of the Society in question, the latter will have no juridical objection to the existence of these States, seeing that its *Droit* will be actualized by them. "Territorial *Droit*" will then coincide with "personal *Droit*," and a member of the Society will never be able to opt out of its *Droit*, everywhere and always the same. But this result will also be attained in the case where the members of the Society would be citizens of a single universal State, which would have absorbed all the others while preserving their common *Droit*. The Society, therefore, will not be juridically opposed to its *Droit* being actualized in and by a domestic *Droit* properly so-called and unique, instead of being actualized by a "private international *Droit*."

This reasoning, however, is only valid when it is a matter of applying Society's *Droit* to its *individual* members, or to collectivities other than the *States* which are part of it. Now these States, being groups of members of the Society, are themselves members of the latter. And if they enter into interaction as such, they are supposed to provoke the intervention of the Third, which would apply to them the general *Droit* of the Society. Some qualified representative of the exclusive juridical group of this Society can play the role of this Third. It therefore always exists, if only in the form of the juridical "public opinion" of the [387] Society in question. And it can also exist in the form of a permanent institution, of an "international Tribunal" (intrasocietal being understood). But as long as the States will be sovereign States, i.e., States in the proper and strong sense of the term, the intervention of the Third will not be irresistible, for the State will always be able to opt out of its judgement by leaving the Society in question. The intervention of the Third can only be irresistible if it is related to the litigants as a governor to the governed.[5] As long as the States remain "autonomous," i.e., precisely as long as they are governors without being governed in their turn, the intervention of the Third will not be irresistible, and therefore *Droit* will only exist in potentiality in relation to the litigants-States— that is, as "public international *Droit*." Now all *Droit* tends to actualize itself fully and completely. The *Droit* of the Society will therefore want to be irresistible even when it is applied to interactions between States that the Society considers as its members. It will also want to actualize itself as "public inter-

---

5. This relation is defined by the fact that the governed cannot refuse to be governed, while the governor may refuse to govern the governed (who is then excluded from the Society).

national *Droit.*" In its juridical aspect, the Society will therefore want to overcome the sovereignty of its members, whomever they are, and will try to give to its juridical relations with them (i.e., to the upholder of the law) the form of a relation between governors and the governed.

This does not necessarily mean that the Society in question wants to constitute itself as a State properly so-called. The State is defined by two qualities: on the one hand, it is a group of friends having a common enemy; on the other hand, it is a group of the governed [who are] governed by governors. Now the allegedly non-political Society does not have enemies by definition: it is therefore not a group of friends, it is not a State in the full sense of the word. But if it is not so itself, it cannot accept either that its members are States in the proper sense of the term, i.e., that they have political enemies; for we have seen that the relations between enemies excludes the intervention of a Third. Now Society is anxious to play the role of juridical Third in the relations between its members. None of its members, therefore, should be the enemy of another.[6] They must not have, therefore, [388] political relations inside the Society, such that in its bosom the members will not be able to enter into interaction in the capacity of sovereign States. At first glance, the member State of the Society could have enemies outside of the Society in question and therefore be a State properly so-called. But if the Society is not *universal,* i.e., if it does not encompass *all* those who are susceptible of being its members, it will have a tendency to extend itself beyond its boundaries: thus, the religious Society that is the Catholic Church wants to encompass humanity as a whole. Therefore, it will set down its relations with the outside, and consequently the relations with this outside for all its members. The latter, therefore, will not be able to be enemies or friends of those who are not part of the Society as they like, just as they cannot be enemies of the members of the Society. And this means that they cannot be sovereign States.[7]

Practically speaking, moreover, the Society will only be able to be apolitical if it is universal; and then all the relations of its members will be domestic—that is, none of them will be able to be a relation between enemies, or a properly political relation. Therefore, it does not include States properly so-called. If Society is not universal, it will have to defend itself against the eventual external enemy— that is, organize itself into a State. And in this case as well it will not be able to

---

6. In principle, Society can accept that a member is the enemy of another member provided that they are enemies in some aspect other than that of member, that they remain "friends" as members of [388] the Society while being enemies as citizens of their respective States. But this is practically impossible. And this is why, in fact, the *Droit* of a non-political Society tends to overcome the political character of its members. In particular, this *Droit* will be essentially "pacifist."

7. A State, member of a given Society, could however freely set down its relations with groups which are not susceptible of becoming members of the aforementioned Society. But since, in fact, every Society tends to encompass humanity as a whole, the freedom in question can only be provisional. Moreover, a non-universal Society necessarily organizes itself into a State, which makes it impossible for its members to be autonomous States; for if a Society excludes *in principle* a part of humanity, it is because it treats it as an *enemy*—that is, it is related to it *politically* or as a State.

tolerate in its bosom autonomous States. Its members, therefore, will only be able to be "States" in the sense that there will be inside of them relations of governors to the governed. One can call them "States," but they are not States properly so-called or "sovereign." They will be States in relation to their citizens, if you will, but they will not be in relation to the outside. Still, they will have to apply as governors to their governed-citizens the common *Droit* of the Society to which they [389] belong. There will then be a *juridical Federation*. And if the Society is itself organized into a State, there will be a *Federation* in the proper sense of the word—that is, a political Federation, a federated State.[8] One can therefore say that if public international *Droit* tends to actualize itself, it can only do so by becoming a *federal* **Droit,** i.e., "public" *domestic Droit*—that is, "constitutional" and "administrative"—of a federated State. As *Droit,* it is imposed by the Federation on its members, just as a domestic *Droit* is imposed by the governors on the governed. And this *Droit* is only "federal" in the sense that certain litigants, namely the federated "States," do not limit themselves to being subject to it, but they apply it themselves in the capacity of governors to their own governed. If the Society is a State properly so-called, it will be a federal *State,* and its members will be *States:* not "sovereign," of course, but "autonomous," if you will (while not being so in relation to the **Droit** that they apply, for this *Droit* will be imposed on them as on the governed). But if the Society (being universal, in actuality or potentiality) is not a political Society or a State, its members will not be so either: there will be a mere "Confederation," "League," or "Union," and so on, of apolitical groups, which actualize as a whole a given *Droit,* which will have nothing to do with what is today called "public international *Droit.*"[9]

§ 57

Let us assume a State where some (domestic) *Droit* is realized. For this *Droit* to exist in actuality, i.e., for the intervention of the State in its capacity as juridical Third to be irresistible, its litigants-citizens must not be able to leave the State without its consent, and no power must come to interpose itself within the State between it and its citizens. In short, for domestic *Droit* to exist in actuality, the State which realizes it must be "sovereign." But if there are sovereign States outside of it, which [390] realize *Droits* other than its own, there will always be a possibility for its litigants to opt out of its judgements by going to the other States. Now, like all *Droit* and all entities in general, the domestic *Droit* being considered will have a tendency to actualize itself completely. At first glance, it seems that the State has three means to actualize its *Droit*. In the first place, it can absolutely isolate itself from all that is outside of it, with-

---

8. A "Federation" differs from an "Alliance" in that it is supposed to be permanent: the federated States can only have a common enemy with which they can only be reconciled in common.

9. One could say that *Droit* in actuality can only be "public" by not being "international," and "international" only by not being "public." Public "international" *Droit* only exists *in actuality* as a *domestic* public *Droit* inside a *federated* State.

drawing into itself. Second, it can conclude juridical treaties with foreigners, which will guarantee either the extradition of its litigants or their judgement abroad according to the *Droit* of their State of origin. Finally, third, the State can impose its *Droit* abroad. Of course, if the State succeeds in isolating itself completely from the rest of the world, one can say that its *Droit* exists in actuality; for its litigants will be effectively unable to opt out of its judgement in these conditions. But even without speaking of the fact that such an isolation (advocated by Plato, for example) is unrealizable in practice, one must reject this solution; for it is in contradiction with itself. Indeed, as every entity tends to actuality, *Droit* wants to propagate itself as much as possible and to be applied to all that is susceptible of being transformed into a juridical situation. Now to be isolated is to renounce juridical expansion. The solution of autarchy, here as elsewhere, is therefore only a stop-gap measure. As for the second solution, it is not satisfying either. To adopt it is to interpose between the State and its litigants the other States, their consent to apply the *Droit* in question. Domestic *Droit* thus becomes a function of international *Droit:* the juridical relations between the State and its litigants imply and presuppose juridical relations between this State and the other sovereign States. Now, by definition, these relations can only exist in potentiality without the irresistible intervention of a Third. The would-be actuality of *Droit* would therefore rest upon a *Droit* in potentiality. Consequently, the *Droit* in question would only exist itself in potentiality. Therefore, the third solution remains: the State, in order to actualize its domestic *Droit,* must want to impose it on all the other States; the domestic *Droit* in question must become the domestic *Droit* of all the States susceptible of entering into interaction with the given State—that is, in the final analysis, of all States in general.[10]

---

10. The fact that *Droit* is not fully actualized clearly appears in certain archaic legislation, which allows the indicted to opt out of the judgement, or the condemned litigant to opt out of the execution of a judgement, by exile: instead of undergoing the penalty, the condemned [391] can leave his country (cf. ancient Roman *Droit,* for example). *Droit* very much exists in this case; for there is a genuine *Droit* in a given Society if its member cannot act contrary to this *Droit* without ceasing to be a member of the aforementioned Society by this very fact. (Thus, there was a *Droit* within the League of Nations, seeing that the State was unable to remain a member of the League and act contrary to its *Droit.* But seeing that it was able to leave freely the League, the *Droit* was only existing in potentiality.) *Droit* exists, therefore, when one must either conform to the law or to the judgement in the case when one has broke the Law, or leave the Society. But if the litigant has the *choice* between these two possibilities, the *Droit* only exists in potentiality: in any case, it is not *fully* actualized; for one must not confuse this *voluntary* exile with obligatory exile, imposed by the judgement. This exile is a genuine penalty, compatible with the actuality of *Droit.* But when the exile is *voluntary,* it is no longer a purely juridical phenomenon; for then it is the litigant who determines (in part) the penalty—that is, the Judgement. The latter is therefore not entirely the work of the *Third;* it is co-determined by one of the *parties;* and to the extent that it is so, it is not juridical. The State which leaves this choice to its litigant, therefore, no longer acts as Third, to the extent that it does so: it acts as a party, while drawing inspiration from "reason of State" or social utility, and not from the sole desire to realize *Droit*—that is, to emphasize a certain ideal of Justice. One can therefore say that in this case alone *Droit* is not fully actualized *in fact,* but that the very *idea* of a fully actual *Droit* has not yet been formed within the State.

[391] As a political entity, the State tends to propagate itself by conquest; it tries to absorb purely and simply foreign States. But as a juridical entity, the State limits itself to imposing abroad its domestic *Droit*. In other words, it tends to create a *Federation* of States or a federal State by becoming itself one of the federated States, the Federation having for a base and for a result the existence of a unique *Droit*, common to all the federated States, and imply-ing—in its "public *Droit*" aspect—an element of "federal *Droit*," regulating the relations of the federated States among themselves, [and] in particular the fed-eral organization of justice. If the Federation is not universal, if it has enemies-States outside, it will have to organize itself into a (federal) State properly so-called. Its integral elements—the federated States—will also have enemies; they will therefore be *States*. But they will always have common enemies and will only be able to be reconciled with them in common: they will therefore not be sovereign States but federated States. However, the Federation will have a tendency to propagate itself as much as possible. At the limit, it will encompass the whole of humanity. Then it will cease being a State in the proper sense of the word, no longer having enemies outside. And the federated States as well will consequently cease to be genuine States. The Federation will then become a simple, worldwide juridical Union [392] (at least in its juridical aspect, which is not the only one).

We thus see that one is led to the same result either by starting from (pub-lic) international *Droit* or by taking for a point of departure domestic *Droit*. By *actualizing itself* fully and completely, the two *Droits* lead to federal *Droit*—that is, to the *domestic Droit* of a federal State or a worldwide Federation. Domes-tic *Droit* existing in actuality implies in its "public" aspect a federal *Droit*, which is nothing other than actualized (public) "international *Droit*." Con-versely, actualized international *Droit* is a federal *Droit*, which is necessarily part of a complete system of domestic *droit*. "Public international *Droit*," therefore, is not a *sui generis Droit*. There is only a single *Droit*, which is domes-tic *Droit*, for *Droit* only exists *in actuality* as domestic *Droit* (the Society which realizes it being, at the limit, Humanity). But to the extent that *Droit* only exists in potentiality and is applied to interactions between sovereign States, one can call it "public international *Droit*." However, this *Droit* only exists by defini-tion in potentiality, and it transforms itself into (federal) domestic *Droit* by being actualized. This is why it tends to overcome itself as international.

B. Public *Droit*

§ 58

Public *Droit* in the proper sense of the word (i.e., excluding penal *Droit*) encompasses constitutional *Droit* and administrative *Droit*. And it is generally said that the first sets down above all the structure of the State as such, while the second determines first and foremost the relations between the State and "individuals," or indeed "private persons [*particuliers*]."

Now, in fact, the Constitution (in the broad sense of the word) is nothing other than the pure and simple *description* of the structure of the State, or its "status," its organization. And it is obvious that such a description, whether it be oral or written, has nothing to do with *Droit.* It is just as little a *Droit* as, for example, the description of the human body in anatomy is a *Droit.* It is simply an observation [393] of what *is,* and not an assertion of what *ought* to be, in conformity with a certain ideal of Justice. Taken in themselves, the structure of a State and the Constitution that expresses it are neither just nor unjust. From the point of view of Justice, all constitutional laws are just as neutral as the law that sets down, for example, the "national colors" of the State, or its name; for by definition, the State (autonomous or sovereign) is isolated and is related only to itself in and by the Constitution. Its interactions with other States are regulated by public *international Droit.* As for "*domestic* public *Droit*" (which alone concerns us here), it considers the State in itself. Now when there is no interaction, nor in general relations between at least two entities, there is neither Justice nor, *a fortiori, Droit.* The Constitution, as (domestic) "public *Droit*" conceives it, is therefore not a *Droit* at all. The Constitution is a Law or a totality (oral or written) of *political* Laws in and by which the State announces to everyone what it is and the way in which it functions. It simply "declares" this to others, as one declares a state of war, for example—that is, by a unilateral act, which excludes the very idea of a Third and the intervention of a Third, able to sanction or annul the "declared" reality. If one says that the Constitution is a *Law,* one must underline that it is a matter of a *political,* and not a *juridical,* Law.

The existence of a Constitution, and of a political *legality* in general, has a very great (political) importance. It has long been noticed (by Montesquieu, for example) that absence of political Laws characterizes "Despotism."[11] The State is "despotic" when the governors treat the governed "as they please" and not in conformity with Laws [that are] fixed and known by all. But this important difference is a difference of degree and not of principle; for every State can change any of its political Laws whatsoever—that is, also amend its Constitution as a whole. Therefore, the State always acts "as it pleases." The difference between the "legal" State and the despotic State is therefore comparable to that between a reflective and an impulsive man, who changes his opinion all the time and does so for no apparent reason—that is, none foreseeable by others. In the "legal" State, the situation is just as little *juridical* as in the "despotic" State: constitutional Law is just as little a "*droit*" or a *juridical* Law as the "arbitrary" decision of the "despot." And this is why a revolution, which is by definition politically [394] *illegal,* cannot be *juridically* condemned. The revolutionary action is in contradiction with the constitutional Law. But this Law not being juridical, the revolutionary action is juridically neutral, and not criminal. If the revolution succeeds, i.e., if it replaces the political Laws that it abol-

---

11. [Ed. See, for example, Montesquieu, *The Spirit of the Laws,* trans. and ed. Anne M. Cohler, Basia Carolyn Miller, and Harold Samuel Stone (Cambridge: Cambridge University Press, 1989), 10, 17–20, 27–30, 59–71.]

ishes with other political Laws, there is nothing to quarrel about, neither political nor juridically. When the revolutionaries "succeed," they become the State—that is, they maintain themselves as autonomous in respect to foreigners (enemies), and as governors in respect to their fellow citizens (friends). They therefore embody the "sovereign" State. Now this State can change its Constitution at will. If the revolution has succeeded, one can say that the State itself has changed its Constitution, and there is nothing to which to object.

One cannot condemn the new Constitution by having recourse to the old; for the latter drew its reality from the will of the State. And it is the same State that now realizes by its altered will the new constitution. If the old one was valid, so also is the new one, and for the same reason. And even if one wanted to oppose the old State to the new, by denying their identity, there would be no *Third* in this interaction between the two States (i.e., between the two consecutive forms of the same State). The situation would have nothing juridical about it; there would be a political Struggle—that is all. For there to be a *Third*, one would have to have recourse to another State. But if another State is supposed to be able to alter as it likes the Constitution of a given State (even by way of a Third), the latter is not a "sovereign" State, i.e., a State properly so-called, and its structure is not a Constitution in the proper sense of the term. To the extent that a "Constitution" is a "litigant" or "subject of *droit*," it is not a genuine Constitution. When there is a *Droit*, there is no *public Droit* in the *constitutional* sense. The constitutional Law that sets down the structure of a State properly so-called has nothing to do with a juridical Law. Or once again, the relations of the State with itself is outside the sphere of *Droit* and even of Justice.[12]

[395] Of course, one can criticize a constitutional Law or even a Constitution as a whole. Thus, a good Constitution should be in agreement with political reality. But if it is not, one can only improve it by making it conform to the reality of the State, and there is no sense in wanting to change this reality under the sole pretext that it does not conform to the Constitution. It should be

---

12. It can happen that a State A makes war on State B because in its opinion B's constitution is unjust, or indeed juridically illegal or illegitimate. But then A does not recognize B as a (sovereign) State. It considers B's governors and the governed as two "private" groups, one of which is acting contrary to its "*droit*." A then intervenes in the capacity of Third and annuls the "illegal" action of the governing group. In other words, A considers B's citizens as its litigants. It must therefore apply to them its *Droit* in actuality. Therefore, A tends to absorb B politically, such [395] that it becomes a sub-political group inside of A. The structure of this group, therefore, is not a Constitution in the proper sense of the term. Therefore, to the extent that a Constitution is subject to a **Droit** and can be called *juridically* legal or illegal, it is not a genuine Constitution—that is, the Constitution of a sovereign State. The *Droit* in question is therefore not a *public* or "constitutional" *Droit*. Likewise, if A is of the opinion that B's Constitution is unjust or juridically illegal in respect to another State C (for example, because it includes in B's territory a portion of C's territory), and if A intervenes to alter the Constitutions of B and C in order to "do justice" to C, A does not treat B and C as sovereign States, and it is therefore not a matter of genuine Constitutions to the extent that there is *Droit*: *Droit* only exists in relation to two sub-political groups B and C inside of State A.

understood that one can also criticize the political reality itself—that is, the given structure of a State. In other words, one can criticize a constitution even if it conforms to the reality that it is supposed to express. But this critique only makes sense if it is strictly *political*. Every Constitution, every political structure of a State, is politically good if it allows the State to maintain itself indefinitely in identity with itself, both externally and internally, and this without having to change the structure, and therefore the Constitution: externally meaning in relation to its enemies; internally meaning indefinitely maintaining the equilibrium between the Governors and the Governed.

Therefore, if constitutional Law is related to the State itself, if it is considered as a Law regulating the structure of the State as such, it is certainly not a *Droit*, for it leaves no place for the existence of a Third. And one cannot even say that it is just or unjust, for it is a matter of an isolated entity, or the relations of an entity to itself, and not an inter-action between two distinct entities. The notions of equality or equivalence, therefore, do not have any claim on the constitutional Law related to the State. And this means that it is outside the sphere of Justice.

Now one often speaks of a "just" and "unjust" Constitution or political structures. If these expressions have a meaning, one must therefore relate constitutional Law not to the State as such, but to "private persons" or [396] "individuals." And indeed "public *Droit*" (above all as "administrative *Droit*") is supposed to govern both the relations between the State and "individuals," and interactions between "individuals" themselves, at least between "individuals" taken as citizens. We must therefore see to what extent "public *Droit*" is a *Droit* when it takes on the indicated aspect.

In order to solve this problem, it is necessary to begin by introducing a distinction that one often forgets to make. It is equally said that the State is related to "individuals" or "private persons." Now, in fact, the "private person" is not necessarily an individual: it can also be a group, some collectivity. Conversely, an "individual" is not only a private person, i.e., a non-citizen, but also a political being, a citizen in the strong sense of the term. It will therefore be necessary to distinguish between citizens (individual or collective, such as political Parties, for example) and private persons (individual or collective, such as a Family, a Church, an economic group, and so on). Man will be a "private person" and will act as such when he does not act politically, i.e., in his capacity as citizen, it being of little importance that he is acting as an animal, as a member of a family, or of an economic, religious, cultural, or another society. And he will be a "citizen" if he acts for purely political motives—that is, as an integral element of his State. One must therefore distinguish: 1) the relations between the State and its citizens; 2) the relations between the State and its private persons; 3) the interactions of citizens among themselves; 4) the interactions of private persons among themselves; [and] 5) the interactions between citizens and private persons. And one must see to what extent "public *Droit*" deals with these five types of relations, and to what extent, dealing with them, it is truly a *Droit*.

Now it is easy to see that, from the point of view that interests us, case 3 reduces to case 1, and case 5 to case 2, such that only cases 1, 2, and 4 remain.

By definition there cannot be conflicts between citizens taken as such. If two citizens act as citizens, they cannot enter into conflict with one another. The interactions between citizens acting as citizens are determined by the very structure of the State, and conversely this structure is realized in and by the civic interactions of citizens. These are therefore regulated by the Constitution (in the broad sense). If the citizens would enter into conflict with one another while acting in conformity with the Constitution, the State could not exist. A viable Constitution must [397] exclude all possibility of conflict between citizens acting as citizens. Now when there are no conflicts possible, there is no place for the intervention of a Third—that is, there is no place for a *Droit*. And seeing that there is no conflict possible, there is no place either for any injustice. One could say that the civic relations between citizens are "just" by definition. But when the very *possibility* of injustice does not exist, there is no justice either (in actuality).[13] To the extent that the Constitution regulates the civic interactions of citizens in a way that excludes all conflict between them, it is not therefore a *Droit,* and it is outside the sphere of Justice.[14]

Therefore, if a citizen acting as citizen enters into civic conflict with another citizen, this means he enters into conflict with the Constitution—that is, with the State itself. Therefore, when there is conflict, i.e., the possibility of a *Droit,* it is in the final analysis a matter of a relation not between two citizens, but between a citizen and the State. One then easily reverts to our case 1 (the action of the citizen this time being politically illegal—that is, revolutionary).

Let us now assume that a man acting as non-citizen enters into conflict with a citizen acting as citizen, i.e., in conformity with the Constitution—that is, in a way that the State is not threatened in its being by this action. The conflict of the non-citizen with the citizen will therefore be a conflict with the State itself, which will defend its own interests by defending its citizen. Generally speaking, the State being nothing other than the totality of its citizens taken as citizens, it must necessarily defend its citizens against every non-citizen: first of all, against the non-citizen in the strong sense of the word, i.e., against the foreigner or enemy; but also against the fellow citizen who would act as non-citizen; and finally, against the non-citizen who would act inside the citizen himself. In all these cases, by a political necessity, the conflict between non-citizen and citizen becomes a conflict between the non-citizen and the State. One therefore effectively reverts to case 2.

[398] As for interactions between non-citizens (case 4), they certainly give rise to conflicts when the State can intervene by way of an impartial and disin-

---

13. When an entity exists in actuality, its opposite also necessarily exists, but in potentiality—that is, as pure possibility. When an entity is *impossible,* its opposite is as well.

14. A Constitution that does not exclude civic conflicts can only exist temporarily; for the State endowed with such a Constitution must perish sooner or later in anarchy. For the State to subsist, the Constitution must be changed in such a way as to exclude all possibility of civic conflicts. This is a *political,* but not a juridical, necessity.

terested Third. This is clearly a sphere where Justice and *Droit* can reign. But this *Droit* is private *Droit,* and it seems that public *Droit* (in the proper sense) has nothing to do with the interactions between non-citizens acting as non-citizens—that is, between "private persons." Indeed, this is very much the way things are if one takes the terms in the strict sense. But one can also reason differently.

In fact, the citizen is also at the same time a non-citizen: first of all, an animal Homo sapiens, then member of a Family, of an economic Society, and so on. The action that he carries out as citizen, therefore, also necessarily affects the non-citizen in him, and consequently the other non-citizens with whom he is interacting. Now suppose that a citizen A acts civically in a legal manner, i.e., conforms to the Constitution, and that he gains from this action a certain benefit as non-citizen—that is, a "private" or "personal [*particulier*]" benefit. Let us suppose that this personal benefit infringes upon the personal interests of a citizen B, and let us assume that B is "in the right [*droit*]" from the point of view of the private *Droit* in force—that is, that A's *personal* action is not conforming to a given ideal of Justice. A's personal action will therefore be unjust. The civic action that provokes it will therefore also be so. And since this action is conforming to the Constitution, i.e., politically legal, the political legality in general of this Constitution itself will be called "unjust." (It will be called "just" in the same sense if it excludes the possibility of analogous cases to the one being considered.) It is in this way and this way alone that a Constitution, which is in itself neither just nor unjust, can be "unjust" or "just": the juridical category of Justice will be able to be applied to the sphere of "public *Droit.*" (However, the idea of Justice will not generate here a **Droit,** for it cannot be applied by an impartial and disinterested Third: there will only be the parties at issue, namely the State and its "public *Droit,*" and the non-civic Society and its private *Droit.*)

Of course, in principle, it is one and the same State that, on the one hand, promulgates its Constitution, i.e., "public *Droit*" in general, and on the other, applies private *Droit.* In other words, in principle, the exclusive political group coincides with the exclusive juridical group. In these conditions, the case mentioned above cannot occur. If it occurred, the State [399] would have to—by *political* necessity, in order to eliminate conflicts between its citizens—either amend the Constitution or change the private *Droit,* in such a way that there would no longer be a possible contradiction between them. But we have seen (Part One, chapter 2) that this is not always the case in fact, and that—temporarily—the two exclusive groups can be disassociated. In this case, the state-sanctioned, private *Droit* will be an "unjust *Droit.*" And since "public *Droit*" shows solidarity with this *Droit,* it will also be called "unjust." There will then be, if you will, a "conflict of *droits,*" a conflict between "just" private *Droit,* i.e., conforming to the ideal of Justice accepted in the exclusive juridical group, and the "public *Droit,*" defining the State which conforms to the ideas of the exclusive political group. Now we have seen that in this case there will be a struggle between the two groups, the juridical group tending either to impose its *Droit* on the State or to become itself an exclusive political group. In the first case, the group will act as a "private person"; in the second, as a citizen (revolutionary or legal). And we have seen that this struggle has nothing juridical about it in itself, given that there is no Third between the parties at issue. The "conflict of *Droits*" is not itself a *Droit:* a given *Droit* does not have any "right"[15] in respect to another. At any rate, this is a matter of relations between the State, and either a citizen or a private person, such that we revert back to cases 1 and 2. When "public *Droit*" may be "just" or "unjust," it is related to relations either between the State and the citizens, or between the State and the private persons. Therefore, it remains for us to see if in these two cases, this would-be "public *Droit*" is truly a **Droit** in the proper sense of the term.

Let us first consider the case where "public *Droit*" regulates the relations between the State and its citizens acting as citizens. The relations between the State and the citizen are then purely political. For example, the State forbids citizens of a certain category from certain posts in the government, the army, or the administrative apparatus (an officer must be from the nobility, for example), against which the affected citizens object. Or again, a citizen wants to obtain the *droit* to vote, which the State has refused him—and so on. Then either one of two things [must hold]. Either the citizen will remain in agreement with the Constitution while defending his political interests—for example, in a Democracy, he will try to get an appropriate law passed in Parliament; or he will enter into conflict with the State as such and will attempt a revolution, having to alter the State so that it responds to his political aspirations. Now it [400] is obvious that in neither case is the situation juridical; for there is not and cannot be a Third between the State and the citizen who wants to alter it, either legally or by revolutionary means. And if the situation is not juridical in the case of conflict between the citizen and his State, it is not either in the case of their agreement. The "public *Droit*" that regulates the relations between the State and its citizens acting politically, i.e., as citizens, is therefore not a genuine *Droit*. The State and the citizen operate here on the same (political) plane, but on this plane there is no place for an impartial and disinterested *Third*—that is, there is no place for any **Droit** whatsoever (precisely because there are no "neutrals" in politics).

Now when the State is interacting with a non-citizen or a "private person," there is no Third either, because in this case the two agents are situated on essentially different planes. In the case of a *conflict* between the State and the private person, i.e., between the political and the private [*privé*], it can therefore only be a matter of mutual exclusion, and not of compromise. All arbitration, all compromise, is therefore impossible, and this means that *Droit* can do nothing in this situation. In particular, the State is politically forced to the pure and simple *suppression* of the "private" element that is opposed to it, and which also tends to suppress it; for the reality of the political entity is nothing

---

15. [Ed. In the original, the English word "right" follows the French word "*droit*" in parentheses.]

other than the *negation* of the "private" entity (as one sees clearly in the case of war, war actualizing the political entity or the State, and annihilating or being able to annihilate the "private" man as such, for example, as an animal).

The relation between the political and the private is analogous to the relation between the human and the animal (the bestial) in man. The interaction, whatever it may be, presupposes an ontological similarity; one can only act on that which is on the same plane of being. Thus, man can only act on the animal and Nature in general—he can only be in inter-action with it—because he himself is an animal, because there is also within him a natural reality. Now if man *can* act on the animal outside him because there is an animal within him, he also *ought* to do so for the same reason: the animal in him (and therefore himself) can only live provided that he is in interaction with the animal outside of him. Man must therefore *use* the animal, [or] Nature in general, through and for [the sake of] the animal in him. But if the animal—outside of man or in man—is opposed to man, i.e., to the human in man, man can only suppress it, and it is this *suppression* [401] of the hostile animal that is his human *reality*. And the same goes for the State and the non-citizen. The State is only real in and by its citizens. Now these citizens are men and as such they are also animals—that is, non-human beings and hence non-political ones, non-citizens, private persons [*particuliers*]. This is why the State needs non-political assets [*valeurs*] in order to exist as a State: first and foremost, biological and economic assets—that is, ultimately children and money. The State as a political entity must therefore *use* the Family and economic Society, and it must consequently be interacting with them. But if the private Family and Society *are opposed* to the State, it must annihilate them (to the extent that they are opposed to it) if it does not want to be annihilated itself. And one sees very well that this "struggle to the death" has nothing to do with a juridical situation; for there is no Third which could simultaneously be neither political nor private [*privé*] (except God). Every human being is necessarily a *party* in a conflict between the political and the private. And this is why the supposedly "public *Droit*" is not a *Droit* at all to the extent that it deals with relations between the State and the non-citizens, whoever they may be.

And this has always been accepted, more or less consciously. When a man deserts the army in order to preserve himself as an animal or as member of a family, or if he betrays the State to protect his economic interests or those of his "class," or indeed those of economic Society as such, one speaks of a "political crime" that is not submitted to ordinary, i.e., truly juridical, Courts. In these cases, the State acts through the intermediary of the political Police, political Tribunals ("High court"), military Tribunals, and so on, and does not go and see Judges properly so-called. And thus, in these cases, the State shows that it is not a matter of *Droit*. Now the case when the State enters into relation with economic Society, for example, or one of its members (by concluding, for example, a procurement "contract"), does not essentially differ from the cases being considered. A commercial "contract" between a private person and the

State has nothing in common with an analogous contract between two private persons. To want to assimilate the State to a private person in these cases is to want to overcome the State as such, leaving in its place only economic Society (which can be "civilized [*policée*]," and thus to imitate the State, while remaining essentially apolitical—that is, quite different from a genuine State). And one has always felt this; for in war time (which *actualizes* the State as a State, i.e., as a *political* entity [402]), one recognizes the "*droit*" of the State not to perform its commercial "contracts." But if the State is not bound by its "contracts" with private persons in wartime, neither is it in peacetime. And indeed, it is not so, for it can always—for political reasons—overcome the Society itself with which—or with a member of which—it concluded a "contract." In any case, no *Third* can come to oppose this and resolve the conflict of the two parties at issue. The relations between private persons and the State acting as a State therefore have nothing juridical about them, and to the extent that they are regulated by a "public *Droit*," this would-be "*Droit*" is not at all a *Droit*, but a political Law that the State can change when and how it sees fit.[16]

When the private person enters into inter-action with the State, he must absolutely submit to the State or seek to overcome the State as such. Now when it is a matter of mutual exclusion (as in war, for example), there is no place for a Third, nor for an arbitration. And there is neither a Third nor arbitration when one of the parties submits absolutely to the other by agreeing in advance to any one of its actions. When there is an *inter-action* between the State and private persons, then, there is no *Droit* possible. Of course, the private person can be independent of the State; but he can only be so when he does not enter into interaction with it, as in the aesthetic sphere, for example. The artist as artist may not be subject to the State because the State does not need him, and to this extent he himself does not need the State (which is only strictly true when the artist creates solely for himself, without communicating his works to anyone else). But then there is no interaction between the private person and the State, and there is then no *Droit* possible either (since *Droit* is an application of the ideal of Justice to *interactions*). In no case, therefore, is there a "public *Droit*" regulating relations between the State and private persons.[17]

---

16. If the State concludes a "contract" abroad with a private person, there will also be no Third; for in case of conflict, the private person in question will only be able to act against the State through the intermediary of his own State. Now the latter will by definition be in solidarity with him against the foreign State; it will therefore be a party and not a Third. And if a State B meddles in interactions between State A and a citizen of A, State A is no longer a "sovereign" State, i.e., a State properly so-called, but a sub-political group in State B: there will then be Droit, but this Droit will not be a "*public Droit.*"

17. Progress consists in the correct delineation of spheres, in [403] particular the political and private spheres. The State must lose interest in all that is not necessary for its political existence, just as apolitical entities must lose interest in the State. (It is here that one considers the problem of the relations between the State and Religion, or indeed the Church.) But this process of delineation obviously has nothing juridical about it, for it is carried out by the parties at issue and not by a Third. And it ends up in an absence of interaction, and not in a **Droit** regulating the relations between the State and private persons.

[403] To the extent that the State is taken as a State, there is then no public *Droit*, it being of little importance whether the State is related to itself ("constitutional *Droit*"), or to its citizens or private persons ("administrative *Droit*"). Generally speaking, there is *Droit* only when it is a matter of relations between private persons. Therefore, if public *Droit* is truly a *Droit*, the State itself must figure in it not as a State but as a "private person." As a State, it should only play the role of Third. Therefore, let us see what this paradoxical situation can mean.

Of course, the State is a "moral person." It does not have itself an animal body. Generally speaking, there is nothing non-state-sanctioned, non-political, "private [*privé*]," or "personal [*particulier*]" about it. But the State can only exist in actuality in and by its citizens, who are not only citizens, but also non-citizens, private persons [*particuliers*]. The State acts in them and by them only to the extent that they act as citizens. Thus, the State is the totality of all its citizens *taken as citizens* and acting as such. More specifically, the State is embodied in the exclusive political Group: the will of this group is the will of the State. And in the narrow sense of the word, the State merges with the collectivity of Governors, recruited from the exclusive Group: the action of this collectivity is the action of the State (the activity of the other citizens only being the *means* of this activity). By definition, the Governors enjoy a political Authority within the exclusive Group, and dominate the other citizens through coercion. If they act politically, i.e., as citizens—as members of the exclusive *political* Group and as a result of the political Authority that they enjoy—they act in the name of the State, which is in unison with them. It is they, then, who set down the structure of the State and the mode of its functioning. In particular, they determine the Constitution of the State and the status of the citizens, as well as the nature of the relations of the citizens with the State and of the State with non-citizens; and also the relations between citizens and non-citizens; and between non-citizens themselves [404] and between citizens themselves. And the totality of political Laws (oral or written) which sets down all this, i.e., "public *Droit*," is not a *Droit*, as we have just seen.

But this is only true as long as the State acts as a State, i.e., as long as the Governors act as such—that is, as citizens. Now they are also necessarily specific private persons [*des personnes privées, des particuliers*], and they act as such. And it is possible that they act as private persons [*particuliers*] while exercising their function as Governors—that is, while believing and giving the impression to others that they are acting as citizens, in the name of the State. Speaking metaphorically, the State itself does not act as a State, but in the capacity of a private person—not as citizen, but as an element of familial, economic, religious, or some other Society. The State properly so-called, therefore, will have to be distinguished from this pseudo-State. And if the latter enters into interaction with the governed, the genuine State will be able to play the role of an impartial and disinterested Third. There will then be a *Droit*, and this *Droit* is nothing other than what is called "public *Droit*." Therefore, it is, if you will, a *Droit* relative to political imposture. It prevents (in principle) private persons from using the State for their private ends, from acting as private persons toward the Governed while giving the impression of acting as citizens in the name of the State, in the capacity of Governors (which they effectively are, moreover).

As long as humanity is not organized into a universal and homogenous State, there are always non-political, familial, economic, religious or some other groups, which have divergent, or indeed incompatible, "personal" interests, and which struggle among themselves on account of these interests. Let us now suppose that one of these groups becomes a political group. Its members then act not only as members of a non-political group (familial, and so on) but also politically, as members of the superimposed political group. This group will aim at the formation of a State. It will be a matter either of creating a new State, or of seizing power in a pre-existing State. In other words, the group in question will have to become an exclusive political Group. And—by definition—the members of the Group will have to *risk their lives* in order to become so (or at the very least, they will have to be ready to do so by threatening a *struggle to the death* with those who would oppose them). Let us assume that they succeed (following an effective victory or because their adversaries refuse battle). In other words, we suppose that the Group succeeds, on the one hand, in preserving itself against foreigners, by [405] making war or by being ready to do so; and on the other hand, it retains this possibility of preserving itself against foreigners by excluding from power a certain number of men whom it nevertheless utilizes in preserving itself (by using coercion), these men forming the excluded political Group.[18] The exclusive group can only succeed by putting out a collectivity of Governors, enjoying a political Authority within the exclusive group, which allows them to use violence against the excluded group. In this case, there will be a State, and the action of this State will be nothing other than the action of the Governors in question. Of course, the latter will act not only according to their political interests (i.e., with a view to preserving themselves as governors of a certain exclusive political group both in respect to foreigners and in respect to the excluded group), but also in order to realize the non-political interests of the group, for example familial or another, to which they also belong (since they created the State or seized power in order to defend these "personal" interests). But it will make no sense to say that the Governors act as private persons, that they defend private interests. In the assumed hypothesis, the interests of the group have become the interests of the State, and the Governors can defend these interests while acting as Governors. It is in this way, for example, that a family can politicize [*s'étatiser*] itself (that of the Frank kings, for example) and become a monarchical *State*. By defending the interests of his family (his "dynasty"), the king does not act as a private person, but as king—that is, as Governor: it is the State that acts in and by him. Likewise, when a familial, economic, or religious, and so on, group forms an aristocratic State, the Gov-

---

18. To simplify things, I suppose that the exclusive group is homogenous in itself, as well as the excluded group. In reality, things are a lot more complicated.

ernors act in the name of the State by defending the interests of the aristocracy—that is, the group in question. And the same goes in oligarchy—and so
on. In all these cases, the Governors set down as they want the status of the State
and citizens, of the Governors and the Governed, and the relations of the Governors with the Governed have nothing juridical about them, seeing that there
is no Third possible here. If the Governed believe themselves injured by the acts
of the Governors, they only have to overcome them as Governors and put themselves in their place. Likewise, if the excluded group believes itself injured by the
exclusive group, it only has to replace it in the State. (And if a foreign [State]
believes itself injured [406] by the State in question, it only has to alter or absorb
it). Now in order to do this, one must act *politically:* either legally or by revolutionary means (or by a war). And all these political interactions have nothing to
do with *Droit,* seeing that they exclude any Third.

Let us now suppose that a Governor (or a collectivity of Governors) acts not
as Governor, i.e., as citizen or representative of the State—as an exclusive *political* Group—but according to specific, private interests [*d'intérêts privés, particuliers*] (which can be either the interests of some group or strictly personal
[*personnels*] interests). This Governor will act as a private person [*particulier*].
If he enters into interaction with the Governed, if he infringes upon their interests, whatever they may be, there will not be a relation between Governor and
the Governed, but between private persons, one of whom is an impostor since
he claims to act as Governor, while in fact, even though he is a Governor, he
acts in the capacity of a private person, according to private interests. These
interests are private because the State has not made them its own, because he
has not imposed them on the State, neither by legal means nor by risking his
life in a revolution (or a war). The Governed who are injured, therefore, do not
need to act *politically* against him, neither legally nor by risking their lives in a
revolutionary (or warlike) struggle. The Governed can have recourse to the
State (i.e., to the Governors acting as Governors) against the Governor who in
reality acts as a private person. The State will in this case be a Third. It will
intervene as Third, and its intervention will reveal whether the Governor had
*the **droit*** to act as he did, or if the Governed had *the **droit*** to oppose his action.
And the totality of legal rules applied by the Third in the cases in question is
going to make up the public *Droit* of the given State (at a given moment).

When the State intervenes in the capacity of Third in the cases in question,
it must rule on two points. In the first place, it must hold that the Governor
acted as a private person and not as Governor; for in the second case, he would
have acted in the name of the State. The State would then be in solidarity with
him; it would therefore be a party and not a Third; and there would not be a
juridical situation, [and] no legal rule applicable. Second, the State must hold
that the Governed was injured by the act of the Governor-impostor (if not,
there would be no reaction, i.e., no interaction to which a legal rule conforming to an ideal of Justice would be applicable), and it must set down the way in
which the criminal or juridically illegal act must be annulled. Public *Droit* will
then have, if you will, two parts.

[407] Now it is obvious that one cannot rule on the first point by scrutinizing the intention of the Governor, if only because he may be acting "in good faith"—that is, he can be mistaken about his intentions and believe that he is acting as a citizen in the name of the State. One must have an objective criterion. And this criterion is given by the Constitution (in the broad sense), by the totality of (political) laws that set down the structure and functioning of the State. If the Governor acted at odds with the Constitution, this means he acted as an impostor, according to personal [*particuliers*] interests, and the State can intervene by way of a Third and eventually annul the act of the Governor-impostor. In themselves constitutional and administrative Laws have nothing juridical about them. But to the extent that they allow a finding that a Governor acted as an impostor, they are part of public *Droit*, such as we have defined it. If you will, they constitute the first part of this *Droit—constitutional* **Droit**.

As for the second part of this *Droit*, it is formed by *administrative* **Droit**. This *Droit* enumerates the cases in which the Governed can consider themselves harmed by the acts of Governors-impostors, and it sets down the way in which these juridically illegal acts must be annulled. Thus, the State will not need to be "provoked" by the injured Governed: it will be able to intervene spontaneously to annul the illegal act of the Governor-impostor.[19] Practically speaking, every anti-constitutional act infringes upon the interest of someone. But if such an act were not infringing upon the interest of anyone, there would not be an interaction between *two* agents, and consequently there would be no *Third*. There would then be no *Droit*, and if the State were to annul the anti-constitutional act all the same, this annulment would be purely political, and not juridical. Administrative *Droit* (and public *Droit* in general), therefore, is only a *Droit* to the extent that acts of Governors-impostors injure the Governed. And it is in this sense that one can say that public *Droit* sets down the rights[20] of the Governed.

But it would be wrong to say that the Governors have *droits* in respect to the State, i.e., in respect to the Governors acting as such; for the State can amend public *Droit* as it likes, by amending its Constitution, for example. Now when it is a matter of a Constitutional amendment [408] (i.e., also of public *Droit*, which implies the latter), *Droit* has nothing more to say since there is no longer a Third possible. However, the Constitution can only be amended by the State itself—that is, by the citizens acting as citizens and not as private persons. The citizens who amend the Constitution must act as Governors—that is, as representatives of the exclusive political Group inside of which they enjoy a political Authority. If not, they will act as impostors, as private persons [*personnes privées*], and they will fall under the grip of public *Droit*, the State intervening

---

19. In practice, the State only intervenes in certain cases if it is provoked by a Governed. Sometimes the Governed must be personally injured in order for the intervention to be possible. But all these variations are only of practical interest.

20. [Ed. In the original, the English word "rights" follows the French word *droits* in parentheses.]

by way of a Third in order to annul their juridically illegal acts. And the Constitution, i.e., public *Droit* (as constitutional *Droit*) allows one to ascertain if one is amending the Constitution as a citizen or not: one can only amend it as a citizen, i.e., legally, by using the means provided for by the Constitution itself. And it should be understood that if one uses these means, one acts politically and not juridically: for here as well, there is no longer a Third. But if one tries to amend the Constitution by illegal means, one acts as a specific private person [*en personne privée, en particulier*], and then one commits a crime of public *Droit*, which will be annulled by the State in its capacity as Third.

[This is true] unless one acts as a revolutionary against the State (i.e., the Governors armed with Authority bestowed by the exclusive political Group). In this case as well there will be no Third, i.e., public *Droit* can no longer be applied; for, by definition, the revolutionary will not act as a specific private person. He will act politically, as a citizen (of the future, post-revolutionary State). Now we have seen that any relations whatsoever between the State and the citizens acting as citizens (legally or by revolutionary, or indeed military, means) have nothing juridical about them. And the fact that the revolutionary acts politically, i.e., as a citizen, is objectively manifested (for here as well the intention does not count, each one being capable of deceiving himself): by *the risk of life* with a view to seizing power—that is, in order to constitute an exclusive political Group (putting out a collectivity of Governors armed with political Authority) which succeeds in preserving itself both against foreigners and against the domestic excluded political group. If the revolutionary fails, he dies; if he succeeds, he becomes Governor. And neither his failure and his downfall, nor his success, have anything juridical about them. This is why, moreover, the authors of an aborted revolution, or one in the process of becoming so, are rarely judged by ordinary Courts. [409] In fact, one cannot apply any *Droit* at all to them. One can only eliminate them politically, by a straightforward police action or by a political Tribunal, which will be a juridical Court in name only—just as the revolutionary Tribunal, which will do away with the agents of the old regime, will have nothing juridical about it.

In short, public *Droit* can only be applied by a State to those who recognize themselves as its citizens, who do not want to change the State as such. This *Droit* allows one to ascertain in which cases Governors act as impostors (i.e., contrary to the structure of the State, but without wanting to alter it) and injure the Governed in so doing; and it determines the way in which the interests thus infringed upon must be restored—that is, the way in which the acts in question of the so-called Governors should be annulled.

§ 59

Public *Droit* is first of all a constitutional *Droit*, and as such it includes the Constitution of the State. Now this Constitution must first and foremost regulate the manner in which it can be changed (for as long as the State is not universal and homogenous, it would be futile to believe that it will not change).

In other words, the Constitution must allow one to notice if the one (or those) who are changing the State are acting as a citizen or private person [*personne privée*], and this without needing to risk one's life in order to do so. If he acts as a citizen, one can say that it is the State that is changing itself. Thus, for example, in the Third Republic [of France] the majority of assembled Senators and Deputies were supposed to act as citizens: if this majority were to amend the State, i.e., its Constitution, one would say that the State changed itself, that it changed "legally." But this is a matter of political, and not juridical, legality. When the State changes itself, there is no Third by definition—that is, no *Droit.* But to the extent that the Constitution allows one to know in which case the men who are changing the State are acting as private persons, i.e., as impostors, against whom one can have recourse to the State, the Constitution is a *Droit,* which sets down the *droit* of the Governed to oppose any change of their status done by impostors—that is, by private persons [*particuliers*] wrongly being thought of as a constituent assembly. This *Droit* is a public *Droit.* In this sense and in this sense alone, therefore, the Constitution is part of this *Droit,* [or] more precisely, of constitutional *Droit.* But since this *Droit* provides [410] that the State can change it as it sees fit (by the action of citizens acting as citizens, i.e., under defined conditions), one cannot say that constitutional *Droit* gives rights[21] to the Governed in relation to the State. Conversely, the State cannot say that it has rights[22] over the Governed; for if they change the State by illegal, i.e., revolutionary, means—by acting politically (as citizens of the future State), by thus risking their lives in order to take power and change the State—their action will not be called criminal in the juridical sense of the word. There will simply be a political struggle, without a possible Third.

Constitutional *Droit* is generally contrasted with administrative *Droit.* But it is generally agreed that the boundaries between these two *Droits* are arbitrary. One could say that constitutional *Droit* sets down the status (and functions) of the Governors who are not at the same time Governed, while administrative *Droit* relates to the Governors who are also Governed—that is, to "Civil Servants" in the narrow sense of the word. But this distinction is rather artificial. To the extent that a Civil Servant, i.e., a Governor, is a Governed, he does not differ from the others who are Governed, who are not Governors. The Civil Servant as well only has *droits* in respect to Governors-impostors, and not in respect to the State—that is, to Governors acting as such, [and] therefore in conformity to constitutional and administrative laws. Administrative Tribunals are distinguished from ordinary Courts by the sole fact that they rule on cases where one of the agents is a Governor: the other can be a mere Governed or a Governed-Governor—that is, a Civil Servant. And there is no theoretical reason at all to create special Tribunals for cases when the Governor at

---

21. [Ed. In the original, the English word "rights" follows the French word *droits* in parentheses.]
22. [Ed. In the original, the English word "rights" follows the French word *droits* in parentheses.]

issue would not be at the same time a Governed: one and the same administrative Tribunal can judge the minister and the lowest-level civil servant, in order to see if they act as Governors-impostors or not.

One could thus distinguish a public *Droit* of structure (of the State and Administrative Apparatuses) and a public *Droit* of function, as one distinguishes anatomy from physiology. But as in the case of the organism, these two aspects make up a single reality; for the organ is only there with a view to its function, and the function is determined by the structure of the organ. Of course, imposture only arises in practice when there is functioning. But to detect imposture [411] one must generally refer not only to legal determinations of functions, but also to administrative structures.

What is more important is that public *Droit* must regulate not only the structures and functions of the State and Administrative Apparatuses, i.e., the Governors, but also those of the citizens taken as citizens, i.e., of the Governed as Governed; for the State itself is nothing but the totality of citizens, these being taken in their *political* being and functions. To set down the status and functioning of citizens is to set down the status and functioning of the State, and conversely.

The status of citizens is freely set down by the State—that is, by the Governors acting as such, or if you will, by the citizens themselves in certain of their political aspects (as a constituent Assembly, for example). This status is therefore not a *Droit* in itself, since there is not a Third that sets down and sanctions it. But it is included in public *Droit* and is thus a *Droit* to the extent that it allows one to see when a man acts as a citizen or as a private person, i.e., also when a Governor acts as an impostor; for the Governor acts as an impostor by definition not only when he is at odds with his own political status, but also when he is at odds with the political status of some Governed.

Thus, for example, the status of the citizen of a modern European State excludes bigamy. A bigamist, therefore, cannot be a citizen, nor act as such. Therefore, if a bigamist wanted to change the Constitution so that the State recognizes bigamy, i.e., if he wanted the State to serve his personal interests as a bigamist, he could not do this (legally); for by definition a bigamist cannot act as a citizen, i.e., as a private person; he could not amend the Constitution of the State without acting as an impostor. Of course, the State can recognize bigamy. But it can only do so (legally) by an action of the citizens acting as citizens—that is, as non-bigamists. And there lies the guarantee—in principle at the very least—that bigamy has been recognized for "reasons of State" and not from private interest. It should be understood that bigamists themselves can also make the State accept bigamy. But then they will have to act as revolutionaries, illegally: they will have to attack the State itself, and they will only be able to do so by risking their lives—which will be the guarantee of the fact that they act not [412] simply as private persons-bigamists, but politically as well, as *citizens*-revolutionaries. And this is what justifies the fact that *Droit* will not be applied in this case, that bigamy will be, if they succeed, a political status just as legal as monogamy, which could also be included in the new public *Droit*.

Now the imaginary case of bigamy brings to our attention a very important point. Every real citizen being a living man, i.e., a non-citizen also, political status must also be related to the non-political being and functioning of citizens. The status of citizens must determine which non-political functionings are compatible or not with political functioning. In other words, the State must establish the norms [governing] relations between the citizen and non-citizen, both outside the citizen and inside the citizen himself. Thus, for example, bigamy belongs exclusively to the status of a member of familial Society. But the State can declare that bigamy is incompatible with citizenship. Now man is first of all an animal. The State must therefore say which animal (Homo sapiens) can be a citizen or exercise any "*droit*" of the citizen. For example, the State may remove the *droit* to vote from children, the insane, women, and so on. Furthermore, man is a member of familial Society, and here as well certain familial relations can be incompatible with citizenship (incest, bigamy, and so on). The same for economic, religious, and other Societies: citizenship can be incompatible with the non-payment of debts, with a certain religious belief, and so on. The State can likewise declare that a citizen cannot be part of a sub- or trans-state political Society: to be a citizen of another State, for example, or a member of the Communist International, and so on.

All variations are possible here, and the State decides [these possibilities] sovereignly. But no State can do without encompassing in the political status of the citizen certain non-political aspects of his being and his functioning. And, as we will see (in part C), this is very important for penal *Droit;* for if a non-political action is compatible with citizenship while being contrary to private (penal) *Droit,* the sentence cannot affect the citizen as citizen. If, for example, the citizen as such has the *droit* to move about, the sentence cannot deprive him of this freedom of mobility. Therefore, if an action brings about a sentence that injures the citizen as citizen, i.e., in his political being and functioning (as voter, for [413] example), it is because the action injures not only a given non-political Society (economic Society, for example) but also the State itself. Therefore, to the extent that the sentence affects the citizen politically, it is delivered by the State not by way of a Third, but as a party. In other words, in this aspect the sentence is not juridical and does not have a *Droit* for a basis. But to the extent that the status of the citizen allows one to ascertain that a Governor (who is at odds with him) is acting as an impostor, which allows the State to apply public *Droit,* this status is part of this *Droit* and is itself a *Droit.* As *Droit,* the status of the citizen sets down the rights[23] of the Governed in respect to the Governors-impostors, but not in respect to the State. Likewise, when a citizen acts contrary to his status of citizen, he injures the State as such: he is not therefore a criminal in the juridical sense of the word, the State being a party and not a Third; he is a political criminal against whom the State acts politically and not juridically.

---

23. [Ed. In the original, the English word "rights" follows the French word *droits* in parentheses.]

Public *Droit*, therefore, necessarily implies laws setting down the structure and functioning not only of the State and its Administrative Apparatuses, i.e., the Governors, but also those of the Governed, taken as Governed by the State—that is, as citizens. To return to our image, anatomy must be completed by histology, and organic physiology by cellular physiology. As for the status of the Governed taken as non-citizens, i.e., private persons [*personnes privées*] (Homo sapiens animals and members of familial, economic, and other Societies), it is part of private *Droit* (civil and penal). But seeing that private *Droit* is state-sanctioned, it is the same State that applies both private *Droit* and public *Droit* in its capacity as Third. This is why private status must be in agreement with political status. Consequently, if a Governor infringes upon the private status of the Governed, by definition he acts as an impostor, just as if he infringed upon the political status. In this sense, therefore, one could say that private status is also part of public *Droit*. This shows that the division between public *Droit* and private *Droit* is artificial to a certain extent: there is basically a single *Droit* (applied by the State). But one can nevertheless bring together under the category of "private *Droit*" all the legal rules that are related to politically "neutral" interactions, i.e., compatible with citizenship, even if they are juridically illegal from the point of view of the *Droit* of an apolitical Society (juridically recognized by the State) that the State [414] applies by way of a Third. In this case, moreover, private *Droit* would reduce to civil *Droit*, in conformity with the classic division of *Droit*.

Be that as it may, public *Droit* is only a **Droit** to the extent that it is related to interactions between the Governed and Governors-impostors. It is only in respect to the latter that the Governed has *rights*,[24] and not in respect to the State, for it can change as it likes all the statuses without there being any possible Third able to oppose or sanction the change nor, consequently, the absence of change—that is, the status itself. This does not mean that the Governed who is injured only has recourse against the Governor-impostor. The State can compensate him. But it will then be a question of a free decision by the State, which will have nothing juridical about it. Public **Droit** only allows the *annulment* of the act of the Governor-impostor (in a way set down by this *Droit*, which can include compensatory damages). If the State wants to punish in addition the guilty Governor, it will then be a party and the punishment will have nothing juridical about it. Likewise, if the State develops solidarity with the Governor, public **Droit** will be unable to prescribe compensation for the Governed who is injured: seeing that the Governor has effectively acted in the name of the State, *Droit* is no longer possible and the Governed has no right[25] at all. The State can certainly compensate him all the same, but the act in itself will then have nothing juridical about it. But it can nevertheless be implied in

---

24. [Ed. In the original, the English word "rights" follows the French word **droits** in parentheses.]
25. [Ed. In the original, the English word "right" follows the French word *droit* in parentheses.]

public *Droit* and thus be a *Droit,* a legal rule; for the law on compensation will allow a determination that the Governor who would refuse to compensate the Governed would act as an impostor. In short, public *Droit* can contain all that it traditionally contains. However, this content must be interpreted in the way which I have just done.

§ 60

If *Droit arises* from the intervention of an impartial and disinterested Third in a (social) interaction between two agents, the relations between these agents and the Third have nothing juridical about them and cannot give rise to the application of a legal rule. These relations can be regulated by (oral or written) Laws, but these procedural Laws will not be juridical laws. In this sense, the "procedural *Droit*" which regulates the status of the Third and its functioning in relation to the litigants is not a genuine **Droit**. It is a [415] unilateral declaration of the Third, a "statement" of his conduct, and no other "Third" (who would be a "fourth") can either annul or sanction this declaration. When *Droit* is state-sanctioned, the Third is the State (or its representative), and it is therefore ultimately the State that decrees procedural Law. Therefore, it is, if you will, a political Law, and not juridical. However, here as well the Third can be an impostor. Supposed to act in an impartial and disinterested manner, he can in fact be interested and partial. In this case, by definition, he will not be a Third, but a party, and one will be able to have recourse to a Third against him.[26] In the case of state-sanctioned *Droit,* he will not be a representative of the State, the Judge-civil servant, but a private person [*particulier*] (impostor), against whom one can have recourse to the State playing the role of an authentic Third. The big question, therefore, is knowing if the person who plays the role of the Third is truly a Third—that is, if he acts as such, in an impartial and disinterested manner, or if he is only pretending to do so by deceiving others, notably the litigants, or indeed, mistaken himself on his own account.

When the Third is an Arbiter freely chosen by the parties, this very choice is supposed to be a guarantee of his authenticity—that is, his impartiality and disinterestedness (his intervention would otherwise not be irresistible, and the *droit* that he declares would therefore only exist in potentiality). But if *Droit* (in actuality) is state sanctioned, i.e., when the Third is imposed on the parties by the State and represents it in the capacity of Civil Servant (properly so-called, or in the sense that his intervention is sanctioned by the State), then the problem arises as to the authenticity or imposture of the Third. It is the same problem with respect to non-juridical Civil Servants in public *Droit*—more precisely in administrative *Droit*. In this sense, therefore, procedural Law is part of the latter (by constituting a special chapter of it). Procedural Law is thus a *Droit*. It allows one to notice the authenticity of the Third; for if the Third

---

26. [Ed. Reading *on pourra faire appel contre lui* for *ne pourra faire appel contre lui* as in the original manuscript.]

acts in violation of this Law, he is by definition an impostor: in his function as Third, he is acting in reality as a private person. The State therefore intervenes as Third in the relations between the "Third"-impostor with the litigants, and it "overturns" his judgment—that is, annuls his intervention, which, at that point, is *juridically* illegal. Procedural *Droit* therefore creates rights[27] of litigants in respect to the State, i.e., in respect to the authentic Third—that is, the Third who conforms to procedural *Droit* (which, [416] in this case, is no longer a *Droit,* but a non-juridical Law).

Procedural *Droit,* therefore, is only a *Droit* to the extent that it allows one to notice the imposture of the Third—that is, the fact that he is not acting in the name of the State, as civil servant or citizen, but in the capacity of a private person [*personne privée*]. This *Droit* is, if you will, the guarantee of the impartiality and disinterestedness of the Third (i.e., of his identity with the State, which is by definition disinterested and impartial in respect to its litigants).[28]

The content of procedural *Droit* (in the narrow sense) is a function of its goal, which is to guarantee the impartiality and disinterestedness of the Third—that is, his authenticity. And it is from this point of view that one must interpret the (state-sanctioned) administration [*réglementation*] of justice.

First of all, [there is] the institution of *Appeal.* But here one must distinguish between two cases. *In the first place,* the two parties, or one of them, can challenge the authenticity of the Third and therefore the validity of his judgment. There will then be a new trial—no longer between the two parties, but between the parties and the Third (suspected of inauthenticity). The State (in the person of the Third of the Appeal) must then see whether the Third truly acted as Third or not. If not, then the appeal will overturn the judgment, which is nothing other than a (juridically illegal) action of a private person [*particulier*]—that is, of a Third-impostor. This is a case of administrative *Droit,* and the Appeal Court is then an administrative Tribunal, similar to other administrative Tribunals and different from juridical Courts. It does not rule on the trial itself—that is, it does not intervene as Third in the interaction of the litigants among themselves. It remands the matter back to the Court of "first instance," where the case is judged again, but with another Third. And this leads us to the second case. *Second,* the impartiality and disinterestedness [of the Third], i.e., the authenticity of the Third, can be guaranteed not only by

---

27. [Ed. In the original, the English word "rights" follows the French word *droits* in parentheses.]

28. The Third, and the State as Third, is juridical Legislator, Judge, and judicial Police. When juridical legislation is the work of the political Government (monarchy, parliament, and so on), the Laws that are related to it are not part of procedural *Droit;* they are implied in constitutional *Droit.* But when juridical Laws are elaborated by the Courts (as in England, for example), one can say that the procedural *Droit* which regulates the functioning of the Courts also guarantees the authenticity of the Third in his capacity as Legislator. Concerning the judicial Police, its regulation can be found either in procedural *Droit* or in administrative *Droit* in the narrow sense. In all cases, procedural *Droit* guarantees the authenticity of the Third taken as Judge. And this is the narrow sense of this term.

the conformity of his [417] conduct to procedural *Droit*, but also by the fact that the judgment does not change when one changes the Third. In this case the Appeal (and the remand to the first proceeding) is nothing other than a change of Third. It is therefore not appropriate to speak of a hierarchy of "proceedings," all of which are on the same plane: there is one and the same Third (the State), and only its "helpers [*supports*]" change in order to guarantee their authenticity. Only in the case of disagreement between two consecutive judgments is it necessary to have recourse to a third, the two concurring judgments being by definition authentic. There must then be at least three proceedings. But it is possible that all three may be in disagreement, which complicates things terribly. This is why, as a matter of convenience, one introduces the idea of a hierarchy of proceedings: the higher [court] is supposed to be more authentic than the lower [court], and the final [court] is authentic by definition. By definition, then, one can stop a trial at some proceeding or another, which will in this case be declared authentic as a matter of course, i.e., truly impartial and disinterested: the State then automatically shows solidarity with it and sanctions its judgment. Let us note, moreover, that in neither of the two cases under consideration is the imposture of the Third necessarily a fraud on his part. He can be in good faith, i.e., believing that he is impartial and disinterested; for he can be mistaken. And, by definition, if his judgment is erroneous, it is because he was either interested or partial, or both at the same time. (And indeed, one can easily be partial even without realizing it; for a "correct" judgment is nothing other than the intervention of an impartial and disinterested Third.) The mistake in judgment, therefore, can only be attributed to the absence of these qualities. Now one is not only "partial" when one has "preferences" for one of the parties; one is also so when one knows the case of one better than the other. A mistake in the proper sense of the word, therefore, is really a "partiality" in justice. Likewise, if the Third does not correctly apply the Law to the given case (correctly established), it is because he is "interested": he acts according to a motive other than to apply the ideal of Justice—that is, by definition, precisely the Law in question. Now, by definition equal, when there is a juridical hierarchy, the higher court is supposed to be more "impartial" and "disinterested" than the lower court. This is why, in the case of disagreement, the "appeal" judgment alone can be considered valid and definitive. When the parties do not appeal, moreover, one can say that there is an arbitration: the parties have [418] come to agreement on the choice of the Third and this agreement is the guarantee (by definition) of his authenticity. But practically speaking, the State (i.e., the appeal court) can intervene all the same, if it notices the inauthenticity of the Third (due to the fact that he acted contrary to procedural *Droit*).

This theory of Appeal also applies to the institution of *pardon*. By definition the leader of the State embodies the State and cannot be an impostor (as long as he remains leader). He can therefore play the role of supreme Third and "overturn" any judgment whatsoever: either by remanding the trial to a lower court, or by ruling himself in a definitive manner. But if he leaves his judgment intact, his "pardon" has nothing juridical about it; for he no longer acts in the capacity of *Third*. He no longer deals with *two* parties; he is only related to *one*, to the losing party, the convict. His pardon is then an (individual) political Law, and has nothing to do with *Droit*—except in the sense that the pardoned one has a **droit** to his pardon, which means that any Governor who would act contrary to the fact that he has been pardoned would by definition act as an impostor, and the pardoned one could appeal against him to the State, the latter then annulling the action of the Governor.

It is the same idea of the guarantee of authenticity of the Third which is at the base of the institution of *Jury*. By definition the Jury is impartial and disinterested. There is then no appeal possible. It is the State which acts through the Jury. And the Jury is an authentic Third, because its members (its "helpers") are "anyone at all" (cf. Part One, chapter 1). Now in fact this guarantee is very precarious. There are, of course, excellent chances that the Jury will be "disinterested" in the common sense of the word. This institution excludes the corruption and influence of Governors-impostors, who would want that the judgment be made according to their interests, which are other than those of Justice. But in another sense the Jury can very easily be "partial" and "interested." A male Jury can be "partial" in respect to a pretty young female litigant; a "bourgeois" Jury can be "interested" in a trial when the criminal strikes a blow at economic Society (theft); and so on. It therefore seems that the solution attempted in Germany is the best. A Third which is somewhere between a professional Judge and Jury seems to provide the maximum guarantee of authenticity: the Jury element makes him "incorruptible" ("disinterested") and the professional element [makes him] "objective" ("impartial"). But it should be understood that the ideal can be closely approximated only in a universal and homogenous State.

One can interpret the institutions [419] of Prosecutor and Defense Counsel[29] from the same point of view. Indeed, one can say that the person of the authentic Third always brings together in himself a Prosecutor, a Defense Counsel, and a Judge-Arbiter. This trinity is only a consequence of the principle *"audiatur et altera pars."*[30] As for the question of knowing if these three elements should be brought together in one person alone or divided among three distinct and "independent" persons, this is a purely practical question.[31] However, if in this interpretation one creates the institution of Prosecutor, one

---

29. [Ed. Kojève here uses the word *Avocat,* which signifies any lawyer who pleads before the courts (or a barrister in British terms). The context, however, seems to indicate the meaning of defense counsel.]

30. [Ed. Literally, "let the other side be heard as well." Common law lawyers will recognize a slightly different Latin tag, *"audi alteram partem."*]

31. [Ed. It should be remembered that in continental judicial systems, the judge is authorized and even required to play an "inquisitorial" role. At times during the proceeding, therefore, he may appear to act as a prosecutor or defense counsel in his questioning, despite the presence of both "independent" (in Kojève's sense) prosecuting and defense counsels in the courtroom.]

must complete it by that of state's Attorney [*Avocat étatique*].[32] And in the majority of cases, a defense counsel is named even if the litigant does not personally retain one. But, in general, the latter can refuse the assistance of a defence counsel. It seems that in this case one would equally have to dispense with the Prosecutor. Or again, if the latter is indispensable, the defense counsel would have to be so also and represent the State in the same way as the Prosecutor.

But one can give to this dual institution a different interpretation. In a civil trial the Third is generally dealing with two lawyers, each of whom represents one of the parties. This "representation" certainly has a practical utility (to which Roman *Droit* had to yield, having originally not admitted "representation"); but it has no theoretical interest at all. The lawyer here is identical with the party he represents. Now in a criminal Trial the party at issue, i.e., the accused, is also generally "represented" by a lawyer, who is identical with him. And this lawyer is opposed by a prosecutor. One could therefore say that the prosecutor is the lawyer of the opposite party, who is also identical with the party he represents. Now we will see (in part C) that in a criminal trial, there is always effectively an "*altera pars*"; for penal *Droit* is nothing other than the intervention of a Third (of the State) in an interaction between a Society (juridically recognized by the State but different from it) and one of its members (individual or collective). One can therefore say that the Prosecutor represents the Society at issue, which—obviously—being a collectivity, a moral person, cannot act personally. Generally speaking, the Prosecutor would represent all those who cannot—in principle—be a party to legal proceedings: the incompetent, for example, and notably minors. He would clearly then be a party, and not a Third, just like the Defense Counsel. But one must say that theoretically this institution, thus conceived, is not necessary (although it may be practically very useful); for the Law fills, as it were, the office of Prosecutor. Society is injured by definition when one of its [420] members acts contrary to the *Droit* of this Society (recognized by the State). Therefore, Society does not need to be "represented" in the criminal trial, since it is the law applied by the Third which "represents" it. Just like the Defense Counsel, therefore, the Prosecutor is a practically useful institution, but without theoretical interest; and this in both possible interpretations.

C. Penal *Droit*

§ 61

Penal or criminal *Droit* is generally included in public *Droit* and contrasted to private *Droit*, which then coincides with civil (in the sense of non-penal) *Droit*. One may wonder if this is truly the case. And the answer will depend on the way in which one interprets penal *Droit*.

---

32. [Ed. The idiomatic American translation is given here; in Britain or other Commonwealth countries, "Crown attorney" would be appropriate.]

Usually, penal *Droit* is included in public *Droit* on the basis that the crime injures the State as such, that it is therefore a matter of an interaction between the criminal and the State. Now the relations between the individual and the State would fall within the competence of public *Droit*. But we have seen that in the cases when the State is injured as such, it is a party and no longer Third, such that there is no longer *Droit* at all. To the extent that the criminal injures the State, the law that is applied to him is very much "public," if you will (i.e., political or social), but there is nothing juridical about it. Thus interpreted, penal *Droit* would not be a *Droit* at all (except to the extent that it allows one to notice that a Governor is acting as an impostor, for then it would be a part of public *Droit*).

In order for (state-sanctioned) penal *Droit* to be a *Droit,* the State must intervene by way of a Third. In other words, the criminal must be in interaction (in his crime) not with the State but with a private person (individual or collective). Like all *Droit* in general, penal *Droit* is therefore a "private" *Droit.* And it is distinguished from civil (private) *Droit* only by the following two points: in the first place, the State annuls the action contrary to penal *Droit* in a "spontaneous" way, while in civil *Droit* it must be "provoked" by the agent injured in the interaction contrary to civil *Droit;* second, the action contrary to penal *Droit* results in [421] a "penalty" or "punishment," while the action contrary to civil *Droit* is annulled by the Third without the agent being punished in addition. Now, we have seen that the "spontaneity" of penal *Droit* is only apparent. In fact, the State is also here "provoked" by the injured party. However, in this case, he is not a member (individual or collective) of a Society (non-political but juridically recognized by the State), but this Society taken as a whole. The latter not being able to "provoke" the Third in fact, the State introduces a convention: it sets down the cases when Society is supposed to be injured and provokes the intervention of the Third, in a (written or oral) penal Code, and it intervenes "spontaneously" every time that someone acts contrary to this Code, in the idea that Society is "provoking" it, being injured by the action in question.[33] What characterizes penal Droit, therefore, is not the "spontaneity" of the intervention of the Third, but the fact that the act annulled by the Third (i.e., the crime) is related to the whole of a Society juridically recognized by the State (but other than the State itself). Now Society taken as a whole can, in principle, be (juridically) injured not only by a "private person" (individual or collective) but also by a Governor (individual or collective, non-governed or governed, i.e., by a Civil Servant), who will in this

---

33. The principle of penal *Droit*, "*Nulla poena nisi lege* [no penalty where there is no law]," means nothing other than the fact that there is no *crime* (and consequently no punishment or judgment) when the act is not contrary to the penal Code; for in this case, by definition, Society has not "provoked" the State, which therefore is not to intervene by way of a Third. And Society does not "provoke" him because it is deemed not to have been injured by the inter-action of which the would-be (but not in fact) criminal act is part—at least it is not injured juridically, i.e., in a way such that the Third consents to intervene to annul the act that injured it.

case be by definition an "impostor."[34] In other words, penal *Droit* can be part not only of private *Droit* but also [422] of public *Droit,* such as we defined it above: there is a penal and civil public *Droit,* just as there is a penal and civil private *Droit.*

If penal *Droit* is related to acts that injure a Society taken as a whole, there are as many species of this *Droit* as there are Societies other than the State, but juridically recognized by the State—that is, Societies such that the State intervenes by way of a Third at the time of their interactions with their members (individual or collective).[35] The nature and number of these Societies vary according to places and epochs, and correspondingly, so does the content of the penal *Droit* of a State. It is generally a question of familial, economic, "worldly," and religious Societies. But generally, modern States do not recognize juridically the latter, and more and more limit their intervention to interactions between "worldly" Society and its members. But it does not seem that the State could juridically ignore the existence of the first two Societies. There will always then be a penal *Droit* of familial Society and a penal *Droit* of economic Society. Generally speaking, there will be as many species of penal *Droit* as species of civil *Droit;* for it is inconceivable that the State would intervene juridically, i.e., in the capacity of Third, in the interactions between the members of a Society (i.e., by applying the civil *Droit* of this Society) without intervening in the interactions between the Society as such and its members (i.e., by applying the corresponding penal *Droit*). But it is possible that the State reserves for itself this last intervention, while having Society itself intervene in the capacity of Third in the interactions between its members. In this case alone penal *Droit* will be fully state-sanctioned. But this distinction does not have theoretical importance, for the *Droit* sanctioned by the State is a state *Droit,* even if it is applied by delegated [agents] who are not civil servants properly so-called.

Now we have seen that the State as State, i.e., as political entity, is itself related to members of certain non-political Societies, since the citizen who [423] realizes the State is necessarily at the same time a member of these Societies: notably

---

34. It is generally said that punishment does not apply to collectivities. But these are rather practical than theoretical arguments to which one refers; for if one recognizes "moral" juridical persons, it is not evident why one cannot also apply to them penal *Droit* in cases when they injure a Society as a whole, even if this person is a collectivity ("Society" or "Association" or an "Institution"). As for the individual moral person (a minor, for example) there still are extra-juridical reasons that make him non-responsible from the penal point of view. But this is a complicated question that I do not want to deal with here.

Practically speaking, a Governor rarely infringes upon the interests of a Society taken as a whole: the "imposture" would be too obvious here. But, in principle, the case is possible.
35. By definition, the members of two distinct Societies cannot enter into inter-action as members of these Societies: religious Society, for example, lacks common ground with economic Society, and so on. But it should be understood that a member of Society A can be at the same time a member of Society B, and consequently injure it: but he will do so as a member of Society B. This is why one can say that penal *Droit* is only related to interactions between a given Society and its members (individual or collective).

familial and economic Societies. This is why the (political) status of the citizen necessarily implies certain elements of the (non-political) statuses of members of these Societies (and—in the past—also religious and "worldly" Societies). To act contrary to these elements of non-political statuses, therefore, is also to act contrary to the political status of the citizen, which is true above all for acts that, being contrary to the status of a member of the given Society, injures this Society as such, taken as a whole. In other words, a lot of acts contrary to penal *Droit* will also be contrary to the political status of the citizen. Or once again, they will injure not only the Society in question but also the State itself. And it is this that leads to the belief and claim that (state-sanctioned) penal *Droit* is related to interactions between the "individual" and the State, which is injured by him. But, once more, to the extent that this is truly so, the penal Law no longer has anything juridical about it and is in no way a *Droit*. The State then intervenes politically (or "socially") as a party, and not juridically, as an impartial and disinterested Third. Practically speaking, these two interventions are intimately linked to one another, seeing that it is the same State (and generally in the person of the same Civil Servant) that intervenes, on the one hand, as State, i.e., politically, and on the other, as Third, i.e., juridically. But theoretically the two interventions are essentially different, and there is only (penal) **Droit** to the extent that it is a matter of the second intervention. And it is even perhaps preferable that the two interventions be separated from one another and be carried out by two different Civil Servants or Courts, of which only one would be called juridical. I will have the opportunity, moreover, to return to this question of the non-juridical aspects or "supplements [*annexes*]" of historical penal *Droit* (§ 63).

Be that as it may, let us suppose that penal *Droit* is related to interactions between a given (non-political) Society and its members, whomever they may be, this interaction giving rise to the intervention of an impartial and disinterested Third (i.e., other than the Society in question itself), and that the action annulled by this Third is "criminal" by definition.[36] Seeing that the Society, being a moral person, [424] is effectively unable to have recourse to the Third

---

36. It seems that the Third can annul not only the action of the member of Society but also that of the Society itself. In other words, there would [424] be not only "criminal" acts of a member of a Society injuring this Society but also "criminal" acts of the Society injuring its member. But this way of speaking does not make sense. If the Society was able to injure its members, it would sooner or later disintegrate: its status, being by definition transitory, cannot therefore be a *Droit,* which is by definition "eternal"—that is, able to maintain itself, in principle, indefinitely in identity with itself. (See my study on Authority [cf. pg. 160n38], where the authority of the Judge, and Justice as such, are related to eternity—that is, to the whole of time. But this question would have to be delved into more fully.) By definition, the action of Society as such benefits Society, [and] therefore also its members taken as members of the Society. But being a moral person, Society can only act through the intermediary of its members. Now they can harm other members, even by supposedly acting in the name of Society. But then they are "impostors," whose action can be annulled by the Third, even if this Third is Society itself, and not the State (Society then acting through authentic representatives). In short, we have here a case of quasi-"public *Droit,*" being related, however, to representatives of a non-political Society, and not to Civil Servants of a State.

(unless it has to this end an authentic representative), he intervenes "spontaneously." This means that the Third intervenes every time that the act of a member of the Society is contrary to an (oral or written) Code, where all the cases of an act that injures Society are set down in a way that it is presumed to have recourse to the Third, who is then obliged to intervene and annul the act if it is really as it seems to be (i.e., "criminal"). This Code is the penal Code (without which there is no crime, no penalty, no intervention of the Third). If the Third who creates and realizes the penal Code in and by his intervention (who creates it by intervening as juridical Legislator and who realizes it by intervening as Judge and judicial Police) is the State itself (not acting politically, but as an impartial and disinterested Third, i.e., with the sole concern to realize a given ideal of Justice), penal *Droit* is a state-sanctioned *Droit,* existing in actuality. If we now bring together all non-political Societies juridically recognized by the State into a single non-political Society that we will call "Society" simply (the "*Bürgerliche Gesellschaft*" of the German writers, in contrast to political Society, called the "State"), we can say that state-sanctioned penal *Droit* is created and realized by the intervention of the State (acting in the capacity of Third) in the interactions between Society as such and its members (individual or collective), in order to annul the acts of the latter to the extent that they effectively injure Society taken as a whole.

[425] This amounts to saying that, when the State applies penal *Droit,* it intervenes "spontaneously," i.e., without effectively being "provoked" by the injured party—that is, by Society. It is "provoked" by the penal Code or *Droit,* which sets down the interests of Society, these interests and therefore this Code or this *Droit* being established by the State itself in its capacity as Third (in its aspect as juridical Legislator).[37] We thus rejoin the classical conception according to which it is the "spontaneity" of the intervention of the State that distinguishes penal *Droit* from civil *Droit.* But as its very name indicates, penal *Droit* is also and above all characterized by the fact that it implies the idea of penalty or punishment. And it is in this way that it is generally characterized. It is therefore a matter of seeing if the two (or three) distinctive characteristics of penal *Droit* coincide. In other words, one must see if, every time the State intervenes "*spontaneously,*" it intervenes in an interaction between *Society* and its member, and if in this case its intervention always results in either a "*punishment*" (or acquittal) of the member in question; and if, conversely, there is a "penalty" only when the State intervenes in an interaction of a member of Society with this Society itself, the State then intervening "spontaneously."

It is only after having shown that the "spontaneous" intervention of the State; the interaction between Society and its member; and the penalty accom-

---

37. **Droit** only exists to the extent that it is a matter of an interest *juridically* recognized by the Third (i.e., here by the State). Society may well have been injured, but if the State does not annul the act that injures it, this act is not criminal. Society has been "materially" but not "juridically" injured. If it has reacted by annulling the act that injured it itself, it did not have *the* **droit** to do so.

panying the annulment of the juridically illegal act, are effectively three insep-arable phenomena, the presence of one of them bringing about the two others, that we can say that the *essential* juridical character of penal *Droit* is due to the fact that it is related to the interactions between Society as such and some one of its members (while civil *Droit* is related to the interactions between two members of Society). And this is what I would like to try to do in the follow-ing section (§ 62). Now, to reach this end, one must start from the uncontested fact of the *penal* character of criminal *Droit*. However, if the penalty charac-terizes a **Droit**, it must be a truly and authentically *juridical* phenomenon. Therefore, it is first of all necessary to establish and analyze it as such. The the-ory of penal *Droit* therefore ultimately boils down to an essentially and specif-ically *juridical* theory [426] of the penal [*peine*]. It is this theory that I now want to attempt to outline.

§ 62

According to our "behaviorist" definition, *Droit* only exists when an (impartial and disinterested) Third intervenes in a (social) interaction between A and B in order to annul B's reaction to A's action. A then has a *right*[38] to his action, and B's action, i.e., his reaction to the act of A, is juridically illicit or ille-gal; it is an "infraction," a "wrong," or a "crime." We will retain this last des-ignation when we speak of penal *Droit*. All juridically illegal action is therefore a negation (or an attempted negation) of a subjective right:[39] it injures some-one *juridically*—that is, it infringes upon someone's *right*.[40] To annul criminal action, therefore, is to annul the juridical injury; to restore or confirm a sub-jective *droit;* [and] to allow the injured person to exercise a *droit*—that is, to behave in conformity with this *droit* without encountering resistance. And the "introspective" definition says to us that the juridical injury, or the crime, is nothing other than the negation either of an equality between A and B, or their equivalence, or, finally, of some synthesis of these two elements, i.e., of equity, in their interactions. In short, criminal action is contrary to a given ideal of Jus-tice, and the Third has as his only goal to make the interactions between A and B again conform to this ideal. If A's subjective *droits* are set down in a Code (or in an objective *Droit*, oral or written), one can define juridically illegal action as an action contrary to this Code, and one can then abstract from the person of A and his action. Given that, taken in itself, every re-action is an action, one can abstract from the fact that the illicit action is a reaction to A's juridically legal action, which tends to annul it. One can consider it as an *action* which is

---

38. [Ed. In the original, the English word "right" follows the French word **droit** in paren-theses.]
39. [Ed. In the original, the English word "right" follows the French phrase *droit subjectif* in parentheses.]
40. [Ed. In the original, the English word "right" follows the French word **droit** in paren-theses.]

contrary to an (objective) Code or *Droit*—that is, by definition, incompatible with someone's subjective *droits*. If the Code sets down the subjective *droits* of an A which is a (non-political) Society taken as a whole, it is a matter of a *penal* Code or *Droit*. And the action contrary to this Code or *Droit* is a *crime*, a *criminal* action. The intervention of the Third (which is "spontaneous") then aims at [427] overcoming or annulling this criminal action (this overcoming implying a "penalty").

Now, like all action in general, criminal action is made up of three essential constitutive elements. Action is first of all the "intention": in this aspect, it is the "motive" that makes the agent act; it is the "goal" that he poses or proposes to himself. (In the action of drinking, for example, the intention is the desire to quench one's thirst—that is, ultimately, to experience a certain contentment in quenching one's thirst.) Second, the action is the "will to act": in this aspect, it is the decision effectively to do this or that thing. (In our example, [it is] the decision to get oneself a glass of water.) Finally, third, the action is the "act": it is in this aspect that it is carried out or is realized, or indeed actualizes itself. ([It is] the act of drinking the glass of water, in our example.) The annulment of an action, therefore, also has three elements or aspects. One annuls the action as "intention," as "will" (to act), and as the effective "act." Now the intention is actualized in and by the will, and the latter in and by the act. It is therefore as act that the action is fully and perfectly actualized. The action that has not yet come to the stage of act remains in a state of potentiality, and the action annulled in its aspect of act is annulled as a whole as actually existing. It is only as act that an action can be part of an *actual* inter-action. In other words, it is only as act that it can annul another *actual* action—that is, *actually* injure an agent. It is the act alone which can overcome an equality or an equivalence (and therefore their synthesis) existing in actuality. As well, by annulling the act that overcomes them, one restores their *actuality*. By intervening in an *actual* inter-action, therefore, the Third is only related to acts, and it is an act that he annuls if the case arises.

Let us now propose a definition. If the Third annuls the action (which is then by definition juridically illicit) in its aspect of "act," this annulment will not be a "penalty" or a "punishment" in the proper sense of the word: one will not say that the agent has been "punished" by the annulment of his action (as act), nor that it was "criminal." There will only be a "penalty" properly so-called when the Third overcomes the action (which will then be "criminal" in the proper sense) either as "intention" or as "will," or finally, as "intention" and "will" at the same time. Now here there are three cases to keep in mind. First of all, the Third can annul the action as intention or will because it never existed [428] as act. Second, he can do it because the action cannot be annulled as an act (this act having taken place). Finally, third, the Third can annul the action as intention and will although he has annulled it as act. It is in this last case that the penalty is particularly apparent. But in truth there is no difference between the penalties in these three cases. Let us note, moreover, that from the *juridical* point of view, the penalty, i.e., the annulment of an "intention" or a "will," is essentially nothing other than the non-penal (or "civil") juridical annulment of an "act." In the two cases, it is a matter of annulling a juridically illicit action—that is, in the final analysis, to reestablish equality or equivalence between the two agents interacting by the suppression of the action (i.e., the re-action) of the one who is tending to annul the action of the other. But from the *ontological* point of view, the penalty differs essentially from non-penal annulment, for the intention and will, being merely potentialities of an action, differ essentially from the *act,* which is the actuality of this same action. And since *Droit* is a *realization* of Justice, determined as such not only by the *ideal* of Justice but also by the *reality* of the interactions to which this ideal is applied, one must take into account in the subdivision of *Droit ontological* distinctions. As well, it is necessary to distinguish *penal Droit* from *Droit* that is not it.

Let us now try to justify our definition by an analysis of some examples. The Third intervenes to annul the reaction of debtor B who opposes the action of creditor A to collect his debt. To simplify things, let us say that the Third annuls B's illicit action by forcing him to pay his debt, put at $100. The fact that B pays the $100 is surely not a penalty; and it is surely B's "act" which is annulled, for neither the Third (nor A) are concerned with B's intention or will. The *act* of non-payment is annulled by the *act* of payment, and not the intention or the will [not] to pay. The act of *non*-payment is annulled by the annulment of its essence, i.e., the "non": it is thus transformed into an act of payment. Generally speaking, an act is annulled by the same act performed, so to speak, in the reverse sense: an act "non-a" by an act "a", and an act "a" by an act "non-a"; the act of not doing it by the act of doing it, and the act of doing it by the act of not doing it. Thus, for example, B breaks A's window and the Third intervenes to force B to pay what it costs to replace the window, put at $10. The act of breaking the window is therefore annulled [429] by the act of not breaking it—that is, of here making it non-broken, of putting it back in its original state, so that everything is as if it had never been broken. Here as well the fact of paying $10 is not a penalty inflicted on B. And here also there is no question of intention or will. One will say that the two cases are cases of civil *Droit* and not penal *Droit.* Let us now suppose that B steals $100 from A—that is, seizes what is juridically the property of A without his consent. And let us assume that in a given *Droit,* the Third intervenes in this case solely to force B to restore to A his $100. There will be no penalty either, and in this *Droit* theft will be a case of civil *Droit.* Now, if every intervention of the Third reduces to restitution, the Third will not be able to intervene when nothing has been stolen. The intention and the will to steal will not provoke any intervention of the Third as long as there is no act of theft. This means that there will be no annulment of the intention or will alone. Let us suppose, by contrast, that (in another *Droit*) the Third does not limit himself to forcing B to restore A's $100, but "annuls" his act of theft by having something else done to him or preventing him from doing something else in addition: by killing him, by mauling his body, by imprisoning him, by making him pay a fine (collected by the Third), and so on.[41] In this case the annulment will incontestable imply a penalty; this will be a case of penal *Droit*.[42] Can one then say that the penalty annuls the intention or the will (in addition to the non-penal annulment of the act)? It very much seems so.

[430] Seeing that B has returned the stolen sum to A, the *status quo ante* has been reestablished; the criminal act has been annulled by its repetition in the reverse sense; and one could say, as in the case of the broken window, that it has not taken place. Therefore, if the Third still intervenes in order to annul B's action, it is because he also wants to annul it in its aspects other than that of "act"—that is, either as "will" or "intention", or finally, in these two aspects at the same time. Now it is obvious, first of all, that the penalty is related to the criminal action taken as "will" (to act). Indeed, if B had taken the $100 from A without his consent, but purely by accident (for example, by bringing it, without knowing it, in the drawer of a piece of furniture bought from A), the Third would not inflict a penalty on B, although the $100 would have to be restored to A. The theft as crime, therefore, is not the fact of seizing a property without (or even against) the owner's consent: it is the (conscious and free) will to do it knowingly [*à bon escient*]. And the penalty is therefore related not to the "act" but to the "will" to steal. If the "act" is annulled by the restitution of the stolen object to its owner, the penalty is supposed to annul the "will" to steal. Now, if this is the way things are, the Third can intervene and inflict a punishment on the thief even if the criminal action has not gone beyond the stage of "will," even if there has only been an attempted theft (aborted for some reason or other).[43] And indeed, one notices that the (penal) *Droit* which annuls a (criminal) action by a penalty inflicts this penalty even if the action in question exists only in the form of a "will" non-actualized in an "act." And the Third (in his aspect of judicial Police) will even intervene so that the will cannot be actualized in an act. But, in the presence of an attempted theft, he will prevent the

---

41. One must not confuse the monetary fine with "compensatory damages," which are a non-penal (civil) annulment of the illicit act. If B has stolen $100 from A, but must pay back $200 to him, this can be a mere restitution. For example, one can reason as follows: B deprived A of $100 during a period of time X; he must therefore restore $100 and the equivalent of the deprivation of $100 during period of time X, which can be another $100; or again, B has to compensate A for losses he sustained from the fact that he was deprived of $100 at a given moment; and so on. Thus, "multiple damages" awards can be awards of civil *Droit*. Likewise, if the debtor is imprisoned (after judgment) by the creditor, this is not a penalty: it is another form of restitution of the debt, a simple (civil) annulment of the illicit *act* of non-payment by an *act* performed in the reverse sense.

42. In principle, one could say that the restitution of the stolen money is part of civil *Droit*, the penalty alone falling within the competence of penal *Droit*. And the victim can effectively "act as a civil party" in a criminal trial. But practically speaking, when the act can be annulled, the civil annulment (of the act) is associated with penal annulment (of intention-will) in a single intervention of the Third, in a single trial called "criminal."

43. [Ed. In fact, in Anglo-American criminal law, it is generally said that guilt requires both a mental element (*mens rea*) as well as an element of action, even in the case when the wrong is an attempt.]

theft from being accomplished, but will nevertheless punish the thief. The Third of penal *Droit*, therefore, is very much related to the action taken as "will." By contrast, when the Third applies (or creates) civil *Droit*, the mere "will" to act (illicitly) will not make him intervene: he will not stop a mere attempt at a civil wrong and will not annul the wrongful action except if it has reached the stage of an "act." And when he intervenes to annul the "act," he does not concern himself with the "will" which brings it into being. Whether it is a matter of *dolus* [fraud] or *culpa* [negligence], the result will be the same: the act alone will be annulled by its repetition in reverse, and it will be so in both cases, without any supplementary penalty.

One can therefore interpret the *punishment* of the thief as an annulment of his criminal "will," of his decision [431] to act in a criminal manner. Thus, if the thief caught in the act (before having been able effectively to conceal the object) is put in prison, this is so that it is impossible for him to have even a "will" to steal (because when the "act" is materially impossible there is no longer a possible "will," by definition, since the "will" is the potentiality of the "act"). Now we have seen that the "will" can be annulled, i.e., punished, even if it is not followed by the act. It can therefore be detached from it. But detached from the act, which is necessarily concrete, i.e., *hic et nunc,* the will (being potentiality) has a general character: it is the will to steal in general. It can therefore be annulled as general, even if it has been actualized in an "act" and even if this act has been annulled (in a non-penal way). One can therefore imprison the thief not only to prevent him from wanting to commit a particular theft but to prevent him from wanting to steal in general. It is in this way that one can interpret the death penalty for the thief, or life imprisonment, or whatever other form of his elimination from the sphere of economic interactions that are able to take the form of a theft. (The mutilation of the right arm can be, as well, interpreted as preventing the criminal will to steal.) As for temporary penalties, such as corporal punishment, prison terms, fines, the penalty of shame alone, and so on, one can give them a psychological or pedagogical interpretation: the penalty is supposed to "reform" the criminal, annulling in him the criminal will by replacing it with a lawful will. But in this case, one must underline that the *juridical* meaning of the penalty resides not in the "moral redress" of the guilty, but solely in the annulment of the criminal will in question, which provoked the intervention of the Third. The Third limits himself to annulling by the penalty the will to steal. Everything that will be done to alter the person of the criminal in its other aspects will have nothing juridical about it. In particular, *Droit* is not to worry about the reformation of a thief condemned to a life sentence, since the will to steal is then annulled as a matter of course.

Therefore, punishment is clearly the annulment of the "will" and not the act. But is it also an annulment of the "intention"? In order to be able to answer this question, one must first get rid of a misunderstanding. It is generally said that intention cannot be punished, and that it does not even have anything juridical about it, because it is inaccessible to the Third. But first, [432] this is not quite exact; and then, this is not the question. The will and even the act can also be in certain cases inaccessible to the Third: a lot of crimes are not discovered and a lot of actual criminals escape punishment. It is a matter of knowing if the Third can want to annul the intention as such in the case when it is known to him and when it can be annulled. And I believe that one must respond affirmatively. Certainly, in the case of theft, the intention is generally not annulled, i.e., punished, as such if it is not actualized either in an act or even in a will. But this is because in this case there is no interaction between the intention of A and B such that B is juridically injured by it: in other words, the mere intention of A overcomes neither equality nor equivalence in the interactions between A and B, if these interactions are such that they can take on the aspect of a theft (B being, moreover, Society, since it must be a matter of crime and punishment). But one can imagine a Society that would be (or would believe itself) injured by the mere "intention" of its member, and if it were juridically recognized by the State, the latter could, by way of a Third, annul this intention, which would then be criminal, and its annulment a penalty. This case occurs in religious Societies, for example. And the penal *Droit* of States that have recognized juridically a religious Society have annulled by appropriate penalties criminal action even in its aspect of "intention," and this even in the case when the intention was actualized neither in an act nor in a will. But the "aspect" of intention in criminal action also intervenes in modern penal *Droit*, when it is a matter of the penal *Droit* of economic or familial Societies, notably in the notion of "aggravating" or "extenuating circumstances." Let us suppose, for example, that A steals B's gun with the intention of preventing B from using it either to kill himself or to kill someone else. There was an act of theft and therefore a will to steal. The Third, by intervening, will annul the act (by a non-penal annulment): the gun (or its equivalent) will be returned to B, [or] it will surely be taken from A. But the thief will be able to plead extenuating circumstances and not be punished. Now the will being manifest, only the intention has been able to overcome annulment by the Third. Therefore, it is because this annulment, i.e., the penalty, was related in this case not to the will but to the intention. (The will, having for its object only a particular theft, which has been committed, cannot be annulled in this case.) And the same goes for aggravating circumstances. The Third annuls [433] an act in a non-penal way, and he also annuls by a penalty the corresponding will. But, due to aggravating circumstances, he increases the penalty. The supplemental penalty can only be related to the intention: it is this that the surplus annuls, the will having already been annulled by the "normal" penalty.[44] The classic case of the mother stealing to feed her children would present no juridical difficulty at all if the Third would not annul with a penalty the criminal intention in addition to the will. This annulment of the intention

---

44. Not all aggravating circumstances are related to the intention. Thus, recidivism is related to the will: the recidivist is punished more because his criminal will is supposed to be more general. There would be a point in defining terminologically juridical phenomena in relation to the intention and distinguishing them from those that relate to the will (or the act).

is, moreover, clearly apparent when, for some reason, the will and the act cannot be annulled. Let us suppose that A assassinates his rival B. The criminal act cannot be annulled (at least in the modern conception), but this is of little importance, since its annulment is not penal by definition (involuntary murder would not be punished)[45] As for the will, it is exhausted in the act that actualized it: A wanted to kill B and he did not want to kill other persons (if so—[if he wanted to kill] another rival, for example—one will also be able to interpret his penalty as an annulment of his criminal will). The will, being actualized, can therefore not be annulled. The Third would consequently be impotent and Justice unrealizable if the action were not capable of being annulled as intention by an appropriate penalty. Now, this is so, for the intention of A was, in the final analysis, to obtain a certain contentment from his action: to *live* without B, and by knowing him dead, to live in a *Society* from which B is excluded, to *reestablish* a *status quo ante* disturbed by B, and so on. Now if the Third *kills* A, or excludes him from *Society,* or *alters* in a certain way his state or status, and so on, he annuls the intention in question. And it is in this way that one must interpret a penalty that is related to the criminal action taken as intention. Of course, the contentment that A drew from the very deed of killing B [434] cannot be annulled, and if all his intention exhausted itself in this contentment, the penalty would no longer make sense when it was related to the intention: for example, if A kills B to save him unnecessary suffering. But it is precisely in this case that one "acquits" the guilty. Now the juridical meaning of acquittal (the criminal act and will being established) is nothing other than the intention's inability to be annulled: it is in this case that the penalty would be called "unjust." Likewise, a sadistic killer could not even be subject to penalty as a non-responsible ill person because his intention (the pleasure caused by the act of killing) cannot be annulled. And if he is punished, the penalty will only annul his will to kill in general. And the same goes for what are called crimes of passion—and so on. Generally speaking, the intention of a crime said to be "disinterested" cannot be annulled, and this is why these criminals are often acquitted—that is, not subject to a penalty. If so, the penalty annuls their generalized will—that is, the will to do it again. But everywhere the criminal "profits" from the crime, it seems "just" that the penalty be such that it also annuls this "profit"—that is, the criminal action as intention, goal, or motive.

Therefore, it seems that punishment properly so-called, in its *juridical* content, annuls not the act, but either the will or the intention, or both at the same time. But can one say that the Third intervenes "spontaneously" every time that he applies a penalty or asks about its application? And is a "spontaneous" inter-

---

45. In fact, one sometimes punishes involuntary murders. But in ancient *Droit* it was not a matter of a penalty (see below): it was a case of civil *Droit.* As for modern *Droit,* one does not punish the murder (the penalty being incomparable to that inflicted on an assassin), i.e., the act of the action, but negligence, imprudence, and so on—that is, a vice of the will. And it is then clearly a case of penal *Droit,* of the same type as a fine for speeding, and so on. One must say, however, that the juridical phenomena in question are not always adequate, nor even authentic.

vention necessarily a case of *penal Droit?* Here as well the analysis of examples seems to suggest an affirmative answer. The intervention is said to be "provoked" when the Third only intervenes when he is solicited by the agent injured (or believing himself so) by the interaction, this agent being by definition a real concrete being, i.e., existing in actuality: an individual or collective member of a Society, and not this Society as such.[46] Now the real agent [435] in actuality can only be injured as such (i.e., as existing *in actuality*) by an actual action, i.e., by an "act." To the extent that the Third is "provoked," he is therefore related to the "act" and neither to the will nor the intention. Conversely, in being related to the "act," the Third cannot intervene "spontaneously"; for the act is juridical, i.e., in particular, susceptible of being annulled in the case when it is revealed to be illicit, only when it effectively injures a subjective *droit* by overcoming either the equality or equivalence of the agents interacting. Now in a real agent in actuality, the injury must also exist in actuality, and the actuality of the injury implies the *consciousness* that he has been injured by this injury. If he does not *declare* himself injured, he is presumed not to *know* that he has been injured, and then he is not so *in actuality*. The Third, therefore, does not have to intervene as long as he is not "provoked" by an explicit declaration of the injury by the one injured. If a creditor[47] does not care about getting reimbursed, the Third does not have to annul the act of non-payment by the debtor. The annulment of the illicit action as "act," therefore, necessarily presupposes a "provocation" of the Third by the one whom the action has injured, and a "provocation" of the Third can only relate him to an "act," which alone will be able to be annulled by him, to the exclusion of the will and leaving intention aside. Neither the will nor the intention can actually injure on their own an agent existing in actuality. The latter cannot therefore claim an injury by intention or will alone, nor consequently "provoke" the Third on that basis. Therefore, if for some reason or another, the Third wants to annul a criminal action as will or intention, he must do so "spontaneously." Conversely, if he intervenes "spontaneously," it is because he is related either to the intention or the act, or to both at the same time, and his annulment will then be a penalty; for an action which is not criminal as intention and will must only be annulled as act—that is, only in the case when it actually injures an actual interest (juridically recognized—that is, a subjective *droit*). Now the *actual* injury necessarily implies the

---

46. I have shown above (Part One) that a collectivity can be considered as a real agent in actuality. As for (non-political) Society taken as a whole (economic, familial, or another Society), it only exists in potentiality. By definition it only exists in actuality as an *autonomous* Society. But then it is a *party* in its relations with its members, which therefore have nothing juridical about them. For there to be *Droit*, a Third must intervene in its relations. But then the Society is no longer autonomous: it is governed by the Society that is represented by the Third. In fact, this Society is the State. The collective will of the Society, therefore, is only actualized in and by the will of the State (which recognizes it juridically). Taken in isolation, therefore, it only exists in potentiality: it cannot [435] *act* as such, as a whole, nor consequently be actually injured in an inter-action.

47. [Ed. Reading *créditeur* for *débiteur*.]

consciousness of the injury—that is, "provocation" of the Third by the one injured. The Third who would annul an *act* without being provoked could therefore annul a juridically legal act—that is, an act which did not actually injure anyone, overcoming neither an equality nor an equivalence in actuality. [436] The supposedly infallible Third, therefore, can only be related "spontaneously" to a will or an intention, or both at the same time.

"Spontaneous intervention of the Third" and "penal *Droit*" are thus clearly one and the same thing. And this *Droit* is necessarily related to the action taken not as act, but as will or intention: it is this that is annulled as such in and by the penalty. But is it really true that penal *Droit* is necessarily related to interactions between a Society taken as a whole and one of its members (individual or collective), and that every interaction of this genre, to the extent that it is followed by the intervention of the Third, is a case of *penal Droit*? The analysis of the examples also yields an affirmative answer to this last question. On the one hand, by definition, the Third only intervenes when there is an inter-action between *two* agents, in order to annul the action of one of them, who injures the subjective *droit* of the other—that is, who overcomes either the equality, or the equivalence, or the synthesis of both, between these agents. On the other hand, we have just seen that a real agent in actuality is in inter-action with neither the will nor the intention, and therefore cannot be injured by them. For there to be penal *Droit*, the criminal action must therefore injure the subjective *droit* of an agent who only exists in potentiality. Conversely, if an agent only exists in potentiality, the action cannot injure him as act, but only as will or intention (which are the action in potentiality, the act being this action in actuality). Therefore, if the Third intervenes in an interaction when one of the agents only exists in potentiality, he can only be related to the action in its aspects of will and intention.[48] Our assertion will therefore be demonstrated if we show that the co-agent who only exists in potentiality is necessarily Society taken as a whole and not one of its members (individual or collective).

Let us first show that a Society which is a subject *of **droit***, taken *as a whole*, can only exist in potentiality.

Society is a collectivity. In one sense a collectivity is nothing other than the whole or the "sum" of it members—that is, of the individuals who constitute it. They [437] alone exist in actuality outside the collectivity and independently of it.[49] The existence of the collectivity, by contrast, depends upon that

---

48. The interaction determines the ontological level. To be related to an act in an interaction is to act in actuality. Now to act in actuality is to exist in actuality. The agent who only exists in potentiality therefore acts virtually and is related in the interaction to the virtual aspect of the action of the other agent—that is, when it is a matter of a social, or indeed human, interaction, to intention and will alone.

49. An entity exists (or is real) *in actuality* when it can enter into inter-action with another entity existing in actuality, the inter-action being capable of going to the limit, up until the annihilation of one by the other. By definition a material entity—a tree or an animal, for example—exists in actuality. The human entity, which can annihilate an animal or be annihilated by it, therefore exists in actuality.

of its individual members: to overcome them is to overcome the collectivity, and it is enough to overcome them as members of the collectivity for the latter to cease to exist. But in another sense the collectivity is more and something different from the "sum" of its members. Here is why. If the collectivity is not Humanity, the being of the individual is not exhausted by his capacity as member of a collectivity: he is this and still something else, for example, a member of another collectivity. Thus, the individual is not only homo economicus, i.e., the member of an economic collectivity, but also an animal, homo religiosus, and so on. The collectivity, as the totality *of its members,* i.e., individuals taken in their capacity as members of the collectivity in question, is therefore something different from the "sum" of individuals taken in the plenitude of their actual reality. But this is not all. Even as members of a collectivity, the individuals differ from one another.[50] Let there be a collectivity of property owners. Not only are its members something else besides owners; they even differ as such among themselves: one has 20 acres, another 40; one has his land here, the other there; and so on. When an individual acts (i.e., actualizes himself) in his capacity as non-owner, this action (and this actual reality) has nothing to do with the collectivity. When he acts as owner, it is as a member of the collectivity that he acts. But if he acts in respect to his personal property, the *hic et nunc* [438] of his possession, he actualizes himself as an individual *member* of the collectivity, differing from all the others and opposed to them (from whence comes the possibility of conflicts). He may, however, act in his capacity of property owner by abstracting from the particularities of his property, by detaching himself from his *hic et nunc.* In other words, he can act as "any given [*quelconque*]" member of the collectivity: another [member], if he acted according to his sole capacity as property owner "in general," will act exactly like him. One will be able to say that in this case the individual acts in the name of the collectivity, that he "represents" it. In other words, the collectivity will be the whole or the "sum" of individuals acting as its members by abstracting from the difference between themselves and the other members. Thus, the collectivity is *something different,* not only from the "sum" of the individuals who make it up, but even from the "sum" of these individuals taken as members of the collectivity, but in

---

50. Existence *in actuality* is an existence *hic et nunc.* Individuals, existing by definition in actuality, therefore necessarily differ from one another, if only by their respective *hic et nunc.* The entity *detached* from its *hic et nunc* exists only in potentiality. It is *action* that connects to the *hic et nunc;* it is this, therefore, that actualizes potentiality. The entity detached from the *hic et nunc* must have a non-material support. This support is words or language (in the very broad sense of a physical phenomenon endowed with "sense" or "meaning"). The act that detaches from the *hic et nunc* is the act of thinking or "speaking" (*Logos*). Only the speaking individual (or "endowed with reason"—*Logos*), therefore, is able to *exist* in potentiality outside of his actual existence, or more exactly, "alongside" of it. He exists and is real: *in actuality,* in the material spatio-temporal world (of the *hic et nunc*); and *in potentiality,* in the universe of discourse (where space is "represented" by the plurality of words and languages—and time, by the unity of their meaning).

their specific differences—that is, as individuals. It will be *something different* because the action of the member acting as "anyone at all," i.e., in the name of the collectivity, can enter into conflict with his own action carried out as an individual member, different from the others. The specific unity of the will and action of the collectivity, i.e., of the collective will and action, is nothing other than the will and action of the individual member of the collectivity, taken as "anyone at all." By definition, as "anyone at all," every individual coincides in his will and action with all the others. Now the individual exists in actuality and can actualize himself by an action properly so-called (capable of leading to the annihilation of an entity existing in actuality, of a material entity, for example). One can therefore say that by acting according to his capacity as "any given" member of the collectivity, the individual actualizes this collectivity as such. And this actual action of the collectivity (i.e., its reality in actuality) will be something different from the action of the individual taken separately from the collectivity or as a member of the collectivity differing from other members—that is, as an individual in the proper sense of the word. Now anyone can act as "any given" member without the action being altered by this fact, from whence comes the possibility of a "representation" of the collectivity. One establishes the individual who is supposed to act as "anyone at all," i.e., "to represent" the collectivity and actualize it in and by his acts: his act will be by definition the act of the collectivity that actualizes it as such.

Now it is possible that a collectivity is a member of another collectivity. [439] For example, the collectivity A of owners of less than 20 acres, and the collectivity B of owners of 20 to 40 acres, may be members of the collectivity C of all property owners. If someone acts as "any given" member of A, i.e., "represents" it, he is not acting as "any given" member of C, and he can enter into conflict with "any given" member of B, who "represents" it. The individual who acts as "any given" member of C abstracts from the differences that separate the "any given" members of A and B. He "represents" C, and C is by definition "disinterested" concerning the conflicts between A and B. The individual who "represents" C can therefore intervene in the capacity of Third in inter-actions between A and B, just as a "representative" of A (or B) can intervene as Third in conflicts between the members of A (or B) who are acting as individual members, according to the *hic et nunc* of their properties. (A *fortiori*, C can be Third in these internal conflicts of A and B.) Now we have seen that the action of an individual member of A (or B) can enter into conflict with the action of "any given" member of A (or B)—that is, with A (or B) himself. And here as well C can intervene by way of a Third. C can, moreover, be a member of another collectivity D—and so on. The collectivity D can be Third in conflicts between C and its members (as well as the members of C themselves).

Let us now suppose that a collectivity (perhaps encompassing other collectivities) is no longer member of a collectivity "of a higher order," belonging to the same "sphere"—let us say to the economic "sphere," for the sake of argument.[51] And let us suppose that the collectivity being considered is not "universal"—that is, that it does not imply the totality of its "sphere." There will then be several "independent" collectivities from the same "sphere," such that the members of the one will not be members of the others.[52] We will call such a collectivity [440] "independent" which is no longer a member of a collectivity of the same "sphere," and which is aligned with other independent or autonomous collectivities of the same "sphere"—a "Society" taken as a whole, [or] an economic Society, for the sake of argument.[53] In a conflict between the Society and its members, there is then no Third possible, and consequently no (penal) **Droit** relating to it. If there is *Droit*, it is because the Society is encompassed by a collectivity (or a Society) belonging to *another* "sphere" than it. The individual who "represents" it, therefore, is not its member ("anyone at all"). And this means that the (actual) action of this individual does not actualize the Society in question as such. This Society, therefore, only exists in potentiality. It is clearly a Society, i.e., a collectivity, seeing that it has "any given" members (a common intention or will—an "idea"); but these members do not act in actuality as such—that is, they cannot push the interaction until the annihilation of the co-agent existing in actuality. Such an actual action is carried out by an individual who represents the collective act, and therefore only actualizes the latter.

It might seem that this reasoning only holds for Society taken as a *subject of droit*. Every subject of *droit* is actualized as such in and by the action of the Third—that is, of another. But the entity that is a subject of *droit* can exist in actuality in another aspect. Thus, the individual exists in actuality as an animal, for example, independently of any action of the Third. Likewise, a collectivity A, member of a collectivity B (from the same sphere) is actualized as a subject of *droit*, in its interaction with its members, only in and by B. But A

---

51. Two collectivities "belong" to the same "sphere" when they *are able* to enter into interaction with one another—that is, when "any given" member of the one can inter-act with "any given" member of the other. By definition, there is no interaction possible between collectivities from different "spheres": for example, a homo religiosus as such does not enter into inter-action with a homo economicus as such. But since a homo religiosus can also simultaneously be a homo economicus, there will in fact be inter-actions: but for the theory, they will take place within the same "sphere."

52. One can say that the "sphere" is a collectivity. But it only exists *for us*, and not for itself. In other words, it is not actualized; for there is no "any given" individual member of the "sphere" able [440] to act as such and thus actualize the "sphere" as such or as a collectivity. The "sphere" is an "ideal" or "abstract" collectivity, which only exists in, by, and for thought, and not in, by, and for action.

53. We have to make this assumption; for if the Society is *universal*, the distinction between civil *Droit* and penal *Droit* loses its meaning. Indeed, a *universal* Society must be *homogenous* (since the lack of homogeneity is actualized in the form of spacial, i.e., territorial, fragmentation, [and] therefore by the absence of universality). And when the Society is homogenous, the members are always "anyone at all." There is then no conflict possible between the Society as such and its members—that is, no case for penal *Droit*. Or, if you will, every conflict between members is a conflict with the Society, and conversely. Civil *Droit* therefore coincides with penal *Droit*.

may be, moreover, an actual reality. A *may* annihilate its individual member (or an aligned collectivity A'). If *Droit* only exists when A renounces [441] this possibility of direct action and has recourse to the Third, there are non-juridical acts of A which actualize it. But in the case we are considering, i.e., when A is a "Society" in the sense indicated, there is no act possible in and by which A can annihilate its individual member, or an aligned collectivity A', supposedly existing in actuality. Indeed, to annihilate A' is to behave as an "Enemy" toward it, and to annihilate an individual member is to behave with respect to him as a "Governor." In actualizing itself, A would therefore simultaneously actualize the category Friend-Enemy and that of Governor-Governed. A would therefore be a *political* Society or a *State* to the extent that it would be *actual*.[54] Therefore, if A is part of a State (which plays, among other things, the role of Third in conflicts between A and the members of A), the State cannot allow A to exist in actuality, for in this case there would be a State within a State, which is absurd and a contradiction in terms. And if A is not part of a State, A itself becomes a State to the extent that it actualizes itself. The non-political (let us say economic) Society, therefore, only exists in actuality as a political Society or State. As Society, it only exists in potentiality. Therefore, when there is an actual or state-sanctioned penal *Droit*, i.e., the intervention of a Third in the interactions between a Society and its members, the Society necessarily exists only in potentiality. The juridical interaction of penal *Droit* (i.e., with Society as such) is necessarily an interaction of an agent existing in actuality (the accused) with an agent which only exists in potentiality and which cannot actualize itself. And Society can be such an agent since it never exists in actuality in the conflicts being considered—that is, when it is a subject of (penal) *Droit*.

It remains to show that all relations of penal *Droit* to an entity which can only exist in potentiality are a relation with a Society (or "Society" in the technical sense indicated above) taken as such. Now we have seen that Society cannot actualize itself as such (i.e., as non-political "Society") because it turns itself [442] into a State by actualizing itself; or again—which amounts to the same thing—because the pre-existing State is opposed to this actualization. But this reasoning no longer applies to a member (individual or collective) of the Society. He does not politicize himself in self-actualization, and the State therefore has no reason at all to oppose his actuality. Society plays, as it were, the role of screen between the State and the members of Society. For the individual and collectivity A, member of a collectivity B, the outside is not an Enemy, since this outside is B and ultimately the corresponding Society. In

---

54. There is a Governor in the proper sense only when the Governed cannot elude the action of the Governor. Now this means that outside the Society is the Enemy; and where there is an Enemy, there is a State. The category Governor-Governed, therefore, only actualizes itself in concert with that of Friend-Enemy—that is, there are Governors properly so-called only in a State (properly so-called). (The universal State, i.e., without Enemies, being necessarily homogenous, the Governor coincides with the Governed, such that one can say that there are no longer Governors.)

wanting to assert themselves, the individual and the collectivity A can only do so by taking account of the fact that they are also members of C and of Society. The individual and A are therefore going to actualize themselves in such a way as to keep Society in existence. Therefore, if the State is in equilibrium with Society, it does not need to balance its relations with the members of this Society, this equilibrium being implied in the very existence of the Society.[55] The actuality of the members of the Society, compatible with the being of the latter, will therefore be able to coexist with the actuality of the State. The member of a Society *can* therefore exist in actuality. Society alone as such exists only in potentiality, not "by chance" or accidentally, but "in principle" or necessarily. To be related to an agent which can only exist in potentiality, therefore, is clearly to be related to Society as such.

Penal *Droit*, which is related to an action injuring an agent existing only in potentiality, is therefore a *Droit* which regulates the relations between Society taken as a whole and its individual and collective members. And one sees that the action aimed at by penal *Droit* is clearly an action taken in its aspects of "intention" and "will." Indeed, Society is nothing other than the being and the action of its "any given" member (ultimately individual)—that is, detached from his *hic et nunc*. Now the action of an agent detached from his *hic et nunc* is also detached from the *hic et nunc*. It does not therefore exist in actuality, it is not an "act": it does not go beyond the stage of its existence in potentiality—that is, it remains at the [443] stage of "will" (or potentiality of the "act") and "intention" (or potentiality of the "will"—that is, potentiality of the potentiality of the "act," or potentiality of the "second degree"). The action of Society as such is nothing more than its "intention" or "will" to act—that is, the intention and will of its "any given" member. The action of Society taken as a whole is its "ideal" or its "directing idea." This idea is set down in its Statute—that is, in the penal Code in particular. And it is the State which *actualizes* this idea by transforming into an "act," the "will" and "intention" of Society. More exactly, it is "any given" individual member of the political Society or the State who actualizes by "acts" the action of "any given" member of the non-political Society, which does not go beyond the stage of intention and will as the action of a member of the Society. The act conforming to this will or intention is carried out by any given member of the State, i.e., by the State as such; the will and intention alone properly belong to any given member of the Society—that is, to this Society as such. Now an act cannot injure an intention or a will. More exactly, the act only injures these latter to the extent that it actualizes a will and

---

55. It should be understood that the State is directly related to the individual taken as citizen—that is, member of the State as political Society. But it can be related to the individual taken as member of a non-political Society through the intermediary of this Society. However, to the extent that the status of the member of this Society is included in the status of citizen, the State must be directly related to the latter (or through the intermediary of *political* sub-collectivities—that is, through the intermediary of the Administrative Apparatuses of the State). The big question, therefore, is knowing what must be included in the status of citizen.

an intention: it is the will and intention which injure a will and an intention. The will and intention alone of a member of Society can therefore injure this Society as a whole (the corresponding act injures the State, such that its annulment has nothing juridical about it). In annulling the action which injures Society, penal *Droit* therefore annuls the action not as act but as intention and will. Now the act, existing in actuality, also injures an actual being—that is, an individual or collective member of Society. But to the extent that one detaches the intention and the will from the act, these go beyond it: the act injures a member of Society, the intention and will can injure Society as a whole. Or once again, the act injures the member of Society taken in his specificity—that is, as different from the other members, in the *hic et nunc* which is proper to him. The will and the intention injure this same member taken as "anyone at all"—that is, as identical to other members. Let us assume that the action of an individual (or of a collectivity existing in actuality) injures as act another individual (or collectivity) taken in its particularity; if it at the same time injures this same individual (or collectivity) taken as "any given" member of Society, it injures Society, i.e., the will and the intention [444] of the Society or "any given" member, and it does so in its aspects of will and intention.

In short, penal *Droit* is related to the action of an individual or collective member of Society to the extent that this action injures this member as "any given" member; and it is only to this extent that the action will eventually be annulled by the Third of penal *Droit*, this annulment then being a "penalty." The criminal action is therefore the action of a "specific" member of Society which injures its "any given" member, this injury being that of a subjective **droit** recognized by the State.

Now for criminal *Droit* to be a **Droit**, for there to be an injury to a *right*[56] of "any given" member, the criminal action (annulled by the penalty) must be at odds with a given ideal *of Justice*. In other words, it must be contrary either to the principle of *equality*, or that of *equivalence*, or finally to some synthesis of these two principles. It remains for us to see, therefore, to what extent this can take place when the action is related to "*any given*" member of Society (i.e., to this Society taken as a whole)—that is, when it is taken not as act, but as will and intention related to another will and intention.

Before discussing this question, it is necessary to stress the fact that the phenomenon of punishment has varied a great deal according to time and place. Not only has the content of *Droit* in general not always and everywhere been the same; the division of this content into penal *Droit* and civil *Droit* has itself varied.

And first of all, despite appearances, penal *Droit* is a relatively late phenomenon, posterior to civil *Droit*. Here is why. One can wonder whether non-political Society ever existed in a pure state, outside of any state organization. In any case, as soon as it is organized into a State, it is as State, as *political* Soci-

---

56. [Ed. In the original, the English word "right" follows the French word **droit** in parentheses.]

ety, that it exists *in actuality*. One could therefore have the impression that non-political Society as such does not exist at all. It breaks down, so to speak, into its elements: its individual and collective members (families, social classes, religious orders, and so on) would seem to have no real bond at all between them, except the political bond that united them as citizens or members of the political Society of the State. The relations of these members with the whole of Society would therefore seem to be relations with the State, which would thus give the impression of being a party in these relations [445] and not a Third. One therefore has the impression that there is no penal *Droit* properly so-called. It is only at the end of a long evolution that one was able to uncover the fact that non-political Society existed all the same—*in potentiality*. It is only then that one understood that the members of Society as such were able to enter into interaction with the Society itself, and not only with the State. It is only then that the latter was able to intervene by way of a Third in these relations. It is then that penal *Droit* was constituted, that the corresponding Codes were elaborated. This constitution was late because it is long and difficult to uncover a reality that only exists in potentiality, above all when it is still covered over by a reality in actuality, as non-political Society is covered over by the State. Originally, the action that *we* call criminal had been annulled by the State either to the extent that it injured a member of Society who existed in actuality, and then it was a matter of civil *Droit* and not punishment; or because this action injured the State itself, and then there was no *Droit* at all. As long as things were like this, there was then no "crime" properly so-called, and consequently neither "punishment" nor penal *Droit:* there was either civil *Droit* or the non-juridical action of the State.[57]

At first glance, archaic *Droit* seems to be, it is true, above all penal. But the fact that it dealt with cases that *we* assign to penal *Droit*, and that it annulled illicit actions by what *we* call penalties, must not lead us astray. From the point of view *of this **Droit***, it was a matter neither of penalty nor crime in the proper sense of the word, i.e., in the meaning *we* attribute to these terms, and which is the true or adequate meaning of the phenomena; for one and the same action can be a case of penal *Droit* or civil *Droit* according to the legal system one is considering. And one and the same way of annulling an illicit action may be either juridical or not, and in the former case, penal or civil. When the State executes its enemy, external or internal, this act of annulment, not being performed by a *Third*, has nothing juridical about it. But even a *juridical* execution may not be a *penalty* properly so-called, being only a civil annulment of the juridically illicit action (and not then *criminal*). If the execution is supposed to annul the illicit action *as an act*, it is a non-penal or civil annulment. Let us take an historical example. [446] There was a time when the actual entity juridically recognized by the State, i.e., the subject of *droit*, was not the individual but the Family. Murder, then, was juridically injuring not the individual killed but his family as a whole. The murderer was overcoming the *status*

---

57. Thus, this explains the fact that Roman penal *Droit* is so much behind civil *Droit*.

quo, which was supposed to have conformed to the principle of equality (for example), by depriving the family of the victim of one of its members. In order to reestablish equality, it was therefore necessary to deprive the family of the criminal of one of its members. This is how the family vendetta worked. When the State took care of this in the capacity of impartial and disinterested Third, the annulment became *juridical.* But it was not *penal.* An *act* was annulled by its repetition in reverse: family B deprived family A of a member; the Third deprived family B of a member and thus reestablished equality in their inter-actions, which had been destroyed by the murder. Now this is a case of civil *Droit.* And this is why the member of B that the Third executed is not neces-sarily the physical killer: it is not a matter of punishing him; it is a matter of reestablishing the equilibrium between families A and B. What counts is the act, and the intention and will to act are of little importance. And only fami-lies A and B are at issue, not Society as a whole. This is why the intervention of the Third in this case is not "spontaneous." Now if the execution is not a penalty, there is nothing surprising about it being able to be replaced by a "fine." And when one considers the *Droit* of *wergild,* one sees very clearly that it is not a matter of penal *Droit. Wergild* is not a "penalty," [and] it is not even a "fine" in the modern sense of the word: it is a simple payment of "compen-satory damages"—that is, the "*civil*" annulment of an illicit act. Practically speaking, it is not the "criminal" himself who pays the *wergild:* in any case the Third does not concern himself with the question of knowing who pays it. And it is not Society as a whole which profits from *wergild;* it is solely the family of the victim. Thus, the Third only intervenes if he is "provoked" by this family. Therefore, [there is] neither a penalty, a "spontaneous" intervention, consid-eration of the intention or will, nor [finally] a relation with Society as a whole: despite appearances, this is clearly a case of civil *Droit.*[58] The situation changed when [447] the *individual* was recognized as a subject of *droit.* Of course, lex talionis (based upon the pure principle of equality) is still a *civil Droit.* If the Third breaks A's arm because A broke B's arm, it is an *act* that he annuls by doing it again in reverse (in order to reestablish equality between A and B). Thus, A's intention and will are of little importance to the Third: the annul-ment will be the same, even if A's act was involuntary or had "justifiable" motives. And it is always only A and B who are at issue. Society as such is not taken into consideration by the Third. As well, he does not yet intervene "spon-taneously." The annulment by lex talionis is therefore not a genuine penalty. However, one eventually had to realize that in the case of *murder,* lex talionis no longer made sense: after A killed B, B not longer existed in actuality. One cannot reestablish equality by bringing B back to life, and by killing A one only

---

58. In certain cases, the State collects a part of the *wergild;* but this is because it felt itself injured by the murder of one of its citizens. (Or again, these are the "costs of justice.") It is not, therefore, in the capacity of Third that it is affected by the *wergild.* This part is clearly a "fine," but it is not juridical—that is, not a "penalty." It is true, however, that the idea of a penalty evolved beginning from this non-juridical fine. It has [447] determined the "spon-taneous" intervention of the State, which ended up by intervening as *Third.*

reestablishes equality in nothingness, which does not make sense.[59] The *act* of A, therefore, cannot be annulled by the Third. Now the Third must annul the action that is clearly illegitimate, since it destroyed an equality. He will therefore try to annul it as will or intention. It is then that the Third will search for criminal will and intention, and its annulment will be a penalty, which will only be applied to the criminal himself, and which will be in addition to the civil annulment in the form of compensation paid to the family of the victim, for example (or to the victim, if he survives the attack). But seeing that B is dead, he does not benefit from the penalty inflicted on A. If it [the penalty] annuls an injury, it is because someone other than B was injured. Now one ends up by understanding that this was Society as such. Thus, the Third inflicts the penalty "spontaneously" according [448] to a penal Code (written or oral), which sets down the status of Society and thus determines the injury. It is then that there is a genuine penal *Droit:* the penalty is in addition to the (eventual) civil damages; it is related to the intention and will of the criminal; the crime is related to Society and the Third intervenes spontaneously. And one thus sees why the penalty and penal *Droit*, in becoming authentic, draw inspiration from the "personalist" and "subjectivist" principle. Civil *Droit* annuls the action as *act*. Now the act is an entity existing in actuality; it can be reached as such; [and] it can be detached from its author: one can annul it as activity [*acte agissant*] or as a done deed [*acte agi*]—that is, in its consequences. This is why a civil wrong is transferable: the act can be annulled by its author or by his heir, for example, who is supposed to develop solidarity with the act in its consequences. Crime, by contrast, is action taken as will and intention—that is, as potentiality. Now potentiality boils down to nothingness once it is detached from its actual support—that is, here, the author of the action. It is in him alone that it can actually be attained and thus annulled. The penalty is therefore necessarily *personal:* one cannot annul a criminal will in the person of the heir, for example. And the penalty is by definition *subjective*, since it is the will and intention of the agent that it annuls, and not the act detached from its "subjective" potentiality.[60] Penal *Droit*, being "personal" and "subjective," is

---

59. Because a $\times$ 0 = b $\times$ 0, a and b being anyone at all, the equality is therefore purely abstract. There was certainly a transitional period: one acknowledged that the dead person did not disappear, that his "soul" survived the death of the body. Then one could think of reestablishing the equality destroyed by the murder by executing the guilty: the soul of B murdered by A equals the soul of A executed by the Third. In this case the execution is not a penalty: it is "civil damages," the annulment of an *act*. But one must have soon understood that the "soul" is on a different ontological plane from the body, such that it does not make sense speaking about an equality between them: an action of the Third in this world cannot equalize an entity in the beyond. As well, the juridical Third reasoned soon enough as if man were absolutely mortal: the "soul" of the dead person was not a subject of *droit* even when, in other respects, one believed in its survival. (One must not confuse the immortal "soul" with purely juridical "survivorship," such as one finds in the *droit* of wills and estates [*tester*], for example. It is the juridically legal action {of the living person} which is supposed to be "eternal.")

60. The Romans saw this difference very clearly. Cf. Giffard, *Précis de droit romain*, vol. II, 169, 213, 327.

therefore opposed to civil *Droit,* which is "impersonal" and "objective." There-fore, when the "penalty" is "impersonal" and "objective," there is not a penalty properly so-called: what *we* call a "penalty" is merely "civil damages" for the *Droit* in question, even if the act of annulment by the Third is the same in both cases.

Be that as it may, we thus return to our last question: penal *Droit* is an authentic **Droit** only if the Third annuls the criminal action in order to reestab-lish either equality, or equivalence, or some synthesis of the two elements, the criminal agent having destroyed them in his (social) interaction with the vic-tim.[61] And we assert that when there is penal *Droit* and penalty properly so-called, the "victim" at [449] issue is solely Society taken as a whole, and that in this case equality and equivalence are destroyed by the will alone or even by the intention alone of the criminal, such that they will not and could not be reestablished except by a (penal) annulment of this will or this intention taken as such.

Of course, criminal action also injures the victim properly so-called, i.e., an entity existing in actuality, who is by definition a *member* (individual or col-lective) of Society. But the being in actuality, let us say the individual, can only be injured actually—that is, by the actual action, or taken as act. The will and intention of the criminal injure the actual victim only to the extent that they are actualized in and by the act. By annulling the act one therefore annuls them to the extent that they have injured the victim. Now it is civil *Droit* which annuls the act. If the action is only related to the actual victim, there is then no penal *Droit:* civil *Droit* annuls the act and in it the will and intention that injured the actual victim. Therefore, if there was a penalty, i.e., an annulment other than that of the act, it is because there was another "victim" (since there is no crime without a victim), a "virtual" victim. And we have seen that this virtual victim (by essence and not by accident) can only be Society taken as a whole, or what is the same thing, its "any given" member, taken as "anyone at all." Civil *Droit* has reestablished the equality or equivalence concerning the actual victim. If the Third intervenes all the same, it is because there is still an equality or equivalence to reestablish, namely that concerning Society or its "any given" member. And it is solely this virtual "victim" that penal *Droit* has in mind. Now it is obvious that Society cannot be injured by the *act:* seeing that it only exists (essentially) in potentiality, only an action in potentiality can be an inter-action with it. And the action in potentiality is precisely the intention or will. When it is a matter of murder, for example, it is not the *act* of killing that injures Society (or its "any given" member). And it does not make any sense to say that Society is injured by the fact that one of its members has been killed; for then it would be absurd to want to reestablish equality by executing the criminal—that is, by depriving Society of another member. What injures

---

61. It should be understood that the Third does not annul *all* inequalities, and so on: he only does so for those which he recognizes juridically as such. But *if* the Third annuls an action, it is solely because it is (according to him) contrary to the principle of equality or equivalence.

it is the murderous will or intention. And this is why the penalty is not applied to an involuntary murderer (or eventually to a murderer with a "justifiable" intention [450]—that is, which does not injure Society).[62] Therefore, if the victim that penal *Droit* has in mind is Society as a whole, the crime is nothing other than the will and intention. It is the criminal will and intention which have overcome the equality or equivalence in interactions between the criminal and Society, or indeed its "any given" member.

This is why penal *Droit* appears when the act cannot be annulled for some reason or other (or is supposed to be such). [This cannot be annulled] because, on the one hand, there has been no act, the action not having gone beyond the stage of will or intention. No member of Society has then been injured. If the Third intervenes, therefore, it is because he has in mind Society as such. And in this case it has obviously been injured only by the will or intention. On the other hand, [this cannot be annulled] because the accomplished act can no longer be overcome, as in the case of murder, bodily injure, rape, and so on.[63] The Third can then only annul the will or intention. But in so doing, he does not give any "satisfaction" to the actual victim. This is because he has in mind another "victim," the virtual victim—that is, Society or its "any given" member. Of course, even if the act can be annulled, and even is annulled, there can still be a penalty. But this is because it is then no longer related to the act, which has already been annulled, but to the will or intention. And it no longer gives satisfaction to the actual victim, who is already satisfied, but to the virtual victim. In all cases of penal *Droit*, there is then the restoration of an equilibrium destroyed by will or intention alone—that is, an equilibrium between an actual agent, a "specific" member of Society, different from all the others, and this Society itself, i.e., its "any given" member.

Let us therefore see in what sense one can say that a will or an intention destroys the equality or equivalence between a "specific" member and "any given" member of Society.

[451] But let us first recall (cf. Part Two) that the general character of penal *Droit* will differ depending upon whether it draws inspiration from the principle of equality alone or that of equivalence alone, or from some synthesis of both principles. And the notion of punishment is going to vary accordingly.

We have seen (Part Two) that the exclusive application of the aristocratic principle of equality yields a penal *Droit* of *lex talionis*. The crime then consists

---

62. There is no inter-action possible between an *act* and Society. The act is always the act of an individual. Now the individual can never annihilate Society by his act (for if he did so, he would annihilate himself). And when there is no annihilation possible, there is no genuine inter-action. The action of the individual, therefore, can only reach Society in his will or intention. The interaction only exists, therefore, between Society, and criminal will and intention.

63. One must not confuse unannulability in principle with the contingent fact that the criminal cannot be punished because he has fled, for example. In civil *Droit*, annulment is also sometimes impossible in fact; the debtor against whom there is a judgment may be insolvent. I have in mind the act that *can* not be annulled, or is supposed to be such for the Third.

in the suppression (by the criminal) of the equality between him and his victim (in their social interactions). The penalty has as its sole purpose the restoration of this equality. The penalty, or the annulment of the criminal action by the Third, then boils down to a restoration of equilibrium between the criminal and the victim. The "quantity" that passed from the victim to the criminal following the crime must be restored to the victim. Or again, if this is impossible, one must remove from the criminal as much as he had removed from the victim so as to reestablish an equilibrium between the two "quantities," which this time will both be less. In the penal *Droit* of lex talionis, it is therefore a matter of a comparison between the criminal and the victim. The two are supposed to have been equal before the crime and must become so again after and through the penalty. The penalty equalizes the members of Society, and therefore is only applied when equality has been destroyed.

The exclusive application of the bourgeois principle of equivalence leads to a different penal *Droit* (cf. Part Two). The members of Society are no longer supposed to be equal. They are only equivalent, finding themselves in conditions that are not equal, but equivalent. Crime, therefore, only destroys equivalence, and the penalty only restores equivalence, and not equality. It is therefore enough that the Third does to the criminal the *equivalent* of what was done to the victim: no need to do *the same thing* to him. Now we have seen that the estimation of equivalence is necessarily "subjectivist." To notice the equivalence between the condition a in which A finds himself, and the condition b of B, it is not enough to compare a and b, or A and B. One must relate a to A and b to B. One thus arrives at the following definition: A and B are equivalent if inside A and B there is equivalence between their respective "*droits*" and "duties"—that is, ultimately, between their "benefits" and "burdens." And since A's benefit is B's burden, and conversely, it is enough to notice equivalence in A alone or B alone. If within any given member the *droits* or benefits and the duties or burdens are equivalent, the ideal of the Justice of equivalence is satisfied, and the [452] Third does not have to intervene. This allows penal *Droit* to abstract, as it were, from the victim and consider only the criminal. The crime is an action that gives the criminal a [certain] benefit without an equivalent burden (which can only take place if there is a victim on whom the crime imposed a burden without an equivalent benefit). The penalty will then aim at reestablishing equivalence. It is by definition a burden. It is a matter of making this burden, whatever it may be, equivalent to the criminal benefit. Penal *Droit* therefore has as its mission to establish equivalence between the crime and the punishment: the condition of the punished criminal must be equivalent (but not necessarily equal) to that of every other member of Society; the equivalence of the members of Society, temporarily destroyed by the crime, will thus be reestablished and the Third will no longer have to intervene. One can therefore say that the crime is related in an immediate manner to the criminal and not the victim (although it is indirectly related to him as well). The punishment is determined not so much by the burden imposed on the victim as by the benefit conferred on the criminal, and which is not compensated in him by a burden. (Thus, a "disinterested" action could not be punished, even if it did not differ from a criminal action when it is related to the victim.)

Generally speaking, the *Droit* of equivalence is "subjectivist": it deals with relations that take place inside an individual, the subject of *droit*. Conversely, all "subjectivist" *Droit* will therefore have a tendency to apply the principle of equivalence rather than that of equality. Now penal *Droit* is always related to intention and will. An act is criminal only if it actualizes a criminal intention or will. It is therefore a matter of relating the act to the will; it is a matter of internal relations within the subject of *droit*. Penal *Droit* will therefore have a tendency to be a *Droit* of equivalence. Penal *Droit* is much more of a "bourgeois" than an "aristocratic" phenomenon: or, more exactly, since real *Droit* is always more or less synthetic, a *Droit* of equity or a *Droit* of the citizen, characterized by a relative predominance of the principle of equivalence. Or once again, penal *Droit* will be relatively more extensive when the Legal system implies more "bourgeois" elements of equivalence. Generally speaking, the penal *Droit* of lex talionis will give way to the penal *Droit* of equivalence between the crime and the punishment.[64]

[453] But whether it is a matter of equality or equivalence in penal *Droit*, it is always a matter of intention or will alone, and the relations between the criminal and Society as such—that is, its "any given" member. It remains for us to see in what sense the will and intention of a "specific" member, differing in his *hic et nunc* from all the others, can overcome his equality or equivalence with "any given" member of Society, and in what sense the penalty can reestablish this equality or equivalence, or their synthesis, considered as "just" by the *Droit*, i.e., by the Third, in question.

Let us first take the case of *equality*. The members of Society are all supposed to be equal among themselves. But, it should be understood, this equality cannot be absolute. In his *hic et nunc*, A necessarily differs from B, who has his own *hic et nunc*. As well, when A is interacting with B, this is not the same thing as when he is interacting with C, or when B is interacting with C, and so on.[65] The members of Society are strictly equal as "any given" members (it is Society itself that is egalitarian); or, if you will, one is "any given" member to the extent that one is *equal* to the other members (while in the Society of equivalence, one is "any given" member to the extent that one is *equivalent* to all the others). A's "specific" action, made from his *hic et nunc*, should never overcome his equal-

---

64. In fact, in aristocratic societies, penal *Droit* is little developed. Either one has recourse to "private vengeance," i.e., to a [453] non-juridical annulment of the crime by the injured *party*, or one applies the *civil Droit* of lex talionis by being content with the juridical annulment through "civil damages" (which generally leads to the civil *Droit* of *wergild*). Generally speaking, therefore, the principle of equality will be applied above all in civil *Droit*. But we will see (in part D, b) that in the sphere of civil *Droit* of economic Society, this is only true for the *Droit* of property and not that of contract.

65. Let us recall, moreover (cf. Part Two), that strictly speaking the equality of the members excludes inter-action between them (which would be pointless). This is why there never has been, in fact, the Justice of pure equality.

ity with *any given* member—that is, create a situation in him that the others would not be able to have, or to obtain, by "specific" actions from their respective *hic et nunc*. If A brings about a certain situation, it must be such that all the members of Society—in principle—could find themselves in the same situation. Or once again, since the being of any given member is set down in and by the "status" of the members of Society, "status" being by definition egalitarian, no one [454] has the *Droit* to act in such a way that his "specific" action is incompatible with this "status," by altering the being set down by it. And the cases when the specific action does so are set down in the penal Code. Now it is not the act of A related to B which can be as an act contrary to this status. In order to overcome equality with *any given* member, A's action must be related not to a specific member B, but to any given member. Now the act can only be related to a specific member. It is therefore in his intention and in his will that the action is related to any given member. The act is *criminal* not because it establishes an inequality between A and B, but because it aims at establishing an inequality between A and *any given* member, i.e., between A and all the other members (or at the very least between a group of members similar or equal to A and all the others)—that is, also between A such as he is supposed to be as any given member and such as he is as a result of his action. The will and intention must therefore extend beyond the act which actualizes them. This act is only the first of a series of other similar acts, the will and intention being fully actualized only by this *series*. The act is therefore criminal only as an element of this *series*. And if the series does not yet exist, the criminal action boils down to the intention alone or the will to realize this series. It is therefore clearly the will which destroys the equality between the criminal and Society, i.e., between the criminal and any given member—therefore also between the criminal as criminal and himself as any given member, since "any given" member is, in particular, also the criminal.

In short, it is the intention and will to *distinguish* oneself from all other members of Society, i.e., from "any given" member, to occupy a "unique" or "privileged" place within Society, that is criminal. And the act is criminal only to the extent that it actualizes this intention and this will. But intention alone suffices to make a criminal of his (individual or collective) relation. One sees this very well in the phenomenon of Athenian ostracism.[66] [455] And the same goes for all cases of egalitarian penal *Droit*. Let us suppose that A commits a theft against B. It is not the act of removing something from B which is crim-

---

66. "Democracy" is not necessarily "bourgeois." In Athens there was still a struggle between the egalitarian aristocratic principle and the bourgeois principle of equivalence. Ostracism is an aristocratic reaction to the inequality introduced by the bourgeois equivalence of the citizens. But this phenomenon is not juridically adequate, for the penalty does not reestablish equality, seeing that it excludes the criminal from Society. Generally speaking, exile and the death penalty (which amount to the same thing) are often measures dictated by practical considerations: it is simpler to cut down a tree that is higher than the others than to trim its height. The death penalty [455], by contrast, has a non-juridical value and is imposed for political "crimes," as we will see in the following section.

inal. It is the intention to do it, whomever B may be, i.e., the intention to be a thief in general; for only this intention touches "any given" member—that is, Society as a whole. Now by definition *everyone* cannot become a thief: there have to be owners capable of being robbed. To want to be a thief is, at the least, to want that Society be divided into two irreducible groups: thieves and victims. In this case there would no longer be "any given" member: one would be either some thief or some victim. The old Society, therefore, would no longer exist: there would be two new Societies (which would probably be at war—that is, would constitute themselves into two sovereign States). One can therefore clearly say that theft (as *theft*, and not as a simple appropriation by A of B's property) injures Society as a whole. And it injures it because it destroys the equality between its members: the thief is not equal to the victim, and this is why theft is incompatible with the (egalitarian) status of "any given" member of Society. Now the penalty can and must restore equality by annulling the theft as theft—that is, as intention and will to steal. Let us assume that the Third puts the thief in prison. One cannot say that his goal is to annul (prevent) theft against a given specific member: perhaps the thief does not have anyone in mind. The penalty annuls (prevents) theft against "any given" member—that is, it annuls the will and intention to steal. The thief in prison has again become equal to the honest member in freedom: nether of them can have the will to steal.[67] The Society made up of honest members in freedom and thieves in prison is therefore egalitarian, and the Third no longer has occasion to intervene. And it is of little importance that it is a matter of prison or something else. What is essential is that equality be established or maintained. The Third must see to it that A in his condition *a* is equal to B in his condition *b*, *a* and *b* being the *hic et nunc* [456] of A and B: despite the difference of the *hic et nunc*, A and B must be equal as any given members of the Society, and this is true both if A and B are honest and if one of them is a thief. And the same goes for all crimes and all penalties. Let us take the case of murder, for example. If A's intention is exhausted in the act of killing B, the Third of *penal Droit* may not intervene: Society is not injured. But if A is a "professional" killer, it is any given member that he has in mind, [and] he injures Society as a whole. And he does so by and in his intention, which extends beyond any concrete *act* of murder. Now here as well this intention destroys the equality of the killer with any given member: as in the case of theft, and much more so, not everyone can be a killer. And here as well the penalty must reestablish equality. Once this equality is reestablished, there is no further reason for a penalty. It is in this way that a punishment can be temporary: if it is enough to overcome the intention or the will which destroy equality, the Third can limit himself to it. If, for exam-

---

67. Juridical honesty is not "moral" honesty. It is possible that the honest person does not steal from fear of imprisonment, just as the thief does not steal because imprisonment "materially" prevents him from doing so. By "intention" and "will," one has to mean not a "dream" or a vague "desire" but a "reasonable" intention—that is, *capable* of being actualized in and by an effective act.

ple, the fact that A paid a fine is enough for his intention to become "honest," the fine will be a sufficient penalty for his crime: "A who paid a fine" will be equal to "B who did not pay a fine"; he will therefore be "any given" member, conform to his "status," and by definition be equal to everyone else.[68]

Let us now move on to the penal *Droit* of *equivalence*. Here, the crime signifies a benefit obtained without an equivalent burden, which implies a negation of equivalence with another member of Society. The penalty that ought to restore this equivalence does so by restoring the equivalence between the benefit and burden in the criminal himself. And, here as well, the intention alone is enough to overcome equivalence. Let us take the case of theft. The thief is not *equal* to the honest member; for in his intention, the thief has at his disposal the property of all the members of Society, while the honest man has at his disposal only his personal property. But the thief is not *equivalent* to the honest [457] man either; for the latter paid for his property, either with money or with his work, while the thief obtained what he has without making equivalent efforts (the effort required to steal having no relation with the value of what one steals, there cannot be a burden "equivalent" to the benefit that the theft procures for the thief). To reestablish equivalence, the Third must therefore introduce a burden into the existence of the thief which is supposed to be equivalent to the benefit he obtains from stealing. Then equivalence will be reestablished and there will not be any reason to want to be a thief rather than something else, rather than an honest man in particular. Crime is therefore, if you will, an "unjust enrichment" but not at the expense of a "specific" member (which would be a case of civil *Droit*), but at the expense of "any given" member—that is, the intention and will to act this way generally. One can also say that the criminal profits from Society (since the "any given" member to which the criminal will is related is Society as a whole) without providing it with "equivalent" services, as do its honest members. The penalty can therefore also consist in the Third forcing the criminal to provide to Society services without gaining benefits from them, from whence comes the idea of "forced labor," for example: as a whole, the condition of "A who committed a crime and works without pay for Society" is "equivalent" to the condition of any given honest member of this Society. Society therefore remains a Society of equivalence even if it includes criminals, provided that they are punished accordingly, for example by being sentenced to forced labor. But if the agent gains no benefit from his action, and acts without the intention to gain benefits, his action may not be annulled as will or intention by the Third—that is, it may not be criminal, despite appearances. Conversely, an apparently legal action of an agent can be criminal if in his intention it is not equivalent to the

---

68. The "equalizing" value of the penalty can also be interpreted in the sense of *lex talionis*. The fact that there is a thief in Society limits the freedom of its honest members, in the sense, for example, that they must guard their belongings, cannot get away, have security expenses, and so on. Now the thief is not limited in his liberty since he is the only thief and cannot steal from himself. Equality will therefore be reestablished if one "does the same" to him, for example, by limiting his freedom of movement (prison), or by taking away a part of his property equal to that which the others spend to guard their belongings (fine).

action of any given member interacting with this agent. Thus, a (bourgeois) penal *Droit* of equivalence can condemn indigence or begging. The act of the beggar does not injure (at least in appearance) any "specific" member of Society, seeing that the ceding of property occurs with the consent of the owner (and from the point of view of egalitarian Justice, the act is even "just," seeing that it tends to equalize conditions). But one can say that the beggar lives without working (by supposing that the act of begging is not a job), while [458] any given member must work in order to live. The intention and will to live without working can therefore be called criminal and annulled by forced labor.[69] With rape, equally, there is an obvious lack of equivalence between the condition of the criminal and that of the victim: the one has only benefits without burdens, the other, burdens without benefits. Likewise for adultery: the husband pays for the benefit of sexual relations with his wife while the criminal has the same benefit without cost.[70] When there is perjury, fraud, racketeering, and so on, equivalence is equally overcome: any given member has the burden of having to struggle with reality (always more or less rebellious) in order to reach his ends, while the criminal succeeds by relying on beneficial fictions that he creates without effort (the act of lying and making up a lie not being considered as an equivalent effort to the result obtained).[71] Finally, sacrilege (and incest) are, as well, contrary to the principle of equivalence; for the divine wrath also affects any given member of Society, who does not gain any benefit from the sacrilegious action, while the criminal is presumed to have committed the sacrilege in order to obtain a benefit.[72] But if the one who commits a sacrilege and gains a benefit has special burdens, equivalent to the benefits the sacrilege provides, this may not be annulled by the Third—that is, he will not be a criminal, [and] this will not be a "sacrilege" in the penal sense of the word. Thus, a priest can commit acts that would be sacrilegious if a layman were to commit them: it is because the priest has special burdens that the lay person does not—and so on.[73]

[459] An action can therefore be criminal either from the point of view of

---

69. It should be understood that the criminal will must be actualized in an act in order to be punished. But the act is only then the sign of the will, and the penalty annuls the latter and not the act. Thus, the beggar is not even required to give back what he received: the act therefore remains non-annulled, and the penalty only annuls the will and intention.

70. This is how Locke justifies the ban on adultery: the husband must pay for a child who is not his. [Ed. This is perhaps an interpretation of Locke's discussion of the family in *Two Treatises of Government*, ed. Peter Laslett (Cambridge: Cambridge University Press, 1988), I: 176–210, II: 303–22.]

71. The lucrative lie is equally contrary to the principle of equality. The liar has at his disposal the real world and the imaginary world, while the honest man, i.e., any given member, is limited to reality. The one therefore has *more* than the other.

72. Here as well there is a negation of equality: the sphere of action of the man determined to commit sacrilege is greater than that of "any given" member.

73. Of course, in this case the divinity accepts the apparently sacrilegious action, which is not so in reality. Thus, Society will not experience any burden. But it is because the divinity adopts the point of view of the Justice of equivalence: it allows the priest to commit acts forbidden to [459] laymen because the priest makes exertions of piety that the layman does not.

the penal *Droit* of equality, or that of the penal *Droit* of equivalence. Or again, it can be condemned by both *Droits* at the same time. But it is also possible that these *Droits* enter into conflict, that an action that is legitimate from the point of view of the one is criminal from the point of view of the other. Now in fact all real penal *Droit* is synthetic, a *Droit* of equity. The criminality of an action, and the meaning and nature of the penalty, will therefore depend on the nature of the synthesis realized by the *Droit* in question. And this is why the analysis of a concrete penal *Droit* is so difficult.

§ 63

Without any doubt, it is always very difficult to "mete out" penalties. What punishment ought one to inflict on the criminal to annul the criminal action— that is, to reestablish equality, equivalence, or both at the same time? It does not seem that one can avoid here altogether a degree of arbitrariness. But this question—of unparalleled importance in the *practice* of penal *Droit*—does not interest us here. We limit ourselves with having defined the goal that the Third of penal *Droit* sets for himself. And we are not dealing with the question of knowing how he chooses to reach this goal in *practice.*

Conversely, practice may be uninterested in our purely theoretical questions. It is of little importance to the criminal whether he is being punished in the proper sense of the term, or merely paying "civil damages," when one cuts off his arm, for example. And it is of little importance in practice whether the penalty restores equality or equivalence, or both at the same time. However, our distinctions, at first glance artificial and subtle, are not without interest even for practice; for they allow the purification of the penal phenomenon of its non-juridical elements, and thus make it authentic and adequate—that is, truly "just" in the juridical sense of the word (it being understood from the point of view of a given ideal of Justice, as long as juridical evolution has not ended).

From the theoretical point of view, our distinctions allow us, I believe, to see clearly into a lot of thorny questions relative to penal *Droit,* and to understand better the historical evolution [460] of this *Droit.* In particular, one can clear up the question of the relations between the juridical notion of penalty and the notions of *vengeance* (vendetta) and *expiation* (retribution).

Inasmuch as it is "private," *vengeance* (the vendetta) certainly has nothing juridical about it, since it is one of the parties at issue which carries it out. But it is felt as a *duty* by the injured family; and it is supposed to be *just,* and not simply beneficial. It therefore seems to be a quasi-juridical phenomenon; it seems to contain a juridical element, if only in an undeveloped state [*en germe*]. Indeed, vengeance is based upon the idea of lex talionis, i.e., ultimately, upon the juridical ideal of equality: it is a matter of doing to the criminal (or to his family) what he did to the victim (or his family) in order to reestablish equality between them, which was destroyed by the crime. It is enough, therefore, that the vengeance be performed not by the injured party, but by an impartial

and disinterested Third, in order for it to become an authentic juridical phenomenon. However, we have seen that if equality is only reestablished between
the criminal and his concrete victim (or his family), it is a matter of civil *Droit*.
And indeed, "state-sanctioned" vengeance generally becomes a *Droit* of
wergild, a "composition"—that is, a "civil damages."[74] But we have also seen
that the crime can destroy the equality between the criminal and "any given"
member of Society. *Any given* member, therefore, may also want to *take revenge*
on the criminal. And indeed, the crime generates the "instinct of revenge" in
still other members of Society than those who were effectively injured by the
crime. Here as well, of course, there will not be any **Droit** as long as any given
member will take revenge himself. But we have seen that this vengeance can be
performed as well by a Third, notably by the State. And one will then have an
authentic case of penal *Droit:* the criminal action will be related to any given
member of Society, i.e., to this Society itself, and it will be annulled as will and
intention. In this sense, one can assert that private vengeance, or vendetta, is
one of the sources of penal *Droit*. And it is not false to say that the penalty is a
"vengeance" of Society or a "public vindication." However, one must underline that vengeance is a source of penal *Droit* only to the extent that it implies
the idea of reestablishing [461] the equality destroyed by the crime, and that it
only becomes an authentic penalty when it is applied by a *Third,* and when
equality is destroyed between the criminal and *any given* member of Society.[75]

As for *expiation,* it is not wrong either to liken it to a penalty. The expression "the criminal has expiated his crime" is too universally widespread not to
contain at least a part of juridical truth. And indeed, one can say that the notion
of expiation is based on the juridical idea of *equivalence.* The criminal has
"expiated" his crime when the punishment has been "equivalent" to this crime.
And it is then that one will say that the penalty was "just." The way in which
this "equivalence" was calculated, moreover, is of little importance. Seeing that
there was a notion of equivalence, the phenomenon can be juridical. But it will

---

74. Certain authors see in "composition" one of the origins of contract. Cf. Decugis, *Les
Étapes du Droit,* 191.
75. Fauconnet, *La Responsabilité,* insists on the fact that crime provokes a strong "collective
emotion": it is because the crime injures not only the victim properly so-called but also "any
given" member of Society. But it is not this "emotion" that founds penal **Droit**: it is the
intervention of a *disinterested* Third (not at all "*moved by emotion* [*ému*]" in principle).
However, the *Droit* applied or created by the Third is felt to be "just" only if it is conforming to the "emotion," if the Third does to the criminal what a member of Society "moved
by emotion" would have done. This "emotion," however, is (quasi) "juridical" or "just"
only to the extent it wants to overcome an inequality or a non-equivalence produced by the
crime.
One speaks of an "*instinct* of revenge." But no animal possesses this "instinct." An animal is going to defend itself, but it is never going to take revenge: neither against the aggressor *after* the aggression, nor against the "near and dear" of the aggressor. Vengeance is therefore a specifically human phenomenon (that implies the ability to abstract from the *hic et
nunc*—that is, the "faculty" of speech and thought). And the human coincides here with the
"juridical": it is the idea of *equality* implicit in the phenomenon of vengeance.

be authentically so, there will be **Droit**, only if the equivalence between the crime and the punishment has been established by an impartial and disinterested Third (this Third, moreover, being capable of being conceived as a divine being). And there will be *penal Droit* only if this equivalence between the crime and the punishment has reestablished the equivalence between the criminal and *any given* member of Society, and not merely between him and the victim properly so-called.

One can therefore say, if you will, that the penalty is both a public "vengeance" and an "expiation" of the crime. But it is only a juridical phenomenon when the criminal action destroys the equality or equivalence between the criminal and any given member of Society, and when it is annulled by a Third, being annulled not as act, but as intention and will.

One cannot therefore say that "private vengeance," [462] that any vengeance whatsoever, is an authentic juridical phenomenon. And the contemporary notion of expiation is not a juridical notion either, in the strict sense of the word. But there is a juridical element in these two phenomena that can and must be drawn from the analysis. Now state-sanctioned penal *Droit*, even modern [*Droit*], is not exempt of non-juridical elements either, and phenomenological analysis aims at eliminating all these impurities. I have attempted to outline in the previous section a purely juridical theory of punishment and consequently of penal *Droit* in general. In this section, I would like to discuss the question of the non-juridical elements that one finds in penal *Droit* and in its interpretation.

I began by discussing theories of "vengeance" and "expiation" because they have often been attacked as anti-juridical in modern times. And I have said in what sense they appear acceptable to me from the strictly juridical point of view. But it seems to me that the theories that one nowadays opposes to them (both in theory and in Codes, and therefore in practice) are not purely juridical either. This is why I would like to discuss briefly the so-called "sociological" Theory (but in reality "medical") of "social hygiene" and the "defense of Society" in its various forms, and the "political" theory of "reason of State," which will provide me an opportunity to speak again about political "crimes." And in discussing these theories I will try to resolve the problem of the death penalty.

Let us begin with the *theory of "social hygiene."*

The goal of the penalty is the "defense of Society" according to this theory. Therefore, the penalty should, on the one hand, render the criminal harmless, and on the other hand, prevent crimes, making them impossible. The first goal is reached either by the elimination of the criminal, by physically preventing him from doing harm, or by rehabilitating the guilty, by psychologically preventing him from committing crimes. As for the second goal, one can equally give it two interpretations. Either the penalty must be severe in order not to have to be applied: it must frighten the criminal and stop his criminal intention; or if one applies it to the criminal, it should stop others, serving as a terrifying example.

If it is Society itself which is being defended by applying the penalty or in acting in some other manner against the criminal, there is no *Droit:* there are only parties, there is no Third. But one can say that there is a [463] Third (the State) which defends Society against the criminal. Of course [this is so]. However, the State will be a *juridical* Third, and there will be (penal) **Droit**, only when the intervention of the Third will aim at restoring either the equality or equivalence destroyed by the crime; if not, the Third will not draw inspiration from the ideal of Justice, and he will not be a *juridical* Third. The State will then defend Society against "criminals" (this word no longer having, moreover, a juridical meaning) like it defends Society against any other "wrongdoers," against malarial mosquitoes, for example. And it is not by chance that the theory of the "defense of Society" speaks of "social *hygiene*" and only wants to see criminals as *ill* persons. Now it has been very correctly observed that crime is quite different from illness, and one clearly distinguishes the ill wrongdoer, the "non-responsible" insane person, from the criminal properly so-called, supposedly having a free and conscience, albeit criminal, will. To put a dangerous insane person in an asylum and sentence a "normal" criminal to prison are two essentially different things. Be that as it may, if the State treats criminals as mere ill persons (socially dangerous), there will not be penal **Droit**, nor a *penalty* in the juridical sense of this word. The measures taken against crime will be mere "administrative measures." It will be up to doctors or to other civil servants to decide about them, and not Judges properly so-called.

Generally speaking, *Droit* only exists when a *Third* intervenes in the interaction between *two* juridically recognized human beings—that is, both of whom exist for the Third taken as Third. There will only be penal *Droit* when the criminal is a juridical person or a subject of *droit* in the same way as the victim. And one can say that the criminal has a **droit** to the penalty, just as the victim has a **droit** to reparation.[76] He has a **droit** to the penalty; for if someone were to try to prevent the infliction of this penalty, the criminal would not need to make efforts to overcome this interference: the Third would undertake to annihilate it.[77] The goal of the Third can never consist in the annulment of the criminal as a juridical person; for if the Third annulled one of the two agents, he would cease to be a *Third:* he would become the *second* agent—that is, a party. The simple fact of eliminating from Society one of its members, therefore, has nothing juridical about it, and the goal of the Third, as Third, cannot [464] consist in such an elimination. The goal of the Third consists *solely* in the restoration of equality or equivalence (or both) between the criminal and any given member—that is, if you will, Society. He must not, therefore, *eliminate*

---

76. Kant insisted very much on this aspect of the question. [Ed. This would seem to be a reference to Hegel, *Philosophy of Right,* 126, rather than to Kant; but cf. Kant, *The Metaphysics of Morals,* trans. Mary Gregor (Cambridge: Cambridge University Press, 1991), 144.]
77. One can even say that the Third defends the criminal, taken as a subject of *droit* or juridical person, against himself, taken as an animal or in general as a non-juridical entity, having no *droits*.

the criminal from Society, but on the contrary reintegrate him, and in any case keep and preserve him there. But he must also keep Society in its identity with itself and in its (postulated) conformity with the given ideal of Justice. And it is the penalty that allows this problem to be resolved. The *punished* criminal is, if you will, comparable to "any given" member of Society: he is equal or equivalent to him in his being and his active behavior.[78] The *punished* criminal, even during the time he undergoes his sentence, remains a member of the Society from the juridical point of view. He is in a juridically recognized inter-action with it, i.e., with any given member, and the Third continues to play the role of *Third* in this interaction between *two* juridical persons, [who are] then supposed to be equal or equivalent. Thus, the Society which includes *punished* criminals remains in conformity with the ideal of Justice that is appropriate to it. One can therefore say, if you will, that the Third "defends" Society by punishing the criminal: it thus prevents the criminal from making this Society not conform to the ideal of Justice that it accepts. But this is a *juridical* "defence," which has nothing to do with the defence of Society against animal wrongdoers, illness, ill persons, and so on. The penalty is, if you will, an "elimination"; but it is an elimination of injustice—that is, of inequality or non-equivalence. And it has a *juridical* meaning only to the extent to which it reestablishes equality or equivalence within Society. And it can only do so by annulling the *intention* and *will* of the criminal, considered "normal" and not "ill." Action against the *body* of the criminal, against the criminal taken as animal, is but a *means* to arrive at this juridical goal. And it is only juridically valid to the extent that it is supposed to arrive there.

   As for the theory of the "rehabilitation" of the criminal, it is juridically valid provided it is correctly interpreted. The goal of the penalty being the annulment of the crime, [465] i.e., criminal *intention* and *will,* this goal is reached if these are replaced in the criminal by an "honest" intention and will. One can therefore say that the penalty aims at the "moral rectification" or "rehabilitation" of the criminal. This is even the ideal of the penalty. But it would be false to say that it has no other goal than this rehabilitation. Here as well, rehabilitation is in reality a means, and not a goal. The goal is the annulment of the injustice that resides in the criminal will, and rehabilitation has a juridical value only to the extent that there is this annulment. But nothing says that the Third cannot annul the will otherwise than by rehabilitation. And if he succeeds, he does not have to worry about this rehabilitation. Of course, from the point of view of *egalitarian* Justice, the annulment of the crime by the rehabilitation of the criminal is superior to all other forms of annulment, for it guarantees a maximum of equality between the members of Society. Indeed, the

---

78. *Droit* is related not to the *hic et nunc,* but to "eternity"—that is, to the *totality* of time. As well, it is the *entire* life of the criminal that is juridically comparable to the *entire* life of any given member. A thief who has committed such a theft and who has undergone such a penalty (prison, for example) is in the whole of his existence equal or equivalent to the honest man who has always been free.

"equality" between the honest man *at liberty* and the criminal *in prison* is entirely relative. But from the point of view of the Justice of equivalence, this reasoning is not essential. It is enough that the penalty be equivalent to the crime, and it is of little importance that it improves the guilty or not. In any case, rehabilitation is only a *juridical* notion to the extent that it annuls the will which has been found criminal by the Third. Anything which goes beyond this annulment no longer has anything juridical about it, and the Third is uninterested (as Third) in a general improvement of the "morality" of the criminal.

Theories of "severe" penalties do not make any *juridical* sense. If severe penalties are enacted in order that they not be applied, these are not penalties properly so-called. They are, if you will, preventative measures of social hygiene, but they have nothing juridical about them. And if the penalty is a genuine penalty, meant to be applied, at the very least in principle, it is only juridically correct provided that it is *equivalent* to the crime, or that it reestablishes *equality* between the criminal and any given citizen (i.e., Society, which is the victim). It would therefore be *unjust* and anti-juridical to apply a harsher penalty to the criminal in order to frighten others. This would infringe upon the **droit** of the criminal to a "just" punishment, and the Third cannot do this by definition. There are then no other *juridical* measures of punishment than those determined by the principles of equivalence or equality.[79]

[466] As for the much debated question of the death penalty in general, it is effectively complicated. It seems that we have resolved it in the negative by saying that the Third cannot *annihilate* the criminal without ceasing to be Third. But what the Third cannot do is to suppress the criminal as a *juridical person*. Now nothing says that the execution of the criminal is such a suppression. It is "civil death" (taken in the absolute sense) or exile (in the ancient sense) which would be anti-juridical, and not the death penalty properly so-called— that is, the annihilation of the criminal in his body, as an animal. If any given member continues to be a juridical member of Society even after his death, the criminal can be so as well. And then there are no longer *juridical* objections to the death penalty (except those that one can make to any penalty that does not aim at the rehabilitation of the criminal and which makes it impossible). The *executed* criminal may—in the totality of his existence—be equal or equivalent to the honest man dead in his bed.[80] A Society which recognizes juridical "survivorship" can therefore admit juridically the death penalty (provided that it does not annihilate the criminal as juridical person). Now *Droit*, being related

---

79. Kant [*Metaphysics of Morals*, 140–1] insisted on this point of view from general "morality." In reality, it is a simple "analytical" consequence of the very *juridical* notion of the penalty. But one must not forget (as do Kant and many others) that the point of view of *equivalence* between the penalty and the crime [466] is not the only one that is juridically possible. There is still that of *equality* between the punished criminal and any given member. It should be understood that the concrete amount of penalties is a difficult question. But it is *another* question.

80. The act of taking the life of the criminal, moreover, can serve to reestablish equivalence or equality with any given member.

to "eternity," i.e., the *totality* of time, has a tendency to admit this juridical sur-vivorship (in principle indefinite, but in fact capable of prescription). And this is why penal *Droit* has generally accepted the idea of the death penalty. How-ever, if this attitude is *juridically* authentic, it nevertheless rests upon a theo-retical (ontological) *mistake*. In fact, there is no afterlife for man (even—*and above all*—in his humanity), who is an *essentially* finite being (and *conscious* of his finitude when he is *fully* humanized—that is, fully self-conscious). In rela-tion to the *human* being, therefore, eternity is nothing other than the totality of human, historical time—that is, constituted by the totality of effective, con-scious, and free human *actions*. In relation to the individual, the *totality* of time is therefore limited by his birth and death. And seeing that *Droit* is a human phenomenon, relative to the human being, it must rest upon the anthropo-logical, and not the theological (i.e., in fact, cosmological [or] "naturalistic") notion of Time, upon [467] the notion of *finite* time, of self-enclosed "eter-nity," of the non-open totality. In other words, *Droit* must limit the juridical being of the subject of *droit* to the effective (i.e., active) life of his support; it then will be necessary to deny juridical survivorship and consequently also renounce the death penalty as a *juridical* means of annulling crime. If modern penal *Droit* has a tendency to renounce the death penalty, it is because mod-ern *Droit* in general tends to eliminate more and more the notion of juridical survivorship or legal heredity. But this is not a purely juridical evolution. *Droit* evolves because man recognizes better and better his finitude and draws all the consequences from it. The *Droit* of man who *knows* himself to be mortal, there-fore, must obviously exclude the notion of juridical survivorship. But as long as men believe in their immortality, *Droit* can recognize it juridically, all the while remaining an authentic *Droit*. And inside *this Droit*, the juridical authen-ticity of the death penalty cannot be disputed.[81]

All that I have just said does not at all mean that Society does not have the ***droit*** to defend itself other than by applying juridical penalties. Leaving aside the "moral" aspect of the question, one can say that Society and the State can do whatever seems fit (seeing that they succeed, by so doing, in keeping them-selves in existence). Thus, the State can "defend" Society by preventative mea-sures, by exemplary "penalties," by attempting "moral rectification" of crimi-

---

81. [This is true] unless one supposes that there is no crime "equivalent" to this penalty, or says that the fact of killing the criminal always contradicts the principle of his equality with any given member. But this is another question—the "unsolvable" question of the amount of the penalty.

One must not confuse the problem of the death penalty with another juridical phenom-enon. If A cannot exercise his right except if B is killed, he has the ***droit*** to kill B—that is, the Third must, in principle, kill B on his behalf. Thus, [we have the following] example: A has the ***droit*** to life; B wants to murder him; A kills B in order to defend himself; or again, the Police intervene and kill B to defend A—that is, spare him the necessary effort to annul B's reaction to A's "legal" action (i.e., his act of living). In this case, the Third must kill B. But this has nothing to do with a *penalty*: it is simply a matter of realizing A's right. [Ed. In this paragraph in the original, the English word "right" twice follows the French word *droit* in parentheses.]

nals, and so on. To say that an insane person is not a *subject of* **droit** and that his incarceration is not a *juridical* penalty does not mean that the State does not have the **droit** to confine him, or to kill him, and so on. In these cases, the act of the State will be *outside* of (penal) *Droit:* therefore, it will be neither according to or contrary to *Droit;* it will be a simple administrative act, which has nothing juridical about it. And nothing prevents the State from treating [468] criminals as insane. However, in this case there will not be penal **Droit**.

There would thus be a point in separating the juridical act of the State acting in the capacity of Third in penal *Droit* from its non-juridical administrative act. Concerning the insane, the juridical Court has only to declare itself incompetent, seeing that there are not the *two* juridical persons necessary for a trial. Then some administrative apparatus will be able to deal with the animal Homo sapiens in question and do what it sees fit. As for the "normal" criminal, the Court should limit itself to imposing the sentence that it considers just and enforcing it. But nothing prevents an administrative apparatus taking another measure, administrative and non-juridical, against the criminal at the same time (or afterwards). And this measure can even be taken automatically: such a juridical penalty corresponds to such and such an administrative measure, which will be added to the penalty, without being a penalty itself. But, in practice, this distinction is difficult to make, seeing that the juridical amount of the penalty is to a large extent indeterminate. Only with [great] difficulty would one know to what extent the penalty is juridical, i.e., destined to annul the crime, and to what extent it pursues a utilitarian goal, thus being a non-juridical administrative measure. And in fact non-juridical considerations are always mixed up with reasons that set down concrete penalties in penal *Droit*.

In particular, these are often utilitarian, "practical," and non-juridical reasons that lead to the death penalty. It seems that in archaic societies the "universal" penalty originally consisted in being made an "outlaw" [*mise "hors la loi"*]. This was equivalent to the annihilation of the criminal as a subject of *droit*, which is juridically inadmissible. But the Third not having the physical means to apply a penalty, being made an outlaw was *in practice* inevitable. By a fiction (justifiable moreover), being made an outlaw was considered as a penalty. Now, in practice, being made an outlaw led either to the death "penalty" or the flight of the criminal, i.e., permanent exile, which amounts to the same thing for Society from the utilitarian point of view. This is why, when the Third began to apply penalties himself, these were at first either a death penalty or exile (the criminal sometimes being able to choose between the two). Once the criminal was killed or exiled, Society once again became—through the elimination—equal or equivalent (according to the case). The Third, therefore, no longer had to intervene, and it might seem [469] that there had been a genuine penalty—that is, the restoration of equality or equivalence by the death penalty or exile. But in reality the suppression of a member of Society is quite different from a *restoration* of the equality overcome by the crime. In fact, there had been no penalty; this truly existed only from the moment that the Third annulled the crime by preserving the criminal in Society as a juridical person (living or dead).

But, supported by the fiction of juridical survivorship, the tradition of the death penalty was maintained (while becoming a genuine penalty). And exile suggested the idea of *life* imprisonment (which can equally be an authentic penalty). And it is from a utilitarian point of view that one debated the benefits of the death penalty and life imprisonment, to which "moral" considerations were later added. It does not seem, therefore, that truly *juridical* reasons generated the institution of the death penalty and life imprisonment, although it has been possible to give these two penalties an authentic juridical form. And it seems that while evolving, penal *Droit* found the means to annul the crime otherwise than by putting the criminal to death or by definitively depriving him of his freedom. And it seems that the synthetic penal *Droit* of equity increasingly seeks to annul crime through a rehabilitation of the criminal. In any case this form of penal annulment is the most consistent with the principle of equality between members of Society. But, once again, the question of the juridical determination of penalties is extremely complicated.

It remains to discuss *the theory of "reason of State."*

I have already discussed the case when the State intervenes to defend Society, and I have said in what sense this "defense" can be juridical: it is only so to the extent that the State, in the capacity of an impartial and disinterested Third, reestablishes through a penalty either equality, or equivalence, or both, between the criminal and Society, i.e., its "any given" given member, by annulling criminal intention and will. But the State can also defend itself as a State. In this case, it will be a matter of a "political" crime. And we should say a few words about it.

It should be understood that when the State defends itself, when the citizen is in (political) interaction with the State as such, the latter cannot be a disinterested Third, and there is then no room for any *Droit* at all. What one calls "political crime," therefore, is not a *crime* in the juridical sense of the word, and the reaction of the State has nothing to do with a *penalty* properly so-called. One cannot therefore say that the State has a [470] **droit** to react against the political offender, nor that it does not have the **droit** to so. Political relations between the State and the citizen are outside the sphere of *Droit* in general. From the *juridical* point of view, the State can therefore act toward the political offender as it sees fit.[82]

Now the analysis of political reactions between the State (taken as such) and the citizens (taken as citizens) shows that in certain cases the reaction of the

---

82. By definition, in case of conflict, the non-citizen must give precedence to the citizen. Consequently, the State does not have to worry about the status of the member of Society. If it wants to act against a political offender, it can do so even if its action is contrary to the status of the citizen taken as a member of Society. However, seeing that it is the same State which intervenes in the capacity of Third in the relations of Society with its members, and thus sanctions their status, there will be good reason to avoid as much as possible conflicts between the State as such, acting politically, and this State taken as juridical Third. "Exceptional measures" are admissible from the juridical point of view, seeing that they are outside the sphere of *Droit*; but the equilibrium of the State requires that these be kept to a minimum.

State against a political offender must take the form of the execution of the latter (which has nothing to do with the death *penalty*).[83] This is the case of "State treason" ("high treason"). We have seen (in part B) that public *Droit* sets down instances when a citizen acts as citizen in the name of the State, either to keep it in identity with itself or to change it. This is what happens when the citizen acts "legally" (from the political point of view)—that is, in conformity to the Constitution. And we have seen that the citizen can also change the State and its Constitution by non-constitutional, i.e., politically illegal or revolutionary, means. In this case, the fact that the citizen acts politically, i.e., as a citizen and not as a private person [*personne privée*] (as an animal or member of Society), is guaranteed by the risk of the life of the citizen: by definition, the man who risks his life in order to act upon the State as State, acts as a citizen—that is, politically, as a revolutionary. The State must therefore try to kill the one who acts upon it in an illegal way. Otherwise, the State would be at the mercy of non-political actions, committed by non-citizens (or by citizens acting in the capacity of non-citizens). Only the risk of life justifies the revolutionary politically, or more exactly, transforms him from political offender into revolutionary. And the political legality of the victorious revolutionary (and of the State that he [471] creates by his revolutionary act) is due to the risk that he ran during the revolution. Now, even in the case of failure, this risk characterizes the revolutionary: in the case of failure, he is a political *offender,* guilty of "high treason," but he is a *political* offender and not a *criminal* in the penal sense of the word, a "common criminal"; he acts as a rebel citizen, but as a citizen all the same. The State must therefore treat him as such. And this is why it must execute him. From the point of view of the State, he is an "Enemy" in the political sense of the word: he is a citizen who is not a citizen of the State (conforming to his political status) and who wants to change it; he is therefore comparable to the external Enemy. Now the interaction of the State with the Enemy as Enemy is a relation of mutual exclusion (of war). If the State is not annihilated by the Enemy, it must annihilate him. In this case, it must execute the rebel citizen. And from the point of view of this citizen, execution by the State is equally vital. If the citizen acts politically (as a revolutionary) against the State, it is because he aspires to "universal recognition" (*an Anerkennen*). He is (at the limit) alone in thinking differently than the State (i.e., "any given" citizen), in acting contrary to the status of citizen. And he wants this status changed in order that it conform with his way of thinking and acting; he wants the State (i.e., any given citizen and—at the limit—all citizens) to change in order that he may be legal, in order that he is "recognized" in his uniqueness. This happens in the case of success: the post-revolutionary State "recognizes" him as a hero, as a "Statesman." But this should also happen in the case of failure (seeing that he has risked his life for this "recognition"). And it is execu-

---

83. Hegel [*Philosophy of Right,* 127–30] insisted on this point. That which follows is an exposition of the Hegelian theory. However, Hegel speaks of penalty and penal *Droit*. In reality, he has in mind purely political wrongs.

tion by the State that allows it to happen to him, for this is also a "universal recognition": the State as a whole is related to him in his uniqueness in and by an effective political act. If the State eliminates him in another fashion, it does not "recognize" him as revolutionary, as citizen. It treats him like the insane, a child, an animal, a non-citizen. The reaction of the State is no longer adequate, no longer conforming to his action. The revolutionary has the political "*droit*" to be suppressed *politically*, and this suppression can only be through execution.[84] Consequently, [472] the State must in certain cases execute *political* offenders, even if the *penal Droit* of this State does not recognize the death penalty.[85]

Now the "common" criminal is also a citizen, although he does not act as citizen when he commits his crime. And if the penalty is related to the non-citizen, to a certain extent it also affects the citizen, since the penalty will ultimately touch the animal which also serves as support for the citizen, from whence comes a possible conflict between the State taken as juridical Third (of penal *Droit*) and this same State as such, which is related to its citizens as citizens. And for the State to be viable, this conflict must be resolved.

I have already had the opportunity to say that the penalty cannot be contrary to the citizen status of the criminal, given that from the point of view of the State (which applies *Droit*) the non-citizen must be subordinated to the citizen. Therefore, if the criminal has not committed any political wrong, the penalty cannot annul his political status. For example, if this status includes freedom of movement, the penalty cannot consist of imprisonment. But we have also seen that the State, in order to be able to exist, must include in the political status of the citizen certain elements of the non-political status of a member of Society. A crime, i.e., an action contrary to "civil" or "social" status, can therefore be at the same time a political wrong, an action contrary to "civic" or "political" status. In this case, the action can result in the alteration of the political status of the agent (for example, he can be deprived of the *droit* to vote, and so on), and the penalty could be applied to him to the extent that it is compatible with his new status. For example, while remaining a citizen, the thief may not enjoy freedom of movement; he could therefore be put in prison. In this case there will be simple "forebearance" [*laisser faire*]: the State as such

---

84. Once again, this political execution has nothing to do with the "death penalty" of penal *Droit*. And this distinction is often made: for example, the common criminal will be hanged, the revolutionary will be shot, and so on. The difference between an "honorable" execution and a shameful death penalty has always been clearly felt. In the case of the death penalty, one suppresses the animal (or the non-citizen), and the citizen is only suppressed, so [472] to speak, by chance. In the case of political execution, on the contrary, it is the citizen who is suppressed as citizen, and it is, so to speak, by chance that one suppresses him by killing the animal that serves him as support. Politically, at first glance, "civic death" alone would suffice: the non-citizen or animal that remains could be preserved alive. But this reasoning is false, seeing that the citizen only creates himself in and by the *risk* of his life. If the revolutionary did not run the risk of being executed by the State (in the case of failure), he would not act as a revolutionary—that is, as a citizen. His "civic death" would then have no meaning.
85. This point of view was adopted in Russia before 1917.

will "forebear" to the State as the Third of penal (or civil) *Droit*. And this "fore-bearance" has nothing juridical about it. [473] Theoretically, the criminal will therefore have to appear before two distinct Administrative Apparatuses: before the juridical Court that passes sentence on him, and before a political Administrative Apparatus, which holds that his political status was altered by his action in such a way that the penalty can be applied to him. But practically speaking, the link can be established automatically. A given action established by the Court automatically brings about such a change of status, and this change is done such that the penalty inflicted by the Court is allowable. In this case a simple (political) Law will be enough, and there would be no need for a second political "Tribunal." And there will be no conflict as long as the exclusive juridical group coincides with the exclusive political group, as long as one and the same exclusive (ruling) group elaborates both the penal *Droit* and the political Law in question.

But the State may not limit itself to mere "forebearance." Seeing that the criminal has acted contrary to his political status, the State can intervene polit-ically against him. It will then be acting as a party—that is, in a non-juridical manner. And in this case a political "Tribunal" distinct from the juridical Court is essential. In other respects, the political Tribunal will be able to act as it sees fit toward the criminal, without worrying about the "*droits*" of the lat-ter; for these *droits* belong to him as a member of Society, i.e., as non-citizen, and they must recede before the citizen and the State in the case of a conflict between them. However, for Justice to be realized (and the State is committed to this in its capacity as Third), the penalty properly so-called must be enforced. Political ("administrative") measures, therefore, can only be added to the penalty and cannot suppress it. This suppression is only juridically admissible in a single case: in the case when the political measure is the execu-tion of the criminal; for in this case the criminal is eliminated from Society, which thus becomes egalitarian or equivalent once again, such that Third no longer has to intervene.[86]

[474] On the one hand, non-juridical ("administrative") measures taken by the State aim at defending the State as such. On the other hand, they aim at defending the citizen against the non-citizen, even when the non-citizen is act-ing in the citizen himself. Therefore, it is this dual goal which determines the nature of the "administrative" measure. If the State is of the opinion that the juridical penalty is insufficient for the political defence of the State, it can add an "administrative" measure to it, which can eventually go as far as execution (which, it should be understood, will not be a "death *penalty*"). It is also pos-

---

86. We have seen that this solution is not perfect from the juridical point of view, since it *suppresses* one of the two parties. This is why the Third should not have recourse to it in its capacity as Third. But if the State does it for political reasons, the Third has no basis to object, since the principal and final result—the "just" character of Society—is attained.

The same reasoning applies to the case when the State acts (non-juridically) according to "public utility," for the "defense of Society." If the utilitarian measure is not an execu-tion, it can only be added to the penalty, without ever being able to suppress it.

sible that the State is of the opinion that the ("just") penalty, on the grounds of its "shameful" nature or for some other reasons (making the *civic* life of the convict impossible, for example), is *absolutely* incompatible with any status whatsoever of the citizen (even reduced to its minimum), incompatible with his "dignity," if you will. In this case as well, the State can exempt the citizen from this penalty through execution. In executing the animal in him, the State defends the citizen against this animal. Now this defence can be preventative: the administrative measure (and even the execution) can be taken before the wrongful action has occurred. But generally speaking, the State will be interested in preserving its citizen as citizen. As well, to the extent that this will be compatible with the security of the State, the administrative measure will aim at the civic rehabilitation of the offender (actual or presumed). At any rate, the administrative measure taken against him allows for his reintegration as citizen (if only as a reduced citizen) in the State. And this is the political "justification" for these measures. However, once again, these political measures have nothing juridical about them. One cannot say the State *does not have the **droit*** to take them. But one cannot say either that it *has the **droit*** to do so. These measures have nothing to do with *Droit* in general, nor consequently with penal *Droit:* therefore, they are not *penalties,* and the execution itself is here only the "supreme measure of political defence" (or "social," if it is a matter of defending not the State as such, i.e., as a political entity, as a collectivity of Friends opposed to a common Enemy, but non-political or civil Society, taken as a whole).

D. Private *Droit*

§ 64

[475] We have seen (chapter 1) that the *Droit* which exists in actuality, being realized by a State, can be divided into public *Droit* and private *Droit.* The matter is one of private *Droit* when neither of the two parties at issue claims to act in the name of the State, when there is no Civil Servant-impostor, even presumed. In private *Droit,* therefore, it is a matter of relations that occur within non-political Society. Now, like public *Droit,* private *Droit* can be either penal or civil. It is *penal* when one of the parties is Society as such—that is, "any given" member of Society. It is *civil* when the two parties are members of Society, taken in their specificity, as different from all the other members.

In this Section, I will only deal with *civil private **Droit**,* i.e., the *Droit* that one generally calls "civil *Droit*" or simply "private *Droit*," these two terms being equivalent.

Penal *Droit* is characterized both by the fact that the intervention of the Third, if it does not lead to an acquittal, results in a penalty, which means that the Third annuls the action as will and intention, and also by the fact that the Third intervenes spontaneously, which means that the criminal action is related to any given member of the Society—that is, Society as such. By contrast, civil *Droit* is characterized in the first place by the absence of punishment, which means that the Third limits himself to annulling the illicit action as act and not as will or intention; and second, by the "provoked" character of the intervention of the Third, which means that the latter does not relate the illicit action to Society as such, i.e., to its any given member, but to a member of Society taken in his specificity.

By definition, therefore, civil *Droit* does not recognize punishment properly so-called. There is at the very most a "reparation of the damage" caused by the illicit action, these "damages" having been sustained by the juridically injured member of Society. Otherwise, the Third's intervention is reduced to the pure and simple annulment of the illicit act, strictly delimited. [476] If A has the subjective *civil* right[87] to act or behave in a certain way, he has it in respect to a determinate B. Only B can injure this *droit* of A by his action or his behavior; for if anyone can injure A's *droit,* this *droit* is not specific to A: anyone can have the same *Droit.* If A's *droit* could have been injured by anyone, it is because this *droit* puts A in (effective or virtual) relation with "any given" member of Society. Now by definition *any given* member has no *specific* relation with A; he has no reason to injure A's *droit* any more than that of any other member—that is, in injuring this *droit* of A, one is not related exclusively to A, but to any given member (subject of this *droit*). In other words, one injures any given member or, which is the same thing, Society as a whole. There is then a case of *penal* and not *civil Droit.* Thus, for example, anyone can steal A's property: and this is a case of penal *Droit.* But only A's debtor B can fail to repay his debt, and he can only not repay it to A: and this is a case of civil *Droit.*[88] A only has subjective civil *droits* in relation to B (A and B capable of being one or several). If A has the (civil) *droit* to act or to behave toward B in a certain way, and if B acts or behaves such that A cannot do so, the Third will intervene to annul B's reaction and thus allow A not to make efforts to overcome B's resistance. This done, the Third withdraws himself from the interaction between A and B, and does not concern himself with the interactions between B and [477] the mem-

---

87. [Ed. In the original, the English word "right" follows the French phrase *droit subjectif* in parentheses.]

88. It should be understood that this does not mean that B is unique in Society: A can have several debtors; "B" will then be their aggregate. What is important is that B has specific relations with A, which he does not have with others. But A and B can be "collectivities," characterized precisely by the specificity of their mutual relations. Of course, it is possible that B wishes to steal a determinate object (a painting, for example) that A alone possesses. But what is specific here is the object and not the owner: the owner A of the object in question can be anyone at all, without the action of the theft being altered (at least in its intention). And this is why it is a case of penal *Droit.* A can be alone in benefiting from a certain *droit,* for example, that of receiving certain signs of respect from all other members. Then any given member can injure this *droit* of A, which belongs only to him. But if B injures this *droit* in acting as any given member, it is the *droit* that he wishes to injure, and not the person of A. Therefore, he wishes to injure Society, which recognizes this *droit* of A. He will injure by his action this Society as such, and there will be a case of penal *Droit.* To the extent that B injures A personally, he no longer acts (only) as any given member, and his act will yield a case of civil *Droit.* In this *civil* aspect, B will owe "compensatory damages" to A, and nothing more.

bers of Society other than A. The relations between B and the other members of Society are therefore not affected by his relations with A; and this is to say that these last relations, even if they implicate the intervention of the Third, do not lead to any *penalty* inflicted on B.

The Third, therefore, is related to B only to the extent that B is related to A. In his relations with A, overseen by the Third, B is supposed to be purely passive—that is, he must behave and act so as not to impede the action and behavior of A toward him, to the extent that A has the (civil) **droit** to do so. If B reacts, the Third annuls his reaction. And this is the whole civil intervention of the Third. Civil *Droit* allows A to act in a certain way with respect to B without being required to make efforts to overcome B's resistance. If such resistance takes place, the Third limits himself to suppressing it, and this suppression is enough to reestablish the *status quo ante* between A and B, which would not give rise to the Third intervening. As for the interactions between A, B, and the other members of Society, they are affected neither by the interaction between A and B, nor by the intervention of the Third in this interaction between A and B.

Now if it is a matter of A and not any other given member of Society, it is because A is taken in his specificity, in his *hic et nunc*—that is, his *actual* (and not virtual) existence. And this *actual* existence manifests itself in and by *acts*. It is in and by his *acts* that A differs from all other members of Society, for these are his acts which *actualize* his potentiality to be by transforming it into a *hic et nunc*, by definition different from all the others. Now the *act* can only be impeded by another *act*, which, by definition, actualizes and specifies a B. The Third can therefore annul by his intervention only the *act* of B—that is, the act of a determinate B and a determinate act of this B. The Third of civil *Droit* is therefore only related to the action of B to the extent that it is actualized in and by an *act*, and he disregards the action taken as will or intention. Of course, the civil *droit* of A toward B can arise from a convention (contract) between A and B—that is, B's intention and will. But when the Third of civil *Droit* intervenes, the convention is already actual; it is transformed by an act into a specific *hic et nunc*. And civil *Droit* only deals with this act: the contract only exists juridically from the moment when it is an "act" concluded between a specific and actual A and B; the mere intention, or will, to contract does not exist for the Third. Of course, the Third can seek the will or intention [478] of the contracting parties in the course of his intervention. But will and intention only interest him to the extent that they are actualized in the corresponding act: what counts is not the will or intention to realize or not to realize a contract; it is the act of making it or not making it. Will and intention determine the nature of this act, but they only intervene to the extent that they are implicated in it: without the act, beyond the act, they are nothing for civil *Droit*. As soon as the Third takes into account will and intention independently, or in addition to their realizations in and by the act, he (also) intervenes as a Third of penal *Droit;* for if the will of B transcends [*dépasse*] his act, it also transcends the person of B and the relations between A and B: it is related to any given member of Society and it is thus within the competence of penal *Droit*. Now, if civil *Droit* is only related to will and intention to the extent that these are implicated in the act, it can be related to the act without taking these into account. This is what takes place when the civil *Droit* of A toward B arises not from a contract between them, but from their status, i.e., not from their wills or intentions but from their very being: thus, for example, when the father has a *droit* to control certain activities of his son, or when the son has a *droit* to inherit from his father. In these cases, the Third only concerns himself with the act (or the actual being in general) and has nothing to do with the intention or the will of the parties at issue. And it should be understood that, here as well, it is only a matter of an interaction between A and B, and not interactions between A, B, and the other members of Society. The Third limits himself to annulling B's illicit reactions to A's actions, the actions and reactions being taken as *acts,* and not as wills or intentions.

However, for the intervention of the Third to be an authentic manifestation of (civil) **Droit***,* it must have as its goal the maintenance or restoration either of equality or equivalence, or both at the same time, between A and B. A has a (civil) **droit** to his action or behavior with respect to B, if this action or behavior maintains equality or equivalence between A and B. And the act of B is illicit if it destroys this equality or equivalence between A and himself. Thus, the act of refusing the repayment of a debt suppresses the equality or equivalence that is supposed to have existed between A and B before the loan, and between A—creditor of B—and B—debtor of A. Likewise, the disobedience of the son suppresses the equivalence that is supposed to have existed between the father and the obedient son, and the attempt of the father [479] to disinherit his son suppresses the equivalence between the situation of the father and of the son expecting an inheritance from his father. Now it is possible that the restoration of the equivalence or equality destroyed by the illicit act may not be achieved by the suppression of this act alone. It is not enough, for example, that the debtor ends by paying his debt; it is possible that the equivalence or equality of the respective situations will only be reestablished if the debtor compensates the creditor for the delay (or annuls the benefit that he gained from delaying payment). In this case the intervention of the Third will result in the payment (in whatever form) of "compensatory damages" to the party whose civil *droits* have been injured. But the act of paying these "compensatory damages" is part of the annulment of the illicit *act,* and this has nothing to do with a *penalty* in the proper sense of the word. The act of having not paid on the very date of the deadline can be annulled by the mere act of paying what is owed. But the act of having defaulted for a year can require, for its annulment, the payment of "compensatory damages" in addition to the debt.

Civil *Droit* is therefore related to action taken as *act.* And the act being a *hic et nunc,* it must be performed by an actual being and be related to such a being. But A and B are taken only in their actual interaction: A as being related in a certain manner to B, and B as being related in a certain manner to A. Thus, one can substitute C for A and D for B, if C and D exist in actuality, and if C and D respectively appropriate the acts in question of A and B. This is why one can assign a receivable[89] and inherit a debt, for example, or sell a contract; for the *act*, existing in actuality, is detached from its potentiality, i.e., here from will and intention (which are at one with their actual relations, i.e., of the person existing in actuality, who possesses them). The act can therefore be attached to another will or intention, to the will or intention of another. But (civil) *droit* is not affected by this substitution of persons: it remains a determinate relation between A and B exclusively, which remains the same if A is replaced by C and B by D. At any rate, civil *Droit* only deals with those beings capable of creating or adopting *acts*—that is, beings existing in actuality, specific beings actualized in a *hic et nunc*. In other words, civil *Droit* is related to interactions between members of Society, and not to interactions with this Society itself—that is, with any given member, without a specific *hic et nunc*. But it should be understood that this actual member of Society is not necessarily [480] a "physical person": it can just as well be a "moral person," individual, collective, or ideal.

Now if it is a matter of relations between *members* of Society, Society as such is not interacting. It is not therefore a party, and can be a Third. Society itself can create and apply civil *Droit*. But if Society is state-sanctioned, (civil) *Droit* will only exist in actuality if it is applied by the State. In this case, the State will act in the name of Society, taken not as party, but as an impartial and disinterested Third. The State will make its own the civil *Droit* of Society, and it is enough for this to be the case that it sanctions the decisions of Society intervening as Third, making them "irresistible."

But whether it is the State or Society that intervenes, they can only intervene on the basis of a "provocation" from the interested parties. Indeed, if the subjective civil *droit* of A is the *droit* of A and not of any given member, it is because this *droit* is not at the same time his duty. He can therefore exercise it or not, as he wishes. If he does not want to exercise it, it is not for the Third to intervene. And the Third can accept that A does not want to exercise his *droit* as long as he does not have recourse to the Third. The specificity of A is his actuality, and his actuality is his *act*. It is therefore the *act* of recourse to the Third, i.e., the "provocation" of his intervention, which actualizes and specifies A as a subject of civil *droit*. If the Third intervened "spontaneously," he would have treated A not as a specific member of Society, capable of being different from all the others, but as any given member, acting as all are supposed to act. In this case, the Third would intervene in the name of penal *Droit*, and not civil *Droit*. And as I have already had the opportunity to say, the non-intervention of the Third does not here mean a renunciation of the reestablishment of suppressed equality or equivalence. If A does not have recourse to the Third, it is because he does not consider himself injured by B's action (admittedly, at least). And in this case he is, effectively, not injured; for it is in his *specificity* that he is sup-

---

89. [Ed. A "receivable" (*créance*) is any money owed as a debt, whether a loan, a contract, and so on.]

posed to be injured when it is a matter of *civil Droit*. And to believe that he is injured, despite his *personal* opinion, is to treat him as *any given* member, [and] therefore to defend something other than his *civil droit*. Civil *Droit* seeks equality or equivalence not between any given members but between A and B; and this is to say that it considers equality and equivalence solely from the point of view of A or B. The equality or equivalence between A and B taken as such cannot be injured by B except if A thinks this [481] to be the case. And the "provocation" of the Third is nothing other than this "opinion" of A.

Civil *Droit* is therefore related to the interactions which take place *within* Society, between its members (individual or collective). But it is clearly necessary that these interactions take place within a *Society* for there to be (civil) *Droit*. Indeed, interactions between animals have nothing juridical about them. Now A or B is more and something different than an animal, he is a truly human being, only to the extent that he is a member of Society. The interaction to which *civil Droit* is related takes place only between A and B, but for this *Droit* to be truly a **Droit**, the interaction to which it is related must be a *social* interaction: A and B must be members of Society and act as such, all the while acting as *specific* members of this Society, and not as any given members.[90] Civil *Droit*, therefore, only exists within Society, and it is related to the social interactions between members of Society.

Now we are aware that there are several types of Societies (encompassed by "*Society*" in the technical sense of the term): familial, economic, worldly, religious, cultural, and so on. A member of a given Society is only able to enter into social interaction with another member of the same Society, taken as such. It should be understood that one and the same individual (or collectivity) can belong simultaneously to several different Societies. But if he acts as a member of a Society, his social action can only affect a member of this same Society (or this Society itself). There are then as many types of social interactions between A and B as there are types of Societies of which A and B are members. In particular, there are as many *civil Droits* as Societies. If A, taken as a (specific) member of a given Society, has the *droit* to act in a certain way toward B, and if B opposes this, the Society in question is going to intervene by way of a Third to annul B's reaction: the Third will then apply or create a civil Legal rule of the Society in question. [482] And the totality of such rules will form the civil *Droit* of this Society.

Now nothing says that different Societies must have one and the same *Droit*, i.e., apply one and the same ideal of Justice; for the human being who actualizes himself within a given Society is not the same being as he who actualizes himself in another Society, even if these two beings have one and the same ani-

---

90. Society is supposed to be something essentially different from an animal association: herd, hive, and so on. I cannot here indicate in what the difference consists. Suffice it to say that relations between animals are *speechless* and relations expressible in speech *by agents in relation* are specifically human. Thus, there is only *Droit* when the interaction is presented to the Third by the interested parties (or their representatives) in a *verbal* form. (The "representative" is supposed to have received—or was *capable of* receiving—*verbal* instructions from the interested parties whom he represents.)

mal Homo sapiens as a basis. To actualize oneself through action as a member of familial Society, for example, is something different from actualizing oneself by acting in economic Society. It is therefore possible that a given familial Society applies an egalitarian ideal of Justice, while economic Society is animated by the ideal of the Justice of equivalence—and so forth. Of course, real *Droit* is always synthetic, based upon the ideal of the Justice of equity. But the nature of this synthesis can differ. Therefore, nothing says that all the civil *Droits* of the Society at a given moment belong to a single legal system. But if the Society is state-sanctioned, all the Societies that belong to it will have a (civil) *Droit* in actuality to the extent that this *Droit* will be state-sanctioned. One and the same State, acting by way of a Third, will therefore apply all the particular civil *Droits*. In order to remain consistent with itself, the State must, therefore, unify these—that is, base them upon the same ideal of Justice. Then the various civil *Droits* will be categories of one and the same Legal System, subdivisions of the civil *Droit* of this System. But in fact the State generally adopts the *Droits* elaborated by Societies. The unity of civil *Droit*, therefore, will be in general entirely relative. The single and unified civil *Droit*, i.e., the truly coherent System, will only exist in the State where all the Societies will have reached the same evolutionary stage. And this will only take place in a Society, and consequently in a State, which is *homogenous*—that is, in the universal State of the definitive future.

In the pages that follow, I will limit myself to saying a few words about only two different possible types of civil *Droit*, which are at present the most important. I will first speak about (a) the **Droit** *of familial Society* and then about (b) the **Droit** *of economic Society*.

a. The Droit of Familial Society

§ 65

[483] It is not a matter here of debating the question of whether it is the State which presupposes the Family, or if it is the Family which presupposes the State (in the broad sense of a social organization other than familial). It is enough to note that, at least nowadays, the Family and the State co-exist: on the one hand, the modern Family lives within a State, of which its members are, in general, citizens; on the other hand, the modern State has not suppressed the Family, and its citizens are, in general, members of Families. And one can note a certain reciprocal autonomy or independence between the Family and the State. Their autonomy is revealed by the fact that they can enter into conflict.[91] The Family is therefore *essentially* something different from the State, familial relations differ *essentially* from political relations, and man taken as member of a Family and consequently of familial Society, is something dif-

---

91. The conflict between the Family and the State is the principal theme of ancient Tragedy, as Hegel [*Phenomenology of Spirit*, 266–94] has shown (see Aeschylus' *Oresteia* and Sophocles' *Antigone*, for example). "Feudalism" is another manifestation of this conflict.

ferent from this same man taken as member of political Society or the State—that is, as citizen. This is why the State "represented" by man taken as citizen can intervene by way of an impartial and disinterested Third not only in interactions between the members of a Family or between Families, but also in the interactions between the members of a Family or a Family, and familial Society taken as such, taken as a whole, "represented" by its "any given" member taken as member of this Society; from whence comes the possibility of a *Droit* of familial Society, civil and penal, existing *in actuality* within a state-sanctioned Society.

But if, on the one hand, being something different from the Family, the State can be disinterested toward it, on the other hand, [the State] needs and is "interested" in its existence: in a certain sense, the State "presupposes" the Family. Indeed, citizens being mortals, the State must be able to replace them. And, until now at the very least, the State itself has not produced [484] its citizens. They have been furnished to it by Families—that is, familial Society. The State is therefore "interested" in the preservation of this Society. It has an interest in every citizen also being a member of familial Society. This is why the status of a member of this Society is, to a certain extent, included by the State in the status of citizen. To the extent that the State intervenes in order to maintain the familial status included in the status of the citizen, it intervenes as an interested party and not as Third: its intervention therefore has nothing juridical about it. But the State is not "interested" in *all* the elements of familial status, and to the extent that it is "disinterested" its intervention can generate or actualize an authentic familial *Droit*, if it intervenes in order to make Justice reign within familial Society. Its intervention, moreover, will be juridical even when it is "interested," if it intervenes not as an interested party, but as a disinterested Third, abstracting as it were from its own interest in the matter. Thus, one and the same act can be annulled by the State in a non-juridical manner as contrary to the status of the citizen, and juridically as contrary to familial status, even if the two statuses have in common the element in question.[92] Of course, in realizing Justice within familial Society, the State maintains it in existence. One can therefore say that it applies Justice because it is interested in the preservation of the Society. But what is important is that the State preserves the Society *by realizing Justice within it* and does not preserve it otherwise. Familial status is not "just" because it preserves familial Society: it preserves it because it is "just"—meaning from the point of view of this Society, i.e., of its any given member (or more exactly, any given member of its exclusive juridical group). If the State were to apply to members of Society an "unjust" status, the Society would end up being dissolved. The State only preserves this Society because it realizes within it [the Society] its valid ideal of jus-

---

92. It should be understood that it will then be difficult to *know for a fact* if the State acts as Third, i.e., juridically, or as Party, i.e., politically. This is why real familial *Droit* often includes juridically unauthentic elements. But that is another question. *In principle*, the distinction proposed is meaningful.

tice. Whether "interested" or not, the intervention of the State therefore realizes in familial Society the ideal of Justice of this Society; one can therefore say that it actualizes the (penal and civil) *Droit* of this Society. And to the [485] extent that familial Society is a *sui generis* human Society, the application (by the State) of a given ideal of Justice to the social interactions characteristic of this Society yields a *sui generis* (penal and civil) *Droit:* familial *Droit.*

Familial *Droit* has as its purpose to make familial Society conform to a certain ideal of Justice: equality, equivalence, or equity. When the ideal of Justice will be applied to interactions between members of familial Society, i.e., the members of a family (individual or collective), or a family, or a group of families, and this Society taken as a whole, i.e., its "any given" member, one will have a case of penal familial *Droit.* As for civil familial *Droit,* it will aim at establishing or reestablishing equality, equivalence, or equity in the social interactions between members of familial Society, taken as members of this Society: that is, first, between members or groups of members of one and the same family; then between one family and its members; further between the members of one family and those of another, or between the members of one family and another family taken as a whole; and finally between two families or two groups of families, the members of the families and the families always being taken in their specificity, in that which distinguishes them from other members and families.

The specificity of familial *Droit* is due to the specificity of familial Society. An ideal of Justice generates *familial Droit* when it is applied to *familial* interactions. We must therefore see what familial Society is as such.

With any doubt, familial interactions are in the final analysis based upon sexuality, which leads to children being brought into the world. As such, sexuality is a biological phenomenon which has nothing specifically human about it. Taken in itself, the animal pairing [*couple*] is just as little a Family as an animal association (herd, hive, and so on) is a State. But if Man is constituted, moreover, as a human being, his biological sexual relations also acquire a human value and become familial relations, just as the association of humanized beings becomes, by the very fact that these beings are human, a human association: a Society or a State. From the moment that the male and female are human beings, they are "husband" and "wife" if they form a "pairing," and this pairing is already [486] a "family."[93] Now man is humanized by Struggle and Work, as Master and Slave. The "pairing" made up of Masters or Slaves, or—more exactly—by a Master or Slave and his companion (with his chil-

---

93. Generally speaking, almost the entire content of human life is a humanization of animal life. What is specifically human, human in a *primary* manner (not derivative), is the Desire for desire—that is, the Desire for recognition, the Struggle which results from it and the Work which is born from the Struggle, with language (or thought: Logos) which this work generates. Everything else is formed by animal life ("psychic": sensation, perception, emotion, desire, and so on), which acquires a human value from the fact that it operates within a humanized life (through Struggle and Work), thus being "self-conscious," and consequently expressible through speech. But the content as self-consciousness is opposed to the

dren) is no longer an animal pairing: it is a human Family. Now Mastery and Servitude generate and include relations between Friends-Enemies. And if man first humanizes himself in actuality as Master, an association of Masters is first of all a political (human) Society—that is, a State (in the broad sense). One can therefore say that the Family presupposes the State: it is within the State that the animal pairing [487] transforms itself into a Family. But on the other hand, the Master and Slave must be born as animals in order to exist, and they are born in and by animal pairing. One can therefore say as well that the State presupposes the pairing, that it exists only to the extent that there are pairings. The State therefore presupposes pairing (as in general man "presupposes" the animal Homo sapiens), but the Family presupposes the State (as human life in general, i.e., self-conscious existence, or what is the same thing, [existence] revealed in and by language or thought, presupposes Work, which presupposes Mastery and the Struggle for recognition). One could also say that there is a simultaneous and parallel humanization of the pairing into the Family and the herd into the State. The Struggle of the Master humanizes animal combats by transforming them into political interactions, the animal association, the herd, thus becoming political Society and finally the State. Within this Society the Work of the Slave humanizes material life and creates economic Society. And inside of the State and economic Society, familial Society constitutes itself through the humanization of sexual life. If you will, one can say with Aristotle that the Family consists of parents, children, *and Slaves*.[94] It is because

---

immediate or brute content (animal in the proper sense), since self-consciousness presupposes—and consequently includes—a *negation* of the brute given (the "instinct of self-preservation"); from whence comes a real transformation of animal life as a result of self-consciousness (or of language, i.e., thought). The "animal" life of a *human* being thus becomes a *human* life, really other than the life of an animal properly so-called. The family, being a *self conscious* animal "pairing" (revealing itself through language), is therefore *really* something different from the pairing properly so-called, formed by animals deprived of self-consciousness (language or thought). As well, the difference can be noticed even by a "behaviorist" method. However, this transformation is derivative and not primary. The Family differs from the pairing because man already differs from the animal, being humanized outside of the pairing by Struggle and Work. The Family is a "dialectical negation" (*Aufhebung*) of the pairing. But it is not in "negating" the pairing (animal sexuality) that man humanizes himself. It is because he is already humanized (by the negation of animal nature in and by Struggle and Work) that man (also) "negates" animal sexual life and thus transforms the pairing into a Family. It is because he is already Master (of a Slave) or Slave (of a Master) that man behaves himself differently toward his woman than the male [animal] toward his female [animal] and becomes "husband" of a "wife." Having "negated" his animal nature in Struggle and Work, man must also "negate" it in sexuality (which is in unity with the animal nature that he negated), and it is this "negation," (secondary or derivative), which humanizes sexuality, transforming it into familial interaction. (The "negation" of animal sexuality is realized and revealed through sexual "taboos." But it is not in "inventing" these taboos, i.e., in humanizing animal sexual life, that man humanizes himself. It is because he has already been humanized by Struggle and Work that he introduces sexual "taboos" and thus humanizes sexual life—in humanizing himself also as male and female.)

94. [Ed. *Politics*, 1252a25–b15.]

the father of the family is a Master possessing Slaves that he is a husband and *family patriarch*[95] and not a male animal with a female and little ones. Being human in his being, i.e., in his action, man is so as well in his sexual activity: by becoming relations between *human* beings, sexual relations (in the broad sense) become *human*, familial relations: a pairing of *human* beings is not an animal "pairing," but a Family.

At first, the "husband" alone is humanized (by becoming—in and by the Struggle—Master or Slave): the wife (who by definition does not participate in the Struggle) remains a female, an animal Homo sapiens. And from the point of view of the humanized husband, she can remain in her animality, provided that she give him (male) children who will become human;[96] [488] for the Master (and man in general) is anxious to have an "heir," i.e., a *human* child, [who is] therefore comparable to his (humanized) father.[97] The goal of the Family (from the point of view of its humanized "leader") is therefore not so much procreation as *education,* i.e., the transformation of a young animal into a human being, supposed to be able to prolong the *action,* i.e., the very being, of his father, who thus "survives" in his heir, and who therefore "defends" him

---

95. [Ed. The original is *père de famille,* which can mean simply father or carry the implication of head of the household. Kojève plays on this expression in this passage to illustrate how the father is not simply a biological father, but in the *human* society of the family, something more. The most elegant way we could find of conveying this in English is the expression *family patriarch.*]

96. In reality the companion of the husband is necessarily a "wife," spouse, and not a female. But she is humanized through the intermediation of the husband (already humanized outside of the Family and independently of his interactions with his wife). The husband, having negated his animality in the Struggle, negates as well the sexual aspect of this animality, in respecting the sexual taboos that he imagines (notably in connection with the Struggle: the sexual taboo has above all the purpose of preserving the military potency of the man). Now, the wife submits to the taboo imposed by the husband: she also therefore negates her animal sexuality and consequently humanizes it by humanizing herself (in her feminine, i.e., sexual, aspect at the very least). This humanization [488] of the wife is mediated by the man (her husband), just as the humanization of the Slave (through Work) is mediated by the Master (and the Struggle), from whence comes a certain analogy between the Wife and the Slave. But the fact of not having struggled is something different from the fact of having abandoned the Struggle (from fear of death), from whence comes an essential difference between the Wife and Slave. But I cannot insist upon this point here.

97. The "heir" is an *Ersatz* for immortality. Man is the sole being who *knows himself* to be finite—that is, mortal. Now *to be aware of* one's end is to transcend it, to overcome it "mentally," from whence comes the desire to overcome it really, to be immortal. Man is therefore the only being who *wants* to be immortal, from whence comes the "myth" (the mistake) of the immortality of his "soul" (distinguished from the body that is known to be mortal), and Religion (Theism). (The endpoint of man's evolution is the acceptance by man of his finitude: irreligious atheism.) And the transposition here below of immortality in the beyond is the idea of the perpetuity of the "soul" immanent in the World, the eternity of the "name," of the "family": the idea of the (male) heir, identified with his father because of the fact that he prolongs the *action* of his father, the action being the very being of man—from whence comes the necessity not only for a young animal, but a *human* child, i.e., *humanized* in and by the Family.

"as himself."[98] Education, like all humanization, is realized and revealed in and by "dialectical negations" of innate animality: rules of hygiene, sexual and dietary taboos, rites of bodily mutilation, paint, clothing, and so on, [and] rites of passage, and so forth. It is the Family that imposes on the child this "negation" of his animal nature and humanizes him through this negation.[99]

It should be understood that the Family does not realize *all* the "negations" that create man from animal. Thus, by definition, the negation that is realized and revealed in and by the Risk of life in a Struggle for recognition (first of all by the Master) takes place outside of the Family, in political Society or the State: man carries it out not as "family son," but in his capacity as citizen.[100] Likewise, humanization through Work (by the Slave [489] first of all) is carried out properly speaking in *economic* Society. The Slave works (in the beginning) in and for the Family: but he is related to the Family taken as an economic, and not a familial, unit. Likewise, the labors of the members of the Family are "familial" only accidentally: one can work without being a member of a Family and one can be a member of a Family without working. Not even all of the "taboos" that negate animality are familial. Religious and worldly Societies also enact taboos (rites, "manners," and so on) and thus participate in the humanization of the child. But there are also sexual taboos (incest, for example) specific to the Family, and there is then a specifically familial humanization of the child. And it is in this specific negating education that the human rationale for the Family resides. Of course (in the beginning, at the very least), the Family also educates the future citizen as well as the future member of economic, religious, worldly, and other Societies: it applies to the child the "taboos" specific to these Societies and the State. But the State and these Societies could have undertaken this themselves, from whence comes frequent conflicts between the Family, on the one hand, and the State and the various Societies, on the other hand, when it concerns the education of the young: familial education (liberal or strict) or religious, state, and so on, education. In principle, familial education has a rationale if the Family has a rationale, and it consists in the preparation—starting from the newborn animal—of a human member of the human Family (of a given type). Now as long as sexuality is to be humanized, i.e., negated in its animal immediacy, there will always be some sort of Family—that is, still something different from

---

98. From this comes the idea of adoption, on the one hand, and "recognition" of the newborn by the father, on the other. The new-born presumed incapable of being humanized (and of "prolonging" the father) may be killed like any other animal (and the daughter, if she is supposed to be incapable of being humanized, humanity being refused to women).

99. Here as well, [we see the] similarity and difference between the Child and the Slave.

100. Now only this Risk truly *actualizes* man's humanity. Man [489] is therefore truly human *in actuality* only in the State, as a member of political Society or a citizen. Man educated within the Family is a citizen *in potentiality,* who *actualizes* himself in and by the State. In this sense, the Family is humanly "subordinate" to the State. A non-state-sanctioned, familial Society cannot wholly and in actuality humanize man. But to the extent that the State is a group of Friends, which co-exists without internal Struggle, it needs a "pacific" humanization of its citizens. It therefore needs the Family, to the extent that humanization without Struggle is carried out in its bosom.

a pairing of male and female animals. And as long as this will be the case, it will be necessary to create (future) members of Families starting from animal new-borns. This negating creation will necessarily have to be carried out within the very bosom of the Family. Be that as it may, the human meaning of the Family is not so much the production of children as their *education*, their transformation [490] into human beings (if only in potentiality) by the negation of their innate animality: first of all (and this is the appropriate "sphere" of familial education), their sexual animality, which transforms the animal new-born into a son, brother, cousin, and so on, as well as into a future father, grandfather, and so on, this transformation being, moreover, valid for both sexes. Of course, the Family produces children, but it only does so in order to educate them, to make them into men.

Now, like every finite being in general, man is only real in actuality inside of the totality of which he is an integral element. This totality is the spatio-temporal Universe and—as a phenomenon—the World where the being in question lives and acts. Man is only real in actuality in his interaction with his World: his being is being-in-the-World (the *In-der-Welt-sein* of Heidegger).[101] As animal, man lives in the natural World, and his innate animal nature is determined by his *topos*, by the place he occupies in the natural World. Now man is humanized in and by the "dialectical negation" of his innate animal nature—that is, of his fixed place in the World or Cosmos. But the human being that he creates by this negation (and which is nothing other than the very *act* of the negation of the natural given) is also only real for him in actuality in a World: in a human or historical World, created starting from the natural World by the negating action of Struggle and Work. And the human being of man is determined by the *topos*, by the place that he occupies in the human, historical, social World. Of course, being free, man can "negate" the social *topos* just as he can negate the natural *topos*. In negating the natural *topos*, he becomes something different from the natural being that he was: he becomes something different from an animal; he becomes a human being. And in negating the given social or historical *topos*, he *becomes* another man. But to the extent that he *is*, he is in a given social and historical *topos*, and he acts starting from this social and historical *hic et nunc*. To create oneself as man and to exist as man is to create a human World and live within this World, occupying a determinate "place" within it.

Therefore, if the Family aims at creating a man starting from the animal new-born (which, generally speaking, it produces itself), it should also create the social *topos* of this man, the World in which he is going to live and act. This World is first of all the familial World. It is the Family which has generated the child and which educates him. This Family has to be a World for the child, a "Universe" in which it is sufficient for him to live. The Family must therefore create a *topos* for the child that is born within it; [491] it must assign him a

---

101. [Ed. Martin Heidegger, *Being and Time*, trans. John Macquarrie and Edward Robinson (New York: Harper and Row, 1962), 401ff.]

"place" in its bosom. But the Family is a "Universe" only for the child. In fact it is part of a larger World, consisting of other families. It must therefore create a *topos* in the World of Families, in familial Society, the child having a well defined *topos* inside this *topos*.

The *topos* of a Family in familial Society is the (hereditary) "patrimony" of this Family, the word patrimony being taken in the broadest sense. And the *topos* of the child within the Family is the "place" that he occupies in relation to this patrimony, concerning both its creation and its consumption, and—last not least[102]—its transmission. The patrimony belongs to the Family as such. If you will, it belongs to the individuals who make up the Family, but only to the extent that they are members of this Family. This patrimony is not only, and not necessarily, a "property," real or personal. It is first and foremost the common *household* [*oeuvre*][103] of the Family, and familial property is only the materialization of this household, which is carried out by Work properly so-called or otherwise. And if one can define the Family by the education of the children that it puts into the world, one can also define it by its household or its "patrimony." The Family is an association of individuals around a common household, a household that the members of the Family produce and "exploit" in common, and which is supposed to maintain itself in existence despite the fact that the individuals who make up the Family change—coming or going. But this household ultimately has as its goal the education of children born within the Family: it is the "site"[104] of this education and the "place" of the members of the Family humanized by familial education.

Of course, generally speaking, the familial household is an economic phenomenon. But economic activity within a Family, as well as economic activity of a Family as Family, are something different from the activity proper to economic Society properly so-called: this is a *familial* activity (in its economic aspect) and not a genuine *economic* activity. In economic Society, interactions take place between isolated individuals, or groups in association for economic purposes. In familial Society, the inter-actions take place between Families, or between individuals taken as members of Families, these Families having as their ultimate goal their preservation as Families which educate their children and create for them a "place" in familial Society. [492] It should be understood

---

102. [Ed. In the original, this phrase is in English.]
103. [Ed. The word *oeuvre* is rather difficult to translate here: while "household" seems most idiomatic, "production" or "works" would perhaps be more literal but also somewhat awkward and even misleading. The idea being expressed is that of a "household" or "house" in the sense of the House of Windsor or the House of Marlborough—household in the sense of suggesting intergenerational stability and continuity in a way that the word household no longer does to our ears. We have decided, therefore, to stick with what might appear to be a slightly anachronistic translation.]
104. [Ed. Reading *lieu* for *lien* as in the original manuscript. What Kojève seems to be doing here is using two very similar words as a turn of the phrase: the family is the "site" in the sense of worksite where the education occurs, as well as the "place," the location of interactions between those so educated. In other words, it is a place where humanity is created and where action between the humans so created occurs.]

that as soon as the familial household has an economic aspect, the Family and its members are generally also members of economic Society, from whence comes interactions and conflicts between familial Society and economic Society. Likewise, the Family and its members are generally members of worldly ("social class"), religious, and other Societies, as well as the State (citizens). The familial household has a value that is economic, social, religious, political, and so on. And the Family creates for its members not only a "place" in familial Society, but also a *topos* in the State and in economic, worldly, and so on, Society. But all these "places" could have been created for the new-born by social entities other than the Family. The *specifically* familial household is that which creates the *topos* within familial Society itself. As "family patriarch," man works (in the broad sense) for his children, i.e., for those who are supposed to "prolong" him (in principle indefinitely) after his death, and not as citizens or members of Society—economic, worldly, and so on—but as "family patriarchs." The *familial* household aims at the perpetuity of the Family as Family: *this* Family. It must assure the familial education of the children—that is, an education such that the new-borns of the family can replace the ancestors within this Family. And since the identity of man presupposes the identity of his world, the familial household must assure the perpetuity of the familial world: the new members, appropriately educated, must be able to live in the same familial world in which their kinsmen lived—that is, in particular, to occupy the same "place" as they within familial Society, to have the same interactions with the totality of other Families, of this Society. The familial household serves education and familial education serves this household: children are educated in order to be able to collaborate in the familial household, which aims at allowing the education of children capable of so collaborating and of putting them in a position to be able to do so effectively. The Family educates its children in order that they educate their own, and the familial household creates the material framework of this perpetual education.

It is nevertheless clear that education and the household do not exhaust the human content of the Family. The latter is not only an association of individuals for the education of children resulting from this association, and [an association] around a household destined to serve education and supposed to be served by the [493] educated children. From all time, one has seen in the Family an association of *love:* between spouse and spouse, parents and children, and so on. And one does not effectively understand the human content of the Family as long as one does not know what human *love* is.

Amorous "interaction" is not an inter-*action*. Love is the attribution of an ("absolute") value not to *action* (or to the being *in actuality*), but to the very *being* as *being* (or "pure" being, in potentiality, if you will, "absolute," outside of all *relations,* i.e., of all *inter*-action, i.e., of all *action*). As was well expressed by Goethe, one loves someone not for what he *does,* but because he *is.* Thus, a mother loves her son not because he has done such and such a thing, and even because he has done such and such a thing to *her,* but simply because he *is* her son: it matters little [whether he is] a "bad son" or a "good son," a "fine man" or a "good for nothing." It is obvious that love so conceived is a specifically human phenomenon: this love presupposes an "abstraction"; it is related to the being as "essence" and not to the *hic et nunc* determined by inter-actions, to existence in actuality. It is only a humanized being, i.e., detached from his natural *hic et nunc* ("animal" or "empirical") that can abstract from the *hic et nunc* of another being, determined by the interactions with his own *hic et nunc*. It is therefore only a prior humanized being (by negation of its animal nature) that can *love* in the indicated sense of the word. But an already human being can love any other being whatsoever (and perhaps even himself, say his soul). And if man starts to love the beings with whom he associates in order to generate children and educate them collaboratively in a common household destined for this education, or equally if in this household he associates with beings that he loves and generates with them children in order to educate them in common, he experiences a *familial* love. The Family could therefore be defined as an association of individuals who *love* one another (at least in principle) and who associate with each other in respect to a common *household* aiming at the *education* of children produced by this association.[105]

[494] From the fact that love is the attribution of a positive value to the very *being* of a man, independently (more or less, of course) of the *action* which

---

105. Man is able to *love* anyone and even anything. He *loves* as soon as he attributes a positive value to the very being of a given entity. Every (positive) "disinterested" relation to a being is "love" and all love is a "disinterested" relation. One can love a thing or an animal. (It is possible that Art is the expression of love of a thing as such: of pure being, i.e., of the "essence," the "idea" of a tree, for example. And music is the expression of love of being as such, [494] ineffable in its abstraction). One can also love man "in general" ("love of one's neighbor" or of "humanity"). But one can also love such a man to the exclusion of all others. One then takes him in his specificity, but by abstracting from the *act* of this specificity—that is, the *action* which actualizes it. Thus, the concept "Napoleon," while applying to only one being, is a *concept*—that is, an entity detached from the *hic et nunc* of the empirical Napoleon. To love "Napoleon" is to relate oneself to the concept "Napoleon"—that is, to his "essence," to his "idea" or to his "being" as such. (This is why the lover "idealizes" the being loved. If he errs in wrongly identifying the "ideal" loved with its *hic et nunc* empirical base, then "love is blind." If he realizes the difference, he will have a tendency to "educate" the base in order to make it conform to his "idea" or "ideal," from whence comes the "platonic love"—which is not necessarily "platonic"—of which Socrates speaks in *The Symposium*. It seems, moreover, that not only does all self-conscious love lead to an "education," but that all spontaneous "education" presupposes love.) One must not conflate love with "sublimated" sexuality (to be "amorous," and so on), which is also specifically human (eroticism). But eroticism can be combined with love, which gives "love" in the contemporary sense of the word. But this "love" has nothing familial about it. If love without eroticism is (in certain cases) "friendship [*amitié*]," the "love [*amour*]" in question is an "erotic friendship [*amitié amoureuse*]": the human basis of "sexual cohabitation [*concubinage*]." [Ed. The expression we translate as erotic friendship is applied in idiomatic French to a relationship, usually between a man and a woman, that is flirtatious and eroticized, characterized more by charm and playfulness than overwhelming passion, and something less than a full-blown affair.] Love only becomes *familial* if it generates children with a view to their *education* and creates a common *household* with a view to this education. And it remains *familial* as long as the beings who love one another are bound to one another by bonds that attach them to this common household—that is, as long as they are "kinsmen." Conversely, a common household, even educative, is not familial as long as

actualizes this being in a *hic et nunc,* i.e., independently of the inter-actions that this man has with me taken in my *hic et nunc,* one can deduce several consequences from this.[106]

[495] The Family has as a physiological basis the birth of children. All the degrees of kinship are calculated starting from this basis. Kinship therefore also exists in the animal realm. But it exists there only "in itself" [and] not "for itself"—that is, *for* the animal itself. It is *we* who know that such an animal is the father, son, brother, and so on, of another: the animal itself does not know this. But the "in itself" is objective, it is a quality of the very being: kinship relations have an ontological nature; they determine the very being of the animal in his ontological relations with the being of other animals. Man (if he is already humanized) can therefore attribute a positive value to kinship as an attribute of *being:* he can *love* his kin as kin. All at once, kinship exists not only "in itself" but also "for itself": it is not only *us,* [but] man *himself* knows that he is the kin

---

the associates do not *love* one another—that is, as long as they do not behave toward one another as "kinsmen." The love between *kinsmen,* moreover, means nothing more than the fact that they mutually attribute to each other a positive value independent of their inter-*actions*—that is, due to the mere fact that they are "kinsmen," that they *are* (as kinsmen). I can despise or even hate my brother. If I give him a thousand dollars *solely* because he is my *brother,* I experience a *familial love* for him. But if I give a thousand dollars to someone *solely* because he has assisted [*collaboré*] in my familial household or contributed to the education of my child, even if I love him moreover, I do not have *familial* love for him: he is not my *kin.* "Familial love" is another word for the phenomenon of "kinship."

106. "The true being of man is his *action*" (Hegel). It is action which is human in man, or which creates the human in him, if one prefers (man *is* only to the extent that he *creates* himself). It follows from this that one cannot *love* the human in man: one can admire it ("recognize" it) or despise it—that is all. But it does not follow that one can only love the animal in man, man as a natural being, the *animal* [495] Homo sapiens (although the purely animal aspect plays a large role in love, even non-sexual). The done action *is* in the same way that things and animals *are.* A house is just as real in actuality as a tree, and it is nevertheless a non-natural human artifact [*oeuvre*]: to love a house is therefore to love a non-natural being. But the house is only human in actuality as long as men *act* humanly: if humanity disappears and houses remain, there will be nothing human in actuality on earth all the same. And the same goes for man himself. He constructs himself like one constructs a house: he is only truly human in the *act* of constructing himself, but the construction is a non-natural being, just like the house. It is "character," "personality," that *are,* like things *are.* One can therefore *love* not only the animal properly so-called in man (his body and physical demeanor and animal "psyche") but also his *human being*—that is, the "cadaver" or "mummy" of his anthropogenic acts. Thus, one can *love* the dead man in the totality of his lived human life, which *is* "eternally" (but not in actuality). One can therefore love "character," "personality," by relating oneself to the man taken in his *being* and not in his action. But one must not forget that "character" is truly human (in actuality) only to the extent that man "negates dialectically" (this "negation," moreover, only being real in actuality to the extent that it creates a reality, i.e., inserts itself into being and becomes a being, i.e., inscribes itself in a "character" and becomes "character"—from whence comes the impossibility and illusion of "romanticism" and the "permanent revolution": time is needed to *realize* a negation and thus to be able to negate it again, and man is mortal). One can therefore *love* the human in man, but the human that one *loves,* being being [*étant être*] and no longer *action,* is no longer human *in actuality:* it is the remembrance of the man that one loves, even in the living [*présent*] man.

of someone and that someone is his kin. And if man does not make do with the theoretical or cognitive attitude, with the fact of *knowing* kinship, but takes toward it an "emotional" and active attitude, by attributing a positive *value* to kinship as such [496] and behaving accordingly, if in a word he "loves" his kinsmen and acts as a result of this "familial love," he is member of a *Family* and behaves as such. And in this he is specifically human. The female may concern herself with her young, defend it, and so on. But she only does so as long as her young sucks on her or, in general, is in effective *interaction* with her. It is not the *being* of the young, the sole fact that he is her son, which determines the behavior of the animal mother. It is the way in which the young behaves toward her. As soon as the inter-action between male and female, between "parents" and children, ceases, animal "kinship" ceases to exist for the animal: the animals become perfect "strangers" to one another and are not "kin" except for *us*. By contrast, the human mother has in respect to her child an attitude that does not depend upon the latter's behavior, upon the inter-action between him and her. It is not the action, it is the *being* of the child, i.e., the fact that it is her child, that determines her behavior. The mother *loves* her child, and therefore the latter is her *child*, a *kin* to her: she is "family matriarch."

And what is true of maternal love is true of familial love in general. In particular, when it is a matter not of camaraderie, friendship, or an erotic liaison, but marriage, i.e., of the Family, one cannot say that two people become husband and wife because they love one another: they love one another (with a familiar love) because they *are* husband and wife. And the same goes for all other bonds of kinship. If the Family is based upon familial love, this love is a simple function of the degree of kinship, it is the fact of attributing a value to kinship as such. Physiological "kinship" is a characteristic of the (natural) being of man, and familial love is the positive value attributed to this characteristic, which determines a specific behavior: familial behavior. Of course, there is no Family without natural, animal, biological "kinship." But this kinship exists only for man, and man alone is capable of attributing to it a value as a characteristic of pure *being*, independent of all action. Man alone is therefore capable of *loving* his kinsmen as kinsmen; he alone is capable of "familial love." And the Family only exists from the moment when the kinsmen who make it up *love* one another as kinsmen and behave accordingly. The Family as a specifically human ("social") phenomenon is the totality of physiological "kinsmen" who *know* they are such and who [497] love one another—that is, attribute a positive value to the fact of being kinsmen and who are determined in their mutual interactions by this love. It is not because they have interactions among themselves of a certain kind that they love one another: they have these interactions because they love one another as kinsmen with a familial love. It is this "familial love" between *kinsmen* which is the base of the "*common household*" of the Family, which aims at the *education* of future or newly arrived kinsmen, i.e., the preservation of kindred *being*, the maintenance of kinship in being and in real existence in actuality. Familial love reveals the "kindred" aspect of being in and by the value which is attributed to it, and the educative familial household actualizes this valorized being by maintaining it in actual existence, this actual existence of kinship-value being nothing other than the Family itself, building block [*élément intégrant*]—in and by interactions with the other Families—of familial Society.[107]

Everyone who is not "kin" is a "stranger" to the Family. But seeing that kinship is a function of being and not action, the same goes for the quality of "stranger." The "stranger," in the sense of "non-kinsman," is a "stranger" on the grounds of his being and not because of his action. And this is why he is not an "Enemy" like the political "stranger,"[108] just as the "kinsman" is not a political "Friend," ally, brother-in-arms, compatriot fellow-citizen. The opposite of Love is Hate, the negative value attributed to *being* as such, the "emotional" negation of being as being, independent of its actualization in and by action. Now, as Carl Schmitt clearly showed (*Über den Begriff des Politischen* [*The Concept of the Political*]), political "enmity" has nothing to do with Hate: there are hatreds between Families but not between States. But between Love and Hate there is indifference, emotional "neutrality," the awareness of a being without negative or positive value. And generally speaking the Family does not hate "strangers," the other (non-kindred) Families: it is indifferent toward them. When, in politics for example, there is inter-*action*, there is no neutrality possible: either one participates in the action of the other, and one is then a Friend, [498] ally, and so on, or one opposes it, and one is then an Enemy. But where Love and Hate rule, i.e., where the relation is not to *action* but to *being,* there is a possibility of neutrality, pure and simple indifference: a being is there, beside another being, without interacting with him. And it is thus that a Family can simply be there, beside other Families, within familial Society. Being based upon (familial) love, the Family is therefore something entirely different from a group of Friends opposed to a common Enemy: it is something entirely different from the State. It is a group of kinsmen who love one another—that is, who attribute a positive value to their being as kinsmen. This group can hate certain groups of "strangers." But generally speaking it will be indifferent toward them. Familial Society can include Families which hate one another and mutually seek to destroy each other in their interaction. But generally speaking this Society is made up of "neutral" Families who, in their mutual indifference, are without reciprocal inter-actions, or again, who are akin and love one another in and by matrimonial exchanges among the young men and women who wed one another. And it is these exchanges which constitute the base of specifically familial inter-actions between Families.

---

107. Familial Society as such is universal. Its subdivisions or "national" familial Societies are not a function of familial life, but of political, economic, religious, cultural, and so on, life. Families form "national" groups because their members are also citizens of national States and members of national economic, religious, and so on, Societies.

108. [Ed. It should be noted that the word we have translated as "stranger"—*étranger*—can mean both "stranger" or "foreigner" depending on the context. We have chosen to translate it consistently in this section as "stranger" so that Kojève's shift between the familial and political contexts can be more precisely tracked.]

If the Family is based upon familial Love, and if this Love, like all Love, attributes a positive value to being and not to action, the distinction of familial love depends solely on the distinction of the *being* of the loved being—that is, the kinsman. The degree of family love is (in principle) proportional to the degree of kinship. And even where this love is insufficient to motivate the educative familial household, even where one will need to apply constraint, force, i.e., a "discipline," i.e., where one will need an Authority capable of mobilizing disciplinary force (since no social, i.e., human, force is truly strong, i.e., efficacious, i.e., durable, unless it rests on an Authority), it is still the Authority of *being*, and not action, to which one will have to resort in the Family. Now the Authority of being is the Authority of the "Father" type: the Authority of the cause, of the author, of the origin and source of what is; the Authority of the past which maintains itself in the present by the sole fact of the ontological "inertia" of being. In the political sphere, it is the Authority of action (of the present) and consequently of the project (of the future), i.e., the Authority of the "Master" and "Leader" type, that is primary. In the familial sphere, by contrast, the first Authority, [499] the grounding Authority, is of the "Father" type (of the past). The Authorities of Judge (of "eternity," i.e., of impartiality), of Leader (who foresees and guides), and of Master (who decides and acts) are derived from that of the Father (who generates being and assures the perpetuity of the past identical with itself). In the State, on the contrary, it is the Authority of the Father (and of the Judge) that is derived from those of Master and Leader (that of the Master being primary).[109] One therefore sees here again an essential difference between the Family and the State. On the one hand, the kinsmen are not Friends opposed to a common Enemy. On the other hand, they are not the Governed who recognize the Authority of the Master and the Leader of the Governors. They are kinsmen who love another according to their degree of kinship, who therefore love above all their common kin, their ancestor, the source and origin of the being to which they attribute a positive value. And if they recognize an Authority (which gives them an *appearance* of political unity, but in fact only a familial unity), it is the Authority F of that "kinsman" *par excellence* that they recognize, and it is this Authority F of *being* as such who is recognized also by non-kindred members of the Family: by slaves, servants, and so on, and—if the case arises—by other Families. Familial organization of the Family is therefore something entirely different from the political organization of the State: the kinsmen subordinate themselves to kinsmen (by love or authority) according to the kinship that determines their being, but they are not properly speaking *governed* by them.

If Love is related to being and not to action, to the act, it does not depend upon the actuality of the loved being—that is, [the beloved is] appreciated as

---

109. See my *Note on Authority* (which it is a matter of completing for the familial sphere [see Part One, chapter 2, note 38 above]). (In the State, the Authority of the Master seems to prevail above all in foreign policy, in relations with the Enemy; that of the Leader in domestic policy, in relations among Friends.)

pure being, independent of his active actualization. If a mother loves her son because he is her son, even if he "behaves badly" toward her, she will also love him if he no longer acts at all—that is, if he is dead, if he no longer exists in actuality (cf. Hegel). "Love is stronger than death" because it abstracts from the action which actualizes being and maintains it in the real *hic et nunc* in actuality or empirically. As pure *being*, past being does not differ from present being: the transition from potentiality to actuality (birth) and the exhaustion of potentiality by actuality (death) do not affect being as such—that is, its "essence." [500] The unborn son and the dead son are sons in the same way as the living son. Death therefore does not affect kinship and does not destroy familial love;[110] from whence comes, on the one hand, the familial cult of death, which is the "religion" of the Family, the manifestation of the religious phenomenon (of affective transcendence, the beyond positively valorized in relation to the here below) in the familial "sphere," and on the other hand, the specifically familial phenomenon of *inheritance* in all its forms.[111] It is not only a matter of economic values in familial inheritance. It is also a matter of the perpetuity of being despite the transitory character of its existential, actual, active manifestation. The being of the father is preserved in the son: they are one and the same being. They differ in and by their actions, but these actions are supposed to actualize the same being, and it is the being alone that counts in and for the Family. In inheriting the being of the father, the son inherits the love which he inspired in others; he inherits also his Authority, his educative function and his relations to the patrimony, the familial household. The son *is* the father in and for the Family, i.e., also in and for familial Society, for other Families. What changes are the active actualities; the essential being remains in identity with itself (from whence comes the "traditionalism" of familial activity: the action of successive generations is supposed to actualize one and the same being, which must therefore remain always the same). Generations pass, but the Family remains. And what remains is the kinship structure of being which is actualized in a common household dedicated to the education of new generations, which will maintain the kinship system in identity with itself, the actual existence of the Family thus being an

---

110. This is why Hegel was able to say in the *Phenomenology* [*of Spirit*, 274] that the daughter (who does not struggle and work) only reveals and realizes her humanity in calmly enduring the death of her parents.

111. It seems that inheritance is manifest in other "spheres" solely because of the fact that the members of political, economic, worldly, religious, and other Societies are also members of familial Society, "kinsmen." *Droit*, being "eternal," easily accepts the idea of inheritance. But the "eternity" of a subjective *droit* is something different from [the idea of] its inheritance. *Droit* does not need another support from the *droits* of the dead. It is the Family that needs an heir who inherits these *droits* from the deceased. As well, to abolish inheritance is not to abolish *Droit*. It is from the Family that *Droit* borrows the fiction of the "survival" of the dead in his heir (his son, for example), which brings about juridical complications in the case of conflict between the will [*volonté*] of the heir and that of the testator.

actualization of the eternal essence of its being—that is, the kinship aspect of the being of its members.

§ 66

[501] Familial Society is immersed in political Society. If the latter is organized into a State, familial Society is, generally speaking, a sub-political society. And there is interpenetration between familial Society and other sub- and trans-political societies: economic, worldly, religious, and so on; for, generally speaking, the member of a Family is at the same time not only a citizen of a national State, but also of an economic, religious, or other Society. Nonetheless, as we have just seen (§ 65), familial Society is a *sui generis* human Society. Its unity is formed by the interactions between Families taken as Families— that is, by familial interactions. In archaic familial Societies, the social unit (the atom) is the Family. In order to reach an individual from the outside, one must pass through the intermediary of the Family to which he belongs, through the intermediary of the leader or representative of this Family, the *pater familias,* for example. These Societies are only acquainted with either intrafamilial or interfamilial interactions: the members of different Families do not have direct interactions among themselves. In a more advanced stage of evolution, familial Society recognizes, it is true (more or less), the autonomy of individuals: they can enter into interactions without going through the intermediary of their respective families or leaders of these families. But the individual is always taken as a member of a family, of "his" family: he acts as husband, father, son, brother, uncle, and so on, and it is also a husband, father, and so on, who reacts. The interaction is only familial to the extent that the agents act and react in their capacity as family members or as families—that is, in the capacity as their "representatives." And familial Society is nothing other than the totality of these familial interactions, which are *sui generis* interactions, seeing that they can only take place where there are Families.

Now we have seen that the Family, as a *sui generis* human phenomenon, presents *three aspects,* which are, moreover, complementary. *In the first place,* the Family is an entity the unity and internal structure of which are determined by relations of *kinship,* to which the members of the Family attribute a positive value and which deal with the very being (and not the acts) of the kindred persons (family love). [502] *Second,* the kinsmen who constitute a Family collaborate (more or less directly) in a common *household,* which is materialized in a "patrimony" (in the broadest sense of the word) and which aims at maintaining the Family in its identity with itself across time—that is, the succession of generations (or, more exactly, the familial household *is* the perpetuity of the Family, its reality in actuality). This is why, *third,* the Family, i.e., the kinsmen who collaborate in the common household, posit as their ultimate and principal goal the *education* (humanization) of future kinsmen, who—generally speaking—are generated within the Family itself (but who can be brought within by adoption). In short, the Family is an educative household achieved in common by kinsmen as kinsmen.

The situation of every member within a Family and the intrafamilial inter-actions of these members are determined, on the one hand, by the "degree of kinship"; on the other hand, by the nature and degree of participation in the common household, by the "degree of familial activity"; and finally, by the role played in familial education—that is, if you will, by the "degree of pedagogical authority." Intrafamilial interactions are generated by kinship, the household, and education; and in turn they generate, maintain, or determine kinship, the household, and education. And the same goes for interfamilial relations (between families or members of families). Either it is a matter of relations of simple coexistence, without mutual impact and consequently without inter-action properly so-called, or, if there is interaction, it creates or destroys the bonds of kinship—that is, relations with the familial household and education.

These familial interactions (inter and intrafamilial) have, as such, nothing juridical about them. But they are *social* interactions, i.e., specifically human, interactions between human beings acting humanly. They can therefore become juridical relations and *sui generis* juridical relations, to the extent that they are *familial* interactions, essentially different from all other social interactions. And this is what takes place when an impartial and disinterested Third intervenes in these interactions. If this Third intervenes to annul the reaction of B (Family or member of a Family acting as such) to an action of A (Family or member of a Family acting as such), A will have a subjective right[112] to his action: the action of A will be juridically [503] legal, that of B illegal. One could then say that in and by his intervention the Third has created or applied a familial legal rule. And the totality of these legal rules will make up a familial *Droit*, existing in actuality when the intervention of the Third has an irresistible character.

We have seen that the irresistibility of the intervention of the Third pre-supposes a state-sanctioned organization of the Society within which the Third intervenes. Familial *Droit*, therefore, can only exist in actuality inside a State, when the Third is in the final analysis a "civil servant" who acts in the name of the State. But to the extent that the Third creates or applies *familial Droit*, he also represents familial Society: he is the representative of the exclusive juridi-cal group of this Society and the State merely sanctions his intervention as rep-resentative of this group. To the extent, however, that the Third represents the State, it is outside of familial Society: it is a Third in respect to this Society. It can therefore intervene also by way of a Third in the interactions between the members of the Society (Families or members of Families) and this Society itself—that is, its any given member ("any given Family" or "any given mem-ber of any given Family"). This is why the familial *Droit* existing in actuality is not only a civil but also penal or criminal *Droit*.

On the other hand, familial *Droit* is only a *Droit* to the extent that the Third

---

112. [Ed. In the original, the English word "right" follows the French phrase *droit subjectif* in parentheses.]

(i.e., the State which is related as Third to the members of familial Society and to this Society itself) intervenes solely to realize a given ideal of Justice (within familial Society, i.e., in its status and its functioning, in familial interactions): the Justice of equality, equivalence, or equity. If the given familial interaction between A and B is conforming to the ideal of Justice accepted by the Third, he will not intervene, except to declare this conformity with a view to the eventual annulment of an act tending to suppress this juridically legal interaction or of its consequences. And if the Third annuls B's action (i.e., more exactly, his reaction to A's action), it is because it destroys either equality, or equivalence, or equity in the relations between B and A, A being either a concrete member of familial Society, different from all the others (a case of civil familial *Droit*) or "any given" member, i.e., the Society itself (a case of penal familial *Droit*).

Of course, like all *Droit*, familial *Droit* results in maintaining (in existence) a certain familial Society [504] in identity with itself. But it is not because it so maintains it that it is a *Droit*. It maintains it because it is an authentic *Droit*—that is, conforming to the ideal of Justice of the exclusive juridical group of this Society. If one wants, *Droit* aims at maintaining a Society in its existence, but only to the extent that this Society is "*just*"—that is, to the extent that it realizes in its status and functioning an ideal of Justice, an ideal of equality, equivalence, or equity.

Now equality, equivalence, or equity must be realized both in the static being of the Society, i.e., in its structure, and in its active being, i.e., in its functioning, in the totality of interactions which are carried out in its bosom. This is why, like all *Droit* in general, (penal and civil) familial *Droit* is just as much a *Droit* of status as a *Droit* of function. There is (familial) status when behavior is determined by the very being of the agent, i.e., by the mere fact of his existence and, since being itself is indifferent to its spatio-temporal actualization, by the mere facts of its birth and death. All the consequences of this mere fact of birth, life, and death for a member of familial Society is part of his familial "status." By contrast, when familial behavior and being are a consequence of action in the proper sense of the word, i.e., of conscious and free action, there is familial "functioning" and a familial *Droit* of function. Thus, for example, the juridical determination of juridical paternity is part of the familial *Droit* of status, while marriage or adoption fall within the competence of the familial *Droit* of function.[113] Con-

---

113. We have said that the relation is not familial if it deals with *action* and not pure and simple *being*. But in marriage, for example, which is really an action or "function," there are two *beings* as such who are united in relation and not two *agents*. It is clear for a so-called marriage of love: the action of marriage unites two beings each of which attributes a value to the pure *being* of the other, independently of his action. But the same goes for specifically familial marriage: a given member of a family unites with a member of another family, because he is a member of this family—that is, on the grounds of the quality of his *being* and not because of his action. Action can cause marriage or divorce but only indirectly: action is supposed to actualize the being to whom one attributes a value, and if it is incompatible with this being one can say that one has been deceived about the being; or again, the action allows the being to be identified. Action has no value in itself; it is only the indicia of being, which alone can have a familial value.

cerning interfamilial relations, moreover, "status" boils down to simple coexistence. As for the "function," it is either [505] marriage or adoption (assuming that there is no kinship bond between the different families). But in intrafamilial relations, "status" and "function" are quite complex (in understanding by the Family the totality of all kinsmen by blood or by marriage, this "extended family" admitting of multiple subdivisions into smaller families). Be that as it may, the (civil and penal) familial *Droit* of status and function exhausts all the possible juridical familial relations—that is, all the cases where a Third can intervene in family life to establish, declare, or reestablish conformity with a certain given ideal of Justice, of equality, equivalence, or equity.

If the phenomenon of the Family presents three essentially complementary aspects, namely *kinship,* the *familial household,* and the procreation and *education* of children, (penal and civil) family *Droit* should have *three* principal *parts.* On the one hand, family *Droit* will have to set down the degrees of kinship within every family and determine the consequences that can be deduced from kinship. On the other hand, this *Droit* will have to define the notion of the familial household and its materialization in and by the patrimony, and determine the relations between kinship and the household in question. Finally, familial *Droit* will have to determine the principles of familial education and connect education both to the familial household and to kinship. Familial *Droit,* in the person of the Third, will have to make equality, equivalence, or equity reign in the sphere of kinship, the familial household, and education within the Family, both in relation to the "status" and relatively to the "function" of the Family.

The "status" of kinship is an aspect of the very being of man. As *"status,"* the degree of kinship is set down by the sole fact of the existence of the individual—that is, by the fact of his birth. Ultimately, the *Droit* of *status* of kinship is a *Droit* of paternity. From the moment that A is recognized as B's son or daughter, all the degrees of kinship between A and the other members of B's family are automatically set down by familial *Droit.* Everything boils down to setting down the extreme limit beyond which biological "kinship" no longer has any juridical value. And in setting down this limit *Droit* can draw inspiration either from the principle of equality, or that of equivalence, or, finally, that of equity. As for the juridical recognition of paternity, it can either be done objectively, or by taking into account to a certain extent the opinion of the interested parties. Generally speaking, juridical paternity and maternity [506] coincide with biological parentage. But given that paternity is always uncertain, *Droit* may take into account the view of the presumed father: the only son or daughter is one accepted as such by the father. This has nothing to do with the adoption or the disowning of a child. The father does not disown his child; he does not recognize such a child as his own. Paternity remains "status." It is not a function of a conscious and voluntary act, either of father or child. It is a function of a relation between the *being* of the father and child, and the view of the father is only an indicia of the existence of this relation.[114] Generally speaking, if A behaves as a father in respect to B, if B reacts against it, and if the Third intervenes to overcome this reaction, it is because A has the ***droit*** to act as father in respect to B, it is because he is his "legitimate" father. Likewise, if A behaves as a son in respect to B, and if the Third annuls B's reaction against it, it is because A is his "legitimate" son. If not, he is B's "natural child," or again, he is not his child at all: in both cases there is no ***droit*** of kinship, no juridically legal kinship, there is no *topos* in familial Society.[115]

If A denies that such a determinate child B is his son, he is related to a specific member of familial Society: he is related to B, and not to C. This is therefore a case of civil familial *Droit*. [507] But if B *is* the "legitimate" son of A, and if A treats him nonetheless as a "stranger," he is related (in an inadequate way) to the son as such, i.e., to a son in general, to any given member of familial Society (taken as "son"). And this is then a case of penal familial *Droit*.[116] It is in this way that incest can be a case of penal familial *Droit*, if having sexual relations means behaving as non-father or non-mother toward one's daughter or son.[117]

---

114. It should be understood that there must be *prior* consent of the father: he must consent to recognize as his child the child he is going to generate with such a woman. But this prior consent, i.e., legitimate marriage, is self-evident when there is a Family, and not sexual cohabitation; for the goal of the Family is the education of future children, which implies their recognition by both parents. [Ed. Sexual cohabitation (*concubinage*) remains a particular status in French civil law.] *Familial Droit,* therefore, only knows [*connaît*] "legitimate" children. Of course, a familial *Droit* can juridically recognize [*reconnaître*] "natural" children. But this is because sexual relations are then assumed to imply the prior consent to educate future children. These relations, therefore, automatically constitute a kind of "legitimate" marriage (without other "formalities"). The principle therefore remains the same: if A is the biological son of B, born *under certain conditions* set down by *Droit,* he is his "legitimate" son, unless B proves that he is not his biological son (this "proof" capable of being reduced to a mere affirmation on his part). *Droit* can limit itself to the mere fact of sexual relations, or again require certain prior ceremonies, an official act, and so on: the situation remains the same. The "natural" child is the child who has no ***droit*** of a son or daughter. If he has these *droits,* he is "legitimate." But these *droits* can vary from one case to another: for example, according to whether there has been or not official prior consent (i.e., an "act of marriage"). If the Third imposes the son on the father, [then] the Family has a forced character, but it is a Family all the same, if the imposed son has the *droit* to call himself son; be educated as a result; and consequently participate in the familial household.

115. It should be understood that a familial *Droit* can include a special status for such familial "displaced persons."

116. Unless he only asserts—on the grounds of his behavior—that Such-and-such "cannot be his son" ("an *unnatural* son"), even if he is his biological son. It is then a matter of a determinate personality—that is, a case of civil familial *Droit*. But then it is a matter of a disavowal, of a disowning: it is therefore a case of the civil familial *Droit* of function and not of status (see below).

117. If behaving as a father, for example, means behaving in a "just" way, i.e., conforming to the principle of equality and equivalence, incest can be excluded from this behavior, because it is contrary to these principles: inequality between children, or between the wife and the daughter, or with other members of Society; or non-equivalence of benefits and burdens; and so on.

As for the **Droit** of *"function" of kinship*, it is related not to being and action as a function of being (of birth), but to action itself and being as a function of this action. But what counts is still being (born of action), and not action (which generates being) as such. The kindred "function" is an action which creates kinship where it did not exist beforehand, or destroys a pre-existing kinship. But familial *Droit* is here related to *kinship* (i.e., to *being*) as created by a conscious and voluntary action, and not to this action itself. This action is either marriage or divorce, either the adoption or the disowning of a son or a daughter.[118]

Let us first consider the positive "function": marriage and adoption. Kinship is here created by a free and voluntary act (bilateral or unilateral). But this action is a function of *being* and not of action, and it generates a quality of *being* as such: a kinship. If the choice is determined by "love," it is by definition a function of the *being* of the one chosen. And if it is a specifically "familial" choice, [508] it is still as a function of *being* that one chooses: one chooses such a member of a family because he is its member.[119] In fact, the choice can be determined by the *actions* of the one chosen. But *familial Droit* does not have to take these motives into account: it only recognizes reasons of "love" or kinship—that is, reasons that come from the very *being* of the one chosen. A chooses Such-and-such (B) for a spouse or adopted child: the being of B being fixed, the choice is valid independently of B's actions. Juridically, one marries So-and-so, daughter of Such-and-such, and so on: one cannot marry someone because she works well, or is honest, and so on. And it is only the qualities of *being* that can be a basis for opposition to a marriage: sex, age, kinship, and so on, and not the *actions* of the candidate. The limits of the act are here set down by the quality of being.

When an act of choice (of two interested persons, or one of them, or a third person) has created a kinship bond between A and B (B becoming spouse or adopted child of A), the bonds of kinship between A and B and the other members of the families of A and B follow automatically.[120] This choice, designating a particular person, is a case of civil familial *Droit*. But to the extent that the person chosen is also "any given member" of familial Society—a member of such a sex, such an age, such a degree of kinship, and so on—the choice is also a case of penal familial *Droit* (of the function of kinship). Thus, the Third can

---

118. To simplify things, I assume that there was no (legal) bond of kinship between the spouses. It is necessary to distinguish between "stranger" families (from the legal point of view) and families that are kindred (legally: by blood or by marriage). The latter make up an "extended family" of which the internal structure is set down by a given familial *Droit:* they can be more or less (juridically) independent from one another.

119. If it is a matter of a "familial displaced person" without any kin, it is to his pure and simple being that the choice is related: it is a choice of "love." If not, the choice has nothing "familial" about it: it is an association of another type and familial *Droit* does not take it into account.

120. It is nevertheless possible that the bonds of kinship between an adoptive child and the members of the adoptive family are different than those between these members and a ("legitimate") biological child of one of them.

not only "ignore" relations with matrimonial aspects (sexual, for example) when they are homosexual or incestuous or take place between minors, but also annul them with a penalty applied to the interested parties. *Droit* can decree [*poser*] that the quality of being which expresses itself through matrimonial kinship is ("ontologically") incompatible with certain other qualities of being, such as sex, age, kinship, race, and so on. And this is because the combination of these qualities would be contrary to the principle of equality, equivalence, or equity, either between the interested parties, or between them and the other members (the any given member) of familial Society. It is in this way that *Droit* can also impose monogamy or permit polygamy (unilateral or bilateral). [509] Here as well, one will only have a case of authentic (penal familial) **Droit** if the Third draws inspiration from an ideal of Justice.

Let us go now to the negative kinship "function": divorce and the disowning of a "legitimate" child, or of a parent by the child. Here it is a matter of *civil* familial *Droit*, given that the interested party denies that *such a determinate person* is his spouse or his child.[121] A does not want to disown *a* spouse or *a* son (father). one cannot divorce because one would like to become a bachelor again or no longer have children. One wants to disown such a *determinate* spouse or son (father). The difficulty is where A invokes the *acts* of B.[122] Now the kinship relations between A and B are relations of *being* to *being* and not to inter-*actions* properly so-called.[123] As well, it is not such an action which is the cause of the disowning, but the ("legal") incompatibility of this action with the kinship quality of *being*: B is not the spouse or the son (father) of A because his acts are incompatible with his *being* of spouse or son (father). A spouse or a son (father) "cannot" behave in this way: despite appearances, B is therefore not spouse or son (father); the Third has only to declare the fact (i.e., the mistake committed). It is not the very *action* of B which forces A to disown him. It is the fact that the *being* of B is not what the being of a spouse or son (father) must be. The action is but the indicia of being and it is being alone that counts. But in fact it is quite diffi-

---

121. When A does not contest that he is spouse or father (son) of B and nevertheless behaves in a way incompatible (from the point of view of the Third) with his capacity as spouse or father (son), in committing an adultery, for example, there will be a case of penal *Droit* (the "penalty," moreover, capable of being reduced to a mere disapprobation on the part of the Third). But a *Droit* can, of course, consider that adultery is compatible with the capacity of the husband (if not the wife).

122. One cannot evoke the disappearance of "love"; for if love attributes a value to *being* and not action, it is by definition "eternal," immutable. One sees this clearly in the case of the son. But "I don't love him anymore" has never been considered a juridical cause for divorce. Certain *Droits* allow divorce by mutual consent or by unilateral decision. But this means that one then allows divorce "without fault." The disappearance of love is never a juridical *cause* for divorce.

123. The case of divorce on grounds of sterility, and so on, presents no difficulty. There was simply a mistake concerning *being*. It is as if one noticed that one had married a man while believing one had married a woman. It is rather the negation of divorce that in this case is difficult to justify. One justifies it by observing that the human goal of the Family is *education* and not procreation. Sterility can therefore be "annulled" by adoption.

cult to distinguish between actions which are or are not compatible with a given being. And this is why the problem of divorce has always been very complex juridically [510] and generally unauthentic. One sees this very well in the case of the disowning of a child, which does not differ in principle from that of divorce. Familial *Droit* only recognizes this disowning grudgingly, so to speak, or simply denies it, even in relation to an adopted child. Now, truth to tell, the very principle of the Family excludes the idea of a kinship bond that is *temporary* or revocable. And this is why familial *Droit* tends to limit the possibilities for divorce.[124] It seems that the juridical authenticity of divorce and the disowning of a kin in general can only be bought at the cost of a "fiction": the fiction of the incompatibility of certain acts with a given quality of the *being* of a person and the mistake about this being, revealed by the acts in question.[125]

Generally speaking, if A behaves as B's spouse [511] and B reacts against this, and if the Third intervenes in order to annul this reaction, this is because A is the "legitimate" spouse of B. And if the Third refuses to intervene, this is because A is not—or is no longer—the spouse of B: there was no marriage, or there was a divorce. The marital *droits* of A are given by the totality of A's actions which would provoke an annulment by the Third of B's reaction to these actions. As for the marital duties of A toward B, these are the marital *droits* of B in respect to A.

Let us now consider the **Droit** *of the familial household* or the Family patrimony.

---

124. "Illegitimate" sexual union leaves the interested parties completely free, and *Droit* can "ignore" it. But where there is Family, i.e., kinship properly so-called with a common household and the education of children, divorce is in principle inadmissible. Those who would want to be able to divorce have only not to marry "legally." The children of "free unions" could be educated by the State (or familial Society). If their biological "parents" keep them, their relations with them will have nothing juridical about them—that is, neither legal kinship nor legal participation in the common household (inheritance), nor legal pedagogical authority.
125. Seeing that the human *being* of man is his *action,* no human act can be incompatible with the *human* being. In the case of divorce, it would therefore only be a matter of an incompatibility of the act with the "natural" being: "a woman who doesn't conduct herself like a woman," and so on. And indeed, this is one of the generally recognized "causes" of divorce (sterility, sexual perversion, illness, and so on). But we have seen (see an earlier footnote) that human action maintains itself as a "human *being*": personality, character, and so on. Certain acts can therefore be incompatible with this "human" being, from whence comes a new possibility for justifying divorce: "change of character," and so on. The big question is knowing to what extent kinship is also a function of "human being," and not only of (biological) "natural being." And the question is further complicated by the fact that the members of familial Society are also citizens and members of other non-political Societies, notably religious Society. Family relations between kinsmen can therefore enter into conflict with the relations of the same persons taken as citizens or members of other Societies, from whence comes a very complicated juridical casuistry. Can two political "enemies" be father and son or husband and wife? For the wife, one avoids the difficulty by assigning her the "nationality" of her husband or by considering her as an apolitical being. But, in the modern world, this is not always possible. And the question of the relationship between political and familial relations remains open, when these relations take place in one and the same person. In reality all these difficulties will only be resolved in the universal and homogenous State. But the familial *Droit* of this State of the future is difficult to predict.

The familial household is attained in common by the members of the Family—that is, by the Family as such. And familial *Droit* first of all determines the nature of this household. It is a matter of knowing to what extent the member of a family is acting on his own account, as an isolated individual, animal, citizen, or member of a Society other than the familial, and to what extent he represents the family in his action, acts in his capacity as member of this family for the sake of the family—that is, all its members. And this delimitation of the familial household has varied a lot according to places and epochs. For modern familial *Droit* the familial household is limited to one part of the economic activity of the members of the family. But in the beginning, the household could also have a political, religious, "worldly" ("class" activity), or another nature, and often it encompassed *all* the activity of the family members, notably all the economic activity of these members (in which case there was no economic Society at all; or again, the latter was made up of families, and not individuals, the interactions between the different families then being not only familial, but also economic in the proper sense of the word: purely economic exchanges between families, for example, but not between individuals).

Having determined the nature of the familial household, *Droit* must also set down the "legitimate" participants in this household. And to the extent that it is a matter of *familial Droit,* this participation must not be set down according to the acts of the participants, but according to their *being.* In other words, the degree of legal participation in the familial household is determined by the degree of kinship of the family members. It is therefore a matter of determining at what degree of kinship the members of an ("extended") family are supposed to no longer participate in the familial household of a given ("nuclear") family. The question is complicated, moreover, because [512] generally speaking more distant kinsmen are connected to the household when certain nearer kinsmen are lacking, and are excluded when these kinsmen exist or appear. It is also here that the question of familial juridical "capacity" arises, which one must distinguish both from non-juridical (for example, political or religious) "capacity" and from juridical "capacity" other than the family (for example, the "capacity" of economic Society). An individual who would otherwise be juridically "capable" (in economic Society, for example) can be burdened by juridical incapacity as a member of a family: as spouse, or as son of a living father, and so on. This incapacity has to do with the participation of the individual in the family household and it is a function of his being (age, sex, kinship, and so on) and not his actions (unless the actions would be "incompatible with being"; see the previous footnote). Instead of saying that familial *Droit* sets down "incapacities," one can also say it sets down the legal authority of the members of the family relative to the familial household. If A contributes in a certain way to the familial household (makes a decision, for example), if B opposes this, and if the Third annuls this opposition (due to the sole fact that it is an opposition of B to the action of A), it is because A enjoys a legal Authority with respect to B in relation to the household; or again, which is the same thing, A is relatively "incapable" in relation to this household. And what goes for the household taken as action also goes for the household taken as static entity, i.e., in particular for the "patrimony": the degree of authority (or incapacity) sets down the degree of freedom to dispose of this patrimony.

Seeing that patrimonial authority (or incapacity) is a function of being and not of action, it is not individualized: it is not so and so who enjoys it, but a father, a son, a husband, and so on, from whence comes the hereditary character of these authorities: in taking the place of the father, the son "inherits" the authority of the father, and so on. And this is true of the household itself, and consequently the patrimony. It belongs in common to the defined totality of kinsmen, which remains identical to itself despite the fact that individuals change, i.e., are born and die: the household and patrimony are related to the "eternal" or "essential" *being* of the family members and not to their actual individuality. This is why the familial *Droit* of the patrimony (or the household) is first and foremost a *Droit* of inheritance (*ab intestat*).[126] The goal of the familial household is the indefinite maintenance of the family in its identity with itself, despite the passing of generations. And this is [513] why the *Droit* of patrimony relates the household to the members of the family (dead, living, or unborn) in such a way that the identity of this family is indefinitely preserved (at least in principle).[127] The will is properly speaking a non-familial juridical institution (above all an institution of the *Droit* of economic Society, where the will is a variety of gift). One could say that the testator bequeaths not in his capacity as member of a Family or of familial Society in general, but in his capacity as member of economic Society, for example.[128] Conversely, one could say that all inheritance is of familial origin: not only because of the truism that there would be no inheritance if there were no family in the sense of conscious paternity or maternity; but because inheritance only makes sense if one relates the inheritance to the very being of the heir and not to his actions. Inheritance has as its basis the notion of the "identity" of *being* between the heir and the testator[129] [of the estate]: the patrimony related to the being of the father is automatically related to the being of the son, since the father and the son are supposed to have one and the same being; now this identification only makes sense if one abstracts from the *acts* of both.[130] *Droit* first seems to have

---

126. [Ed. Literally, intestate, or without making a will. This expression signifies a right of inheritance that does not depend on the will of the deceased but rather follows from the status of the heir as heir, i.e., the kinship relation between the deceased and the heir. As Kojève will go on to explain, he views inheritance through the will of the deceased as an economic, not a familial, legal institution.]

127. The perpetuity of the Family is symbolized and manifested by the "surname," from whence comes a familial *Droit* of the name: a subdivision of the *Droit* of patrimony or the household.

128. If the will is made for the benefit of a member of a family, taken as such, it is a familial act. But in principle the *familial* will is only there for correcting the inevitable imperfections of the *Droit* of inheritance *ab intestat*.

129. [Ed. Reading *testateur* for *légataire*.]

130. From this comes the absurdity of the inheritance of political power, essentially *active* and *acting*.

sanctioned the principle of inheritance of the familial household. And starting from familial *Droit,* the idea of inheritance passed into the *Droit* of economic, religious, and so on, Society: thus a son can inherit the activity of the father that the latter had not had as father or member of familial Society, but as member of economic or religious Society, for example.

Like all *droit* in general, familial *Droit* of the household is, on the one hand, a *Droit* of status, and on the other, a *Droit* of function.[131] The *Droit* of status considers the household as a given, static entity (patrimony) and determines the relations of the members of the family with this household to the extent that these relations are a function of the very being of these [514] members: by the sole fact of their life, their death, or their birth. But in its dynamic aspect the household falls within the competence of the *Droit* of function. This *droit* is related to the acts that constitute the household, which alter, increase, or diminish the patrimony (as patrimony). Now, one of the principal sources of active, i.e., voluntary, alteration of the structure of the household and the participation of members of the family in this household is marriage (and to a much lesser extent adoption), from whence comes the juridical notion of a *contract* of marriage (all contract falling within the competence of the *Droit* of function). There is *contract* when there is a conscious and voluntary interaction, and there is a contract of *marriage* (contract of *familial Droit*) when the interaction has in mind the creation (or the alteration) of a familial household (a patrimony). Now marriage itself is a function of the being and not the actions of the future spouses, while contract properly so-called puts *actions* properly so-called in relation. The contract of marriage is therefore a *sui generis* contract, where the action—the object of the contract—is a function of the being of the contracting parties. This is why freedom of contract cannot be absolute here:[132] only the actions compatible with the *being* of the contracting parties will be accepted, i.e., here with their quality as spouse; it is not only the "will" of the contracting parties which is "law" for them, but also the quality of their being. Now if action (being negator of the given) is infinitely variable (as Descartes already saw: it is as "will" that man is infinite), being has fixed qualities (and limited [*dénombrables*] as "essential"), from whence comes the fact that familial *Droit* offers to the interested parties a small number of types of contracts of marriage (if not a single type, as is often the case). The Third intervenes only when the "patrimonial" action is conforming to the familial *being* of the agent—that is, in particular, when the interaction is anticipated by a "legal" type of familial contract.[133]

When the interactions between A and B relative to the familial household (to the patrimony) are "personal," the Third applies or creates *civil* patrimonial

---

131. If one takes these terms in the narrow sense, one can say that the *Droit* of the household is a *Droit* of function, while that of the *patrimony* is a *Droit* of status.

132. It is not, moreover, anywhere else. Cf. (b) below.

133. The invalidity of different familial contracts of the legal type is something different from the invalidity of "immoral" contracts (for example, economic), and so on.

familial *Droit*. And this is generally the case; for in the interactions relative to the household, a member of the family generally has in mind such and such a determinate member of *his* family and not a member of *any given* family or *any given* member (individual or [515] Family) of familial Society. But if A's patrimonial action is supposed to injure any given member of familial Society (individual or Family), and if the Third intervenes, there will be a case of *penal* patrimonial familial *Droit*. But it should be understood that this distinction is to a large extent arbitrary and familial *Droit* has varied a great deal in this regard.

Generally speaking, like in all *Droit*, the Third of patrimonial *Droit* intervenes according to a certain ideal of Justice. When this ideal is egalitarian, the *ab intestat* division [of property] will be equal: all those who participate in the inheritance will do so in equal parts. Likewise, there will be no degrees of patrimonial authority or incapacity. Either a member of the family will have no *droit* relative to the patrimony, or he will have them all (the ancient Roman *pater familias*, for example, who deals only with "incompetents," with "*alieni juris*" within his family): the members of a family and familial Society are juridically equal; either they are not subjects of familial *droit* ("*alieni juris*"), or they all have the same subjective *droits* (the "*patria potestas* [paternal power]"). By contrast, when the ideal of equivalence (or equity) is applied, all familial inequalities are possible, provided that the situations of all the members of a Family or of familial Society in general are equivalent to each other, which will take place if in every member his familial *droits* are equivalent to his familial duties. In egalitarian (aristocratic) familial *Droit*, members [who are] equal in the plenitude of their *droits* do not (in principle) have duties to members equal in the absence of all *droits*. In the familial *Droit* of equivalence, the members of familial Society and the Family are fundamentally unequal from the juridical point of view. As for the familial *Droit* of equity, it combines both principles: the members of the Family and of familial Society are supposed to be *equal*, but have *duties* equivalent to their *droits*—that is, equivalent, reciprocal *droits* and duties. However, the presence of children in familial Society makes impossible any strict equality between its members. Juridical equality between parents and (young) children can only exist when the State (or familial Society, sanctioned by the State) controls the relations between children and parents, playing the role of "guardian" [or] "representative" of the child in respect of the parents. Equality is only possible between the members of familial Society taken as "individual moral persons." And it is toward this solution that familial *Droit* seems to be evolving.

[516] It remains to say something about the *familial* **Droit** *of education*, which is, moreover, inseparable from the *Droit* of kinship and the *Droit* of the household or patrimony, [which are] equally inseparable.

It is here that the question arises of the "age of minority," or its counterpart, "pedagogical authority." On account of his very being (age, sex, degree of kinship, and so on) certain members of familial Society are placed under the moral or pedagogical authority of certain other members: the son under the authority of the father, for example. Familial education, moreover, should be understood in a very broad sense: it is the totality of actions of the Family which aim at the transformation of the animal new-born into a human being, member of the Family. Thus, for example, familial pedagogical supervision can extend to the entire life of certain members of the Family, women for example. A father can retain all his life his pedagogical authority over his children, and so on. In particular, parents often have the *droit* to decide on the marriage of their children, at least up to a certain age (which does not coincide with the age of "legal puberty"). Given that the existing members of the Family have the *droit* (and the duty) to create members who are called upon to replace them, either through procreation, adoption, or marriage, but in all these cases by submitting them to the appropriate pedagogical transformation, it is natural that they should have the *droit* to determine (or co-determine) the marriage of members of the Family.[134]

Moreover, one must not conflate familial Authority as such with its *juridical* aspect. The fact that the members of a family recognize the pedagogical authority of another member has in itself nothing juridical about it. One can only say that A has pedagogical **droits** over B, a juridically legal pedagogical Authority, if a Third intervenes in order to annul B's reaction to A's (pedagogical) action. Thus, formerly in France, the institution of *lettres de cachet* was a juridical recognition of paternal pedagogical authority.[135] But it should be understood that *Droit* can [517] recognize pedagogical Authority in very different ways. The essential thing is that A be able to exercise his pedagogical action over B without having to make an effort (in principle) to overcome the eventual resistance of B. If it is a Third who annuls this resistance, A has a familial pedagogical **droit** over B.

The distinguishing feature of familial education is the creation of a member of the Family, capable of replacing the departing members without the identity of the Family being broken. But in fact the Family does not generally limit itself to creating members of familial Society starting from new-borns (of the animal species Homo sapiens). By its educative activity it also creates citizens and members of Societies other than familial Society: economic or religious Society, for example, when it is the case that the members of familial Society are also members of these Societies. But in principle this education of citizens and members of non-familial Society has nothing to do with the Family: it is not a *familial* education properly so-called; it is of no concern to *familial Droit*. Political education can (and should) be carried out in and by the State, just as

---

134. Formerly in French *Droit*, the son who married without the consent of his father could be disinherited. The idea is that a son who is not conforming to the full extent with the pedagogical stamp of his parents has not become a (human) member of the Family capable of replacing the old generation. He is therefore excluded from the Family (from the familial household and patrimony) as insufficiently "humanized," or at the very least, insufficiently "familialized." Thus, a biological "son" who is clinically "retarded" may not be a son in the eyes of familial *Droit*.

135. [Ed. Kojève would seem to be making a joke here about absolutism, because *lettres de cachet* were orders for imprisonment or banishment without trial under Royal seal.]

economic, religious, and so on, Society itself can educate its members. Indeed, this is what one also observes. Thus, in primitive societies, the civic education of the citizen, which culminates in "rites of passage," comes to supplement properly familial education. And in more evolved States, military service and secondary or higher instruction are nothing other than a political pedagogical action that educates the citizen outside of the Family and in addition to properly familial education. But the limits between the Family and the State and the other Societies are difficult to establish; there are generally conflicts present between familial education and political education, or non-familial education in general. And it is the familial *Droit* of education which is called upon to set down the limits of properly familial education by determining the limits of the pedagogical authority of the Family. It seems that at the limit the Family must submit to the control of the State in all that concerns civic education—that is, the creation of *citizens* from non-citizens (animals or members of non-political Society). But it also seems that the Family has a pedagogical sphere of its own: this is the creation of future members of familial Society capable of maintaining it indefinitely in its identity with itself.

The familial *Droit* of education is also divisible into a [518] *Droit* of status and a *Droit* of function. As pedagogical Authority is a function of being, i.e., of age, sex, kinship, and so on, it is set down by the *Droit* of status. But pedagogical activity as activity and inter-action falls within the competence of the *Droit* of function.

One can also distinguish here as well between a civil and criminal *Droit* of familial pedagogy. But, as always, this distinction is difficult to make and is to a great extent arbitrary. The principle remains the same: it is a matter of civil *Droit* when there is a pedagogical interaction between two "specific" members of familial Society; but when a specific member is related pedagogically to a supposedly "any given" member, one has a case of the penal familial *Droit* of education.[136]

---

136. Generally speaking, all familial *Droit* is in a certain sense a *civil Droit;* for when A is related to B taken as his *kinsman,* he is related to *this* kinsman and not to *any given* member. And this is why familial *Droit* is generally included in "civil *Droit.*" However, there have been, and there still are, cases of familial *Droit* that incontrovertibly have a penal character: the punishment of adultery, for example, or of incest, as well as the "corruption of minors," and so on. Adultery poses no difficulties, seeing that the two adulterers are not kindred. One can therefore say that the adulterer seduced any given "someone else's wife," any given married woman. One can compare adultery to theft. Likewise, "corruption" is comparable to rape, for example—that is, to violence inflicted on "any given member" of familial Society. But the interpretation of the punishment of incest is more delicate (and this is also a legal rule in the process of disappearing). One could say that A is punished because he slept not with such a woman who is, so to speak, by chance, his mother, but with his mother, who is by chance such a woman. Incest is therefore committed, as it were, with "any given mother" and the criminal intention is toward "the mother," and not "this woman." But this is a subtlety difficult to sustain. In fact, incest has been punished because it brought divine punishment upon the whole of familial Society. It would therefore be an injury of the interests of this Society as such by one of its members, which is clearly—on this hypothesis—a case of penal *Droit.* And it is in this way that one must also interpret the

It should be understood that the familial *Droit* of education is only an authentic *Droit* to the extent that the Third intervenes in the pedagogical interactions between the members of familial Society with the sole concern of realizing in this [519] Society and by these interactions a certain ideal of Justice: equality, equivalence, or equity. An egalitarian *Droit* will not admit degrees of pedagogical Authority: the subjects of familial *droit* will all have the same Authority, while those who have none will not be recognized as subjects, at the very least not as subjects of the familial *Droit* of education. But the *Droit* of equivalence can admit all possible inequalities, compatible with the principle of equivalence of situations—that is, equivalence of pedagogical *droits* and duties. Finally, the *Droit* of equity will have to combine these two principles: equality of *droits* and their equivalence with duties. But when there are young children, equality can only exist provided that one views the child as an "individual moral person" who exercises pedagogical *droits*, equal to those of others and equivalent to corresponding duties, not personally, but by the intermediary of a third, who can be the Third of the familial *Droit* of education.

b. The Droit of Economic Society

§ 67

If familial Society has as its *biological* basis the sexuality of the animal Homo sapiens and his child-rearing necessities, the *biological* basis of economic Society is given by the necessity for this animal to eat. But, just as the sexuality of an already humanized being is something different from animal sexuality, his food also differs from purely "natural" food. Here as well this difference is realized and revealed in and by Negativity: there one has the phenomenon of rape (unknown among animals, where the female never resists if she is able to have sexual relations, and where she is not desired by the male if she is not in this state), sexual "perversions" and "taboos" (which at the limit result in the asceticism of chastity); here [one has] food digested independently of biological need and even contrary to this need, the artificial preparation of dishes (cooking, spices, and so on) and dietary "taboos" (which at the limit result in fasting, which can go as far as death). And since Negativity generates language (*Logos*), man also differs from the animal (even of the species Homo sapiens)

---

punishment of homosexuality (between consenting adults) and of "bestiality." In all these cases (and in the assumed hypothesis) there is a lack of equality or equivalence between the homosexual, incestuous, or "bestial" member of familial Society and its "any given member": for example, as a result of criminal action, everyone has burdens, but the criminal alone has an additional "benefit" (pleasure); or again, there is no equality once the criminal indulges in that from which others refrain. [Ed. It should be noted that what Kojève means here by "incest" is not sexual abuse of children, which would count as "corruption of minors," when it was not a case of rape as such; he clearly means sexual relations between consenting adults who happen to have some degree of consanguinity. In fact, Kojève is right to imply that what is terrible about sexual abuse is not consanguinity as such, but the vulnerability of the child in respect to the adult parent.]

by the fact that he does not limit himself [520] to having sexual relations and eating, but he *speaks* about his sexuality and diet, these also becoming a function of the discourse that is related to them.

But in addition to the biological or animal source, there is also a specifically human source of economic Society, namely Work (and Exchange, which results from it). In the final analysis, the autonomy of economic Society in general and its *Droit* in particular rests upon the essential difference between the humanization of the animal of the species Homo sapiens by the Struggle for recognition and that [which occurs] by Work (which emerges out of this Struggle and presupposes it, moreover). The Struggle is, if you will, a social (or, more exactly, anthropogenic or sociogenic) interaction, an interaction between two human beings, acting as such. But given that it is a relation of mutual exclusion or, more exactly, of an intentional reciprocal annihilation, the Struggle itself does not create social interactions properly so-called (those between Master and Slave being a *result* of the Struggle, which presuppose its termination): it does not found as such a Society. But individuals can associate in and for a Struggle against a common Enemy.[137] And this association by and for Struggle generates a group of Friends having a common Enemy, i.e., a political Society and ultimately a State (to the extent that the interaction between the participants in the Struggle against the common Enemy is also a relation between Governors and the Governed—that is, to the extent that the group recognizes a political Authority). In the State (and in political Society in general), individuals are interacting by participating in some way or other in the Struggle for recognition. But if individuals enter into interaction as Workers, they constitute an *economic Society*. This is why one can say that if the socialization of the Struggle generates the State, the socialization of Work generates economic Society.[138]

---

137. This association itself has nothing specifically human about it: it also exists among "social" animals. It becomes a human Society by the fact that every associated member struggles for "prestige" alone, for "recognition"—that is, "humanly," for non-biological reasons.

138. We will see that Property presupposes in the final analysis the Struggle: it is the Struggle for recognition that transforms the biological fact of possession into recognized *property* (and—finally—recognized by a Third, i.e., juridically). Now there is no economic Society (nor *Droit*) without property (individual or collective: but socialist economic Society recognizes "personal property"). It [521] seems, therefore, that economic Society and *Droit* are based upon the Struggle. But we will see that there is no economic Society properly so-called without the *Exchange* of property. Now we will equally see that Exchange presupposes Work: the property suitable for exchange is generated by Work and not by the Struggle. In this sense, therefore, economic Society and its *Droit* presuppose Work, and it is from this that their specificity and autonomy with respect to the State emerges. But on the other hand, Work presupposes the Struggle, from whence comes the complexity of the relations between economic Society and the State, of which I will speak in § 70. In short, one must attribute an autonomy to economic Society to the extent that one attributes an autonomy to Work in relation to the Struggle. And it is clearly necessary to do so, since universal history is nothing other than a "dialectic" of Struggle and Work, i.e., of Master and Slave, which is "synthesized" in and by the Citizen, in whom Struggle and Work coincide.

[521] More exactly, the State based (more or less) exclusively upon the Struggle and the relations that emerge from it is an aristocratic State, a State of Masters (where some—the Governed—recognize the political Authority of others—the Governors—or those Administered recognize the political, i.e., "administrative" or "governmental," Authority of the Administrators).[139] Now, in such an aristocratic State, Work is done by Slaves, who are not politically recognized as citizens of the State (neither as Governing citizens nor even as governed citizens). To the extent that economic Society is constituted by interactions based upon Work, it therefore has nothing to do with the aristocratic State, nor with the State in general, to the extent that the latter is based upon the Struggle. But economic Society exists within the State. Furthermore, the Master determines as he pleases the existence of the Slave. Therefore, if the (aristocratic) State is represented by the Masters, and if economic Society is made up of Slaves, the State determines the existence of the latter and economic Society has no autonomous existence. But if the Masters, i.e., the State in general, recognize the members of the Society, if not politically at least economically, it will be (to a certain extent) autonomous in respect to [522] the State. And since economic Society, based upon Work, differs essentially from the (aristocratic) State based upon the Struggle, this Society will tend to assert its autonomy in respect to this State, and the State, if it does not deny its existence, will tend to recognize its autonomy. Now if social (economic) interactions within the Society based upon Work give rise to the intervention of an impartial and disinterested Third (taken within this very Society), there will be a specific *Droit* of economic Society. And the State will have to recognize the autonomy of this *Droit* if it recognizes the autonomy of the Society. To the extent that the State sanctions this *Droit* (or creates and applies it through its Civil Servant, the Third not being able to be part of the Society), it will exist in actuality, as the *civil* Droit of economic Society. And since the State recognizes the *autonomy* of the Society, there will also be a *penal* Droit of economic Society, the State intervening by way of a Third not only in (economic) interactions between "specific" members (individual or collective) of the Society, but also between these members and the Society itself—that is, its "any given member." And the State will be able to do so even if it recognizes politically the members of economic Society—that is, even if these members are at the same time citizens of the State. It is enough that the State distinguishes between the individual taken as a citizen (i.e., in his relation to the Struggle) and this same individual taken as a member of economic Society (i.e., in his relation to Work).

---

139. It is possible that the Governed are not Masters properly so-called, the latter all being "Governors"—the "dominant" or "ruling [*gouvernante*] class." The Governed are perhaps those formerly conquered, quasi-Slaves, politically recognized by their conquerors, the Masters—that is, Citizens (to be [*en germe*] and "for us"). In aristocratic States, *all* Masters would therefore belong to the "exclusive political group," i.e., to the group of Governors, and the Governed, "the excluded political group," would be made up of Slaves, "metics," "plebeians," and so on, who have no political "*droit*," who are (administered) "subjects" and not (governed) *citizens*.

If Work is done by a Slave properly so-called, work does not generate any juridical phenomenon. By definition, the relation of the Worker with the thing, "the raw material," Nature, has nothing to do with *Droit*, which is only related to *social* interactions, to relations between two human beings. Now in his relations with other men (Masters), the Slave is not recognized as a human being; he is not a "juridical person," a "subject of *droit*." "For us" and in truth, Work humanizes man, but as long as it is a matter of a Slave, this humanity created in and by Work is not "recognized"; in particular, is not recognized juridically. But if one recognizes (for whatever reason) the humanity of the Worker as Worker, he can become a subject of *droit*, namely a subject of the *Droit* of the Society based upon Work—that is, the *Droit* of economic Society. Now, to recognize the humanity of someone is also to recognize him [523] politically, to a certain extent. Seeing that there are no "neutrals" in politics, the being recognized as human is necessarily either Friend or Enemy. Between Enemies there is no *Droit* possible. But there are no Friends without *Droit*. To recognize the humanity of the Worker and treat him as a Friend, is (more or less) to recognize him as citizen (if only as a Governed).[140] Now, if the State recognizes as citizen the Worker, it is because it is no longer based exclusively upon the Struggle (as with the aristocratic State) but also upon Work.[141] In these conditions, the status of citizen will also be related to his capacity as Worker, and generally speaking, as member of economic Society. Thus, for example, citizenship will be a function of the citizen's wealth: a State with "poll taxes on voting"—and so on. To the extent that this is so, the ("political-economic") status will have nothing juridical about it. But seeing that every State also has the Struggle as a base, while economic Society is *exclusively* based upon Work, the State and this Society will never entirely coincide: the status of citizen and the status of member of economic Society, as well as the functions of the two, will never completely overlap. This is why there is a certain autonomy of economic Society in respect to the State. And this is why there is a specific (civil) and autonomous (whether state-sanctioned or not) *Droit* of this Society, as well as a *penal Droit* of economic Society, where the State plays the role of a *Third* in respect to this Society, which it can do by reason of the autonomy of the latter.[142]

Hegel has shown[143] that just like the Struggle for recognition, Work humanizes man, transforms the animal of the species Homo sapiens into a truly human

---

140. It should be recalled that every real man is never purely a Master or Slave, but always more or less a Citizen.

141. In reality, there are no pure aristocratic States. And, by definition, there are no States based *exclusively* upon Work. But the relations between the Struggle and Work as foundations of the State vary according to places and epochs.

142. The question of the relations between the State and economic Society will be discussed in § 70. It is there that the question will be raised concerning the *Droit* of economic Society in the universal and homogenous ("socialist") State, which, being the State of the Citizen, realizes the (perfect) synthesis of Struggle and Work.

143. See my "Autonomy and Dependence of Self-Consciousness" in *Mesures*.

being. Work, moreover, presupposes the Struggle. The vanquished, who renounces the pursuit of the Struggle from fear of death, becomes the Slave of the victor, his Master. It is the Master who requires the Slave to work for him: the Slave [524] works against his instinct, without biological profit for himself, through fear of the Master who embodies in his eyes his death. Through the conscious and voluntary Risk of life for a non-biological goal, for Recognition, the Master has realized and revealed his autonomy, his liberty, his independence in respect to his animal nature, i.e., in relation to Nature in general, to which the Slave is enslaved, who prefers (animal) life to (specifically human) Recognition. This is why the Master inserts the Slave between himself and Nature. Everything that is determined by Nature in the interaction between man and Nature, everything that enslaves man to matter, is related to the Slave, who molds through his Work the "raw material," the natural *given*. By contrast, the Master dominates Nature and gets it to serve him through the intermediary of the Slave. He consumes the products of Work without needing to work himself, for he consumes the products of the Work of the Slave. Now these products have been produced to serve man: the artifact is a "humanized" material, negated as the natural given and molded by and for man. By living in a technological World, prepared for him by the Slave, the Master does not live as an animal within Nature but as a human being in a cultural World. It is the Slave who transforms by his Work the natural World into a cultural or human World, but it is the Master who profits from it and who lives humanly in his World, adapted to his humanity. And one can say that it is the humanity of the Master, generated in and by the Risk, which is objectively realized and revealed as the cultural World, created by the Work of the Slave, who depends upon the Master because of the Risk accepted by the latter.

But the Slave is not an animal pure and simple either. He also has engaged in a Struggle for recognition; he also has therefore desired a desire, has experienced anthropogenic Desire. Of course, he renounced the Struggle through fear of death. But it is a Struggle *for recognition* that he renounced, not a biological struggle for food or sex. In the terror (*Furcht*) of death, the Slave saw that which the Master, who had only to overcome a simple fear (*Angst*) of danger, did not: he saw his essential finitude; he understood that Recognition presupposed biological life; he sensed that death was absolute Nothingness [*Néant*], pure or abstract Negativity—a Nothing [*Rien*]. The terror of death has therefore humanized the Slave, even if he was forced to renounce the *Recognition* of his humanity, i.e., its *actualization* or *objectification;* for the animal that *knows* itself to be finite [525] or mortal is no longer an animal: it is a human being, if only in potentiality, a being who *aspires* to the infinite, to immortality (from whence comes Religion and its "dualism," the notion of "transcendence"). And this is why death is embodied for him not in Nature, which kills the animal (illness, various accidents, or old age), but in the Master, in a human being, in a being who goes to the very end of the Struggle to the death for Recognition. And this is why, in submitting to death, the Slave does not submit to Nature, but to Man, to the Master, to his Master. This is also why this submission, this dependence, leads to Work for the Slave; for the Master, on which his life depends, does not kill him and is not content to let him be: he forces him to work and to work for him. Now to work for the Master, to work for another, to exert effort without profiting from the results, is to act against animal nature, against his biological interests: it is to negate his innate animal nature, and consequently to negate Nature in general, the natural given. This is why the Slave transforms Nature by his Work. He negates it, and the revealed or objective reality of this negation is the artefact, the technological or cultural World, the humanized or human World. Of course, the Slave does not profit from this World that he produces. But if he is not part of it, like the Master, as consumer, he nevertheless is part of it as producer: and being part of a humanized or human World, he is himself humanized or human: he humanizes himself in and by his (productive) Work. In "molding" the "raw material," the Slave-worker "molds" himself: to the extent that he works he *is* human.

By his Work, the Slave (and man in general) frees himself from his dependence with respect to Nature, the spatio-temporal material given, since he negates it, transforms it into an artifact, creating in its place a technological reality—that is, humanized or human. He abstracts, so to speak, from the given reality in its specific *hic et nunc,* from the "this" which is "here and now." If his animal body is, for example, stopped by the *hic et nunc* of a river, his human being of Worker "abstracts" from this *hic et nunc,* in constructing, say, a canoe: he replaces the given natural *hic et nunc* by a technological *hic et nunc* created by his Work. By working, man therefore lives in a universe other than that of the given *hic et nunc.* Now, to preserve objective reality while abstracting from the natural *hic et nunc,* in detaching it [objective reality] from it [the natural *hic et nunc*], is to violate the essence of existence; it is to conceive [526] reality in and by a concept (*Logos*). In working, man thinks and speaks. And it is in thinking and speaking that he works; for the artifact is a *concept* realized by Work, which negates the raw given. And this is why the artifact is independent of the natural *hic et nunc,* of its *topos* in the Cosmos of Nature, in particular, the *hic et nunc* of the technological producer, of his body, his animal being.

This independence, this autonomy of the artifact, i.e., of the concept realized and revealed by Work in respect to the natural *hic et nunc,* is realized and manifested first of all by the fact that the Master alienates from the Slave the Product of the Slave's Work, and appropriates it to himself. The artifact is attached not to the body, to the animality of the Slave-worker, but to his humanity: to the concept-discourse (*Logos*) and the conscious will that generates and realizes the concept-project. Therefore, to the extent that the Worker is a Slave; to the extent his will is that of the Master; [and] to the extent he executes the "project" of the latter through his Work, the product of this Work, the artifact, is attached to the Master; it is the Master to whom it "belongs." But if for some reason the Worker ceases to be a Slave properly so-called, if he has a will of his own, an autonomous concept-project, if Society or the State recognize his autonomy as a Worker, the product of his Work will belong to him (it being of little importance whether he is recognized as citizen or quasi-citizen, bourgeois, or only as a member of economic Society). And this product, like any product of Work, will be just as alienable from the natural *hic et nunc,* in particular the *hic et nunc* of the producer himself, as the product of slave labor was alienable and transferrable [*détachable et rattachable*] to the Master. Now this "conceptual" ("logical") character of the product, its independence from the natural *hic et nunc,* is realized and revealed objectively in and by *Exchange.* It is because the products of the Work of A and B are alienable from the *hic et nunc* of A and B, that A can *exchange* the product of his work for that of the work of B. And this Exchange of the products of Work realizes and reveals the specifically human character of these products and of Work itself: for there is only Exchange when there is genuine Work, and this is why there is no Exchange in the animal world.[144]

[527] On the one hand, Work attaches, links the Worker to the thing, to the raw material, to the given *hic et nunc,* which determines the nature of the Work: one works differently to make an axe than to manufacture a canoe. But on the other hand, this same Work liberates the Worker from the given, natural *hic et nunc:* the man-animal is strictly a land-dweller; the man-worker can also live under the water and in the air, from whence comes a dual consequence of Work for the Worker. On the one hand, there is a *specialization* of Work and the Worker, determined by the "matter" and the "raw material": this is the aspect of Work which is a function of the given thing and [the task] to be done. On the other hand, there is a *universalization* of Work and the Worker: to the extent that Work transcends and negates the given, it is not dependent on it, nor consequently is the Worker; the "needs" of the latter are not an exclusive function of his innate animal nature; they go beyond or can go beyond ([and] therefore will one day end up going beyond) this nature and its animal "instincts"; and they are not set down either by the nature of his Work. This is why Work can vary indefinitely as a function of human needs, which are not set down by the already existing Work, and this is also why needs can vary indefinitely as a function of Work, which generates the need even among those who are not doing it themselves, by the sole existence of his product, by the "offer" of exchange. Being alienable from the *hic et nunc* of the Worker, Work can generate a need which did not exist previously in the given *hic et nunc* both among this Worker and elsewhere. And a new need can generate a new Work both among the Worker who experiences it himself and among one who does not experience it. In other words, it is not only Work that makes Exchange *possible:* it makes it necessary as well. The Worker specialized in his Work and universalized in his needs can only satisfy them by exchanging the products of his specialized Work for other specialized products of Work.

The product of Work taken as an object of exchange, i.e., as alienated from the *hic et nunc,* both the *hic et nunc* of the Worker and that of its own material

---

144. One finds among certain animals a "work" in common and even a kind of "division of labor." But one never finds exchange properly so-called—that is, commerce. And this is the proof that there is no Work either in the proper sense of the term—that is, the active realization of a "project," of a concept conceived before its real existence.

content, is ultimately realized and revealed as *Money* or *Value*. The price of the product of Work (and ultimately of everything, to the extent that it is related to Work: as "raw material" to mold, or as the product of a "virtual," possible Work, and so on) is the material symbol of its conceptual essence, of the concept-project realized [528] by Work. (This is why one ends up no longer selling *this* axe, and so on, but *an* axe or *axes*.) Now, if Value is the product of Work taken as an object of exchange, the Price of something is a function, on the one hand, of the quality of the Work invested in it, and on the other hand, of the possibilities for exchange that it offers. A thing that "costs no work" "costs" nothing or is "worth" nothing, and a thing that one cannot or does not want to exchange for another is "priceless" (in general or for the one who possesses it). Price is therefore determined by production and the market, or by production in light of the market. And *economic Society* is in the final analysis nothing other than a *Market*—that is, the "place" where exchanges of products of Work occur. Thus, the specific *Droit* of this Society, *economic **Droit***, is the *Droit* that is applied to social interactions aiming at the exchange of artifacts. It is to these interactions that this *Droit* applies a given ideal of Justice.

Droit is only applied to *social* relations, to interactions between two *human* beings. Therefore, to the extent that Work (as production) puts man in interaction with Nature (the "raw material"), it has nothing juridical about it. Of course, there are also interactions between Workers taken as producers (and not as agents of exchange [*échangistes*] or "merchants"); there is a Work in common, a collaboration in and by Work. And these are quasi-social interactions.[145] But if the interaction between men (the Workers) is determined by the given thing—a tree that can only be moved by several persons together, and so on— it is not a *social* interaction properly so-called—that is, specifically human. The interaction becomes truly *social* only to the extent that it is determined by the thing *to be done*, by the concept-project—that is, by the *result* of common Work. Now, to be related to the result of Work is to alienate oneself from the given *hic et nunc*, from the raw material and the Work already carried out. Those who participate in collective work participate in its product. But it is not necessarily the part produced by A that comes back to him: A can receive the part produced by B, and B, that produced by A. There is then an *exchange* (virtual at the very least) between the products of the Work of the participants in a common undertaking [*oeuvre*]. And this means that all *collective* work is ultimately compensated by a [529] *Salary*. Everything occurs as if every participant drew a Salary in money and spent it entirely on buying a part of the product of this Work. And there is a *social* (that is, "subject to law" [*justiciable*]) interaction between Workers associated in a single Work only to the extent that there is an *exchange* (if only among themselves) of the (virtual) products of their Work.[146]

---

145. Let us note, however, that this sort of interaction also exists among animals.

146. It is possible that an "entrepreneur" takes a part of the Salary of the Workers as his profit. But this is because his "work" costs more, it being of little importance whether it is little or nothing as Work properly so-called—that is, productive. It can have a great value as an object of exchange or "capital." But the analysis of this question cannot be done here.

Economic society is clearly, therefore, a Market, and its *Droit* a *Droit* of Exchange (of the products of Work). Men working side by side do not constitute by this fact an (economic) *Society*, nor even those who work at one and the same undertaking. There is economic Society and economic *Droit* only when individuals (or collectivities) enter into interaction with a view to *exchanging* the products of their work. Without Work there is no Exchange possible, but without Exchange Work is not a truly social phenomenon, to which a *Droit* could be applied—that is, an ideal of Justice.[147]

In the final analysis, economic Society and its *Droit* are based upon the (specifically human) phenomenon of Exchange. Now in order for a thing (in the broad sense) to become an object of exchange, it must be, on the one hand, linked to a human being (individual or collective), and on the other hand, be alienated or alienable from the *hic et nunc* of this being, of the human being taken as a natural being (from his "body" in the broad sense). This link between the "essences" or "concepts" of the thing and man, combined with the independence of their spatio-temporal "existence," is realized and revealed as *Property* (which is something entirely different from *Possession*, or "physical," natural belonging, noticeable also in Nature among animals). Indeed, Property *belongs to* the owner, but it is *alienable* from his *hic et nunc* (capable of being in the possession of another), and it can therefore become an object of exchange. One can therefore say that there is no Exchange without Property. Consequently, it is Property that is [530] the ultimate basis and foundation of economic Society and its specific *Droit*. Economic Society is a group of Owners who enter into interaction as Owners. And as I have already said, and as is universally acknowledged nowadays, Property is only a juridical (and social) phenomenon to the extent that it generates *interactions* between human beings (taken as Owners or non-Owners). That which is juridical is not the relation between the Owner and his Property, but that between the Owner of such a thing and the non-Owners of this thing (as well as between Owners and non-Owners in general). Now the social relations generated by Property as such are relations of mutual exclusion (as Owners), or, more exactly, of simple co-existence (between Owners, or between Owners and non-Owners). These relations are not inter-actions properly so-called: they therefore do not found a genuine Society and do not give rise to a *Droit* properly so-called. There is genuine (economic) inter action only when there is *exchange* of property, when the properties are alienated or are at least alienable.[148] Consequently,

---

147. This is why the familial household is not enough to constitute the Family as a (familial) social entity. It is necessary that this household be accomplished by *kinsmen*. Now the "kinship" in economic Society is represented by Exchange: the contract of exchange links the members of economic Society as kinship (and the contract of kinship) links the members of familial Society.

148. [Ed. Previously in this section, Kojève has used the word *détachable* to denote alienability of property; now he uses the word *aliénable*. We have used the idiomatic legal English "alienable" to translate both French words, since they apparently denote the same idea.]

we were right to say that economic Society and its *Droit* are based upon the phenomenon of Exchange. But it must be added that Exchange presupposes Property. And one can say that if there is no Exchange without Property, there is no Property properly so-called either without Exchange, or at least without possible or virtual Exchange. In any case, Property becomes a truly social and juridical phenomenon only when it generates Exchange: as a social and juridical entity, a property is always an object of virtual or real exchange. A totality of Owners who would never exchange their properties would not constitute an economic Society, and their relations of simple co-existence without (economic) interaction would not have generated an economic *Droit*.[149]

The *Droit* of economic Society is therefore necessarily at the same time a *Droit* of Property and a *Droit* of Exchange, Property being considered by *Droit* as the condition *sine qua non* of Exchange, and Exchange (virtual, at least) as a corollary or necessary consequence of Property. Moreover, the term Exchange should be [531] taken in a very broad sense: it concerns any inter-*actions* between Owners taken as Owners (other than relations of simple co-existence, the exclusion of non-owners from the property of the owner). These inter-actions are realized and manifested in the form of *Obligations,* which acquire a juridical character when they are sanctioned by an impartial and disinterested Third, who has just annulled the reactions of the party who is bound [*obligé*] to the actions of the party to whom a duty is owed [*obligeant*] which result from the obligation. When the Obligation is voluntary in the sense that it is willed (or supposed to be willed) by the party who is bound and the party to whom a duty is owed, it is a matter of *Contract* (or *quasi-Contract,* when the will is unilateral). When the Obligation is involuntary in the sense that it not willed by either the party who is bound or the party to whom the duty is owed, it is a matter of *Delict* (or *quasi-Delict*). The *Droit* of economic Society is therefore, on the one hand, a **Droit** *of Obligations:* contractual (or quasi-contractual) and delictual (or quasi-delictual). On the other hand, it is a **Droit** *of Property,* Property being considered the condition *sine qua non* of Obligations, as that which renders Obligations possible. Now, the possibility of Obligations is also what one calls (economic) juridical "capacity," the ability to contract (economic) obligations. Therefore, the economic *Droit* of Obligations also implies a *Droit* of economic capacity. And since Obligations presupposes Property, the capacity to bind [*s'obliger*] oneself presupposes that of being or becoming an owner. He who is incapable of being an owner is by definition incapable of binding himself. But one can be capable of being an owner while being (more or less) incapable of binding oneself. One must therefore distinguish

---

149. Even theft is a kind of prohibited, illicit Exchange. The right of Property does not make sense without a juridical ban on theft. Now, to assume the possibility of theft is to admit the possibility of an Exchange, [and] therefore also of a juridically legal Exchange. [Ed. In the original, the English word "right" follows the French word *droit* in parentheses.]

between a *Droit* of capacity included in the *Droit* of Property from the *Droit* of capacity which is part of the *Droit* of Obligations.[150]

One can say that, generally speaking, the *Droit* of Property is a *Droit* of *status,* while the *Droit* of Obligations is a *Droit* of *function;* for it is enough to *be* (in the present, or even in the past or the future) to be an Owner, while one must *act* in order to be bound and to bind. But just as in Property there is an aspect of "status" properly so-called—a purely static element—and a dynamic element—an aspect of "function"—there is also in Obligations [532] a properly functional or active aspect and a status-like [*statutaire*], relatively passive aspect. One could therefore distinguish between a *Droit* of status and a *Droit* of function both in the *Droit* of Property and that of Obligations properly so-called.

Be that as it may, the *Droit* of Property and the *Droit* of Obligations constitute two distinct branches of the general *Droit* of economic Society. I will therefore speak about them separately, commencing with the former (§ 68).

But when it is a matter of Property or Obligations, there is (economic) *Droit* only to the extent that there is an intervention of an impartial and disinterested Third, who intervenes with the sole concern to realize a certain ideal of Justice in the social economic interactions within a given (economic) Society. And, as always, this ideal can be either that of equality or that of equivalence, or finally, that of their synthesis (more or less perfect)—that is, of equity. In addition to aristocratic, and servile or bourgeois economic *Droits* (which, moreover, never exist in their pure state), there is also then an economic *Droit* of the Citizen, which exists in very different forms.[151]

§ 68

Property and the notion of Property (which is, moreover, the same thing since there is no unrecognized Property) are constituted in and by the anthropogenic Struggle for recognition.[152] Risk and Struggle, ending in Recognition (*Anerken-*

---

150. Given that Property only makes juridical sense as a possibility of Exchange, i.e., of Obligations, the capacity for property always implies a certain capacity for obligations. But for there to be Exchange, an *action* must be added to the *fact* of Property. This is why the capacity for obligations does not coincide with that of property.

151. I will speak about the "absolute" *Droit* of the Citizen in § 70—that is, about the economic *Droit* of the universal and homogenous State of the future.

152. [Ed. Throughout this section, we will translate the French word *propriété* as either property or ownership, depending on the context. While we generally prefer to translate any key term by a single English equivalent, not to make the distinction in this case would make it difficult for the reader to understand Kojève's fundamental point in unpacking property *droit* or the concept of property, namely that ownership and possession are separate phenomena, only the former being a genuinely juridical phenomenon, while the latter is not in itself of juridical significance (unless it plays a role in establishing a "convention" with respect to the determination of ownership, which is also central to the juridical notion of property). If we were to translate *propriété* as property when Kojève is distinguishing between ownership and possession, this fundamental claim would be harder for the reader to grasp.]

nen) of the victor, also and by this very fact end in the recognition of his possession (*Besitz*) as his "Property" (*Eigentum*). One could even acknowledge that the
"first" Struggle is engaged in for the recognition of a Property: A struggles against
B and risks his life so that B recognizes a thing (in the broad sense) as A's "property," to which B consequently has "no *droit.*" Animals struggle for the physical
possession of a "thing" (food, female, and so on). Men, as human beings, struggle
so that a "thing" (that they may already possess in fact) is *recognized* as their "property." Thus, man does not struggle to possess such and such a woman: he struggles so that such and such a woman (that he possesses or not) is recognized as "his
woman," so that one recognizes [533] his "exclusive *droits*" to this woman, so that
one accepts her as his "property" and as his alone. And seeing that this is the very
fact of recognition, the notion of property that counts, the "thing" and its effective possession can be absent: the "thing" can be an "abstraction" without utility,
or indeed without biological reality (a title, for example, or a name, a "medal,"
and so on), and possession can be alienated from the property: the property of the
owner can be—and remain—in the possession of the non-owner.

   However, the recognition of a property and of a man as owner is something
different from Recognition properly so-called—that is, the recognition of the
human reality and dignity of a man. Recognition is generated by the risk of life
for a non-biological end, and it is this same risk which *creates* the human being
from the animal Homo Sapiens (and in this animal). Thus, to renounce this risk
is to renounce human reality (in actuality) and its recognition: it is to accept a
unilateral recognition, it is to become a Slave, the Slave of the one who has
accepted the risk until the very end. But to refuse to risk his life for the recognition of a property is not to refuse all (anti-biological) risk in general: it is to refuse
to risk his life as a function of a particularity, of such and such a given "thing" (in
the broadest sense). Thus, B can be ready to struggle with A for the Recognition
of his human dignity, but he may refuse to risk his life in a struggle with A for the
recognition of the "*droit* of property" over such and such a woman, for example,
or such and such other determinate "thing." Therefore, if A is ready to run this
determinate risk with respect to a "thing" and B is not, B will recognize by his
refusal of risk that A is the *owner* of the thing in question. B renounces all his
"*droits*" relative to this thing: in respect to it, he is like A's Slave—but only relative to this thing, since B is ready to risk his life in a struggle with A either for total
Recognition, or even eventually for the recognition of another "thing" as his
property. Likewise, A can refuse to risk his life in their struggle for the ownership
of another thing. In renouncing all risk, the Slave renounces all recognition—that
is, in particular, he renounces being recognized as owner in general and therefore
as owner of a determinate thing. In recognizing his victor as his Master, he also
recognizes him as owner and as "absolute" owner, [534] as owner of *every*
"thing," himself included.[153] But if a Master A renounces struggling against
another Master B for the ownership of the thing *b*, B being ready to do so, A only

---

153. In relation to his Slave, the Master is owner of *all* things: he is "master of the world." If his
"*droits*" are limited, if he is only owner of *certain* things, it is only in relation to other Masters.

recognizes B as owner of the thing *b*, and it is only in relation to this thing that he "submits" to B[154] and accepts a unilateral recognition. A can, moreover, recognize the humanity, or indeed the "mastery" of B, without having struggled with him, simply because he knows that B has risked his life in a Struggle for recognition with C, having made C his Slave. And if A refuses to struggle with B for the ownership of this Slave C, he recognizes B not only as a Master—and therefore as an owner in general—but also as the owner of Slave C. Being thus B's "Slave" in relation to C, A is not C's Master: he has "no *droit*" over him; he unilaterally recognizes B as owner of C, without being recognized by B[155] as an owner of C. But to be a Master and be recognized as such, and therefore as owner, A must equally have a Slave D. And B must recognize A as owner of D, by renouncing all *droits* over this D. Thus, one cannot be Master without being owner, but one can be so without being owner of such and such given thing. One must know and be able to risk one's life for Recognition and for the ownership of one given thing, but one can renounce risking one's life for the ownership of another thing. But to refuse every risk is to renounce Mastery and at the same time ownership in general (which does not mean depriving oneself of all *possession*).[156]

[535] It is by utilizing the idea of the Struggle for recognition of property (which presupposes the Struggle for Recognition in general) that one must interpret the property *droit* of "first occupant." It is not the fact of *possessing* a thing, nor the fact of possessing it *first*, which creates a property *droit*, which transforms biological *possession* into human *property*. The "occupant"—and in particular the "first occupant"—has a *property droit* only to the extent that he is supposed to have been willing to risk his life for the sake of the thing that he "occupies," while others are supposed to have refused this risk for the thing "occupied." When there is a genuine *struggle* for ownership, there is war ("private" or "national") and *Droit* has nothing to do with it. The Third of the *Droit* of property only intervenes when A wants to deprive B of his property without wanting to risk his life in order to do so.[157] But the Third may not wait for the effective

---

154. [Ed. Reading *B* for *A*.]

155. [Ed. Reading *B* for *A*.]

156. The total risk of life being the same for everyone, all Masters are alike as Masters, from whence comes the "universalism" of the Master, the absence of "individuality" and "particularity" in him. But the risk for ownership is a "determinate" risk: a risk for such and such thing and not for such and such other thing. Masters are therefore different as Owners. The "particularism" and "individualism" of the Master therefore comes from private property. It is therefore a function of the thing, of the *topos* in the natural world. This is not a truly human particularity or individuality. By contrast, the Slave "particularizes" himself by Work: he therefore *humanizes* himself by particularizing himself. This is why his "*individuality*" does not need to be a function of private property. To be an "individual," it is enough for him to be *universally* recognized in his *particularity* as a Worker. The "individuality" of the Master, by contrast, is only the *universal* recognition of his *property* (particular, i.e., "private"). It is not, therefore, a fully human or humanized "individuality": [535] as a specifically human being, he is only a Master—that is, "universal."

157. A thief, robber, and so on, can risk his life *in fact*. But this risk is not his *goal*. And it is for the *possession* that he risks his life, not for *ownership*. He therefore risks his life as an animal and this is why *this* risk does not create any *droit*.

Struggle. He can create conventions. Thus, for example, he can accept that the "first occupant" does not have to struggle against anyone, seeing that no one has expressed his will to struggle for the ownership of the thing in question by "occupying" it. On the other hand, he can assume that every first "occupant" is ready to risk his life to preserve the ownership of the thing that he "occupies." Finally, the State can forbid struggles for determinate things ("private wars"). Then no one will be able to attack the "first occupant" and one will be able to maintain indefinitely the fiction that he is ready to struggle for the ownership of the thing "occupied." Struggles being ruled out, every attempt to deprive him of this property will be capable of being considered juridically illegal.[158]

[536] Property is linked to a given thing. But seeing that the Struggle (which founds the *droit* of property) is waged for *ownership* and not for possession, the recognized owner may not be the possessor of the thing which is his property. Generally speaking, the accent is on ownership (of the thing) and not on the thing (which is a property, effectively possessed or not). One risks one's life to be *owner* of the thing, and since this risk is total, thus the same for all, all have the same "*droit* of property." All are equal as owners; they differ only by the things which are their property, but not by the *droit* of property. On the other hand, the Risk for Recognition being the same for everyone, and Recognition being nothing other than the objectification of this risk, all Masters are equal as "recognized," as Masters. Being equal as Masters and as Owners, it is natural that all Masters have the same property.[159] Now things differ from one another, from whence comes the *collective* character of specifically aristocratic property: it is a *collective* ownership with *equal* participation of all the co-owners. Each can *possess* a *different* part from that of the others. But each has *the same droit* of *property* over the totality of things of which the collectivity is owner. Thus, all are equal as *owners,* both subjectively and objectively, all having the same property, while differing as *possessors.* A group of Masters (a Fam-

---

158. But the owner must *want* to risk his life for his property. He must therefore effectively risk it if the opportunity presents itself. Now, even if the State forbids "private wars," there are always national wars, which threaten the property of a State, i.e., of its citizens—that is, also of the owner in question. As owner, he must therefore participate in war, from whence comes the idea of excluding (as in Rome) from the army "proletarians" without property. (Even modern wars affect [*touchent*]—indirectly—private property, since they impoverish the State: in defending the "capitalist" State, every citizen-owner therefore also defends his own property *droit*—this defense, moreover, having nothing juridical about it). But military service can also be detached from the *droit* of (private) property: States also struggle for Recognition, and every [536] citizen, recognized by the State as citizen, must take part in this Struggle for pure prestige. Moreover, there are in fact no "proletarians" properly so-called: every citizen, every man who is not the Slave of another, is always "owner," if only of his body and the work that this body can provide.

159. It might seem that A can risk his life to be owner of more things than B. But then A risks his life for *possession* (of more women, more food, and so on) and not for *ownership*—unless property becomes a symbol of Recognition: the nobility of the rich and the riches of the nobleman. But then one struggles for Recognition in general, and Property is no longer but a means. Riches are, moreover, an already "bourgeois" phenomenon: the nobleman through his riches is "Citizen" and not Master properly so-called.

ily not become a State [*non étatisée*], but autonomous; or a "Nation": clan, tribe, and so on) is owner of a totality of things: all struggle in common against the Enemy for this collective property, and each is an owner of the totality to the same extent as the others. Moreover, it is of little importance that they "exploit" the collective property in common or that each is possessor (temporarily or even permanently) of a [537] distinct part of the totality of the property (drawing of shares by lots, redistribution of shares, on so on).

Beside this collective property there is, of course, "personal property": the body [*corps*], first of all, and all that "goes with [*fait corps*]" this body (clothes, arms, women, and so on.) Here possession coincides with ownership.[160] And here a refusal of Struggle is equivalent to a renunciation of Recognition: for the body and that which goes with it is the very basis of being recognized, since there is no human being outside of the animal. Recognition therefore implies recognition of "personal property." But this is just as little a "private property" in the proper ("bourgeois") sense of the word as "collective property." Neither of them signifies a genuine inter-action (and therefore a possible conflict) between the "non-owner" and the "possessor-user [*usufruitier*]." "Personal property" is inalienable even as possession. And "collective property" is only *possessed* by co-*owners*.

Generally speaking, when there are no exchanges between owners, the very *Droit* of property boils down to very little. It only sanctions this absence of exchange by annulling illicit "exchange"—theft, kidnapping, poaching, and so on: every exchange, every change of ownership, if "private wars" are forbidden; all change [of ownership] without prior struggle for ownership, if these wars are allowed. The *Droit* of property is then a penal *Droit*; for seeing that it is a matter of ownership and not possession, the nature of the illegally acquired thing has no importance. It is a matter of "any given thing" and consequently of "any given owner." The thief therefore injures the Society of owners as a whole. This is why the Third intervenes "spontaneously" and annuls the action as intention and will—that is, in and by a penalty.[161]

Now, in a truly aristocratic Society, when the owners are equal not only because they have the same **droit** of property but also because they have equal properties, there is no place for an Exchange between owners. Concerning "personal property," the *Droit* of property therefore effectively reduces to the penal *Droit* [538] which annuls theft (in the broad sense). There are, so to speak, no juridically lawful inter-actions between "personal" owners. But inter-actions exist between the co-owners of "collective property." It is therefore to this property that the *civil Droit* of property is related.[162] It is within the owner-collective that the question arises of relations between (equal) property

---

160. There can be loans among friends. But this is quite different from a "lease." In this "loan," possession is without importance. In the "lease," it matters just as much as with ownership, and this is why there is payment.

161. The thief wants to *possess* a determinate thing. But since ownership is not linked to such a thing, he injures "any given" owner by stealing this thing.

162. "Collective property" is in fact above all real [*foncière*]. This is why for archaic civil *Droit* of property (and also Roman *Droit*, which also inspired the French Civil Code), prop-

and possession (of different shares), as well as the "succession" of property. Not being linked to the *hic et nunc* of the thing, property is transmissible, in particular by the means of inheritance. But the aristocratic *Droit* of property must always suppose the will of the owner to struggle for his property (from whence comes the exclusion of women, for example). As for the relation between ownership and possession (division of shares, and so on), it is a matter of acting such that the inevitable inequality of possession does not destroy the purported equality of ownership (from whence comes drawing of shares by lots, complex division of collective lands, redistribution, and so on). And it is still the same principle that governs the distribution of economic authority within the collectivity (recruitment of the economic "leader" and his control by the co-owners).

Very early on, and perhaps even from the beginning, collective aristocratic property has the character of a family estate [*une propriété familiale*]. The civil *Droit* of property therefore made its appearance above all as a *Droit* of familial Society, namely as the *Droit* of the familial household. The property *Droit* of economic Society applies only to interactions between Families (or between isolated individuals) taken as owners. Now in an aristocratic Society where the owners (individual or collective) are not only equal in *droit* but also in fact, these ("civil") interactions boil down to very little. Therefore, the civil aristocratic *Droit* of property has a very restricted content.

Essentially, this *Droit* deals with a) the co-existence of properties; b) the acquisition; and c) the loss of property. Property is juridically legal only if it can *coexist* with other properties—without suppressing them as such (nor as possession) [and] without being suppressed by [539] them—from whence comes the *Droit* of the limits of property (the "sacred" character of limits [*bornes*]) and the *Droit* of easements [*servitudes*]:[163] he who does not want to (or cannot) struggle for the property of another must recognized the limits of the latter and render its existence possible by recognizing certain restrictions to his [own] property, indispensable to the existence of the other property ("easements"). As for acquisition (other than by Exchange, which falls within the competence of the *Droit* of obligations), there is either the *Droit* of first occupant, or that of conquest, or finally inheritance. But these are only three variations of the principle of the Struggle for property. Conquest is this Strug-

---

erty properly so-called is first and foremost "immovable [*immeuble*]." Originally, "movable [*meuble*]" property is above all "personal" and as such does not give rise to inter-actions between owners, such that there is no possible application for a *Droit*.

163. [Ed. A *servitude* is an acquired legal right to use another's property, or a part thereof, for a specific purpose—a classic example would be the right of B to use a footpath across A's property that allows B access to a commons, a highway, a drinking well, and so on, from his own property. At common law such rights are typically called easements, and we have so translated. Easements can be acquired through long usage that is not contested by the owner of the property being used; such rights are also transmitted with the property itself, so that if A sells his or her property to C, B now has the easement against C, who must recognize it.]

gle pure and simple. The first occupation is equivalent to the will to struggle for the property against new claimants, without the possibility of struggling against former owners, seeing they are non-existent. As for the heir (to the extent that he is not a kinsman, in which case it is a matter of Familial *Droit*), he is supposed to have made his own the will to struggle of the former owner from whom he has inherited (this is the idea that is at the basis of the hereditary fief, to the extent that it is not a "living" [*bénéfice*],[164] in which case the heir inherits the fief because he inherits the function that the fief compensates). Now, when the State forbids private war for property, the latter becomes "eternal," "not subject to prescription [*imprescriptible*]." It belongs forever to the "first occupant," or more exactly to the "latest occupant"—that is, to he who was owner at the moment when struggles for property (or at least for *this* property) were forbidden. To the extent that *Droit* recognizes the "survival" of man in his heir, "eternal" property becomes an hereditary property. There remains the loss of property, which is nothing other than "prescription"—that is, the acquisition by the new owner. Here as well it is the idea of the Struggle for property that is fundamental. The owner who does not claim his property during a certain time x is supposed to have renounced the struggle for it. On the other hand, the possessor is supposed to have the will to struggle (here is the deep meaning of the notion of the *animus* [mind or will] of the possessor in Roman *Droit*). Everything therefore boils down to the will to struggle, and this is why this struggle was the first "proof" of ownership (later interpreted as "judgment of God": cf. the Roman procedure with the spear, the praetor arriving as by chance and separating those struggling to the death for a property). All contestation of property without the will to struggle is null by definition. And this is why appropriation by theft, which excludes struggle by definition (seeing that the thief hides his action), is annulled "spontaneously" [540] by the Third. "Civil" contestation before the Third is equivalent to a bilateral will to struggle. Now this struggle being forbidden by the State, the Third has only to determine the "first occupant" or heir—that is, he whose will to struggle is recognized as a matter of course, unless there is "prescription." The will of the other is without significance, seeing that actual [*effective*] struggle is forbidden. But seeing that both are ready to struggle, they are equal as owners. The difference, therefore, only concerns a determinate thing, a specific property. This is a case of civil *Droit*, and not of penal *Droit*, where the thief, refusing the Struggle, denies the very principle of property and therefore injures the whole of the (economic) Society of owners.

There still remains the problem of usufruct (in the broad sense)—that is, the distinction between possession and ownership pure and simple. But usufruct is an obligation. One is therefore in the sphere of the *Droit* of obliga-

---

164. [Ed. Here Kojève may be thinking of certain ecclesiastical properties, where religious responsibilities were inherited with the land; thus, we translate *bénéfice* as "living." A "living" might also exist when the heir was expected to perform duties of military protection, i.e., for the king or feudal lord, in consequence of inheriting the estate.]

tions. The *Droit* of property only sets down the basis, the necessary but not sufficient condition, of usufruct. Seeing that ownership is something essentially different from possession, nothing prevents distinguishing them juridically: an owner remains owner even if he is no longer (for some reason or other) in possession of his property; it suffices that he be ready to struggle for it (taken as property). The purely negative fact that the possessor does not become owner due to the mere fact of possession is established by the *Droit* of property. But the positive relations between the owner and the possessor-user (i.e., beneficiary of the owner's consent to his possession), are established by the *Droit* of obligations (§ 69).

In short, the aristocratic *Droit* of property is based upon the idea of Struggle for property. And this is why this *droit* does not allow for different degrees [of ownership]: either one has no *droit* of property (having renounced the struggle altogether, i.e., in becoming Slave), or one has all these *droits* (when one accepts the risk, i.e., when one is Master). Thus, children, women, in general those who are deemed not to have been able to struggle for a property, are not recognized as its owner. Now, since the Struggle is the basis of Mastery, and since in aristocratic Society only the Master is juridical subject, every juridical subject is subject of the plenitude of the *droits* of property: only *alieni juris* do not possess these *droits;* but this is because they are not juridical persons, not (or not yet) having access to Mastery, i.e. ultimately to the Struggle, [541] and therefore to the struggle for property. Of course, as long as this struggle lasts, there is no place for a Third and there is then no *Droit*. The **Droit** of property only appears once the State forbids struggles for property—that is, "private wars." But this (aristocratic) *Droit* is nonetheless based upon the idea of this struggle, upon its "possibility," upon "virtual" struggle. *Juridical* property is "*eternal*" because *Droit* presupposes the ban on the actual [*effective*] Struggle, capable of removing property from its owner. But the owner is only owner (not a mere possessor) because he is supposed to have the *will* to struggle to the death for his property, if the (hypothetical) opportunity were to present itself. And the entire content of the aristocratic *Droit* of property can be deduced from this principle: the will to struggle without the possibility of struggle. The absence of this will (or the legal presumption of this absence) in the owner leads to "prescription" by the possessor—to "theft": one can neither be owner nor become one without a recognized will to struggle to the death for property—that is, to place oneself in the same situation as the challenger [*prétendant*]. The acquisition or maintenance of property without struggle is contrary to the aristocratic ideal of egalitarian Justice. And this is why the aristocratic *Droit* of property cannot accept it. The equality of owners is in the final analysis based upon the absolute equality of the risk of their lives.

Such are the principles of the *aristocratic* **Droit** *of property*. Property is a function of Risk, which is the same for all, from whence comes the egalitarian principle according to which each must have property equal to the others. Now, when there is equality between owners there are, so to speak, no interactions, no exchanges between them, and consequently no contracts or obligations in general. Therefore, *aristocratic economic* **Droit** in the main boils down to the *Droit* of property, and this itself boils down to very little, as we have seen. *Bourgeois economic* **Droit**, by contrast, is first and foremost a *Droit* of Exchange or Obligations, for property is fundamentally unequal in bourgeois economic Society, which renders economic exchanges indispensable. One can even say that Property is nothing other than the condition *sine qua non* of Obligations: Property can be defined as that which can be exchanged, creating obligations between the agents of exchange [*échangeants*]. Not only is there no Exchange possible without Property, but one can say that there is no Property either properly so-called without Exchange, at [542] least without possible or virtual Exchange. One cannot bind oneself if one is not Owner, at least in potentiality, and one is bound, at least virtually, by the very fact that one is Owner.[165] Thus, the bourgeois *Droit* of property is, as it were, only an introduction to the *Droit* of obligations, which represents close to the entirety of bourgeois economic *Droit*.

This difference is due to the fact that the *bourgeois* **Droit** *of property* is based upon an entirely different principle than the corresponding aristocratic *Droit*, [the latter] based upon the idea of Struggle and Risk.

Bourgeois *Droit* is the *Droit* of the Slave, or more exactly, of the Slave recognized as a juridical person—that is, as a human being, [and] therefore of the Slave become Citizen. But in the Citizen-bourgeois the servile element greatly predominates over that of mastery. The Bourgeois is a *recognized* Slave, but recognized in his *servitude* (despite there being no more Masters properly so-called: the Bourgeois is a Slave without a human-Master, who therefore is seeking a Master and who finds it at first in God, and then in Capital, which he "serves"). Now, by definition, the Slave does not struggle and it is not through a Struggle that his property comes to him. It can only come to him through his Work. As well, from the point of view of bourgeois *Droit*, the sole source of Property is Work: either the work of producing the thing, or an exchange of work for a thing.

Generally speaking, bourgeois *Droit* is based upon the ideal of the Justice of equivalence: every *droit* is supposed to be equivalent to a duty that is connected to it, and conversely, the "*droit*" corresponding to some benefit or other, the "duty" to a burden. Therefore, if Property is a "*droit*," or indeed a "benefit," one needs, in order that it be "just," an equivalent "duty" that is connected to it, or a "burden" in general. And this "duty" is, on the one hand, the Work which generates Property, and on the other hand, the Obligations that Property creates once it exists (taxation, for example, and so on). Therefore, Property must first of all be equivalent to the Work effort provided by the one who acquires it. Every Property presupposes an equivalent Work provided by the

---

165. Of course, one can say that aristocratic Property also includes an Obligation: an "easement," for example. But aristocratic obligation is related to other concrete properties, while bourgeois obligation is related to economic Society as a whole and is linked to Property as such: taxation, for example.

Owner, and every Work effort generates an [543] equivalent Property. Every man who has made (manufactured) a thing is the owner of this thing (or the virtual owner of an equivalent thing, that he can acquire by exchange).[166] On the other hand, the enjoyment of a property being a "*droit*" or a benefit, it must be accompanied by an equivalent "duty" or burden: every Owner has obligations equivalent to it that flow from the very fact of ownership, and that a non-owner does not have: Property is just as much a "duty" as a "*droit.*" Thus, when the Property requires a continuous effort to maintain it, it is the owner who is supposed to provide it (or to provide the equivalent).

Now equivalence does not at all imply equality. And the work effort provided by one can differ from that provided by another; their properties can be unequal. And the inequality of properties is going to generate Exchange and Obligations. Thus, Property which is a function of Work is essentially a Property to exchange. And the very *Droit* of property is going to define the latter such that it can serve as a basis for Exchange, Contract, and Obligations in general, which is possible, seeing that Property, being quite different from possession, is not linked to the *hic et nunc* of the thing: the owners remain identical to themselves as owners, even if they exchange the things they possess in the capacity of owners. A is owner of a thing *a*, and B of another thing *b*. In both cases, once *droits* and duties linked to the ownership of the thing are equivalent, nothing will be changed from the point of view of the *Droit* of property if A becomes owner of *b*, and B of *a;* for what counts is not the *possession* of such and such thing, but ownership—that is, a totality of *droits* or benefits equivalent to a totality of duties or burdens, or indeed of the invested work effort.

In the bourgeois *Droit* of property, the coexistence of owners is not only static, as in the corresponding aristocratic *Droit*, but also dynamic. Not only must a given property allow the existence of other properties (limits to property, [544] easements, and so on), it must also be exchangeable with these other properties, for the benefits that it embodies are only real to the extent that they can be exchanged against other properties (equivalent, but of another kind [*nature*]). This is here a necessary consequence of specialization, of the division of labor, and therefore of the specification of the property produced by this work. He who produces shoes can only take advantage of the property produced if he can exchange it (at least in part) for clothes, food, and so on. Now Property as exchangeable is ultimately represented by money. As well, the bourgeois *Droit* of property is related above all to value, to the price of the thing of which one is owner, and not the thing itself. That which is guaranteed by the Third is the ownership of the *value* of the things of which one is owner. As for the things themselves, the State can oblige the owner to alienate them, either

---

166. The term "Work" must be taken in a broad sense. It can also mean "intellectual work," from whence comes the *droit* of "intellectual property." As for the "make [*firme*]," the "brand [*marque*]," and so on, these "abstract" properties symbolize a Work invested by their owner. When Work does not create material entities, property is connected to "ideal" entities, to symbols of Work: the name and reputation of a business, for example, a patent, the brand of a product, and so on.

by exchanging them for other things, or by selling them for money (ban on stockpiling, expropriations, and so on). Money thus becomes the direct equivalent of work, while the thing produced by this work can be alienated from it. At the limit, one can say that money becomes the only property juridically recognized: one cannot take away the monetary equivalent of the property of the owner, but one can very well dispossess him of the things he possesses in the capacity of owner: it suffices to pay him for them.

As for the acquisition of bourgeois property (aside from exchange), it occurs not by Struggle but by Work. As well, the "first occupant" only becomes owner due to the work that he has invested in the thing occupied, and the fact that he is "first" only means that no one before him invested work in the thing in question. Thus, the "proof" of ownership boils down to the proof of work invested, the *animus* of the possessor being here his will to work the possessed thing. Likewise, the heir can only succeed the former owner provided that he accepts the "duties" bound to the property, in particular to continue the work connected to the thing of which he is owner. And since work provided by one individual is not necessarily equal (or equivalent) to that provided by another, nothing *a priori* says that the heir has the *droit* to the same property as that of he from whom he has inherited.[167] This is why [545] in the final analysis the notion of hereditary property is foreign to the bourgeois *Droit* of property (from whence comes succession duties [*taxes élevées sur les successions*], and so on). The continuity of property is only justified to the extent that there is continuity of obligations which are linked to it (taxes [*impôts*], for example). But the source of ownership ultimately being Work, all acquisition without corresponding work, i.e., acquisition by inheritance as well, is basically juridically illicit.[168]

The loss of property is here the result of the abandonment of work that is connected to it. "Prescription" means nothing other than the fact that the owner has not worked his property (during a [period of] time x). He has therefore lost his *droit* of ownership. And if the possessor has (during this time) invested in the possession the work which is connected to it as property, he becomes owner of that which he possesses. (The *animus* is here not only the will or the intention but the act of working.)

As for theft, and so on, it is a matter of an acquisition without equivalent work (the effort of the thief not being work properly so-called, since it creates nothing, does not negate the given, does not transform a "raw material," does not "mold"

---

167. The risk in the struggle for property is, by contrast, always the same. This is why the heir who accepts the eventual struggle has the *droit* to the entirety of the inheritance.
168. The will to struggle can exist even when the struggle is forbidden by the State. The inheritance of aristocratic property, therefore, does make sense. But Work being allowed, the mere "will" of the worker is not enough. The heir must therefore provide a work equivalent to the value of the inheritance to become owner of it. But then there is no longer inheritance: the "heir" has himself produced his property by his work. Bourgeois inheritance is therefore in fact inheritance of the "means of production," of the *possibility* of a determinate work: on such a field, which such tools, and so on. And if this "possibility" is provided by a third, notably by the State, the inheritance of property no longer has a reason to exist.

the thing). And seeing that there is a negation of the very principle of bourgeois property, based upon Work, the thief injures bourgeois economic Society as a whole. Seeing that he acquires without work, he can acquire anything whatsoever, any given thing, [and] therefore the property of any given owner. Therefore, theft is here also a case of *penal Droit* of property. As for civil *Droit,* it only deals with the relationship between a given work and a specific, determinate property. Seeing that someone has provided a determinate quantity of Work, he has a *droit* to "any given" corresponding property: therefore, he does not injure "any given" owner by effectively acquiring it. But it is possible that he injures a "specific" owner [546] in acquiring his property instead of acquiring that of another (equivalent). In this case the Third will be able to intervene, but he will apply *civil Droit.*

Contrary to the Risk in the Struggle, Work effort admits of distinctions and degrees, from whence comes distinctions both objective and subjective in the bourgeois *droit* of property. Not only can the properties of different owners be different and unequal, the one having something more and something else than he has; the very *droit* of ownership admits of variations and degrees: the juridical "capacity" of owner is not the same for everyone. Thus, for example, someone can be the legitimate owner of a personal estate [*biens meubles*], without being able to be the real [*foncier*] owner, in which case he will be deemed unable or unwilling to work the land. Generally speaking, the juridical "capacity" of ownership is a function of the capacity for work.

By its very essence, Work *particularizes* man by humanizing him (and therefore *individualizes* him, to the extent that his human *particularity* is recognized *universally*). It also therefore particularizes him as owner: bourgeois property born from work is "particularistic" and not collective, as the aristocratic property generated by the Struggle. Property created by work is bound to the particularity of the Worker: it is to him, to the exclusion of all others—that is, of all those who have not participated in the production. But while not being collective, bourgeois property also differs from aristocratic "personal" property; for it does not go with the body of the owner. Being essentially exchangeable, it is alienable from him and remains his even in being effectively alienated. This property is therefore a "private property" in the proper sense of the term. The owner may not be the possessor of his property: he nevertheless remains its owner and he is alone in being so. And it is this "private property" which is the genuine basis of Contract and Obligations in general, just as conversely it only makes sense as a result of this (effective or virtual) Obligation.[169]

---

169. In principle, the owner remains owner because he is supposed to provide a work equivalent to that which he would have provided if he had remained possessor of his property. As for the user, he is supposed to gain a property equivalent to the work that he invested in the thing of which he is only the possessor. But in fact, it is rarely like this. Bourgeois *Droit* manages by dint of "formal" subtleties. Furthermore, as we will immediately see, there is an (imperfect) synthesis of the bourgeois principle with [547] the aristocratic principle (or more exactly, with a "fiction" of this principle), which yields "capitalist" bourgeois *Droit*— the first (imperfect) sketch of the *Droit* of the Citizen relative to Property: the property acquired without Work (and without Struggle) is "formally" likened to aristocratic

[547] The *property* **Droit** *of the Citizen* is a synthesis of the corresponding aristocratic and bourgeois *Droits.*

Thus, in the first place, this *Droit* preserves, on the one hand, the aristocratic notion of Property exempt from all "duty" and not destined for Exchange—that is, independent of all Obligation (it is the "personal property" of the perfect synthetic *Droit,* i.e., socialist). On the other hand, this *Droit* is also familiar with bourgeois Property, understood as a simple premise of Obligations, destined for Exchange and equivalent to a corresponding "duty" (it is the "collective" or "social property," "state-sanctioned," and so on, of socialist *Droit:* to participate in collective property is to participate in collective work). Second, this *Droit* reunites equality with equivalence. Thus, in its perfect form, it admits the equality of properties (and *droits* of property), but among each the *droit* of property is accompanied by a duty which is equivalent to it. And the maintenance of the principle of equivalence allows one to preserve the notion of money, value, and price, the equality of properties capable of being limited to that of their values. Third, the *Droit* of the Citizen is also a synthesis of the principles of Struggle and Work. It is Work which generates Property and it is by working that one becomes Owner. But the Owner is supposed to have to defend his Property with arms in hand if the necessity presents itself: in case of a war, for example, which injures collective property and consequently the properties of the co-owners. Finally, fourth, Property recognized by this *Droit* is as much collective as individual: not only because alongside collective or "social" property there is a "personal property," but also because participation in collective property is strictly individual. The unit of economic Society is here the individual and not the Family or any other given social group.

In the beginning, moreover, the synthesis of the *Droit* of the Citizen is still imperfect, or indeed "abstract" or purely "formal"—that is, if you will, erroneous. One has "bourgeois" *Droit* [548] properly so-called or the "capitalist" *Droit* of property. On the one hand, this *Droit* likens ("capitalist") Property to aristocratic Property, seeing that it admits that the latter can be acquired and possessed without Work. But on the other hand, this same Property is likened to bourgeois Property, seeing that it can be acquired and kept without a Struggle and even without the will to Struggle. This pseudo-synthesis is purely "formal": the absence of Struggle is likened to Work, which in reality is missing, just as the absence of Work is likened to the Struggle, which in fact no longer exists either. But it tallies very well with the "unauthentic" existence of the Bourgeois himself, who is a Slave without a Master, [who is] from the formal point of view likened to the Master, seeing that he does not have one (although he has not freed himself from the Master by a revolutionary Struggle and therefore does not participate in authentic Mastery, based upon the Risk in the Struggle for recognition). Now, not struggling on the grounds of his servitude, the Bourgeois believes [himself] capable of not working on the grounds of his would-be Mastery (i.e.,

---

property (acquired by the Struggle or the will to Struggle), which does not include any "duty," in particular a duty to work, and which is "eternal," or indeed hereditary.

in fact, because he no longer has a Master who forces him to work, if not God or "Capital" itself). And this pseudo-synthesis allows one to combine ("abstractly" or "formally") in capitalist Property the characteristics of aristocratic and bourgeois Property, the combination being carried out for the benefit of the Owner. Just like aristocratic Property, capitalist Property is supposed to be "eternal"— that is, hereditary. But being individual like bourgeois Property, the succession is absolutely arbitrary (the *droit* to make out one's will as one likes), all the more so because the heir inherits neither from a will to struggle nor from a duty to work. Likewise, being likened to bourgeois *Droit*, the capitalist *Droit* of property is not at all egalitarian: it admits the inequality of Properties both in fact and in *droit*. But, by being likened to aristocratic *Droit*, this *Droit* tends to free the *droit* of property from all the duties that bourgeois *Droit* attaches to it. Just like the latter, Property is reduced to its monetary value. But this "abstract" property is likened to aristocratic Property: its exchange is not a duty and the coexistence of properties can be purely static. And it is in this sense that Property becomes "Capital": a movable likened to an immovable, if you will (or an immovable likened to a movable, when Capital is real). Exchange not being required, it can be bought: Property-Capital carries a revenue by transforming itself into exchange Capital, [549] the loan of Capital being bought at so many percent.[170]

This "capitalist" synthesis, being imperfect, admits of an infinity of degrees. There is then a large number of capitalist *Droits* of property. But in their historical evolution (in their "dialectic"), these *Droits* tend to one and the same limit: to the perfect (and consequently immutable) synthesis of the aristocratic and bourgeois principles in the socialist *Droit* of property, which is part of the Legal System of the *Droit* of the Citizen of the universal and homogenous State of the future. I will say a few words about this in the final section of this work (§ 70).

§ 69

Let us now see what the second part of the *Droit* of economic Society is— that is, the **Droit** *of obligations,* or if you will, the exchange of properties.[171]

---

170. By contrast, the property of the worker, produced by his work, is interpreted according to the principles of bourgeois *Droit*: its exchange is obligatory and therefore is not bought; the worker who exchanges the product of his work for another product only receives the strict equivalent of the work that he delivered. As for the capitalist, he may not exchange his property—that is, his capital. If he does so, he then gets a premium for his consent to exchange: one gives back to him his capital plus interest. This is why one can only call "Capital" in the proper sense the property that the owner can shield from exchange: it is that which remains to him after he has covered his costs of personal consumption.

171. [Ed. It must be recalled that the French word *délit* can mean both "wrong" and "delict," depending on context. Moreover, when Kojève uses *délit* to mean "delict," it can refer to the general branch of obligations including both delict and quasi-delict, or in the narrower sense to something like an intentional torts (e.g., battery and defamation). The context should make clear whether Kojève is using delict in the broader sense, as including quasi-delict, or the narrower one, as distinguished from quasi-delict (e.g., negligence).]

First of all, let us recall that *Droit* only exists when there is an intervention of a Third in a social interaction. The interactions between human beings to which the *Droit* of obligations (contract and delict) can be applied have, in themselves, nothing juridical about them. The fact of contracting a debt, of renting a house, or of breaking a neighbor's window, and so on, have nothing to do with *Droit*. These are only social, or indeed economic, interactions, which *may* become juridical relations between subjects of *droit,* but which may just as easily remain outside of the juridical sphere. An economic social interaction only becomes a juridical situation starting from the moment when an impartial and disinterested Third intervenes in this interaction in order to overcome the reaction of one of the two agents against the action of the other. If A promises to reimburse B on such a date for an amount he borrowed, this relation between A and B is not yet juridical. It is only so when a Third is supposed to intervene in order to overcome [550] B's opposition if A acts (on the appointed date) to take away from B the amount owed to him by A.[172] The convention between A and B is a juridical relation only to the extent that it implies the possibility of an intervention of the Third. A *juridical* obligation (contract or delict), therefore, necessarily contains two elements: a relation between the agents interacting and the acceptance of this relation by the Third. One says that the obligation has the force of law for the interested parties, for it is rightly [*justement*] sanctioned by a Third (who embodies the juridical "law"): if A has an obligation toward B, and if he does not perform it, it is the Third who will force him to do so and not B himself, and this only to the extent that A's obligation toward B is a *juridical* obligation (a contract or a delict). The Third intervenes not because A promised something to B or because B thinks that A owes him something, but because *the Third has recognized* A's obligation toward B: it is not because there is an obligation of A toward B that the Third intervenes; it is because he intervenes that there is an obligation in the juridical sense of the term (contract or delict). This is why the so-called "natural" obligation (for example, a gambling debt in modern society) is not a juridical phenomenon if the creditor [*obligeant*] takes no "action" against the debtor [*obligé*].[173] And if the payment of a "natural" obligation is considered as a *payment* (and not as a gift), and if it cannot be "repeated," it is because the (voluntary) *payment* of a "natural" obligation is a juridical act sanctioned by the Third. But the obligation itself has nothing juridical about it as long as the debtor has not complied.

By definition, the *Droit* of obligations of economic Society is a *civil Droit.* In other words, the Third only intervenes here in economic interactions between two specific members of economic Society, taken as these members in their

---

172. [Ed. Reading *la somme due à lui par A* for *la somme due par lui à A.*]
173. [Ed. The words *obligeant* and *obligé* have the narrow meaning of "creditor" and "debtor," as well as the much wider meaning of the "the one (or party) to whom a duty is owed" and the "the one (or party) who is bound." They will be translated in both ways depending on the context.]

respective *hic et nunc.* A is "bound" [*obligé*] to B when he is a concrete member of economic Society, differing from all the others, and not "any" given member representing Society as such taken as a whole. This is why a (reciprocal or unilateral) obligation between A and B does not at all affect a given [*déterminé*] C, or "any" other member, i.e., the Society itself: a contract has no effect toward the Thirds. Of course, A can bind B to benefit another person C: for example, B can borrow money from A with the obligation to repay it to C. But then there are, in reality, two obligations: either B's obligation toward A [551] and A's obligation toward C, or B's obligation toward A and B's obligation toward C. Or once again, A and C [could] form a collective moral person to whom B is bound (and whose status is set down in the contract between A and B). At any rate, it is a matter of relations between specific members of economic Society, who do not at all affect this Society itself (at least in principle)— that is, any given member. The fact that the obligation between A and B has "the force of law" for A and B, but does not have any effect for the thirds, proves that A and B are absolutely isolated from the rest of the Society in and by this obligation: they constitute a sort of "State within a State." Their interaction reaches no one else and is affected by no one other than themselves. Now this precisely means that we are in the presence of a case of *civil Droit.* If A owes B money, this only concerns A and B, but not any given member of the Society—that is, this Society as such. The latter can therefore intervene by way of a disinterested Third in the obligation between A and B. But this Third will not intervene "spontaneously": he will only intervene if A or B are injured, which can only manifest itself to the Third by a "provocation" coming from A or B. Likewise, by intervening and annulling the action (of A, for example), the Third will limit himself to annulling it as an act, for only the act (and not the intention or will) can injure a specific member (A or B) of the Society: the intention and will are related to "any given" member, whereas this member is not affected by the obligation in question and cannot therefore be injured as a result of it. Thus, compensatory damages—that by which the annulment carried out by the Third can be expressed—have nothing to do with a penalty. Quite simply, the refusal of the debtor to comply for the benefit of the creditor has altered his obligation by adding compensatory damages to it. The Third, by requiring the debtor to pay the debt and damages, limits himself to overcoming his [the debtor's] reaction to the creditor's action, [who was] attempting to recuperate the debt—that is, the former debt plus damages. And this new debt is only claimed [*touché*] by the creditor and not by "any given" member, i.e., by the Society itself: the damages are not a fine—that is, a penalty.

The Third therefore limits himself to having the obligation enforced, or generally speaking, to annulling the injury to the creditor coming from the behavior of the recalcitrant debtor. The debt paid late, but increased by compensatory damages, does not at all differ from the debt simply restored [552] on the appointed date. And this is why all juridical economic obligations have a tendency to turn into *financial* obligations. A is bound not toward any given member but toward B, in his *hic et nunc;* and A is not bound (toward B) as any given member, but in his *hic et nunc,* to the extent that this *hic et nunc* is deter-mined by that of B. Therefore, it is only a part of A which is bound, and a part alienable from A taken as any given member of the Society, this member not being bound toward B. A is only bound in and by what he has that is purely and strictly "personal," but which is alienable from his "person." He is only bound by and in his "having"—that is, ultimately in and by his "private prop-erty." And this is why one can say that it is only A's private property which is bound and not A himself. If A loses his property, he is no longer bound, for without this property, A is no longer the A who was bound and who had this property. But if A recovers the lost property (or its equivalent), he is again bound. On the other hand, the one who inherits A's property as being A's property also inherits the obligation bound to this property—that is, to a *hic et nunc* (of A) involving the aforementioned property.[174]

[553] Obligations in economic *Droit* are therefore by definition a case of civil *Droit.* Through some of its aspects, however, it is similar to cases of penal *Droit,* where "any given" member intervenes—that is, economic Society itself. Thus, an obligation is juridically nil (non-existent) if it has a (juridically) "illicit cause." In other words, A and B, who are bound, are not absolutely iso-lated from Society, and their obligation is supposed to be able to affect thirds—that is, "any given" member. But the difficulty here is only apparent, and one is very much in the sphere of civil *Droit.* An obligation is said to have an "illicit cause" when it is supposed to injure (or, in general, to affect, "to interest") *any given* member of (economic) Society, if only in the person of the debtor (or the creditor). Now, by definition, the obligation (in the proper sense) is a relation between two *specific* members. To the extent that it is related to *any given* mem-ber (i.e., to Society as such), it is not an "obligation" in the proper sense of the

---

174. There has been, and there still is, a lot of vagueness in these questions. Previous *Droit* was annulling the obligation with the death of the debtor because this *Droit* was connecting the obligation to the *concrete person* of the debtor (from whence also comes physical restraint, prison or slavery for debts, and so on). This was conforming to the principle of civil *Droit:* the obligation was related to A and B, and not to any given members—that is, not to C or D (heirs of A and B, for example). But in fact, there was an antinomy, for the *person* is also any given member of the Society, who by definition is not affected by the oblig-ation. One has therefore abolished prison for debts, and so on, which were also fatally affect-ing any given member in the person of the debtor. Obligation has been related to the pri-vate property of the debtor. As the debtor, therefore, A was considered as "any given member having such and such private property." Now, the heir of this property is also "any given member possessing this property": he is also therefore bound just as A was. And see-ing that A's property can be alienated from him, it can also be so from his own *hic et nunc.* What is bound, therefore, is not such and such a property but its equivalent in money, to the extent that this equivalent is connected to the debtor. In certain *Droits,* the non-restitu-tion of a "deposit" is considered as a case of penal *Droit;* this is because one must distinguish two aspects. The one—the civil aspect—is the non-restitution of the deposit (which is then a simple debt), which is annulled (after "being provoked") by the annulment of the act alone (restitution plus eventual compensatory damages); the other aspect is the *theft* of another's property (by chance "entrusted" to the thief), and this is a case of penal *Droit,* which injures any given member.

term. It does not exist, therefore, in the eyes of the third; it does not have any juridical reality; it is "nil," as they say. And this is why it does not have any juridical effect: in particular, it cannot be ascribed to its authors. Not existing, it cannot be *annulled:* in particular, it cannot be annulled in and by a penalty. An obligation, therefore, must be such that a *specific* member can contract it without affecting (injuring) *any given* member, even if this member is affected in his person. A "lawful" obligation is only supposed to affect the one who contracts it, the contracting party being taken as a *specific* member of economic Society. It is only in this case that Society (or the State, which represents Society) can intervene in the capacity of an impartial and disinterested Third, and that, consequently, the obligation exists as a juridical entity.

It is said that the exercise of a right[175] cannot create obligations (by a delictual act). By saying this, one has reasoned in the following way. To have a *droit* is to have one toward *any given* member of the Society. By exercising it, one cannot injure *this* member by definition. Therefore, by exercising his *droit*, A cannot injure a *specific* member B either, nor consequently be bound toward him. But in reality an obligation is only related to the interaction between two *specific* members, which does not affect *any given* member. The action which creates the obligation, therefore, is by definition indifferent for Society—that is, for any given member [554], i.e., for anyone other than A and B. In the aspect where it is taken, therefore, this action is not A's *droit* in respect to any given member, since there is no interaction between them. If the action follows from A's *droit* in respect to B, it certainly cannot create an obligation toward B. But what is a *droit* in respect to any given member may not be a *droit* in respect to a specific member B. And in this case, the action can bind A toward B; for what does not injure any given member can very well injure a specific member in his *hic et nunc*. However, if A's action only affects B, it is for B to reveal it as injuring him: it is B who must "provoke" the Third and provide proof of the injury. Of course, by exercising his valid *droit* in respect to any given member, A cannot injure the latter, and he cannot therefore injure B as any given member. But if A directs his action not at any given member but exclusively at B in his *hic et nunc*, he is not exercising his *droit*. He can therefore injure B and contract an obligation toward him (if the Third intervenes upon B's provocation).[176]

There are, of course, interactions sanctioned by the Third which are related to any given member of economic Society—that is, to this Society as a whole. But these interactions then have nothing to do with the obligations that we are considering here. If A is bound in a delictual way toward any given member,

---

175. [Ed. In the original, the English word "right" follows the French word *droit* in parentheses.]

176. Thus, for example, to show a "spirit of bickering" is not to exercise his *droit* of juridical action against any given member but to want to harm B, and him only. Now, general *Droit* is not directed at B. The action in question [*en justice*] against B, taken as B, is not therefore a *droit*. Likewise, to build a wall which blocks the neighbor's light is related to this neighbor, and not to any given member.

one has a case of penal *Droit;* but this "obligation" or "wrong," which is in reality a crime, has nothing to do with the civil Wrong of the *Droit* of economic Society. Civil Delict only exists when the delictual action is related (or was supposed to be related) solely to a specific member of economic Society taken as such in his *hic et nunc.* Likewise, if a convention sanctioned by the Third binds any given members, or a specific member with any given member, this convention has nothing to do with the civil Contract of economic *Droit.* It is still a case of penal *Droit,* based upon the general status (static or dynamic) of economic Society. Civil Contract is an interaction between two specific members of this Society [555] taken as such in their respective *hic et nunc.* And it is only Contract and Delict properly so-called, i.e., civil economic Obligations, that will be discussed in this section.

The *Droit* of Obligations properly so-called is part of the *Droit* of economic Society, which means that Obligation itself has an economic character. Familial "wrongs" and "contracts," for example, have nothing to do with obligation. In particular, the act which binds the husband and his wife has nothing of a Contract about it, properly so-called. At the very most, the economic relations between spouses can give rise to a Contract. And still, it is necessary that the contracting parties be taken as members of economic Society and not of familial Society—that is, for example, not as husband and wife.

Therefore, (contractual or delictual) Obligations only exist when there is an (economic) social interaction between specific members of economic Society taken as these members, but in the specificity of their *hic et nunc;* this means that an Obligation can only take place between Owners acting as such. The *Droit* of Obligations implies and presupposes the *Droit* of Property. Obligations only bind the one bound as an Owner.

The notions of owner and Property, moreover, should be taken here in a very broad sense. The debtor may be the owner only of his body, but in this case he should be considered as a genuine owner of this body. The conception of body-property, moreover, has nothing artificial about it. Still today, a woman commonly sells her hair, and one can sell his own corpse to medical science [*au théâtre anatomique*]. The prostitute and movie extra rent their bodies, and the worker sells the product of his body—the physical effort that this body provides. He is only the owner of the product of this effort to the extent that he is owner of his body, and not a Slave, for example. It is also because the body has been considered as the property of the debtor that there have been imprisonments and slavery for debts, for example. The big question is to know if the body belongs to the "juridical person" taken as any given member of the Society or as a specific member. And it is in the first case alone that it is juridically absurd to bind the body of the debtor, since the obligation is only related to the specific member. Be that as it may, a being deprived of all property, even that of his own [556] body, cannot be bound, neither by contract nor because of a wrong. This was the case of the Slave.

Property, however, is a necessary but not a sufficient cause of Obligations. Taken in itself, Property does not generate any contract or delict. For there to be any Obligation at all, there must be an inter-*action* between two human beings acting as Owners. Or again, if you will, there must be an *Exchange* of Properties. One also says that Obligation presupposes a "will." This is true to the extent that all effective acts presuppose a will to act and an intention. This is why the Third will have to ask about intention and will in order to know if there has been a genuine inter-*action*, without which there cannot be an obligation. Thus, a case of necessity [*force majeure*] does not create obligation precisely because there has not been genuine action—that is, conscious and voluntary [action]. But seeing that the interaction in the Obligation has taken place between two *specific* members taken in their *hic et nunc*, it [the interaction] only intervenes in its spatio-temporal actuality—that is, as an *act*. The intention and will, therefore, only intervene in the *Droit* of Obligations to the extent that they are realized and actualized as an act. And one thus sees again that this *Droit* is a civil *Droit*: it is the act alone which will be annulled by the Third, and he will only annul the intention and will to the extent that they are actualized in the act. But this act will only be annulled if it actualizes the corresponding intention and will; for it is only in this case that it is a specific act between two specific members—that is, an act capable of generating an obligation. There is no Obligation without Exchange, and there is no Exchange without conscious and voluntary action—that is, without an act generated by a will arising from an intention.

Property, therefore, can only found an Obligation to the extent that it is exchangeable. Now the essentially exchangeable Property is ultimately money. Consequently, all Obligation tends to become a monetary obligation: what does not have, or is not supposed to have, a monetary equivalent cannot be bound. Thus, when the body is considered as inalienable (unsaleable), it cannot be bound, and there can no longer be prison for debts, nor being sold into slavery as a result of an obligation. Generally speaking, an Obligation not performed can only be annulled by the Third by a payment of compensatory damages assessed in money.

[557] The *Droit* of Property is in the main a *Droit* of status. By contrast, the *Droit* of Obligations, which is related solely to inter-*actions*, is a *Droit* of function. Now the *Droit* of status is above all based upon the principle of equality, while the *Droit* of function bases itself above all upon the principle of equivalence; for equality makes Exchange useless, and in Exchange there is generally an equivalence and not an equality of what one exchanges. The *Droit* of Obligations is therefore in the main a bourgeois *Droit*, based upon the ideal of the Justice of equivalence. What is important in Obligation is that the benefits of the one who is bound are equivalent to his burdens, just as the benefits of the one to whom a duty is owed are equivalent to his burdens; from this one deduces the equivalence of benefits (and burdens) of the one to whom a duty is owed and the one who is bound.

However, the principle of equality is not absent from the *Droit* of Obligations, which—like all real *Droit*—is a Droit of equity, of the synthesis of equality and equivalence. If there is not a strictly aristocratic *Droit* of Obligations (seeing that there is not, so to speak, economic Exchange in purely aristocratic Society), there is an aristocratic element in the real *Droit* of Obligations.

In the final analysis, human phenomena in general, and consequently juridical phenomena, revert back to the "first" anthropogenic Struggle for recognition (cf. Part Two). This Struggle is, if you will, the first "Obligation," [or] more exactly, the first "Contract." The man who enters the Struggle imperils the life of his adversary, but by this very fact he begins to imperil his own life. It is this *equality* of conditions which realizes and reveals the Justice aspect—the juridical side—of the Struggle, and of anthropogenesis in general—that is, of specifically human existence itself. From the aristocratic point of view, i.e., for the Master, an interaction can only be truly human, i.e., just and consequently juridically valid, provided that the two co-agents find themselves in the same situation, in equal conditions. A Contract, and an Obligation in general, therefore, can only take place between *equals,* and the one who is bound must find himself, at the moment when he contracts the obligation, in the same general situation as the one to whom a duty is owed. Now this "aristocratic" aspect of Obligation is encountered in the synthetic *Droit* of Obligations, i.e., in all real *Droit,* and in particular in modern *Droit.* Here as well the co-agents of an obligation are supposed to be equal at the moment of the birth [558] of the obligation, and to find themselves in the same general situation. An obligation which necessarily presupposes an inequality of the situations of the co-agents is juridically "nil"—that is, it does not exist as an Obligation properly so-called. Thus, for example, if A does violence to B, B is no longer in the same situation as A; the "obligation" that B contracts toward A in this situation is "nil." Likewise, [the same situation occurs] if A is in a state of ignorance [*d'erreur*] while B acts with full knowledge of the facts—and so on.[177] This is why the incapable [person] cannot bind himself to the extent that he is incapable—that is, supposed to find himself in a general situation different from that of the co-agent enjoying the plenitude of *droits.*[178]

It should be understood that the Struggle is an "obligation" only in the very broad sense of the word. This "obligation," while having a juridical aspect (cf. the *Droit* of war), has nothing to do with the economic Obligation we are studying. At the very most, it is one of the distant sources of these Obligations properly so-called. And in general, the aristocratic *Droit* of equality only intervenes as such a distant source in the *Droit* of Obligations. The same thus applies to the fundamental principle of aristocratic Justice and *Droit*—that is, of the ideal of equality with oneself, which is expressed, among other ways, by the fundamental aristocratic duty of keeping one's promise. The Master is sup-

---

177. Moreover, violence, ignorance, and so on, annul the obligation because it must be an inter-action—that is, an action properly so-called, [and] therefore a conscious and voluntary action.

178. But being "eternal," *Droit* is related to the whole life of the individual. An incapable [person] can therefore bind himself to the extent that he is supposed to become "capable" subsequently in his life. Taken as a whole, the situation of the adult [*majeur*] (who has been a minor) is equal to that of the minor (who will be an adult).

posed to be faithful to the "sworn oath" because he is supposed to remain a Master—that is, to be kept in identity with himself despite variations of the *hic et nunc*. If he has given "his word" at a given moment and in given circumstances, he must keep it at all times and in all circumstances: if not, he depends upon the natural *hic et nunc*, [and] he is not truly human—that is, he is not genuinely a Master. Now the "sworn oath" is one of the sources of Obligation, and in particular of Contract properly so-called. If it is not a sufficient condition, at least it is necessary for all contract. However, to the extent that Contract is a phenomenon of *private Droit*, it is only related to a given [*déterminée*] interaction between two [559] specific members, A and B, of economic Society. In order to observe a contract, therefore, it is not a matter of maintaining the identity of A and B taken as any given members, nor even the identity of A and B taken as A and B. It is enough that A remains identical to himself in his relation of obligation with B, and conversely. If A (or B) maintains this identity, B (or A) cannot annul it: he should also remain identical to himself in his relation of obligation with A (or B).[179] When the Third intervenes in an Obligation, it is also the principle of equality (or equivalence) with himself that inspires him: he often intervenes in order to force someone to keep his promise, in order to sanction the "sworn oath." But in the real synthetic *Droit* of Obligations, this "identity" is only one of the elements at issue, and it can be mitigated by others (for example, if the contract is revealed as too burdensome for one of the parties—that is, if it is "unjust" from the point of view of the bourgeois Justice of equivalence). Be that as it may, if the identity of A with himself is a "duty," in general or in relation to B, this identity of A is also B's "*droit*": if B acts so that A is kept in identity with himself, and if A reacts against it, the Third will annul this reaction. The upholding of an obligation is therefore a *droit*, a juridical phenomenon.

But the aristocratic "sworn oath" only generates an Obligation properly so-called if it is related to an exchange of property. Now in the *Droit* of aristocratic Society, this exchange can only take place on the basis of equality; but the equality of properties makes all exchange useless (or at the very least, less frequent and not at all necessary). This is why aristocratic Society is not familiar with, so to speak, the *Droit* of obligations. In the Potlatch, however, one of the distant sources of Contract has been discovered.[180] Now, the Potlatch is very much an aristocratic phenomenon (to the extent that a real Society can be so [i.e., aristocratic]). The

---

179. In the bourgeois *Droit* of obligations, this principle of *identity* with oneself is replaced by that of the *equivalence* of the new attitude with the previous one, and with that of the co-agent. This is why bourgeois obligation (contract, for example) is a lot more flexible than aristocratic obligation. The Aristocrat "keeps his word" in all cases; the Bourgeois can alter his engagements according to his circumstances, provided that the altered obligation is equivalent to the previous one and remains equivalent to that of his partner. The "formalism" of the *Droit* of obligations is an element of aristocratic *Droit*: the "form" [*formule*] frees the obligation from the *hic et nunc* and makes it immutable.

180. Cf. [Georges] Davy, *La Foi Jurée* [(Paris: Librairie Félix Alcan, 1922), reprinted by Arno Press, New York, 1975].

Potlatch is a [560] Gift. Now in aristocratic Society, the Gift only makes sense if it is supposed to establish or reestablish equality between the donor and the donee. To give something to someone, therefore, is to assume or give the impression that one is superior to the one to whom one gives. It is therefore to admit implicitly that he is not a Master in the proper sense of the word, seeing that all genuine Masters are supposed to be equal. The one who has received the Gift must therefore repay it in order to demonstrate his Mastery—that is, his humanity.[181] Thus, the Potlatch is in fact an exchange of property of a contractual type; and this is why one sees there the (aristocratic) origin of (bourgeois) commerce and the (bourgeois, or indeed synthetic) *Droit* of obligations. But the Potlatch properly so-called is not yet a juridical phenomenon, seeing that it does not give rise to the intervention of a Third. At the very most, it is a "source" of the *Droit* of obligations, and a rather distant source. The fact nonetheless remains that the principle of the Potlatch, i.e., equality, is an integral element (albeit secondary) of the real synthetic *Droit* of obligations. An obligation can be juridically "nil" if it ends up in too great an inequality between the bound parties.

Just like Contract or aristocratic pseudo-contract, aristocratic Delict is also based upon the principle of equality. If A, by his action toward B, destroyed the equality between himself and B (by "decreasing" B), he is supposed to have to reestablish it. Likewise, if the interaction between A and B has "decreased" A, it is B who must reestablish the destroyed equality. In the two cases, there is a delictual obligation. And it should be understood that for there to be (civil) Delict properly so-called, equality must only intervene as a relation between A and B, and not relative to "any given" member (in which case there would be crime and not wrong). Now in truly aristocratic Society, any given members are supposed to be equal. By destroying his equality with B, A therefore destroys his equality with any given member. This is why in aristocratic Society, there are no genuine civil Wrongs, all "wrong" being in reality a crime.[182] The equalizing delictual Obligation [561] only becomes a straightforward case of civil *Droit* when it is a matter of reestablishing the equality destroyed between A and B taken in their specificity—that is, when the equality of any given members is no longer postulated. But in this case, Society is bourgeois;

---

181. To refuse the Gift is either to offend the donor, by making him understand that one has more than him, or to be humiliated, by showing that one is not capable of reciprocating the gift, which is needed for consumption.

182. Of course, in archaic *Droit*, the person injured must "provoke" the Third. But it does not follow that this is a case of civil *Droit*. The person injured acts in the capacity of any given member, as "prosecutor," by reporting the crime (which—by chance—concerns him). The distinction between a "provoked" and "spontaneous" intervention of the Third only makes sense when the latter exists. Now it generally does not exist in archaic *Droit*. [561] But to the extent that the *Droit* of lex talionis is a civil *Droit*, and when equality is replaced by equivalence—by the practice of *Wergild*—one can say that it is a matter of the *Droit* of Obligations. It has even been said that the credit extended by the family of the murder victim to the family of the murderer concerning the payment of *Wergild* is one of the sources of Contract. At any rate, *Wergild* can be likened to the compensatory damages paid following a civil Wrong.

it is based upon the principle of equivalence and not upon that of equality. And in this Society Obligation itself will be based upon the principle of equivalence, and the Delict will arise from an elimination of the equivalence between A and B, and not their equality. But the fact nonetheless remains that the real synthetic *Droit* of obligations also draws inspiration from, in certain cases or aspects, the aristocratic principle of equality, both when it is a matter of Contract and when it is a question of Delict.

But once again, the *Droit* of obligations is essentially a bourgeois *Droit*, not a *Droit* of the citizen with a predominance of the bourgeois element: it has for a principal base the Justice of equivalence and not that of equality. This *Droit* is a *Droit* of the Exchange of property, and Exchange presupposes in fact the inequality of owners, just as a Property generated by Work—that is, specified by the latter. Not being enough for all the needs of the owner, this property moves him to Exchange. Now Property [that is] unequal and based upon Work is an essentially bourgeois phenomenon, which naturally adapts itself to the Justice of equivalence and thus generates a *Droit* of obligations based upon this principle.

Property based upon Work is supposed to be a benefit equivalent to the burden of the effort which produced it. To work—to make an effort—is thus to give oneself a "receivable" [*se constituer une "créance"*]. If A worked for B, their situation can only become equivalent if B provides A an equivalent property for his effort: ultimately, a given sum of money. One can therefore see in the work provided one of the direct principal sources of Obligation, namely Contract.[183] One could say that the "first" [562] genuine Contract was a labor contract, setting down a salary: having worked for B, B ought to pay A the equivalent of the work provided; having provided B a Property, B ought to work for A or provide him an equivalent of work which corresponds to the property received. In the latter case, B will have exchanged his property for A's property. And if A and B themselves produce their properties by their work, a partial exchange of their properties will sooner or later be necessary for them. This Exchange of Property can be considered as the second direct principal source of Obligation, notably of Contract properly so-called (barter, sale, and so on). [Because] Exchange in the final analysis presupposes Work, the equivalence of properties exchanged in the obligation will be, on the one hand, determined by the work necessary for their production: A's property will be equivalent to B's if the work provided by A to produce his property is equivalent to the work required from B for his property. But Obligation also presupposes Exchange, either of one work for another work, or of work for a property, or finally of two properties. The exchange value of what is exchanged will also have to be taken into consideration when the Third determines the equivalence in an Obliga-

---

183. If A provides his work to any given member, i.e., to Society as such, there is also an "obligation" for Society to pay him. But this is then a case, if you will, of penal *Droit*. In any case, in (civil) Obligation properly so-called, A provides his work for the benefit of [562] B, taken in his specificity, in his *hic et nunc*. This is why the obligation is established between A and B's "private property."

tion. Now this "exchange value" is determined by the law of supply and demand—that is, by the respective scarcity of the exchanged entities. The global value is established by the quantity of work invested and by the exchange value. And the equivalence of two values is ultimately expressed by the equality of their price in money. The entities exchanged in an Obligation, therefore, must have the same price.[184]

Generally speaking, contractual obligation is juridically valid (not "nil") only if there is equivalence between the obligations of those bound. The Third (of the bourgeois *Droit* of Obligations) will only intervene when B requires from A the economic equivalence [563] of what he provided A. If this equivalence does not take place, the Obligation is "illicit," or indeed "nil"—that is, non-existent as juridical obligation. Thus, A can require nothing from B if he has provided him nothing, and he cannot knowingly require more than the equivalent of what he has provided, from whence comes the prohibition on "unjust enrichment." If making an effort gives [one] the *droit* to obtain an equivalent, the obtaining of something without an equivalent effort is a wrong. The Third will therefore annul this wrong by eliminating the obtaining and reestablishing the equivalence of conditions by the restitution of the equivalence between the burdens and benefits. Unjust enrichment is a genre of Wrong where A enriches himself at the expense of B without having made an equivalent effort. The Third eliminates the injustice by reestablishing the equivalence of burdens and benefits of A and B. As for Delict properly so-called, it will take place when A's conduct is going to provoke burdens in B, without B being able to have real or possible benefits as a result of A's very conduct. In other words, Delict will exist when there is no Contract between A and B—that is, when A and B are not supposed to be interacting. If this interaction nevertheless takes place, and if as a result of this "illegal" interaction B has burdens, the interaction will be annulled by the Third through A paying B compensatory damages equivalent to his burdens. By contrast, if the "illegal" interaction (in the non-contractual sense) between A and B, where A is alone in acting in the proper sense of the word, results in a benefit for B, the interaction will be annulled by the Third, who will remove from B the benefits obtained without effort (without genuine action on his part) and which constitute an "unjust enrichment."

But in all these cases, it is a matter of *civil Droit*—that is, relations between A and B taken in their specificity. It is between A and B that there is or is not

---

184. The *equality* of price is not an *equality* properly so-called but an *equivalence;* for the price implies the "exchange value," which does not establish equality but—in principle—the economic equivalence of two entities: property or work. A's work may be less than B's work; their products will have the same price, i.e., will be economically equivalent, if the exchange value of A's product is superior to that of B's product. Thus, for example, cash can have an exchange value greater than a product or productive work. There will still be economic equivalence, and the Obligation will be "just" from the point of view of bourgeois *Droit;* however, there is no equality, such that for aristocratic *Droit,* the Obligation will be "unjust," or indeed "nil."

equivalence, and not between any given members. Consequently, it is for A
and B to notice if an absence of equivalence takes place, and to demonstrate
this to the Third. When neither A nor B happens to "provoke" the Third, he
does not intervene: the silence of the interested parties is a proof of the existence of equivalence in their relation of obligation; and where B does not
protest, there is no wrong of A against B. This is why A may make a free gift to
B; in this case, one says that A gains a "moral" benefit from the gift. But the
Third does not have to worry about that. Seeing that A and B do not "provoke"
the Third in the event of A making a gift to B, there is by definition economic
equivalence [564] between the act of giving and that of receiving, even if this
equivalence remains hidden, inaccessible to the thirds, and in particular to the
Third of the *Droit* of Obligations.

All *Droit* of Obligations of economic Society deals with two fundamental
types of Obligations: *Contract* and *Delict.*

Contract exists when there is an inter-*action* properly so-called between A
and B—that is, when A acts with a view to B's reaction, and B with a view to
A's reaction. Now the genuine action is conscious and voluntary. This is why
one says that in a Contract there is an "agreement of two wills." But the "wills,"
i.e., the wills to act, and the intentions only intervene here to the extent that
they determine the acts and are actualized in and by these acts. Contract is an
actual inter-action; these are two (conscious and voluntary) *acts* which mutually condition one another; and they are supposed to be equal or equivalent. In
quasi-contract, it is true, the action seems to be unilateral. When A makes a gift
to B, or when A manages B's affairs without a mandate on his part, it seems
that there is no action of B—that is, no inter-action. But this is only an illusion. In the case of the gift, the quasi-contract only exists starting from the
moment B accepted the gift, and this acceptance is a conscious and voluntary
action (a reaction). And if B can resort to the Third in order to obtain the gift
promised but still not delivered, it is because he is supposed to have accepted
it at the very moment when it had been promised. Therefore, there has been
an inter-action, or an agreement of two wills determining two acts. And in the
case of management [of B's affairs by A], B is also supposed to have accepted
it at the moment when it was taking place. Now, to accept it is to conclude a
contract and to acknowledge by this very fact the principle of equivalence (or
equality), from whence comes B's obligation to pay A an equivalent of the
effort made and the result obtained by this effort. If not, there would be an
unjust enrichment by A—that is, a sort of wrong toward B, and consequently
an obligation to annul it by a payment of equivalent compensatory damages.
Because it is a matter of contract or quasi-contract, there is always then an
inter-action properly so-called between A and B, the act of interaction being
intentional and voluntary both with A and B.

By contrast, when there is a *Delict* of A toward B, there is very much a genuine action on the part of A, i.e., a conscious (or intentional) and voluntary act,
but B neither acts nor reacts in the proper sense of the word: he remains purely
passive. A throws a rock, for example; B is stuck with possessing a [565] win-

dow broken by this rock. Now, if A's action causes a burden to B, this burden cannot be compensated for by a benefit to B, seeing that he does not act—that is, does not consciously and voluntarily participate in A's action. By this event, B finds himself in an "unjust" situation, for the sum of his burdens now exceeds the sum of his benefits (by assuming, as one must do, that these sums were equivalent before A's action). One must therefore compensate for the resulting burden caused [by A] by an equivalent benefit. In our example, one must pay B for his broken window. Now it is not any given member who has caused the burden, but A. It is up to A, therefore, to fix it, and not to any given member— that is, to Society. Of course, A did not want to break the window, to cause B damage; but he did want to act as he did, and he acted in his specificity, in his *hic et nunc*. It is therefore up to him, in his specificity, in his *hic et nunc*, to fix the damage; for if he acted voluntarily in this fashion, it is because he gained, or thought he could gain, a benefit from his act, a benefit for him in his specificity. A (real or expected) benefit for A is therefore set against a burden for B. In order to reestablish the equivalence, A must compensate for the resultant. The "theory of strict liability [*risque*]," therefore, is right to eliminate all elements of "fault" from the notion of Delict. It is enough that A has acted in the proper sense of the term—that is, performed a voluntary and (conscious) intentional act. If not, there would be no Delict, no Obligation: for example, a case of "necessity." If A has *acted,* and if a consequence of his act (foreseen or not, wanted or not) harmed others, A is bound toward the injured person; if he harmed [someone] without *acting,* he is not responsible (even if he foresaw the injury and wanted to harm [the other person]). Thus, for example, if A has typhus and infects B by the sole fact that he coexists with him, he is not bound toward B. But if A has a venereal disease and infects B by performing a (voluntary and conscious) sexual *act,* he is responsible and owes compensatory damages (supposing that B did not consent to a sexual interaction with a *diseased* A). Of course, in practice it is often difficult to know if there has been a genuine *action* of A, or a case of "necessity," a consequence of the sole fact of A's passive existence. And this is why the Third can speak of "fault," "negligence," and so on; for when there has been "fault," and so on, there certainly has been an *action* properly so-called, and consequently an obligation (in the case of the injury of others). What matters is not the "fault" or "negligence," but solely the [566] fact of the *action.* For the same reason, one can distinguish between wrong properly so-called, when there is a will to harm, and the quasi-wrong, when this will is presumed to be lacking: for when there has been a will to harm, there has certainly been a *will* to act—that is, an action properly so-called, an intentional and voluntary act. But here as well, it is not the will to *harm* that matters, but solely the *will* as such. Whether A wanted to break B's window or whether he did so "by chance," the obligation will be the same: it is to pay for the broken window. In the first case, however, it will not be a question of "necessity," while in the second case, this question will have to be raised.

Generally speaking, Delict is a de facto interaction between A and B, when A alone genuinely acts, [and] B remains passive, limiting himself to existing. If this interaction (forcible from B's point of view) does not destroy B's equivalence, nor that between A and B, the Third's intervention does not take place, and there is no Delict, no Obligation. If so, the Third will intervene in order to reestablish the equivalence (or equality), either by making A pay, if B has been injured, or by making B pay, if he has been enriched "unjustly" by the (unwanted) interaction with A. At any rate, the interaction (unilateral as regards the will) only takes place between A and B, taken in their specificity. It is very much then a case of civil *Droit*.

One can say, if you will, that Contract is a *Droit* of function, while Delict is a *Droit* of status. Indeed, for there to be a contractual obligation between A and B, the two must *act* in the proper sense of the term, or in any case, have the intention to act or want to act. But in order to benefit from a delictual obligation, B does not need to act: it is enough for him to exist, to realize passively by his very being a certain status, which guarantees to him among other things his equivalence (or equality) with A. But taken as a whole, the *Droit* of Obligations is nevertheless a *Droit* of function, in contrast to the *Droit* of property, which is a *Droit* of status: for there even to be Delict, there must be an action properly so-called from the side of the one who delictually binds himself. Simple, purely passive coexistence cannot generate any Obligation, while [it may] create Property relations.

One can say that A's delict in respect to B is the manifestation of a conflict between A's action (or function) and B's status. Now, one can wonder if, in order to be bound in delict, A must not accept or recognize beforehand B's status (as well his own status in its relations with that of B, A's status also being [567] recognized by B). Now this reciprocal recognition could be interpreted as a sort of Contract between A and B. The Delict, which presupposes a status, would therefore presuppose a Contract, for all Status is supposed to arise from a Contract. This is the theory of the "social Contract," which will now be briefly discussed.

Seeing that Obligation is a *civil* phenomenon, it is not based upon a contract between A and *any given* member of (economic) Society; for, by definition, the wrongful action does not at all affect this member: it only injures B taken in his specificity. But A could conclude a contract with any given member (i.e., with Society as such), by which he would promise to respect the equivalence (or equality) of conditions of all the members taken in their specificity—that is, in particular that of B. If A has the will or only the intention of not keeping this commitment toward any given member, i.e., of injuring any member whatsoever of the Society, he commits a crime and falls into the grip of penal *Droit*. But if A maintains this general commitment and only injures B, taken in his specificity, it is a case of civil *Droit*, of an Obligation toward B. By performing this Obligation, by paying the compensatory damages in question, A performs his contract with any given member: he is therefore in agreement with penal *Droit*. And if he annuls the wrongful act by the payment of damages, he will also be in agreement with civil *Droit*.

But is it really true that there is such a "social Contract"? Can one say that there is a *Contract* between a specific member of the Society and this Society itself, i.e., its any given member, in which the contracting parties accept certain burdens equivalent to a certain benefit—for example, A promising to respect B's status because B respects his own, making efforts to support the Society in order that it supports and protects him, and so on? One could, it seems, assert this when A's membership to a given (economic) Society is the result of an action properly so-called on his part, when A consciously and voluntarily joins the Society, being able not to do so. But when A is part of the Society as a result of his existence alone—by the fact of his birth, for example— the notion of Contract seems inapplicable. It is more a matter of a Status connected to the very being of the interested party and not to his action, to the "function" of this being. There are then Statuses independent of all Contract, but all Contract presupposes one Status or another—to say [568] the very least, the one which makes the contracting parties subjects of *droit*, juridical persons.

There are collectivities, or indeed "Societies," formed by a free agreement of their members. One says that these Societies are based upon a Contract, upon a "social Contract," if you will. But German authors[185] have rightly insisted upon the difference between such a "social Contract," which they call *Vereinbarung* (i.e., Convention), and Contract properly so-called (*Vertrag*). In a Contract there is an inter-action between A and B, while the Convention aims at the creation of a common action of A and B, of an "agreement of wills" with a view to an interaction (contractual, for example) between the collectivity (A plus B) and another (individual or collective) agent C.[186] The Convention creates the collectivity in its *being*, and it creates it as a juridical person if the Convention is recognized by the Third. As for Contract, it is the *function* or *action* of the collectivity created by the Convention. One can thus say that in and by the Convention the members (consciously and voluntarily) recognize their collective *status*, the status of each of them in their relations with the statuses of the other members.

The "social Contract," therefore, can only be a Convention in the sense indicated: it is not a Contract properly so-called. One cannot therefore say that all Delict presupposes a Contract. One must say that all Obligation, wrongful or contractual, presupposes a juridical status, which is the manifestation or result of a Convention. (As for Delict, it is independent of all Contract: on the contrary, there is only Delict properly so-called by A in respect to B to the extent that there is no Contract between A and B.) The big question is knowing if all Status (and therefore all Obligation) necessarily presupposes a Convention in the proper sense of the term. And this is the problem of the "social Contract."

---

185. Notably [Georg] Jellinek. Cf. Sternberg, *Allgemeine Rechtslehre*, vol. II, 38.

186. The "collective contract" does not essentially differ from an individual contract: the contract between A and B remains the same if A and B are individuals or collectivities. In the latter case, there have been prior *Conventions* between the members of A (and B). But this Convention being given, A is comparable to an individual: it is a (moral collective) juridical person, which is capable, among other things, of concluding Contracts, or indeed of committing Delicts (and even crimes, although the latter point is not universally accepted—wrongly, it seems).

There is a genuine Convention only when the status of the members of the Society is consciously and freely (voluntarily [569]) accepted by them—that is, when they would have been able not to accept it and when they can, having accepted it, relinquish it again (under certain conditions). This is the case of "Societies," i.e., of collectivities of civil *Droit* (and it is Conventions which form them, which are comparable to Contracts and are part of the *Droit* of Obligations): no one at all is forced to belong from the sole fact of his existence (from birth, for example), and every member can leave the collectivity when he sees fit. This is because he takes part only in his specificity, and not as any given member of the (economic) Society properly so-called—that is, global.[187] But if the Society is autonomous, its members belong to it according to their *being*, and they cannot leave it as a result of an *action*—that is, a will. In this case, therefore, it makes no sense to speak of a Convention, and still less of a "social *Contract*." There is a Status which is connected to the very being of the members and which does not depend upon their actions, their will, their recognition of status. Now, when belonging to Society is optional, the *Droit* of this Society only exists in potentiality. On the contrary, far from founding an *actual Droit*, Convention excludes it. *Droit* exists *in actuality* only when there is no Convention, when the Status is connected to the being and not the will or the action. But *Droit in potentiality* ultimately presupposes a Convention (at least a Convention of the members of the exclusive juridical group). And since actual *Droit* actualizes virtual *Droit*, all *Droit* presupposes a Convention in the final analysis (forming a collectivity that realizes the *Droit* in question). In order to be actualized, therefore, *Droit* transforms the Convention, or if you will, the "Contract," into Status. The juridical evolution is here going from Contract to Status, and not from Status to Contract, as Sumner Maine wanted. But this Status is a status of [570] *any given* member of (economic) Society.[188] It does not therefore affect the specific member in his

---

187. A cannot break the Convention by a unilateral act of will: he cannot leave the collectivity as its member, but he can leave it as (any given) member of the global economic Society. As member of the Collectivity, i.e., in his specificity as a member of a given collectivity, A is therefore distinct from himself taken as any given member of the economic Society— that is, he only takes part in the collectivity by a "severable membership," i.e., by a property, and ultimately by the presumed equivalent of a property. He cannot then remove his property entered in a collectivity by a convention. But "he himself," i.e., himself as member of the global economic Society, can remove himself from the collectivity. And this is why the collectivity is "conventional," or if you will, "contractual": a collectivity of private civil *Droit*.

188. In fact, economic Society only becomes obligatory for its members to the extent that it is state-sanctioned: [and] this is because the member of the Society is a citizen of a (national) State who cannot leave it as he pleases. This has nothing juridical about it. But the Third does not have to worry about it. What matters for him is that he is dealing with a Status and not a Convention (Contract). If the contract between A and B is contrary to the status of A and B, it is nil; if A's action is contrary to B's status, it is a wrong. The origin of the status does not interest the Third. He knows that his intervention, based upon this status, is "irresistible"—that is all. Moreover, the relation between the Third and his litigants has nothing juridical about it by definition, seeing that there is no other "Third" in the interaction between the Third and his litigants.

specificity. He can therefore conclude a Contract with another specific member to the extent that the Contract is compatible with the Status. This Contract will be a Contract of civil *Droit*. Now any given member may more or less coincide with the specific member. In other words, (inherited) Status can leave a more or less wide margin for (voluntary) Contract: the being of a member of the Society may more or less determine his action. Now historical evolution increased this margin more and more; and this is what Sumner Maine had in mind. "Social Contract" (i.e., the acceptance of a common Enemy and the recognition of an Authority), or more exactly social Convention, yielded the place to a (social) Status; but this Status determines less and less the specific member. (Practically speaking, the activities of individuals become less and less inherited.) This means that the sphere of civil Contract becomes more and more extended (and it is of little importance that there is a tendency to become *collective* instead of being *individual*). But if Status leaves the field free to the *activity* of the specific member, it continues to govern his passive *being*, from whence comes the existence of wrongful Obligation: the *action* of a specific member is a Delict if it is contrary to the status of the *being* of another specific member. It all boils down, therefore, to knowing what is part of the *being* of the specific member and what is a function of his *action*. Now the preservation of life is part of the being. Status can therefore guarantee to the specific member the preservation of his life—that is, for example, the work necessary to this preservation, from whence comes a "*droit to work*." And to the extent that work is supposed to preserve life—the very being of the worker—it is implied in his status, from whence comes a "labor Code," and so on. It could therefore seem that the (recent) evolution is again going from Contract to Status. But to [571] the extent that the kind [*mode*] of work is not *hereditary*, there is a labor *contract* (collective or not), and not a *status* properly so-called.[189] However, this contract (like all contract) must be in agreement with status, from whence comes *prescribed* types of contracts (like "marriage contracts," for example). But these are nevertheless types of *contracts*. However, to the extent that action (contractual or not) is at odds with being (determined by status), it is wrongful. And if it is at odds with the being of *any given* member of the Society, it is even criminal, from whence comes a semblance of the predominance of status over contract.[190]

---

189. This is the difference between a socialist Society and the late Roman Empire, for example, where professions were *hereditary*.

190. In a *homogenous* Society (i.e., socialist), the specificity of the members is diminished, seeing their real equality. This is why civil Contract between specific members tends to coincide with relations between any given members, based upon their status. In this sense, one can say that Socialism replaces (civil) Contract with a Status. But this is not because the socialist *Droit* (of the Citizen) is contrary to Contract; it is simply because the homogenous Society, like all aristocratic Society, makes the majority of contracts of bourgeois Society useless: equals have few things to exchange, whereas Obligation presupposes exchange. But the principle of Contract is preserved in the sense that all the specificity of the members tends to become contractual and not status-like (i.e., hereditary). See § 70.

To summarize, one can say that the *Droit* of Obligations of bourgeois economic Society comprises Conventions, Contracts, and Delicts. There is Convention (*Vereinbarung*) when A freely promises, and with full knowledge of the facts, to conform to a specific status that he has in common with the other members of the collectivity based upon the Convention in question. This conventional status only affects the specific member A of economic Society—that is, he is related to (a part of) his property that can be converted into money. But this specificity is set down by the status, and the Third can intervene in order to force A to respect it. *Convention* is an agreement with a view to a common action. As for *Contract* properly so-called, it is an inter-action between two specific members (individual or collective) A and B. Finally, *Wrong* is a unilateral action by A which affects B in his specificity. If this action injures B, it is a *Wrong* by A in the narrow sense of the term. If it brings B a benefit, there is an *unjust Enrichment* by B—that is, a sort of Wrong by B. One can therefore say that civil Wrong in the broad sense (in line with Contract and Convention) is either a Wrong in the proper sense, or an unjust Enrichment.

[572] In all these cases, it is a matter of *civil Droit*, i.e., of relations between members of economic Society taken in their specificity, which does not affect any given member—that is, the Society itself. This is why all Obligations (conventional, contractual, or wrongful) must be in agreement with the Status of any given member—that is, be carried out in the margin left free by this status. On the other hand, Obligations, in order to have a juridical existence, i.e., in order to have genuine Obligations, must be conforming to the principle of Justice acknowledged by the (economic) Society where they take place—that is, in bourgeois Society, to the principle of equivalence, namely the equivalence between specific members taken in their specificity, or once again, the equivalence between the specific "*droits*" and the specific "duties" in the one who contracts one Obligation or another. The benefits that A gains (or believes to be able to gain) from his action must be equivalent to the burdens caused by this very action. In the case of an interaction (mutually consented or unilaterally imposed), this is only so when there is an equivalence between the benefits and burdens of A, on the one hand, and those of B, on the other. The Third will only intervene in the Obligation in order to establish, maintain, or reestablish such an equivalence between two specific members to the extent that the equivalence is a function of Obligation.

It is from this general notion of the equivalence between specific members that all bourgeois *Droit* of Obligations can be deduced. Any Obligation whatsoever is supposed to establish, maintain, or reestablish a specific, particular equivalence between two members of economic Society. This equivalence being *specific*, it can be alienated from the (postulated) general equivalence of any given members. This means that it is a matter of equivalence between private properties that can be converted into money (the word property being taken in its broadest sense). It is solely this property which is affected by the Obligation.

This general principle allows one to solve the problem of *the transfer of Obligations*. To the extent that A's specificity, affected by the Obligation, passes to another member B of economic Society, B is bound by the Obligation in question. But B can only be bound by A's Obligation if he accepts the specificity of A at issue. Practically speaking, since the specificity in question is realized and revealed in the form of a property that can be converted into money, B is only [573] bound to the extent that he accepts A's property—or at least the part affected by the Obligation. Thus, by refusing the inheritance, the heir (testamentary or *ab intestat*) is freed from the Obligation. But if B accepts A's specificity, even if A's property is insufficient to pay the Obligation, B has accepted the latter and is responsible in his own specificity, i.e., with all his property; for his specificity (property) then implies that of A.

As for *the prescription of Obligations,* it is also based upon the principle of equivalence. Either one can say that by the sole fact of the length of the Obligation the equivalence between A and B has been reestablished without A or B having to do something in conformity to the Obligation; or one can admit that if B has not "provoked" the Third because of the non-performance of A's Obligation, this is because his situation has been equivalent to that of A without A having needed to do something—that is, to perform the Obligation. In other words, Obligation is juridically non-existent or nil seeing that there has not been the elimination of equivalence. The idea is basically the following. Society is supposed to be based upon the equivalence of its members. If it functions normally, it is because this equivalence exists. Therefore, if an Obligation has been able not to have been performed, without social life being disturbed, it is because it was useless, equivalence having existed without it. This means that it is "nil," that it does not exist juridically. It is juridically nil because it cannot be justified from the point of view of the Justice of equivalence.

The question of *the capacity for an Obligation* remains. Seeing that Obligations are related to the *specificity* of the member of economic Society, the capacity in question is nothing other than the capacity of this specificity. No one can be bound other than the one who can be a *specific* member of economic Society, and only to the extent that he can be so. Now, ultimately, the specificity of economic Society is expressed by private property—that is, alienable from the owner while being his exclusive property. In order to be able to be bound, one must be able to be an Owner, on the one hand, and one must be able to alienate one's Property, on the other. It can therefore also be said that the capacity for Obligation is a capacity for the Exchange of property—that is, for economic action properly so-called. It can depend upon age, sex, the state of (physical or moral) health, and so on.

There is then an aristocratic *Droit* of Obligations based upon the principle of equality between the specific members of [574] economic Society, and a bourgeois *Droit* of Obligations based upon the principle of the equivalence of these members. But these two *Droits* never exist in a pure state. All real *Droit* of Obligations is a synthetic *Droit,* a *Droit* of the Citizen based upon the principle of equity, which synthesizes equality and equivalence—not only in the sense that in all real *Droit* there are egalitarian Obligations alongside Obligations of equivalence, but also because in all real Obligation there is an aspect of equality and an aspect of equivalence. All real Obligation is an Obligation of equity. In every Obligation there is an egalitarian, or indeed aristocratic, aspect: the equality of conditions from the start, the identity with oneself (the "sworn oath"), the principle of the Potlatch; and there is also an aspect of equivalence: the equivalence between benefits and burdens of each one, the equivalence of benefits and burdens of one and the other, the equivalence of exchanged properties (the equivalence of work and the product, of price and the merchandise, and so on). Now, in this coexistence, in this synthesis of the two principles, the one is always tempered by the other: equality must put up with equivalence, and equivalence with equality. And before becoming perfect, i.e., immutable or "absolute," the synthesis implies a greater or lesser predominance of one of the two principles, from whence comes a practically infinite diversity of the *Droit* of Obligations, of which the ones are rather "bourgeois" and the other "aristocratic." The predominance of one of the two principles provokes a reaction from the other, which—by becoming predominate—provokes in its turn the reaction of the first. And this dialectic persists until the perfect equilibrium, i.e., stable and definitive, [is] realized in the "absolute" *Droit* of Obligations, which is the *Droit* of the economic Society of the universal and homogenous State of the future (which may never be realized, given the finitude of human existence).[191]

It not a question of analyzing here the various possibilities of synthesis in the *Droit* of economic Society, in particular in that of Obligation. In order to determine this, I will only say a few words about "absolute" economic *Droit*— that is, the *Droit* of the economic Society of the universal and homogenous State.

§ 70

[575] Economic Society is a Society of Owners who enter into interactions as Owners. Therefore, if in the universal and homogenous State, i.e., in the socialist Empire, there are no longer Owners, there will no longer be an economic Society distinct from the State (or from political Society), and consequently no *Droit* of the economic Society—in particular, no *Droit* of Property and Obligations.[192] Now, for there no longer to be Owners, man (the individual) must cease to be the very owner of his own body.[193] In other words, the citizen of the Empire will be comparable to the Slave in aristocratic Society. He

---

191. An entity which is *never* realized is impossible. A thing which is necessarily realized during an infinite time is possible. But it may only remain possible during a finite time, if it is not realized during this time.

192. If the Family is preserved, there will be a civil *Droit*, if only the *Droit* of familial Society.

193. If one realizes—by some remote chance—a *strict* equality of all citizens of the Empire, the notion of Property will no longer make sense, even concerning the body itself. If all are truly equal, the difference between mine and yours is empty of content, [and] it is purely "formal": it is therefore without actual reality. But in fact, absolute equality is impossible, seeing that every real entity *differs* from all the others, if only by its *hic et nunc*.

will differ from the Slave, however, seeing that he does not have a Master, his "Master" being the State, i.e., himself as well, since the State is universal and homogenous, since it implies all and each one, and each one in the same way as all the others. One can also say that the specific member of the Society will be the "Slave" of any given member—that is, of himself as well taken as any given member. At the very least, he will be so economically: his body, with all its belongings, will be "the thing" of any given member—that is, of the State. On the economic plane, then, there will be no human *specificity, recognized* as such, in particular, juridically recognized. There will be no economic *Droit* relating to specificity: there will be no civil *Droit* of the economic Society.

But will it truly be like this?

Of course, one cannot make predictions concerning human reality on account of man's "freedom"—that is, the fact that his being is nothing other than his action, which may or may not take place in a given time, in particular in [576] the time that human history is going to last.[194] But one can assume, or if one prefers, stipulate that the Empire will retain the phenomenon of Property, if only by preserving the idea of property constituted by the owner's own body. Now this is enough for there to be an economic Society distinct from the State, and consequently a *Droit* of this Society, a private economic *Droit* of Property and Obligations.

Indeed, if each one is Owner of his body, he will also be [Owner] of the belongings of the latter, of what is connected to this body, being used to keep it in existence (clothes, food, and so on).[195] Now bodies are necessarily different, as are all spatio-temporal, material entities: they are different by the "this" of their *hic et nunc*. The belongings of the bodies will therefore be different as well: they will be different according to bodily differences—that is, [differences] of "natures," "characters," "tastes," and so on. The body with its belongings constitute the "personal Property" of the individual. And to the extent

---

194. The "possible" is what is *necessarily* realized during an *infinite* time; the "impossible," what will *never* be realized. During (any) finite time at all, an entity can remain in the state of mere "possibility," which means that it is not realized during the given time, but will necessarily be realized in the infinite time taken as a whole. But human reality is essentially *finite*. The notion of the "possible," therefore, does not apply. What is not realized during (finite) History will never be realized, for after the end of History there will no longer be anything human. But one cannot say that this has been "impossible" because it is only during a *finite* time that this was not realized. And one cannot say either that what is realized in this finite time was "possible," since by definition this was not able to use [*disposer*] an infinite time in order to be realized. The human reality, therefore, is not the realization (actualization) of a "possibility" (a "potential"); and the reality which does not presuppose a possibility, the act which does not actualize a potential, is a free reality, an act of freedom, real freedom in actuality. One can only "deduce" human reality afterwards—that is, one can only understand or explain it, but not foresee it. And one understands or explains it by Dialectic, where the Thesis precedes the Antithesis which presupposes it, and where the Synthesis integrates the two after they have been realized.

195. [Because] it is a *human* body, its existence is therefore *human*: clothes must not only be warm, they must be pretty, fashionable, and so on—likewise, the food must be good, and so on.

that this Property is alienable, it will lend itself to Exchange and even require it, seeing that these Properties differ from one another.[196] Now, where there is Property and [577] the possible Exchange of Property, there is a *Droit* of Property and obligations (conventional, contractual, and delictual). Thus, for example, one can join together with several [persons] in order to build a park or garden, or rent antique furniture, or exchange paintings that one has made for sculptures done by another; or once again, one can maim another's body or a possession of his body by an act to which he did not agree.

Personal Property presupposes a specificity which distinguishes one individual from all who are not him: his body. And it implies a possibility of specific relations between the specificities of individuals: interactions between their bodies. Conversely, personal Property (connected to the body) generates specificities—a body clothed differently, fed differently, and so on, than another—and specific relations between these specificities—exchange of clothes, of food, and so on. These specific interactions, being interactions between specificities, do not affect, by definition, the agents taken as "any given members," equal to others. In other words, they do not affect the Society as such, nor consequently the State, the Empire. Economic Society or the State can therefore intervene in the capacity of a disinterested and impartial Third in these specific economic interactions. There will then be an economic (civil) private *Droit*. And this *Droit* will be the *Droit* of an economic Society different from the State, of the Society formed by the Owners acting as Owners—that is, here, in their specificity, as "personal Owners."

It is said that in the socialist Empire all belongs to the State, that it is the only Owner.[197] But this may be false. It is possible that *personal* Property be kept, and that only the non-specific or the non-specified "belongs" to the State (it being understood that it is not its [the State's] Property in the juridical sense of the term). What is related to "any given" citizen taken as such will be the Property of no one. But what is connected to the citizen taken in his *specificity* may very well be his (personal) Property—provided that, of course, this personal Property does not at all affect "any given" citizen, or deprive him of anything above all (and does not enrich him at all). Thus, for example, the "means of production," which are related to "any given" consumer and producer, [578] can be excluded from the *Droit* of property, i.e., "belong" to the State, or indeed to "any given" citizen—that is, also to consumers and producers taken not in their specificity but in what they have in common, universally. But a product connected to a specific body by consumption may be considered as a possession of this body—that is, as a "personal Property" of the individual, of the citizen possessing this body in fact and juridically. The piece of cheese I have already swal-

---

196. Even the body properly so-called is, if you will, alienable: one can sell it after death or while living (it can be sold to a sadist, [577] in order that he kills it in ten years). The function of the body (work, sexuality, and so on) is certainly alienable, as well as all the "belongings."
197. The notion of Property then does not make any sense—in any case, not any juridical sense, seeing that a Third is no longer possible.

lowed is clearly "mine": no one has the *droit* to take it from my stomach. In that case, then, the cheese I have grasped in order to swallow is also "mine"; and the cheese that I have "acquired" in some way or another is equally mine.

Now in the socialist—universal and homogenous—Empire, all are citizens, and all the citizens are strictly equal and equivalent (abstracting from children and the insane: but I am not discussing this difficult question). Citizens as citizens, therefore, do not have any specificity. Specificity shows itself in the Society, or if one prefers, creates this Society: civil Society, the *bürgerliche Gesellschaft.* When specificity is realized and revealed as (personal) Property ([i.e.,] of the body and its belongings), it is a matter of economic Society. Any given member is a personal Owner as such. And all citizens (children and the insane aside) are such an Owner—that is, any given member of economic Society. But in the specificity of his Property, the citizen is a specific member of economic Society to which the private civil *Droit* of this Society is applied, realized by the Society in its capacity as a Third, or by the State in the name of the Society. As for the relation with any given member of economic Society, i.e., as for the private penal *Droit* of this Society, it is the State which realizes it in its capacity as Third in relation to this Society itself.[198]

Let us suppose that a citizen makes paintings.[199] He does this for his pleasure. But he paints too many to keep them all. Now one cannot say that he has worked for any given member of Society, who is required to take them from him; for this member may not like paintings or his [579] paintings. Therefore, he does not work for Society as such, and still less for the State. The State does not have to acquire his paintings. But it is possible that another member of Society—as a result of his specificity or "taste"—wants to acquire his painting by exchanging it for an alienable, personal property—that is, for money, his money. Why would he not be able to do it? Now, with a view to this possible client, Society (or the "State," if one prefers) can take the paintings that the painter wants to exchange in trust, and give them to the client while handing over the price to the painter. The Society will thus serve as a simple agent (paid by a levy on the price paid for the painting). And the case can be generalized. Society as a whole (in the person of the Civil Servant) may serve as an intermediary in the exchanges of personal properties of its specific members. There will be a Contract (of sales, lease, and so on) between two specific members, mediated by any given member—that is, by Society as such. And this very Society, being a disinterested Third in the Contract, can play the role of juridical Third and juridically sanction this Contract.

There will then be a totality of economic interactions between the citizens of the Empire taken not as Citizens but as personal Owners, and this totality

---

198. If the specificity of the individual is still realized and revealed by his "kinship," there will be in addition to economic Society a familial Society as well and a private (civil and penal) *Droit* of the Society. But I will not discuss this question here.
199. For simplicity's sake, one can assume that he does it during his leisure hours, after having finished the required work of the citizen.

will constitute economic Society. And to the extent that the members of this Society will act not as (personal) Owners in general, [being] anyone at all, but in their specificity, in the specific nature of the (personal) Property of each one, their interactions, if they provoke the intervention of Society (or the State) in the capacity of juridical Third, they are going to generate and realize a private civil *Droit* of the economic Society—in particular, a *Droit* of Obligations. Let it be understood [that this is only true] to the extent that their interactions do not affect the Citizen of the Empire at all—that is, to the extent that they are compatible with the status of the latter.[200]

Let us not forget, moreover, that the socialist Empire is a *universal* and *homogenous* State: this means, on the one hand, that it has no [580] Enemy, does not make war; on the other hand, because of its homogeneity, there is not in it an exclusive political Group, i.e., relations between Governors and the Governed (although there is a distinction between Administrators and the Administered). In other words, the Empire will be deprived of the two essential characteristics of the State. It will not have, so to speak, any political "interest." It will be "disinterested" in respect to its Citizens. This is why it will be able to continue to play the role of the juridical Third in respect to them. And one can even say that only the Empire will be able to play this role in a truly perfect way, without conflicts between the ideal of Justice and "reason of State." The Citizen of the Empire will not be a Warrior; and he will be neither Governor nor the Governed. He will only be a Citizen in and by his equality and equivalence with others, with *all* the others, all men in general. To be a Citizen, therefore, will be nothing other than being a human being in the full and strong sense of the term. And the Status of the Citizen will be the "status" of the human being as such. The State will have to see to it that this status is maintained.[201] In relation to this Status, the State will not be a Third; but it will be so in relation to all that is not included in this Status. It will therefore be a Third of private *Droit*. And practically speaking, it will be nothing else. It will have to see to it that the *specific* interactions of citizens are compatible with the Status of any given citizen. Now they will be so if they conform to the *Droit* in force. The activity of the universal and homogenous State, therefore, will boil down to a juridical activity. It will not be "interested" in *specific* interactions (economic or familial, for example) between its Citizens; and it will have to see to it that interactions between Citizens preserve this "specific" character—that is, does not affect "any given" Citizen, or indeed the State as such. As for any given citizens and their interactions, the State will not have to intervene there (polit-

---

200. In itself, this (political) Status will have nothing juridical about it; but it receives a juridical character to the extent that one applies public *Droit* to it, in the sense indicated above. Thus, the Status of a citizen can imply, for example, the requirement of working x hours a day according to the instructions of the State (or the economic Society). No Contract will then be able to free someone from this work. But work carried out apart from the required work may be the object of a Contract of private *Droit*.

201. If, for example, the human being can only be realized in and by Work, the State will see to it that all citizens work, under conditions set down by the State.

ically, for here it is no longer disinterested, it is no longer a Third, but a party), for there will not be, in principle, conflict in these interactions: the universality and homogeneity of the Empire being given, the State will find itself neither in the presence of national conflicts (external wars) nor social conflicts (revolutions and civil wars). As long as the Citizen will act in his capacity as Citizen, i.e., as *any given* member of the community, [581] or according to his human being, he will not be able to enter into conflict with another Citizen acting likewise. There will certainly be conflicts between Citizens taken in their specificity—that is, not as Citizens but as (specific) members of the (economic or another) Society. But these conflicts will be resolved by the State acting by way of the Third of the (private) *Droit* of the Society. Therefore, the State will be nothing other than a Judge. But this Judge will be a State, seeing that its intervention will have an irresistible character. In other words, (private) socialist *Droit* will exist *in actuality*. And only the *Droit* of the Empire will be truly actual, seeing that the universality of the Empire alone rules out all possibility of escaping its judgement.

The socialist Empire, therefore, accepts the existence of an economic Society and of a civil and penal (private) *Droit* of this Society existing in actuality—that is, sanctioned by the State acting as Third. And this socialist *Droit* of economic Society will be divided into the *Droit* of property and the *Droit* of obligations.

First, let us see what the **Droit** *of property* can be —that is, the Property recognized by socialist *Droit*.

The State does not have Property in the juridical sense of the word, for there is no Third capable of recognizing and sanctioning its *droits* as Owner. By contrast, Society (notably economic Society) can have a Property juridically recognized by the State in its capacity as Third—that is, if you will, a collective Property. However, the collectivity is here formed by any given members of the economic Society taken as such. The Property of the Society is the Property of its any given member. All attempts to "specify" this Property, all efforts by a specific member to appropriate the Property of the Society, will be annulled by the Third. One will then have a case of penal *Droit* of economic Society. Now any given members being by definition equal (and equivalent), an Exchange of Property between them will not take place. The Property of any given member is therefore unalienable; it does not have any monetary value; and it cannot be the object of an Obligation (conventional, contractual, or wrongful). As for the (specific) Property of a specific member, it is alienable from its owner. It therefore has a monetary value and can be the object of one Obligation or another. It can become collective following a Convention which joins specific members together in their specificity. It can be exchanged as a result [582] of a Contract (sold or rented). Finally, it can be alienated in order to annul a civil Delict, or indeed an unjust Enrichment. But this specific, alienable Property is not a "private Property" in the sense of bourgeois or "capitalist" *Droit*: it is solely a "personal Property," which means that the Property is always connected to the "person" of the Owner—that is, ultimately to (the specificity of) his body, to a "possession" of his body. Of course, a personal Property can be alienated from A's body, but solely to be immediately connected to B's body. Personal Property, therefore, does not have an *autonomous* existence comparable to that of "Capital," of private Property ("deprived of personal support"—that is, corporeal). One can *exchange* two personal Properties, definitively (barter) or temporarily (rent). But one cannot take back former property with something else extra, without having provided an equivalent work for this extra.

Practically speaking, Property is personal when it is not hereditary. The *Droit* of property of the socialist economic Society, therefore, is not familiar with economic inheritance, it does not recognize wills (while acknowledging gifts). And this is enough for there not to be an accumulation of property and for personal Property not to be turned into an impersonal "Capital."[202]

Let us now see what socialist Obligation can be.

Seeing that there is no autonomous or capitalistic "private Property," there will not be any Obligation of the capitalist type. Obligation will be connected to property as in capitalist *Droit,* and not to the person of the debtor taken as a whole: there will be no imprisonment for debts, and so on. But the bound Property will be connected to the person of the Owner—that is, to his body. The obligation will therefore disappear with this body: there will be no hereditary transfer of obligation, for the simple reason that there will be no hereditary transfer of bound property. But the latter will remain bound after the death of the owner. The specificity disappearing, the property belongs to any given member—that is, to economic Society [583] as a whole, as well as the obligation connected to this property. But an Obligation can be assigned [*cédée*]—that is, exchanged for another.

Generally speaking, all *Droit* of "bourgeois" and "aristocratic" obligations will be maintained to the extent that it is related to personal Property. By a Convention, personal properties will be able to be shared; and a Contract will be able to provoke their (definitive or temporary) exchange. Finally, a Wrong will allow a personal property of one owner to go to another, as well as allow an unjust Enrichment.

The Exchange (conventional, contractual, or wrongful) of personal Properties will have the character of barter: one Property will be alienated from one owner in order to be "immediately" connected to another. But this transfer will be mediated by economic Society (by the "State"): if A's alienated property remains in the hands of Society for a certain time before being connected to B, this is not important, for during this time the Property ceases to be specific—

---

202. If there is a familial Society, i.e., Kinship, in the socialist Empire, all inheritance cannot be ruled out. And if the socialist Family has the task of educating its members (or a part of this education), one must accept the existence of a familial household, [which is] by definition hereditary. To the extent that this household implies a Property, this will be equally hereditary. But I am not discussing this question here, speaking only about economic Society.

that is, able to be bound [*obligeable*] (or even a Property in general, if it is the State which keeps it). What is essential is that there is no property that is susceptible of being bound and that is nevertheless not connected to a specific member of the Society. Otherwise, as in bourgeois *Droit*, the exchanged properties must be equivalent, they must have the same value or the same price, calculated according to the work which has been invested in them and their "exchange value," governed by the law of supply and demand, or indeed of (objective or subjective) scarcity.

Just as in "bourgeois" economic Society, all Property will ultimately be an (equivalent) product of the Work of the Owner. But just as in "aristocratic" Society, Properties will be equal between them. But in this synthetic Society, equality will be tempered by equivalence. Any given members of economic Society will be strictly equal. There will be, in other words, a minimum of required Work equal for all. But an optional, supplementary Work will be accepted—and consequently, an equivalent personal Property. It is solely this surplus which will be alienable in fact—that is, convertible into money. Thus, there will not be strict *monetary* equality. But there will be an equivalence between the money possessed and the work provided to have it. Within this margin, therefore, personal Properties will not be identical, neither quantitatively nor qualitatively—this even less so because they [584] will result from Work, necessarily specific [and] specialized, from whence comes a necessity for Exchange, i.e., the existence of money, a price, and a *Droit* of Exchange— that is, of economic Obligation. As for the required Property stemming from required Work, it can be excluded from all Obligation [and] from all exchange, from whence comes the uselessness of converting it into money, of setting its price. It is the Property of any given member of economic Society: to touch it is therefore to commit a crime.

To close, let us see if the Society (and the State) of the socialist Empire is based upon a "social Contract (Convention)" or upon a "Status."

On the one hand, it is very much a matter of a Status, determined by the very being of the individual and independent of his action: the Status of a member of the socialist Society and State is a function of birth. For the State and Society being *universal*, the individual has nowhere to go: he can no longer escape his Status, [and] he is subjected to it from the sole fact of his birth, of his very being. But on the other hand, this Status is also a "social Contract," or more exactly a "social Convention," for this Society and this State are "democratic." It is a function of the "will," of free, i.e., conscious and voluntary, action of all and of each: of *all*, since the Society is *universal* [and] encompasses the whole of humanity; of *each*, since it is *homogenous*, with each one acting as the others act (the Society and State being the action and the being of *any given* member, these members being strictly equal and equivalent). Difference only appears in and by the specificity of the members, but by definition it does not affect any given member nor his Status—that is, Society itself. Being equal, any given members come to an agreement, and their agreement is Society. This Society is very much the result of a universal *Convention* between equals. But seeing that all are equal from the sole fact of their birth, this Convention is just as much a *Status:* it is more status-like than all the Statuses of national and heterogenous Societies. But this Status is also more conventional than all the limited and heterogenous Conventions; for no one submits to it without voluntarily and consciously accepting it (children and the insane aside). The Empire therefore synthesizes Status and Convention, just as its *Droit* synthesizes equality and equivalence. And this is why this *Droit* is familiar with Statuses just as much as Contracts or Obligations in general: the Statuses of any given members and the Obligations of specific members. [585] And if Obligations must be in agreement with the Statuses, the latter must leave a place for Obligations.

Thus, for example, the Status of any given member can imply the *droit* and duty of working under certain conditions: *droit* and duty freely consented to but sanctioned by the State in the capacity of Third—that is, *juridical droits* and duties.[203] But the *specificity* of Work is not set down by Status: occupations are not hereditary [but] depend upon the will or action—not the being—of individuals. And this means that this specificity—like all specificities—is set down by a Contract.[204] The specificity of work (and therefore of Property, and so on) of each is set down by Contracts between workers, by Obligations of private (civil) *Droit*. And it matters little that these Contracts are "collective" or "individual," that they are concluded directly between the interested parties, or mediated by Society (the State). What is essential is that Society plays the role of a Third (arbiter, judge, lawyer, trade union, and so on), that it is not interested as such. If this is the case, there will be a private civil *Droit* of the economic Society: a *Droit* of work-Property or property-Work, and a *Droit* of Obligations, of the Exchange of personal Properties born from this specific work: of conventional, contractual, or wrongful Exchange.

Therefore, Contract is here status-like, and Status contractual or conventional. In other words, being is function, and function is being. And it is in this very thing that humanity is realized and actualized; for "the true being of man is his action" [586] (Hegel), and the action of man really exists in actuality and is revealed as human, non-natural, cultural, [and] historical being.

---

203. No longer having to defend itself against an Enemy, the State is not "interested" as a State in economic life (nor in the number of the population). It can therefore intervene as Third, i.e., in order to realize an ideal of Justice, of humanity, and not for "reasons of State." For the State, the idle person can die of hunger if he wants. What is essential is that he does not *live* without working—that is, he does not have benefits without equivalent burdens. Of course, the decrease of the population and the laziness of individuals is going to lower the "standard" of living. But this standard only touches the specificity of individuals: the State, therefore, is not interested. If it maintains and sanctions it, it does so by way of the Third; for even if, by some remote chance, all the citizens wanted to die of hunger rather than work, the State would not be affected politically as a State, seeing that it does not have an Enemy and does not imply Governors. Now the State is "interested" in its preservation only to the extent that its existence is threatened either by an external Enemy or by a revolt of the Governed.

204. It is solely in this that Socialism differs from the Statism of the late Roman Empire, Egypt, the kingdom of the Incas, and so on: there, even specificity was status-like.

Historical evolution, therefore, is going from Convention to Status, and thence to their "socialist" synthesis in and by the universal and homogenous State. The first Societies and the first States are born from Conventions: it is a Convention which creates the first collectivity which is opposed to a common Enemy and which recognizes the (political) Authority of governing from one of its members (or a group of its members). But this conventional State is limited; it has an external Enemy, a world which is not this State. And it is not homogenous, for an exclusive political group of Governors is opposed to an excluded political group of the Governed. Now, by its very essence, the State longs for universality and homogeneity. This is why Convention tends to turn itself into Status: one is a citizen not because one wants it but because one *is,* because one exists as a human being. However, in fact, all are not citizens and all are not so to the same extent, from whence comes the character of constraint connected to Status, the oppression of its hereditary character. There are men hereditarily excluded from this Status, [who are] also excluded [from a place] within the Status of Governors, from whence comes external and internal wars—Revolutions and political changes in general. And this war-like and revolutionary dialectic will last as long as there are men excluded from a given political Status and as long as all those who submit to it are not "satisfied" (*befriedigt*) with it—that is, as long as they will feel their inheritance as a burden. But when the Status is the same for all, and when all freely accept it, change is no longer possible. And this Status, infinitely "static [*statutaire*]" in its immutable and universal character, is also infinitely "conventional," seeing that it "satisfies" those who submit to it, such that they do not submit to it but voluntarily create and maintain it, in and by their actions, which are their very being. Being hereditary like all genuine Status, it is freely consented to like all true Convention. The Dialectic of Status and Convention (Contract), therefore, leads to the end of history, with the universal and homogenous State—to a definitive synthesis where status like *being* is identified with conventional *action,* and where active convention solidifies itself into a truly [*réellement*] existing status in actuality in its identity with itself.

Index

About the Author and Translators

Alexandre Kojève was born in Moscow on May 11, 1902, into a well-to-do bourgeois family (his uncle was the painter Vassily Kandinski). Kojève escaped from Russia in 1920 and spent the first half of the decade in Germany, where he completed his dissertation on the religious philosophy of Vladimir Soloviev under the supervision of Karl Jaspers. Toward the end of 1926, Kojève traveled to Paris where he continued his studies and in 1933, he took over Alexandre Koyré's seminar on Hegel's *Phenomonology of Spirit* at the Ecole Pratique des Hautes Etudes, lecturing on this one book until 1939. Kojève's seminar achieved an exceptional notoriety: not only was Kojève's interpretation of the *Phenomonology* recognized as compelling (albeit controversial), but the people who attended and were subsequently influenced by his lectures reads like a veritable who's who list of future French intellectuals. Raymond Aron, Georges Bataille, André Breton, Gaston Fessard, Jacques Lacan, Maurice Merleau-Ponty, Eric Weil, and others attended Kojève's seminar at various times and many of them attested to the power of his interpretation. In 1940, Kojève was drafted into the French army but did not see any combat, and being unable to leave France the following year, he spent the course of the war in Marseilles. Kojève wrote the *Esquisse* during the summer of 1943 in Gramat, France, by which time he was working for the Resistance in various capacities. With the help of Robert Marjolin, Kojève secured a job in the Direction des relations économiques extérieures after the war, and for the next twenty years, he was instrumental in helping to shape France's foreign trade and economic policy. Although Kojève continued to publish occasionally, many of his longer and more detailed studies in the history of philosophy and political thought were published posthumously. He died of a heart attack in 1968 while giving a speech in Brussels before a meeting of the Common Market.

Bryan-Paul Frost is assistant professor of political science at the University of Louisiana at Lafayette. He received his B.A. from St. John's College in Santa Fe and his M.A. and Ph.D. from the University of Toronto. He is the author of articles on Alexandre Kojève, Raymond Aron, Cato the Younger, Cato the

Elder, and Cicero. Professor Frost is currently working on a study of Aristotle's *Rhetoric* and civic education, completing a book on Kojève's political philosophy, and co-editing a volume of essays entitled *History of American Political Thought*.

Robert Howse is professor of law at the University of Michigan Law School and a member of the World Trade Institute in Bern, Switzerland. He has taught at the University of Toronto, Harvard Law School, and the Academy of European Law, European University Institute in Florence, Italy. He holds degrees from the University of Toronto and Harvard Law School. Professor Howse has been a consultant or adviser to institutions as diverse as the Organization for Economic Cooperation and Development (OECD), the Canadian Standards Association, and the International Centre for Human Rights and Democratic Development. He is the author of numerous works on world trade law, globalization, and legal and political philosophy.